Interdisciplinary perspectives on modern history

Editors
Robert Fogel and Stephan Thernstrom

Mammon and the pursuit of Empire

Mammon and the pursuit of Empire

The political economy of British imperialism, 1860–1912

LANCE E. DAVIS
and
ROBERT A. HUTTENBACK
with the assistance of Susan Gray Davis

The right of the
University of Cambridge
to print and sell
all manner of books
was granted by
Henry VIII in 1534.
The University has printed
and published continuously
since 1584.

CAMBRIDGE UNIVERSITY PRESS

Cambridge
London   New York   New Rochelle
Melbourne   Sydney

Published by the Press Syndicate of the University of Cambridge
The Pitt Building, Trumpington Street, Cambridge CB2 1RP
32 East 57th Street, New York, NY 10022, USA
10 Stamford Road, Oakleigh, Melbourne 3166, Australia

First published 1986

Printed in the United States of America

Library of Congress Cataloging-in-Publication Data
Davis, Lance E., 1928–
Mammon and the pursuit of Empire.
(Interdisciplinary perspectives on modern history)
Bibliography: p.
1. Great Britain – Colonies – Economic conditions.
2. Great Britain – Colonies – Economic policy.
I. Huttenback, Robert A.   II. Title.   III. Series.
HC259.D38   1986   330.9171′241   86–2649

British Library Cataloguing in Publication Data
Davis, Lance
Mammon and the pursuit of Empire : the political
economy of British imperialism, 1860–1912. –
(Interdisciplinary perspectives on modern history)
1. Economics – Great Britain – History
2. Imperialism – History   3. Great Britain –
Colonies – Economic conditions
I. Title   II. Huttenback, Robert   III. Series
325′.32′0941   HC255

ISBN 0 521 23611 8

Contents

v

Preface

Hard by Westminster, font of British power, and on the Thames Embankment, stands the statue of Boadicea – Queen of the Iceni, who died in 61 A.D., "after leading her people against the Roman Invader" as the words on the statue's base relate. On the obverse side, another inscription manifests the virtues of the dictum, "if you can't beat them join them," for it intones:

> Regions Caesar never knew
> Thy Posterity shall sway.

And indeed they did.

This book deals with an aspect of the remarkable expansion of an island nation into the far reaches of the earth. Its completion has consumed better than a decade and has taken the authors into all manner of unlikely places. Official records are by and large kept in known and accessible archives. Private papers and company records are frequently a different matter. Thus the imperatives of research required work in an abandoned meat-packing plant that was virtually without light and furniture and where even in the middle of summer the temperature numbed the extremities. In one case the relevant documents pertaining to a still-existing firm were under the floorboards of the managing director's office. Vickers provided a penthouse and the records of Lloyds Bank were kept in the specie room under the constant gaze of television cameras.

Through it all, the authors received the support of a vast multitude of people and institutions and they are duly grateful. Special thanks are due not only to Susan Davis but to Curtis Mosso, without whose genius in the area of computer programming the authors would still be mired in unresolved data problems, and to Benjamin Kamhi, their prime research assistant, who patiently endured many difficult moments. Other research assistants included Charlotte Atkins, Eli Azar, Marta Burg, Meredyth Cable, Richard Castro, Gerald Czuleger, Richard Dulaney, Robin Fleming, Guy Gadbois, Matt Gallman, Catherine Garnett, Alan Gin, Moira Hill, Charles Keene, Tina Kelly, Peter Liss, Kathy Loh, Catherine Lolov, Michael Lowrie, Rudy Lucero, Kathrine Mack, Margaret McCandless, Larry Miller, Collette Moulton, Jennifer Owen, Christine Partridge, Sandra Petersen, Rebecca Rothenberg, Bret Roy, Dianna Schulte, Natalie Seaman, Claus Suverkropp, Howard Tarre, Rob Taylor, Tulsi Uprety, Bruce Vogen, and Andrea Woodward.

A great corps of wonderful secretaries and word processors not only typed and retyped the manuscript, but managed to keep vast mounds of data in some sort of order. Among them were Connie Friedman, Joy Hansen, Charlene Heinz, Cheryl Kelly, Ellen Kennedy, Susan Paruolo, Ann Sonstelie, Edith Taylor, and Barbara Yandell.

Finally, many individuals and institutions gave generously of their time and deserve both great thanks and recognition. Although this list is not exhaustive their ranks include Mr. J. Lingwood and Mr. Colin Turnack, Pacific Steam Navigation Company; Mr. R. Evan, Council of Foreign Bondholders; Miss B. Ramsbotham, National Coal Board; Mr. T. D. Scrase, Gittins and Co., Stock and Sharebrokers; Mr. Allan F. Mack, Manchester Chamber of Commerce and Industry; Mr. E. F. Holman, the Merseyside Chamber of Commerce and Industry; Mr. A. A. Duncan, Glasgow Chamber of Commerce; Mr. R. G. Donkin, the Foreign and Colonial Investment Trust Co., Ltd.; Mr. Colin Allflatt, Brooke Bond Liebig Ltd.; Mr. W. A. L. Seaman, County Record Office, Tyne and Wear County Council; Mr. J. R. Knight, the Stock Exchange, London; Mr. J. G. Curtis, Matheson and Co., Ltd.; Mr. J. Claydon, Cambridge University Library; Mr. J. L. Cleland, Reference and Access, Commonwealth Archives Office; Mr. James Mair and Ms. Dorothy Lemon, Sidlaw Industries; Mr. John Barker and Mrs. Auld, University of Dundee Library; Mr. Edward Kaye, United Africa Company; Mr. Michael Moss and Ms. Elsbeth Simpson, Glasgow University Library; Mr. John Goodchild, Wakefield Central Library; Mr. Peter Kale, Company Records Office; Miss J. M. R. Campbell, National Westminster Bank Limited; Mr. R. A. Hobson, Lloyds Bank International; Ms. R. Vermette and Mr. Eric Swanik, Legislative Library, Winnipeg; Mr. C. Arden-Clark, UAC International; Mr. J. Hare, the Courage Brewing Company; Mr. C. Bruce Fergusson, Public Archives of Nova Scotia; Dr. J. Neville Bartlett, King's College; Mr. Ronald Stevens, Kleinwort, Benson Limited; Ms. Mary McRae, Archives Office of Tasmania; Mr. G. R. Cavendish, Commonwealth Archives Office; Mr. H. Adolphe, Archives Office, Mauritius; Mr. F. Burnham Gill, Department of Tourism, Newfoundland; Ms. Margaret Medcalf, Battye Library; Mr. W. D. Walls, Place Bell Canada; Dr. B. J. T. Leverton, Natal Archives Depot; Mr. M. E. Freeland, Reserve Bank of Australia; Mr. L. J. Hanley, Commonwealth Archives Office; Mr. Freeman Clowery, Bank of Montreal; Mr. B. T. Burne, Commonwealth Archives Office; Mr. J. H. Davies, Chief, Cape Archives Depot; Mr.

P. D. Wilson, Queensland State Archives; Mr. J. H. Love, State Library of South Australia; Mr. O. R. Davie, National Archives, Wellington; Mr. D. J. Cross, the Archives Authority of New South Wales; Mr. Clinton V. Black, the Jamaica Archives; Mr. H. J. Robertson, University of Cape Town; Mr. A. P. Skerman, Commonwealth Archives Office; Mr. D. R. Allen, City of Westminster Chamber of Commerce; Mr. L. C. Arkell, Donnington Brewery; Mr. H. T. Holman, Public Archives, Prince Edward Island; Ms. Joan Smith, Liverpool University Library; Mr. Peter Emerson, British Steel Corp.; Mr. John Hill, Bristol City Lines; and Mr. E. G. Fielding, Vickers Ltd.

Particular gratitude is owed to Mr. Edwin Green, Archivist, Midlands Bank Ltd.; Mr. Derek Charman, Corporation Archivist, British Steel; Mr. F. Page, Crown Agents, Millbank; Mr. A. W. Abbott, Crown Agents, Millbank; Mr. Thomas W. Shaw, Keeper of Printed Books, Guildhall Library, London; Professor Peter Payne, University of Aberdeen, Scotland; and Professor Anthony Slaven, Department of Economics History, University of Glasgow.

Many libraries and their staffs lent assistance to the project, including those of the Universities of California at Berkeley, Los Angeles, and Santa Barbara; the California Institute of Technology; Oxford and Cambridge Universities; Rhodes House; the Universities of Hull, Glasgow, Birmingham, Nottingham, Leeds, and Liverpool; Imperial and University Colleges of London University; the libraries of the Institute of Historical Research, the India Office, the British Museum, the former Colonial Office and the Guild Hall. Special thanks are also due to the Center for Advanced Study in the Behavioral Sciences, in Stanford, California.

Research was conducted in virtually every British archive, most notably in the Public Record Office and its English and Scottish Company Record Offices, the archives of the coal and steel industries, and county and city record offices throughout the length and breadth of Great Britain.

Thanks are due H. M. Stationery Office for permission to use Crown copyright material. In its final stages, the manuscript was the object of discussion at the annual All University of California Economic History Conference, held in May 1983. The remarks made at that time were extremely useful. In addition, warm thanks are due to many others who read and commented on the manuscript. Their numbers include Professors Stanley Engerman, John S. Galbraith, D. K. Fieldhouse, Richard Kesner, Michael Edelstein, Gary Cox, Donald McCloskey, Roger Louis, Richard Sylla, Roger Noll, Peter McClelland, David Galenson, Roderick Flood, Kenneth Sokoloff, and Charlotte Ericksen. Ron Twisdale undertook the complex task of preparing the index.

Cliometric research is painfully expensive and the authors are grateful for the financial support received from the National Endowment for the Humanities (Contract No. RO–27612–77–1415), the National Science Foundation (Contract No. SOC–7809080 and BNS–8011494), the California Institute of Technology, and the University of California.

1 The British Empire and the economics of imperialism: an introductory statement

I. Introduction

Few questions have engendered as much reappraisal, reinterpretation and recasting as Western imperialism in the late nineteenth century. At this moment, three-quarters of the way through the 1980s, a majority of the countries represented in the United Nations blame imperialism for the poverty, illiteracy, and the generally unsettled condition of the Third World. In Britain, the political left still finds in the imperial past some of the explanation for slow economic growth; and Argentina continues to press irredentist land claims to an imperial relic in the South Atlantic past the point of war. Nor have professional historians ignored the alleged implications of imperialism. Indeed, it is difficult to find a single economic or political historian of modern Britain who has not had something to say about the British imperial experience or the relationship between overseas finance and the climacteric in the domestic economy.

The fact that four generations of historians have been mesmerized by imperialism in theory and practice suggests that the last word may never be written. In this book, no attempt is made to reach a moral judgment on the imperial process, to differentiate between the settling of essentially unpeopled lands and the conquest of populated ones, nor to measure the social or psychic effects that the colonial experiment had on inhabitants of the imperial domain or, for that matter, on the British themselves. Rather, this is essentially a work of economic history, although at times it might better be described as political economy.

The focus is the "profitability of Empire" in the five decades preceding the First World War, and on the identity of what might be termed the players in the imperial game. To that end, data have been collected on the direction and volume of portfolio finance that passed through the London capital market between 1865 and 1914; the rates of return earned by firms operating at home, in the Empire, and abroad; the composition of government receipts and expenditures in those same three loci; the identities of the investors whose main concern was the Empire; and the politicians whose votes shaped the Empire.

1

As a work of economic and political history, the focus of this work is quite narrow. It has been argued that in the late nineteenth century the British Empire was a political instrument designed to increase business profits, and that incomes in the United Kingdom (at least some incomes) reflected these "exploitive" profits. At the same time, the literature argues, preoccupation with Empire diverted capital from the domestic economy, making British industry increasingly noncompetitive and as a consequence less profitable. It is our hope that the ensuing pages will help to determine whether or not these propositions are true.

Imperialism is a vast subject and one that touches on any number of very important issues. This work makes no attempt to be exhaustive or to treat even all the important questions that are raised by the nature of the imperial relationship. It deals only with the British Empire, and there is no attempt to examine any others. Questions concerning the French or Germans in the nineteenth century or America or Russia in the twentieth are well beyond the scope of this endeavor. The primary focus is on the effect of the imperial system on Britain, not on the Empire or its inhabitants. Dependency theories have assumed an important place in the literature on development, but little effort is made here to assess the impact of the political economic system on indigenous populations or economies. As far as Britain is concerned, the effort is again severely limited. Economics hold the center of this stage, but even that subject is not dealt with comprehensively. No attempt, for example, is made to explain the growth or maintenance of an empire. Interest is limited to an examination of the role that profits may have played in motivating the political policies designed to continue and strengthen imperial ties. Once more, the examination of the effects of the Empire does not include an analysis of the long-term impact on British society and its psyche.

In the area of economics, the work examines in detail the rate of return on Empire investment, the flows of capital that underwrote those returns, the costs inherent in maintaining or expanding that Empire, the groups that paid the costs, and those that reaped the economic benefits. The study, however, touches only briefly on the subject of trade, and addresses not at all the effects of induced changes in the terms of trade and on the direction and rate of labor migration. Finally, the discussion is limited to the "formal" as opposed to the "informal" Empire.

This extended caveat is not meant to minimize either the nature of this undertaking or the importance of questions that fall outside its scope. It is a statement of the limits of the present work and a recognition of the many very important questions that arise from the imperial connection that have not been examined in detail. Finally, it is an admission of the fact that, if it is not impossible, it is at least very difficult to do everything.

II. Imperial theories

Any work that claims to deal with the development of empire cannot help but be concerned with the motives for grasping and holding an empire; in the literature, indeed, these motives are legion. There are geopolitical explanations for particular acts of conquest, although attempts to generalize from those experiences have not proved too enlightening. The turbulent frontier hypothesis is one example of such a geopolitical theory. It conjectures that if an area of order is surrounded by a zone of disorder, the government of the former must eventually, for its own protection, conquer the latter. Thus, empires would tend to advance their frontiers until they reach some great natural barrier or the borders of another stable power. The British experience in India can be advanced as evidence of the influence of the turbulent frontier.[1] On the subcontinent, the argument runs, the British, through the medium of the East India Company, were willing (so long as the Mogul Empire was strong) to restrict their activities to trading stations like Surat, Bombay, and Madras. With the decline of Mogul power, however, the Company was "forced" to raise military forces to quell the anarchy in the surrounding countryside; and political annexation was the inexorable next step. The final northern frontiers of British India rested along the lofty barrier of the Himalayas and the borders of the great Russian and Chinese Empires. In the West, however, less definite geographical and political limits caused constant frontier fluctuations and frequent British interference in the affairs of "turbulent" Afghanistan.

If there is a dearth of truly political theories, the same cannot be said for other conceptual frameworks. In recent years much debate has centered on the concept of "informal empire" and the influence of free trade on the establishment of British hegemony in so many parts of the world. A great deal of the discussion was vitalized by a controversial article by John Gallagher and Ronald Robinson, entitled simply "Imperialism and Free Trade." It is the classic statement on informal empire and implies that formal empire or the acquisition of territory was a last resort; that the British government much preferred to support British business in what were in essence client states.

Social scientists are seldom silent on any issue, and they too have entered the intellectual fray. They have, for example, found the motivation for imperial expansion in the precepts of social Darwinism or rooted in the nature of society and the human animal. Joseph Schumpeter claimed that imperialism was a social atavism not prompted by economic reason or national interest, but purely by "the objectless disposition on the part of a state to unlimited forcible expansion," – a tendency encouraged, according to David Landes, by "the disparity of force between Europe and the rest of the world . . . that created the opportunity and possibility of dominion."[2] Or as Hilaire Belloc put it: "Whatever happens we have got the maxim gun and they have not." Similarly, but at the other end of the sociological scale, humanitarianism rather than atavistic behavior has been advanced as an explanation of imperial adventures. In West and South Africa it is argued, the British antislavery movement virtually forced the government to acquire unwanted territory in order to protect the native population. It could be considered the "bearing of the white man's burden" in the most positive sense. More recently, social imperialism, the marriage of social reform and aggressive expansionism, has been the focus of increased discussion.

Other theories rest on individual or social psychology for their inspiration. Examples abound; and among these, those that assume irrationality was the driving force behind the advance of empire must be given their place. How else, it can be argued, can we explain the strange triumphs of mindless ambition and the insane desire to "paint the map red" or whatever other color was the manifestation of the national ego? Again, in an age of slow communications, the "man on the spot" could, it is conjectured, influence events according to his own designs, unrestrained by the wishes of the home government; and empire, thus, might be considered the result of a series of idiosyncratic decisions. Cecil Rhodes in South Africa, Frederick Lugard in East Africa and Charles Napier in India are all cited as examples of this phenomenon; and the British government was allegedly presented in each case with territory it would much rather have done without. One cannot leave this particular discussion without mention of Charles "Chinese" Gordon, who, by stubbornly disobeying orders and thereby bringing about not only his own death but the massacre of the entire garrison of Khartoum, so aroused the passions of the British populace that the government was forced to acquire a province, the conquest of which it had tried studiously to avoid. But irrationality is always hard to stomach as historical explanation. Thus, Robinson and Gallagher reenter the debate to explain the so-called "scramble for Africa" by using South Africa, Egypt, and the route to India as the necessary touchstones.

However, probably the most diverse and numerous group of imperial theorists are the economic determinists. They deprecate the influence of geopolitics, of social and psychological forces, and of the "man on the spot." To them frontier turbulence might have provided opportunities, but it was the potential profits that set the rate of imperial expansion. Men and women might love war and strive mightily to save their fellows, but it was profit that dictated the battles to be fought and the societies to be rescued. As for the imperial proconsul, he was merely the pawn, albeit often an unwitting one, of the financiers and the bankers at home. To the economic determinists, the expansion of empire was consciously decreed by a small coterie of capitalists associated with the stock exchange and the great banks of England. As J. A. Hobson put it in his classic statement:

> In view of the part which the non-economic factors of patriotism, adventure, military enterprise, political ambition, and philanthropy play in imperial expansion, it may appear to impute to financiers so much power as to take a too narrowly economic view of history. And it is true that the motor-power of Imperialism is not chiefly financial: finance is rather the governor of the imperial engine directing the energy and determining its work: it does not constitute the fuel of the engine, nor does it generate the power. Finance manipulates the patriotic forces which politicians, soldiers, philanthropists, and traders generate; the enthusiasm for expansion which issues from these sources, though strong and genuine, is irregular and blind; the financial interest has those qualities of concentration and clear-sighted calculation which are needed to set Imperialism to work. An ambitious statesman, a frontier soldier, an overzealous missionary, a pushing trader, may suggest or even initiate a step of imperial expansion, may assist in educating patriotic public opinion to the urgent need of some fresh advance, but the final determination rests with the financial power.[3]

Lenin put Hobson's agents of the financial power to his own use when he wrote, "... all these have given birth to those distinctive characteristics of imperialism which compel us to define it as parasitic or decaying capitalism...."[4]

And Bernard Shaw, probably not aware that he was an economic determinist, wrote, as only an Irishman could, that an Englishman

> ... is never at a loss for an effective moral attitude. As the great champion of freedom and national independence, he conquers

> and annexes half the world, and calls it Colonization. When he
> wants a new market for his adulterated Manchester goods, he
> sends a missionary to teach the natives the Gospel of Peace. The
> natives kill the missionary: he flies to arms in defence of Chris-
> tianity, fights for it, conquers for it; and takes the market as a
> reward from heaven. . . . His watchword is always Duty; and he
> never forgets that the nation which lets its duty get on the op-
> posite side of its interest is lost. . . . [5]

Even the explorer H. M. Stanley belonged to the ranks of the
economic determinists.

> There are forty millions of people beyond the gateway to the
> Congo, [he wrote] and the cotton spinners of Manchester are
> waiting to clothe them. Birmingham foundries are gleaming with
> the red metal that will presently be made into ironwork for them
> and the trinkets that shall adorn those dusky bosoms, and the
> ministers of Christ are zealous to bring them, the poor benighted
> heathen, into the Christian fold. [6]

What a happy marriage of the spiritual and the material!

Many missionaries in Africa, notably David Livingstone, envis-
aged a union of commerce and Christianity – "those two pioneers of
civilization" – as the salvation of Africa. In 1857, in a speech at Cambridge, Livingstone exhorted his audience "to direct your attention
to Africa. I know that in a few years I shall be cut off in that country,
which is now open; do not let it be shut again! I go back to Africa to
try to make an open path for commerce and Christianity. . . . " [7]

Economic determinists of the Leninist persuasion find the hand
of the financier everywhere, even in the acquisition of areas that
were at best marginal, like the humid and inhospitable lands of West
Africa. To them, imperialism was a symptom of the final crisis of
capitalism, the time when the competition for protected markets that
were needed to absorb the increasing domestic production was at
its height. Consequently, they argued, the control of markets, even
those that would have been considered worthless in previous decades, became necessary for survival.

Of all the explanations of empire, none is more compelling than
the one concerned with economic gain. Regardless of the weight
given to the importance of the various motives for imperial expansion, few doubt that, once hegemony was established, economics
(if not economic determinism) emerged as an important force in
questions of imperial governance and continuity. British authorities
were constantly worried about the costs of Empire. As early as 1828
one of the directors of the East India Company wrote the governor-
general:

The expenses of [the Indian establishment] are now under consideration and I trust that they may be greatly reduced without
injury to the public interest – and I would fain hope and believe
that under your Lordship's administration, if Peace and Tran-
quillity be preserved in India, the embarrassments in which the
Company's affairs are now involved will be removed and that we
shall be able to render a good account of our government of India
both as respects our Financial and Political administration.[8]

And for the years under study, almost every colonial governor,
whether in India, Canada, or West Africa, received similar instruc-
tions. Whitehall consistently opposed the assumption of any new
responsibilities – at least when they threatened to become a drain
on the exchequer. And yet, this attitude does not appear to have
prevented lands that were clearly unprofitable (at least in the public
sense) from coming under the British flag.

While it would be perfectly appropriate to measure any or all the
various factors associated with imperialism, this work centers largely
on the economic ones, not only because of their intrinsic importance
but because the kind of quantitative data needed for the analysis
are available. That is not true for other aspects of imperial theory,
and our task is to determine whether and to what degree Britain's
prosperity in the late nineteenth century was dependent on its economic and political relations with the Empire.

III. The growth and development of the Empire

While the search for profits may have underlain the growth of Empire, the mechanism that is supposed to have connected the cause
with the effect is sometimes obscure. It has been said with at least
the spirit of truth that the British Empire was founded in a fit of
absence of mind, and that the largely ad hoc development of the
overseas extensions of Britain itself owed more to traditional British
pragmatism than to any master plan emanating from the corridors
of Whitehall. In 1926, Lord Balfour defined the lengthy imperial
experience by contending that the Empire "considered as a whole
. . . defies classification and bears no resemblance to any other political organization which now exists or has ever yet been tried."[9]

This unique hybrid enjoyed at least two incarnations. The so-called
First Empire was limited largely to North America and the Caribbean. There, the desire to rid the home islands of religious and
political dissidents combined with a mercantilist doctrine of state to
allow settlers to plant the British flag on the eastern seaboard of the

continent and on the sugar islands of the West Indies. It was an empire of settlement – of colonies peopled by British immigrants – and it died, to all intents and purposes, with the American Revolution. The Second British Empire, whose birth coincided with the death throes of the first, was founded, if for any rational reason, on ambitions for increased foreign trade. Ideally, it was to have been a chain of trading posts protected by strategically placed naval bases. The attainment of wealth through commerce was to have been its purpose, but the profits were not to have been diminished by the expense of colonization and the costs of warfare that had proved so frustrating in North America. Constitutional developments in the Second Empire spawned the Empire–Commonwealth. Dating from the 1850s, it established a dichotomy between the increasingly autonomous colonies of the white settlement and the dependent possessions.

A policy designed to lead to profits without costs may have been rational, but the pattern of actual development did not follow the anticipated path. The West Indian sugar islands remained of major economic significance; however, profits were unattainable without administrative expense. An imperial connection with North America was unavoidable because Canada – ironically acquired to protect the lands further south, now gone – was still part of the Empire. In the Southern Hemisphere, Australia and New Zealand were rediscovered and occupied, and the population explosion of the nineteenth century peopled these new possessions with British immigrants. In India, the stable structure of the Mogul Empire, under whose aegis the East India Company had once securely conducted business, had collapsed, and that development created a vacuum into which the British felt themselves forced to move. Thus, the Second Empire was no less free of cost than the first – Canada, Australia, New Zealand, and the administration of other lands all demanded the expenditure of resources.

Once committed, however reluctantly and unwillingly, questions of communication and access could not be avoided by the home authorities and their servants in the field. Consequently, the British ship of state set sail on a whole new troubled sea when the Cape of Good Hope was wrested from the Dutch in 1814. The conquest was designed to facilitate the journey to India; and similar considerations, this time to protect the Suez Canal route to the East, led to the establishment of British control in Egypt. Nor, as it turned out, was British hegemony in Africa limited to the Cape and Egypt. Over the course of the nineteenth century, a variety of factors prompted continued expansion throughout the continent – into

East, West, and Central Africa and into the Sudan. Inadvertence, greed, humanitarianism, personal ambition, missionary zeal, fear of foreign intervention, and that curious phenomenon, "prestige imperialism," which toward the end of the century whetted the British appetite for expansion – all may have played their parts. In addition to new possessions in Africa, the nineteenth century saw northwest India; the Malayan archipelago; Brunei, Sarawak, and Hong Kong; Cyprus; Fiji, Tonga, and the islands of the Western Pacific Group; Mauritius, the Seychelles, and, to all intents and purposes, Egypt coming under the Crown (see Appendixes 1.1 and 1.2).

Commercial companies, religious dissidents, planters, and adventurers were at least as important in extending the bounds of Empire as the soldiers and sailors of the monarch. Indeed, until the third quarter of the nineteenth century the whole enterprise prompted either ennui or outright hostility in Britain itself. As late as 1865 Sir Charles Adderley, the British colonial reformer and Parliament's most eloquent anti-imperial spokesman, had asserted in the House that the four British possessions on the West Coast of Africa wasted a million pounds a year. The attempt to create a "civilized" Negro community in Sierra Leone, he claimed, had failed; the Gold Coast had involved the British government in several unjustifiable wars; and the trade of Gambia and Lagos was at best negligible.[10] The Committee on West African Affairs, a Parliamentary select committee, created in response to Adderley's protest, recommended:

> All further extension of territory or assumption of government, or new treaties offering protection to native tribes, would be inexpedient .... The object of our policy should be to encourage in the natives the exercise of those qualities which may render it possible for us more and more to transfer to them the administration of all the governments, with a view to our ultimate withdrawal from all, except probably Sierra Leone.[11]

By 1866, the Colonial Secretary, Edward Cardwell, was able to report that the West African establishments had been drastically reduced.[12]

It was only six years later that Disraeli rose in London's great Crystal Palace to attack the anti-imperial bias of Gladstone's Liberal Party. He urged his listeners to take pride in an empire "which may become the source of incalculable strength and happiness to this land." And he issued a stentorian challenge to his audience.

> Will [you], [he asked] be content to be a comfortable England, modeled and moulded upon Continental principles and meeting in due course an inevitable fate, or ... will [you] be a great coun-

try, an Imperial country, a country where your sons, when they
rise, rise to paramount positions, and obtain not merely the esteem of their countrymen, but the respect of the world.[13]

Disraeli's words did not fall on deaf ears. The Conservative Party
consciously used empire as an election issue and was swept into
power on a wave of votes from the newly enfranchised urban working class, to whom the vicarious pleasure of ruling an empire upon
which the sun literally never set appeared to offset a more logical
loyalty to the Liberals.

Even then, however, public enthusiasm was usually no more
matched by official elation than it had been earlier. The Treasury
continued to rail against the costs of empire, and debates on imperial
and particularly Indian issues were calculated to empty the halls of
Parliament. Besides, the growth of colonial responsibilities somehow
ran counter to the burgeoning of liberalism and later, humanitarianism, in Britain itself, and this dilemma required the development
of an administrative doctrine and a philosophical foundation in keeping with the prevailing climate of public opinion – no easy matter.

The period of high imperialism lasted little more than two and a
half decades. It began at the Crystal Palace and ended at Mafeking.
The Boer War, fought against a gallant and badly outnumbered foe
and for gold rather than virtue, seemed to many to strip away what
aura of moral rectitude was attached to the concept of empire. The
costs of imperial glory also rose. During this brief span of years the
British entered into intense rivalry with the French and the Germans,
and several times a major war was narrowly averted. It is a testimony
to the degree to which imperialism developed a mindless force of
its own that far more territory was added to the British Empire during
the administration of the anti-imperialist Gladstone than during the
government of the expansionist Disraeli.[14] The Liberals added territory at the rate of 87,000 square miles per year in power, compared
to the Conservatives' paltry 5,300.

The new Empire as it grew was far from homogeneous. On the
one hand there were the colonies of white settlement, Canada, the
Australian colonies, New Zealand, and in some sense, South Africa;
on the other, colonies of the so-called dependent Empire, predominantly nonwhite, centered at first in Asia but including by the end
of the century large tracts of Africa.[15] (See Appendix 1.1.) The latter
group could again be divided into colonies, protectorates, and protected states. Colonies, or Crown Colonies, as they came to be
known, developed a form of government with a powerful governor
advised by an appointed executive council and working with, but
not responsible to, a legislative council. The proportion of elected

to "official" members on that council varied from colony to colony. In most colonies, the council gradually developed into an increasingly representative legislative assembly, acting either unicamerally or as the lower house in a bicameral legislature where the executive council constituted the upper.

That the dependent Empire (and particularly India) should remain under the close scrutiny of Whitehall was never questioned until well into the twentieth century. Indeed it had been the original intention of the British authorities to follow the same philosophy not only for the dependent Empire but for those lands peopled largely by those of European descent as well. It was generally assumed that the loss of the American colonies had been due to the benign neglect that had allowed the colonists to assume they had rights and privileges that were, in effect, vested in the Crown and Parliament. Consequently, those in power tended to agree with the words of William Knox, a former undersecretary in the Colonial Department, when he stated, "It was better to have no colonies at all than not to have them subservient to the maritime strength and commercial interests of Great Britain."[16] Based on this reasoning, Canada, the only remaining colony of significance, was kept under a tight reign in the years following the American Revolution.

The revolts that broke out in both Upper and Lower Canada in 1837 caused a shock wave to run through the British body politic. Inattention had brought on the American Revolution, and now close control had seemingly produced the same result in Canada. This dilemma was solved by an estimably pragmatic strategem. It was called "responsible government" and, as propounded by Lord Durham in his report of 1839, was really simplicity itself.

> Every purpose of popular control might be combined with every advantage of vesting the immediate choice of advisers in the Crown were the Colonial Governor to be instructed to secure the cooperation of the Assembly in his policy, by entrusting its administration to such men as could command a majority; and if he were given to understand that he need count on no aid from home in any difference with the Assembly, that should not directly involve the relations between the mother country and the Colony. . . .[17]

Essentially, the formula implied colonial self-government; and, although Durham reserved to London control over the sale of public lands, tariffs, and foreign affairs, the first two limitations went by the boards immediately, and the last as soon as the colony found it in its best interests.

Responsible government was established in Canada in 1847 and quickly spread to the other colonies of white settlement. If the goal of the British government was colonial self-sufficiency, responsible government would seem to have been the ideal solution. Increased autonomy, however, allowed colonial legislatures to reject British requests for financial support in what London assumed was a shared responsibility – the administration and defense of the Empire. The more affluent parts of the dependent Empire were not in such a happy position, but ultimately it was British taxpayers and, to a lesser extent, those of India, Ceylon, Singapore, and Hong Kong who shouldered most of the burden.

The reluctance with which Britain developed administrative mechanisms to preside over its empire was perhaps best captured by the history of the physical premises from whence imperial authority flowed. Until the third quarter of the nineteenth century, the Colonial Office was located at 14 Downing Street and a single house further west. The buildings were gloomy and so damp that the basements where many of the staff worked had to be pumped out daily. In order to help stabilize the structures, records were packed into the walls and foundations; and fires had to be kept burning twenty-four hours a day to stop the files from dissolving. Sound passed unimpeded through the walls, and by the 1860s ominous groanings and frequent tremors led to the fear that the edifices would soon be reduced to heaps of rubble.

Again, the administrative structure of the Colonial Office itself seemed to match its architectural history. In 1801 the position of Secretary of State for War and Colonies was created, and responsibility for imperial affairs was transferred from the Home Office to this agency. The marriage of war and colonies was not a happy one. The concerns of the secretary of state were dominated by military matters. The situation was improved in 1806, when an extra undersecretary with jurisdiction over military affairs was appointed. As a consequence, the original appointee was left free to devote his energies to colonial matters. Six years later the Colonial Office was recognized as a distinct unit, although the responsibilities associated with military operations technically remained with it until the creation of the fourth secretary of state (war) in 1854.

From 1825, the table of organization of the Colonial Office, in addition to the secretary of state and the parliamentary undersecretary, called for a permanent undersecretary, a chief clerk, 17 clerks, a counsel, a librarian and his assistant, a registrar and his assistant, a private secretary for the secretary of state, a precis writer, 2 office keepers, 2 porters, and a housekeeper – for a total of 31. Yet, as late as 1849, the actual staff numbered but 23 and, even in 1907, the total was only 125. Reforms in 1850 and 1870 altered the staffing schedule, but the division of work into a general plus four geographical departments – the North American, the West Indian, the Australian, and the African and Mediterranean – remained essentially unaltered. The first decade of the twentieth century saw one further refinement: the bifurcation of the Colonial Office into a Crown Colonies and a Dominions Division.[18]

Ancillary administrative agencies associated with the Colonial Office included the Land and Emigration Board and the Crown Agents. Between 1840 and 1878 the former agency was charged with administering the sale of Crown lands and assisting in the administration of emigration policies. The latter grew out of a decision in 1858 that the numerous and largely independent Agents General of the Crown Colonies, who as Colonial Office appointees represented individual colonies in business, finance, and purchasing, were to be reconstituted as a joint body known as the Crown Agents for the Colonies. With the rise of the self-governing colonies, the Agents' main concern became the Crown Colonies, while the more autonomous entities were encouraged to appoint their own representatives in London.

In the field, the executive arm of the Colonial Office was the governor. In the colonies of the dependent Empire, though often assisted by advisory and protolegislative councils, his powers were at times close to absolute; however, the degree of his primacy varied from colony to colony. In those colonies with responsible government, the governor represented his imperial masters in London and acted as a ceremonial head of state subject to policies developed by his ministers.

In terms of numbers, the British Empire was run by very few people, and mainly middle-class ones, at that. It was hardly the great system of outdoor relief for the upper classes suggested by George Cornwall Lewis. For example, the Colonial Office list for 1892 numbers about 2,400, and the total thirty years previous had been less than 1,000. Included were not only the mighty but second clerks, second-class inspectors, cashiers, cadets, a sub–distributor of stamps, a compiler of labor ordinances, the interpreter to the resident magistrate in Durban, a "landing waiter" in Antigua, bishops, minor prelates, some military officers, and a considerable number of retired personnel. In addition, virtually all elected and appointed indigenous officials of the colonial governments were included – the mayors of small towns and functionaries of provincial county halls – as well as living persons who at some time had been associated with the colonial service but no longer were. The India Office list for 1896 included some 3,000 persons (2,000 in 1886) roughly comparable in status to those on the Colonial Office list, and many of them were Indian. Thus, the British Empire at the apogee of its existence was managed by less than 6,000 souls! Nor is the story of the effect of the Empire on employment much altered if the 75,000-odd troops stationed in India and the 45,000 serving in the colonies are added to the total. Whatever can be said about the financial burden of Empire, it would seem to have provided a lot of ego enhancement without major additions to the civil list.

India was the single most visible jewel in the imperial crown. It was an empire in itself and was too massive and complex an undertaking ever to fall under the aegis of the Colonial Office. Until 1858, the British dominions in India were governed through the fiat of the East India Company, its directors, and "secret committee," although the real power lay with the Board of Control for India, an organ of the British government. The Company's chief officer on the subcontinent was the governor-general. At the end of the Mutiny, the Company's charter was revoked and India came directly under the Crown. The India Office became the new governing agency in Britain and through the governor-general, now also a viceroy, it administered British India directly and the Princely States indirectly. The secretary of state for India assumed the duties heretofore carried out by the chairman of the board of control, and he gained membership in the cabinet. The secretary was advised by a council, and certain of his decisions had to be made "in Council."

The organization of the India Office was largely analogous to that of the Colonial Office. A permanent and parliamentary undersecretary assisted the secretary, as did an assistant secretary, who served also as clerk of the Council. Most of the office's departments corresponded to committees of the Council (Finance, Political, Military, Revenue and Statistics, Judicial and Public Works, and Stores) and each was staffed by a secretary, an assistant-secretary, and several clerks. There was also a director-general of the stores department, an accountant general, a registrar, superintendent of records, director of funds, legal advisor, librarian, and several others. An auditor was attached to the office, and his appointment had to be countersigned by the Chancellor of the Exchequer.

India was the Treasury's ideal. It conducted its affairs as that agency thought a British dependency should. Having no effective form of self-government, it was legally at the mercy of whatever policies its British governors and the authorities in Whitehall might devise. India underwrote all of its own administrative costs. There were no occasions, as in other dependent possessions, when a bare treasure chamber necessitated a British subsidy. So sui generis was India's position within the British Empire that even the heart of the devoutest "Little Englander" – that dedicated opponent of virtually all things imperial – was inclined to beat a little faster at the thought of Union Jack flying over the battlements of Fort St. George, Fort St. David, or one of the subcontinent's other bastions of Empire.

India's uniqueness provided both the government of India and the India Office considerable independence from the Treasury. The Colonial Office was not so fortunate, but once established it moved to capture what it judged to be its rightful domain not only from the Treasury but from Customs, the Post Office, and the Board of Ordinance – offices that still maintained their own officials in the colonies. Eventually, most of these jurisdictional problems were solved. The Treasury, most ancient and powerful of government agencies, however, proved a stubborn exception. Organized into a finance and four "control" divisions, it exerted in theory virtually absolute power over British expenditures both foreign and domestic. It was this claim to omnipotence in the financial sphere that led to conflict with many government offices, but particularly with the Colonial Office. In fact, Treasury control was less all-encompassing than that agency tried to assume, and the Colonial Office was in time able to establish some degree of independence from its Argus-eyed rival.

As Gladstone pointed out when he was first Lord of the Treasury and Chancellor of the Exchequer: "We are only one department side by side with others, with very limited powers; it is more after all by moral suasion . . . that our influence is exercised, than by any large power we have."[19] The Treasury was not empowered to question departmental policy, only the financial arrangements supporting that policy. But it would be illusory to think that ensuring the most efficient and economical method of implementing a policy decision did not affect policy itself.

When all is said and done, the Treasury's chief power lay in obstruction. One minister, and certainly a combination of several, could usually frustrate the exchequer at the cabinet level, if not before, but success required both energy and coordination. Robert Kubicek further explains the Treasury's real source of power as follows:

> The Treasury's role in control of expenditure was presumably subsidiary to that of Parliament. Yet, departmental estimates could not be submitted to the political arena until approved by one of the Treasury's control divisions. The spending departments had to accept the Treasury's decisions on proposed new

expenditures, subject only to reversal by the cabinet. An auxiliary branch, the comptroller and auditor-general's department, examined the manner in which the funds allocated were spent.[20]

Imperial expenditures were less easily controlled by the Treasury than domestic ones. Colonies could not be allowed to go bankrupt, and the financial status of most Crown Colonies was usually precarious. They were dependent on an uncertain local revenue that was frequently not only insufficient to pay the governor's salary but allowed absolutely no contingency for emergencies. As a result, British support was often required. In case of financial distress, the usual instrument of imperial assistance was the grant-in-aid. This subvention was awarded either to supplement a colony's general revenue or for some specific purpose. Grants-in-aid were an exception to the general rules that imperial funds could only be spent on items enumerated in parliamentary votes and that all accounts had to be balanced by year end.

For colonies with responsible government, imperially guaranteed loans rather than grants-in-aid were the key to development. The Cabinet and Parliament alone held the power to undertake an imperial guarantee, and the Treasury's role was largely a supervisory one. It oversaw colonial compliance with the regulations regarding the establishment of a sinking fund and the rules for repayment.

Until the last third of the nineteenth century, the Treasury theoretically controlled the revenue and expenditure of Crown Colonies. Annual estimates were prepared by departmental officers in the colony and were approved successively by the colonial financial officers, the governor (with the advice of the Executive and Legislative Councils), and the Treasury. Only then was the estimate reported to Parliament. No expenditure was to be incurred without prior Treasury approval.

As the power of the Colonial Office increased, fewer parliamentary returns were demanded from the colonies, and Treasury control decreased. By 1868, while the Treasury supervised the accounts of eighteen Crown Colonies, eighteen others fell under the gaze of the Colonial Office alone. Whether a colony came under Treasury or Colonial Office control was largely a matter of historical accident. The audit of the accounts of all colonies was left by law to the discretion of the Treasury, but that agency in turn agreed, so long as no imperial (i.e., British) monies were involved, to delegate the authority to the Colonial Office. Treasury audit of Crown Colony accounts was thus confined to those colonies receiving grants-in-aid. Even then, however, colonies with grants designated for specific purposes – governor's salary, colonial steamers, mail service –

needed only to forward a yearly abstract for purpose of examination.[21] Treasury control, after March, 1870, was limited to matters of imperial concern. No subject dealing with Crown Colonies was to be referred to the Treasury "except such as would be equally referred in Colonies of equal importance which possess representative institutions."[22]

On the other hand, the Treasury was still charged with supervising the annual estimates, particularly any increases in the civil establishment, of Crown Colonies receiving grants-in-aid in support of their general revenues. Supervision continued for two years after those grants had been terminated. In the case of those colonies that had not received grants in support of their general revenue but that owed money to the Home Government, had received aid in the form of a guaranteed loan, or had been awarded a specific grant-in-aid, the Colonial Office had only to furnish the Treasury with an annual statement of revenue, expenditure, and public debt.

Despite the increased colonial and Colonial Office independence, no item seemed too minute to escape the Treasury's gimlet-eyed functionaries, whether in the estimates, later requests for augmentations, or in the actual record of expenditures. It took some eight years for the Treasury to accept an accommodation regarding the accounts of Sir Theophilus Shepstone, who had led an expedition into the Transvaal in 1877. Shepstone had had the temerity to charge his official account for presents given to native chiefs: "My Lords can only express their astonishment," an aroused Treasury wrote to the Colonial Office, "that any officer should have imagined that coats, hair brushes and fishing guards, and the like would be passed without explanation, nor can they admit the explanation now offered to be satisfactory."[23] When in 1885 the Transvaal duly paid the British Government £7546.17.6 due on a loan, the Treasury promptly complained (and in error) that the payment was four pence short!! "My Lords request," the Treasury archly wrote the Colonial Office, "that the High Commissioner in South Africa might be instructed to call upon the Transvaal Government to apply this additional sum of 4d on the next occasion of payment."[24]

Although the engraving of a public seal for the government of British Guiana was in time sanctioned, the Treasury still wished to determine why the estimates for the screw press, copper counters, and box was £5.5 more than had previously been paid by St. Kitts and Nevis. With estimable moral rectitude, the Treasury concluded: " . . . My Lords are not prepared to sanction new items which cannot be warranted by recent precedent, and would ask an explanation for the increase of charges to which they refer."[25] Nor, despite the

history of British humanitarianism, did the Treasury ever sanction
the payment of fifteen shillings and two pence to Gambia ". . . on
account of the maintenance of a liberated African woman."[26] But
the Treasury was not always small minded. In 1893, for example, it
agreed to the appropriation of an additional £5 per month to hire
an extra night guard for the Mafeking jail:

> The description given in the enclosure to your letter of the escape
> from a cell in which five men were confined of two prisoners,
> one of whom had two wooden legs, by making a hole through
> or under a 14 inch brick cell wall, with the handle of a bucket,
> convinces My Lords that a single Gaoler cannot keep the prisoners
> under proper supervision at night without assistance.[27]

Perhaps the Treasury's obdurate determination to emerge trium-
phant on matters of minutiae was rooted in the almost constant
frustration it encountered on questions of greater moment. The appropriate level of a colony's military contribution was a source of
constant dispute, and it all too often produced a conflict between
the Treasury and the Colonial Office at home and between Her
Majesty's Government and the colony abroad. In the Treasury's
eyes, colonial contributions were always too low. When hostilities,
whether local, and hence exclusively a colonial responsibility, or
partly of imperial significance, erupted the colonies seemed never
to pay their appropriate share. In the end the Treasury was nearly
always forced to acquiesce in settlements with which it was totally
out of sympathy. ". . . Colonies are under a natural temptation,"
the Lords of the Treasury averred, "to prefer that the pacification
of their native neighbours should be accomplished by means of an
armed expedition at the cost of the mother country, rather than by
measures of conciliation at the expense of the colony. . . ."[28]

Nor was colonial (not to mention Colonial Office) recalcitrance in
the Treasury's eyes limited to the military sphere. The same viola-
tions of "accepted imperial financial dogma" occurred on the civil
stage as well. In January, 1888, for example, the Treasury wrote the
Colonial Office:

> Their Lordships will view with regret the refusal of the Colony
> of Vancouver Island to pay back advances made in 1859–65 for
> lighthouses in the shore of the Straits of Juan de Fuca. They are
> willing to write off the debt in actuality but they want to keep it
> on record as a warning to the Treasury that actual security must
> be taken from the government of dependencies for the repayment
> of a loan, since the instance now under consideration shows that
> a promise to pay may not be observed.[29]

If the Treasury rarely carried the day on arguments involving military or civil expenditures, it also received little support in its attempts to reduce the salaries of colonial officials in times of economic depression. At one point, however, Fiji at least acted in the recommended manner, and the Treasury was able to write approvingly:

> The financial history of Fiji affords a striking illustration, on the one hand, of the danger of increasing establishments on the faith of continuing prosperity, and, on the other, as my Lords are happy to add, of the success with which circumstances of great depression can be met by resolute self-denial and a spirit of independence.

Furthermore, when and if it became possible to restore the former salary levels, the Treasury recommended it should be made clear that the continuance of the higher rate was

> . . . dependent on the prosperity of the colony, and no restoration should be permitted until the whole of the floating debt has been redeemed and a scheme has been set on foot for repaying the imperial loan.[30]

Some evidence on the success of the Treasury in guarding the public purse from those who would squander resources on excessive administrative expenses can be seen in Table 1.1.[31] Britain maintained, in per capita terms, about the same level of administrative expenses as a typical developed country. However, while foreign-developed countries had seen expenditures increase by 50 percent in the years after 1880, there is little movement in the United Kingdom series until the very end of the period. In 1908, Winston Churchill wrote to Asquith, then the prime minister,

> . . . the expenditure of less than ten million a year not upon relief but upon machinery and thrift stimuli would make England a different country for the poor . . . . I say thrust a big slice of Bismarckianism over the whole underside of our industrial system . . . .[32]

The machinery to which Churchill referred was administrative, and the heeding of his advice resulted in an increase of administrative costs. All in all, of the sixteen economically developed countries outside the British Empire (see Appendix 1.3), twelve expended less on average than the United Kingdom over the years 1860–1912. Of the four that did not (France, Germany, the Netherlands, and Italy), two spent at more than twice the British average, that is to say that

TABLE 1.1A

ADMINISTRATIVE EXPENDITURES BY HOME, EMPIRE AND FOREIGN GOVERNMENT
(Railroads and Cost of Tax Collection Excluded)

	(£'s Per Capita)							(Percent of Total Expenditures Railroads not Included)						
	UKN	RG	DC*	India	PSts	FD	FU	UKN	RG	DC*	India	PSts	FD	FU
PANEL I: COLONY WEIGHTS														
1860-64	.13	.30	.23	.01	.04	.08	.12	6.2	11.6	23.8	3.1	22.5	8.9	23.1
1865-69	.12	.35	.22	.01	.04	.08	.09	6.0	12.9	21.2	3.5	24.6	8.4	15.4
1870-74	.09	.25	.18	.02	.06	.08	.10	5.0	9.6	17.8	4.3	20.4	7.3	16.8
1875-79	.11	.18	.16	.02	.05	.07	.08	5.1	7.3	19.0	3.6	27.0	6.7	14.9
1880-84	.23	.21	.15	.02	.06	.10	.17	9.2	5.1	16.1	4.0	22.4	7.2	16.1
1885-89	.15	.30	.15	.01	.07	.14	.13	5.2	5.2	13.6	4.4	29.1	7.5	11.0
1890-94	.12	.30	.14	.01	.05	.14	.07	4.3	5.0	11.2	4.2	23.0	7.6	12.6
1895-99	.12	.33	.12	.01	.06	.16	.13	3.5	4.4	11.6	4.2	23.8	7.9	15.9
1900-04	.12	.35	.12	.01	.05	.15	.08	2.5	5.6	11.6	4.6	17.4	7.1	14.3
1905-09	.14	.19	.10	.01	.05	.15	.12	3.5	6.0	11.2	4.6	18.5	6.5	14.7
1910-12	.39	.15	.09	.01	.05	.13	.13	9.6	4.9	9.7	5.1	16.6	5.6	14.6
AVG(d)	.15	.27	.15	.01	.05	.12	.12	5.3	7.1	15.4	4.1	22.5	7.4	15.9
PANEL II: POPULATION WEIGHTS														
1860-64	.13	.13	.11	.01	.04	.06	.11	6.2	7.9	17.0	3.1	21.8	7.3	29.0
1865-69	.12	.16	.08	.01	.04	.08	.13	6.0	9.4	12.7	3.5	21.8	8.2	28.0
1870-74	.09	.17	.07	.02	.03	.10	.12	5.0	9.3	10.6	4.3	18.1	9.7	30.6
1875-79	.11	.13	.07	.02	.03	.08	.10	5.1	5.6	11.0	3.6	17.4	8.2	21.7
1880-84	.23	.15	.08	.02	.04	.10	.06	9.2	4.7	10.6	4.0	17.6	9.1	13.5
1885-89	.15	.19	.08	.01	.04	.15	.07	5.2	5.1	10.0	4.4	14.4	9.6	12.5
1890-94	.12	.17	.08	.01	.03	.16	.07	4.3	4.8	9.1	4.2	12.2	9.6	13.2
1895-99	.12	.18	.06	.01	.03	.18	.07	3.5	4.3	8.5	4.2	12.4	8.4	11.9
1900-04	.12	.21	.05	.01	.04	.16	.09	2.5	4.7	9.6	4.6	13.1	8.1	12.1
1905-09	.14	.13	.04	.01	.03	.13	.10	3.5	3.8	8.4	4.6	12.8	6.5	10.2
1910-12	.39	.09	.04	.01	.03	.15	.09	9.6	2.6	8.4	5.1	13.0	6.7	8.4
AVG(d)	.15	.16	.07	.01	.04	.12	.09	5.3	5.8	10.6	4.1	15.9	8.3	17.5

*Top and bottom 5 percent of colonies removed.

UKN: United Kingdom National   PSts: Indian Princely States
RG: Responsible Government   FD: Foreign Developed Countries
DG: Dependent Colonies   FU: Foreign Underdeveloped Countries

the entire period they spent almost as much as Britain did in the last few years.[33]

In the Empire outside of India the scenario turns on the weights chosen to average expenditures across colonies. If each colony is given equal weight, the penchant for administration seems, despite the Treasury, to have come earlier and stayed later. The colonies with responsible government appear to have spent at levels not quite twice those prevailing in Britain and more than twice the levels in the two foreign sectors. The dependent colonies display levels about equal to those in the United Kingdom and slightly above the two foreign sectors. Only one country (the Netherlands) spent as much as the average of the colonies with responsible government; although there was substantial intercolonial variation. Among these

TABLE 1.1B

ADMINISTRATIVE EXPENDITURES BY HOME, EMPIRE AND FOREIGN GOVERNMENT
(Railroads Excluded, but Cost of Tax Collection Included)

	(£'s Per Capita)							(Percent of Total Expenditures Railroads not Included)					
	UKN	RG	DC*	India	PSts	FD	FU	UKN	RG	DC*	India	PSts	FD	FU

PANEL I: COLONY WEIGHTS

1860-64	.20	.36	.28	.04	.05	.14	.22	9.8	14.6	27.3	11.4	25.9	19.0	34.1
1865-69	.19	.41	.26	.04	.05	.16	.13	9.5	16.0	24.5	11.1	29.8	20.1	24.5
1870-74	.16	.31	.21	.05	.09	.14	.13	8.7	13.0	20.7	11.4	28.5	16.4	23.8
1875-79	.18	.24	.19	.05	.06	.14	.11	8.5	9.7	21.8	10.9	34.5	14.9	22.3
1880-84	.30	.28	.18	.05	.07	.20	.24	12.3	7.1	19.0	11.5	27.2	16.3	24.6
1885-89	.23	.38	.19	.04	.09	.29	.21	8.2	7.0	17.2	16.5	34.0	16.6	20.4
1890-94	.20	.38	.20	.03	.06	.29	.17	7.2	6.8	15.3	14.8	27.6	15.9	22.3
1895-99	.21	.42	.17	.03	.07	.32	.20	6.0	6.0	14.9	14.6	29.5	15.6	24.7
1900-04	.20	.42	.16	.04	.06	.32	.16	4.2	7.0	14.5	15.7	24.3	14.6	23.4
1905-09	.22	.25	.13	.04	.06	.31	.21	5.7	8.2	13.9	15.9	24.0	13.3	24.4
1910-12	.48	.22	.12	.03	.07	.28	.24	11.7	7.2	12.1	15.4	22.4	11.5	24.2
AVG(d)	.23	.34	.19	.04	.07	.23	.18	8.2	9.4	18.5	13.5	28.2	16.0	24.4

PANEL II: POPULATION WEIGHTS

1860-64	.20	.18	.15	.04	.05	.13	.15	9.8	11.0	22.9	11.4	28.1	15.9	39.1
1865-69	.19	.22	.11	.04	.05	.17	.15	9.5	12.7	17.7	11.1	29.2	17.0	33.2
1870-74	.16	.22	.10	.05	.04	.17	.14	8.7	11.8	15.3	11.4	26.1	17.3	35.3
1875-79	.18	.17	.10	.05	.04	.14	.12	8.5	7.6	15.8	10.9	24.6	15.1	27.1
1880-84	.30	.20	.11	.05	.05	.17	.10	12.3	6.4	15.0	11.5	23.2	15.4	21.7
1885-89	.23	.26	.11	.04	.05	.26	.11	8.2	7.0	14.2	16.5	19.6	16.7	19.8
1890-94	.20	.24	.11	.03	.04	.30	.11	7.2	6.6	12.8	14.8	17.2	17.6	19.6
1895-99	.21	.26	.09	.03	.04	.36	.10	6.0	6.1	12.2	14.6	17.9	17.9	16.9
1900-04	.20	.27	.06	.04	.06	.35	.13	4.2	6.1	12.3	15.7	18.7	17.9	17.8
1905-09	.22	.19	.05	.04	.04	.31	.16	5.7	5.5	10.7	15.9	17.1	15.1	16.5
1910-12	.48	.15	.05	.03	.04	.29	.15	11.7	4.3	10.5	15.4	17.4	13.3	13.2
AVG(d)	.23	.22	.10	.04	.05	.24	.13	8.2	7.9	14.6	13.5	21.8	16.2	23.8

*Top and bottom 5 percent of colonies removed.

UKN: United Kingdom National
RG: Responsible Government
DG: Dependent Colonies
PSts: Indian Princely States
FD: Foreign Developed Countries
FU: Foreign Underdeveloped Countries

colonies where, of course, Treasury control was absent, those in Australia averaged £.35, New Zealand £.25, South Africa £.16, and North America £.08. The reader should bear in mind that while to a substantial degree Canada was administered at the local and provincial level, even in Newfoundland the figure was only £.12. In the dependent colonies, the level of administrative expenditure appears to roughly correlate with seniority in the Empire. The highest levels were in the Caribbean and the West Coast of Africa, the lowest in the new African and Asian colonies.

If, however, the averages reflect population weights, the Treasury's performance appears far better. By that measure, even with no supervisor, the colonies with responsible government were spending at rates only about equal to those at home and about a quarter more than the foreign developed nations. The difference is in substantial part caused by the treatment of the six Australian colonies, colonies that were characterized by very expensive administrations. In the dependent colonies the change of weights also yields a very different story. In part the lower figures reflect some economies of scale in administration but in part it also appears to reflect the Treasury's ability to keep expenditures in the largest colonies under very tight control. Moreover, there was a substantial decrease in per capita administrative expenditures over time, and the colonies appear to have spent about a third less than the countries in the foreign underdeveloped sector. A comparison of the two series suggests that the Treasury was at times very efficient, but in the older and smaller colonies it seems not to have exerted the control accepted history would lead one to believe prevailed. For example, the average administrative expenditure was £.54 in Gambia, £.53 in Bermuda, and £.42 in Gibraltar.

In India, stylized stories of the *Raj* to the contrary, there is no question that administrative expenditures were very low. The Indian government on average spent only about £.01 per person per year, and administration absorbed only slightly more than 4 percent of the government of India's budget. These figures are much below the levels observed in the underdeveloped world, and about one-fourth those of the Princely States. The economies of scale can be seen clearly from a comparison of India with the rest of the dependent Empire. The coefficient of the (population)^2 term of a regression on per capita administrative expense for the dependent colonies is both negative and significant.[34] The tendency toward "thin" administration is demonstrated by a comparison of the number of employees per capita serving the India and Colonial Offices in the mid-90s. Given the relative populations of India and the rest of the Empire and the observed economies of scale, one would expect that the number of India Office employees per capita in the field would have been about one-half the number serving the Colonial Office. In fact, the ratio was less than one-fourth.[35]

Table 1.1B displays comparative administrative expenses, this time including the costs of tax collection. In most cases, this adjustment makes little difference. But in the case of India, per capita administrative expenses rise from £.01 to £.04 and, as a percentage of governmental budget, from 4.1 to 13.5. The explanation lies only in part in the increased attention devoted to revenue collection after the uprising of 1858. The 1908 edition of the *Imperial Gazeteer of India* contends that "... since the days of the Mutiny, India has been equipped with the apparatus of a modern civilised state." What was left unsaid was the decision by the government of India, for political reasons, to maintain in addition the apparatus associated with an archaic, complex, and highly traditional society. Much of the increased expense associated with raising taxes in the latter part of the century resulted from the superimposition of a "modern apparatus" on such existing taxes as the United Provinces' *patwari cess* – an assessment that did little save support village revenue officers. The consequence was both a very complicated tax structure and considerable duplication!

To assume that the Colonial Office judged the Treasury to be nothing more than an unattractive nuisance would be a mistake. It was rarely averse to using supposed Treasury opposition as the pretext for disallowing certain items in the colonial estimates. In 1891, Charles Lucas, then private secretary to the permanent undersecretary in the Colonial Office, Sir Robert Herbert, wrote on the question of the Ceylon military contribution:

> Of late, as far as I can judge, the leading people in the colony have been more and more regarding [the Colonial Office] as their friend, and it is very important to maintain such a feeling. I incline to think less harm would be done in the long run if a larger increase were exacted, after it had been made patent that the Colonial Office had made its stand and been overborne . . . . [36]

Interagency rivalry in Britain itself was only one of the complexities underlying imperial governance. Of greater importance was the relationship between the parent country and its often unruly offspring. Although most of the colonies of the dependent Empire enjoyed legislative institutions, they tended to be advisory, and the governor and the Colonial Office remained very much in control. In those possessions blessed with responsible government, however, the governor was at best a constitutional monarch. Technically, he enjoyed a veto over colonial legislation or the power to refer it to London "for the signification of Her Majesty's pleasure." However, these rights were invoked but rarely and then usually with disastrous results. Still, the knowledge that in theory the British Government retained very real powers over legislation could well have caused considerable resentment and a very real sense of subservience in the dominions.

To prevent the development of stress and to relieve these feelings of frustration and inferiority, the British in 1887 established a new institution. As a part of the celebration of Queen Victoria's Golden Jubilee, the British government invited delegates from the Crown Colonies and Dominions to a conference in London.[37] This assemblage was the first of the Imperial Conferences (then called Colonial

Conferences). The conferences (soon limited to the Dominions alone) provided an institutional mechanism for introducing structural change into the political matrix and became in many ways the key to the survival of the Empire. Of all the areas of common concern, Foreign Affairs remained most directly under the control of the British government. To a large extent this monopoly was the product of the Dominions' assumption that, since they shouldered virtually none of the costs of defense, nonconsultation on international questions meant noninvolvement. World War I was to prove how very wrong they had been.

This sketch then, in brief, captures the essence of the British Empire that evolved in the nineteenth century, and these were the institutions that shaped both economic and political behavior. They established the context of Empire and the environment in which the business and political communities met, competed, and cooperated to produce what can be termed the "British imperial experience."

IV. The study

The study of the profitability of Empire begins with an examination of the flows of long-term finance through the London market. Here, the relative importance of domestic and Empire finance, the demands that competed for British savings, is assessed. Chapter 3 develops an analysis of the private rates of return on home, foreign, and Empire finance. It not only provides estimates of the overall private "profitability of Empire" but attempts to identify those industries that yielded the highest returns. Chapter 4 examines the patterns of government expenditure in an effort to discover if the official organs of the British government (the governors, their councils, the Colonial and India Offices, and Parliament) set public expenditures in a manner designed to favor British business. Chapters 5 and 6 provide an estimate of the British "subsidy" to the Empire. The former deals explicitly with the defense component of that subsidy, the latter with the remainder (interest, loans, grants-in-aid, mail, and telegraph subsidies). Chapter 7 draws on a sample of stockholders to identify the investors who placed their funds in firms primarily doing business in the Empire and contrasts them with those who invested in domestic and foreign enterprises. Chapter 8 examines the tax receipts in Britain and the colonies in an attempt to identify the groups in the Empire who would have been forced to shoulder an increased tax burden had the imperial subsidy been removed, and those in Britain itself who actually paid the taxes that supported the subsidy. Chapter 9 deals with relations between unions, business (individual companies), chambers of commerce, trade associations, etc., and the House of Commons. It also treats patterns of parliamentary support for imperial affairs in the context of class, party, and constituency; and Chapter 10 provides a summary of the preceding discussions.

One final caveat. What did happen can only be explained by contrasting the events that did occur with those that did not. Since almost anything "might" have happened, the specification of the "correct" counterfactual is a critical ingredient of any historical analysis. Professor Edelstein, for example, in his work on the gains of imperialism, has suggested two possible counterfactual models: the "marginal nonimperialist" and the "strong nonimperialist."[38] The former assumes a world where a colony becomes independent at the moment the attempt is made to measure the gains, and the latter that the colony had been independent of British rule throughout modern economic history.

The ability to make "strong" or elaborate counterfactual arguments, however, depends on the ability to model an elaborate world, and then to deduce the effects of some assumed change in a precise manner. In the case of the British Empire the specification of a dynamic multisectional world is not very difficult, but requires a far more elaborate mathematical model than any yet conceived. What would, for example, have been the position of India if the British had never set foot on the subcontinent? Would there have been a single Indian economy, a vast number of small states, or, perhaps, Portuguese or French rule? Does absence of Empire imply not only the want of a political connection, but also the absence of western European migration? How, under these conditions, should Australia and New Zealand be modeled – as similar to the United States or as completely undeveloped primitive islands?

In the absence of a formal, well-specified model of global development, the problem of constructing an appropriate counterfactual argument is at least difficult, and probably impossible. It is, of course, always possible to assume one's own conclusions, but such assumptions, although logically valid, do not appear to move the level of discourse forward in a useful fashion. In this book, reasonably appropriate ad hoc counterfactuals are used which are often suggested by the previous literature. Given the current state of theoretical knowledge, it is rarely useful to do more.[39] At least the problems inherent in the use of such ad hoc counterfactuals are immediately apparent, and it is sometimes possible to evaluate the sensitivity of a given conclusion to reasonable variations in the counterfactual assumptions.

APPENDIX 1.1

THE GROWTH OF EMPIRE

Colony Name	Date Added*	In Empire 1860	Change 1860-69	Change 1870-79	Change 1880-89	Change 1890-99	Change 1900-09	From	To
		(1,000s of Square Miles)						Dates for Which Financial Records Are Included	
A. Responsible Government									
1. Australia	1901	(2,974.6)							
a. New South Wales(1)		310.4						1860	1902
b. Queensland(1)		670.5						1860	1902
c. South Australia(1)		380.1						1860	1902
d. South Australia(2) (Northern Territory)		523.6						1887	1902
e. Tasmania(1)		26.2						1860	1902
f. Victoria(1)		87.9						1860	1902
g. Western Australia(1)		975.9						1860	1902
2. Canada	1867	(3,894.7)						1867	1913
a. Nova Scotia(3)		21.4							
b. New Brunswick(3)		28.0							
c. Ontario(3)		260.9							
d. Quebec(3)		351.9							
e. Manitoba(5)		238.7							
f. British Columbia(6)		357.6							
g. Prince Edward Island(7)		2.2							
h. Alberta(8)		253.5							
i. Saskatchewan(8)		250.7							
j. Yukon		207.1							
k. Northwest Territory(4)		1,922.7							
3. Newfoundland		(162.7)							
a. Newfoundland		42.7							
b. Labrador		120.0							
4. New Zealand		103.3							
5. Union of South Africa	1910	(473.2)						1911	1912
a. Cape Colony		277.0						1860	1910
b. Natal		35.4						1860	1910
c. Orange River	1900						50.4	1902	1910
d. Transvaal	1902						110.4	1903	1910
B. India									
a. British India		1,097.8		53.8			38.7	1860	1913
b. Princely States		675.3		78.0				1860	1913
C. Dependent Colonies									
1. Asia									
a. Ceylon		25.3						1860	1912
b. Straights Settlements		1.6						1864	1912
c. Labuan		0.0						1860	1906
d. Hong Kong		0.4						1860	1912
e. Federated Malay States	1896							1895	1912
(1) Perak	1874			7.9				1882	1894
(2) Selangor	1874			3.2				1883	1894
(3) Sugei-Ujong	1875-76			2.6				1891	1895
(4) Pahang	1887				14.0			1891	1894
(5) Negri-Sembilan	1874-89							1883	1894
f. North Borneo	1881				31.1			1891	1912
g. Brunei	1888				2.6				
h. Sarawak	1888				42.0			1896	1912
i. Unfederated Malay States	1909								
(1) Kelantan	1909						5.0		
(2) Trenggam	1909						6.0		
(3) Kedah	1909						3.2		
(4) Perlis	1909						.3		
(5) Johore	1885				9.0				
j. Weihei	1898					.3			
2. Pacific									
a. Fiji	1874			7.4				1876	1912
b. British New Guinea	1884				90.5			1889	1912
c. British Solomon Islands	1893					14.6		1898	1913
d. Gilbert & Ellice Isle	1896-99					.2		1896	1912
e. Tonga	1900						.4	1905	1912
3. Africa									
a. Ascencion & St. Helena		.1						1860	1912
b. Gambia		4.0						1860	1912
c. Sierra Leone		30.0						1860	1912
d. Gold Coast		91.7						1860	1912
e. Lagos	1861			28.6				1868	1906
f. Basutoland	1868			11.7				1877	1913
g. Egypt	1882				400.0			1882	1913
h. Somali Coast Protect.	1884				68.0			1898	1913
i. Bechuanaland	1885				275.0			1897	1913
j. Niger Coast & So.Nigeria	1885				91.9			1868	1912

APPENDIX 1.1   (Continued)

(1,000's of Square Miles)

Colony Name	Date Added	In Empire 1860	Change 1860-69	Change 1870-79	Change 1880-89	Change 1890-99	Change 1900-09	Dates for Which Financial Records Are Included From	To
k. Northern Nigeria	1885				276.0			1901	1913
l. Zanzibar	1890					1.0		1892	1912
m. Southern Rhodesia	1890					37.9		1905	1912
n. Nyasaland	1891					291.0			
o. Northern Rhodesia	1893					148.6		1904	1912
p. Uganda	1893					110.3		1895	1913
q. Kenya (Br. East Africa)	1895					245.1		1896	1913
r. Sudan	1898					1,014.6			
s. Swaziland	1903						6.7	1905	1913
4. Indian Ocean									
a. Aden (inc Perim & Socotra)		10.4							
b. Mauritius		.8						1860	1912
c. Seychelles		.2						1886	1912
5. Europe									
a. Gibralter		.0						1860	1913
b. Malta		.1						1860	1913
c. Ionian Islands		.7	-.7					1860	1863
d. Cyprus	1878			3.6				1879	1913
6. Carribean and South America									
a. Antigua		.2						1867	1913
b. Bahamas		4.4						1860	1913
c. Barbadoes		.2						1860	1912
d. Bermuda		.0						1860	1912
e. British Guinea		89.5						1860	1912
f. British Honduras		8.6						1860	1913
g. British Virgin Islands		.1						1860	1913
h. Dominica		.3						1860	1913
i. Falkland Islands		4.6						1860	1913
j. Grenada		.1						1860	1913
k. Jamaica		4.5						1860	1913
l. Monteserrat		.0						1860	1913
m. St. Kitts-Nevis-Anquilla		.2						1860	1913
n. St. Lucia		.2						1860	1913
o. St. Vincent		.2						1860	1913
p. Tabago		.1						1860	1913
q. Trinidad		1.9						1860	1913
r. Turks Island		.2						1860	1912
s. Virgin Islands		.1						1860	1913

Total Responsible Government		7,477.7					160.4	7,608.1	
Total India		1,773.1		131.8			38.7	1,943.6	
Total Dependent Colonies		280.7	39.6	24.7	940.1	1,863.6	21.6	3,170.3	
Total		9,501.5	39.6	156.5	940.1	1,863.6	220.7	12,722.0	
% Change			0.4	1.6	9.7	17.5	1.8	33.9	

*In the case of colonies with responsible government, the date when this status was attained.

(1) a+b+c+e+f+g into Commonwealth 1901	(4) Into Dominion of Canada 1869	(7) Into Dominion of Canada 1873
(2) Into Commonwealth 1911	(5) Into Dominion of Canada 1870	(8) Into Dominion of Canada 1905
(3) Into Dominion of Canada 1867	(6) Into Dominion of Canada 1871	

APPENDIX 1.2
EMPIRE POPULATION BY STATUS

	UK	RG	DC	India	Dependent Colonies	Overseas Empire	Total	UK	RG	DC	India	Dependent Empire
	(in 1,000s)							(Percents)				
1862	29,245	5,434	3,647	139,360	143,007	148,441	177,686	16.5	3.1	2.1	78.4	80.5
67	30,409	5,961	4,319	148,674	152,993	188,954	189,363	16.1	3.1	2.3	78.5	80.8
1872	31,874	7,018	5,399	160,788	166,187	173,205	205,079	15.5	3.4	2.6	78.4	81.0
77	33,576	7,834	6,167	177,702	183,869	191,703	225,279	14.9	3.5	2.7	78.9	81.6
1882	35,206	8,801	13,800	209,017	222,822	231,623	266,824	13.2	3.3	5.2	78.3	83.5
87	36,598	9,795	15,342	260,741	276,083	285,878	322,476	11.3	3.0	4.8	80.9	85.6
1892	38,134	10,876	18,337	288,683	307,020	317,896	356,030	10.7	3.1	5.2	81.1	86.2
97	39,937	12,258	25,993	292,207	318,200	330,458	370,395	10.8	3.3	7.0	78.9	85.9
1902	41,483	14,331	39,405	296,453	335,858	350,189	391,672	10.6	3.7	10.1	75.7	85.7
07	43,737	21,877	46,258	301,795	348,043	369,930	413,667	10.6	5.3	11.2	73.0	84.1
1912	45,436	24,186	51,852	322,441	374,293	398,479	443,915	10.2	5.4	11.7	72.6	84.3

UK: United Kingdom
RG: Responsible Government
DG: Dependent Colonies

NOTE: Anglo Egyptian Sudan is not included. If it were the 1902 Dependent Empire figure would be increased to about 2,000,000; the 1907 figure by about 2,500,000; and the 1912 by about 3,000,000.

APPENDIX 1.3

Foreign Countries and Indian Princely States
Data From Which for the Years Indicated are Used in this Study

COUNTRIES   YEARS

Foreign Developed
     Austria-Hungary   1860-1912
     Belgium   1860-1914
     Denmark   1860-1913
     France   1860-1912
     Germany   1871-1912
     Italy   1864-1913
     Japan   1900-1913
     Netherlands   1860-1868; 1881-1905
     Norway   1890-1913
     Portugal   1861-1914
     Prussia   1860-1868
     Russia   1860-1912
     Spain   1860-1913
     Sweden   1860-1913
     Switzerland   1860-1868; 1896-1899
     United States of America   1860-1913

Foreign Undeveloped
     Argentina   1863-1913
     Brazil   1860-1912
     Bulgaria   1905-1912
     Colombia   1873-1913
     Costa Rica   1868-1913
     Ecuador   1885-1904
     Egypt   1880; 1881
     El Salvador   1900-1913
     Guatemala   1869-1913
     Haiti   1892; 1893
     Honduras   1888-1913
     Japan   1868-1899
     Liberia   1892-1912
     Mexico   1869-1913
     Nicaragua   1895-1912
     Paraguay   1887-1914
     Peru   1860-1872; 1885-1913
     Romania   1883-1890
     Santo Domingo   1884; 1891; 1901-1912
     Serbia   1907-1911
     Siam   1894-1912
     Tunisia   1896-1912
     Turkey   1860-1913
     Uruguay   1880-1913
     Venezuela   1884-1913

Indian Princely States
     Ali-Rajpur   1888-1897; 1909-1913
     Baroda   1880-1912
     Barwani   1888-1897
     Cochin   1889-1913
     Dhar   1888-1897; 1912-1913
     Hyderabad   1884-1912
     Jamkhandi   1889-1913
     Jhabua   1888-1897
     Jobat   1888-1897; 1912-1913
     Kapurthala   1874-1889
     Kolhapur   1874-1913
     Manipur   1893-1913
     Mysore   1861-1912
     Pudukkottai   1879-1913
     Rampur   1892-1898; 1909-1913
     Savantvadi   1870-1912
     Teri   1893-1913
     Travancore   1865-1913

2 The export of British finance: 1865–1914

I. Introduction

In the late nineteenth century a tourist might view the Crystal Palace or the Tower Bridge as evidence of Britain's development. If that tourist were a businessman from the American Midwest or the German Ruhr he would be likely to equate power and development with sparks from the forges of Cleveland or the sound of riveting from the shipyards of the Clyde. It was, however, the City that drew the attention of the foreign "men of money," be they J. P. Morgan, the American financier, or Gustav von Meuissen, the president of the Darmstadtler Bank. Christened the eighth wonder of the modern world, the City provided the link that bound the vast accumulations of Victorian savings to investments in locations as disparate as the Midlands, the Midwest, and the Mid-Pacific. It was to the City that Andrew Carnegie had turned to finance his first steel enterprise, and it was there, too, that the Nizam of Hyderabad had gone for funds to finance his railway in the hills of South Central India. Nor was the market limited to overseas investment; it also continued to fuel the engines of domestic industrial growth. Vickers, for example, drew extensively on the City to finance its growth from a small specialty steel producer on the River Don to the armament giant of the early twentieth century.

Perhaps even more important, the interest and profits generated by these investments flowed back into London and were a major source of the prosperity that characterized the British economy. Schumpeter, in discussing the "third Kondratieff" – a cycle caused, in most of the world, by the innovation of electricity and electrical equipment – noted that "the English case presents a striking contrast." So striking were its features, that he labeled the period the "neomercantilist" Kondratieff.[1]

> The strong increase in capital exports . . . complements this. Foreign and particularly colonial enterprise and lending was the dominant feature of the period. Rubber, oil, South African gold and diamonds, Egyptian cotton, sugar, irrigation, South American (Argentinian) land developments, the financing of Japan and colonial communities (municipalities, particularly Canadian) afford examples of the way in which England, more than through

30

domestic development, took part in the industrial process which carried the Kondratieff prosperity. The London money market concerned itself mainly with foreign and colonial issues to an extent never equaled in England or in any other country. The great issuing houses in particular, almost exclusively cultivated this business, managing, sometimes rigging, the market for it.[2]

Schumpeter wrote just before the outbreak of the Second World War, but the importance of the London market was well understood by contemporaries as well. Among the classical economists, both Mill and Marx had worried about the effects of overseas capital transfers. To the former the flow provided a means to increase the supply of cheap food, establish markets for British manufacturers, and arrest the decline in the rate of profit in England:

> Thus the exportation of capital is an agent of great efficiency in extending the field for that which remains and it may be said truly that up to a certain point the more capital that we send away the more we shall possess and be able to retain at home.[3]

Marx too noted the flow, and surprisingly not only was his analysis similar to Mill's, but so were his conclusions.

> If capital is sent to foreign countries, it is not done because there is absolutely no employment at home. It is done because it can be employed at a higher rate in the foreign country .... These higher rates of profits ... sent home ... enter into the equalization of the general rate of profit and keep it up to that extent.[4]

Nor did Marx argue that the increased foreign rate was necessarily dependent on exploitation. While such exploitation was one possible cause, there was also, he argued, a substantial probability that the difference was due merely to the transitory monopoly profits attributed to the innovation of new production techniques in the underdeveloped country, "in the same way a manufacturer who exploits a new invention before it becomes general undersells his competitors and yet sells his commodities above their individual value."[5]

Alfred Marshall shared the view of Mill and Marx that foreign investment contributed positively to domestic welfare, although he admitted that there were numerous advantages to domestic commitments. On balance, however, it was clear to Marshall that overseas investment, in particular investment in the colonies, was very attractive since "Capital is abundant in England; and she has few openings in which it can be made to yield a very high return."[6] Like Marx, Marshall saw the high overseas rates as a temporary phenomenon resting on rents attached to new lands and new processes.

As the relative position of the British economy shifted, so economists' views on the utility of capital exports also changed. Few, however, doubted that the exports redounded to the benefit of the recipients; their concerns were with the impact of those transfers on the domestic economy. It was not until the present century that such investments came to be viewed by some as an unmitigated evil, injuring both the lender and the borrower.

Hardly had the Boer War ended than J. A. Hobson launched an attack on all things imperial beginning with the oft-quoted remark that "Although the new Imperialism has been bad business for the nation, it has been good business for certain classes and certain trades within the nation."[7] Hobson's conclusions have provided the basis for three-quarters of a century of neo-Marxist rhetoric. Engels wrote " . . . colonization today is merely a subsidiary of the stock exchange." Rosa Luxemburg argued that "Imperialism is the political expression of the accumulation of capital." But it was Lenin whose definition of imperialism included " . . . the merging of bank capital with industrial capital, and the creation on the basis of this 'financial capital' of a financial oligarchy, [and] the export of capital which has been extremely important as distinguished from the export of commodities . . . . "[8] It was also Lenin who focused his attention on the concentration of British overseas finance in the Empire. He argued "The principal sphere of investment of British capital are the British colonies," and he put the Empire's share at almost 50 percent.[9]

Recognition of the importance of capital outflows was not limited to academic economists and critics of the system. Contemporary politicians took note of the phenomenon and speculated about its impact on the British economy. Joseph Chamberlain, for example, was convinced that capital transfers were the sinews of Empire, and that prosperity both overseas and at home rested on a continuation of those flows. Lenin may have gone too far when he concluded that "leading British bourgeois politicians fully appreciated the connection between what might be called purely economic and the political-social roots of imperialism."[10] Chamberlain, however, certainly espoused the principle that Empire should be a source of monetary profit to the parent country; and he believed that those profits should be supported by substantial capital transfers, even if those transfers had to be subsidized. In a famous Birmingham address he laid the basis for the policy of that "creative imperialism" he attempted to effect during his tenure at the Colonial Office. To Chamberlain it was

> . . . not enough to occupy certain great spaces of the world's surface unless you can make the best of them, unless you are willing to develop them. We are the landlords of a great estate; it is the duty of the landlord to develop his estate. . . . In my opinion, it

would be the wisest course for the government of this country
to use British capital and British credit in order to create an instrument of trade in all . . . new important countries.[11]

Of course, Treasury objections severely constrained official actions,
but the issue was important and it did produce a plethora of policy
recommendations and at least some monetary subsidies.[12]

In the absence of a firm statistical base, it was clearly impossible
for J. A. Hobson, Lenin, or even Chamberlain to provide an accurate
assessment of the role of the London capital market. In 1914, C. K.
Hobson in his analysis of financial exports provided a partial foundation. Since that time understanding of the subject has been advanced by the endeavors of Feis, Jenks, Cairncross, Segal, and
Simon.[13] While others have also concerned themselves with the level
of capital export, this group has approached the question through
examination of the issues of financial instruments. To Jenks this
implied the detailed study of hundreds of individual issues, but to
Segal and Simon, as to Hobson, it involved the scrutiny of the financial press, which for nineteenth-century Britain meant the *Investor's Monthly Manual, The Stock Exchange Annual Yearbook,* and
Burdett's Official Intelligencer.

This chapter reworks those sources, provides some substantial
revisions of the general conclusion of the earlier work, and, more
importantly, extends those previous studies in several new directions. Since there is no straightforward relationship between financial issues and capital transfers, any approach presuming such a
relationship has been severely criticized; and as research produced
more direct estimates of capital transfers, academic interest has
shifted away from the scrutiny of financial issues. For this chapter
the criticism is irrelevant, since the focus is on the financial investments actually made by the British; and the new-issues series do
provide a record of the actual composition of new paper investment.

The shift in economists' attention from finance to capital is not
surprising. For the great majority of questions it is the level of the
real flows that is important, and the earlier excursion into finance
was engendered almost solely by a desire to acquire an adequate
proxy for those real transfers. From the point of view of certain
questions in economic history, however (and the political economy
of imperialism is one of those questions), it is the financial rather
than the real flows that are more relevant. For economists the most
important questions concern the magnitude of the transfers from
the United Kingdom to the rest of the world. For questions involving
finance capitalism as outlined by Lenin and Hobson, the central
issues involve the financial relations between the domestic and over-

seas sectors. Use of real rather than financial data for this latter purpose raises at least two serious problems.

First, use of real flows may distort the analysis because of the way investments are distributed between the home and overseas markets. Consider two firms. Both raise £1,000,000 on the London capital market; however, one invests the entire amount in tea plantations in Assam, while the other divides its new resources between similar plantations and distribution facilities in the United Kingdom. The first firm has invested twice as much overseas as the second, but an analysis based on capital transfers would miss the fact that ceteris paribus both firms have an equal interest in maintaining an Empire connection (i.e., both have £1,000,000 at risk, and the level of that risk may be related to the strength of the Empire connection).

A second source of distortion rests on the treatment of "rolling over" in the calculation of capital transfers. Consider a firm that sells shares worth £100,000 in a Colorado cattle ranch in the 1870s. A few years later the enterprise is sold to American interests, and the proceeds are invested in a new enterprise in the Canadian prairies. The real capital series show an overseas transfer at the time of the first investment, but the figures are not affected by the second transaction. From the point of view of British Empire relations, however, it is only the latter transaction that is relevant. The financial data, on the other hand, would reflect both stock issues, and, although overstating the total amount of capital transferred, provide an accurate assessment of the amount of finance made available to the United States in the 1870s and to the Empire a few years later. From the point of view of this work, it matters little whether the source of those funds was new savings or disentanglements from past accumulations, whether it represented new overseas transfers or merely the rolling over of funds long since in place outside the British Isles.

The new-issues series provide an imperfect but superior index of imperial economic activity and probably a better measure of the connection between Britain and the Empire. Some feeling for the differences between the two measures can be obtained by a comparison of the new foreign lending figures used by Edelstein with the annual series of capital called up.[14]

Reliance on the financial series is not to deny that for some purposes the length of the investment may well be important; this point has recently been made (somewhat obliquely) by D. C. M. Platt.[15] If the financial series are used to estimate the amount of portfolio finance in place at any one time, it is necessary to know not only the annual volume but the maturity of those issues as well. The amount of American railroad finance held by the British public in 1914 is not the sum of the issues from 1830 to 1914, but that total *less* repayments. To the extent that there were significant differences in the maturities of home, foreign, and Empire issues, it is misleading to use the simple sum as an index of the total finance transferred. External evidence, however, suggests that to the degree there were significant differences, it was domestic issues that had the longest maturities.[16] Thus such summary totals, although inflated, minimize the importance of the domestic component and provide a maximum estimate of the proportion of foreign and Empire transfers. It is in this latter context that they are used in this analysis.

The figures cited in this study do not include the finance transferred by nonpublic companies, by some public companies floating issues on provincial exchanges, and by direct investment. It is possible that inclusion of those omitted transfers might have changed the results. Subsidiary evidence, however, indicates that the omissions tended to be concentrated in domestic issues. The provincial exchanges were inclined to specialize in domestic securities, and the bulk of private offerings were domestic. Taken together, these factors suggest that the estimates of the proportion of foreign and Empire securities can be viewed as providing a maximum evaluation of their actual importance to the British market. Moreover, what overseas flows there were appear to have been relatively small and fairly closely correlated with the reported measure. Thus, it appears unlikely that the general conclusions would have been much altered if allowance for the omitted transfers had been made. Still the caveat remains: this chapter is entitled "the export of finance" not "the export of capital." It focuses on the spatial and industrial distribution of finance, not on the amount raised by the British savers nor on the level of the accumulated total of overseas finance.

The series are drawn from the same financial press on which C. K. Hobson and Segal and Simon based their work, but some earlier errors have been corrected. Both spatial and industrial distributions have been analyzed and the Empire has been divided into those colonies with responsible government and the dependent Empire. The series should be viewed as an index of the capital calls, and the actual totals are almost certainly higher than the figures reported.

The basic tables provide three alternative measures of the financial flows. The "minimum" series includes only those issues that are (1) actually reported and (2) reported as taken up entirely within the United Kingdom. The "intermediate" series is also limited to "entirely taken up in the United Kingdom" issues, but, in addition to those enumerated in the minimum series, includes adjustments for calls whose presence can be inferred from existing reports.[17] Finally, the "maximum" series includes calls reported as "partly abroad" issues, adjusted for inferred nonreported calls.

Given the focus on the spatial and industrial distribution of finance, no attempt has been made to adjust these figures, either for those portions of issues reported as sold on the UK market alone that were purchased by overseas residents, nor for the foreign and Empire securities initially held in the United Kingdom but later repatriated. D. C. M. Platt has recently concluded that these omissions were important for a study of capital transfer, particularly after the turn of the century, and that a correction for them could reduce the estimates of the British holdings of overseas symbolic capital at the outbreak of the First World War by more than 40 percent.[18] Neither omission is directly relevant for this study, and the latter not at all. To the extent that a portion of the initial offerings passed immediately into colonial or foreign hands, the British contribution (as opposed to that of the London capital market) to colonial and foreign finance is overstated. A study of the stockholders from a sample of such corporations suggests that about 16 percent of foreign securities were foreign-held, and about 2.5 percent of colonial shares were held by foreigners and an additional 8 percent by Empire residents.[19] Such purchases do not, however, appear to have biased the conclusions about the spatial and industrial distributions of "British" funds.

While the data thus produced differ in some ways from the general outlines proposed first by C. K. Hobson and revised by Segal–Simon and Simon, the primary purpose of this exercise is not to replace one set of estimates with another – the differences are relatively minor – but to expand the coverage of those earlier series, and to make it possible to provide a quantitative estimate of the extent and character of "financial imperialism." Simon and Segal extended Hobson's aggregate by providing a continent-by-continent breakdown of financial flows, and some estimates of the industrial composition of those flows. It is possible to refine those estimates further and provide: (1) a measure of the industrial distribution of the flows to each continent, and (2) a measure of the size and the industrial composition of the financial transfers to the UK domestic market and to each part of the Empire (that is, to the colonies with responsible government, dependent colonies, and to India). This latter breakdown is a necessary prerequisite if the goal is an accurate assessment of the neo-Marxist view of the late nineteenth century.

Since C. K. Hobson's estimates are based on "capital created" rather than "capital called," it is difficult to provide an exact comparison; however, a simple regression suggests that there is a high degree of association between Hobson's figures and all of the three new series (depending on the series chosen, the correlation coefficients range from .77 to .83). A more direct comparison is available with the Segal-Simon and Simon estimates. The correlation coefficients for the minimum and intermediate series are .92 and .93, respectively, but the maximum series suggests a slightly lower degree of association (.82). Since Simon has allocated the partly abroad issues between Britain and the rest of the world, it is probably not surprising that his estimates fall, in general, between the minimum and maximum estimates. Over the entire fifty years, although subject to substantial year-to-year variation, the minimum estimate is something more than three-quarters of the Segal–Simon/Simon figure, the intermediate about equal (97 percent, but almost exactly equal after 1885), and the maximum about 17 percent higher (only 3 percent after 1885). The differences between these and the earlier estimates appear significant only in two half-decades, 1895–99 and 1910–14. In the former instance the Segal–Simon/Simon figures are about 12 percent above the "maximum" figure, and in the latter about half that amount. Although the way in which the Simon data are reported make direct comparisons difficult, it appears that the major source of the differences in the period 1895–99 rests in the Empire agriculture and extractive estimates, particularly those for North America, but to a lesser extent those for Africa, Asia, and Australasia as well. In the last quinquennium the major differences appear to have been in the estimates for Europe and North America (the differences are about the same for Empire and foreign sectors), and about half of the total discrepancy can be accounted for by the estimate for the agriculture and extractive sector.[20]

II. The data: gross flows

With the exception of the 1870s, when French War Loans and U.S. Treasury borrowing bloat the maximum series, the three estimates indicate similar trends in the volume of total finance.[21] In the interest of simplicity, and given the underlying similarity, the remainder of this discussion is cast largely in terms of the minimum series. Annual flows averaged something less than £40 million per year in the late 1860s, rose to about £55 million in the early 1870s, and to more than £90 million between 1875 and 1884. From then until the end of the century the annual total fluctuated between £70 and £85 million, but thereafter increased steadily. It was more than £130 million in 1900–4, £145 million in 1905–9 and £175 million in 1910–14. In "real" pounds of 1913 (that is adjusted for changes in the price level), those total flows averaged £40 million over the decade 1865–74; £75 million in 1875–84; £98 million in 1885–94; £130 million in 1895–1904, and £173 million over the last pre-war decade.

Clearly, the British market directed a vast quantity of finance into a myriad of activities throughout the world. To put these aggregate figures into perspective, during the peak years (the late 1880s and the immediate pre-war period) the market handled about £4.5 each year for every man, woman, and child in England, Scotland, and Wales; and, even in the periods of low activity, the average was in excess of £1.5. Since national income amounted on average to only about £40 per person per year, it is easy to see why Lenin spoke of "Finance Capitalism."

Europe may well have been the world's banker, but Britain was the majority stockholder in that enterprise. For capital as opposed to finance, it is estimated that Britain accounted for 75 percent of all international movements in 1900, and although its share declined thereafter, it was still in excess of 40 percent in 1913. In the case of foreign investment in the United States, for example, the United Kingdom's share of total foreign investment is estimated to have been 80 percent in 1880, 72 percent in 1900, and 59 percent in 1913.[22] Despite these figures, it is necessary to examine the spatial and industrial composition of the financial flows before it is possible to conclude that *Empire* finance either played an important role in underwriting British prosperity or served to drain funds away from the domestic enterprise, or provided the foundation of finance imperialism in the Hobson–Lenin–Chamberlain sense of the word (see Chart 2.1).

Table 2.1 divides the total flows into their domestic, foreign, and Empire components. Over the entire fifty-year period, about 42 percent of the minimum total went to the foreign sector, somewhat less than a third remained at home, and the remaining quarter supported Empire activities. The distribution between home and overseas finance is quite consistent with C. K. Hobson's earlier estimate of one-third home and two-thirds abroad. There are, however, probably some differences in the foreign–Empire distribution of the overseas component between these estimates and those of other authors. Lenin put the Empire's share at just less than 50 percent, while Simon places the figure at slightly more than 40 percent. That latter figure is not far different from the minimum estimate (39 percent), but it is substantially higher than the one-third figure implied by the intermediate and maximum estimates.

The overall averages, while providing some feeling for magni-

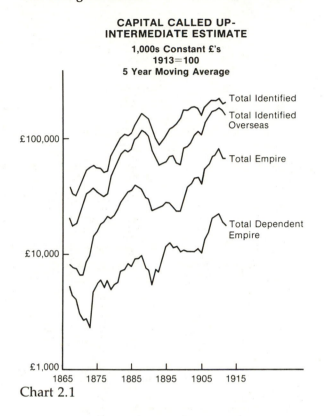

CAPITAL CALLED UP-
INTERMEDIATE ESTIMATE

1,000s Constant £'s
1913=100
5 Year Moving Average

Chart 2.1

tudes, mask some important facets of the transfer process. Traditional historiography, for example, asserts that late-Victorian industry was starved by lack of new investment, as the nation's capital streamed abroad. While there is no simple relation between finance and capital, there is still no evidence in these data to indicate that the domestic economy suffered financial deprivation because of overseas demand. From 1880 to 1904 the domestic economy received more than 35 percent of the total available finance, and for the last decade the fraction was almost one-half. Moreover, in the private sector (domestic private industry is, after all, the subject of the conventional interpretation), the result is even clearer. The domestic average for the entire period is nearly 40 percent. The variety of enterprises funded suggests that the market was at least as willing to finance the new growth industries as the traditional iron and textile firms, and an examination of domestic borrowing suggests that they were able to borrow at rates only slightly above the consol rate – rates that were much below the charges levied on overseas or Empire firms.

TABLE 2.1

CAPITAL CALLED UP 1865-1914

(1,000s £'s)

ALL CAPITAL

	UNITED KINGDOM			FOREIGN			EMPIRE		
	Total	Private	Govt	Total	Private	Govt	Total	Private	Govt
	(1) MINIMUM ESTIMATE								
1865-69	91,964	90,530	1,434	64,315	34,782	29,533	41,126	29,332	11,794
1870-74	106,634	99,487	7,147	127,526	86,789	40,737	45,029	21,566	23,463
1875-79	88,874	70,016	18,858	56,093	27,332	28,761	86,465	13,355	73,110
1880-84	119,433	94,299	25,134	188,669	113,271	75,398	115,334	38,926	76,408
1885-89	142,396	126,122	16,274	241,012	163,431	77,581	132,928	46,419	86,509
1890-94	109,164	90,256	18,908	153,444	97,953	55,491	82,507	24,938	57,569
1895-99	176,743	155,036	21,707	143,992	75,189	68,803	81,004	50,571	30,433
1900-04	331,604	152,975	178,629	179,597	139,180	40,417	142,400	58,006	84,349
1905-09	135,774	96,984	38,790	361,762	247,334	114,428	221,008	134,203	86,805
1910-14	184,921	113,431	71,490	422,090	296,937	125,153	278,443	144,667	133,776
TOTAL	1,487,507	1,089,136	398,371	1,938,501	1,282,198	656,302	1,226,239	561,983	664,261
AVG	148,750	108,914	39,837	193,850	128,199	65,630	122,624	55,987	66,426
	(2) INTERMEDIATE ESTIMATE								
1865-69	129,449	128,015	1,434	87,192	50,031	37,161	53,172	41,295	11,877
1870-74	113,634	106,487	7,147	131,288	90,551	40,737	46,257	22,794	23,463
1875-79	106,328	87,470	18,858	61,967	28,673	33,294	88,813	15,541	73,272
1880-84	135,537	106,871	28,666	224,020	124,163	99,857	122,532	41,258	81,274
1885-89	171,554	151,973	19,581	290,443	195,731	94,712	148,458	53,494	94,964
1890-94	151,089	127,440	23,649	219,323	143,835	75,488	113,002	44,523	68,479
1895-99	231,638	202,811	28,827	184,895	99,976	94,919	113,103	72,815	40,288
1900-04	396,715	199,712	197,003	216,181	157,256	58,925	179,031	78,750	100,281
1905-09	173,902	127,081	46,821	483,503	320,555	162,948	270,991	162,983	108,008
1910-14	218,547	143,922	74,625	558,670	377,301	181,369	352,494	185,818	166,676
TOTAL	1,828,393	1,381,782	446,611	2,467,481	1,588,072	879,410	1,148,851	719,271	768,582
AVG	182,839	138,178	44,661	246,748	158,787	87,941	148,785	71,716	76,858
	(3) MAXIMUM ESTIMATE								
1865-69	129,449	128,015	1,434	188,527	64,792	123,735	53,397	41,520	11,877
1870-74	113,700	106,553	7,147	494,971	130,035	364,936	47,014	23,551	23,463
1875-79	106,328	87,470	18,858	303,422	34,970	268,452	91,313	15,541	75,772
1880-84	135,537	106,871	28,666	262,303	134,628	127,675	122,555	41,281	81,274
1885-89	171,691	151,973	19,718	307,127	198,274	108,853	148,583	53,619	94,964
1890-94	151,089	127,440	23,649	233,633	148,804	84,829	113,188	44,624	68,564
1895-99	231,759	202,932	28,827	209,731	103,865	105,866	113,536	73,229	40,307
1900-04	396,765	199,762	197,003	218,846	157,604	61,242	179,160	78,863	100,297
1905-09	173,911	127,090	46,821	493,569	327,519	166,050	281,609	170,009	111,600
1910-14	218,624	143,999	74,625	560,954	379,118	181,836	355,137	185,835	169,302
TOTAL	1,828,853	1,382,105	446,748	3,273,083	1,679,609	1,593,474	1,505,488	728,072	777,420
AVG	182,885	138,211	44,675	327,308	167,940	159,347	150,549	72,596	77,742

It must be remembered that arguments based on the concept of finance imperialism concentrate on the fraction of British finance that went into the Empire.[23] Over the entire fifty years from 1865 to 1914, the proportion is about 25 percent of the total (see Chart 2.2), but that average is biased upwards by the transfers made during the last decade. For the period before 1900, about which Hobson

| | TOTAL | | EMPIRE | | | | | | | | | |
| | | | RESPONSIBLE GOVERNMENT | | | DEPENDENT COLONIES | | | INDIA | | |
Total	Private	Govt	Total	Private	Govt	Total	Private	Govt	Total	Private	Govt
197,405	154,644	42,761	14,144	3,962	10,182	4,539	2,927	1,612	22,443	22,443	0
279,189	207,842	71,347	30,910	13,069	17,841	2,248	1,701	547	11,871	6,796	5,075
231,432	110,703	120,729	62,338	9,460	42,878	1,219	521	698	22,908	3,374	19,534
423,436	246,496	176,940	85,628	24,882	60,746	7,131	3,773	3,358	22,575	10,271	12,304
516,336	335,972	180,364	100,356	33,812	66,544	6,804	5,093	1,711	25,768	7,514	18,254
345,115	213,147	131,968	57,478	19,820	37,658	4,407	2,275	2,132	20,622	2,843	17,779
401,739	280,796	120,943	45,234	24,151	21,083	16,271	14,387	1,884	19,499	12,033	7,466
653,601	350,161	303,440	105,533	33,537	71,996	16,959	12,957	4,002	19,908	11,512	8,396
718,544	478,521	240,023	162,720	104,856	67,864	20,870	14,053	6,817	37,418	15,294	22,124
885,454	555,035	330,419	207,836	101,866	105,970	34,550	26,396	8,154	36,057	16,405	19,652
652,244	2,933,317	1,718,934	872,174	369,415	502,762	114,998	84,083	30,915	239,069	108,485	130,584
465,224	293,100	171,893	87,217	36,730	50,276	11,500	8,408	3,092	23,907	10,849	13,058
269,813	219,341	50,472	16,326	6,061	10,265	5,885	4,273	1,612	30,961	30,961	0
291,179	219,832	71,347	31,172	13,331	17,841	2,383	1,836	547	12,702	7,627	5,075
257,108	131,684	125,424	63,038	9,998	53,040	1,219	521	698	24,556	5,022	19,534
482,089	272,292	209,797	91,207	26,525	64,682	7,364	3,976	3,388	23,961	10,757	13,204
610,455	401,198	209,257	110,071	37,874	72,197	8,258	6,426	1,832	30,129	9,194	20,935
483,414	315,798	167,616	82,411	36,331	46,080	6,926	3,770	3,156	23,665	4,422	19,243
539,636	375,602	164,034	63,139	37,190	25,949	22,750	19,346	3,404	27,214	16,279	10,935
791,927	435,718	356,209	128,987	43,229	85,758	25,082	20,058	5,024	24,962	15,463	9,499
928,396	610,619	317,777	195,481	122,207	73,274	28,862	20,076	8,786	46,648	20,700	25,948
129,711	707,041	422,670	263,418	127,918	135,500	47,384	37,198	10,186	41,692	20,702	20,990
783,725	3,689,125	2,094,603	1,045,251	460,664	584,586	156,113	117,480	38,633	286,489	141,127	145,363
578,373	368,681	209,460	104,525	45,855	58,459	15,611	11,748	3,863	26,489	14,113	14,536
371,373	234,327	137,046	16,326	6,061	10,265	6,110	4,498	1,612	30,961	30,961	0
655,685	260,139	395,546	32,729	13,888	17,841	2,583	2,036	547	12,702	7,627	5,075
501,063	137,981	363,082	63,038	9,998	53,040	1,219	521	698	27,056	5,022	22,034
520,395	282,780	237,615	91,230	26,548	64,682	7,364	3,976	3,388	23,961	10,757	13,204
627,401	403,866	223,535	110,196	37,999	72,197	8,258	6,426	1,832	30,129	9,194	20,935
497,910	320,868	177,042	82,562	36,432	46,130	6,961	3,770	3,191	23,665	4,422	19,243
555,026	380,026	175,000	63,538	37,589	25,949	22,765	19,361	3,404	27,233	16,279	10,954
794,771	436,229	358,542	129,116	43,342	85,774	25,082	20,058	5,024	24,962	15,463	9,499
949,089	624,618	324,471	196,822	123,548	73,274	38,139	25,761	12,378	46,648	20,700	25,948
134,715	708,952	425,763	263,435	127,935	135,500	50,010	37,198	12,812	41,692	20,702	20,990
607,424	3,789,786	2,817,642	1,047,991	463,340	584,652	168,490	123,605	44,886	289,009	141,127	147,882
660,742	378,747	281,764	104,799	46,123	58,465	16,849	12,361	4,489	28,901	14,113	14,788

wrote and Lenin paraphrased, the proportion is only about one in five. Furthermore, of either fraction, only one-third went to the dependent Empire and the rest to the colonies with responsible government. In terms of private finance, while foreign firms received almost 45 percent and domestic, 40, *all* Empire firms absorbed less than one-fifth of the total, and only about one pound in eight in the

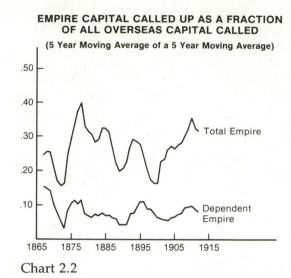

**EMPIRE CAPITAL CALLED UP AS A FRACTION
OF ALL OVERSEAS CAPITAL CALLED**

(5 Year Moving Average of a 5 Year Moving Average)

Chart 2.2

year before 1900. Moreover, the dependent governments received only about a third of that Empire total. The domestic share, on the other hand, was above 40 percent in every decade until 1905 when it declined in response to a wave of finance directed toward the foreign sector and the self-governing colonies. In the case of government finance the story is different. The foreign sector received something less than 40 percent; the Empire's share ballooned to about the same level; but that of the domestic economy fell to just less than a quarter. Of the governmental total, however, only about one pound in eleven went to India and the dependent colonies (see Table 2.2).

The picture is clear. Britain was indeed a major supplier of the world's finance; but, apart from the last decade, the Empire was not a major recipient of those funds. Despite the Empire's more significant role in the market for government finance, there is little evidence that at any time, at least before 1905, it provided a significant alternative for private funds pushed out of Britain by low domestic returns, or a fertile ground for investment at high "exploitative monopolistic" rates.

These observations are confirmed by a closer examination of the funds that did move into the Empire. Of that total, the regions with responsible government received over 70 percent.[24] Of the remaining fraction, India received about two-thirds and the dependent colonies the remainder. As a fraction of all (home, foreign, and Empire) finance, the colonies with responsible government garnered about

20, India 5, and the other dependent possessions a little more than 2 percent. Limiting observation to private finance reduces further the role of the Empire in general, and of the dependent Empire in particular. The share of the colonies with responsible government falls from 19 to 13 percent, India to less than 4, and the dependent colonies to under 3 percent of the total.

III. The data: geographic distribution

Table 2.3 provides a geographic breakdown of the financial flows, and Table 2.4 shows the distribution between the Empire and foreign sectors for each continent.[25] Overall, the allocation of finance by continent is similar to that of Simon's earlier study; however, there are some noticeable differences. As one would expect, the treatment of partially called issues produces some substantial differences in Europe (and to a lesser extent in North America in the late 1870s). There are, however, other differences as well. In particular the Simon series appears to underestimate somewhat the proportion of finance flowing to South America, and to overestimate the proportion directed toward Asia and Africa. Analysis suggests that these differences may be explained in part by the taxonomy, although Simon is not clear on his methods. In the present study, Asiatic Russia was assigned to Europe, and Central America placed in the Southern Hemisphere. A rough reassignment of those two areas (Central America is easily shifted, but the Russian adjustment was limited to a transfer of the Trans-Siberian Railroad from Europe to Russia) reduces much of the South American and Asiatic discrepancy, but it still leaves the problem of Africa unresolved. In that case the differences are concentrated in the decade 1895 to 1904, but the source of that difference is not easily discovered.[26]

The United Kingdom aside, the North American continent was the most important recipient of British finance; it attracted a quarter of all British finance and slightly more than a third of the overseas total. It was, however, the foreign sector (largely the United States) that early drew the bulk of the funds, although that domination all but disappeared in the present century. The United States and Mexico accounted for more than three-quarters of the total before 1905, but only about half thereafter.

Of the Empire total, almost all went to what is now Canada. The increase in the Empire's share during the late 1880s and again in the last decade was largely associated with increased investment in Canadian railroads. In the 1880s, the Canadian Pacific and the Grand Trunk of Canada were the major recipients of London funds, but a

TABLE 2.2

PERCENT OF PUBLIC AND PRIVATE OF ALL CAPITAL CALLED UP 1865-1914

(1,000s £'s)

	United Kingdom		Foreign		Total Empire		Total		Responsible Government		Dependent Colonies		India	
	Private	Govt	Private	Govt	Private	Govt	Private	Govt	Private	Govt	Private	Govt	Private	Govt
(1) MINIMUM ESTIMATE														
1865-69	98.4	1.6	54.3	45.7	71.3	28.7	78.4	21.6	28.0	72.0	64.5	35.5	100.0	0.0
1870-74	93.3	6.7	68.1	31.9	47.9	52.1	74.4	25.6	42.3	57.7	75.7	24.3	57.2	42.8
1875-79	78.8	21.2	48.7	51.3	15.4	84.6	47.8	52.2	15.2	84.8	42.7	57.3	14.7	85.3
1880-84	79.0	21.0	60.0	40.0	33.8	66.2	58.2	41.8	29.1	70.9	52.9	47.1	45.5	54.5
1885-89	88.6	11.4	67.8	32.2	34.9	65.1	65.1	34.9	33.7	66.3	74.8	25.2	29.2	70.8
1890-94	82.7	17.3	63.8	36.2	30.2	69.8	61.8	38.2	34.5	65.5	51.6	48.4	13.8	86.2
1895-99	87.7	12.3	52.2	47.8	62.5	37.5	69.9	30.1	53.4	46.6	88.5	11.5	61.7	38.3
1900-04	46.1	53.9	77.5	22.5	40.7	59.3	53.6	46.4	31.8	68.2	76.4	23.6	57.8	42.2
1905-09	71.4	28.6	68.4	31.6	60.7	39.3	66.6	33.4	64.4	35.6	67.3	32.7	40.9	59.1
1910-14	61.3	38.7	70.3	29.7	52.0	48.0	62.7	37.3	49.0	51.0	76.4	23.6	45.5	54.5
AVG L	73.2	26.8	66.1	33.9	45.7	54.3	63.0	37.0	42.2	57.8	73.1	26.9	45.4	54.6
AVG(d)	78.7	21.3	63.1	36.9	44.8	55.2	63.8	36.2	36.9	63.1	67.1	32.9	46.6	53.4
(2) INTERMEDIATE ESTIMATE														
1865-69	98.9	1.1	57.9	42.1	77.7	22.3	81.4	18.6	37.1	62.9	72.6	27.4	100.0	0.0
1870-74	93.7	6.3	69.0	31.0	49.3	50.7	75.5	24.5	42.8	57.2	77.0	23.0	60.0	40.0
1875-79	82.3	17.7	46.3	53.7	17.5	82.5	51.2	48.8	15.9	84.1	42.7	57.3	20.5	79.5
1880-84	78.9	21.1	55.4	44.6	33.7	66.3	56.5	43.5	29.1	70.9	54.0	46.0	44.9	55.1
1885-89	88.6	11.4	67.4	32.6	36.0	64.0	65.7	34.3	34.4	65.6	77.8	22.2	30.5	69.5
1890-94	84.3	15.7	65.6	34.4	39.4	60.6	65.3	34.7	44.1	55.9	54.4	45.6	18.7	81.3

1895-99	87.6	12.4	51.3	48.7	64.4	35.6	69.6	30.4	58.9	41.1	85.1	14.9	59.8	40.2
1900-04	50.3	49.7	72.7	27.3	44.0	56.0	55.0	45.0	33.5	66.5	80.0	20.0	61.9	38.1
1905-09	73.1	26.9	66.3	33.7	60.1	39.9	65.8	34.2	62.5	37.5	69.6	30.4	44.4	55.6
1910-14	65.9	34.1	67.5	32.5	52.7	47.3	62.6	37.4	48.6	51.4	78.5	21.5	49.7	50.3
AVG L	75.6	24.4	64.4	35.6	48.3	51.7	63.8	36.2	44.0	56.0	75.3	24.7	49.3	50.7
AVG(d)	80.3	19.7	61.9	38.1	47.4	52.6	64.8	35.2	39.7	60.3	69.2	30.8	49.0	51.0

(3) MAXIMUM ESTIMATE

1865-69	98.9	1.1	34.8	65.2	77.8	22.2	63.2	36.8	37.1	62.9	73.6	26.4	100.0	0.0
1870-74	93.7	6.3	26.3	73.7	50.1	49.9	39.7	60.3	43.8	56.2	78.8	21.2	60.0	40.0
1875-79	82.3	17.7	11.5	88.5	17.0	83.0	27.5	72.5	15.9	84.1	42.7	57.3	18.6	81.4
1880-84	78.9	21.1	51.3	48.7	33.7	66.3	54.3	45.7	29.1	70.9	54.0	46.0	44.9	55.1
1885-89	88.5	11.5	64.6	35.4	36.1	63.9	64.4	35.6	34.5	65.5	77.8	22.2	30.5	69.5
1890-94	84.3	15.7	63.7	36.3	39.4	60.6	64.4	35.6	44.1	55.9	54.2	45.8	18.7	81.3
1895-99	87.6	12.4	49.5	50.5	64.5	35.5	68.5	31.5	59.2	40.8	85.1	14.9	59.8	40.2
1900-04	50.3	49.7	72.0	28.0	44.0	56.0	54.9	45.1	33.6	66.4	80.0	20.0	61.9	38.1
1905-09	73.1	26.9	66.6	33.6	60.4	39.6	65.8	34.2	62.8	37.2	67.5	32.5	44.4	55.6
1910-14	65.9	34.1	67.6	32.4	52.3	47.7	62.5	37.5	48.6	51.4	74.4	25.6	49.7	50.3
AVG L	75.6	24.4	51.3	48.7	48.3	51.7	57.3	42.7	44.1	55.9	73.4	26.6	48.8	51.2
AVG(d)	80.3	19.7	50.7	49.3	47.4	52.6	56.5	43.5	39.9	60.1	68.8	31.2	48.8	51.2

TABLE 2.3

ALL CAPITAL CALLED UP BY CONTINENT

(1,000s £'s)

	United Kingdom	Europe	North America	South America & Caribbean	Africa	Asia	Australia & Pacific	Unknown	Total
(1) MINIMUM ESTIMATE									
1865-69	91,964	20,036	19,049	16,896	11,702	26,366	11,714	2,001	199,728
1870-74	106,634	20,584	70,484	46,702	2,803	19,578	15,200	2,641	284,626
1875-79	88,873	11,185	40,913	12,601	16,349	26,434	35,075	1,122	232,552
1880-84	119,432	73,349	85,583	41,275	18,814	27,581	57,451	3,381	426,866
1885-89	142,396	29,767	90,914	128,895	20,266	36,017	68,251	4,177	520,683
1890-94	109,164	27,013	77,900	42,589	20,254	33,224	34,944	1,298	346,386
1895-99	176,757	42,930	32,894	29,304	33,823	51,639	34,494	1,983	403,824
1900-04	331,604	19,003	113,869	34,326	89,082	39,137	26,580	553	654,154
1905-09	135,774	41,307	241,281	124,717	56,207	96,634	22,576	2,181	720,677
1910-14	184,921	64,800	286,910	153,930	40,898	85,908	68,119	3,463	888,949
TOTAL	1,487,519	349,974	1,059,797	631,235	310,198	442,518	374,404	22,800	4,678,445
AVG	148,752	34,997	105,980	63,124	31,020	44,252	37,440	2,280	467,845
(2) MAXIMUM ESTIMATE									
1865-69	129,449	105,826	30,130	23,084	24,291	46,605	13,111	2,489	374,985
1870-74	113,700	172,092	195,840	70,028	35,505	56,115	15,200	2,641	661,121
1875-79	106,328	43,909	251,374	13,833	16,349	33,645	35,625	1,152	502,215
1880-84	135,537	124,152	95,286	53,223	21,477	30,567	60,203	3,527	523,972
1885-89	171,691	54,353	103,546	158,214	23,244	41,540	74,983	4,212	631,783
1890-94	151,089	48,649	113,794	60,965	27,798	44,440	51,148	1,652	499,535
1895-99	231,773	52,561	56,500	42,470	44,923	76,216	50,686	2,497	557,626
1900-04	396,765	30,395	122,242	47,670	112,117	48,889	36,692	567	795,337
1905-09	173,911	58,318	303,734	168,998	75,587	137,953	30,535	3,072	952,108
1910-14	218,624	107,644	353,636	205,080	52,464	112,862	84,441	5,531	1,140,282
TOTAL	1,828,867	797,899	1,626,082	843,565	433,755	628,832	452,624	27,340	6,638,964
AVG	182,887	79,790	162,608	84,357	43,376	62,883	45,262	2,734	663,896

46

number of smaller lines, including the Atlantic and Northwestern; the Midland of Canada; the Ontario and Quebec; the Qu Appelle, Long Lake, and Saskatchewan; the Quebec Central; the Quebec and St. John; and the Western Countries (Nova Scotia) also funded issues in excess of £100,000. After the turn of the century, the largest volume of securities was issued by the Canadian Pacific, the Grand Trunk of Canada, the Grand Trunk Pacific, and the Canadian Northern. Again, however, access to the London market was not limited to those firms. Railroads such as the Edmonton, Dunvegan, and British Columbia; the Pacific Great Eastern; the Terminal Cities; and the Atlantic, Quebec, and Western also received substantial transfusions.

The history of Canadian growth after Confederation is well known, and Edelstein's penetrating study neatly summarizes the interaction between international capital movements and Canadian development. All that need be emphasized here is that the financial data provide vivid support for the picture he provides. Edelstein concludes that throughout the period 1867 to 1915 Canada depended very heavily on foreign capital imports. His estimates indicate that at the time of Confederation one-half of gross domestic capital formation was financed from abroad, and that the fraction declined to approximately one-third by 1890, but then rose again to its previous peak by the outbreak of the First World War. The latter surge was triggered by the opening of commercial wheat production on the prairies, but it was reinforced by a wave of industrial investment resting on Canadian tariff and patent policy, and by investment in the second and third transcontinental railroads. The latter apparently absorbed between 7 and 8 percent of Canadian GNP in the immediate pre-war decades.[27] The financial data identify and enhance these results. They pinpoint the railroad finance that underwrote the links that tied the prairies to Eastern and European markets in the late 1870s and the 1880s and the outpouring of railroad and industrial issues that flooded the London market after 1902.

Below the border, the development of domestic capital markets reduced American dependence on British finance and contributed to the decline in the continent's receipts. The North American total had reached about £18 million a year in the decade 1880–9, but it had fallen to less than half that amount ten years later. In the immediate pre-war period, however, the flows again increased. The United States and Mexico received £272 million, and the Canadians tapped the British market for an additional £257 million; together these amounted to an average of almost £53 million a year.

In terms of the total volume of overseas finance, South and Central

TABLE 2.4

CAPITAL CALLED UP BY CONTINENT AND TYPE OF GOVERNMENT (MINIMUM)

(1,000s £'s)

AFRICA

	FOREIGN			TOTAL EMPIRE			TOTAL			RESPONSIBLE GOVERNMENT			DEPENDENT COLONIES			INDIA		
	Total	Private	Govt	Total	Private	Govt	Total	Private	Govt	Total	Private	Govt	Total	Private	Govt	Total	Private	Govt
1865-69	10,000	1,267	8,733	1,702	306	1,396	11,702	1,573	10,129	173	60	113	1,529	246	1,283	NOT APPLICABLE		
1870-74	2,041	1,956	85	763	619	144	2,804	2,575	229	192	98	94	571	521	50			
1875-79	7,254	454	6,800	9,095	80	9,015	16,349	534	15,815	8,965	50	8,915	130	30	100			
1880-84	3,992	3,892	100	14,822	3,109	11,713	18,814	7,001	11,813	13,658	1,945	11,713	1,164	1,164	0			
1885-89	15,722	4,902	10,820	4,545	2,567	1,978	20,267	7,469	12,798	2,330	625	1,705	2,215	1,942	273			
1890-94	12,894	5,249	7,645	7,360	2,080	5,280	20,254	7,329	12,925	6,251	1,577	4,674	1,109	503	606			
1895-99	17,020	15,404	1,616	16,803	10,678	6,125	33,823	26,082	7,741	7,179	1,587	5,592	9,624	9,091	533			
1900-04	9,564	7,738	1,826	79,518	26,740	52,778	89,082	34,478	54,604	67,419	17,215	50,204	12,099	9,525	2,574			
1905-09	19,604	16,533	3,071	36,600	15,937	20,663	56,204	32,470	23,734	24,362	9,208	15,154	12,238	6,729	5,509			
1910-14	21,774	13,784	7,990	19,100	12,535	6,565	40,874	26,319	14,555	1,371	953	418	17,729	11,582	6,147			
TOTAL	119,865	71,179	48,686	190,308	74,651	115,657	310,173	145,830	164,343	131,900	33,318	98,582	58,408	41,333	17,075			
AVG	11,987	7,118	4,869	19,031	7,465	11,566	31,017	14,583	16,434	13,190	3,332	9,858	5,841	4,133	1,708			

ASIA

	FOREIGN			TOTAL EMPIRE			TOTAL			RESPONSIBLE GOVERNMENT			DEPENDENT COLONIES			INDIA		
	Total	Private	Govt	Total	Private	Govt	Total	Private	Govt	Total	Private	Govt	Total	Private	Govt	Total	Private	Govt
1865-69	2,854	1,036	1,818	23,513	23,314	199	26,367	24,350	2,017	NOT APPLICABLE			1,070	871	199	22,443	22,443	0
1870-74	7,009	3,626	3,383	12,569	7,494	5,075	19,578	11,120	8,458				698	698		11,871	6,796	5,075
1875-79	3,044	169	2,875	23,390	3,649	19,741	26,434	3,818	22,616				482	275	207	22,908	3,374	19,534
1880-84	1,779	1,688	91	25,802	11,734	14,068	27,581	13,422	14,159				3,227	1,463	1,764	22,575	10,271	12,304
1885-89	8,680	4,945	3,735	27,337	8,792	18,545	36,017	13,737	22,280				1,569	1,278	291	25,768	7,514	18,254
1890-94	10,148	4,527	5,621	23,077	4,143	18,934	33,225	8,670	24,555				2,455	1,300	1,155	20,622	2,843	17,779
1895-99	30,384	1,461	28,923	21,256	13,396	7,860	51,640	14,857	36,783				1,757	1,363	394	19,499	12,033	7,466
1900-04	15,207	1,450	13,757	23,930	14,211	9,719	39,137	15,661	23,476				4,022	2,699	1,323	19,908	11,512	8,396
1905-09	51,653	8,927	42,726	44,981	21,619	23,362	96,634	30,546	66,088				7,563	6,325	1,238	37,418	15,294	22,124
1910-14	35,670	13,964	21,706	50,239	28,882	21,357	85,909	42,846	43,063				14,182	12,477	1,705	36,057	16,405	19,652
TOTAL	166,428	41,793	124,635	276,094	137,234	138,860	442,522	179,027	263,495				37,025	28,749	8,276	239,069	108,485	130,584
AVG	16,643	4,179	12,464	27,609	13,723	13,886	44,252	17,903	26,350				3,702	2,875	828	23,907	10,849	13,058

AUSTRALIA/PACIFIC

	FOREIGN			TOTAL EMPIRE			TOTAL			RESPONSIBLE GOVERNMENT			DEPENDENT COLONIES			INDIA		
	Total	Private	Govt	Total	Private	Govt	Total	Private	Govt	Total	Private	Govt	Total	Private	Govt	Total	Private	Govt
1865-69	0	0	0	11,704	1,860	9,844	11,704	1,860	9,844	10,756	912	9,844	948	948	0	NOT APPLICABLE		
1870-74	0	0	0	12,405	3,013	9,392	12,405	3,013	9,392	12,405	3,013	9,392	0	0	0			
1875-79	0	0	0	35,075	3,897	31,178	35,075	3,897	31,178	34,703	3,720	30,983	372	177	195			
1880-84	259	63	196	57,401	11,344	46,057	57,401	11,344	46,057	55,976	10,558	45,418	1,425	786	639			
1885-89	40	40	0	67,972	13,456	54,516	68,231	13,519	54,712	66,042	12,190	53,852	1,930	1,266	664			
1890-94	375	375	0	34,904	9,519	25,385	34,944	9,559	25,385	34,904	9,519	25,385						
1895-99	86	86	0	34,106	21,357	12,749	34,481	21,732	12,749	31,474	19,038	12,436	2,632	2,319	313			
1900-04	13	13	0	26,494	6,545	19,949	26,580	6,631	19,949	26,277	6,328	19,949	217	217	0			
1905-09	360	360	0	22,563	6,286	16,277	22,576	6,299	16,277	22,344	6,067	16,277	219	219	0			
1910-14				67,731	11,226	56,505	68,091	11,586	56,505	67,361	10,856	56,505	370	370	0			
TOTAL	1,133	937	196	370,355	88,503	281,852	371,488	89,440	282,048	362,242	82,201	280,041	8,113	6,302	1,811			
AVG	113	94	20	37,036	8,850	28,205	37,149	8,944	28,205	36,224	8,220	28,004	811	630	181			

	CARIBBEAN & SOUTH AMERICA																	
1865-69	16,476	5,464	11,012	420	390	30	16,896	5,854	11,042				420	390	30			
1870-74	46,083	17,416	28,667	619	122	497	46,702	17,538	29,164				619	122	497			
1875-79	12,406	4,215	8,191	196	0	196	12,602	4,215	8,387				196	0	196			
1880-84	40,058	29,629	10,429	1,217	262	955	41,275	29,891	11,384				1,217	262	955			
1885-89	127,969	82,788	45,181	927	443	484	128,896	83,231	45,665	NOT			927	443	484	NOT		
1890-94	42,009	28,317	13,692	581	210	371	42,590	28,527	14,063				581	210	371			
1895-99	27,488	16,854	10,634	1,816	1,172	644	29,304	18,026	11,278	APPLICABLE			1,816	1,172	644	APPLICABLE		
1900-04	33,706	24,642	9,064	620	515	105	34,326	25,157	9,169				620	515	105			
1905-09	124,532	87,206	37,326	185	115	70	124,717	87,321	37,396				185	115	70			
1910-14	152,924	103,738	49,186	1,007	704	303	153,931	104,442	49,489				1,007	704	303			
TOTAL	623,651	400,269	223,382	7,588	3,933	3,655	631,239	404,202	227,037				7,588	3,933	3,655			
AVG	62,365	40,006	22,338	759	393	366	63,124	40,400	22,704				759	393	366			
	EUROPE																	
1865-69	19,676	13,367	6,309	360	360	0	20,036	13,727	6,309				360	360	0			
1870-74	20,224	16,690	3,534	360	360	0	20,584	17,050	3,534				360	360	0			
1875-79	11,147	3,011	8,136	39	39	0	11,186	3,050	8,136				39	39	0			
1880-84	73,289	8,780	64,509	60	60	0	73,349	8,840	64,509				60	60	0			
1885-89	29,480	14,069	15,411	137	137	0	29,617	14,206	15,411	NOT			137	137	0	NOT		
1890-94	26,750	5,226	21,524	263	263	0	27,013	5,489	21,524				263	263	0			
1895-99	42,931	18,075	24,856	0	0	0	42,931	18,075	24,856	APPLICABLE			0	0	0	APPLICABLE		
1900-04	19,003	3,632	15,371	0	0	0	19,003	3,632	15,371				0	0	0			
1905-09	41,276	17,060	24,216	32	32	0	41,308	17,092	24,216				32	32	0			
1910-14	64,800	22,263	42,537	0	0	0	64,800	22,263	42,537				0	0	0			
TOTAL	348,576	122,173	226,403	1,251	1,251	0	349,827	123,424	226,403				1,251	1,251	0			
AVG	34,857	12,186	22,640	125	125	0	34,983	12,311	22,640				125	125	0			
	NORTH AMERICA																	
1865-69	15,623	13,962	1,661	3,428	3,103	325	19,051	17,065	1,986	3,215	2,990	225	213	113	100			
1870-74	52,170	47,102	5,068	18,314	9,959	8,355	70,484	57,061	13,423	18,314	9,959	8,355	0	0	0			
1875-79	22,242	19,483	2,759	18,670	5,690	12,980	40,912	25,173	15,739	18,670	5,690	12,980	0	0	0			
1880-84	69,551	69,282	269	16,033	12,418	3,615	85,584	81,700	3,884	15,995	12,380	3,615	38	38	0			
1885-89	58,903	56,665	2,238	32,012	21,025	10,987	90,915	77,690	13,225	31,984	20,997	10,987	28	28	0	NOT		
1890-94	61,604	54,595	7,009	16,296	8,698	7,598	77,900	63,293	14,607	16,296	8,698	7,598	0	0	0			
1895-99	25,796	23,021	2,775	7,098	4,044	3,054	32,894	27,065	5,829	6,581	3,527	3,054	517	517	0	APPLICABLE		
1900-04	102,032	101,632	400	11,837	9,994	1,843	113,869	111,626	2,243	11,837	9,994	1,843	0	0	0			
1905-09	124,686	117,596	7,090	116,595	90,163	26,432	241,281	207,759	33,522	115,963	89,531	26,432	632	632	--			
1910-14	146,564	142,829	3,735	140,346	91,299	49,047	286,910	234,128	52,782	139,099	90,052	49,047	1,247	1,247	0			
TOTAL	679,171	646,167	33,004	380,629	256,393	124,236	1,059,800	902,560	157,240	377,954	253,818	124,136	2,675	2,575	100			
AVG	67,917	64,617	3,300	38,063	25,428	12,424	105,980	90,045	15,724	37,795	25,171	12,414	268	258	0			

America (including the Caribbean) ranked second. As early as 1873, British companies controlled almost three-quarters of the Argentine railway network, and that interest was reflected in the flows of finance. Over the full period the southern continent received about 14 percent of all finance.[28] That proportion was, however, subject to wide variation. After absorbing almost a quarter of all finance in the late 1880s, for example, it received only 7 percent in the decade of the 1890s. During both surges and recessions, however, the formal Empire received only a tiny fraction (about 1 percent). Taking the two continents together, the Western Hemisphere absorbed about two-fifths of all London-based finance and more than half of the overseas total. Of that total, the foreign sector received more than three-quarters and Canada almost an additional third. The dependent colonies together drew only about half of 1 percent.

Europe stood fifth among the continents, if the minimum measure is employed. For the entire period, by even the latter measure, it drew about £1 in 12 of the total volume of identified finance. Of that £350 million, only £1.3 million went to Britain's European colonies (Gibraltar, Cyprus, and Malta). Thus, of the three "Western" continents (regions that accounted for almost two-thirds of overseas finance), the foreign sector received about four-fifths of the total. Canada (and the colonies that went to make up Canada) was the destination of an additional 20 percent, and the dependent Empire drew far less than 1 percent.

On the three remaining continents, regions that absorbed less than 25 percent of all (and slightly over a third of overseas) finance, the story was somewhat different. Of the three, Asia received the largest share, and although the foreign sector could hardly be termed insignificant, more than 60 percent went to the Empire. India was the major Empire beneficiary, although the subcontinent's share declined from almost the entire Empire total to less than £3 in 4 as the tin and rubber industries on the Malay peninsula began to tap the London market.

The development of Japan, together with China's increasing attractiveness as an area for foreign investment, reduced the Empire's dominance of the continent's total. The foreign sector accounted for only about £1 in 8 between 1865 and 1885, but for almost four times that proportion in the last pre-war decade. In that latter period, government borrowing involved the national governments of Japan, China, and Siam, and cities like Tokyo, Nagoya, Osaka, and Yokahama. In the private sector there were railroad issues of the Imperial China, the Manila, and the Philippine railroads; financial issues from the Industrial Bank of Japan and the National Bank of China; and the agriculture and extractive issues of firms like the Anglo-Dutch plantations of Java, the Chinese Engineering and Mining Company, the Hayeop (Dutch Borneo) Rubber Estates, the Mendaris (Sumatra) Rubber and Produce Estates, and the Royal Dutch Company for the Working of Petroleum Wells in the Netherlands Indies.

Of all the continents, none was more clearly a British financial preserve than Oceania (Australia, New Zealand, etc.). Although only sparsely populated (fewer than six million inhabitants compared to some seven million residents of greater London), it received almost 8 percent of all finance, a figure that by some measures was equal to Europe's. From the 1860s to the 1890s, investment boomed and a large portion of that new capital (a fraction ranging from about a quarter in the 1870s and 1890s to almost a half in the 1860s and 1880s) was financed by loans and other financial transfers from the United Kingdom. The financial flow rose to more than £13 million a year in the latter half of the 1880s and in the peak decade (the 1880s) accounted for almost one-fifth of all Britain's overseas finance. On a per capita basis, Britain contributed more to Oceania than to any other continent; and almost all went to the Empire.

Unlike Canada, in Australasia, while there were some private issues, the majority of the transfers were public. In the Dominion about one-third of the total was governmental; in the Commonwealth the figure was more than three-fourths and in the boom decade of the 1880s it was over four-fifths. Given the independent attitude of the Australasian governments and the horror with which the British government greeted each new financial issue, it can hardly be argued that it was the British who were forcing their savings on an unwilling set of colonists. In 1875 Lord Carnarvon, Secretary of State for the Colonies, wrote to W. H. Smith: "I am not surprised that you are rather startled at the Treasury at the financial speed at which New Zealand is travelling. At the same time the crisis may not come yet . . . ."[29] Australia and New Zealand had voracious financial appetites. The dependent colonies, however, received very little; £39 of every £40 went either to colonies with responsible government, or to those (like Western Australia) about to achieve that status.

Finally, there is Africa, along with India the inspiration for most of the imperial rhetoric. Imperialism there may well have been, but it does not appear to have been finance imperialism. The continent ranks last among the overseas recipients, and the figure is as large as it is (about 10 percent) only because of the heavy flows between 1895 and 1909. Nor were the bulk of those flows directed toward the dependent Empire. While the reshuffling of allegiances that followed the Boer War blurs the distinctions between foreign, responsible, and dependent regions, some trends can be distinguished. Over the entire fifty-year period, the foreign sector received almost 40 percent of African finance – a total that would have been even higher had the Transvaal and the Orange Free State not been absorbed into the Empire in 1902.[30] The Empire's share was divided between responsible and dependent governments in a ratio of about two to one, if the two newly acquired colonies are classified as responsibly governed in the years from 1902 to 1906. In no year before 1895 did the dependent Empire in Africa absorb as much as £1 million, and the average for the entire period was only about a third of that figure.

Europe, the Western Hemisphere, and Australasia provide little comfort to the prophets of finance imperialism, if that term is understood to imply major financial transfers to parts of the dependent Empire. Only Lenin even among the neo-Marxists argues that Britain had substantial exploitative control over the self-governing colonies. Certainly the British were under no illusion about their ability to affect governmental policy in the self-governing colonies, even when those policies directly affected Great Britain. As early as 1871 Kimberley lamented that "the effect of the New Zealand [tariff] Bill would undoubtedly be that New Zealand might admit Sydney made shoes free and charge any duty she pleased on shoes from Northhampton,"[31] but admitted nothing could be done. Similar comments were common not only on tariff issues but on such widely diverse enterprises as loan repayments, provision for the common defense, and attempts by those colonial governments to expand their economic and political power into neighboring territories. If any evidence is to be found to support the concept of financial imperialism, it must refer to Asia or Africa. Yet little more than 16 percent of all finance was transferred to these two continents; and of that amount, well under half was directed toward India and the dependent colonies. Even in the twentieth century when those latter flows peaked, they accounted for only one-tenth of all finance passing through the British capital market. If, as Hobson argued, "final determination rests with the financial power," or, as Lenin concluded, "British bourgeois politicians fully appreciated the connection between what might be called the purely economic and the political-social roots of imperialism," it is unclear why the Empire developed as it did.[32]

TABLE 2.5

CAPITAL CALLED UP BY INDUSTRY (ALL LOCATIONS)
(MINIMUM)

	A&E	Finance	Mfg	Public Utilities	T&S	Transp	Unknown	Total Private	Total Govt	Total
					1,000s £'s					
1865-69	5,604	28,570	9,836	8,291	4,773	95,508	1,755	154,337	42,761	197,098
1870-74	16,721	30,982	20,329	15,580	5,146	123,024	1,497	213,279	71,348	284,627
1875-79	1,842	16,759	5,703	6,057	3,621	76,984	859	111,825	120,728	232,553
1880-84	20,354	37,140	14,345	10,051	7,099	159,059	1,879	249,927	176,940	426,867
1885-89	29,698	52,338	62,053	11,556	11,524	169,336	3,814	340,319	180,364	520,683
1890-94	16,917	40,035	31,639	7,022	15,203	100,766	2,836	214,418	131,969	346,387
1895-99	40,436	36,754	80,450	10,649	27,223	83,864	3,424	282,800	120,943	403,743
1900-04	25,198	45,765	47,457	17,475	13,812	199,419	1,589	350,715	303,440	654,155
1905-09	38,059	53,917	32,078	27,685	16,082	309,277	3,558	480,656	240,023	720,679
1910-14	65,730	87,969	61,350	37,063	18,777	282,427	5,214	558,530	330,419	888,949
TOTAL	260,559	430,229	365,240	151,429	123,260	1,599,664	26,425	2,956,806	1,718,935	4,675,741
AVG	26,056	43,023	36,524	15,143	12,326	159,966	2,643	295,681	171,894	167,574
					PERCENTS					
1865-69	2.8	14.5	5.0	4.2	2.4	48.5	0.9	78.3	21.7	
1870-74	5.9	10.9	7.1	5.5	1.8	43.2	0.5	74.9	25.1	
1875-79	0.8	7.2	2.5	2.6	1.6	33.1	0.4	48.1	51.9	
1880-84	4.8	8.7	3.4	2.4	1.7	37.3	0.4	58.5	41.3	
1885-89	5.7	10.1	11.9	2.2	2.2	32.5	0.7	65.4	34.7	
1890-94	4.9	11.6	9.1	2.0	4.4	29.1	0.8	61.9	38.1	
1895-99	10.0	9.1	19.9	2.6	6.7	20.8	0.8	69.9	30.1	
1900-04	3.9	7.0	7.3	2.7	2.1	30.5	0.2	53.6	46.3	
1905-09	5.3	7.5	4.5	3.8	2.2	42.9	0.5	66.7	33.3	
1910-14	7.4	9.9	6.9	4.2	2.1	31.8	0.6	62.8	37.1	
TOTAL	5.6	9.2	7.8	3.2	2.6	34.2	0.6	63.2	36.8	
AVG	5.1	9.6	7.8	3.2	2.7	35.0	0.6	64.0	36.0	

A&E: Agriculture & Extractive   Mfg: Manufacturing   Transp: Transportation
Govt: Government   T&S: Trade & Services

IV. The data: industrial composition

How did British finance distribute itself across the industrial spectrum? (See Tables 2.5 and 2.6.) Neither Jenks nor C. K. Hobson made a systematic attempt to answer this question, but Segal and Simon made a first hesitant step in this direction. In their 1961 article they provide an industrial profile drawn across eight industries for the total of all issues covered by their thirty-year study. In his extension of their joint work, Simon provides annual estimates from 1865 to 1914 but, unfortunately, adopts a different taxonomy – one that includes only three sectors (social overhead, extractive, and manufacturing) and explicitly excludes "real estate, defence, and miscellaneous." Both Segal–Simon and Simon alone include both private and government issues in their industrial classification; the inclusion of the latter class raises severe technical problems.

The classification scheme adopted for this study is narrower but, it is hoped, more easily comprehensible. First, at the highest level, issues were classified either as public or private. There was no attempt to include a "mixed" category since it appeared impossible to delineate such a class of securities with any precision. Any issue emanating from any level of government was classified as "government," but any issue originating in the private sector (even issues

TABLE 2.6

CAPITAL CALLED BY TYPE OF GOVERNMENT AND INDUSTRY (MINIMUM)

(1,000s £'s)

	A&E	Finance	Mfg	Public Utilities	T&S	Transp	Unknown	Total Private	Total Govt	Total
					UNITED KINGDOM					
1865-69	1,564	18,929	8,442	1,310	3,610	55,617	1,060	90,532	1,434	91,966
1870-74	4,315	16,875	15,531	3,129	4,337	54,415	885	99,487	7,147	106,634
1875-79	572	11,497	4,715	2,012	3,161	47,816	242	70,015	18,858	88,873
1880-84	2,325	17,481	10,436	3,974	5,560	53,890	633	94,299	25,134	119,433
1885-89	6,149	29,872	49,354	2,623	9,138	27,215	1,771	126,122	16,274	142,396
1890-94	3,224	18,656	24,638	4,589	14,035	23,629	1,485	90,256	18,908	109,164
1895-99	2,773	13,477	68,007	7,695	24,388	36,565	2,131	155,036	21,707	176,743
1900-04	1,082	27,950	41,303	14,290	11,136	56,680	535	152,976	178,629	331,605
1905-09	1,214	23,292	22,053	10,600	8,984	29,168	1,674	96,985	38,790	135,775
1910-14	2,957	42,291	33,247	7,335	11,454	14,519	1,626	113,429	71,490	184,919
TOTAL	26,175	220,320	277,726	57,557	95,803	399,514	12,042	1,089,137	398,371	1,487,508
YR AVG	2,727	22,950	28,930	5,996	9,979	41,616	1,254	113,452	41,497	154,949
					FOREIGN					
1865-69	1,526	5,141	548	4,345	580	22,427	10	34,577	29,533	64,110
1870-74	10,336	9,438	3,975	9,371	736	52,902	32	86,790	40,737	127,527
1875-79	791	1,661	863	2,880	307	20,799	30	27,331	28,761	56,092
1880-84	8,119	10,202	2,496	3,145	584	88,603	123	113,272	75,398	188,670
1885-89	15,186	11,152	10,828	7,001	1,866	116,947	452	163,432	77,581	241,013
1890-94	10,076	12,271	6,266	1,468	558	66,807	507	97,953	55,491	153,444
1895-99	20,340	6,991	10,714	2,108	1,158	33,702	176	75,189	68,803	143,992
1900-04	4,547	7,927	3,710	1,507	625	120,603	261	139,180	40,417	179,597
1905-09	19,516	18,884	5,421	13,556	5,751	183,593	613	247,334	114,428	361,762
1910-14	32,890	23,230	16,322	21,692	2,896	197,836	2,073	296,939	125,153	422,092
TOTAL	123,327	106,897	61,143	67,073	15,061	904,219	4,277	1,281,997	656,302	1,938,299
YR AVG	12,333	10,690	6,114	6,707	1,506	90,422	428	128,200	65,630	193,830
					ALL EMPIRE					
1865-69	2,160	4,323	335	2,523	584	17,275	20	27,220	11,794	39,014
1870-74	1,436	640	662	3,050	72	15,706	0	21,566	23,464	45,030
1875-79	303	3,280	65	1,157	35	8,343	172	13,355	73,120	86,465
1880-84	9,014	9,076	791	2,826	745	16,241	233	38,926	76,408	115,334
1885-89	7,197	10,740	869	1,863	394	25,174	181	46,418	86,509	132,927
1890-94	3,281	9,005	527	916	556	10,330	324	24,939	57,569	82,508
1895-99	17,065	15,858	1,367	834	1,466	13,598	383	50,571	30,433	81,004
1900-04	19,490	9,853	2,382	1,673	2,042	22,136	431	58,007	84,394	142,401
1905-09	17,023	11,451	4,191	3,513	1,331	96,407	287	134,203	86,805	221,008
1910-14	28,107	21,849	11,719	7,871	4,402	69,879	839	144,666	133,776	278,442
TOTAL	105,076	96,075	22,908	26,226	11,627	295,089	2,870	559,871	664,262	1,224,133
YR AVG	10,945	10,008	2,386	2,732	1,211	30,739	299	58,320	69,194	127,514
					RESPONSIBLE GOVERNMENT					
1865-69	134	775	60	0	60	821	0	1,850	10,182	12,032
1870-74	1,201	231	589	1,200	0	9,849	0	13,070	17,841	30,911
1875-79	98	2,936	10	685	0	5,560	172	9,461	52,878	62,339
1880-84	4,858	6,741	504	1,867	695	10,144	73	24,882	60,746	85,628
1885-89	4,444	8,587	677	859	323	18,870	52	33,812	66,544	100,356
1890-94	1,969	7,442	499	916	543	8,127	324	19,820	37,658	57,478
1895-99	10,272	8,594	1,142	315	1,235	2,251	344	24,153	21,083	145,236
1900-04	14,637	3,324	2,164	1,495	810	10,753	353	33,536	71,996	105,532
1905-09	10,028	4,906	3,803	1,950	548	83,416	205	104,856	57,864	162,720
1910-14	12,896	16,018	11,187	6,247	1,062	53,701	756	101,867	105,970	207,837
TOTAL	60,537	59,554	20,635	15,534	5,276	203,492	2,279	367,307	502,762	870,069
YR AVG	6,306	6,204	2,149	1,618	550	21,197	237	38,261	52,371	90,632
					DEPENDENT COLONIES					
1865-69	1,338	701	176	400	0	293	20	2,928	1,612	4,540
1870-74	149	209	45	844	12	442	0	1,701	547	2,248
1875-79	105	344	0	7	30	35	0	521	698	1,219
1880-84	877	1,833	56	48	50	760	149	3,773	3,358	7,131
1885-89	1,670	1,507	0	864	71	943	39	5,094	1,711	6,805
1890-94	558	1,121	0	0	7	588	0	2,274	2,132	4,406
1895-99	3,902	7,128	125	260	232	2,710	29	14,386	1,884	16,270
1900-04	2,970	6,322	100	92	242	3,154	77	12,957	4,002	16,959
1905-09	5,559	5,545	61	1,006	100	1,699	82	14,052	6,817	20,869
1910-14	14,195	5,831	329	1,460	290	4,216	74	26,395	8,154	34,549
TOTAL	31,323	30,541	892	4,981	1,034	14,840	470	84,081	30,915	114,996
YR AVG	3,262	3,181	93	519	108	1,546	49	8,758	3,220	11,979

TABLE 2.6 (Continued)

	A&E	Finance	Mfg	Public Utilities	T&S	Transp	Unknown	Total Private	Total Govt	Total
					INDIA					
1865-69	689	2,847	100	2,123	524	16,161	0	22,444	0	22,444
1870-74	86	200	29	1,006	60	5,415	0	6,796	5,075	11,871
1875-79	100	0	55	465	5	2,748	0	3,373	19,534	22,907
1880-84	3,279	502	231	911	0	5,337	11	10,271	12,304	22,575
1885-89	1,084	646	193	140	0	5,361	90	7,514	18,254	25,768
1890-94	753	441	28	--	6	1,614	0	2,842	17,779	20,621
1895-99	2,891	136	100	258	0	8,637	10	12,032	7,466	19,498
1900-04	1,884	206	118	85	990	8,229	0	11,512	8,396	19,908
1905-09	1,435	1,000	326	558	682	11,293	0	15,294	22,124	37,418
1910-14	1,016	0	204	164	3,049	11,963	9	16,405	19,652	36,057
TOTAL	13,217	5,978	1,384	5,710	5,316	76,758	120	108,483	130,584	239,067
YR AVG	1,377	623	144	595	554	7,995	12	11,300	13,602	24,903
					UNKNOWN					
1865-69	355	178	511	113	0	190	665	2,012	0	2,012
1870-74	634	4,030	161	30	0	0	581	5,436	0	5,436
1875-79	176	322	59	8	117	25	415	1,122	0	1,122
1880-84	895	382	623	106	210	325	890	3,431	0	3,431
1885-89	1,166	575	1,002	69	126	0	1,410	4,348	0	4,348
1890-94	337	103	208	50	54	0	520	1,272	0	1,272
1895-99	258	428	362	13	211	0	733	2,005	0	2,005
1900-04	79	35	62	5	9	0	362	552	0	552
1905-09	307	290	413	16	16	108	984	2,134	0	2,134
1910-14	1,776	599	63	165	25	193	676	3,497	0	3,497
TOTAL	5,983	6,942	3,464	575	768	841	7,236	25,809	0	25,809
YR AVG	623	723	361	60	80	87	754	2,688	0	2,688

Dash (--) = No Data

A&E:	Agriculture & Extractive	Mfg:	Manufacturing	Transp: Transportation
Govt:	Government	T&S:	Trade & Services	

with government guarantees) was termed a private one. Secondly, no attempt was made to classify government issues by use; they were termed government whether the funds were "used" to pay public servants, to build railways, or to fight wars.[33] Finally, the private sector was further subdivided into six superindustries: agriculture and extractive, manufacturing, trade and services, finance and real estate, public utilities, and transportation.

Because of the different bases of classification it is impossible to compare these estimates with Simon's series, and a comparison with the Segal–Simon "all years all issues" estimate should be accompanied by a set of clear caveats. If, for example, it is assumed that the public-works sector is entirely government and that nine-tenths of the "all other" sector should be similarly assigned, then the two sets appear to yield quite similar results for the thirty-year period 1865–94.[34] The current study permits a more detailed analysis of the industrial composition of the flows by political sector – a classification that has not previously been available.

About two-thirds of all issues were private, and more than half of private finance went into transport, a figure that translates into about one-third of all finance.[35] The proportions were even higher during the first two decades, as the British financed not only European and American railroads but domestic lines as well. The list of the world's railways that turned to the London market for financial support is very long. Between 1865 and 1880, for example, it included such famous names as the Caledonian; the three Greats (Eastern, Northern, and Western); the Midlands; the North British; and the South Eastern in the United Kingdom. The list also included the B&O, the Erie, the Milwaukee, the New York Central, the Katy, the Pennsy, the Reading, the Southern Pacific, and the Union Pacific in the United States; and the Charkof-Azoff, the Dutch Rhenish, the Orel-Vitebsk, the Roumanian, the Southern Austria, and the Orleans and Chalons in Europe. The market also provided substantial funds for railways whose names were never household words and which have long since faded into history; for example, the Cuxhaven, the Des Moines Valley, the Dunaburk and Witepsk, the Edinburgh and Bathgate, the Keokuk and Kansas City, the Plymouth, the Kankakee and Pacific, and the Taff Vale.

The fraction of total finance accounted for by transportation declined somewhat as those networks in Europe, Britain, and the United States neared completion, but it rose once again as construction boomed in the parts of the Empire with responsible government. That latter surge was largely concentrated in Canada, but there were major issues from Australia (the Midlands and Western Australia) and South Africa [the New Cape Central and the Vryheid (Natal)]. Over the fifty-year period, hardly less than £1.6 billion (British) were directed toward the transport sector, and of that total almost all (97 percent) went to railways.

No other industrial sector attracted nearly as much private capital as the railways, although finance did command about one-fourth as much. Manufacturing ranked third. Relatively unimportant until the mid-1880s, it represented a substantial draw on the total thereafter; and in the late 1890s it drew an average of £16 million a year – just less than a fifth of all finance. The sector's importance declined in the first decade of the present century, but rose again just before the outbreak of the First World War. Of the other three private industrial sectors, agriculture and extractive absorbed approximately 8 percent; public utilities, some 5 percent; and trade and services, about 4 percent of the private total.

Although the government absorbed only one-fourth of domestic finance, the average for the foreign sector was about one-third, and in the Empire it was well above half. The explanation for the comparatively high proportion of government in overseas finance reflects in part the relative difficulty of marketing foreign private issues, and in part marked differences in the composition of demand. The former is, however, a consideration that must have had implications for the public–private mix in both countries and colonies far removed from the London financial center.

There are some sharp contrasts between the composition of the total financial flows and the streams received by the domestic, foreign, and Empire sectors; and these differences are important for any understanding of the financial roots of imperialism, but they have not previously been examined systematically (see Tables 2.7 and 2.8). The data presented are estimates of the relative proportion of finance flowing into the six private industrial sectors in the home, foreign, and Empire markets as compared with the averages of those flows in the total. For example, an Empire transport figure of 150 indicates that, as a proportion of all flows, transport in the Empire was one and a half times as important as that industry was in the market in general. Similarly, a UK figure of 70 would indicate that in Britain transport issues were only 70 percent as important as they were in the "world" market. In the domestic market, the agriculture and extractive category was only about one-fourth as important as it was in the all-finance total, and over time the domestic index fell. Similarly, transport's share of the home market was substantially below the all-finance average total, and it is marked by a strong negative trend, a trend that reflected the virtual completion of the domestic railway network. Before 1890 domestic public utilities issues appeared less frequently than the all-finance averages, but over the succeeding two decades they became much more prominent. Much of domestic gas and water investment antedates 1865; however, the diffusion of electricity, slow by United States and German but fast by world standards, raised the domestic sector's share in the first decade of the twentieth century. In the home country, three other industries all reflect proportions well in excess of the average: finance almost half again as much, and trade and services and manufacturing more than twice that level.

In the foreign sector, the indices for finance, manufacturing, and trade and services are well below the average, and none appear to have been increasing. Public utilities stand almost at the all-finance average; and the agriculture and extractive industry only slightly above, a bias that seems to reflect popular perceptions of the latter industry's profit potential at the time. In the years immediately after the American Civil War, British investors, it is alleged, proved particularly susceptible to the lure of the American West. Any Englishman interested in Western mining – so the story goes – was considered a sitting duck by native sharpshooters. After one particularly shady transaction, a noted London financial journal wrote

TABLE 2.7*

INDUSTRY RELATIVES BY TYPE OF GOVERNMENT

(1,000s £'s)

UNITED KINGDOM

	A&E	Finance	Mfg	PU	T&S	Transp
1865-69	51	114	155	27	127	100
1870-74	56	131	161	42	165	92
1875-79	54	107	131	53	130	98
1880-84	31	124	199	104	202	89
1885-89	57	154	212	61	209	43
1890-94	46	110	183	154	219	55
1895-99	13	67	154	131	157	79
1900-04	10	140	199	187	185	65
1905-09	16	214	344	189	276	47
1910-14	23	230	265	97	299	25
ALL YRS	27	138	206	104	210	68

EMPIRE

	A&E	Finance	Mfg	PU	T&S	Transp
1865-69	217	80	19	183	70	96
1870-74	86	23	32	189	32	123
1875-79	151	215	10	158	26	90
1880-84	293	156	36	180	89	65
1885-89	183	150	11	117	29	108
1890-94	169	193	16	122	31	88
1895-99	236	242	9	44	38	90
1900-04	468	130	30	58	89	67
1905-09	161	76	47	45	30	111
1910-14	169	105	73	82	90	95
ALL YRS	214	118	33	92	50	97

FOREIGN

	A&E	Finance	Mfg	PU	T&S	Transp
1865-69	129	81	26	230	53	105
1870-74	154	84	47	144	32	103
1875-79	192	40	62	193	33	109
1880-84	91	60	40	69	18	121
1885-89	109	44	36	125	33	142
1890-94	132	67	43	45	8	144
1895-99	189	72	50	74	15	150
1900-04	46	44	20	22	11	152
1905-09	100	68	33	95	69	115
1910-14	96	48	50	110	29	131
ALL YRS	109	57	39	102	29	130

INDIA

	A&E	Finance	Mfg	PU	T&S	Transp
1865-69	90	69	7	174	74	117
1870-74	16	23	4	198	33	135
1875-79	198	0	32	252	4	117
1880-84	404	33	40	220	0	81
1885-89	170	56	14	55	0	142
1890-94	341	83	7	--	3	120
1895-99	168	9	3	57	0	240
1900-04	228	14	8	15	218	126
1905-09	119	58	32	63	133	114
1910-14	54	0	11	15	550	143
ALL YRS	139	38	10	104	117	131

RESPONSIBLE GOVERNMENT

	A&E	Finance	Mfg	PU	T&S	Transp
1865-69	99	107	25	0	48	34
1870-74	119	14	46	123	0	127
1875-79	69	203	2	133	0	85
1880-84	247	182	36	186	96	63
1885-89	155	165	11	74	28	111
1890-94	128	200	17	140	39	87
1895-99	297	275	17	34	51	31
1900-04	608	76	48	89	61	56
1905-09	121	42	55	32	16	123
1910-14	110	97	99	92	31	104
ALL YRS	188	111	45	82	33	102

DEPENDENT COLONIES

	A&E	Finance	Mfg	PU	T&S	Transp
1865-69	1,346	131	99	252	0	16
1870-74	113	95	27	663	27	44
1875-79	1,344	431	0	23	166	10
1880-84	295	326	26	32	45	31
1885-89	386	192	0	496	40	37
1890-94	316	263	3	0	4	55
1895-99	190	383	0	48	16	63
1900-04	320	374	6	14	47	43
1905-09	501	352	7	124	21	19
1910-14	467	136	11	83	33	31
ALL YRS	424	249	9	116	29	33

* % in Government
  % in Total

A&E: Agriculture & Extractive   T&S: Trade & Services
Mfg: Manufacturing   Transp: Transportation
PU: Public Utilities

Dash (--) = No Data

NOTE: Issues recorded with no amount called have been excluded.

TABLE 2.8

CAPITAL CALLED UP BY INDUSTRIES AND BY TYPE OF GOVERNMENT (MINIMUM)

(1,000s £'s)

(A) AGRICULTURE & EXTRACTIVE

	United Kingdom	Foreign	Total Empire	Responsible Government	Dependent Colonies	India	Total
1865-69	1,564	1,526	2,160	134	1,338	689	5,250
1870-74	4,315	10,336	1,436	1,201	149	86	16,087
1875-79	572	791	303	98	105	100	1,666
1880-84	2,325	8,119	9,014	4,858	877	3,279	19,458
1885-89	6,149	15,186	7,197	4,444	1,670	1,084	28,532
1890-94	3,224	10,076	3,281	1,969	558	753	16,581
1895-99	2,773	20,340	17,065	10,272	3,902	2,891	40,178
1900-04	1,082	4,547	19,490	14,637	2,970	1,884	25,119
1905-09	1,214	19,516	17,023	10,028	5,559	1,435	37,753
1910-14	2,957	32,890	28,107	12,896	14,195	1,016	63,954
TOTAL	26,175	123,327	105,076	60,537	31,323	13,118	254,458
YR AVG	2,618	12,333	10,508	6,054	3,132	1,322	25,458

(B) FINANCE

	United Kingdom	Foreign	Total Empire	Responsible Government	Dependent Colonies	India	Total
1865-69	18,929	5,141	4,323	775	701	2,847	28,393
1870-74	16,875	9,438	640	231	209	200	26,953
1875-79	11,497	1,661	3,280	2,936	344	0	16,438
1880-84	17,481	10,202	9,076	6,741	1,833	502	36,759
1885-89	29,872	11,152	10,740	8,587	1,507	646	51,764
1890-94	18,656	12,271	9,005	7,442	1,121	441	39,932
1895-99	13,477	6,991	15,858	8,594	7,128	136	36,326
1900-04	27,950	7,927	9,853	3,324	6,322	206	45,730
1905-09	23,292	18,884	11,451	4,906	5,545	1,000	53,627
1910-14	42,291	23,230	21,849	16,018	5,831	0	87,370
TOTAL	220,320	106,897	96,075	59,554	30,541	5,978	423,292
YR AVG	22,032	10,690	9,607	5,955	3,054	598	42,329

(C) MANUFACTURING

	United Kingdom	Foreign	Total Empire	Responsible Government	Dependent Colonies	India	Total
1865-69	8,442	548	335	60	176	100	9,325
1870-74	15,531	3,975	662	589	45	29	20,168
1875-79	4,715	863	65	10	0	55	5,643
1880-84	10,436	2,496	791	504	56	231	13,723
1885-89	49,354	10,828	869	677	0	193	61,051
1890-94	24,638	6,266	527	499	0	28	31,431
1895-99	68,007	10,714	1,367	1,142	125	100	80,088
1900-04	41,303	3,710	2,382	2,164	100	118	47,395
1905-09	22,053	5,421	4,191	3,803	61	326	31,665
1910-14	33,247	16,322	11,719	11,187	329	204	61,288
TOTAL	277,726	61,143	22,908	20,635	892	1,384	361,777
YR AVG	27,773	6,114	2,291	2,064	89	138	36,178

(D) PUBLIC UTILITIES

	United Kingdom	Foreign	Total Empire	Responsible Government	Dependent Colonies	India	Total
1865-69	1,310	4,345	2,523	0	400	2,123	8,178
1870-74	3,129	9,371	3,050	1,200	844	1,006	15,550
1875-79	2,012	2,880	1,157	685	7	465	6,049
1880-84	3,974	3,145	2,826	1,867	48	911	9,945
1885-89	2,623	7,001	1,863	859	864	140	11,487
1890-94	4,589	1,468	916	916	0	--	6,973
1895-99	7,695	2,108	834	315	260	258	10,637
1900-04	14,290	1,507	1,673	1,495	92	85	17,470
1905-09	10,660	13,556	3,513	1,950	1,006	558	27,669
1910-14	7,335	21,692	7,871	6,247	1,460	164	36,898
TOTAL	57,557	67,073	26,226	15,534	4,981	5,710	150,856
YR AVG	5,756	6,707	2,623	1,553	498	571	15,086

(E) TRADE & SERVICES

	United Kingdom	Foreign	Total Empire	Responsible Government	Dependent Colonies	India	Total
1865-69	3,610	580	584	60	0	524	4,774
1870-74	4,337	736	72	0	12	60	5,145
1875-79	3,161	307	35	0	30	5	3,503
1880-84	5,560	584	745	695	50	0	6,889
1885-89	9,138	1,866	394	323	71	0	11,398
1890-94	14,035	558	556	543	7	6	15,149
1895-99	24,388	1,158	1,466	1,235	232	0	27,012
1900-04	11,136	625	2,042	810	242	990	13,803
1905-09	8,984	5,751	1,331	548	100	682	16,066
1910-14	11,454	2,896	4,402	1,062	290	3,049	18,752
TOTAL	95,803	15,061	11,627	5,276	1,034	5,316	122,491
YR AVG	9,580	1,506	1,163	528	103	532	12,249

(F) TRANSPORTATION

	United Kingdom	Foreign	Total Empire	Responsible Government	Dependent Colonies	India	Total
1865-69	55,617	22,427	17,275	821	293	16,161	95,319
1870-74	54,415	52,902	15,706	9,849	442	5,415	123,023
1875-79	47,816	20,799	8,343	5,560	35	2,748	76,958
1880-84	53,890	88,603	16,241	10,144	760	5,337	158,734
1885-89	27,215	116,947	25,174	18,870	943	5,361	169,336
1890-94	23,629	66,807	10,330	8,127	588	1,614	100,766
1895-99	36,565	33,702	13,598	2,251	2,710	8,637	83,865
1900-04	56,680	120,603	22,136	10,753	3,154	8,229	199,419
1905-09	29,168	183,593	96,407	83,416	1,699	11,293	309,168
1910-14	14,519	197,836	69,879	53,701	4,216	11,963	282,234
TOTAL	399,514	904,219	295,089	203,492	14,840	76,758	1,598,822
YR AVG	39,951	90,422	29,509	20,349	1,494	7,676	159,882

that the British investors involved had fallen victim to "gold extract-ing with a vengeance."[36] The *Statist* of July 18, 1885 noted that, "When novices meddle with foreign or colonial mines, they play to lose. American mines," the journal continued, "were not very re-munerative. They are got up exclusively for export."[37]

American cattle ranching, too, seemed to have fired the British investor's imagination. Profitable in the late 1870s and early 1880s, British-owned cattle companies had by the end of the century suf-fered major financial reverses. The loss to British investors between 1884 and 1900 has been placed at about $18,000,000.[38]

In the case of transport, the foreign sector received more than what could be termed its "fair" share. Over time the index rose from 1880 to the mid-1890s, but declined somewhat after 1905. Again, American railways exerted an almost hypnotic effect on the British investor. As late as 1865 there had not been an American railway stock or bond on the British market, but twenty years later British involvement was so great that a collapse in American railway se-curities resulted in a depression throughout Britain.[39]

Railway investment in South American Railways was also heavy, particularly in Argentina.[40] The Peruvian Corporation, a British firm, for example, counted among its holdings no less than eight of Peru's railways. As in the United States, investment patterns were often more enthusiastic than wise. In reference to the Chimbote Railway, the corporation's records point out:

> In the early days of the Corporation hope was always held out that as soon as various coal deposits were reached there would be im-mediate traffic for the railway. In practice, however, the first coal deposit reached ... proved quite worthless and the same was found to be the case with the coal deposits at Huallancana .... [41]

Once more, the Central Railway was conceived in part to serve the Cerro de Pasco silver mines, but due to wrong-headed intransigence the corporation lost that concession even before the line was com-pleted. As the company records admit:

> It is evident that the Corporation had abundant opportunity and power to retain this concession to construct the railway and open up the mines but all this was allowed to fall in other hands. [To add insult to injury copper was discovered] ... the existence of which the original concessionaries had no idea.... [42]

In the Empire, manufacturing and trade and services both received substantially smaller fractions of total finance than world levels. Empire transport, however, received funds in proportions that were more or less "typical," and the sector's share of finance stood above the general average. That latter figure reflects in large part the issues of the financial, land, and investment companies that inflated the sector's total, particularly in the last three decades of the century. Those firms were closely tied to land and depended for their profits on well-defined property rights. Similarly, Empire agriculture and extractive firms received much more than their proportionate shares, and the sector's share was particularly large in the decade 1896 to 1905. That surge was associated not with agriculture but with mining (particularly gold mining). Although the list of firms included those as familiar as De Beers, it was dominated by names with a "get rich quick" aura, including, for example, the Ivanhoe, the World's Treasure, and the Corsair.

While the Empire played third fiddle to the home and foreign sectors in terms of total resources drawn from the Victorian financial markets, it displayed a greater-than-average affinity for finance and for agriculture and extractive issues. In the colonies with responsible government the agriculture and extractive industries drew substantially above-average proportions of finance, but these indices were well below those displayed by the dependent colonies. In the case of finance, the self-governing colonies received somewhat more than average amounts; however, that inflated figure largely reflects the boom in Australasian land and development companies in the decade and a half after 1875, and the similar activities in South Africa in the 1890s. In transport, the self-governing colonies received about "typical" proportions, and while somewhat above all-Empire averages in manufacturing, they were below that figure for trade and commerce. For public utilities, on the other hand, the fractions received were below the world, the all-Empire, and the foreign-sector averages. In summary, it appears that in the areas of the Empire with responsible government (and they were parts of the Empire that attracted the greatest absolute levels of finance), the stream of private finance tended to be directed toward the agriculture and extractive industries, toward finance, and, to a lesser degree, toward transport.

Although the dependent colonies received only 2.5 percent of all private finance, the industrial composition was quite different from the patterns prevailing either in the self-governing portions of the Empire or in India. In manufacturing, trade and services, and transport, the dependent colonies received substantially less than normal proportions, and there is no evidence of an upward trend in any of the three series. In the agriculture and extractive industries, in the public utilities, and in finance, the dependent colonies drew proportions well above Empire and all-world levels. For finance, the fifty-year average was almost two and a half times, and for agriculture and extractive, it was more than four times typical proportions; and those levels were almost as high at the end of the period as they had been at the beginning. Intrasectoral analysis indicates that it was the financial, land, and development component that produced the inflated finance figure. Thus, it appears that in the dependent colonies, finance imperialism, to the degree that it existed, was intimately connected to the possession of land and a legal structure that gave British investors the right to relatively unfettered exercise of their ownership privileges.

In India, the other part of the dependent Empire, transport and agriculture and extractive industries drew relative shares of finance almost 50 percent above the world average. In the latter industry, the major transfusions occurred during the two and a half decades between 1880 and 1905; but at both the beginning and the end of the period, the subcontinent drew less than normal proportions. While tea, rubber, and even oil companies contributed to that rise, the greatest impetus came from the financial demands of the Indian gold fields. Thus, while firms like the Assam Oil Company, the Consolidated Tea and Lands Company, the Imperial Tea Company, and the India Rubber Estates all managed to market issues with values between £100,000 and £1,000,000, the Gold Fields of Mysore drew £691,000; the Mysore Reef Gold, £500,000; the Kempinkote Gold Field, £275,000; and even firms with names like Coromandel, Dharwai, and Jibutil floated issues of over £100,000.

Transport remained vital throughout the period, and railroads were almost as important a component of private finance in India as they were in the foreign sector (the index for both was 129). On the subcontinent, railroad finance was bolstered immeasurably by government's guarantee of interest payments. From 1859 to 1869 the guarantee stood at 5 percent, and even the modified scheme initiated in 1879 left the figure at 4 percent which, given the current rate on government bonds of 3.1 percent, was no mean inducement to a potential investor.

To summarize: the concept of finance imperialism, insofar as it had substance at all, must have been linked to the agriculture and extractive sector throughout the dependent Empire; to the financial, land, and development component of the finance industry in the dependent colonies; and to railroads in India.

Relative measures suggest something about tendencies, and perhaps about relative profit rates; however, the Hobson-Lenin argument does not hinge on such tendencies, but on the magnitude of finance directed toward the Empire. From the relative measures it may be possible to infer that some Empire activities were more profitable than others (and those inferences may suggest something about the nature of imperialism), but the total magnitude of the transfers must be examined if one is to conclude that exploitative profits drove the imperial engine (see Tables 2.9A and 2.9B). It is, after all, total profit, not the rate of profit, that is relevant to the argument; and on that point, the evidence is much more ambiguous.

In the case of the agriculture and extractive sector, while almost one-half of the total flow went into the foreign sector, the Empire's share was just above 40 percent. Of that figure, about two-fifths went to the dependent colonies and India, and the proportion shows some tendency to increase over time, although those gains were concentrated in the dependent colonies. Still, the amount of agriculture and extractive finance channeled to colonies with responsible government was substantial (about a quarter of the total), and the foreign sector's share was larger than the entire Empire total. Thus, although the dependent Empire may well have been a lucrative area for agricultural and extractive investment, it is clear that political dominance, although perhaps useful, was not a necessary prerequisite.

In the case of finance, the home market received more than one-half the total funds, the foreign sector about one-quarter, and the Empire the remainder, divided in a proportion of three to two between self-governing and dependent sectors. For manufacturing, the Empire was unimportant, and the dependent portion insignificant. The entire Empire drew hardly more than 5 percent, although that fraction tripled in the last pre-war decade. Of that total, nine-tenths went to the colonies with responsible government, leaving hardly more than .5 percent for both India and the dependent colonies. Even in the final decade, when the Empire's fraction was almost one-fifth, it was Canada, growing behind substantial tariff barriers, that drew the major share. While both the Australian Smelting Company and Ohlssons' Cape Brewery appear on the list of Empire firms issuing blocks of securities valued at more than £100,000 in the years after 1905, 36 of those 38 firms were located in the North American dominion. The Imperial Tobacco Company of Canada by itself attracted £2,635,000; and, although no other firm received as much, a greater total was received by the Dominion's embryonic steel industry (Algoma Steel, Canada Iron, Dominion Iron and Steel, and the Steel Company of Canada).

The Empire's share of all trade and service finance was less than 10 percent, but, of that sum, the dependent Empire drew more than half. The dependent colonies received only a tiny fraction, but India alone drew more than all of the colonies with responsible government.

TABLE 2.9A

CAPITAL CALLED UP, INDUSTRIES BY CONTINENTS - ALL GOVERNMENTS

(1,000s £'s)

AFRICA

	A&E	Finance	Mfg	PU	T&S	Trans	Unknown	Total Private	Govt	Total
1865-69	78	709	0	0	560	227	0	1,574	10,129	11,703
1870-74	117	1,349	0	510	12	586	0	2,574	229	2,803
1875-79	54	250	0	200	32	0	0	534	15,815	16,349
1880-84	1,827	2,576	104	688	194	1,400	213	7,002	11,813	18,815
1885-89	3,113	1,860	153	998	135	1,154	56	7,469	12,798	20,267
1890-94	4,731	1,451	91	271	170	603	13	7,330	12,926	20,256
1895-99	9,916	9,781	376	308	698	4,899	111	26,081	7,741	33,822
1900-04	12,839	13,782	3,006	396	934	3,248	274	34,479	54,604	89,083
1905-09	12,052	14,570	1,207	1,181	251	2,976	236	32,473	23,735	56,208
1910-14	13,782	6,747	481	1,579	258	3,439	58	26,344	14,554	40,898
TOTAL	58,509	53,075	5,418	6,123	3,242	18,532	961	145,860	164,344	310,204
YR AVG	1,170	1,061	108	122	64	371	19	2,917	3,287	6,204

ASIA

	A&E	Finance	Mfg	PU	T&S	Trans	Unknown	Total Private	Govt	Total
1865-69	1,394	2,997	275	2,693	524	16,467	0	24,350	2,017	26,367
1870-74	149	2,187	74	2,564	98	6,049	0	11,121	8,458	19,579
1875-79	206	2,170	141	513	0	2,784	0	3,819	22,616	26,435
1880-84	3,685	1,688	355	946	0	6,721	27	13,422	14,159	27,581
1885-89	2,050	2,058	233	213	40	9,050	93	13,737	22,280	36,017
1890-94	1,561	2,161	44	4	10	4,793	96	8,669	24,556	33,225
1895-99	3,881	491	297	258	11	9,909	10	14,857	36,782	51,639
1900-04	2,986	1,388	118	85	990	9,955	140	15,662	23,476	39,138
1905-09	5,811	3,928	483	558	702	18,939	126	30,547	66,087	96,634
1910-14	15,846	2,177	1,922	873	3,086	18,880	61	42,845	43,063	85,908
TOTAL	37,569	19,245	3,942	8,707	5,466	103,547	553	179,029	263,494	442,523
YR AVG	751	385	79	174	109	2,071	11	3,581	5,269	8,850

AUSTRALIA/PACIFIC

	A&E	Finance	Mfg	PU	T&S	Trans	Unknown	Total Private	Govt	Total
1865-69	443	1,180	60	0	0	168	20	1,871	9,844	11,715
1870-74	436	3,004	349	540	0	1,479	0	5,808	9,392	15,200
1875-79	80	2,947	10	688	0	0	172	3,897	31,178	35,075
1880-84	3,155	4,887	412	1,019	670	1,178	73	11,394	46,058	57,452
1885-89	3,193	7,896	200	384	264	1,591	12	13,540	54,711	68,251
1890-94	921	6,325	406	452	456	685	314	9,559	25,385	34,944
1895-99	10,063	8,841	725	66	731	1,008	311	21,745	12,749	34,494
1900-04	3,448	656	98	1,391	108	844	86	6,631	19,949	26,580
1905-09	3,941	1,504	149	60	496	149	1	6,300	16,277	22,577
1910-14	3,158	6,307	84	399	113	1,476	76	11,613	56,505	68,118
TOTAL	28,838	43,547	2,493	4,999	2,838	8,578	1,065	92,358	282,048	374,406
YR AVG	577	871	50	100	57	172	21	1,847	5,641	7,488

NORTH AMERICA

	A&E	Finance	Mfg	PU	T&S	Trans	Unknown	Total Private	Govt	Total
1865-69	573	1,052	0	1,858	32	11,437	0	14,952	1,986	16,938
1870-74	5,324	2,322	2,508	2,122	0	44,785	0	57,061	13,423	70,484
1875-79	238	819	320	2,261	38	21,498	10	25,174	15,739	40,913
1880-84	5,572	7,718	984	736	110	66,570	342	81,700	3,884	85,584
1885-89	5,096	6,006	8,839	2,214	87	55,106	303	77,690	13,225	90,915
1890-94	3,929	927	5,096	287	64	45,687	58	63,293	14,607	77,900
1895-99	4,588	2,166	2,620	817	343	16,471	85	27,063	5,829	32,892
1900-04	2,871	1,918	374	596	178	105,604	193	111,626	2,243	113,869
1905-09	6,876	3,354	4,386	12,026	453	180,472		207,760	33,522	241,282
1910-14	18,406	14,460	20,376	18,201	1,104	160,525	1,057	234,129	52,781	286,910
TOTAL	53,473	47,742	45,503	41,118	2,409	708,155	2,048	900,448	157,239	1,057,687
YR AVG	1,069	955	910	822	48	14,163	41	18,009	3,144	21,154

SOUTH AMERICA, CENTRAL AMERICA & CARIBBEAN

	A&E	Finance	Mfg	PU	T&S	Trans	Unknown	Total Private	Govt	Total
1865-69	839	466	355	461	0	3,517	10	5,648	11,042	16,690
1870-74	1,341	889	193	3,359	25	11,709	20	17,536	29,165	46,701
1875-79	141	599	350	177	84	2,864	0	4,215	8,387	12,602
1880-84	1,758	1,154	646	636	145	25,540	13	29,892	11,384	41,276
1885-89	7,080	3,640	821	4,742	1,265	65,564	120	83,232	45,665	128,897
1890-94	1,530	3,413	322	658	143	22,386	75	28,527	14,063	42,590
1895-99	3,001	305	1,981	1,209	221	11,233		17,950	11,278	29,228
1900-04	756	21	982	494	15	22,783	106	25,157	9,169	34,326
1905-09	3,639	6,812	718	1,746	338	74,035	34	87,322	37,396	124,718
1910-14	4,371	10,299	2,330	5,839	2,246	78,989	368	104,442	49,488	153,930
TOTAL	24,456	27,598	8,698	19,321	4,482	318,620	746	403,921	227,037	630,958
YR AVG	489	552	174	386	90	6,372	15	8,078	4,541	12,619

EUROPE

	A&E	Finance	Mfg	PU	T&S	Trans	Unknown	Total Private	Govt	Total
1865-69	360	3,071	193	1,856	48	7,886	0	13,414	6,309	19,723
1870-74	4,404	3,120	1,514	3,326	674	4,001	11	17,050	3,534	20,584
1875-79	375	3,155	108	1,198	186	1,996	30	3,048	8,136	11,184
1880-84	1,187	1,254	787	1,947	210	3,436	8	8,841	64,509	73,350
1885-89	1,852	452	1,602	315	470	9,657	31	14,356	15,411	29,767
1890-94	685	1,277	834	712	244	2,983	69	5,489	21,524	27,013
1895-99	5,957	15	6,082	291	621	3,779		18,076	24,856	42,932
1900-04	1,138	167	1,515	218	441	305		3,632	15,371	19,003
1905-09	4,221	5,117	2,670	1,449	4,841	3,430	314	17,092	24,216	41,308
1910-14	5,419		2,873	2,666	491	4,405	1,293	22,264	42,537	64,801
TOTAL	25,598	14,628	18,178	12,978	8,226	41,878	1,776	123,262	226,403	349,665
YR AVG	512	293	364	260	165	838	36	2,465	4,528	6,993

A&E: Agriculture & Extractive   PU: Public Utilities   Trans: Transportation
Mfg: Manufacturing   T&S: Trade & Services

64

TABLE 2.9B

CAPITAL CALLED UP, INDUSTRIES BY CONTINENT & GOVERNMENT

(1,000s £'s)

ASIA – FOREIGN

	A&E	Finance	Mfg	PU	T&S	Trans	Unknown	Total Private	Govt	Total
1865-69	150	150	0	530	0	206	0	1,036	1,818	2,854
1870-74	30	1,819	0	1,208	38	532	0	3,627	3,383	7,010
1875-79	0	0	86	48	0	36	0	170	2,875	3,045
1880-84	96	50	124	35	15	1,384	3	1,689	91	1,780
1885-89	323	908	40	57	0	3,599	96	4,945	3,735	8,680
1890-94	468	875	16	4	0	3,068	0	4,527	5,621	10,148
1895-99	226	25	180	0	0	1,030	0	1,461	28,923	30,384
1900-04	8	1,069	0	0	0	233	140	1,450	13,757	15,207
1905-09	1,080	1,021	156	0	19	6,576	75	8,927	42,726	51,653
1910-14	4,686	131	1,582	710	4	6,831	20	13,964	21,706	35,670
TOTAL	7,067	6,048	2,184	2,592	76	23,495	334	41,796	124,635	166,431
YR AVG	141	121	44	52	2	470	7	836	2,493	3,329

ASIA – INDIA

	A&E	Finance	Mfg	PU	T&S	Trans	Unknown	Total Private	Govt	Total
1865-69	689	2,847	100	2,123	524	16,161	0	22,444	0	22,444
1870-74	86	200	29	1,006	60	5,415	0	6,796	5,075	11,871
1875-79	100	0	55	465	5	2,748	0	3,373	19,534	22,907
1880-84	3,279	502	231	911	0	5,337	11	10,271	12,304	22,575
1885-89	1,084	646	193	140	6	5,361	90	7,514	18,254	25,768
1890-94	753	441	28	0	0	1,614	0	2,842	17,779	20,621
1895-99	2,891	136	100	258	0	8,637	10	12,032	7,466	19,498
1900-04	1,884	206	118	85	990	8,229	0	11,512	8,396	19,908
1905-09	1,435	1,000	326	558	682	11,293	0	15,294	22,124	37,418
1910-14	1,016	0	204	164	3,049	11,963	9	16,405	19,652	36,057
TOTAL	13,217	5,978	1,384	5,710	5,316	76,758	120	108,483	130,584	239,067
YR AVG	265	120	28	114	106	1,535	2	2,170	2,612	4,781

ASIA – DEPENDENT COLONIES

	A&E	Finance	Mfg	PU	T&S	Trans	Unknown	Total Private	Govt	Total
1865-69	555	0	176	40	0	100	0	871	199	1,070
1870-74	33	169	45	350	0	102	0	699	0	699
1875-79	105	170	0	0	0	0	0	275	207	482
1880-84	310	1,136	0	16	0	0	0	1,462	1,764	3,226
1885-89	644	504	16	0	25	90	0	1,279	291	1,570
1890-94	341	844	0	0	4	111	0	1,300	1,155	2,455
1895-99	763	330	0	0	11	243	16	1,363	394	1,757
1900-04	1,094	112	0	0	0	1,493	0	2,699	1,323	4,022
1905-09	3,297	1,907	0	0	0	1,070	51	6,325	1,238	7,563
1910-14	10,144	2,046	136	0	33	86	32	12,477	1,705	14,182
TOTAL	17,286	7,218	373	406	73	3,295	99	28,750	8,276	37,026
YR AVG	346	145	7	8	1	66	2	575	166	741

AFRICA – FOREIGN

	A&E	Finance	Mfg	PU	T&S	Trans	Unknown	Total Private	Govt	Total
1865-69	30	540	0	0	500	197	0	1,267	8,733	10,000
1870-74	56	1,228	0	410	0	203	0	1,957	85	2,042
1875-79	54	200	0	200	0	0	0	454	6,800	7,254
1880-84	792	2,221	36	215	119	430	80	3,893	100	3,993
1885-89	2,341	1,528	67	225	50	661	30	4,902	10,820	15,722
1890-94	3,515	897	23	37	167	598	13	5,250	7,645	12,895
1895-99	7,987	3,459	198	194	299	3,173	95	15,405	1,616	17,021
1900-04	944	4,904	867	208	0	811	4	7,738	1,826	9,564
1905-09	4,597	8,956	344	99	99	2,293	146	16,534	3,071	19,605
1910-14	10,053	3,263	132	221	67	67	48	13,784	7,990	21,774
TOTAL	30,369	27,256	1,667	1,809	1,234	8,433	416	71,184	48,686	119,870
YR AVG	607	545	33	36	25	169		1,424	974	2,397

AFRICA – RESPONSIBLE GOVERNMENT

	A&E	Finance	Mfg	PU	T&S	Trans	Unknown	Total Private	Govt	Total
1865-69	0	0	0	0	60	0	0	60	113	173
1870-74	0	22	0	0	0	76	0	98	94	192
1875-79	0	50	0	0	0	50	0	50	8,915	8,965
1880-84	831	278	68	473	25	270	0	1,945	11,713	13,658
1885-89	341	68	86	40	39	50	0	624	1,705	2,329
1890-94	998	277	67	234	0	166	0	1,576	4,674	6,250
1895-99	199	834	179	137	209	1,259	192	1,587	5,592	7,179
1900-04	10,174	2,723	2,039	98	692	683	67	17,216	50,204	67,420
1905-09	5,322	2,129	856	0	53	375	259	9,208	15,154	24,362
1910-14	374	40	164	982	1,078	2,879	5	953	418	1,371
TOTAL	18,239	6,421	3,459	982	1,078	2,879		33,317	98,582	131,899
YR AVG	365	128	69	20	22	58		666	1,972	2,638

AFRICA – DEPENDENT COLONIES

	A&E	Finance	Mfg	PU	T&S	Trans	Unknown	Total Private	Govt	Total
1865-69	48	169	0	0	0	30	0	247	1,283	1,530
1870-74	61	40	0	100	12	308	0	521	50	571
1875-79	0	0	0	0	30	0	0	30	100	130
1880-84	204	78	0	733	50	700	133	1,165	0	1,165
1885-89	430	264	0	0	46	443	26	1,942	273	2,215
1890-94	218	277	0	0	3	5	0	503	606	1,109
1895-99	1,730	5,488	0	106	190	1,560	16	9,090	533	9,623
1900-04	1,721	6,156	100	51	242	1,179	77	9,526	2,574	12,100
1905-09	2,134	3,486	6	985	100		19	6,730	5,509	12,239
1910-14	3,356	3,444	160	1,358	258	2,998	280	11,583	6,147	17,730
TOTAL	9,902	19,402	266	3,333	931	7,223		41,337	17,075	58,412
YR AVG	198	388	5	67	19	144	6	827	342	1,168

TABLE 2.9B (Continued)

AUSTRALIA/PACIFIC - FOREIGN

	A&E	Finance	Mfg	PU	T&S	Trans	Unknown	Total Private	Govt	Total
1865-69	--	--	--	--	--	--	--	--	--	--
1870-74	--	--	--	--	--	--	--	--	--	--
1875-79	--	--	--	--	--	--	--	--	--	--
1880-84	--	--	--	--	--	--	--	--	--	--
1885-89	0	0	0	0	0	63	0	63	196	259
1890-94	40	0	0	0	0	0	0	40	0	40
1895-99	375	0	0	0	0	0	0	375	0	375
1900-04	38	0	0	49	0	0	0	87	0	87
1905-09	13	0	0	0	0	0	0	13	0	13
1910-14	360	0	0	0	0	0	0	360	0	360
TOTAL	826	0	0	49	0	63	0	938	196	1,134
YR AVG	28			2		2		31	7	38

AUSTRALIA/PACIFIC - RESPONSIBLE GOVERNMENT

	A&E	Finance	Mfg	PU	T&S	Trans	Unknown	Total Private	Govt	Total
1865-69	98	750	60	0	0	5	0	913	9,844	10,757
1870-74	436	209	349	540	0	1,479	0	3,013	9,392	12,405
1875-79	80	2,773	10	685	0	0	172	3,720	30,983	34,703
1880-84	2,946	4,305	367	1,019	670	1,178	73	10,558	45,418	55,976
1885-89	2,954	7,137	200	384	264	1,253	0	12,192	53,852	66,044
1890-94	881	6,325	406	452	456	685	314	9,519	25,385	34,904
1895-99	8,810	7,528	616	66	700	1,008	311	19,039	12,436	31,475
1900-04	3,289	602	98	1,301	108	844	86	6,328	19,949	26,277
1905-09	3,860	1,429	94	39	496	149	1	6,068	16,277	22,345
1910-14	2,775	5,978	51	386	113	1,476	76	10,855	56,505	67,360
TOTAL	26,129	37,036	2,251	4,872	2,807	8,077	1,033	82,205	280,041	362,246
YR AVG	523	741	45	97	56	162	21	1,644	5,601	7,245

AUSTRALIA/PACIFIC - DEPENDENT COLONIES

	A&E	Finance	Mfg	PU	T&S	Trans	Unknown	Total Private	Govt	Total
1865-69	345	420	0	0	0	163	20	948	0	948
1870-74	--	--	--	--	--	--	--	--	--	--
1875-79	0	174	0	3	0	0	0	177	195	372
1880-84	160	581	45	0	0	0	0	786	639	1,425
1885-89	239	739	0	0	0	275	12	1,265	664	1,929
1890-94	--	--	--	--	--	--	--	--	--	--
1895-99	878	1,301	109	0	31	0	0	2,319	313	2,632
1900-04	122	55	0	41	0	0	0	218	0	218
1905-09	68	75	55	21	0	0	0	219	0	219
1910-14	23	301	33	13	0	0	0	370	0	370
TOTAL	1,835	3,646	242	78	31	438	32	6,302	1,811	8,113
YR AVG	37	73	5	2	1	9	1	126	36	162

NORTH AMERICA - FOREIGN

	A&E	Finance	Mfg	PU	T&S	Trans	Unknown	Total Private	Govt	Total
1865-69	537	914	0	1,858	32	10,621	0	13,962	1,661	15,623
1870-74	4,560	2,322	2,268	1,462	0	36,490	0	47,102	5,068	52,170
1875-79	220	707	320	2,261	38	15,938	0	19,484	2,759	22,243
1880-84	4,491	5,523	914	361	110	57,873	10	69,282	269	69,551
1885-89	3,919	4,624	8,447	1,778	67	37,539	290	56,664	2,238	58,902
1890-94	3,339	7,086	5,070	58	4	38,245	293	54,595	7,009	61,604
1895-99	3,307	1,933	2,273	483	18	14,994	13	23,021	2,775	25,796
1900-04	1,696	1,918	346	538	169	96,954	10	101,631	400	102,031
1905-09	6,029	1,932	1,532	10,263	453	97,330	56	117,595	7,090	124,685
1910-14	8,578	4,426	9,404	12,345	155	107,543	378	142,829	3,735	146,564
TOTAL	37,176	31,385	30,574	31,407	1,046	513,527	1,050	646,165	33,004	679,169
YR AVG	744	628	611	628	21	10,271	21	12,923	660	13,583

NORTH AMERICA - RESPONSIBLE GOVERNMENT

	A&E	Finance	Mfg	PU	T&S	Trans	Unknown	Total Private	Govt	Total
1865-69	36	25	0	0	0	816	0	877	225	1,102
1870-74	764	0	240	660	0	8,295	0	9,959	8,355	18,314
1875-79	18	113	0	0	0	5,560	0	5,691	12,980	18,671
1880-84	1,081	2,158	70	375	0	8,697	0	12,381	3,615	15,996
1885-89	1,149	1,382	392	436	20	17,567	52	20,998	10,987	31,985
1890-94	90	840	26	230	60	7,442	10	8,698	7,598	16,296
1895-99	1,262	233	347	249	326	1,077	33	3,527	3,054	6,581
1900-04	1,175	0	27	58	9	8,650	75	9,994	1,843	11,837
1905-09	847	1,347	2,853	1,763	0	82,584	137	89,531	26,432	115,963
1910-14	9,748	9,999	10,927	5,856	994	51,849	679	90,052	49,047	139,099
TOTAL	16,170	16,097	14,882	9,627	1,409	192,537	986	251,708	124,136	375,844
YR AVG	323	322	298	193	28	3,851	20	5,034	2,483	7,517

NORTH AMERICA - DEPENDENT COLONIES

	A&E	Finance	Mfg	PU	T&S	Trans	Unknown	Total Private	Govt	Total
1865-69	0	113	0	0	0	0	0	113	100	213
1870-74	--	--	--	--	--	--	--	--	--	--
1875-79	--	--	--	--	--	--	--	--	--	--
1880-84	0	38	0	0	0	0	0	38	0	38
1885-89	28	0	0	0	0	0	0	28	0	28
1890-94	--	--	--	--	--	--	--	--	--	--
1895-99	19	0	0	85	0	400	13	517	0	517
1900-04	--	--	--	--	--	--	--	--	--	--
1905-09	0	74	0	0	0	558	0	632	0	632
1910-14	80	35	0	0	0	1,132	0	1,247	0	1,247
TOTAL	127	260	0	85	0	2,090	13	2,575	100	2,675
YR AVG	4	9	0	3	0	70	0	86	3	89

EUROPE — FOREIGN

	A&E	Finance	Mfg	PU	T&S	Trans	Unknown	Total Private	Govt	Total
1865-69	360	3,071	193	1,496	48	7,886	0	13,054	6,309	19,363
1870-74	4,404	3,120	1,514	2,996	674	3,971	11	16,690	3,534	20,224
1875-79	375	155	108	195	186	1,961	30	3,010	8,136	11,146
1880-84	1,187	1,254	787	1,947	210	3,376	20	8,781	64,509	73,290
1885-89	1,852	452	1,452	313	470	9,522	8	14,069	15,411	29,480
1890-94	685	0	834	712	244	2,720	31	5,226	21,524	26,750
1895-99	5,957	1,277	6,082	291	621	3,779	69	18,076	24,856	42,932
1900-04	1,138	15	1,515	218	441	305	0	3,632	15,371	19,003
1905-09	4,221	167	2,670	1,449	4,841	3,398	314	17,060	24,216	41,276
1910-14	5,419	5,117	2,873	2,666	491	4,405	1,293	22,264	42,537	64,801
TOTAL	25,598	14,628	18,028	12,283	8,226	41,323	1,776	121,862	226,403	348,265
YR AVG	512	293	361	246	165	826	36	2,437	4,528	6,965

EUROPE — DEPENDENT COLONIES

	A&E	Finance	Mfg	PU	T&S	Trans	Unknown	Total Private	Govt	Total
1865-69	0	0	0	360	0	0	0	360	0	360
1870-74	0	0	0	330	0	30	0	360	0	360
1875-79	0	0	0	4	0	35	0	39	0	39
1880-84	0	0	0	0	0	60	0	60	0	60
1885-89	0	0	0	2	0	135	0	137	0	137
1890-94	0	0	0	0	0	263	0	263	0	263
1895-99	--	--	--	--	--	--	--	--	--	--
1900-04	--	--	--	--	--	--	--	--	--	--
1905-09	0	0	0	0	0	32	0	32	--	32
1910-14	--	--	--	--	--	--	--	--	0	--
TOTAL	0	0	0	696	0	555	0	1,251	0	1,251
YR AVG	0	0	0	20	0	16	0	36	0	36

SOUTH AMERICA — FOREIGN

	A&E	Finance	Mfg	PU	T&S	Trans	Unknown	Total Private	Govt	Total
1865-69	449	466	355	461	0	3,517	10	5,258	11,012	16,270
1870-74	1,286	889	193	3,295	25	11,707	20	17,415	28,667	46,082
1875-79	141	599	350	177	84	2,864	0	4,215	8,191	12,406
1880-84	1,554	1,154	635	588	145	25,540	13	29,629	10,429	40,058
1885-89	6,751	3,640	821	4,628	1,265	65,564	120	82,789	45,181	127,970
1890-94	1,530	3,413	322	658	143	22,176	75	28,317	13,692	42,009
1895-99	2,489	297	1,981	1,140	221	10,726	0	16,854	10,634	27,488
1900-04	723	21	982	494	15	22,301	106	24,642	9,064	33,706
1905-09	3,578	6,809	718	1,746	338	73,996	21	87,206	37,326	124,532
1910-14	3,794	10,294	2,330	5,750	2,246	78,989	334	103,737	49,186	152,923
TOTAL	22,295	27,582	8,687	18,937	4,482	317,380	699	400,062	223,382	623,444
YR AVG	446	552	174	397	90	6,348	14	8,001	4,468	12,469

SOUTH AMERICA — DEPENDENT COLONIES

	A&E	Finance	Mfg	PU	T&S	Trans	Unknown	Total Private	Govt	Total
1865-69	390	0	0	0	0	0	0	390	30	420
1870-74	55	0	0	64	0	3	0	122	497	619
1875-79	0	0	11	0	0	0	0	0	196	196
1880-84	204	0	0	48	0	0	0	263	955	1,218
1885-89	329	0	0	114	0	0	0	443	484	927
1890-94	0	0	0	0	0	210	0	210	371	581
1895-99	512	8	0	69	0	507	0	1,096	644	1,740
1900-04	33	0	0	0	0	482	0	515	105	620
1905-09	61	3	0	0	0	39	12	115	70	185
1910-14	577	5	0	89	0	0	33	704	303	1,007
TOTAL	2,161	16	0	384	0	1,241	45	3,858	3,655	7,513
YR AVG	43	0	0	8	0	25	5	77	73	150

Dash (--) = No Data

A&E: Agriculture & Extractive PU: Public Utilities Trans: Transportation
Mfg: Manufacturing T&S: Trade & Services

That latter somewhat surprising result was the product of the last five years of the study when the subcontinent drew over £3,000,000 in trade finance – the role played by Shell Oil being particularly important.

The home market absorbed about two-fifths of the funds destined for the public utilities, and the foreign sector somewhat more. Of the remaining fifth, the self-governing colonies received about 60 percent and the dependent regions 40 percent. If, however, the years 1910–14 are excluded – a quinquennium that saw the colonies with responsible government absorbing an eighth of all public-utility finance – the dependent Empire outdrew its self-governing equivalent.[43]

For transport, foreign-sector demand was by far the most important. It accounted for about a third of the total before 1880, and over 60 percent thereafter. United Kingdom receipts averaged another 25 percent, but still the Empire received almost one-fifth, and that share increased substantially after the turn of the century. While the bulk of the flows went to colonies with responsible government, something less than a third went to the dependent Empire, almost all of the latter going to India.

The Empire received almost 40 percent of all government finance, and while more than three-quarters was accounted for by the issues of responsible governments, almost £1 in 10 was destined for the dependent Empire. Of that sum, India received somewhat less than 8 percent and the dependent colonies slightly less than 2. As with the agriculture and extractive, transport, and the public-utility industries in the private sector, it appears that the continued stability of the financial instruments of the governments of the dependent Empire may have been an important consideration for the few, if not the many, British investors.

V. The data: the industrial composition of regional finance

The examination of the industrial and geographic composition of the flows of finance provide evidence that at some times, in some places, and in some industries, the dependent Empire might have exerted noticeable pressure on British investors and the London financial community. A further breakdown of the "financial flows" makes it possible to isolate those "times and places" where arguments about the exploitative nature of "finance capitalism" may not be patently false.

In the first place, the economic needs of an area, and therefore the region's demand for finance, are not the same in every country. Instead of an all-world standard, the flows of funds to the dependent empire could better be measured against continent-wide, not world-wide, standards (see Table 2.10). In the second place, an examination of the geographic distribution of flows strongly indicates that "those places" (where finance imperialism might have reigned) could only be in Africa or Asia. The dependent colonies in Europe, North and South America, and Australasia drew less than .5 percent of all London-based finance; and no matter how profitable those investments were, it is inconceivable that they could have had any noticeable impact on the British economy. The dependent empire in Africa and Asia absorbed a little more than 7 percent of the total. Expropriation or dramatic changes in the yields of those issues might well have had an impact on Britain, and certainly they would have been felt in the financial centers.

Although the total level of African finance amounted to only slightly more than 1 percent of the total, there were important differences between the flows destined for the dependent colonies and those that went to the other political regions on the African continent. Despite the lure of King Solomon's mines and later agricultural expansion in East Africa, the first decade aside, the relative proportions of finance received by the dependent colonies (60) was well below the continent-wide average and even further below the proportions received by the colonies with responsible government. Although the totals were not large, the shares of public utilities (193), transport (138), and finance (129) received by those dependent colonies were well above the all-continent average, and the share of trade and services slightly above it. The finance totals in Africa, as elsewhere, are inflated by receipts of the financial, land, and development firms.

In Asia, the dependent colonies and India developed differently. For the former, the proportion of agriculture and extractive finance was high, almost three times the continent average, and it accounted for almost half of all the finance received by those colonies. Finance, too, was well above continent averages and accounted for about a fifth of the total transfers to those colonies. Again, it was land and the land-related industries that inflated the total.

The flows to the agriculture and extractive sector were a much smaller proportion of the total finance in India than elsewhere in the Asian dependent Empire (only £1 in 5 as compared with almost .5). Although India's total private financial receipts were five times those of the dependent colonies, the total amount of agriculture and extractive finance was only about three-fourths that received by those colonial possessions. The trade and services proportion was, however, more than one and a half times the Asian average; and,

TABLE 2.10

INDUSTRIAL PROFILES BY CONTINENT*

(Africa & Asia Only)

AFRICA - FOREIGN

	A&E	Finance	Mfg	Public Utilities	Trade & Services	Trans	Total Private	Govt
1865-69	48	95	0	0	111	108	95	101
1870-74	64	126	0	106	0	46	104	51
1875-79	118	94	0	118	0	0	191	97
1880-84	78	155	60	56	111	55	262	4
1885-89	115	125	70	34	56	87	85	109
1890-94	104	86	33	19	139	139	112	93
1895-99	136	60	93	108	70	110	117	41
1900-04	33	159	129	245	0	112	209	37
1905-09	75	121	57	17	75	151	146	31
1910-14	139	93	56	27	0	4	98	103
TOTAL	106	105	62	600	77	93	126	77

AFRICA - RESPONSIBLE GOVERNMENT

	A&E	Finance	Mfg	Public Utilities	Trade & Services	Trans	Total Private	Govt
1865-69	0	0	0	0	281	0	259	75
1870-74	0	43	0	0	0	340	56	598
1875-79	0	214	0	0	0	0	18	103
1880-84	164	39	233	248	46	70	38	137
1885-89	131	44	690	48	350	52	73	116
1890-94	98	89	358	400	0	0	70	117
1895-99	33	140	807	0	489	56	29	340
1900-04	159	40	136	73	148	78	66	122
1905-09	156	51	251	31	75	80	65	147
1910-14	75	16	56	0	0	300	108	86
TOTAL	136	53	281	69	145	68	54	141

AFRICA - DEPENDENT COLONIES

	A&E	Finance	Mfg	Public Utilities	Trade & Services	Trans	Total Private	Govt
1865-69	388	152	0	0	0	84	120	97
1870-74	260	15	0	97	460	259	99	107
1875-79	0	0	0	0	1,786	0	700	80
1880-84	67	18	0	0	154	301	269	0
1885-89	53	55	0	281	133	147	238	19
1890-94	67	278	0	0	26	12	125	86
1895-99	50	161	0	100	78	91	123	24
1900-04	49	162	11	45	93	132	203	35
1905-09	85	115	3	406	188	0	95	107
1910-14	55	116	78	195	220	198	101	97
TOTAL	60	129	16	193	105	138	151	55

ASIA - FOREIGN

	A&E	Finance	Mfg	Public Utilities	Trade & Services	Trans	Total Private	Govt
1865-69	254	118	0	461	0	29	39	838
1870-74	62	255	0	144	111	27	91	112
1875-79	21	0	1,368	210	0	29	39	110
1880-84	44	24	281	30	100	163	195	10
1885-89	57	123	47	75	0	110	150	69
1890-94	59	78	80	192	0	123	171	75
1895-99	3	52	615	0	0	106	17	134
1900-04	64	828	0	0	9	25	24	151
1905-09	91	88	106	255	0	119	55	121
1910-14	80	18	251	127	6	111	78	123
TOTAL	80	136	236	127	6	97	62	126

ASIA - INDIA

	A&E	Finance	Mfg	Public Utilities	Trade & Services	Trans	Total Private	Govt
1865-69	54	103	36	86	105	107	108	0
1870-74	100	15	57	64	100	147	101	99
1875-79	56	0	43	103	100	112	102	100
1880-84	116	39	85	127	0	104	93	106
1885-89	97	57	153	119	0	108	77	114
1890-94	147	62	200	0	200	103	53	117
1895-99	92	33	40	124	0	108	214	54
1900-04	86	20	125	140	137	112	145	70
1905-09	49	50	131	200	196	119	129	86
1910-14	17	0	27	50	258	165	91	109
TOTAL	58	51	59	108	158	122	112	92

ASIA - DEPENDENT COLONIES

	A&E	Finance	Mfg	Public Utilities	Trade & Services	Trans	Total Private	Govt
1865-69	1118	0	1836	41	0	17	88	245
1870-74	362	123	914	217	0	27	176	0
1875-79	707	1373	0	0	0	0	397	50
1880-84	77	617	0	0	0	0	93	107
1885-89	338	263	0	81	667	11	214	30
1890-94	146	261	0	0	300	15	203	64
1895-99	215	733	60	0	300	27	269	31
1900-04	212	46	0	0	0	87	168	55
1905-09	274	234	0	0	0	27	265	24
1910-14	220	322	24	0	4	2	176	24
TOTAL	286	235	59	29	10	20	192	38

A&E: Agriculture & Extractive
Mfg: Manufacturing
Trans: Transportation
Govt: Government

*For Industries: % in Sector of Total Private
                   % in Continent of Total Private

For Total Private and Total Government: % in Sector Total
                                          % in Continent Total

perhaps most important, the fraction flowing to transport finance was one and a quarter times the foreign and almost six times the share of the dependent colonies. Public utilities drew somewhat more than typical proportions. Lastly, the share of government issues in total Indian finance was almost twice the level that prevailed in the dependent colonies of Asia and Africa, although because of foreign borrowing it fell somewhat below the continent average (92).

VI. Conclusion

If the First Empire attracted traders and planters who left Britain to earn their fortunes in the far-flung corners of the imperial domain, its later incarnation is alleged to have appealed to investors who supported entrepreneurs in their attempts to open new markets for the products of British industry and who organized new sources of raw materials for the factories at home. No doubt the romance of Empire and the lure of distant places played their part; and it is not possible to deny that to many the City, with its satchel of Empire securities, appeared far more dynamic and exciting than the bicycle factories of the Midlands. With few exceptions, however, the dependent Empire did not draw large quantities of British finance.

By almost any standards, the London securities market was remarkable for the scale of its activity. The sales of new issues alone amounted to £34 billion (British) in 1865 and £192 billion (British) in 1914; to put it another way, the sales came to £1.5 in 1865 and £4.5 in 1914 for every man, woman, and child in the United Kingdom. Over that fifty-year period, the British markets directed close to £5 billion of new finance to government and businesses across the entire globe. While Britain itself was the recipient of almost one-third of the total, the remainder poured across the seas. The question, however, still remains: Granted that finance was important both to the British economic process and to the psychological well-being of the middle and upper classes, how important was the Empire to the British economy and the body politic? To answer this question, attention should be directed to those flows that might have been affected by the imperial connection and should exclude the fraction of foreign and domestic finance. The British economy's share was about 30 percent of the total for the entire period. The foreign portion comes to at least another 45 percent.

Nevertheless, the £1.2 billion that did go to the Empire was no small sum. It is, however, a figure that cannot be taken at face value. Given the ability of the colonies with responsible government to bend the political process to their own ends, there was little chance for British capitalists to garner more than competitive returns. Those colonies consistently refused to pay for even their share of imperial expenditures, they failed to favor British imports, and they continually pressed the British government to engage in political adventures where the economic profits, if they existed at all, redounded to the benefit of the colonies. The self-governing colonies together accounted for an additional 17 percent of all new issues. Thus, taken together, the domestic economy, foreign governments, and colonies with responsible government accounted for more than 90 percent of the new funds that passed through the British capital markets. Less than 10 percent went to the dependent Empire. That sum was not, however, distributed evenly across the globe. Of £355 million, Asia drew more than three-quarters and Africa an additional sixth. Oceania absorbed only about 2 percent, if Western Australia and the Northern Territories are included among colonies with responsible government; and the dependent colonies in North, Central, and South America, the Caribbean, and Europe together received about the same share. In aggregate terms, it appears that the dependent Empire received such a small share of the capital flows that, under any reasonable set of assumptions, a redirection of those resources to other parts of the world would have only trivially affected the realized rate of return. Moreover, if recent history presents any clue, even if those dependent areas had been independent, they would have continued to attract some British finance.

If the dependent Empire was alluring to British financiers and savers, the attraction was clearly limited. To the degree that it existed at all, it appears to have been connected in India with transport and, to a lesser degree, with trade and public utilities. In the dependent colonies, the appeal appears to have been associated with investments in the agriculture and extractive industries, with finance and government of lesser importance. There are, however, no grounds for thinking that, in terms of the volume of finance alone, the dependent Empire could have played an important role in shaping the British economy. For some persons it might well have been important, but the few investments involved would have had to yield spectacular profits to have provided the engine to drive either the domestic economy or the British political machine.

3 British business and the profits from Empire

I. The setting

" . . . Protection is quite gone," Queen Victoria wrote her uncle, the Belgian king, in 1852, and to all intents and purposes it was.[1] The nation was embarking on a new course that connoted a change in the British economy – an economy that was just approaching the apogee of its relative power. Before 1850, the economic progress had been largely domestic, but thereafter the area of expansion was much broader, encompassing not only the United Kingdom, but the Empire and most of the rest of the world.

Textiles, the extractive industries, and iron lay at the heart of Britain's midcentury predominance, and these same industries led the shift from domestic to world markets. In 1839, the country had produced just over half a million tons of pig iron; by 1913 that figure had risen tenfold. Of more direct relevance, in the first year only one-sixth of the total had been directed toward the export market; but by the end of the period, exports absorbed almost one-half of output.

In the case of coal, output quadrupled in the sixty years after 1854; and exports, which had amounted to barely 5 percent at the beginning, accounted for more than 25 percent of all output in 1913. Over the same period, although cotton textile production did not quite triple, exports more than quadrupled. It is not that the domestic market was dormant, but rather that, in the overseas market, British business had found a new source of strength. Dominance in iron and, later, steel led to similar pre-eminence in shipbuilding and weaponry, and the economic infrastructure that supported manufacturing superiority led also to leadership in world commerce and banking.

The great burgeoning of commercial, industrial, and manufacturing activity in Victorian Britain demanded that increased attention be paid to questions of business organization in general; and the redirection of activity from Britain to the lands overseas called for more scrutiny of the question of limited liability in particular. For an economy expanding on the basis of new technologies which were often characterized by increasing returns to scale, the private or family firm often lacked sufficient access to finance to permit the

73

successful exploitation of those opportunities. Moreover, as the focus of business moved abroad it became increasingly difficult to convince investors to make commitments that had no limits on liability. Legislation in 1844 was less than perfect. The Act of 1856 established "effective general Limited Liability," but it was the Companies Act of 1862 that was, in fact, the necessary and vital vehicle. Under that law any seven or more associates, provided their objects were lawful, might constitute themselves a company with limited liability by simply subscribing to a memorandum of association.

British entrepreneurs took advantage of the new statutes, but perhaps not as rapidly as might have been predicted. Between 1856 and 1862 an average of 382 corporate charters were granted each year; in the following decade the figure rose to 699. Over the next ten years the annual figure was 1,126; for the period 1883–92, 2,142, followed by 4,002 in the 1890s, and 5,386 in the decade 1903 through 1912. The delay in adopting the new institutional framework was less marked among recently formed concerns than among the old family enterprises, and it was much more prevalent among firms doing business in the foreign and empire sectors than those operating in Scotland or the Midlands. Even when old family-held firms did take corporate charters, control tended to remain in the hands of a few. The Cunard Line, for example, became a limited company in 1878; but 60 percent of the equity remained in the hands of three families.[2]

Clapham points out that, as late as the mid-1880s, while limited liability had gained great favor among firms concerned with coal, iron, and engineering, the vast majority of manufacturing firms were still family businesses.[3] That bias is also apparent in the classification scheme used by the London Stock Exchange which, after all, limited its dealings in the private sector to the issues of corporations. As late as 1900, although iron, coal, and steel firms were listed in one separate category and brewing and distilling in another, all the other industries that make up the manufacturing and commercial sector were combined into a single classification. Wool, cotton, linen, silk, lace, hosiery, cutlery, pottery, bicycle manufacture, retail, and wholesale trade were still in the main privately controlled enterprises; and even brewing did not become largely public until the end of the 1880s.

II. The problem

Such was the business environment in the third decade of Victoria's reign, as British entrepreneurs began with increasing frequency to turn to overseas activities. The contribution that British capital made to the development of the overseas economy in the late nineteenth and early twentieth centuries has been discussed. As Cairncross's and Imlah's data as interpreted by Michael Edelstein have shown, over the half century that preceded the outbreak of the First World War, capital exports from Britain amounted to more than 5 percent of that nation's gross national product, and by the end of the period those exports accounted for about £3 in every 4 of its national savings.[4] The outflow probably represents the largest absolute voluntary capital transfer in the history of the world. It is clear that had the British saver chosen to invest accumulations in a different manner, the course of development both in England and abroad would have been very different.

Most of the flow of capital was directed not toward the Empire (with the possible exception of Canada) but toward the United States and Latin America; and of the one-fourth that was Empire-bound, the vast majority of the resources went to the colonies of white settlement, not to the dependent Empire. Thus, it is still not clear what part British capitalism played in the development of the Empire, or conversely, what role the Empire played in the development of British capitalism. The latter question is the concern of this chapter. At the same time that capital exports surged, despite the attraction of Empire, the lure of exotic markets, and the task of financing the world's railroad network, the domestic economy continued to attract a very significant portion of the finance that passed through the nation's formal capital markets and almost all of the funds that bypassed those markets.

The statistical portrait seems very clear, but it does not appear to be the picture painted by Hobson and Lenin, nor, for that matter, the one drawn by Shaw and Stanley.[5] To Hobson and Lenin, resource exhaustion, a poor distribution of the gains of economic growth, and a decline in opportunities at home drove profits lower; and the business community, in an attempt to recover those lost profits in protected markets, used its political influence to promote imperial development. The Shaw–Stanley scenario is slightly different, but the last act is much the same. "Those dusky bosoms" represented new markets with a potential demand for British products that, if captured, could yield profits far in excess of the ones available at home or in the parts of the world not controlled by Whitehall. To effect this result, say Shaw and Stanley, business used its influence to develop and perhaps extend the area under British control. The first scenario might be viewed as hegemony by push and the second as Empire by pull, but both attribute the development and persistence of the British Empire to a rational economic calculation: a calculation that indicated investment in the political structure of Empire would be profitable.

Both, in short, rested on the assumption that profits in Empire were higher than those available elsewhere, or that the resources to be tapped in the colonized areas were so valuable that their exploitation would raise the world profit rate substantially. That the capital directed toward the dependent Empire was a relatively small fraction of the total casts some doubt on the Shaw–Stanley scenario, and the apparent vitality of the domestic economy carries a similar message for the Hobson–Lenin argument. Still, at the beginning of the twentieth century, there were only 46 million residents of the British Isles; and it may have been that the Empire, while employing only a tiny fraction of the total available finance, yielded very high returns. Thus, the high income levels observed in the United Kingdom may have been maintained by Empire profits, while the finance that flowed into the domestic and foreign economies was merely the surplus that could not be absorbed at the "monopolistic and exploitative rates" that prevailed within the Empire.

To examine this argument, it is not sufficient merely to measure the capital flows. It is also necessary to compare the profits that were attainable in the Empire with those that would have been available in the domestic and foreign sectors, had the Empire not existed. The questions then become: (1) Was it rational for the British to invest in the legal and political structure required to maintain an Empire, and (2), if it was a rational decision, to whom did the benefits accrue? Arguments based on ex ante beliefs are always difficult to answer, since most evidence is by definition ex post; and it is always possible to argue that a decision was in fact rational, given a set of expectations that could have been but were not realized. Consequently, "facts," no matter now compelling, can never provide proof; however, historical circumstances sometimes make it possible to make inferences about ex ante expectations from ex post evidence. The political and economic decisions about the Empire were made over more than half a century, and while British financial history is replete with speculative "bubbles," none lasted forever. Both business people and investors did learn. Hence, the realized returns on home, empire, and foreign investments, although providing direct evidence only on actual profits, do also give indirect evidence on the *expected* long-run returns from these ventures.

Such relative returns on alternative investments provide at least indirect evidence on two important questions. First, were such returns sufficient to make the average British subject in the United

Kingdom better off than he or she would have been had the Empire not existed? Second, were they great enough to make at least some more affluent, even if the average Briton did not benefit and may, in fact, have been made poorer? If the answer to either question is yes, then one cannot deny the possibility that it was the search for economic profits that underwrote the Empire. Moreover, if the answer to the first question is no but the answer to the second, yes, then the scope of the inquiry must be expanded to include the British political arena, if the nature of the imperial enterprise is to be understood.

In either case, the initial step is to test the strict economic argument that returns in the Empire were greater than those available at home. The second step involves a comparison of Empire and domestic returns with those available abroad, that is, outside the Empire. Any repatriation of Empire investments would certainly have driven domestic rates down, and one might argue that the Empire was important not because rates were higher than those available at home, but because the Empire kept domestic rates higher than they otherwise would have been. The threat of a repatriation disaster would have been greatly mitigated if there had existed a third alternative (the foreign sector) to provide an effective substitute for Empire investment. Investments in the foreign sector did not impose financial exactions on the British taxpayer, although those parallel levies may have appeared as costs to British investors; and the third-alternative opportunities were readily available to the British businessperson and investor in the nineteenth century. Moreover, the third alternative, encompassing as it did most of the rest of the world, was very large.

Another word of warning: The observed rates of return are average rates, and the usual hypothesis concerning the economic rationale for Empire are cast in terms of marginals. It might have been true that while the average rate of return on domestic investment was higher than the average Empire rate, the marginal rate (the return on the last project undertaken) might have been higher in the Empire. Unfortunately, it is almost impossible to observe marginal rates; however, for the major thrust of *this* question – Did the Empire pay? – the appropriate measure is the average, not the marginal. After all, it is the average rate that reflects the earnings of British investors. Moreover, even if interest is centered on the causes of the expansion, where it is the marginal returns that are central, two considerations make it likely that in the long run the average rates are reasonable proxies for the marginals. In the first place, marginal and average rates are not unrelated; and they do tend to move together. This relationship is particularly close when the level of new investment is large relative to the existing capital stock. Such a description, of course, captures fairly accurately much of Empire investment and a great deal of domestic investment in the commercial and industrial sector, where rates were highest. In the second place, the very large size and the varied nature of the foreign sector suggests that rates would fall only gradually as investment expanded; and to the extent that foreign enterprise could absorb large blocks of domestic capital without precipitating a dramatic decline in rates, it would have prevented the realized marginal return on domestic investment from declining precipitously.

If Empire returns were higher than domestic or foreign, some individuals almost certainly benefited from the investment in Empire. If the profits were enough greater than the alternatives to remain the investment of choice, even after the social costs (defense, for example) had been deducted, then it appears that the average Briton could have benefited; and the only question remaining is why the returns were not distributed in a more equitable fashion. If they were not high enough to make Empire investment appear profitable after all costs were charged, questions about mechanism become important. How large, then, were the profits that accrued to the businesspeople who chose to employ their capital in India, Australia, Canada, or Lagos; and how do these profits compare with those earned by their contemporaries who chose, instead, to direct their energies toward the Midlands, the United States, or Argentina?

III. The literature

The question of the relative returns on home and foreign investment has interested scholars at least as long as the political implications of these activities have been a subject of discussion. As early as 1909, George Paish concerned himself with the returns on British imperial and foreign investment; and R. A. Lehfeldt measured the returns on home, colonial, and foreign bonds in 1913.[6] Lehfeldt's estimate for home and Empire returns (3.6 percent for the Empire and 3.4 percent for Britain over the years 1888–1909) casts doubt on the assumption that the Empire was a lucrative and protected area for British investment. For the years 1888 through 1914, he found that rates on foreign bonds averaged over one percentage point higher than domestic, but Empire rates were only slightly, and not significantly, higher. Some forty years later, Alexander Cairncross, working with data provided by R. L. Nash in 1880, estimated the returns on some classes of home and foreign investment for the decade

1870–80.[7] Although his data indicate that rates on Empire bonds were higher than those on British consuls, his conclusions do not differ substantially from Lehfeldt's.

As interesting and suggestive as these findings are, they provide little solid information on the questions at hand: What were the relative productivities of the investments in the three sectors? Both Lehfeldt's and Cairncross's figures are rates of return on financial assets. In each case the numerator is the yield, and the denominator the market value, of the paper assets. To the extent that capital markets operate efficiently, the market value of the numerator should adjust to equate the yields on all equally risky assets. For example, the decline in the ratio of colonial to British bonds between the 1870–80 period revealed by Cairncross (1.4:1), and the 1898–1914 period reported by Lehfeldt (1:1), almost certainly reflects little about changes in the profitability of government enterprises but merely the greater perceived safety of colonial issues after the passage of the Colonial Stocks Act of 1900. That act made the British government the guarantor of colonial issues.[8]

Economists have recognized that the so-called market problem makes it very difficult to use financial rates of return to measure the profitability of an enterprise. Assume, for example, that a firm discovers a new process that allows it to manufacture a product much more cheaply than its rivals. Investors seeking a higher than normal rate of return rush to buy it. As they bid against each other, the market price of the firm's shares rises until the ratio of the firm's earnings to the market value of the securities is exactly the same as the ratio for every other equally risky firm. It will pay an investor to continue to bid up the price of the shares as long as returns from the firm are above the rate on comparable alternative investments. Despite the fact that the returns earned by the new stockholders are not more than the average for the industry, the firm is still relatively profitable, if the basis for calculation is the original, rather than the current, market value of the shares. The extra profits have been captured by the original stockholders whose investments were made at the prices that prevailed before the innovation. Their earnings are calculated on the basis of the original prices; or if they have sold their holdings, their profits include a large capital gain.

Similarly, if a firm suffers from poor management and earns below-average returns, the market value of its securities will decline until the financial rate of return is once again equalized. In this case, it is the original shareholders who earn less than market returns. If the calculation is made on the basis of the price they paid for the securities, they have earned less than "normal," or if they have sold their shares, they have absorbed the capital losses. Thus, the market rate of return provides a measure of the earnings an investor can expect to make from investing in a particular class of firm, but it tells us nothing about the productivity of the resources that were committed to that enterprise.

For the British economy in the late nineteenth century, the problem of financial returns has been thoroughly explored by Michael Edelstein in his insightful study of returns on portfolio investments.[9] He examines the returns on a sample of securities over the years 1870–1914 and concludes that, after adjustment for risk, overseas investment on the average paid better than domestic. That overall differential rested, however, on quite high relative returns in the years 1875 to 1885 and 1895 to 1910. Edelstein is well aware of the problems of financial returns, and he explicitly attempts to finesse this dilemma by arguing that the financial rates are proxies for the real. That is, the market was not perfect and, after adjustment for risk, the transitory rate differentials can be taken as evidence of real productivity differences – differences that lasted until the market recognized the change in opportunities and adjusted.

Edelstein may well be correct, and his work is certainly a marked improvement over that of his predecessors. His conclusions, however, while suggesting that there were profitable opportunities for overseas investment, imply nothing about the profitability of Empire investment. To infer something about that, an attempt has been made to disentangle the foreign and Empire components of Edelstein's averages (see Table 3.1). To the extent that this effort is successful, his figures indicate that, while colonial firms were more profitable than domestic, they were substantially less profitable than foreign. Moreover, if the period 1896 to 1909 – years of very low domestic returns – are dropped, returns at home were somewhat higher than colonial in railroads and banking equity; slightly lower on railroad debentures; and substantially lower only in the social-overhead sector. Overall, there is little evidence to indicate that financial investment in Empire was particularly profitable, whether the yardstick is domestic or foreign rates of return.

The market problem can be finessed in another, quite different manner. If it were possible to determine accurately the resources committed to a typical enterprise and the resulting returns, it would be simple to obtain an unambiguous measure of relative profitability. In principle, the new gauge would be superior to the instruments that use financial returns as proxies for real returns. In practice, however, it is very difficult to measure either the resources invested or the revenues accrued. Accountants do attempt to provide such

TABLE 3.1

ESTIMATES OF REALIZED RATES OF RETURN: EDELSTEIN

(Percents)

	1870-76	1877-86	1887-96	1897-1909	1910-13	1870-1913	Colonial /Foreign	1879-96 and 1910-13	Index UK=100
			RAILROAD EQUITY						
UK	11.19	5.19	6.87	-.83	1.51	4.41		6.61	100
Colonial	5.46	8.22	6.46	1.48	3.94	5.00	.65	6.47	98
Foreign	6.78	12.58	4.97	9.31	-1.30	7.70		7.02	106
			RAILROAD DEBENTURES						
UK	6.01	5.09	5.95	.64	1.25	3.77		5.08	100
Colonial	4.63	6.71	5.40	2.69	2.17	4.48	.78	5.23	103
Foreign	6.16	7.48	5.53	5.43	1.92	5.72		5.84	115
			BANKING EQUITY						
UK	10.75	7.00	7.85	4.46	-.56	6.35		7.15	100
Colonial	11.15	8.34	4.82	8.82	1.97	7.55	1.19	7.01	98
Foreign	4.66	5.10	7.68	8.57	1.94	6.35		5.42	75
			SOCIAL OVERHEAD EQUITY						
UK	7.94	7.65	6.28	.81	6.08	5.22		7.07	100
Colonial	9.84	8.21	7.35	6.51	5.18	7.50	.92	7.91	112
Foreign	5.95	12.54	6.99	4.30		8.13		8.61	122

SOURCE: M. Edelstein, "Realized Rates of Return on U.K. Home and Overseas Portfolio Investment in the Age of High Imperialism." Mimeographed. New York: Queens College, CUNY, 1975.

information to owners and management; and, while their reports are at times suspect, the data they furnish, to the extent it is correct, provides a basis for this alternative measure. Moreover, while often flawed, their data are usually collected in a reasonably consistent fashion, a consistency, in late nineteenth-century Britain, that extended not only temporally for a particular company, but across firms in the same industry as well. Thus, a profit measure based on firm accounting records, although not without problems, does provide a consistent measure of returns not distorted by "market" adjustments. To that end, the focus of the study is shifted from the financial markets to individual firms and their accounts.

IV. Rates of return by industry

The measures presented in the remainder of this chapter are based on the records of 482 British firms (see Appendix 3.1). These 482 firms operated either at home, in the Empire, or in the rest of the world. All were British owned or British chartered and therefore represented a viable set of investment alternatives to the British saver. Of the 482 concerns, 241 are chosen from a random sample of corporations whose shares were traded on the London Stock Exchange sometime between 1883 and 1912.[10] For these firms, the financial data are drawn from the reports they filed more or less annually with the Exchange.[11] Usually, these reports were the annual statements presented to their stockholders.

The second group of firms (234 in number) includes partnerships and sole proprietorships, as well as corporations; and it provides records of their business successes during the years 1860–82 as well as between 1883–1912.[12] Selection, however, is based on no systematic sampling, unless one believes that choice based on the existence and availability of records provides a random sample of the firms that operated in the past. The specific firms were included only because some portion of their original records exist and are available for analysis. These documents include correspondence, minute books, original ledgers and journals, and published reports (all are not, unfortunately, available for every firm).

Finally, a third group includes seven British domestic railways. Their financial records were taken from the annual reports to the British government. The only basis for the choice of those seven firms was an attempt to gain a modicum of regional representation.

For the group of 234, whenever possible, estimates of the rate of return were constructed from the firm's original financial sources and those estimates were then compared with the published financial data. On occasion, these comparisons uncovered systematic differences between nineteenth-century and current accounting practices. For example, stated profits were at times below "actual" returns because of high interest payments to owners on their loans to the firm, substantial management bonuses when the managers were also the owners, payments of large fees to directors or debenture trustees, inclusions as costs items (dividends, for instance) that no modern accountant would so classify, and of transfers of revenue to reserves that bore only the faintest business justification (the dividend-guarantee fund or the "standard-reserve fund," to cite only two). On the other hand there are almost equally numerous instances of "bending" the accounts to increase the stated level of profits. There are examples of zero-interest loans from owners, skipped trustee and director payments, and the exclusion of legitimate business expenses (bad debts, for example) from profit calculations. In addition, the treatment of depreciation provided considerable opportunity to move profits in any desired direction, although British firms do appear to have had a more consistent policy than their nineteenth-century American counterparts.

Most of the measures presented in this chapter are estimates of the rate of "profit," rather than the rate of return to all capital claimants. Although it is possible to argue that under some conditions the latter measure might appear more appropriate, at least two considerations are important enough to dictate the choice of a profit measure. On the intellectual level, it was the search for profits that allegedly led businessmen to turn their attention to the Empire. On a more practical level, employment of a profit measure makes it possible to argue symetrically about returns and the structure of ownership. In nineteenth-century Britain, most bonds were bearer bonds. Stockholder lists survive and contain the names and addresses of the men and women who put their savings at risk. There are, however, few surviving lists of bondholders – the owner of a bond made out to "bearer" remained anonymous even to the issuing corporation. Only a careful study of an individual's assets can uncover his or her bondholdings – and in Britain (except for Scotland) even the probate records cannot support such a study.

In the measures reported in this chapter, attempts were made to make accounting practices consistent across firms. In addition, when some "unusual" practice – a practice that appears widespread in a particular industry – was discovered, records of all firms in the industry, including those in the stockholder sample, were adjusted. Since there is more than an element of arbitrariness in these determinations, a number of alternative estimates have been calculated; but differences between the series do not appear to be related to location.[13]

The denominator of the profit measures is the value of the firm's assets, but even that concept is not without some substantial ambiguity. Accountants value many of a firm's assets (inventories, accounts receivable, and cash, to cite three) at current prices. Fixed assets (plant and equipment) are, however, traditionally valued at historical cost; and if the prices of capital goods change, the difference in the method of treatment can create problems. For the period in question, the Sauerbeck–Statist price index declines from 100 in the early 1860s to 61 in 1896 and then rises to 85 in 1912. The inclusion of "good will" among a firm's assets also presents problems. Good will appears most often on a firm's balance sheet after a private company has gone public, and it reflects the fact that the market value of the firm was higher than the accounting value of its assets (that is, it represented the discounted stream of capital gains that the investors believe would be realized because the firm was earning more than normal profits).

Fixed assets were converted from historic to current values by adjusting the reported figures for price changes. In every year the stock of fixed assets held at the beginning of the year was revalued in current prices; any change in assets over the course of the year was assumed to have been valued at current prices. The plant and

TABLE 3.2

RATES OF RETURN - HIGH UNWEIGHTED
COMMERCIAL BANKS

	UK	Foreign	Empire
1860-64	2.3	2.3	
1865-69	2.2	2.8	
1870-74	2.2	1.6	
1875-79	1.6	0.8	
1880-84	1.5	1.8	1.1
1885-89	1.4	2.0	1.3
1890-94	1.3	1.6	0.9
1894-99	1.2	1.3	1.5
1900-04	1.2	1.0	1.4
1905-09	1.2	1.3	1.5
1910-12	1.3	1.1	1.5
AVERAGE	1.6 (1.3)*	1.6 (1.5)*	1.3

*Figures in parentheses are 1880-1912.

equipment is assumed to have been acquired uniformly over the life of the firm to date, with a thirty-year depreciation period (an average of fifty years for structures, and ten years for equipment). Because of differences in accounting practices, assets were initially included at their gross rather than net (of depreciation) value, but they have all been depreciated over a thirty-year period.

The book value of good will was deducted from the total value of assets. This adjustment has the effect of producing a measure of profit that does not take account of capital gains (or losses). Only one series (high) is reported here; however, it should be reiterated that, as far as home, Empire, and foreign differentials are concerned, there is no evidence that the conclusions are dependent on the choice of profit measure or on the set of accounting adjustments.

The firms included in the sample vary greatly in size – there are companies with total assets of less than £100, and others with assets in the millions. Any average causes something to be lost. If each firm is taken as a single observation, a small filemaker counts as heavily as Vickers in the iron and steel average, and if some form of weights is employed (assets, for example) the filemaker gets lost in the calculation. Only the unweighted series are reported, but the thrust of the conclusions would not be blunted if the weighted ones were substituted. The calculations presented in Tables 3.2 through 3.13 are rates of return calculated by dividing the estimated profit figure by total assets, less depreciation and good will.[14]

Because of the interindustry differences in capital structures, these measures are not particularly useful for examining all-industry profitability, but they provide a very powerful tool for comparing returns of firms with similar structures. If firms in an industry very heavily dependent on borrowed, as opposed to equity, funds are compared with firms in a different industry (the contrast is most marked be-

TABLE 3.3

RATES OF RETURN - HIGH UNWEIGHTED
FINANCIAL, LAND AND DEVELOPMENT

	UK	Foreign	Empire
1860-64		16.4	
1865-69		3.3	8.3
1870-74		5.6	6.6
1875-79		-0.7	0.7
1880-84	2.1	9.1	4.3
1885-89	2.2	10.7	4.3
1890-94	1.5	-1.4	2.3
1895-99	2.0	1.7	1.4
1900-04	2.1	-1.0	-1.8
1905-09	2.1	2.6	2.4
1910-12	1.6	1.5	3.5
AVERAGE	2.0	4.5 (3.4)*	3.2 (2.3)*

*After 1880.

TABLE 3.4

RATES OF RETURN - HIGH UNWEIGHTED
FINANCIAL TRUSTS

	UK	Foreign	Empire
1860-64			
1865-69			
1870-74			
1875-79			
1880-84		5.3	
1885-89	2.1	4.8	
1890-94	1.1	3.2	3.7
1895-99	0.9	2.4	4.8
1900-04	0.7	3.3	1.5
1905-09	1.9	3.9	1.6
1910-12	2.9	3.6	2.8
AVERAGE	1.5 (1.4)*	3.8 (3.3)*	2.9

*After 1890.

TABLE 3.5

RATES OF RETURN - HIGH UNWEIGHTED
BREWERIES AND DISTILLERIES

	UK	Foreign	Empire
1860-64	9.6		
1965-69	7.6		
1870-74	14.6		
1875-79	19.9		
1880-84	10.8		
1885-89	10.4		
1890-94	6.6	2.9	8.2
1895-99	7.8	2.6	7.7
1900-04	5.3	3.7	5.6
1905-09	4.6	5.2	3.6
1910-12	5.1	9.6	3.2
AVERAGE	9.5 (5.9)*	4.4	5.9

*After 1890.

tween commercial banking and the commercial and industrial sector), they display very low relative returns. The evidence indicates that, within industries, capital structures were reasonably comparable across locations. Thus, the analysis begins with an examination of the relative earnings of the home, Empire, and foreign firms in

TABLE 3.6

RATES OF RETURN - HIGH UNWEIGHTED
COMMERCIAL AND INDUSTRIAL

	UK	Foreign	Empire
1860-64	13.3	11.6	17.8
1865-69	11.4	11.3	15.6
1870-74	15.5	12.0	12.1
1875-79	14.0	10.6	15.9
1880-84	13.3	7.6	12.2
1885-89	14.5	29.7	7.3
1890-94	11.3	6.3	5.3
1895-99	10.8	22.5	5.6
1900-04	7.1	8.1	7.5
1905-09	7.2	2.9	6.7
1910-12	7.9	7.5	8.7
AVERAGE	11.6 (10.7)*	12.0 (12.4)*	10.5 (7.5)*

*After 1880.

TABLE 3.7

RATES OF RETURN - HIGH UNWEIGHTED
IRON AND STEEL

	UK	Foreign	Empire
1860-64	11.1		
1865-69	10.3		
1870-74	17.5		
1875-79	9.0		
1880-84	10.3	4.5	
1885-89	10.3	3.5	4.1
1890-94	8.4	6.3	-2.0
1895-99	10.0	2.8	-0.3
1900-04	9.0	2.3	5.6
1905-09	7.3	2.4	7.1
1910-12	8.0	6.7	4.3
AVERAGE	10.2 (8.9)*	3.9 (3.8)*	3.1

*After 1885.

TABLE 3.8

RATES OF RETURN - HIGH UNWEIGHTED
RAILROADS

	UK	Foreign	Empire
1860-64	4.3	--	
1865-69	3.2	4.7	
1870-74	3.5	6.7	
1875-79	3.0	9.4	
1880-84	3.8	7.2	0.1
1885-89	2.8	8.2	2.8
1890-94	3.0	5.4	2.9
1895-99	3.1	4.4	2.1
1900-04	2.6	3.8	1.4
1905-09	2.6	5.0	1.9
1910-12	2.6	6.6	3.1
AVERAGE	3.2 (2.8)*	6.1 (5.5)*	2.0 (2.3)*

*After 1885.

each industry. The question of overall rates of return on home, Empire, and foreign investment is deferred until later. In the remainder of this section, all figures refer to the "high" unweighted rates of return on assets, and all comparisons of interlocation profitability refer to a single industry only (see Appendix 3.2).

TABLE 3.9

RATES OF RETURN - HIGH UNWEIGHTED
SHIPPING

	UK	Foreign	Empire
1860-64		8.9	
1865-69		4.4	
1870-74		13.9	
1875-79		6.6	
1880-84		7.1	2.6
1885-89		7.4	4.2
1890-94	6.8	5.2	-4.8
1895-99	5.8	8.3	14.4
1900-04	8.5	8.1	5.4
1905-09	5.3	4.1	3.8
1910-12	6.8	7.2	7.5
AVERAGE	6.6	7.4 (6.5)*	4.6 (5.1)*

*After 1890.

TABLE 3.10

RATES OF RETURN - HIGH UNWEIGHTED
TRAMS AND OMNIBUSES

	UK	Foreign	Empire
1860-64	0.2		
1865-69	4.3		
1870-74	0.1		
1875-79	3.1		
1880-84	5.5	3.8	5.2
1885-89	5.6	4.7	-0.4
1890-94	6.9	5.4	-0.8
1895-99	9.5	3.0	1.2
1900-04	4.6	2.7	3.1
1905-09	-0.2	3.6	4.5
1910-12	2.0	3.1	7.6
AVERAGE	3.8 (5.0)*	3.8	2.9

*After 1880.

TABLE 3.11

RATES OF RETURN - HIGH UNWEIGHTED
GAS AND ELECTRICITY

	UK	Foreign	Empire
1860-64	7.8		
1865-69	9.0		
1870-74	6.9		
1875-79	8.7		
1880-84	8.7		6.1
1885-89	9.7		7.6
1890-94	10.1		7.8
1895-99	10.2	5.9	8.6
1900-04	7.3	6.5	6.8
1905-09	6.1	6.2	8.5
1910-12	6.7	5.5	9.6
AVERAGE	8.4 (7.7)* (8.5)**	6.1	7.8 (8.2)*

*After 1895.
**After 1880.

A. Banking

In the case of banking, foreign earnings after 1880 dominated those at home, but there was little to choose between home
and Empire. Given the relatively low interest rates prevailing in

TABLE 3.12

RATES OF RETURN - HIGH UNWEIGHTED
WATERWORKS

	UK	Foreign	Empire
1860-64	5.8		
1865-69	8.1		
1870-74	7.4		
1875-79	8.8	0.5	
1880-84	9.0	0.2	2.4
1885-89	11.6	6.9	15.5
1890-94	11.7	4.7	12.5
1895-99	13.6	4.2	12.9
1900-04	6.8	5.0	12.7
1905-09	6.1	5.3	11.5
1910-12	7.1	5.6	13.1
AVERAGE	8.8 (9.7)*	4.5 (5.3)*	13.0

*After 1885.

TABLE 3.13

RATES OF RETURN - HIGH UNWEIGHTED
EXTRACTIVE AND AGRICULTURE

	UK	Foreign	Empire
1860-64	3.5		4.5
1865-69	11.7		-0.2
1870-74	10.2		17.1
1875-79	0.9	11.0	19.6
1880-84	6.1	9.4	13.5
1885-89	7.4	16.4	9.4
1890-94	14.9	15.2	10.2
1895-99	9.3	10.8	8.6
1900-04	19.4	15.3	6.6
1905-09	8.6	15.8	10.5
1910-12	8.9	23.3	12.5
AVERAGE	9.2 (9.5)*	14.2	10.1 (11.3)*

*After 1875.

Britain and the importance of interest earnings in profits, it is worthy of note that the colonial rates were not higher than they were.[15] Over the entire period, domestic rates averaged 1.6 percent; but in the years after 1880 the figure was only 1.3. In the foreign sector, rates averaged 1.6 percent, and in the years after 1880 the figure was 1.5. Early data for colonial banks is limited, but in the period 1880–1912 they, like those at home, averaged a return of 1.3 percent.

Domestic rates declined between the early 1870s and the mid-1880s, a period that saw a widespread introduction of branch banking, an innovation that rooted out the last vestiges of locational monopolies in the United Kingdom. From 1890 onward, however, the rates show little evidence of trend. Rates in the colonial and foreign sectors are certainly more variable than domestic, but they, too, display little evidence of any long-term movement. The somewhat higher returns attached to foreign investment after 1880 suggest that the British business community might well have been interested in expanding that segment of its investment activities.

The giant of the domestic industry was the Midland Bank. Its guiding genius was Edward H. Holden, the chairman and general manager. Holden joined the bank as an accountant in 1881, became joint general manager ten years later, and general manager in 1897. Between 1883, when he began to have a substantive voice in the bank's management, and 1912, the Midland absorbed 54 other banks, opened 650 branches and saw its assets increase from £2.5 to almost £100 million. Over the thirty-year period the Midland's returns were almost one-fifth higher than the average of the other domestic banks included in the study, and success invited imitation. In 1886 there had been 320 joint stock banks with 2,500 branches. In 1912 the total number of banks had dropped to 32, but they had 7,000 branches. Of the 32, 20 had more than 100 and 3 in excess of 500 branches. In 1881, the Midland had ranked in the lower half of the 320 in terms of size; by 1912 it was by far the largest.

B. Financial, land, and development

The financial, land, and development firms should be correctly viewed as assets trusts. In the same way that trusts held portfolios of paper securities, the financial, land, and development companies held portfolios of properties for development and resale. They were the growth industry of the late nineteenth century, and growth was almost certainly postulated on their earlier profitability. In both the Empire and foreign sectors, land and development companies were quite profitable in the years before 1880 (the former averaged 6.2 and the latter 5.1 percent). Empire companies invested most heavily in Canada, Australia, and New Zealand while those in the foreign sector directed the bulk of their attention toward South America. In both instances, the most profitable property tended to be used in the agriculture and the extractive industries.

Success attracted imitators, and even the United Kingdom appeared fertile ground for land speculation. There the most lucrative investments appear to have been in commercial and residential building in the rapidly growing cities, and, of these, London was the recipient of more than its share of attention. For the years after 1880, foreign returns outstripped both domestic and Empire, but the profits on overseas investments were substantially more variable.

C. Financial trusts

Like their twentieth-century counterparts, the nineteenth-century trusts held symbolic capital issues. Some were specialized (the Rolling Stock Trust, for example) and some general (Colonial and General Trust, to name one). The pattern of returns tends to reflect the interest rates prevailing in the three sectors. Trusts that concentrated their investments in the United Kingdom earned the lowest returns; nor does there appear to have been any long-term movement in their earnings. Those with major commitments in the Empire did about twice as well as their domestic counterparts, and those in the foreign sector did about two and a half times as well. In the twentieth century, however, Empire returns were probably no higher than domestic; and the disappearance of the differential almost certainly reflects the trustee status granted colonial issues. It is totally absent in the case of foreign returns; those returns were, although somewhat lower than Empire in the 1890s, twice as high in the present century.

D. Breweries and distilleries

In the 1880s, breweries and distilleries were split off from the catchall group, commercial and industrial. By that time, improvement in quality-control techniques made it possible to greatly increase the scale of brewing just when the Liberals – a party committed to at least some limited form of prohibition – were attempting to forceably reduce the number of licensed public houses. Taken together, these antagonistic forces induced breweries to integrate vertically in order to gain a firm grip on their retail outlets. Companies that had the financial resources to buy choice retail locations tended to survive, others did not. This need for finance forced many of the breweries to turn to the formal capital market, and the late 1880s saw a large increase in the number and size of brewing issues.

From the 1860s to the mid-1880s, domestic returns in brewing differed but little from those earned in other manufacturing and trading enterprises and not at all from the industries not characterized by technical or market innovation. Returns averaged 13.5 in the commercial and industrial sector, 12.5 in brewing and distilling, and 11.5 in iron and steel. Over the ensuing quarter century, however, despite substantial technical developments in brewing, the average for brewing and distilling was 7.0, compared with 10.5 and 9.6 for the other two sectors. The downward trend in returns can be attributed to the capital losses suffered as a consequence of the reduction in the number of retail licenses, and to the increased prices that firms were forced to pay for the remaining licensed locations. The former represents a net loss to British business, the latter merely a redistribution from the brewing to the retail sector; but both were the products of the social rather than the economic policies of the governing Liberal party.

Gray and Sons, Maldon appears to have remained highly profitable, returning 13.2 percent in 1890–9 and 10.2 percent in the next decade, but it was the exception rather than the rule. The much larger Flower and Sons, for example, lost 2.5 percent per year with assets of more than £1,000,000 in the three years after 1909. Abroad, the picture is somewhat different. While foreign-sector returns were not high (from 1890 onward they were less than those available at home), that statistic is somewhat misleading. Foreign profits were biased downward by particularly low returns in the 1890s, a decade that saw British entrepreneurs buying what at times appears to have been almost every foreign brewery that came on the market; reorganizing those firms; and, then, selling their shares to British investors. Over the longer period these investments proved to be moderately remunerative. The American-based Goebel Brewing Company, for instance, earned 4.5 percent in the half decade 1890–5, but 15.5 percent in the years 1905–12. Overall, returns in the last three years were 9.6 percent, almost twice domestic and five times Empire returns. In the Empire, although the overall trend is downward, returns were equal to those in the domestic and higher than those returned by the foreign sector.

E. Commercial and industrial

If, in an attempt to discover something about the potential for growth or the "spirit of the economy," interest is focused on the total number and variety of firms, as opposed to the size of individual enterprises, then the commercial and industrial sector is almost certainly the most significant. Perhaps the single most important fact to be learned from the behavior of these firms does not concern the Empire, but rather the much maligned domestic economy. Industrial and commercial enterprises performed far better than conventional wisdom has indicated, and while there is evidence of a long-run decline in returns, it is no more rapid than the fall in foreign returns and less rapid than the decline in Empire returns. For the entire period domestic returns in the commercial and industrial sector averaged 11.6 percent. While the figure was almost 14 percent from 1865 to 1890, it was above 10 percent from then until the turn of the century. It was only in the years from 1900 to 1912 that the rate fell below that level, and even then it averaged more than 7 percent.

For the entire period, there is little to choose between the performance of the foreign and the domestic sectors; the average return was about 12 percent for both. In the Empire, the figures were substantially different. Although the average was 10.5 percent, profits were very high over the first two and one-half decades (almost 15 percent) but much lower thereafter. From 1880 onward, they averaged less than 8 percent in contrast with 11 and 12 percent in the other sectors.

A more detailed examination of the individual firms suggests an explanation for the remarkably buoyant domestic returns – the rise of a set of firms serving the growing mass consumer market. It was a phenomenon that (with the exception of a few, like Liebig's Extract of Meat) did not seem to exist, at least for the British investor in the Empire and foreign sectors. The Maypole Dairy, for example, served the London metropolitan area. From 1895 to 1909 the company returned 23 percent on an asset base that grew from a quarter of a million pounds to three times that amount. Between 1890 and 1894, eleven domestic commercial and industrial firms reported returns that averaged more than 9 percent (the high was 43), and in the next quinquennium there were eighteen. In contrast to the performance of other industries, while overall profits did fall, returns (to some firms, at least) remained high. The years 1900–09 saw sixteen firms reporting more than 9 percent, while the high was 58 percent.

Far from stagnating, the domestic economy was very lively. That effervescence is nowhere better captured than in the variety of the enterprises that were launched. Some firms succeeded and some did not, but the range of activities must have surprised any visitor. The De La Rue Company printed postage stamps, and in one year-and-a-half period alone (November 1879 to July 1881), produced almost one and a half billion. On the other hand, vitality did not always imply profitability – a conclusion that is supported by the history of the Metropolitan Tower Construction Company. The firm was chartered to erect an exact replica of the Eiffel Tower in the London suburb of Wembley. (Another was planned for Chicago.) Although construction never proceeded further than the second stage, that much was completed. There, high in the air, a dance floor was erected and a public bar opened. The half-finished structure, the noise, and the bibulous crowd so annoyed the neighbors that the authorities withdrew the company's liquor license. That final straw doomed the faltering enterprise to extinction, and in August, 1906, the directors ordered that their dream, now deemed a "public eyesore," be dismantled.[16]

Glasgow-based Alley Maclellan was incorporated in the first years of the twentieth century and provides another example of the diversity, but not necessarily the success, of British industry. Although the corporate charter gave the managers permission to act as engineers, iron founders, brass founders, shipbuilders, marine engineers, electrical engineers, smiths, boilermakers, galvanizers, pattern makers, merchants, and metallurgists, the company's actual purpose was to manufacture a "steam waggon."

At the more successful end of the spectrum was Huntley and Palmers, the Reading biscuit manufacturer. The firm was founded in 1857 and soon became a leader in the mass distribution of bakery products. Early growth was based on the innovation of aerated bread; and by the 1860s, the firm was returning 24 percent per year on its £102,000 asset base. In 1889 the company produced the first chocolate biscuit, the "Chocolate Table," but, as often happens, while early innovation led to profits, imitation was swift. In the next five years, annual returns averaged more than 30 percent, but thereafter they fell rapidly. The firm celebrated its fiftieth anniversary with a great jubilee extravaganza and, in an attempt to regain leadership in the biscuit field, introduced a new product, the "Tilia." Unfortunately, that innovation was never accepted by the public. The company's annual report for 1911 indicated that business was still reasonably lucrative but that the high profits of the 1890s were a thing of the past.

In the early decades of the study, Empire profits, particularly those earned by the diversified trading firms, were very high, although investment was not large. For the years between 1860 and 1864 Cox Brothers returned 22 percent on assets of £136,000; Leon and Sons, 16 percent on £43,000; and F & A Swanzy, over 16 percent on £59,000. With increased competition, however, profits declined, and it was the mid-1890s before there were signs of revival. In that second surge, the leaders were again based in the dependent Empire. In the last five years of the nineteenth century, Leon and Sons earned 14 percent on assets of £131,000; the Royal Niger Company returned almost 18 percent on assets valued at about a million pounds; the Falkland Island Meat Company, 10 percent on £209,000; and the Gowrock Ropeworks, more than 9 percent on £307,000. These latter returns provide little evidence of lucrative exploitative manipulation. They were good, but certainly not unique.

The Tarkwa Trading Company did business on the Gold Coast, and it provides an example of a fairly successful colonial enterprise. The general meeting of May 7, 1908, reviewed some of the company's achievements. "It is only five years since we started this business in Tarkwa with very small capital of £2,500 cash, of which upwards to £1,000 was expended in preliminary expenses and buildings at Tarkwa."[17] The business proved to be a success from the start and in spite of the great disadvantage "of insufficient capital and considerable competition, our most formidable competition has ceased to exist, and nearly all the European trade is in our hands. We have now upwards to £30,000 invested in our business."[18] In the years between 1910 and 1912 the company averaged a return of nearly 10 percent on its assets which now totaled £61,000.

Some domestic and Empire firms were successful and so were some that operated in the foreign sector. The Liebig Extract of Meat Company was organized in 1867 with an initial capitalization of £500,000. Its object was to manufacture on a large scale the pure and genuine "extractum which had been developed by Baron Liebig and Professor Pettenkoffer." " . . . One pound of meat extract," the prospectus asserted, "contained the soluable part of thirty pounds of the finest meat, free from fat and gelatine." The makers claimed that less than one-half a teaspoon of extract dissolved in half a pint of hot water "makes at once strong beef tea or mutton broth." Furthermore, one pound of extract together with some bread and potatoes could provide a hearty soup for 130 men at only a penny a serving. At first the undertaking was extremely profitable. In those early years, before the advent of refrigeration, South American cattle were valued for their hides alone, and the meat was literally left on the pampas to rot. With the discovery of the extract, those heretofore waste products could be put to valuable use, and, as demand increased, Liebig turned to cattle ranching. By the turn of the century the company owned vast herds of cattle in both South America and Africa.

As every investor learns, profits induce imitation, and rivals soon appeared on the scene. At the same time, the introduction of the refrigerator ship made it possible to ship beef, and this raised the price of the firm's major resource requirement. Liebig's annual report for 1886 lamented the decline in profits and reported the increase in the number of "fake" extracts. Despite continual attempts to improve the product (in 1897, for example, the firm retained the services of Sir Henry E. Roscoe, Fellow of the Royal Society), rivals did not disappear. In 1900, the managers plaintively reported that: "All these competitors wish to profit from the enormous amount we have spent on advertising . . . . They generally imitate our package as nearly as possible. In order to protect the public as much as possible, we have been obliged to adopt an additional trademark for our jars, making conspicuous the word LEMCO, the initials of Liebig's Extract of Meat Company. Being an easy word to remember, we hope that it will in large correct the evil of substitution."[19]

Other competitors posed greater threats. Dr. E. Kemmerich ran a successful meat extract business for several years before he was taken over by Liebig. More threatening was Dr. George L. Johnston, who in 1877 introduced "Johnston's Fluid Beef." Because of technical difficulties, Liebig had been capable of selling its product only in bulk while Johnston was able to package Fluid Beef in small bottles and thus gain direct access to the mass consumer market. Johnston's chief asset, however, was not his product but rather its name, Bovril. The public seemed to find that appellation particularly seductive, combining, as it did, connotations of bovine and virile. Liebig admitted that "the invention of the weird word must now be considered as a stroke of brilliant inspiration."[20] In 1901, Liebig countered with a new name of its own, OXO, but it never appeared to attain the same level of public appeal as its competitor; and Liebig, while strong in Britain itself, had a difficult time selling either LEMCO or OXO on the continent. Finally, in 1911 Liebig developed the OXO (bouillon) cube. The extract, now packaged in dry form, gave the firm access to the entire market. It could be sold in quantities small enough to cost only a penny, and it was, thus, accessible to working-class budgets. Parity had now been achieved, and OXO with its little cube and Bovril with its happy name were able to pursue their separate but successful paths.

Antony Gibbs's South American venture is an interesting example of a British enterprise in a foreign environment, and its history underscores the dependence of such undertakings on the good offices of the local government. A substantial fraction of the firm's operations involved the guano and nitrate trades, and the resulting connection with the land and, therefore, property rights involved the company in both the internal politics and the international disputes of Chile. In 1902, after Great Britain had successfully arbitrated a boundary dispute between that country and Argentina, Gibbs was involved in the resale of four battleships that the two nations had bought when it seemed that their dispute would erupt into war. Two were sold to the Japanese; but it took time, tact, and pressure to convince the British Admiralty that it should buy the two remaining vessels, built, as they were, to South American specifications and unlike anything the Royal Navy had ordered in the past or might ever want to acquire in the future.

By 1911, Chile again was interested in expanding its navy. In particular, they desired a battleship of the dreadnought class. Once more the good offices of Antony Gibbs and Company were sought. This time a letter was addressed to the Japanese ambassador in London. "We should be greatly obliged," the note read, "if your Excellency would kindly let us know whether the Japanese government were in a position to offer us a Battleship such as would be likely to meet the requirements of our friends and we beg that your Excellency will favour us with an early reply."[21] Not surprisingly, the Japanese answered in the negative, and there the matter rested.[22]

F. Iron and steel

Iron and steel, so the tale goes, performed poorly in the late Victorian period. If stylized facts are to be believed, the British domestic iron- and steelmakers were very slow to adopt the most modern technological practices. Donald McClosky has already cast substantial doubt on this version of the story, and the rate-of-return data tend to reinforce his reinterpretation.[23] Although domestic returns in iron and steel were lower than those available in the commercial and industrial sector, the difference was not great; moreover, after the turn of the century the comparison is quite favorable. Overall, the industry averaged 10.2 percent, as compared with 9.5 in brewing and 11.6 in commercial and industrial. For the years after 1880 the figures were 9.1, 7.6, and 10.7, and in the twentieth century they were 8.1, 5.0, and 7.3. The profitability of individual firms provides further evidence on financial success. The Anderston foundry, for example, earned almost 30 percent in the last half of both the 1860s and the 1870s. More significantly, that colossus of the future, Vickers, recorded a profit of 12 percent on assets of more than £400,000 in the former quinquennium. The name Vickers had initially made its appearance in 1829 with the organization of Naylor, Hutchinson and Vickers, a firm that soon became Naylor, Vickers and Company. The company's origins lay in steel, but its future depended on diversification: into specialty steel, armaments, armor plating, and naval construction. In 1867, the partnership was turned into a limited company under the name Vickers, Sons and Company, Ltd.; and its first acquisition, the Naval Construction and Armaments Company, bringing with it the Barrow Shipbuilding Company, established the new directions. These added subsidiaries were important for the firm's growth between 1870 and 1900, but of even greater significance was the acquisition of the Maxim, Rodenfelt Guns and Ammunition Company. With that takeover, Vickers and its tentacles reached into the far corners of the globe. In 1860, Vickers's assets were less than £500,000, but by the turn of the century they were four times that large.

In the years between 1890 and 1894, nine domestic iron and steel firms (out of a total of twenty-eight) earned more than 9 (and as much as 24) percent; and between then and the end of the century, twelve surpassed the 9-percent threshold. The new century saw some decline, but four firms earned more in the succeeding quinquennium and eight in the three years ending in 1912. While there were profitable firms there were also, of course, some that were far less successful. James and George Thompson, for example, lost on average 1 percent in the last half of the 1880s, but that was an improvement on the 2.5- and 4-percent losses recorded in the two previous quinquennia.

Abroad, the record stood in stark contrast. In the thirty-three years after 1880, domestic firms averaged 9.1 percent, but foreign ones only 3.9; and even that figure rests on the very strong performance of the foreign industry in the last three years. It appears unlikely that these figures reflect the true profitability of *foreign* enterprises abroad. There are, for example, no German and only one American firm. The British-controlled firms in the foreign sector were located in places like Russia and Spain. In the Empire for the years after 1885, returns averaged only 3 percent. In the twentieth century, however, when domestic earnings were 8.1 percent, and foreign, 3.4 percent, the Empire firms, while not matching the domestic performance, still returned 5.9 percent.

G. Railroads [24]

Long considered a leading sector in the economy's development, the railroads in England were, as has been argued in the American context, the nation's first big business. The British initially built railroads at home and then turned their attention to the rest of the world. They were almost solely responsible for the South American rail network and for initial developments in Asia and the Middle East as well. In addition, British capital provided a substantial fraction of the finance that underwrote construction in North America and Europe. In the Empire, Indian railroad policy has been the object of considerable criticism, but the British were also intimately involved in laying rails in the self-governing colonies and in building what rail lines there were in Africa.

In the United Kingdom, profits averaged more than 3 percent. Empire returns were lower (in the years after 1885 they averaged 2.3 percent, compared with a domestic average of 2.8); and only in the last three years before 1912 do returns exceed those at home. If there were large profits to be earned in Empire railroad investment, it appears that they were captured by shippers, or, perhaps, by consumers (or maybe by managers and workers). Despite the "quasi-monopolistic" position that the railroads held in most of the dependent Empire, there is nothing to indicate that these roads enjoyed better returns than the railroads in Britain, where routes were quite competitive and regulation relatively stringent.

Foreign railroads were more profitable, if the criterion is Empire or domestic performance. It has been said, and only partly in jest, that the British paid for the American railroad network three times in the nineteenth century. For forty-eight years between 1865 and 1912, foreign roads averaged 6.1 percent; and, even for the post–1885 period, the figure approaches twice the domestic and more than twice the Empire average. The markets in South and Central America that were opened by British-built and -financed railroads were profitable, and the railroads captured a part of the profits. For example, in the last half of the 1880s, the Sao Paolo Brazilian Railroad returned 12 percent on its £3.1 million asset base; and the Tehuan-tapec National Railway earned 10 percent on its £5.6 million in the years between 1910 and 1912.

H. *Shipping*

Given the ease of substitution between investment in ship-ping activities, it is not surprising that there is relatively little dif-ference in the rates of return between the foreign and domestic sectors, and probably between those two and the imperial as well. For the period after 1890, domestic shipping returned 6.6; foreign, 6.5; and Empire, 5.1. These returns, supported by a steady stream of government subsidies, were sufficient to underwrite a continued flow of investment into an economic activity that was obviously of vital concern to the island nation.

The Cunard Company provides an excellent example of a rather rare phenomenon in nineteenth-century Britain – close government–business cooperation. The relationship was based on the govern-ment's desire to maintain good communications with its far-flung Empire and on the threat of a war to the island's supplies. The company's directors announced, in 1902, that an agreement had been concluded with the government that provided for a 2.5-percent loan (in that year the rate on consols was 2.9 percent) to pay for two high-speed vessels for the Atlantic trade (the *Mauretania* and *Lusi-tania*).[25] In addition, the government agreed to pay an annual sub-vention of £150,000 from the date that the ships came into operation.[26] In return, the company would hold all the ships in its fleet available for government charter. At a later date the company also agreed to prevent any foreigner from becoming a director of the company and to require that all masters, engineers, officers of the watch, and three-fourths of the crew be British subjects. All officers on Cunard vessels were to be members of the Royal Navy Reserve, and the two subsidized steamers would be equipped to carry guns. The agreement was to last twenty years, and, during that time, the Cunard management agreed that the firm would remain a purely British enterprise.

I. Trams and omnibuses

In most of the developed world, commercialization was linked with urbanization; and, in the· late nineteenth century, the world's most commercialized country was also its most urbanized. In 1850, over one-half of Britain's population lived in cities, a level not reached in the United States until 1920. The demand for urban transport in the United Kingdom was high, and a series of new techniques provided opportunities for significant entrepreneurial activity. By the turn of the century in London, four very different technologies competed for the traveler's shilling.

There were firms that operated horse-drawn trams (the precursor of the street car). These companies, although competitive on the margins, maintained routes that were largely noncompetitive. They operated under government charter with some local control of rates; and, if chartered after 1870, they faced possible compulsory government purchase after twenty-one years of operation. Second, dating from the 1860s, were the undergrounds. The District, Metropolitan, and Circle Lines operated steam trains in tunnels directly beneath the streets. (The Circle Line, although allegedly using smokeless coal, was known among its customers as the Sewer Line.) They too were dependent on government charter, and they too faced the threat of compulsory purchase and possible rate regulation. Third, there were the "Tubes," the electrified subways. First chartered in the 1880s, they began operations at the end of the century. Although they were also dependent on parliamentary licensing, they appear to have developed in spite of, rather than because of, government encouragement.

Finally, there were the omnibus companies. These firms ran horse-drawn (later gas-driven) buses on the city streets and operated with minimum government control. The intrusion of the latter technology into the London market touched off competitive rate wars and an erosion of returns after the turn of the century. The subways and trams had been slow to innovate and willing to profit from their position as near natural monopolies. They made few attempts to coordinate schedules, and as late as 1897 horses continued to pull over 90 percent of the trams. By that date, in the United States electrification had replaced almost 90 percent of the horse-drawn vehicles. If the firms that operated the traditional forms of transport had been lethargic and slow to adopt new techniques, the unregulated omnibuses were not. They quickly adopted coordinated schedules, and they were very prompt in replacing equine with gasoline power. If one believes the qualitative records, it is possible to conclude that technological change was almost too swift. These firms brought motor busses to the London streets in 1900 (seven years before the Model T) when the threat of obsolescence was so great that they felt required to adopt six-month to two-year depreciation schedules.

On average, domestic and foreign rates of return were higher than those for firms located in the Empire (the averages for comparable years were 5.0, 3.8, and 2.9 percent). The British figure, however, is an average of relatively high earnings of the 1880s and 1890s and of much lower returns in the present century. Abroad, the time path was different. Between 1880 and 1899, when domestic firms were earning almost 7, their foreign counterparts were returning a little over 4, and Empire firms slightly less than 2 percent. In the present century, when domestic firms returned slightly over 2, those that were foreign-based earned over 3, and Empire firms more than 5 percent. The foreign sector probably proved somewhat more profitable than the domestic after the turn of the century, and it almost certainly was not substantially less so. In the areas penetrated by the British overseas firms (largely in Central and South America) urban growth was slower, but there does not appear to have been the same fierce intertechnological competition.

In the Empire, British firms did very well in the later years. Higher returns were associated with the newly electrified tramways operating as monopolies (either naturally or through charter) in the cities of Canada, Australia, India, and South Africa. As in the foreign sector, within the Empire there appears to have been less intertechnological competition. The profitability of natural monopolies was blunted at home (by regulation and intertechnological competition) and abroad (by political decisions that tended to favor home consumers over foreign profits), but these forces were less powerful in the Empire. The slow growth of urban areas probably reduced the incentives for external competition, at least in the dependent Empire, and the political structure was possibly favorably biased toward outside investors – at least those from the parent country.

J. Gas and electricity

Gas companies were natural monopolies; and, although their profits appear to deny it, they were among the first activities subject to governmental regulation. Domestic gas and light firms averaged greater than 8 percent return over the entire period and relatively high earnings were not unusual. The Commercial Gas Company (London), for example, averaged a return of more than 9 percent over the fifteen years between 1875 and 1889. Even in the years after 1905 when the profitability of the whole industry decreased, the Wolverhampton Company averaged a return of 13.5 percent annually and the comparable figure for the Brentford Gas Company was 11 percent. Gas manufacture in the United Kingdom was technically very advanced, but despite changes in the regulatory constraints that permitted firms to earn higher profits if their prices fell, progress was slower after the advent of regulation.[27] Moreover, although development was slow, electricity began to undercut the monopoly of gas in lighting. In 1890, although electricity had captured a third of the U.S. urban lighting market, it had made no appreciable inroads in Britain. Ten years later, at a time when 60 percent of U.S. urban consumers used electricity, the British proportion had barely reached 10.[28] This slow growth reflected not only the early technological superiority of gas, but also increasingly stringent government regulation and the political machinations of the hostile and well-entrenched gas firms. Of those companies whose records were studied, most expended resources attempting to block the charters of electric companies that might have competed with them directly, and many appear to have devoted at least some effort in attempting to impede almost any proposed electric charter. Only one concern, the Barnett Gas, sought a charter that would permit it to expand into electric service.

Even clearly profitable innovations were not costless, and for both gas and electric companies political expenditures reduced profits. From 1875 to 1885, the gas and electric companies averaged returns of 8.7 percent, while from 1910–1912 they earned 5.5 (gas and electric companies together returned 6.7 percent).

Abroad, the story was somewhat different. After 1895 the three sectors averaged 7.7 (domestic), 6.1 (foreign), and 8.2 (Empire). In the foreign sector, while formal regulation developed more slowly than in the United Kingdom, firms still depended on government charters and were subject to political pressure. British-owned public utilities in Rosario, Argentina, are a case in point. There, the end of war with Paraguay and the rise of Buenos Aires as a rival port led to acute xenophobia and placed the British-controlled companies under constant local pressure with little or no hope of relief.[29] Profits, as a consequence, were sporadic and elusive.

K. Waterworks

A similar structure but a slightly different time path underlies the pattern of returns of the third natural monopoly. Electricity was an excellent substitute for gas, and omnibuses a good one for trams. There were no substitutes for water. Domestic rates were high for most of the nineteenth century and only dropped in the twentieth. In contrast, foreign-sector returns were much lower in the nineteenth century, but less so in the twentieth. In the Empire, earnings were substantially higher than at home and much higher than in those overseas cities not in the Empire.

L. Extractive and agriculture

Because control of property rights might have made it possible for British investors to earn very high returns, the fiscal success of the agriculture and extractive sector could prove crucial to any argument concerning rates of return and the economics of Empire. The extractive and agricultural category is an amalgam of the stock exchange's mining and tea and coffee industries, combined with the coal firms from the iron, coal, and steel classification, and agricultural and extractive enterprises (particularly nitrate) from the commercial and industrial list. The history of these firms confirms the hypothesis that property rights and profits were related. Although Empire rates were lower than foreign, they were higher than domestic and much higher after 1870. In comparative periods (e.g., 1875 to 1912) Empire firms returned 11.3, foreign 14.2, and domestic 9.5 percent. Although domestic returns were volatile, the level of profit does not appear to have eroded over time, and it compares favorably with earnings in other domestic industries. That result depends to a large extent on the profits earned by British coal mines. Although resource exhaustion may have become a factor, collieries continued to be relatively profitable until the new century was well underway, and they were particularly profitable during the Boer War.

In the foreign sector, as a group the most profitable companies dealt in nitrate (Liverpool Nitrate, for example, averaged a 23 percent return from 1885 to 1912), but the most consistent success was the Consett Spanish Iron Company. The firm was not large (its total assets hovered around £70,000), but from 1880 to 1912 its earnings averaged almost 40 percent, and in no year were they less than 15.

In the Empire, in the later years, it was the South African gold mines that contributed the most heavily to the industry's well-being; but earlier it had been the tea and coffee companies of India and Ceylon. In both cases, firms that entered the market early did well; those that followed, much less so. To the extent that the existence of the Empire made it possible to acquire and maintain the property rights that underlay those profits, the political structure of Empire contributed to British prosperity. Empire concerns had the advantage of a certain stable set of political rules, and those rules protected them. They were not required to invest the resources that South American nitrate firms had to commit to the protection of their property rights in a less than hospitable political environment. The experience of the foreign sector, however, suggests that such a political connection, although certainly helpful, was not a necessary condition for success.

A review of returns in the Empire indicates that in banking there was little to differentiate profit in areas under British control from earnings in the other two sectors. Among financial, land, and development companies, foreign returns were considerably greater than either those in the Empire or in Britain. The twentieth century aside, Empire financial trusts did about twice as well as British, although only about two-thirds as well as foreign. Empire breweries and distillers returned profits about equal to those available at home; however, both were better than foreign.

In terms of sample size, the commercial and industrial category is by far the largest and because of its role in the economy it should probably be deemed the most significant. There, the supposedly sluggish domestic economy appears to have performed much better than conventional wisdom has asserted. Over the entire period the rate of return was 11 percent, and it fell significantly below that figure only in the last thirteen years. Foreign-based firms earned 12 percent overall, but at only half that level in the twentieth century. Early entry into a largely noncompetitive environment allowed Empire companies to earn almost 15 percent over the first twenty-five years, but increased competition induced a substantial decline in profitability and led to a fifty-three years' average of a still respectable 10.5 percent.

Again, conventional wisdom suggests that domestic iron and steel were in the doldrums in the late nineteenth century. British firms, however, earned over twice as much as foreign ones; and their average of more than 10 percent was much higher than the 3 percent returned by Empire firms after 1884. Returns on British railways were about 3 percent after 1880; Empire roads for the same period averaged two-thirds that figure and foreign roads close to twice as much. Shipping returns for the three sectors show little difference, and the same is true for trams and omnibuses. In the late nineteenth century, domestic gas and electricity companies outstripped imperial and foreign firms, but by 1905 foreign concerns had narrowed the margin and Empire firms surpassed them both. A similar pattern emerges from the history of waterworks; but there Empire returns rose to twice domestic in the new century.

Nor did British domestic firms fare very badly in the extractive and agricultural sector. Foreign ones, often investing in the highly profitable South American nitrate fields, showed profits of over 14 percent. Empire firms, with the gold of South Africa and Western Australia and the tea of India and Burma at their command, brought an average return of more than 10 percent; but the average domestic return was in excess of 9 percent.

V. Interindustry comparison

The measure of profitability that has been employed is the rate of return on the adjusted book value of assets. To the extent that firms in the same industry faced similar technologies and competed in the same capital markets, it provides a reasonably consistent and fairly unambiguous measure of the underlying productivity of the resources committed to a particular economic activity. As attention is directed away from the industry to higher forms of aggregation, the assumption of similar capital structures becomes less tenable, and the measure a less reliable indicator of relative returns.

Unfortunately, the historical rhetoric has in large measure been cast in terms of the rate of return. Perhaps more importantly, in most industries Empire investment was not particularly profitable, although it was in some; and returns there may have been sufficient to make the imperial adventure, on net, a profitable investment. Some measure of average rate of return on home, foreign, and Empire investment is obviously required; however, it should be recognized that there are flaws in any such measure and that any index probably raises at least as many questions as it answers. Given the problems inherent in attempts to merge firms into industries and industries into an economy, the reader should tread warily indeed.[30]

The discussion in this section, a comparison of returns across industries, focuses on the returns earned on investment in equity.[31]

The subsequent section, an examination of the rate of return, uses three different measures. Across all industries the unweighted domestic returns on equity for the two decades 1860–79 averaged 12.2 percent; for the following thirty-three years, the figure is 8.3 percent. Comparable averages for the foreign sector are 11.4 and 7.1 percent, and for the Empire, 15.4 and 6.7 percent. If for each of these latter years (the data are sparse in the earlier years) clusters of the most and least profitable firms are examined, some patterns emerge – patterns that reinforce and extend the previous analysis. For each decade a most-profitable industry is one that has at minimum twice as many firms among the total sample's most profitable 20 percent as statistical normality would dictate, and a least-profitable industry is one with twice the expected representation among the bottom fifth of firms surveyed. By this criterion an industry could, if it had both very profitable and very unprofitable firms, be both a "most" and a "least" profitable one.

In the 1880s, total domestic returns averaged 9.8; foreign, 7.5; and Empire, 5.4 percent. In that decade, the commercial and industrial industry, led by such firms as De La Rue and Samuel Courtauld, was the most profitable domestic activity. In the foreign sector, it was agriculture and extractive, but in the Empire, no industry meets the established criterion. Among the least profitable were British financial trusts; foreign telephones and telegraphs; and, mirroring the most-profitable list, foreign agriculture and extractive firms. In the Empire, it was railroads and waterworks that performed relatively poorly.

During the next decade (the 1890s) returns averaged 7.8, 5.5, and 5.3 percent in the three locations. The most-profitable domestic industries were agriculture and extractive and commercial and industrial. No foreign industry meets the most-profitable criterion, but in the Empire, agriculture and extractive, breweries and distilleries, and waterworks made the list. The unsuccessful industries included domestic financial, land, and development companies, financial trusts, and canals and docks; foreign breweries and distilleries, railroads, and shipping lines; and imperial canals and docks, financial, land, and development companies, iron and steelworks, shipping lines, and trams and omnibuses.

Finally, in the years 1900–9, average returns were 7.4, 7.1, and 7.4 percent. British banks and agriculture and extractive firms were among the most profitable. The same status was claimed by foreign agriculture and extractive firms, and brewing and distilleries, and by shipping lines in the Empire. The "least" profitable category was dominated at home by financial, land, and development companies and by trams and omnibuses; by foreign canals and docks, financial, land and development companies and iron and steelworks; and in the empire by breweries and distilleries, financial, land, and development companies and financial trusts.

VI. General measures of profitability

The analysis in this section is based on three different measures of "the" rate of return and all are flawed. They are: (1) the rate of return to all capital claims, (2) the rate of return on the book value of equity, and (3) the rate of return on "adjusted assets" for firms in the goods producing sector.[32]

The first measure is based on the assumptions that all firms are equally risky and that the total return to all capital claims is independent of industry. The second, that this peculiar measure captures what the returns on equity investment would have been, if some had not been garnered as capital gains by previous owners. The third, that the goods producing sectors (merged because they have similar capital structures and chosen because they are quite diverse and well represented in the sample) do reflect economic trends in the economy as a whole. It should also be borne in mind that none of the averages is weighted and that they measure only the composition of firms included in the study, not the actual structure of British, foreign, or Empire economic activity and investment.[33]

There are differences in level, and at times the measures diverge markedly. For example, the surge in foreign earnings in the late 1870s and early 1880s is more apparent in the goods-producing sector than in either of the other averages, and the domestic increase associated with the Boer War is less apparent when the focus is narrowed to exclude coal mining. Despite these differences, the overall patterns are similar. In the case of all three measures the overall trend is downward, and the rate of decrease is higher for foreign than domestic and greater for Empire than for foreign. Of more importance, the return on domestic investment, however measured, was certainly not below and likely substantially above the return on Empire activities from at least the early 1880s to the end of the Boer War (see Tables 3.14 and 3.15 and Charts 3.1, 3.2 and 3.3).

It must be remembered that the number of Empire firms in the study is relatively small in the years before 1880 and includes a substantial fraction of "pioneer" enterprises (firms operating in newly opened regions). At the same time, the foreign firms in those early years tended to operate in already established markets and the same was true for the domestic concerns. Thus, sample selection

TABLE 3.14

MOST AND LEAST PROFITABLE INDUSTRIES BY LOCATION AND DECADES[1]

Date	Home	Foreign	Empire
		(A) MOST PROFITABLE	
1860-69	Banks		C&I
1870-79	I&S		Banks; A&E
1880-89	C&I	A&E	
1890-99	C&I; A&E		B&D; WWK; A&E
1900-09	Banks; A&E	A&E	B&D; Shipping
		(B) LEAST PROFITABLE	
1860-69	T&O; C&D	Shipping; FL&D	
1870-79	A&E; T&O	FL&D	Banks
1880-89	FTrst	T&T; A&E	RRs; WWK
1890-99	C&D; FTrst; FL&D	B&D; RRs; FL&D; Shipping; C&D	I&S; Shipping; T&O; C&D; FL&D
1900-09	FL&D; T&O	FL&D; I&S	FL&D; B&D; FTrst

NOTE: Only firms with at least four years' data in a decade were included.

[1] Most = twice as many + firms top 20% as expected;
Least = twice as many + firms bottom 20% as expected.

A&E:	Agricultural & Extractive	G&L:	Gas & Light
Banks:	Commercial Banks	I&S:	Iron & Steel
B&D:	Breweries & Distilleries	RRs:	Railroads
C&D:	Canals & Docks	T&T:	Telephones & Telegraphs
C&I	Commercial & Industrial	T&O:	Trams & Omnibuses
FL&D:	Financial, Land & Development	WWK:	Waterworks
FTrst:	Financial Trusts		

TABLE 3.15

	RATES OF RETURN									RETURN RELATIVES								
	Adjusted Goods Producing			Adjusted Equity			All Claims on Capital			FOR/UK			EMP/UK			EMP/FOR		
	UK	FOR	EMP	UK	FOR	EMP	UK	FOR	EMP	CC	AE	GP	CC	AE	GP	CC	AE	GP
1860-64	12.8	11.7	18.4	12.5	22.5	26.4	5.0	9.2	11.7	184	180	91	234	211	144	127	117	157
1865-69	10.0	11.0	15.0	13.2	16.5	17.5	5.0	4.8	9.9	96	125	110	198	133	150	206	106	136
1870-74	15.2	11.5	11.5	19.4	18.6	16.2	7.8	7.4	9.0	95	96	76	115	84	76	122	87	100
1875-79	9.9	9.5	15.3	12.7	10.5	29.0	5.5	4.3	12.4	78	83	155	225	228	155	288	276	161
1880-84	9.7	6.2	10.3	12.7	7.6	10.5	5.6	3.0	5.6	54	603	655	100	83	106	187	138	166
1885-89	10.1	19.1	6.2	12.1	11.6	8.6	6.0	6.1	3.3	102	96	189	55	71	61	54	74	32
1890-94	7.6	4.4	4.1	11.6	7.1	6.3	5.8	3.6	2.6	62	61	58	45	54	54	72	89	93
1895-99	8.1	6.7	4.5	12.7	7.4	7.2	7.5	3.6	3.7	48	58	83	49	57	56	103	97	67
1900-04	6.2	4.1	6.0	12.0	9.3	7.7	5.6	3.5	2.5	63	78	66	45	64	97	71	83	146
1905-09	6.0	2.8	5.6	10.0	10.8	9.0	3.6	3.9	3.7	108	108	47	103	90	93	95	83	200
1910-12	6.3	6.5	6.8	11.8	17.3	10.7	4.3	5.6	4.7	130	147	103	109	91	108	84	62	105
AVG	9.4	8.0	9.5	12.8	12.5	13.7	5.7	5.0	6.3	88	98	101	111	107	101	126	110	100
1860-84	11.5	10.0	14.5	14.1	15.1	19.9	5.8	5.8	9.7	100	107	87	167	141	126	167	132	145
1885-1912	7.5	6.2	5.4	11.7	10.1	8.1	5.5	5.3	3.3	78	86	83	60	69	72	77	80	87

UK:	United Kingdom	CC:	All Claims on Capital
FOR:	Foreign Countries	AE:	Adjusted Equity
EMP:	Empire	GP:	Goods Producing

may have biased the results; however, it appears difficult to reject the conclusion that the Empire was "good business" for the British businessman until the early 1880s; and that conclusion holds whether the yardstick is foreign or domestic returns. Although the result depends somewhat on the measure chosen, it would seem that in those halcyon years Empire returns were about a third greater than domestic and something more than half as large as foreign.

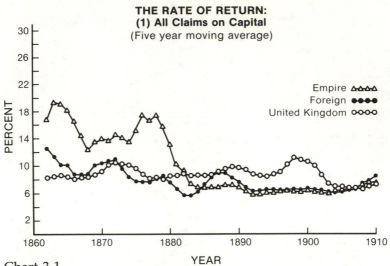

Chart 3.1

Chart 3.2

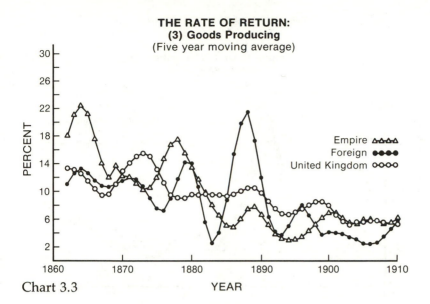

Chart 3.3

That finding is reversed over the last twenty years of the nineteenth and the first few years of the twentieth century. In those later years Empire firms were substantially less profitable than domestic, and somewhat less profitable than foreign. In the last decade, however, the domestic advantage had disappeared and Empire returns were, if anything, slightly higher.

As the "crisis of capitalism" approached (and the rate of profit at home was declining – albeit slowly) it does not appear that the Empire represented any better, and perhaps not even as good, an alternative as the foreign sector; and neither appears to have been as attractive as the domestic economy. Again, while there is no way of knowing what the marginal return on investment may have been, given the size of the foreign sector and the returns there relative to those in the Empire, it seems unlikely that, even on the margin, the Empire would have appeared a much more attractive alternative.

All three measures are presented in Chart 3.4, and returns in the Empire are compared to those available at home. The three patterns are similar. Empire profits were very high in the early years, but that pattern was reversed in about 1880. From that time on, British firms were more profitable than their Empire counterparts; however, at the end of the period relative Empire rates were rising, and for the years after 1905, there is little to choose between the two sectors. While it is necessary to treat these data with great care, it is difficult to imagine how the central finding – that after 1880, although the

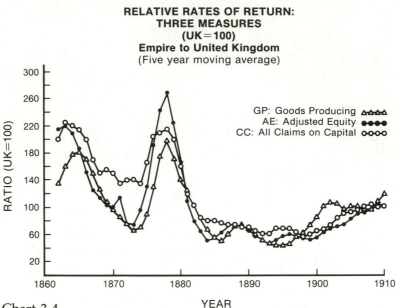

Chart 3.4

Empire may have remained good business for some, on average it was almost certainly less rewarding than domestic alternatives – could be reversed.

One conclusion seems apparent. No matter how profitable the Empire was in the early decades, it was much less so later. Examination of the qualitative evidence indicates that when new areas were opened, there were opportunities for substantial profits; but in most instances competition eroded those opportunities in a relatively short period of time. Little is known about pioneer firms in the foreign sector, and it would be interesting to examine a larger number of firms operating in the American West or in South and Central America in the years before 1880. If the profits of those firms were substantially below those available in the Empire, then it could be argued that, for a time at least, the Empire did make a difference. Be that as it may, for the general investor in the years after 1880, the Empire was probably a snare and a delusion – a flame not worth the candle.

APPENDIX 3.1

FIRMS, DATA FROM WHICH IS UTILIZED IN THE STUDY

A. Random Sample of Corporations Whose Shares were Traded on the London Stock Exchange, 1883-1912

Aberdeen Cattle & Farm Produce Association
Acol Collieries
African & United Supply & Cold Storage
African City Properties Trust
African Lakes Trading Corp.
Alexandria Water Co.
Allynugger Tea Co.
Amazon Telegraph Co.
American Trust Co.
Anamalay Coffee Co. Ltd.
Anglo Californian Bank
Anglo Egyptian Bank
Anibiri Wassau Exploration
Anterior Matabele Gold Mines
Antwerp Tivoli Breweries
Ardilla Copper Mines
Ashton Vale Iron Co.
Assets Founders' Share Co.
Auckland Electric Tramways
Australian Chilling & Freezing
Azoff Coal Co.
Bank of Mauritius
Bank of Tarapaca & London
Bankers' Investment Trust
Barran, John & Sons
Bell's Asbestos Co.
Bengal Iron & Steel Co.
Bengal Nagpur Railroad
Beyrouth Water Works
Bolivar Railroad
Bombay Gas Co.
Bombay Tea Co.
Booth Steamship Co.
Boston Consolidated Copper & Gold Mining Co.
Bradford Banking Co.
Brahmapootra Tea Co.
Brazilian Street Railroad
Bridgetown & St. Andrews Railroad Co.
Bright's Light & Power
British Columbia Canning
British Columbia Electric Railway
British Columbia Telephones
Buenos Ayres Gas Co.
Buenos Ayres Southern Dock
Bulawayo Water Works
Burgon & Ball
Bute Shipbuilding, Engineering & Dock Co.
Calcutta Electric Supply Corp.
Calcutta Tramways
Calico Printers Assoc.
Cambrian Consolidated Mines
Cape Asbestos Co.
Cardiff District & Penarth Harbour Tramway
Cardiff Junction Dry Dock & Engineering Co.
Carrizal Share Trust Ltd.
Carter, Milner & Bird
Carthagena & Herrerias Steam Tramway
Cedar Valley Land & Cattle Co.
Chesapeake & Ohio Steamship Co.
Chiapas Zone Exploration
Chicago Breweries
Chile Telephone Co.
Chilean National Ammunition Co.
Chinese Engineering & Mining Co.
Chubwa Tea Co. of Assam
Clitters United Mine
Colombo Electric Tramways & Lighting
Colombo Gas & Water Co.
Colonial Securities Trust
Combined Rhodesia Syndicate
Consolidated Rand Rhodesia Trust & General Exploration Co.
Consolidated South Rand Mines Deep Ltd.
Consolidated Water Works of Rosario
Cornish Adventurers
Cornish Bank
Costa Rica Electric Light & Traction Co.
Costa Rica Railroad Co.
Daira Sanieh Sugar Corp.
Dalgety & Co.
Deary & Co.
Delhi & London Bank
Dindicolle & Gaudin

(A. continued)

Dominion Breweries
Dominion Carpet Co.
Dorman, Long & Co.
East India Coal Co. Ltd.
East India Tramways
Eastern Extension Australasia & China Telegraph Co.
Eastern Mortgage & Agency Co.
Edinburgh North American Investment
Emu Bay & Mount Bischoff Railway
Falkland Islands Meat
Floating Dock Co. of St. Thomas
Foreign & Colonial Investment Trust
Franco African Exploration & Investment Co.
Friary Holroyd's & Healy's Brewery
Glamorgan Public House Trust
Gleesons Success Gold Mines Ltd.
Globe Telegraph & Trust Co.
Goebel Brewing Co. Ltd.
Gold Ore Treatment Co. of West Australia
Goomera Tea Estates
Great Boulder Proprietory Gold Mines
Great Western of Brazil Railroad
Halifax Brewery
Halifax Graving Dock
Harmony Proprietory Co.
Hart & Levy
Heritable Investment Bank
Hood & Moore's Stores
Huon Timber Co.
Imperial Tramway Co.
Indian Midlands Railway
Indianapolis Breweries
International Bank of London
International Lighting Assoc.
International Line Steamship
Kalgoorlie Electric Power & Lighting
Kanan Devan Hills Produce Co.
Kimberley Waterworks Co.
Klerksdorf Estates
Klip Colliery
La Capital Tramways Co.
Labuan & Borneo Ltd.
Lagunas Syndicate
Lancashire & Yorkshire Bank
Land Mortgage Bank of North Western America
Lands Trust Co.
Lea Bridge District Gas, Light & Coke
Leicester Real Property
Linkwood Glenlivet Distilleries
Liverpool & North Wales Steamship Co.
Liverpool Commercial Investment Co.
Liverpool Nitrate
London & Hanseatic Bank
London & San Francisco Bank
London & South Western Bank
London Bank of Australia
London House Trust
London Paris & American Bank
London Platino Brazilian Telegraph Co.
Lucia Silver Mines
Main Colliery Co. Ltd.
Majuli Tea Co.
Malayan (Pahang) Exploration Co.
Malta & Mediterranean Gas Co.
Manitoba Mortgage & Investment Co.
Marbella Iron Co.
Marianao & Havana RR
Mashonaland RR Co.
Maxim, H. Electrical & Engineering
Maypole Dairy
Melbourne Brewery & Distillery
Mercantile Bank of India
Mercantile Pontoon Co.
Merchants Trust
Mersey Forge
Metropolitan Coal Co. of Sydney
Mexican Electric Tramways
Mexican Electric Works
Middleburg Steam Coal & Coke
Mining Investment Co. of Glasgow
Mona & Parys Mines
Montevideo Water Works
Montserrat Co.
Mount Carbon Co.
Natal Steam Coal Co.
Natal Zululand RR
National Bank of New Zealand

(A. continued)

New Cape Central
New Cimbula Co.
New Ravenswood
New Theatre Cambridge
New Zealand Mines Trust
Newbury's Ltd.
Nitrate Producers Steamship
Nitrate Railways Co.
Noakhali (Bengal) Railway Co.
North Alabama Assets Co.
North Borneo Trading
North Cachar Tea Co.
North Eastern Banking Co.
Nottingham Brewery
Ocean Minerals
Ohlsson's Cape Breweries
Orient Produce Co.
Orient Steam Navigation Co.
Oriental Gas Co.
Parchoca Iron Ore & RR Co.
Parish Lighting
Peking Syndicate
Portsmouth United Brewery
Provincial Tramways Co.
Queensland Smelting Co.
Railway Rolling Stock Trust
Railways & Metropolitan Omnibus
Rand Central Electric Co.
Reynolds Bros.
Rhodesia Breweries
Rhodesia Gold Reefs (Purdon's) Ltd.
River Plate Gas Co.
Riverside Gold Mines
Rohilkund & Kumaon RR
Royal Niger Co.
Russian Engineering Co.
Salar del Carmen Nitrate Syndicate
San Francisco Brewery
San Jacinto Land Co.
Seville Water Works
Shanghai Waterworks Co.
Sheffield Forge & Rolling Mills Co.
Smith's Dock Co. Ltd.
South African Brewery
South African General Syndicate
South African Lighting Assoc. Ltd.
South African Super Aeration
Southern Coal Co. of New South Wales
Southern Mahratta Railroad
Spencer, Turner & Boldero
St. Pauli Breweries
Stroud Brewery Co.
Sydney Harbour Collieries
Tarkway Whim Gold Syndicate
Trust & Agency Co. of Australasia
Tyne Pontoons & Dry Docks
United Trust Co.
Val de Travers Asphalt Co.
Warner Estates
Weardale Lead Co.
West Coast of Africa Oil & Fuel Co.
West Prussian Mining Co.
West's Patent Press
Western Australia Proprietary Gold Mines
Western Railway of Santa Fe
White Pass & Yukon RR
Wrexham Gas & Coke Co.
Wynaad Tea Co.
Yangtse Valley Co.
York Tramways Co.
Yorkshire Electric Power Syndicate
Yorkshire Indigo Scarlet & Colour Dye

B. Companies with more Complete Records, 1860-1912

Aberdare & Aberaman Consumers Gas Co.
African Association Ltd.
Alison, James & Sons.
Alley Mclelland Ltd.
Alliance Investment Co.
American Hawaiian Steamship
American Investment Trust
Anderson & Robertson Ltd.
Anderston Foundry
Anglo-Russian Cotton Mills
Arroll, William & Co.
Ashanti Goldfields Corp.

(B. continued)

Assam Co.
Associated Omnibus Co. Ltd.
Barclay, Curle & Co.
Barclay, Perkins & Co.
Barnet District Gas & Water
Barry Dock Cottage Co.
Bathurst Trading Co.
Baxter Bros. & Co., Ltd.
Beardmore, William
Bell, Thomas & Sons
Benson, Robert & Co.
Bertram, James & Sons
Birmingham Small Arms & Metal
Black Dyke Mills
Blaenavon Co.
Bolckow, Vaughan & Co.
Brentford Gas Co.
Bridgend Gas & Water
Bristol City Lines
British Slate Co. Ltd.
Brooke-Bond Tea
Brynmawr & Blaina Gas Co.
Burgess, John & Son
Burnyeat, Brown & Co.
Calder & Hubble Navigation
Calder Navigation
Carlton Main Colliery
Carney & Barrow
Carney & Barrow II
Champdany Jute
Cheltenham Original Breweries
Chilworth Gunpowder Co.
City and West End Properties
City of London Gaslight & Coke
City Bank
Clifton & Kersley Coal Co.
Clydebank Engineering & Shipbuilding
Colville Steel
Commercial Gas Co.
Connock Chase Colliery Co.
Consett Iron Co.
Consett Spanish Iron Ore Co.
Cook, Thomas
Copland & Lye
Cossall Colliery
Courage & Co.
Courtauld, Samuel & Co.
Cox Bros.
Cumberland Union Bank
Cunard Steamship
Darlington Forge
Davey, Paxman & Co.
De La Rue Co.
Dowanhill Estate
Dowlais Iron Co.
Dudley Gas Co.
Duston Iron Ore
Eagle Oil Co.
Eagle Oil Transport Co.
East Cannock Colliery
Economic Life Assurance Soc.
Edmund Swaithe Colliery Co. Ltd.
Ellis & Everard Ltd. II
Ellis, Joseph & Sons (Ellis and Everard I)
Extract Wool & Merino Co.
F. Kendall & Sons
Fairfield Shipbuilding & Engineering
Farnham United Brewery
Finlay Clarke & Co.
Finley, James
Fish, J. Ltd.
Fitton & Sons
Flintshire Oil & Cannel
Flower & Sons Ltd.
Ford-Ayrton
Fordham, E.K. & H.
Foreign, American & General Investment Trust
Fox, Samuel & Co.
Fulham Pottery Co.
Gas Light & Coke
General Hydraulic Power Co.
Gibbs, William - Australia
Gibbs, William - Liverpool
Gibbs, William - South American
Giggal & Clay
Gilroy & Sons
Glasgow Steamshipping Co.
Glenanvon Gawr Collieries

(B. continued)

Gold Coast Machinery & Trading
Gowrock Ropeworks
Grand Junction Canal
Gray & Sons - Chelmsford
Gray & Sons, Maldon
Great Central Gas Consumer Co.
Greg & Greg Mill
Grierson, Robert & Co.
Hadden & Co.
Hallamshire Steel & File Co.
Hammersmith & City RR
Hampstead Colliery
Hardy & Padimore
Harrow & Stanmore Gas
Harrow Electric Light & Power
Hartley, John & Sons
Hepworth, J & Sons
Hills Plymouth & Co., Ltd.
Hirst, George & Sons
Hodgsons Kingston Brewery
Hopewell Tea
Horseley Co.
Huddersfield Banking
Hull Dock Co.
Hunt & Winterbotham
Huntley & Palmers
Huth & Co.--Valparaiso
Ibbotson Bros. & Co.
Indemnity Mutual Marine Assurance
International Financial Society
Isleworth Brewery
Jacquard
Jessop Bros.
John Foster & Sons
Jowett, Robert & Sons
Kendall (Lille)
Kleinwort, Drake & Cohen
Lautaro Nitrate
Lee, Nephew & Sons
Leon & Sons
Liebig Extract of Meat
Lister & Co.
Little, David
London Assurance Co.
London General Omnibus
London Joint Stock Bank
London Road Car Co.
London, Buenos Ayres, and River Plate Bank
   (Lloyd's Bank International)
Lovell, J & Sons
Macclesfield Silk Manufacturing Co.
Maciver, W. B. & Co.
Main, A & J
Metropolitan District Railway
Metropolitan Tower Construction
Mexican Mines of el Oro
Midlands Bank
Mitchell Main Colliery
Nettlefold's Ltd.
New Charleston Colliery
New Zealand & Australia Land Co.
Newstead Colliery Ltd.
Noakes & Co.
North & South Wales Bank
North Metropolitan Electric Power Supply
North Metropolitan Power Distribution Co.
North Metropolitan Tram
Northern Assurance Co.
Ocean Coal & Wilsons Ltd.
Ocean Marine Insurance Co.
Orr Ewing & Co.
Pacific Steam Navigation Co.
Palatine Insurance Co.
Peek, Frean & Co.
Pennycook Patent Glazing & Engineering
Peruvian Corporation
Phillips, J & B
Pirie, Alexander & Sons
Quarry Bank Mill
Ramsden, T & Sons
Redbourne Hill Co.
Reffel Bexley Brewery
Roper, J. G. & Sons
Royal Brewery Brentford
Royal Mail Steam Packet
Royston Water Co.
Sandwell Park Colliery

(B. continued)

Sao Paolo Brazilian RR
Sheepsbridge Coal & Iron
Shotts Iron Works
Sloane, William & Co.
South Durham Steel & Iron
Spears & Jackson
Spen Valley Brewing Co.
Spencer, John Ltd.
Stavely Coal & Iron
Steel Co. of Scotland
Sterling, William & Sons
Stewarts & Lloyds
Sun Fire Insurance
Sunderland & South Shields Water
Swanzy, F & A
Tarapaca Nitrate Co.
Tarkwa Trading Co.
Tehuantepec National Railway
Tenbury Wells Improvement Co.
Tetley Brewery
Theatre Royal Leicester
Thompson, James & George
Thwaites & Reed
Tod, John & Sons
Townsend, Eli
Turnbull Co.
Tyser Line
Veracruz Electric Light Power and Traction
Veracruz Land & Cattle
Vickers, Sons & Maxim Ltd.
Walker, Harry
Walsall Wood Colliery
Wardle & Davenport
Wearmouth Coal Co.
Wembly Park Estates
West Riding Steam Ploughing, Cultivating, and Threshing Co.
Western Railroad of Havana
Wharcliffe Colliery
Whitechapel & Bow Railway
Whitworth, W. G. Armstrong
Wiggins Teape & Co.
Wilkins, R. F.
Wolverhampton Gas
Woolley Coal Co.
Wordie & Co.
Wordie Property Co.
Yorkshire & Derbyshire Coal & Iron
Yorkshire Banking Co.

C. **British Railways**

Caledonian Railway (Scotland)
Furness Railway (England)
Great Central Railway (late Manch. Sheff. Linc.)
Great Eastern Railway (England)
Great Northern Railway of Ireland
London and Northwestern Railway
Midland Railway (England)

Appendix 3.2

APPENDIX 3.2

UNWEIGHTED RATES OF RETURN FOR INDUSTRIES, BY DECADE

RATE 2 (HIGH)

	1 COMMERCIAL BANKING			2 BREWERIES & DISTILLERIES			3 CANALS & DOCKS			4 COMMERCIAL & INDUSTRIAL			5 FINANCIAL, LAND & INVESTMENT		
	UK	FOR	EMP	UK	FOR	EMP	UK	FOR	EMP	UK	FOR	EMP	UK	FOR	EMP
1860-65	2.3	2.3	--	9.6	--	--	--	--	--	13.3	11.6	17.8	--	16.4	--
1865-69	2.2	2.8	--	7.6	--	--	4.8	--	--	11.4	11.3	15.6	--	3.3	8.3
1970-74	2.2	1.6	--	14.6	--	--	4.6	--	--	15.5	12.0	12.1	--	5.6	6.6
1875-79	1.6	0.8	--	19.9	--	--	7.1	--	--	14.0	10.6	15.9	--	-0.7	0.7
1880-84	1.5	1.8	1.1	10.8	--	--	7.9	2.9	--	13.3	7.6	12.2	2.1	9.1	4.3
1885-89	1.4	2.0	1.3	10.4	--	--	4.4	2.2	-1.0	14.5	29.7	7.3	2.2	10.7	4.3
1890-94	1.3	1.6	0.9	6.6	2.9	8.2	5.3	2.1	-0.3	11.3	6.3	5.3	1.5	-1.4	2.3
1895-99	1.2	1.3	1.5	7.8	2.6	7.7	6.5	7.6	-0.5	10.8	22.5	5.6	2.0	1.7	1.4
1900-04	1.2	1.0	1.4	5.3	3.7	5.6	5.7	4.0	4.3	7.1	8.1	7.5	2.1	-1.0	-1.8
1905-09	1.2	1.3	1.5	4.6	5.2	3.6	5.1	3.3	2.4	7.2	2.9	6.7	2.1	2.6	2.4
1910-12	1.3	1.1	1.5	5.1	9.6	3.2	6.4	-0.2	1.3	7.9	7.5	8.7	1.6	1.5	3.5
AVG	1.4	1.6	1.2	6.5	2.1	7.2	3.2	0.6	0.6	9.5	7.7	7.8	2.0	4.0	2.9

	6 FINANCIAL TRUSTS			7 GAS & LIGHT			8 IRON, COAL & STEEL			10 RAILROADS			11 SHIPPING		
	UK	FOR	EMP	UK	FOR	EMP	UK	FOR	EMP	UK	FOR	EMP	UK	FOR	EMP
1860-64	--	--	--	7.8	--	--	11.1	--	--	4.3	--	--	--	8.9	--
1865-69	--	--	--	9.0	--	--	10.3	--	--	3.2	4.7	--	--	4.4	--
1870-74	--	--	--	9.0	--	--	17.5	--	--	3.5	6.7	--	--	13.9	--
1875-79	--	--	--	8.7	--	--	9.0	--	--	3.0	9.4	--	--	6.6	--
1880-84	--	5.3	--	8.7	--	6.1	10.3	4.5	-19.3	3.8	7.2	0.1	--	7.1	2.6
1885-89	2.1	4.8	--	9.7	--	7.6	10.3	3.5	4.1	2.8	8.2	2.8	--	7.4	4.2
1890-94	1.1	3.2	3.7	10.1	--	7.8	8.4	6.3	-2.0	3.0	5.4	2.9	6.8	5.2	-4.8
1895-99	0.9	2.4	4.8	10.2	5.9	8.6	10.0	2.8	-0.3	3.1	4.4	2.1	5.8	8.3	14.4
1900-04	0.7	3.3	1.5	7.3	6.5	6.8	9.0	2.3	5.6	2.6	3.8	1.4	8.5	8.1	5.4
1905-09	1.9	3.9	1.6	6.1	6.2	8.5	7.3	2.4	7.1	2.6	5.0	1.9	5.3	4.1	3.8
1910-12	2.9	3.6	2.8	6.7	5.5	9.6	8.0	6.7	4.3	2.6	6.6	3.1	6.8	7.2	7.5
AVG	2.4	4.3	3.1	6.4	5.6	5.3	7.9	5.4	-0.6	2.9	5.7	1.5	5.0	3.3	2.6

	13 TELEPHONES & TELEGRAPHS			14 TRAMWAYS & OMNIBUSES			15 WATERWORKS			17 AGRICULTURE & EXTRACTION		
	UK	FOR	EMP	UK	FOR	EMP	UK	FOR	EMP	UK	FOR	EMP
1860-65	--	--	--	0.2	--	--	5.8	--	--	3.5	--	4.5
1865-69	--	--	--	4.3	--	--	8.1	--	--	11.7	--	-0.2
1970-74	--	--	--	0.1	--	--	7.4	--	--	10.2	--	17.1
1875-79	--	--	--	3.1	--	--	8.8	0.5	--	0.9	11.0	19.6
1880-84	--	1.8	5.8	5.5	3.8	5.2	9.0	0.2	2.4	6.1	9.4	13.5
1885-89	--	3.7	7.6	5.6	4.7	-0.4	11.6	6.9	15.5	7.4	16.4	9.4
1890-94	--	4.1	11.2	6.9	5.4	0.8	11.7	4.7	12.5	14.9	15.2	10.2
1895-99	--	2.5	13.9	9.5	3.0	1.2	13.6	4.2	12.9	9.3	10.8	8.6
1900-04	--	3.9	8.0	4.6	2.7	3.1	6.8	5.0	12.7	19.4	15.3	6.6
1905-09	--	8.3	8.1	-0.2	3.6	4.5	6.1	5.3	11.5	8.6	15.8	10.5
1910-12	--	12.6	8.9	2.0	3.1	7.6	7.1	5.6	13.1	8.9	23.3	12.5
AVG		3.0	6.1	1.7	2.4	2.6	5.6	3.7	7.1	8.5	6.6	7.4

Dash(--) = No Data

4 Government expenditure in support of business

I. Introduction

While investments in the dependent Empire never loomed large in the total British portfolio, they were almost certainly a sizeable fraction of some individuals' holdings; and investments in those parts of the Empire with responsible government were important to a significantly larger number. In terms of the private sector, in the later decades those investments, while on average yielding less than returns available at home, may have been slightly more profitable than other overseas alternatives, and they were certainly not substantially less so. Nevertheless, at some times and in some places and industries, imperial investments were relatively profitable regardless of the measures chosen. Moreover, even those investments that appear relatively unprofitable shared with their more lucrative counterparts the fruits of government expenditures in support of business.

Aerospace engineers in El Segundo, California, and dairy farmers in Grundy Center, Iowa, well recognize that business profits are not unrelated to government policy, and there is no evidence to suggest that in the nineteenth century British businesspeople were any less astute. If a California engineer or an Iowa farmer were asked about such government policies they would most likely respond in terms of the impact of the B–1 bomber on aircraft sales or of price supports on butter prices. Today, however, government policies are far more pervasive, and their influence on all aspects of economic life is taken for granted. In an earlier age the "responsibilities of government" were less clearly recognized, and the costs of some services devolved on the business community when the government chose not to provide them. The evidence indicates that nineteenth-century businesspeople realized that if the government could be made to assume "its responsibilities" any number of "free" services could be produced that would drastically reduce the costs of doing business.

A smoothly functioning legal system makes it possible to enforce contracts cheaply and to effect transactions that would otherwise have proved prohibitively expensive. Governmentally underwritten military and police forces mean that business does not have to carry the cost of private armies and guards to protect property. The East

118

India Company, for example, had among its costs of operation not only a very large army but a naval force as well. If the government built roads and maintained postal and telegraph services, private transaction and marketing costs were much reduced, and so the story goes. The British Empire was a political system, and it should, in principle, have been possible to arrange affairs to produce a pattern of expenditures that would provide support to private business and at the same time charge costs to others.

In the foreign sector, the British investor had little influence over the amount government chose to spend in support of business nor was there any easy way to shift the burden imposed by those expenditures. In the Empire, however, it may have been possible to increase the level of support and transfer the costs either to the colonial or to the British taxpayer. To the degree that British business could influence colonial governments to adopt such policies, the level of private profits in the Empire was higher than it would otherwise have been, and losses, when they occurred, lower.

Investment in "business" overhead capital includes not only the traditional additions to the real capital stock, but a number of items not always included in the standard social accounts. The real capital inventory involves roads, bridges, buildings, railroads, gas and waterworks, sewage systems, lighthouses, harbors, rabbit fences, and a host of other kinds of physical capital. In the nontraditional category are counted the expenditures made to increase the productivity of labor (education, public health, and the support of immigration), and those that maintain and enforce property rights (police, the courts, and probably a portion of military expenditures). In addition to overhead capital the business sector benefits from a myriad of other policies that substitute government expenditure for private cost. Such policies include, for example, production subsidies and governmental funding for institutions such as agricultural marketing boards and information services.

To say that the political structure of Empire could have been used to manipulate expenditures for the benefit of British business is not to argue that it did. To answer *that* question it is necessary to examine the level and composition of Empire expenditures. It should be obvious, however, that no figure on road expenditures in Ceylon has much significance when examined in isolation, and it can contribute to an answer to the underlying question only if analyzed in the context of the fiscal behavior of other governments. The data on the functional distribution of expenditures presented in this chapter encompass, therefore, the United Kingdom, India, fifteen colonies with responsible government, fifty-nine colonies and protectorates in some form of dependent status, eighteen Indian Princely States, sixteen foreign countries classed as developed and twenty-five categorized as underdeveloped.

A complete enumeration of the colonies and countries can be found in Appendixes 1.1, 1.2, and 1.3 to Chapter 1, and a discussion of the data and its inherent problems, in Appendix 4.1. One important caveat should, however, be borne in mind. These are data from national (or colonial) units, and do not include the expenditures at all political levels. In the case of the United States, for example, the data are for federal expenditures and exclude those of states, counties, and cities. The smaller or less developed the political unit, the more likely it is that expenditures will be centralized. Thus comparisons between units of very different size or state of development tend to be distorted. In an attempt to permit the reader to assess the degree of bias, figures for United Kingdom "national" (UKN) and "total" (UKT) expenditures are included for the cash-expenditure category.

A second question arises over the selection of the measure of "typical" behavior. For England or India there are no problems, but for those sectors made up of more than a single political entity, there are questions about the appropriate measure of "average" spending. If each unit (colony or country) is included in a simple average, the results may be different than if those units are combined in some other fashion.

Table 4.1 provides some indication of the possible differences. Panel A shows both colony-weighted and population-weighted averages for total spending as a fraction of expenditures in the United Kingdom.[1] Panel B displays the ratio of the unweighted to the weighted averages for those same totals. For the Princely States and the foreign-developed sector, although there are differences in some years, in general the two measures give about the same results. For the colonies with responsible government and the dependent colonies the difference on average was about 70 percent and for the foreign-underdeveloped sector, 30 percent. In most instances the colony-weighted figures are much higher than the population-weighted ones. That difference can in large measure be attributed to the fact that while spending is unbounded upward it can't fall below zero. Clearly the more heterogeneous the units the greater the disparity is likely to be. For the colonies with responsible government, before 1900 the six Australian colonies carried more than one-half of the weight in the colony-weighted average and they pushed that average upward. In the case of the dependent colonies the differences can be traced in part to the very heterogeneous nature

TABLE 4.1

GOVERNMENT EXPENDITURE RELATIVES

(Railroads Out)

Decade	PANEL A: (UK = 100) Responsible Government CWT	PWT	Dependent Colonies CWT	PWT	India	Princely States CWT	PWT	Foreign Developed CWT	PWT	Foreign Under-developed CWT	PWT	PANEL B: RATIO CWT/PWT RG	DC	India	PSts	FD	FU
1860-64	128	77	50	30	16	8	8	40	43	31	19	166	167	100	100	93	163
1865-69	142	84	55	32	19	8	9	48	51	27	23	169	172	100	89	94	117
1870-74	167	101	54	33	22	14	9	52	53	29	22	165	164	100	156	98	132
1875-79	172	108	42	29	20	10	10	49	44	25	21	159	145	100	100	111	119
1880-84	188	135	41	30	17	10	10	53	47	38	18	139	137	100	100	113	211
1885-89	234	133	43	29	8	9	9	62	56	33	21	176	148	100	100	111	157
1890-94	248	130	56	32	7	8	9	63	62	29	19	191	175	100	89	102	153
1895-99	259	117	37	21	6	7	8	61	61	25	18	221	176	100	88	100	139
1900-04	177	89	23	11	5	5	5	41	39	15	14	199	209	100	100	105	107
1905-09	92	88	28	12	6	7	6	58	53	26	27	105	233	100	117	109	96
1910-12	91	87	28	12	6	8	6	58	53	28	21	105	233	100	133	109	133
AVG	176	104	39	23	10	8	8	53	51	28	20	168	176	100	105	103	139

CWT: Colony Weight   DC: Dependent Colonies   FD: Foreign Developed Countries
PWT: Population Weight   PSts: Indian Princely States   FU: Foreign Underdeveloped Countries
RG: Responsible Government

of the group (there is a very great deal of difference between Hong Kong and Bermuda on the one hand and Northern Rhodesia and Swaziland on the other), and in part to the growing importance in the population-weighted calculations of the Central and East African colonies. In those colonies, the population estimates were frequently blind guesses (and they were often very large figures).

There is of course no "right" answer to the question of the appropriate measure, and it is possible to make a compelling case for a simple average, an average using population, or perhaps for one using yet some other set of weights. For that reason, both the population-weighted and the unweighted averages are presented. The choice of measure does not appear to affect the direction of the argument, but it does affect the thrust.

In the following pages, total expenditures and four subclasses (law and justice, public works, science and human capital, and direct business support) are examined in detail: the total because it provides an index of the role of government in the economy; the others because they include most of the business supporting activities.[2] Law and justice reflect the expenses incurred in maintaining property rights and enforcing contracts. Public works are, railroads aside, the real capital component of social overhead investment. Railroads were sometimes government owned, on other occasions privately held or, yet again, jointly owned; and their inclusion distorts inter-country comparisons. Still, government expenditure on railroad construction was often large; therefore, public works are examined both with and without the capital expenditures on railroads. "Science and human capital" picks up the nontraditional capital components of the infrastructure. The category includes expenditures on education, science, medicine, charity, relief, immigration and even religion.[3] Expenditures in direct support of business include not only such administrative departments as labor and commerce, but subsidies or any other expenditures made in support of agriculture, manufacturing, commerce, or mining.

II. The pattern of expenditure

In the late nineteenth and early twentieth centuries, total per capita expenditures in Great Britain were high, if the standard is other independent countries (Table 4.2). Excluding railroads, UK national expenditures averaged £2.92 over the period covered by this study, and they reached £5.03 in the period 1900–4. Comparable figures for Germany were £1.28; France, £2.87; and the United States, £1.36. The United Kingdom level is almost twice that of the average developed country, although France spent nearly as much.

In the Empire, however, the colonies with responsible government spent at rates slightly above the British, if the measure is the population-weighted index, and at rates more than half again as high, if the colony weights are used. For all colonies in that happy state, the annual per capita colony-weighted average was £5.10; however, the propensity for "big government" was not equally strong throughout the Empire. The expenditures averaged £6.38 in the six Australian colonies (but only £4.94 after the formation of the Commonwealth), £6.39 in New Zealand, £2.43 in South Africa, and £1.55 in North America.

If per capita expenditure is any measure of the role of the government in the economy, the Australasian pattern is unmatched anywhere in the world. Even in Tasmania, the colony with the lowest levels of spending, the rate was almost one and one-half times that in the United Kingdom. Given that the per capita Australian gross national product averaged less than £50 annually, these colonies maintained government structures of nearly contemporary proportions.[4]

In the dependent Empire, the story is mixed, but on average, expenditures were relatively high. Among the dependent colonies the colony-weighted average was £1.13, and the population-weighted one £.66. Those figures are low when compared with the United Kingdom, but at least 10 percent higher than the comparable measure for the underdeveloped countries. In the case of India the average is much lower (£.30), but while below that of the underdeveloped countries, it is 30 percent higher than the levels observed

TABLE 4.2

TOTAL GOVERNMENT EXPENDITURES

(£'s Per Capita)

	UKN	UKT	RG	(RAILROADS OUT) DC	India	PSts	FD	FU	UKN	UKT	RG	(RAILROADS IN) DC	India	PSts	FD	FU
								PANEL A:	COLONY WEIGHTS							
1860-64	2.08	--	2.66	1.03	.33	.16	.84	.64	2.08	--	2.80	1.03	.38	.16	.88	.69
1865-69	2.01	2.39	2.86	1.10	.38	.17	.97	.55	2.01	2.39	3.11	1.10	.44	.17	1.05	.60
1870-74	1.86	2.78	3.10	1.00	.40	.26	.96	.54	1.86	2.78	3.53	1.02	.46	.26	1.04	.67
1875-79	2.09	3.46	3.59	.88	.42	.20	1.02	.52	2.09	3.46	4.44	.90	.49	.20	1.06	.56
1880-84	2.40	3.99	4.50	.98	.41	.25	1.27	.92	2.40	3.99	5.90	1.00	.51	.25	1.32	.97
1885-89	2.84	4.79	6.64	1.21	.23	.25	1.75	.94	2.84	4.79	8.94	1.27	.33	.25	1.81	.99
1890-94	2.82	5.02	6.98	1.57	.19	.23	1.79	.81	2.82	5.02	9.44	1.65	.25	.23	1.86	.85
1895-99	3.50	6.49	9.05	1.31	.21	.25	2.12	.89	3.50	6.49	11.92	1.36	.29	.25	2.21	1.05
1900-04	5.03	8.90	8.88	1.17	.23	.27	2.05	.76	5.03	8.90	11.57	1.24	.33	.28	2.15	.80
1905-09	3.86	8.28	3.56	1.10	.24	.28	2.24	1.02	3.86*	8.28	4.84	1.18	.36	.28	2.37	1.10
1910-12	4.11	8.56	3.75	1.15	.23	.32	2.38	1.16	4.11	8.56	5.06	1.24	.34	.33	2.52	1.26
AVG(d)	2.92	5.34	5.10	1.13	.30	.23	1.55	.78	2.92	5.03	6.56	1.18	.38	.24	1.63	.85
								PANEL B:	POPULATION WEIGHTS							
1860-64	2.08	--	1.60	.63	.33	.17	.89	.39	2.08	--	1.75	.64	.38	.17	.90	.40
1865-69	2.01	2.39	1.69	.65	.38	.18	1.03	.47	2.01	2.39	1.79	.68	.44	.18	1.08	.49
1870-74	1.86	2.78	1.87	.62	.40	.16	.98	.40	1.86	2.78	2.04	.65	.46	.16	1.00	.44
1875-79	2.09	3.46	2.26	.60	.42	.20	.93	.43	2.09	3.46	2.73	.65	.49	.20	.94	.46
1880-84	2.40	3.99	3.25	.71	.41	.25	1.12	.44	2.40	3.99	4.16	.78	.51	.25	1.14	.49
1885-89	2.84	4.79	3.77	.83	.23	.25	1.59	.60	2.84	4.79	5.47	.89	.33	.26	1.62	.65
1890-94	2.82	5.02	3.67	.91	.19	.26	1.74	.54	2.82	5.02	5.15	.99	.25	.27	1.80	.59
1895-99	3.50	6.49	4.11	.72	.21	.27	2.12	.63	3.50	6.49	5.43	.81	.29	.28	2.22	.72
1900-04	5.03	8.90	4.49	.53	.23	.27	1.94	.72	5.03	8.90	6.14	.61	.33	.29	2.00	.77
1905-09	3.86	8.28	3.41	.48	.24	.25	2.05	1.03	3.86	8.28	4.77	.55	.36	.26	2.13	1.12
1910-12	4.11	8.56	3.59	.48	.23	.25	2.19	.88	4.11	8.56	5.01	.64	.34	.25	2.39	.95
AVG(d)	2.92	5.34	3.04	.66	.30	.23	1.49	.59	2.92	5.03	4.00	.72	.38	.24	1.55	.64

Dash (--) = No Data

UKN:	United Kingdom National	PSts:	Indian Princely States
UKT:	United Kingdom Total	FD:	Foreign Developed Countries
RG:	Responsible Government	FU:	Foreign Underdeveloped Countries
DC:	Dependent Colonies		

in the Princely States – although after 1885, expenditures were higher in these states. Throughout the Empire, India aside, governments (regardless of their level of constitutional development) tended to spend at levels higher than those independent countries in comparable stages of development.

A. Law and justice

A casual inspection of the budgets of the dependent colonies could lead to the conclusion that British imperialism should be viewed not as a political but as a moral institution designed to bring temperance to the "uncivilized" masses of the underdeveloped world. For many colonies the liquor tax was a significant source of revenue; and police, jails, and courts were among the major items of expenditure. Moreover, a surprisingly large fraction of the legal effort was devoted to the arrest, conviction, and incarceration of inebriates. Levity aside, the Empire was marked by relatively high levels of expenditure on law and justice, and some substantial fraction of those expenditures provided the legal sinews that tied a decentralized economy together. A system of law and justice that

TABLE 4.3

GOVERNMENT EXPENDITURE: LAW & JUSTICE

	(£'s PER CAPITA)								(PERCENTAGES OF BUDGET; RAILROADS OUT)							
	UKN	UKT	RG	DC	India	PSts	FD	FU	UKN	UKT	RG	DC	India	PSts	FD	FU
						PANEL A:	COLONY WEIGHTS									
1860-64	.10	--	.39	.19	.03	.01	.04	.04	4.7	--	15.6	19.1	7.8	8.1	5.0	5.0
1865-69	.11	.13	.35	.20	.03	.01	.11	.03	5.3	5.4	14.5	19.7	7.5	8.0	6.6	5.9
1870-74	.12	.18	.32	.19	.03	.01	.04	.03	6.4	6.3	12.2	19.7	6.5	6.0	4.5	5.4
1875-79	.15	.23	.39	.17	.03	.01	.04	.03	7.0	6.6	10.7	19.9	6.2	7.7	4.1	6.0
1880-84	.18	.28	.44	.17	.03	.02	.05	.04	7.5	6.9	10.4	17.3	6.6	6.3	4.0	6.1
1885-89	.21	.33	.71	.21	.02	.02	.06	.05	7.4	7.0	10.5	18.6	10.3	10.1	3.4	6.7
1890-94	.14	.29	.63	.24	.02	.02	.06	.07	5.1	5.8	9.3	17.3	10.8	11.3	3.8	10.7
1895-99	.13	.30	.67	.23	.02	.02	.07	.04	3.8	4.7	8.1	16.2	10.4	10.4	3.4	6.6
1900-04	.12	.29	.69	.18	.02	.02	.08	.06	2.5	3.3	8.8	15.0	10.4	8.9	3.7	9.6
1905-09	.11	.30	.33	.16	.03	.02	.08	.07	2.9	3.6	10.8	14.5	11.0	8.6	3.8	8.5
1910-12	.11	.29	.35	.16	.03	.02	.10	.07	2.7	3.4	12.0	13.2	11.9	7.1	3.9	7.3
AVG(d)	.14	.26	.48	.19	.03	.02	.07	.05	5.1	5.4	11.1	17.5	8.9	8.5	4.2	7.1
						PANEL B:	POPULATION WEIGHTS									
1860-64	.10	--	.22	.12	.03	.02	.03	.02	4.7	--	13.6	18.8	7.8	11.3	3.4	4.7
1865-69	.11	.13	.19	.12	.03	.02	.05	.02	5.3	5.4	11.5	18.6	7.5	10.7	5.4	3.7
1870-74	.12	.18	.13	.12	.03	.02	.03	.02	6.4	6.3	7.2	19.4	6.5	10.8	2.7	4.3
1875-79	.15	.23	.19	.11	.03	.02	.02	.03	7.0	6.6	8.3	18.4	6.2	10.0	2.6	6.2
1880-84	.18	.28	.24	.14	.03	.02	.03	.03	7.5	6.9	7.5	19.3	6.6	8.4	2.4	7.9
1885-89	.21	.33	.30	.15	.02	.02	.03	.05	7.4	7.0	7.8	17.7	10.3	9.5	2.0	8.0
1890-94	.14	.29	.29	.14	.02	.02	.04	.04	5.1	5.8	7.9	15.5	10.8	9.2	2.1	7.7
1895-99	.13	.30	.32	.11	.02	.03	.05	.04	3.8	4.7	7.8	15.2	10.4	9.8	2.3	6.1
1900-04	.12	.29	.36	.07	.02	.03	.05	.05	2.5	3.3	8.0	12.5	10.4	9.7	2.4	6.6
1905-09	.11	.30	.27	.06	.03	.03	.05	.07	2.9	3.6	8.0	12.3	11.0	9.9	2.4	6.6
1910-12	.11	.29	.26	.06	.03	.02	.07	.05	2.7	3.4	7.2	11.9	11.9	9.5	3.0	4.6
AVG(d)	.14	.26	.25	.11	.03	.02	.04	.04	5.1	5.3	8.7	16.5	8.9	9.9	2.8	6.1

Dash (--) = No Data

UKN: United Kingdom National	PSts: Indian Princely States
UKT: United Kingdom Total	FD: Foreign Developed Countries
RG: Responsible Government	FU: Foreign Underdeveloped Countries
DC: Dependent Colonies	

provides for the definition and enforcement of a set of property rights and that provides for both civil and criminal enforcement of these rights is an almost necessary precondition for an operating free-enterprise economy. When British businesspeople ventured into foreign markets, they were at times required to make substantial "side payments" to assure that the local authorities enforced the businesspeople's alleged property rights; and even these payments were frequently insufficient to keep these rights from being "redefined," not infrequently in the middle of a business transaction. When the costs of the resources required to establish and enforce property rights are transferred to society as a whole, the private rate of return is increased. In the Empire, rights were both well defined and enforced – at society's expense – and the external evidence indicates that the benefits were substantial. While they accrued in part to local citizens, they also worked to the benefit of British businesspeople who, unlike their Empire counterparts, paid few of the costs.

In the United Kingdom, expenditures on law and justice averaged about £.14 (£.26 for all levels) per person per year - a figure that represented about 5 percent of all expenditures (see Table 4.3). These

figures were somewhat higher than the £.04 to £.07 that characterized the expenditures of an average developed country, and of those
countries, only Belgium spent more and Portugal, Denmark, and
the Netherlands as much as 60 percent, of the United Kingdom
figure. Even the United Kingdom expenditures appear small when
compared with those of the colonies with responsible government.
There the average annual expenditure was £.48 per capita (more
than 11 percent of the total) in the colony-weighted average and
£.25 even in the population-weighted one. In this case, while the
Australasian average was high, that region was not alone in diverting
resources into the area of law and justice. The six original Australian
colonies averaged £.60, but Tasmania spent no more than £.32, and
three others fell between £.43 and £.56. New Zealand spent only
£.41 and Australia but £.35. Moreover, while expenditures in Western Australia were £1.12, the highest in the world, the Transvaal
(£.77) was second. The African colonies averaged about £.40, and
only in North America was the average below the level in the
United Kingdom. Even there, Newfoundland spent almost as
much (£.13), and Canada (£.07) – despite the absence of provincial
expenditures – was slightly above the developed-country average.
  In the dependent Empire the scenario was repeated, but the emphasis was perhaps even stronger. In underdeveloped countries
there appears to have been growing concern for law and order (if
not justice). Expenditures in support of these ends were hardly below the level in the developed nations, and the fraction of total expenditures, substantially higher. In the dependent colonies, the
colony-weighted average figure was £.19, 17 percent of the total
(and even the population-weighted figure was £.11). While that
number is biased upward by a few colonies which spent at very
high levels (the Falkland Islands spent £.57, Gibraltar £.52, British
Honduras £.49, and Hong Kong £.39), it was also held down by
the most underdeveloped colonies where the army served as the
police force (in East and Central Africa the average was less than
£.03). In West Africa and the Caribbean, where British rule had
been long in place and where distinct military forces existed, the
expenditures tended to be compressed between £.10 and £.25
(twenty-five colonies fell into this range). Among the nations in
the "underdeveloped" category only three spent more than £.10,
and of those one spent £.11 and another £.12. In the dependent
Empire the arm of justice was certainly both long and strong.
  The Indian data might lead one to quite different conclusions. If
the standard is the Princely States then India's per capita figure of
£.03 is about half again their average, but the proportion of the Indian

budget is but little higher than the share of expenditures that law and justice commanded in those States. Moreover, when the measure is the average underdeveloped country, the Indian percentage figure is somewhat higher, but the per capita figure is lower. In fact, India exceeded only five of the twenty-five countries (Colombia, Costa Rica, Japan, Liberia and Venezuela) in its level of expenditure for law and justice. While there may have been economies of scale in the provision of justice and, perhaps, the local courts were more important on the subcontinent, expenditure levels were low, and the explanation of that situation unclear. The qualitative evidence indicates that the legal system operated well and that property rights were defined and protected.

B. Public works

Institutional overhead can increase private profits, but so can investment in real capital. When the costs of all physical improvements are assessed directly against the business sector, private profits plummet – a lesson learned at some cost by investors in the late chartered companies. When the services of the capital are available at less than full cost, business firms capture a part of those savings and profits respond accordingly. The infrastructure supporting railroads and telegraphs was at least partly charged to users, but there was little direct connection between use and the incidence of the costs of the roads, bridges, and canals that constituted an important fraction of public-works expenditures. How well did the Empire supply its citizens (and perhaps British businesspeople as well) with the services of the stock of physical capital?

In the United Kingdom the contribution appears quite low when compared with the foreign-developed category; however, that conclusion rests at least in part on a statistical artifact (Table 4.4). The data are drawn from national budgets, and in the United Kingdom a substantial portion of the public-works expenditures was made at the local level. The effect of that distribution of authority is apparent in the UKT-column figure. Since the other developed countries have not been similarly adjusted, the average of £.56 cannot be used for comparison, but it does represent the total actually spent in the United Kingdom, and it suggests that the £.06 to £.15 comparison with foreign-developed countries understates the relative level of domestic expenditures. Conversely, it should be borne in mind that there were no government expenditures on railroads in the United Kingdom – something that was not true in many of the other developed countries. In the 1860s, when government support for the railroads had been suggested, it was rejected not only because it would "depress the price of government securities" but because it would "tend to give us [the government] by degrees a control over the proceedings of the companies, and throw upon us a considerable but ill defined and imperfect responsibility for the management of the Railway," a responsibility that the British government was unwilling to assume.[5] Other nations were less hesitant.

In Britain private enterprise (although often regulated) continued to operate most public utilities considerably longer than in many other developed countries, but times were changing. While railroads were still beyond reach, the government was in the process of nationalizing the telegraphs. As Sir Stafford Northcote, the President of the Board of Trade (later the Secretary of State for India and still later Lord Iddesleigh), said in writing to Disraeli,

> As a general rule one looks doubtfully at proposals that the government should carry on business on its own account but . . . the telegraph is treading on the heels of the post office and it is quite possible that a few improvements of detail might make it a possible rival. . . .[6]

In 1878 the government did take over the telegraphs and, within the span of only a few years, transformed what had been a profitable enterprise into a perpetual drain on the Treasury. Hence, it was perhaps just as well that the government did not accept responsibility for the railroads. Whatever the case, if railroads are included in the public-works figure, the United Kingdom fares less well in comparison to other developed countries: £.06 as compared to £.18.

In those parts of the Empire with responsible government, there was far less hesitation to turn to government to complete the social overhead structure. While a typical developed country spent about £.15 per person per year on all public works, excluding railroads, the colonies with responsible government were spending somewhere between £.59 (population weights) and £.99 (colony weighted). If railroads are added, the average for a developed country rises to about £.20, but the responsible-colony figure reaches more than £1.00 (the two measures are £1.76 and £1.08). Even without the railroads, whereas a typical developed country spent less than 10 percent of its budget on public works, the average self-governing colony committed almost twice that figure.

In the case of expenditure on public works, the Australasian colonies were again the most active. Excluding railroads, the six Australian colonies averaged £1.60 per person per year; New Zealand, £1.10; the South African colonies, £.43; Canada, £.25; and New-

TABLE 4.4A

GOVERNMENT EXPENDITURE: PUBLIC WORKS

(£'s Per Capita)

			(RAILROADS OUT)								(RAILROADS IN)				
	UKN	UKT	RG	DC	India	PSts	FD	FU	UKN	UKT	RG	DC	India	PSts	FD	FU
					PANEL A:	COLONY WEIGHTS										
1860-64	.03	--	.70	.14	.02	.02	.05	.01	.03	--	.82	.14	.03	.02	.07	.06
1865-69	.04	.12	.54	.15	.02	.02	.06	.02	.04	.12	.72	.15	.03	.02	.12	.06
1870-74	.06	.25	.74	.13	.03	.03	.06	.02	.06	.25	1.08	.13	.04	.03	.12	.15
1875-79	.11	.39	.75	.11	.04	.03	.10	.04	.11	.39	1.40	.12	.06	.03	.12	.07
1880-84	.06	.39	1.23	.16	.04	.03	.16	.06	.06	.39	2.22	.17	.10	.04	.20	.11
1885-89	.07	.47	1.43	.23	.02	.03	.17	.07	.07	.47	3.00	.23	.07	.03	.21	.11
1890-94	.05	.47	1.10	.35	.02	.04	.17	.05	.05	.47	2.55	.37	.05	.05	.22	.08
1895-99	.06	.68	1.61	.26	.02	.04	.23	.09	.06	.68	2.98	.26	.05	.04	.29	.23
1900-04	.06	1.10	1.56	.22	.02	.04	.23	.08	.06	1.10	2.35	.24	.06	.05	.28	.10
1905-09	.07	.93	.49	.21	.03	.05	.25	.12	.07	.93	.92	.22	.08	.05	.34	.17
1910-12	.10	.94	.49	.24	.03	.05	.25	.12	.10	.94	1.06	.26	.07	.05	.33	.17
AVG(d)	.06	.56	.99	.20	.03	.03	.15	.06	.06	.56	1.76	.21	.06	.04	.20	.12
					PANEL B:	POPULATION WEIGHTS										
1860-64	.03	--	.38	.09	.02	.02	.05	.00	.03	--	.51	.09	.03	.02	.05	.01
1865-69	.04	.12	.31	.10	.02	.02	.06	.00	.04	.12	.36	.10	.03	.02	.10	.03
1870-74	.06	.25	.46	.11	.03	.02	.05	.01	.06	.25	.57	.13	.04	.02	.07	.04
1875-79	.11	.39	.44	.11	.04	.03	.06	.01	.11	.39	.78	.14	.06	.03	.07	.03
1880-84	.06	.39	.84	.15	.04	.03	.13	.03	.06	.39	1.48	.16	.10	.04	.14	.07
1885-89	.07	.47	.87	.18	.02	.03	.14	.04	.07	.47	2.06	.20	.07	.03	.16	.09
1890-94	.05	.47	.66	.26	.02	.04	.14	.03	.05	.47	1.52	.30	.05	.04	.18	.07
1895-99	.06	.68	.72	.18	.02	.03	.22	.06	.06	.68	1.20	.23	.05	.04	.32	.14
1900-04	.06	1.10	.84	.12	.02	.04	.21	.08	.06	1.10	1.36	.17	.06	.04	.28	.10
1905-09	.07	.93	.49	.12	.03	.04	.22	.14	.07	.93	.93	.15	.08	.04	.30	.19
1910-12	.10	.94	.47	.11	.03	.04	.27	.11	.10	.94	1.08	.23	.07	.04	.33	.15
AVG(d)	.06	.56	.59	.14	.03	.03	.14	.04	.06	.06	1.08	.17	.06	.03	.18	.08

Dash (--) = No Data

UKN: United Kingdom National   PSts: Indian Princely States
UKT: United Kingdom Total   FD: Foreign Developed Countries
RG: Responsible Government   FU: Foreign Underdeveloped Countries
DC: Dependent Colonies

foundland, £.37. When railroads are added, all numbers increase – Australia to £2.99, New Zealand to £1.97, South Africa to £.63, and Canada to £.38. The levels attained in Oceania – levels that were more than three times those spent in an average developed country whether or not railroads are considered – are striking. The nearest foreign rival to those colonies was Belgium, a country with a centralized public-works function, and Belgium spent only £.59.

There is considerable question as to the motivation that underlay the expenditure patterns in the colonies with responsible government. They were growing rapidly, their population was young, and they had had a much shorter history over which they could have accumulated a stock of social overhead capital. Thus, form of government or Empire status aside, they could be expected to devote a greater fraction of their current resources to such investment than older, long-settled areas. Still, the levels are so very much higher than those observed elsewhere, that it appears unlikely that age alone can account for the difference. For example, over the years 1870 to 1900 in the Pacific region of the United States – a young and rapidly developing area – the federal government spent £.10 and the states an additional £.07 per capita per year on social overhead

TABLE 4.4B

GOVERNMENT EXPENDITURE: PUBLIC WORKS

(Percents)

	UKN	UKT	RG	(RAILROADS OUT) DC	India	PSts	FD	FU	UKN	UKT	RG	(RAILROADS IN) DC	India	PSts	FD	FU
								PANEL A:	COLONY WEIGHTS							
1860-64	1.4	--	20.3	11.4	7.1	13.1	6.0	2.0	1.4	--	21.8	11.3	6.7	13.1	6.8	7.6
1865-69	2.1	4.3	15.2	13.0	6.6	13.2	6.8	4.1	2.1	4.3	16.7	12.9	6.1	13.2	9.5	8.9
1870-74	3.3	9.0	19.2	13.0	7.9	13.5	6.3	6.7	3.3	9.0	21.8	13.1	8.4	13.5	9.3	15.9
1875-79	5.3	11.3	16.9	11.9	9.7	14.7	7.5	8.4	5.3	11.3	21.7	12.1	12.2	14.7	9.3	13.8
1880-84	2.6	9.7	22.6	15.2	10.9	15.7	9.9	10.0	2.6	9.7	29.5	15.3	18.2	16.5	12.9	15.4
1885-89	2.5	9.8	22.0	16.2	9.5	12.9	8.4	8.0	2.5	9.8	31.1	16.0	22.4	12.9	11.0	11.2
1890-94	1.8	9.3	19.0	20.9	9.8	16.4	8.4	6.7	1.8	9.3	27.6	20.9	18.2	17.0	10.9	9.1
1895-99	1.7	10.5	20.4	16.7	8.9	15.5	9.0	9.4	1.7	10.5	24.1	16.5	17.6	16.2	11.3	13.1
1900-04	1.3	12.4	19.7	16.9	10.5	16.6	9.5	9.2	1.3	12.4	22.3	16.9	19.2	18.6	11.5	11.3
1905-09	1.8	11.2	14.0	17.5	11.8	16.9	9.6	9.4	1.8	11.2	18.6	17.3	21.4	17.8	12.4	12.2
1910-12	2.4	10.9	14.4	18.2	12.3	16.5	10.0	8.4	2.4	10.9	21.3	18.8	19.3	17.3	12.2	11.1
AVG(d)	2.4	9.8	18.7	15.4	9.4	14.9	8.2	7.4	2.4	9.8	23.4	15.4	15.3	15.5	10.6	11.8
								PANEL B:	POPULATION WEIGHTS							
1860-64	1.4	--	23.6	14.5	7.1	11.9	5.2	0.2	1.4	--	28.9	14.3	6.7	11.9	5.5	3.1
1865-69	2.1	4.3	18.3	15.8	6.6	13.0	6.0	1.0	2.1	4.3	20.1	15.1	6.1	13.0	9.5	5.0
1870-74	3.3	9.0	24.0	18.2	7.9	12.1	5.5	2.6	3.3	9.0	27.6	19.9	8.4	12.1	6.9	9.6
1875-79	5.3	11.3	19.6	19.0	9.7	15.3	6.9	3.1	5.3	11.3	28.1	21.6	12.2	15.6	7.6	7.8
1880-84	2.6	9.7	24.6	20.4	10.9	12.3	11.5	6.0	2.6	9.7	34.2	21.0	18.2	14.2	12.7	13.5
1885-89	2.5	9.8	23.2	22.2	9.5	11.2	8.6	6.1	2.5	9.8	37.4	22.2	22.4	11.0	10.0	13.1
1890-94	1.8	9.3	18.0	28.5	9.8	14.3	7.7	6.1	1.8	9.3	28.8	30.0	18.2	14.2	9.9	12.5
1895-99	1.7	10.5	17.4	24.5	8.9	11.9	10.2	9.8	1.7	10.5	21.9	28.3	17.6	12.4	14.3	17.9
1900-04	1.3	12.4	18.8	22.3	10.5	14.3	10.9	10.4	1.3	12.4	22.2	27.1	19.2	14.9	13.7	13.2
1905-09	1.8	11.2	14.4	24.3	11.8	14.6	10.9	13.4	1.8	11.2	19.4	26.5	21.4	14.9	14.1	16.9
1910-12	2.4	10.9	13.1	22.7	12.3	15.4	12.5	9.1	2.4	10.9	21.5	34.6	19.3	15.9	14.5	11.6
AVG(d)	2.4	10.9	19.8	21.1	9.4	13.3	8.6	6.1	2.4	9.8	26.6	23.3	15.3	13.6	10.7	11.3

Dash (--) = No Data

UKN: United Kingdom National   PSts: Indian Princely States
UKT: United Kingdom Total   FD: Foreign Developed Countries
RG: Responsible Government   FU: Foreign Underdeveloped Countries
DC: Dependent Colonies

capital.[7] It appears reasonable to conclude that the colonies with responsible government, and particularly those in Oceania, displayed a strong inclination to devote funds to public investment; and, while a desire to increase business profits may not have been the reason for their behavior, it should be clear that the business community benefited.

In the dependent Empire there was again a marked difference between the colonies and India. In the former, there was a sharp increase in the colony-weighted spending levels after 1884 but no long-term change in the population-weighted measure. Overall those colonies spent £.20 (increased to £.21 by the addition of railroads) if the colony-weighted measure is chosen. The population-weighted measures are £.14 and £.17 – a fifth of all expenditures. These figures, while paling in comparison to Australia and New Zealand, still stand out when compared to the £.06 per capita and 7 percent of total expenditure that was typical of the underdeveloped countries and compares more than favorably with the £.15 and 8 percent of the developed ones. Inclusion of the railroads, however, makes the contrast somewhat less dramatic; but even in that case, colonial levels were very much higher than the underdeveloped countries and almost equal to the developed. Foreign countries do, however, display a more rapid rate of increase. In the Empire, there appears to have been no single official policy on public works. The distribution of expenditures among the dependent colonies was very wide. While the colony-weighted average expenditure was £.20, eighteen spent less than £.04, and twelve others between £.04 and £.10.

In any given colony, it appears that the level of expenditure depended in large measure on the policies of the particular colonial government, although these policies were at times modified by Whitehall. Certainly Milner, while in South Africa, viewed public works as a necessary investment. In a letter to Randolph Churchill he wrote:

> It is essential that we should start with the recognition of two fundamental principles: the first is a liberal expenditure on the development of the new colonies as a condition precedent to that great expansion of revenue to which we must look if they are, besides providing for their own growth needs, to share the burden of the British war debt. No great growth of revenue is possible without such expenditures.[8]

But it is not clear how much support he received from London. Similarly, the attempt by the British government to push particular development plans at times brought howls of protest even from the British plying their trade in the colonies. For example, the West African trader, John Holt, when speaking of government policies toward the West African Railways, referred to "These vampires of our colonies who are in Downing Street and . . . care not what becomes of them."[9] Still, between the local governors and their advisors and the central administration in London, the dependent colonies structured their public-sector expenditures to yield a substantial block of real capital.

In India, few subjects attracted more official attention than the public-works department. From the 1860s until the turn of the century two debates raged: Should public works be undertaken by the public or private sectors, and within the public sector what was the appropriate level and composition of public investment? Of the two, the former occupied more of the policy makers' attention. As early as 1865 John Lawrence, then viceroy, wrote:

> I am strongly under the opinion that the government should undertake such work itself. For social, financial, and even political reasons, I consider this to be the right course. With all its shortcomings I believe it could be shown that the Public Works De-

partment can – and does – work cheaper than private companies. I consider that with all precaution, private companies by the pressure they can bring to bear on government, both at home and in India, will force us into an arrangement and engagement injurious to the state and the people.[10]

In a subsequent letter to Northcote, Lawrence reiterated, "There is nothing which a company can do, which the state cannot do better and cheaper."[11]

However, financial problems soon tempered these strong convictions. Lawrence realized that, despite his preference for state enterprise, he would accept private initiatives "rather than have no more canals . . . ," and he recognized that course "is the only mode of raising additional revenue to which there will be no murmur."[12] Nor were the concerns all financial and political. Questions were frequently raised about the efficiency of the public sector. In 1868, Northcote worried, "whether anything can be devised to supply the loss of the keen stimulous of self interest, which makes the private adventurer direct all his energies . . . ."[13] But the old policies persisted. Ten years later Lord Lytton, the viceroy wrote: " . . . The public works department of the government of India has always been, when left to itself, the most extravagant, the worst managed, and altogether the least satisfactory branch of our administration."[14]

Despite the strong commitment of some, such as Lawrence, to a socialized public-works system, that ideal eroded in the face of political, financial, and efficiency arguments. In 1881 Devonshire at the India Office wrote to the viceroy, Lord Ripon:

> I see a considerable disinclination to the admission of private enterprise in India Railways in the council here, and probably the same feeling exists more strongly in India. There is sure to be soon a strong protest and reaction against the restruction of expenditure on useful public works, and it seems to me the only ground on which we should be able to take our stand will be that by restructuring our own operations we will be giving a fair field to private enterprise.[15]

And Ripon himself wrote,

> There are two possible modes of doing so [financing railroads to prevent famines]. We may either devote to this purpose a much larger annual sum of money, raised either by taxation or borrowing, or we may once again appeal to private enterprise to do the work for us. Which of these two methods shall we adopt? I am strongly of the opinion that it is to the latter that we should turn.[16]

But established bureaucracies have lives of their own, and policy changes are effected at best slowly. In 1899, Lord Curzon, now in the viceregal chair, wrote Northcote at the India Office,

> ...I find a perfect chorus of dissatisfaction as to the manner in which the [public works] department reviews and treats offers of railway construction that come from responsible quarters in England and India. I saw yesterday a small private deputation of merchants who gave me specific cases .... The outcry in the papers is unanimous, bitter and strong .... [17]

The Indian expenditure data reflect the ebbs and flows of policy concerning public works and the role of the private as opposed to the public sector in building them. Railway construction in India commenced in about 1850 and was for a number of years carried out by British joint-stock companies who were guaranteed a 5-percent profit on their capital outlay and half of the surplus profits. In 1870 the government of India, reflecting Lawrence's conviction, changed its policy. Thereafter new railway lines were to be built through the direct agency of the state. The resources available to the government proved inadequate, and in 1880 the *Raj* once again turned to the private sector. Three different classes of contracts were designed, but all provided that the guaranteed interest not exceed 4 percent and gave the shareholders less than half the surplus profits. In addition, lines built under these new contracts were to become the property of the government after twenty years.

When all is said and done, India spent on public works at a lower rate than the underdeveloped countries and at a level similar to the Princely States. Moreover, unlike the other sectors, where expenditures rose over time, in India they peaked in the early 1880s and declined thereafter. In terms of percentage of budget, the Indian average was one-quarter higher than the figure for the underdeveloped countries, but only two-thirds of the average of the Princely States. Inclusion of railroads raises the Indian levels substantially. The same adjustment, however, pushes the foreign-underdeveloped indices upward as well, and India's relative position changes but little. It does, however, boost expenditures above those in the Princely States.[18] Even the inclusion of the railroads does not do full justice to India, for the figures still do not reflect the level of investment bound up in the state subsidy to "private" railroad investment.

In comparison with underdeveloped countries, if public but not subsidized private railroads are included, India spent more than eight of the underdeveloped countries and more than half of the

Princely States. Even without railroads, expenditures were greater than in several Caribbean, Central, and South American countries – El Salvador and Peru, for example – and some large but not budgetarily centralized countries (e.g., Japan and Turkey). In India a deliberate change of policy in the 1880s appears to have altered substantially the level of government contribution to the "nation's" capital stock. That change was in part a response to political pressure from business groups in Britain, but it was in large measure dictated by financial exigencies.

The physical capital component of the infrastructure was heavily socialized in the colonies with responsible government and, by a different yardstick, in the dependent colonies as well. In India the levels were lower. Even there, however, per capita investment exceeded the figures for the poorest underdeveloped nations. Imperial businesspeople were advantageously placed to draw on the investments of society, and that conclusion holds before consideration is given to the subsidy provided by government guarantees to the "private" Indian railroads.

C. Human capital

Investment can take a variety of forms and not all yield physical capital. Among the nontraditional components are the resources devoted to human capital. The term is a broad one encompassing expenditures on food, clothing, and housing for children in the years before they can become productive, on public health and medicine which permit people to work longer and harder, on formal education and on-the-job training, and on distribution schemes that prevent or mitigate famines and pestilence. While a part of these costs are always borne by the worker or the worker's family, economic development has been linked with some movement toward socialization. In the absence of slavery, generalized investment in human capital by private firms is seldom profitable; and for a complex series of reasons, even individuals tend to invest in themselves at less than optimum levels. Failing some form of government involvement, the level of investment in human capital is almost always less than optimal, and the productivity of the economy suffers accordingly.

In the United Kingdom expenditures at the national level in the early years were very low in absolute terms, but about equal to expenditures elsewhere in the developed world (see Table 4.5). Beginning in the mid–1870s, however, they rise rapidly, and by 1912 they average £.66 per person per year. Overall the fifty-two-year

TABLE 4.5

GOVERNMENT EXPENDITURE: HUMAN CAPITAL

	(£'s PER CAPITA)								(PERCENTS: RAILROADS OUT)							
	UKN	UKT	RG	DC	India	PSts	FD	FU	UKN	UKT	RG	DC	India	PSts	FD	FU
PANEL A: COLONY WEIGHTS																
1860-64	.05	--	.31	.18	.00	.01	.04	.02	2.3	--	14.5	16.7	1.2	6.4	4.5	4.0
1865-69	.04	.14	.29	.17	.01	.02	.04	.01	1.9	4.8	12.8	15.6	1.7	11.7	4.2	3.1
1870-74	.05	.29	.34	.16	.01	.03	.04	.02	2.8	10.4	12.6	16.2	2.7	10.8	4.3	2.7
1875-79	.08	.44	.48	.15	.02	.02	.05	.03	4.0	12.7	12.6	17.3	4.2	11.5	4.6	5.1
1880-84	.12	.53	.60	.16	.01	.02	.06	.06	4.9	13.3	12.9	16.2	2.6	9.1	5.1	5.7
1885-89	.17	.68	.76	.20	.01	.03	.09	.08	6.0	14.2	12.4	16.7	4.1	10.7	5.4	7.7
1890-94	.23	.80	.66	.23	.01	.02	.10	.06	8.0	15.8	11.4	15.9	4.2	10.5	5.9	7.7
1895-99	.35	1.18	.70	.22	.01	.03	.12	.07	9.9	18.2	9.9	14.9	6.2	10.5	5.6	7.2
1900-04	.37	1.41	.82	.19	.02	.03	.13	.05	7.6	16.0	12.1	13.2	7.6	10.9	5.9	6.8
1905-09	.45	1.84	.50	.18	.01	.03	.14	.10	11.6	22.2	14.1	13.9	5.9	10.3	6.3	8.6
1910-12	.66	2.02	.56	.19	.01	.04	.18	.10	16.1	23.6	15.1	14.1	5.9	11.0	7.1	8.3
AVG(d)	.22	.89	.55	.18	.01	.02	.09	.05	6.5	14.8	12.7	15.6	4.1	10.3	5.3	6.0
PANEL B: POPULATION WEIGHTS																
1860-64	.05	--	.17	.11	.00	.01	.03	.02	2.3	--	10.7	18.0	1.2	4.5	3.1	4.3
1865-69	.04	.14	.15	.11	.01	.02	.03	.01	1.9	4.8	8.6	16.5	1.7	8.7	2.7	3.1
1870-74	.05	.29	.16	.11	.01	.02	.03	.01	2.8	10.4	8.2	17.6	2.7	10.6	3.2	2.1
1875-79	.08	.44	.25	.12	.02	.03	.03	.02	4.0	12.7	11.0	19.2	4.2	14.2	3.4	4.6
1880-84	.12	.53	.34	.13	.01	.02	.05	.02	4.9	13.3	10.5	18.0	2.6	9.1	4.2	5.1
1885-89	.17	.68	.42	.14	.01	.02	.07	.04	6.0	14.2	11.3	17.0	4.1	6.9	4.4	6.6
1890-94	.23	.80	.39	.15	.01	.02	.07	.03	8.0	15.8	10.6	16.1	4.2	7.3	4.0	6.4
1895-99	.35	1.18	.42	.12	.01	.02	.10	.04	9.9	18.2	10.1	16.3	6.2	8.2	4.9	5.9
1900-04	.37	1.41	.52	.07	.02	.02	.09	.04	7.6	16.0	11.6	13.0	7.6	8.0	4.6	5.9
1905-09	.45	1.84	.40	.06	.01	.02	.10	.10	11.6	22.2	11.9	12.3	5.9	9.3	4.9	9.5
1910-12	.66	2.02	.55	.06	.01	.03	.12	.07	16.1	23.6	15.1	12.8	5.9	10.5	5.3	11.3
AVG(d)	.22	.89	.33	.11	.01	.02	.06	.04	6.5	13.4	10.7	16.2	4.2	8.9	4.0	5.8

Dash (--) = No Data)

UKN:	United Kingdom National	PSts:	Indian Princely States
UKT:	United Kingdom Total	FD:	Foreign Developed Countries
RG:	Responsible Government	FU:	Foreign Underdeveloped Countries
DC:	Dependent Colonies		

average was £.22 – something in excess of 6 percent of all expenditures. By the most favorable measure (the country-weighted one) initial expenditures in the developed countries were about equal to those in Britain, and those in the underdeveloped sector about half that level. Like the UK levels, both rise over time; but abroad, the rate of growth was much slower. Overall, foreign-developed countries averaged £.09 and underdeveloped ones £.05 (the figures are £.06 and £.04 if the population-weighted measure is chosen). In terms of total budget, the underdeveloped countries spent slightly less than the British (a larger fraction early, a smaller one later), and the developed countries a little less than that (more than the British early, much less later). In many ways these are the least reliable series because of the differences in the level of government assigned responsibility for education. Among the developed countries only France and Sweden spent at levels about equal to the United Kingdom. The German and U.S. figures were low, at least in part because almost all expenditures were made by state and local authorities. State and local expenditures on education were, for example, £.75 in the United States in 1902, and £.79 in Prussia in 1911.[19]

In the Empire outside of India the levels of expenditure were surprisingly high. In the colonies with responsible government, the all-years colony-weighted average was £.55, two and one-half times the British national figure; and the population-weighted figure, at £.33, was about one and one-half times as large. Even in the decades of the 1860s the colony-weighted average was £.31 – more than the British fifty-two-year average – and the population-weighted figure, £.17. Among those colonies, New Zealand averaged £.84, the six Australian colonies followed with £.76, and for Australia after 1902 the figure was £.77. The South African average was £.31, and in North America, Canada expended only £.06 per person but Newfoundland spent £.33.

Both the colonies with responsible government and those in a more dependent status devoted about £1 in 8 of their total governmental expenditure to activities relating to human capital. That figure is approximately twice as much as the fraction in the United Kingdom or either foreign sector. In the case of the dependent colonies, the colony-weighted expenditure averaged about £.18 and the population-weighted one about £.11. These figures appear small in comparison with the responsibly governed colonies, but very high if the standard is the underdeveloped countries (or the developed countries for that matter). Again the wide range of expenditures suggests that the actual policies tended to reflect the views of individual governors and their advisors rather than any coherent centralized scheme. While twenty-six of the colonies spent less than £.05, twenty-two spent more than £.20; that latter group included Mauritius, Malta, British Guiana, and almost all of the Caribbean Islands.

If Britain committed some resources to human capital, and the colonies in the Empire relatively more, the same could not be said for India. Overall the Indian government spent only £.01 per person per year (about 4 percent of all expenditures), while even the Princely States were spending £.02, more than 10 percent of their budgets. Among independent underdeveloped countries only one spent less, and neighboring Siam spent £.11 and 6 percent of its budget. Moreover, while the trend almost everywhere was upward, there is little evidence of movement in the Indian series.

Nor were the British unaware of the low level of expenditures on human capital in India.[20] In 1871 Lord Mayo wrote to Argyll at the India Office concerning education,

> I know that millions have been spent and will be spent which might have been and could be spent in . . . elevating the children of the soil. We have done much but we could do a great deal more – it is, however, impossible unless we spend less on the interests and more on the people.[21]

Ten years later the dissatisfactions were similar. At that time Ripon wrote to Gladstone:

> ... I am also engaged in what can be done to extend and improve our system of primary education. A good deal has been done to encourage higher education here, but elementary education has been too much neglected .... [22]

And soon thereafter a memorandum from Randolph Churchill lamented:

> ... everyday brings to our notice fresh objects for which public education is most desirable – take the development of primary education alone, in which much has been done for an Asiatic country, the educational means are still significantly deficient as compared with any civilized standard. [23]

But despite the concerns that both the political rhetoric and the data uniquely manifest, policy did not change. Rather Hardinge wrote in 1911:

> Our educational policy in this country has yet to be formed. At the present moment we are anxious to spend money on technical education at the same time Gokhale and some of his followers advocate very strongly free primary education which they would like to make compulsory .... I cannot help but feel that, apart from their desire for educational advantages for the people, they have the idea at the back of their heads that education will create unrest among a class without whom they feel that no movement in the country can acquire any serious force .... [24]

In India it appears that political concerns and a general disinclination to spend money combined to warp the structure of social overhead investment in a way that could well have redounded against profits and productivity.

D. Direct government support for business: manufacturing, agriculture, and natural resources

Today no one is surprised when even those governments most committed to private enterprise devote a significant block of their resources to providing direct support to business. That commitment, however, grew up rather slowly over the course of the late nineteenth century. In the United Kingdom, for example, trade and industry did not emerge as a separately reported category of expenditures until 1928, although of course there were expenditures toward those ends much earlier. In other nations the activities were officially acknowledged sooner, but similar caveats apply. For these reasons, the reader should view these figures as a minimum estimate of the levels of government support. In the United Kingdom the identified undertakings absorbed on average £.07 per capita per year but £.13 in the last twelve years. In the developed countries the comparable figures were £.05 and £.09, and among the underdeveloped countries, £.04 and £.08 (see Table 4.6). For both the developed and undeveloped countries the fraction of budget was about 5 percent.

In the Empire, the colonies with responsible government seem to have discovered the value of business-supporting expenditures long before anyone else was more than dimly aware of their possible advantages. Over the entire fifty-two-year period they absorbed about 8 percent of those colonies' budget, and by the end of the period the figure was more than a tenth. These percentages translate into colony-weighted per capita expenditure levels of £.46 for the all-years average (£.27 for the population-weighted measure). Among the colonies with responsible government, New Zealand averaged £.95, the six Australian colonies £.51 (Australia after 1903, £.48), and the South African colonies £.24. Newfoundland spent £.16, Canada £.12.

Even the dependent colonies, while spending at a much lower level than their more autonomous fellows, still averaged at least as much as either the industrialized or the underdeveloped countries, although by the end of the period they were probably spending somewhat less. In these colonies the government felt little compunction about expenditures directed toward improving business. For example in 1908, Walter Davidson, Governor of the Seychelles, reported:

> The Agricultural Board sent in a series of unanimous resolutions asking that the surplus revenues of the colony be invested in loans to planters. They have my hearty sympathy, as long as the Loan Board is the Governor and the Executive Council, so there can be no hanky panky or bad debts. I hold that investments locally to develop land bearing interest at 6 percent are better value than 3 percent gilt edged securities at home .... [25]

The highest levels of these direct business-supporting activities were in the Falklands, Trinidad, and Bermuda but twenty-eight dependent colonies spent more than £.05. At the other end of the scale,

TABLE 4.6

GOVERNMENT EXPENDITURES ON DIRECT BUSINESS SUPPORT

(£'s Per Capita)

			RAILROADS OUT								RAILROADS IN			
	UKT	RG	DC	India	PSts	FD	FU	UKT	RG	DC	India	PSts	FD	FU
						POPULATION WEIGHTED								
1860-64	--	.13	.05	.00	.00	.02	.02	--	.13	1.05	.00	.00	.02	.02
1865-69	.01	.13	.05	.00	.00	.03	.02	.01	.13	.05	.00	.00	.03	.02
1870-74	.03	.13	.05	.00	.00	.02	.02	.03	.13	.05	.00	.00	.02	.02
1875-79	.04	.21	.05	.00	.00	.02	.02	.04	.21	1.05	.00	.00	.02	.02
1880-84	.04	.22	.05	.00	.02	.03	.02	.04	.22	2.25	.00	.02	.03	.02
1885-89	.05	.29	.06	.00	.02	.06	.03	.05	.29	3.06	.00	.02	.06	.03
1890-94	.06	.27	.06	.00	.02	.06	.03	.06	.27	2.06	.00	.02	.06	.03
1895-99	.08	.35	.05	.00	.02	.07	.04	.08	.35	2.05	.00	.02	.07	.04
1900-04	.10	.46	.04	.00	.02	.06	.06	.10	.46	2.04	.00	.02	.06	.06
1905-09	.13	.39	.04	.00	.02	.07	.11	.13	.39	1.04	.00	.02	.07	.11
1910-12	.18	.41	.04	.00	.02	.09	.10	.18	.41	2.04	.00	.02	.09	.10
AVG(d)	.07	.27	.05	.00	.01	.05	.04	.07	.27	.05	.00	.01	.05	.04
						COLONY WEIGHTED								
1860-64	--	.25	.06	.00	.00	.03	.02	--	.25	1.06	.00	.00	.03	.02
1865-69	.01	.27	.07	.00	.00	.03	.02	.01	.27	1.07	.00	.00	.03	.02
1870-74	.03	.24	.06	.00	.00	.02	.02	.03	.24	1.06	.00	.00	.02	.02
1875-79	.04	.34	.05	.00	.00	.03	.02	.04	.34	2.05	.00	.00	.03	.02
1880-84	.04	.37	.05	.00	.01	.05	.02	.04	.37	3.05	.00	.01	.05	.02
1885-89	.05	.55	.07	.00	.01	.07	.04	.05	.55	4.07	.00	.01	.07	.04
1890-94	.06	.56	.09	.00	.01	.08	.03	.06	.56	4.09	.00	.01	.08	.03
1895-99	.08	.83	.07	.00	.01	.09	.06	.08	.83	5.07	.00	.01	.09	.06
1900-04	.10	.74	.07	.00	.03	.09	.04	.10	.74	4.07	.00	.03	.09	.04
1905-09	.13	.47	.08	.00	.02	.10	.07	.13	.47	2.08	.00	.02	.10	.07
1910-12	.18	.49	.09	.00	.02	.11	.08	.18	.49	2.09	.00	.02	.11	.08
AVG(d)	.07	.46	.07	.00	.01	.06	.04	.07	.46	.07	.00	.01	.06	.04

(Percent of Budget)

			RAILROADS OUT								RAILROADS IN			
	UKT	RG	DC	India	PSts	FD	FU	UKT	RG	DC	India	PSts	FD	FU
						POPULATION WEIGHTED								
1860-64	--	8.2	8.0	0.7	0.2	2.3	6.4	--	7.5	7.9	0.6	0.2	2.2	6.2
1865-69	0.4	7.8	8.1	0.6	2.0	3.4	4.3	0.4	7.3	7.8	0.5	2.0	3.2	4.1
1870-74	0.9	7.1	8.6	0.4	1.7	2.1	4.3	0.9	6.5	8.1	0.3	1.7	2.1	3.9
1875-79	1.1	9.5	7.8	0.6	1.7	2.7	5.4	1.1	7.9	7.2	0.5	1.7	2.6	5.0
1880-84	1.1	6.9	7.5	0.5	7.7	2.8	4.9	1.1	5.4	6.8	0.4	7.5	2.8	4.5
1885-89	1.1	7.7	6.7	0.2	7.5	3.7	5.7	1.1	5.3	6.2	0.1	7.2	3.6	5.2
1890-94	1.2	7.5	6.9	0.2	8.6	3.4	5.1	1.2	5.4	6.4	0.2	8.2	3.3	4.6
1895-99	1.2	8.6	7.3	0.2	8.4	3.3	6.7	1.2	6.5	6.5	0.1	8.0	3.2	5.9
1900-04	1.1	10.1	7.3	0.2	9.0	3.3	7.6	1.1	7.4	6.4	0.2	8.6	3.2	7.1
1905-09	1.6	11.5	8.5	0.3	9.7	3.5	10.6	1.6	8.2	7.5	0.2	9.4	3.3	9.7
1910-12	2.1	11.4	8.9	0.3	8.0	4.3	8.2	2.1	8.2	6.7	0.2	7.9	4.0	7.6
AVG(d)	1.1	8.7	7.8	0.4	5.9	3.1	6.3	1.1	6.8	7.1	0.3	5.7	3.0	5.8
						COLONY WEIGHTED								
1860-64	--	8.9	3.8	0.7	0.1	3.5	5.2	--	8.6	3.8	0.6	0.1	3.4	4.9
1865-69	0.4	8.4	4.1	0.6	2.0	4.4	3.9	0.4	8.0	4.1	0.5	2.0	4.1	3.8
1870-74	0.9	7.0	4.8	0.4	0.8	2.7	3.2	0.9	6.4	4.7	0.3	0.8	2.6	3.0
1875-79	1.1	8.9	4.6	0.6	0.9	2.5	3.7	1.1	7.8	4.5	0.5	0.9	2.5	3.5
1880-84	1.1	9.6	5.1	0.5	3.5	3.3	3.1	1.1	7.9	4.9	0.4	3.4	3.1	2.9
1885-89	1.1	8.5	5.6	0.2	2.2	3.7	3.4	1.1	6.2	5.4	0.1	2.1	3.6	3.1
1890-94	1.2	8.5	5.3	0.2	2.8	3.9	3.8	1.2	6.1	5.1	0.2	2.8	3.7	3.5
1895-99	1.2	8.3	6.9	0.2	3.4	3.8	3.9	1.2	6.2	6.7	0.1	3.3	3.6	3.3
1900-04	1.1	8.4	8.6	0.2	7.2	4.2	3.2	1.1	6.5	8.4	0.2	6.8	4.1	3.0
1905-09	1.6	11.2	8.9	0.3	6.8	4.6	4.1	1.6	8.3	8.5	0.2	6.6	4.3	3.7
1910-12	2.1	12.5	8.4	0.3	5.1	4.3	4.6	2.1	9.6	7.9	0.2	5.0	4.2	4.2
AVG(d)	1.1	9.0	5.9	0.4	3.1	3.7	3.9	1.1	7.3	5.7	0.3	3.0	3.5	3.5

Dash (--) = No Data

UKT:	United Kingdom Total	PSts:	Princely States
RG:	Responsible Government	FD:	Foreign Developed Countries
DC:	Dependent Colonies	FU:	Foreign Underdeveloped Countries

thirteen spent £.01 or less. The explanation of the spread in expenditures is difficult to discover. However, there does appear to be some loose correlation with development. Most of the larger Caribbean islands, Hong Kong, the Straits, and similar settlements are in the top half of the list, while the African colonies and the small Caribbean islands make up the bulk of the bottom.

While government support in the dependent colonies was substantial by the standards of the underdeveloped world, the same was not true for India. On the subcontinent few resources except those budgeted for transport appear to have been committed directly to the support of any business. In the early years there were some expenditures in support of private irrigation schemes, but they were never large. In 1882 the government moved briefly and tentatively into the business sector:

> The government of India have for some time past had under special consideration the importance of developing the iron industry in India. The Bengal Iron Works have consequently been purchased for the sum Rs 4, 30, 761 (£43,000). His excellency the Governor General in Council is now pleased that they will be retransferred for that sum together with any indispensable outlays to any parties who may establish satisfactorily that they are in possession of sufficient skill and resources and bona fide prepared to carry on the manufacture of iron and steel . . . . [26]

It was, however, a step from which there was almost immediate withdrawal. Later, when a scheme for an agricultural bank was proposed all Minto could write was:

> . . . I very much wish we could induce the people of India to invest more money in undertakings in their own country . . . . On the face of it there is much in its [the Agricultural Bank's] favour. The intention of relieving the agriculturist from debt and enabling him to borrow at a lower rate than at present is excellent, but one is thrown back on the fact that this is to be done by English speculators counting on a rate of interest – a very high one according to English ideas – to be gleaned from India and safeguarded by guarantees from the government of India . . . . [27]

The contrast with Davidson's letter is instructive. Even the governments of the Princely States expended more on direct business support than the Indian government. They spent at a rate that, although below the dependent Empire, was still well above India. In India the government was apparently committed to laissez faire (a strange contrast with the early attitudes toward public works), or perhaps only to not spending money; and periodic famines made it nearly impossible to carry out any systematic program, no matter how the politicians felt. Whatever the reason, there is no evidence that the government of India or the India Office ever skewed the budget in a way that would have made British investment particularly profitable.

III. Conclusion

Table 4.7 summarizes the expenditures in support of business. It is possible to use the data as evidence that governments in the Empire biased their expenditures in the direction of the private sector; however, the results are not quite those the critics of Empire might have expected.

In the United Kingdom the national annual per capita expenditures averaged £.42. That figure is higher than the average for foreign-developed countries; however, given the relative development of the United Kingdom among the developed nations, it appears likely that a substantial portion of the difference reflects that position rather than a major difference in "taste." The United Kingdom and the foreign-developed series display similar trends and, as a fraction of total expenditure, those foreign countries appear to have devoted more "effort" to business-supporting activities.

In the Empire, at least in those parts with responsible government, there is evidence of such a taste difference. In the "railroad-out" case, the colony-weighted average on business-supporting activities is six times the home level and even the population-weighted average is over three times as high. If railways are included, those measures rise to 8 and 4.5. Of course, a part of the difference can be traced to the allocation of functions between governmental levels. If the total (national plus local) expenditure figure for the United Kingdom is used, the ratio for the colony-weighted figure falls to 1.4, and for the population-weighted average to less than one (.8). That comparison is, of course, overdrawn since expenditures by cities and subcolonial units are excluded from the colonial figures. Thus the colonies with responsible government do appear to have displayed considerable inclination to support their own, or perhaps even British, business.

In the dependent colonies the evidence of a taste difference appears almost equally strong. Levels of spending were less than in colonies with responsible government, but were probably as high as the national totals in the United Kingdom. The colony-weighted estimate averaged £.64 without railroads and even when weighted by population the figure was £.39. Moreover, those colonies devoted on the average more than one-half of their total budgets to these

TABLE 4.7

GRAND TOTAL FOR DIRECT SUPPORT OF BUSINESS

(£'s Per Capita)

	RAILROADS OUT								RAILROADS IN							
	UKN	UKT	RG	DC	India	PSts	FD	FU	UKN	UKT	RG	DC	India	PSts	FD	FU
	POPULATION WEIGHTED															
1860-64	.18	--	.87	.34	.06	.05	.12	.06	.18	--	1.00	.34	.06	.05	.13	.07
1865-69	.19	.40	.77	.35	.06	.06	.17	.05	.19	.40	.82	.35	.06	.06	.21	.07
1870-74	.23	.74	.86	.36	.07	.06	.13	.05	.23	.74	.98	.38	.08	.06	.15	.08
1875-79	.34	1.10	1.06	.36	.09	.08	.15	.08	.34	1.10	1.40	.39	.11	.08	.15	.10
1880-84	.36	1.24	1.60	.44	.08	.09	.23	.10	.36	1.24	2.24	.46	.13	.10	.25	.15
1885-89	.45	1.54	1.82	.51	.06	.09	.30	.15	.45	1.54	3.00	.52	.11	.09	.32	.20
1890-94	.42	1.61	1.60	.60	.05	.10	.30	.13	.42	1.61	2.46	.63	.07	.10	.35	.17
1895-99	.54	2.25	1.78	.45	.05	.10	.44	.17	.54	2.25	2.27	.50	.09	.11	.54	.26
1900-04	.56	2.91	2.10	.29	.07	.11	.41	.22	.56	2.91	2.62	.34	.10	.12	.47	.24
1905-09	.63	3.20	1.54	.27	.07	.11	.44	.41	.63	3.20	1.98	.30	.12	.11	.52	.46
1910-12	.87	3.43	1.66	.27	.07	.11	.54	.32	.87	3.43	2.28	.39	.11	.11	.60	.36
AVG(d)	.42	1.78	1.42	.39	.07	.09	.29	.16	.42	1.78	1.90	.42	.09	.09	.33	.19
	COLONY WEIGHTED															
1860-64	.18	--	1.59	.54	.06	.05	.16	.09	.18	--	1.71	.54	.06	.05	.17	.13
1865-69	.19	.40	1.42	.57	.06	.06	.25	.08	.19	.40	1.60	.57	.06	.06	.31	.12
1870-74	.23	.74	1.58	.52	.07	.07	.17	.08	.23	.74	1.93	.53	.08	.07	.23	.21
1875-79	.34	1.10	1.88	.47	.09	.07	.21	.12	.34	1.10	2.52	.48	.11	.07	.24	.15
1880-84	.36	1.24	2.57	.54	.08	.08	.32	.18	.36	1.24	3.57	.55	.13	.09	.37	.23
1885-89	.45	1.54	3.37	.70	.06	.09	.39	.22	.45	1.54	4.93	.73	.11	.09	.43	.26
1890-94	.42	1.61	2.92	.95	.05	.10	.41	.21	.42	1.61	4.38	.97	.07	.10	.46	.24
1895-99	.54	2.25	3.80	.78	.05	.10	.51	.25	.54	2.25	5.17	.81	.09	.10	.57	.39
1900-04	.56	2.91	3.74	.67	.07	.11	.52	.22	.56	2.91	4.53	.71	.10	.12	.57	.24
1905-09	.63	3.20	1.79	.65	.07	.12	.59	.35	.63	3.20	2.22	.67	.12	.12	.68	.39
1910-12	.87	3.43	1.88	.67	.07	.12	.63	.37	.87	3.43	2.45	.70	.11	.12	.71	.42
AVG(d)	.42	1.78	2.43	.64	.07	.09	.37	.19	.42	1.78	3.21	.66	.09	.09	.42	.25

Dash (--) = No Data

UKN:	United Kingdom National	PSts:	Indian Princely States
UKT:	United Kingdom Total	FD:	Foreign Developed Countries
RG:	Responsible Government	FU:	Foreign Underdeveloped Countries
DC:	Dependent Colonies		

activities. That proportion is slightly above the levels found in the colonies with responsible government, and it is much above levels in the United Kingdom or either foreign sector.

In India, the evidence runs in the other direction. The average level of expenditures is much below that of the foreign-underdeveloped sector, but, as a fraction of the total, the "effort" is not dissimilar. More compellingly, in both absolute and relative terms, India spent less on public works, human capital, the legal structure, and resources than did the Princely States. These data, when coupled with the qualitative evidence, indicate that the relevant governmental policies were less the product of pressure from British business than of the government of India's perception of local needs.

In the responsibly governed Empire, where Britain had almost no voice in policy, expenditures were by far the greatest. In those dependent colonies where local citizens had at least some access to the political process the expenditure levels were highest, but in possessions where that access was minimal (even though they may well have been potentially the most productive from the British businessperson's viewpoint) they were lowest. Of the fifteen dependent colonies with average expenditures of more than £.90, five were in the Caribbean, seven were other island colonies (Falklands, St. Helena, Gibraltar, Hong Kong, Malta, Tonga, and Mauritius), and the other three were on the Malay Peninsula (the Federated Malay States, Selangor, and Perak). Only in Hong Kong, the Federated Malay States, and Tonga does it appear that these expenditures primarily served a foreign business community, and in the latter case the European community was not British but Australasian. Conversely, of the twenty colonies that spent less than £.20, thirteen were in West, Central, or East Africa – areas of alleged economic imperialism. Finally, on the Indian subcontinent (where the voice of British business should have been easily heard) per capita expenditures fell at the thirtieth percentile of the dependent-colony list (44 above, 1 equal, and 19 below) and over time those expenditures appear to have been trendless. Little more was spent in the twentieth century than in the 1860s. On the other hand, in the United Kingdom the ratio of last- to first-decade expenditures was almost 5, in the foreign-developed sector it was 4, for the underdeveloped sector it was 5, and even in the Princely States it was more than 2. To the extent that the British business community had any political interest or influence, it does not appear to have used it effectively, and it seems to have been particularly ineffective in India.

The analysis of expenditure patterns cannot deny the allegation that the British warped the political process to bolster the profits of their business community. On the other hand, it does not confirm the charge. If the British government had set out to effect such a policy, the political mechanism should have produced quite different results. Political control was great in India, and least effective in the colonies with responsible government. Therefore the evidence of manipulation (the level of expenditures in support of business) should have been strong in India and weak in the colonies of white settlement. The actual facts are otherwise. Evidence of government influence on behalf of business is weakest in India, where political control was almost absolute. Next come the dependent colonies, where there was often at least some local consultation. Finally, government involvement is the most significant in those colonies where British political control was the least evident. Thus, an alternative explanation appears in order. Yes, government may well have warped the political process to aid business, but it was the local, not the British, business community. British business did, of course, benefit, but it appears that the British government itself was, at most, marginally involved.

APPENDIX 4.1

The data presented in this chapter are estimates of the functional distribution of the expenditures of the United Kingdom, India, 15 colonies with responsible government, 59 colonies at various levels of autonomy or dependency, 18 Indian Princely States, 16 foreign countries classified as developed, and 25 listed as underdeveloped. Interest is centered on the business-supporting activities of government, and the functional taxonomy reflects that emphasis. The reader should, however, be aware of some potential pitfalls in the data.

First, as to classification: The United Kingdom in our context refers to England, Wales, and Scotland but not Ireland. India includes all areas governed through the India Office. The colonies with responsible government are those enumerated in Chapter 1, Appendix 1.1, and the rest are placed among the dependent colonies. Egypt is included as a dependent colony after 1881. The foreign-developed classification incorporates most of western Europe (including Greece, Spain, and Portugal), Russia, the United States of America, and Japan after 1900. In the underdeveloped category are some countries in eastern Europe (Serbia, Romania, and Bulgaria), a number in Central and South America (including Haiti and Santo Domingo), Siam, Liberia, Japan (before 1900), Tunisia, and Egypt (before 1882). A full enumeration of countries and classifications can be found in Appendix 1.3.

The list of countries is not complete, and the criterion for inclusion was solely the availability of data.

As to functional categorization, while a serious attempt was made to be as consistent as possible, the effort was not always successful. As the budget data were not originally gathered with this purpose in mind, it is likely that there are some misclassifications. In the case of the British Empire, the sources were official reports, and independent checks on the original data indicate that classifications were similar both between colonies and over time. For the foreign countries, however, considerable adjustment and estimation were necessary to produce the data that are the basis of this analysis.

Sources also vary as to reliability. The data on the non-Indian empire are drawn from the Colonial Blue Books (the annual reports of the colonial governors to the Colonial Office). The Indian budgets are taken from the annual reports of the India Office to Parliament. In neither case is there any reason to doubt the reliability of the data. As to the foreign countries, the data are drawn from a wide variety of sources, and they almost certainly reflect a considerable range of accuracy. The sources include historical statistics when available, the annual British compilation of foreign statistics, the commercial reports of the British diplomatic corps, monographs on the finances of specific countries, the annual reports of the Council of Foreign Bondholders, and as a last resort, the *Statesman's Yearbook*. While the data for the developed countries is probably reasonably accurate, that for the underdeveloped ones is less so. Not infrequently the "estimates" rather than the actual expenditures were used; but a probably greater source of error lies in the sometimes propagandistic nature of the "official budgets." At times they appear designed not to reflect the actual level of expenditure but to frighten suspected aggressors or to allay the fears of potential lenders.

Currencies have been converted to British pounds on the basis of prevailing exchange rates. For gold-standard countries they are accurate, and the silver-depreciation calculations are acceptable. The South American currency depreciations, however, cast some doubt on the accuracy of the rates on those paper currencies. The data reported have been adjusted for inflation on the best available price indices, but here too lies a source of potential error.

Finally, and perhaps most importantly, the reader should note that the budgets represent those of the national or colonial governments and hence do not reflect data for all the political units within the borders of the country or colony in question. Inclusion of the expenditures of states, cities, provinces, rabbit districts, and what have you would have provided a more accurate measure of government activity; however, those data are almost nonexistent. In the case of the United States, for example, although the first government estimate of state and local finance was made in 1902, figures were not collected on a regular basis until 1912. The national expenditure figures are at best an index of the total size and composition of the public sector, but even this index should be viewed with a jaundiced eye. The smaller (in population or geographical size) and the less developed the political unit, the greater the fraction of total expenditures carried out at the national (or colonial) level. Comparisons between countries or colonies of very different levels of development or size produce substantial distortions. To provide some measure of these problems, the expenditures of the United Kingdom after 1868 are reported in both national (UKN) and total (UKT) terms.* Despite the above caveats, the data appear to provide some very useful clues about the nature of governmental behavior.

---

*Thus in the case of the United Kingdom in the years 1910–12, "national" expenditures were 48 percent of all government expenditure. In contrast, in the less centralized states, the figure for the United States in 1902 was 34 percent and for the Germans in 1912, 35 percent.

5   The costs of defending an empire: the British and colonial taxpayer

I. The struggle for colonial involvement

The Empire was an attractive alternative to British investors in part because of the subsidy supplied by the British taxpayers. Guaranteed loans, grants-in-aid of official salaries, public works, and disaster relief all served to reduce the financial burden on the colonies and hence increased the potential return to the investor. Of all the subsidies enjoyed by the colonies, none was more lucrative than that for defense.

In the early history of the Empire there was a certain air of official indifference associated with questions of cost and the military. It was only when the drain on the British exchequer engendered by the colonial phases of the Anglo–French wars became apparent that British officials began seriously considering the financial burdens of imperial defense. Eighteenth-century attempts at transferring those costs to the Empire were both clumsy and ineffectual and cost the Crown the original American colonies. Constitutional developments in the next century complicated matters still further. In the mid-nineteenth century most of the colonies of white settlement were granted responsible government – a status that implied a paradox. Responsible government loosened the bands that tied the colonies to Great Britain and lifted the hand of Whitehall from most areas of government. Colonial legislatures were required to underwrite the costs of purely domestic services, but they could not be forced to share the burden of imperial – that is, empire-wide – expenses. The self-governing colonies saw little advantage in supporting an imperial defense establishment. They were convinced the British taxpayer would assume that responsibility if they did not, and in large measure they were correct.

The struggle over the defense burden was fought in two areas: overseas, between the colonies and the British government, and domestically, between the Treasury – guardian of the public purse – and the Colonial Office. Only the latter seemed to understand that the preservation of the British Empire was intimately linked with the happiness of white British subjects, and that attempts to coerce that group would quite likely produce other Lexingtons and Concords, not to mention Yorktowns.

Parliament usually was more concerned with the costs of the Em-

145

pire than with any glories it might impart to the British Crown. In a debate of March 30, 1860, for instance, Sir Charles Adderley rose in the Commons to complain of the high cost of imperial defense. He asserted Great Britain contributed £4,000,000 to the maintenance of security while the colonies contributed less than £40,000. "Why," he asked, "should the colonies be exempted from paying for their own defense?" Parliamentary emotions on the question of defense expenditures ran surprisingly high. Again, it was Adderley who captured the prevailing spirit when he averred that "it was absolutely unparalleled in the history of the world that any portion of an empire – colonial, provincial or otherwise – should be so exempted in purse and person from the cost of its own defences" as was a British colony.[1]

Reflecting the Commons's concern, a Colonial Office committee in 1860 urged that the colonies be deemed militarily self-sufficient and should, therefore, not expect to draw on domestic resources. Words alone, however, did not satisfy Parliament. On March 5, 1861, Arthur Mills moved for the creation of a select committee on colonial military expenditure. The only sure way of retaining the colonies, he contended, was to enable them both to govern and defend themselves. The committee was duly appointed with Mills as chairman, and it grappled with the issues in detail. Evidence before the body indicated that there were more than 44,000 troops (over a third of the total British armed forces) stationed in colonial garrisons. Slightly more than half of these were in Malta, Gibraltar, Bermuda, Halifax, St. Helena, and Mauritius, stations that were considered particularly vital for defense purposes and designated "imperial fortresses." The rest of the imperial army was scattered throughout the Empire with heaviest concentrations in New Zealand, beset with Maori problems, and South Africa, involved in incessant wars with the indigenous African tribes. The British exchequer contributed £1,715,000 toward the cost of those forces and the colonies £370,000.[2] The committee's final report was filed on March 4, 1862. It accepted the British government's responsibility for military expenses arising from imperial policy; but for internal order, the report placed that "main responsibility" on the colonies.[3]

With the advent of responsible government, the affected colonies lost British subsidies for internal administration but were in return able to refuse aid on matters of general imperial concern. It was a case of point-counterpoint as to what constituted an "imperial" as opposed to a purely local concern, and the colonies were never loathe to exploit that ambiguity. In 1900, for instance, New Zealand appealed for British assistance in the construction of harbor defenses contending that it was a matter of imperial consequence. The prime minister, Richard Seddon, wrote:

> ... the chief drawback has been the finding of the capital required for the completion of our harbour defences, the equipment of the defence forces, the purchase of great and small arms and ammunition .... I therefore, with much reason, urge that it would be of advantage to the Mother Country ... if the monies required ... were raised by the Imperial authorities and advanced to the colony .... There would ... be the direct advantages to the Imperial authorities and the Empire in having a reserve force established ready for any contingency that might arise ... [4]

In general, Her Majesty's government took the position that land defenses were the sole responsibility of the local government and that Empire-wide expenses, such as the navy, should be shared; but it was a stance with which the colonies took strenuous issue.

The controversy over the definition of imperial responsibility spilled over to the offices in Whitehall as well. In 1886, when the Colonial Office favored the expenditure of British funds for the defenses of Table Bay, Simonstown, and Cape Town, the Treasury stood stoutly in opposition and urged the abandonment of all work if the colony did not agree to pay the costs.[5] Robert Meade, one of the assistant undersecretaries at the Colonial Office, reached close to the heart of the matter when he contended,

> Defence is an ambiguous word in relation to a colony like the Cape with 1) a large native population, and 2) a seaboard liable to attack by enemies in war. If we claim in general terms that the Imperial troops are there for 'defence,' and that the colony ought to pay their cost, the colony might in turn claim to make use of them in native wars, which would be a losing bargain for the home government in the end, and might lead to incalculable expenses.[6]

Whatever ambivalence may have been aroused vis-a-vis the responsibilities of the self-governing colonies, the same ought not be said for the dependent Empire – at least as far as official opinion in London was concerned. The absence of viable representative institutions, ones that in the self-governing colonies provided protection against even reasonable demands from Whitehall, should have made it easy to raise funds for imperial defense from colonial revenues. In addition, that many of these colonies depended on parliamentary subsidies and nonrepayable grants-in-aid should have made them particularly vulnerable. Actually, the British government was able to exact at least some contributions from a few of the dependencies:

India, Ceylon, Mauritius, Hong Kong, and the Straits Settlements all made not insubstantial payments; but the colonies of white settlement remained largely immune. As Edward Cardwell, the Secretary of State for War, wrote George Granville at the Colonial Office in 1869:

> ... It is not, I think satisfactory to Parliament ... that the Australian colonies and the Cape ... shall contribute at a much lower rate than is required from Ceylon, a Crown Colony, or that the Dominion of Canada, the most powerful and not the least prosperous of Her Majesty's possessions shall ... be an exception to the rule which requires contributions from the colonies.[7]

Because of the recognized unfairness of the allocation, Parliament and the Colonial Office moved to redress the balance, but not, perhaps, in the manner that the Treasury would have preferred. Both politicians and Colonial Office bureaucrats realized that Mauritius only had defense costs because it was a "fortress" in an Empire it never chose to join and whose shipping it had been elected to protect. When the Treasury, in 1889, attempted to increase the military charge upon Hong Kong, the Colonial Office resisted. They pointed out that the island was endangered only because it was a coaling station and naval depot from which vessels bound for China and Japan were protected in a

> ... trade which is mainly independent of H. Kong and which is carried on for the benefit of the mother country and the British taxpayer .... The 'British taxpayer' who plays so large a part in the Treasury position, is probably the only person who is strongly interested in the defence of Hong Kong. The Island produces nothing, and the defence of it is the defence of British trade .... "[8]

Similarly, Sir W. H. Gregory, a former Governor of Ceylon, wrote the Colonial Office in 1891, "The defence of Ceylon, is the defence of English supremacy against the substitution of some other European power's; it is not the defence of an independent state."[9]

The Treasury for its part persisted in equating the responsibilities of British and colonial taxpayers. As a consequence, conflicts between it and the Colonial Office were common and not infrequently had to be decided at the Cabinet level. Correspondence between the two offices could be vituperous. At one point the Colonial Office petulantly wrote the Treasury "to express his Lordship's regret that the unusual language employed respecting himself and a former Secretary of State as well as officers of this department" precluded any action of a nature desired by the Treasury being taken.[10] When the Treasury, in its turn, accused the Colonial Office of placing excessive and unjustifiable burdens on the British taxpayer, the Colonial Office remarked, "This is a serious charge for one public office to make against another. . . . It is without foundation . . . and scurrilous."[11]

Regardless of the Treasury or their state of constitutional development, all colonies were advantageously positioned when it came to paying for actual hostilities. Wars were not infrequent along the imperial borders, and the initial expenses were almost always paid by the local governor from the treasury chest, a fund of several hundred thousand pounds spread through the Empire for public services and emergencies.[12] Once the imperial monies had been expended, the British Treasury usually enjoyed but small success in recouping its monetary advances.

Sierra Leone, for instance, was singularly reluctant to pay the expenses of military operations conducted in the colony during the years 1898 and 1899. The total sum advanced exceeded £45,000, and the colony was expected to pay an initial installment of £10,000 followed by annual payment of £5,000 until the debt was discharged. At the end of 1900, the War Office wrote the Treasury: "It will be seen . . . that no remittance can at present be expected, even in respect of the first installment. I am to add that it is not clear why additional expenditure has been incurred on other services within the colony."[13] Despite the absence of strong representative institutions, Sierra Leone was able to resist War Office pressure to contribute a yearly sum toward its own defense, even with an annual budgetary surplus of £20,000. As an indication of the difficulties Whitehall encountered with even the least redoubtable of colonies, it is to be noted that Sierra Leone did not disgorge any monies until 1905, and then only two-thirds of the sum demanded.[14]

At another level, and as a surprise to some, the cooperation of Sir George Goldie and the Royal Niger Company was hard to enlist. Salisbury complained that "the company's troops will take their orders from him [Goldie] and not from us . . . . What we want is not his assistance but his men to act as Queen's troops and take their orders like any other . . . ."[15] To make matters worse, Goldie assumed that it was the British government's responsibility to protect the company's territory. Lord Sanderson, at the Foreign Office, wrote, "I do not know where Goldie finds his doctrine that the Charter implies that Her Majesty's government will undertake to defend the Company's territory against all European powers."[16]

Even the smallest victory seemed hard to gain. During the 1862 war in Gambia, the Treasury wrote the Colonial Office: "Milords are of opinion that no sufficient case has been made for our relieving

the Government of Gambia from colonial expenses incurred in connection with the war against the king of Badiboo."[17] The fine of
£2,400 which had been imposed on the offending monarch would
have effectively paid for the war, but the governor had already
remitted three-fourths of the mulct when the king signed a treaty
guaranteeing free trade within his territory. In this case the Treasury
eventually recouped its losses, but not quickly or easily.[18]

But "success" was the exception rather than the rule. Thus, despite protest, the British taxpayer bore the entire £900,000 cost of
the Ashanti War of 1873–4. Again, in 1878, Sir Michael Hicks-Beach,
the Secretary of State for the colonies, wrote Sir Bartle Frere in South
Africa:

> There is . . . one reason in favour of keeping the peace to which
> I do not think I have much adverted and that is the question of
> cost . . . . We shall make Natal bear some of the cost already in-
> curred on account of Zulu affairs and if there is a war, she must
> bear more. I hope you will impress this clearly on the people
> there at once.[19]

Nevertheless, the Zulu War broke out in 1879, and, as a temporary
expedient, the expenses were defrayed by the British government.
Peace came, but not repayment. Only one-fourth of the £1,000,000
cost of the hostilities was ever squeezed from a reluctant Natal. Sir
Garnett Wolseley in frustration wrote to Hicks-Beach:

> This little puffed up council has command of the purse strings
> as fully as the House of Commons has at home, and its members
> are more puffed up with an idea of importance even than your
> English country member is . . . . If you want any money from them
> for imperial purposes, you can only get it as a bargain by giving
> them something in return . . . .[20]

Similarly, the Treasury was never able to gain full recompense
from Cape Colony for its share of the £1,750,000 cost of the Ninth
Frontier or Border War.[21] The governor, Sir Bartle Frere, had anticipated difficulty. He urged the Colonial Office merely to send him
a dispatch containing the amount due, and the monies would then
be forthcoming. He only cautioned Whitehall that, "in doing this,
please remember how very sensitive colonists are and have the dispatch worded as little as possible in the imperative mood . . . ."[22]
But London was clearly not sympathetic enough. Six months later
the governor wrote, " . . . the colonists here are incensed at the want
of appreciation of the efforts they have made . . . to provide for their
own defence . . . ."[23] As late as January 1882, the Treasury was still
trying to collect some portion of the debt, but the lowered demand

of £216,363 was still considered excessive by the colonists. As a consequence the Treasury, in defeat, wrote the Colonial Office: "My Lords will consent to accept £150,000 in full discharge of the debt. . . ."[24]

When the Cape ceased to make its £10,000 annual contribution toward the upkeep of the imperial garrison in the colony, the Treasury could only reserve the right to reopen the subject and lament, "My Lords cannot, however leave unnoticed the implication . . . that a colony should not be called upon to contribute towards the cost of a force maintained as an imperial garrison within its territory, with this opinion Milords cannot agree."[25] Even a colony as insignificant as Bermuda was able to refuse successfully a Treasury request for a military contribution.[26]

The total cost of the Boer War to the imperial exchequer came to £217,166,000. Most was paid by the British taxpayer, but, for years thereafter, the colonies and the home country continued to wrangle over the apportionment of expenses. In 1908 the Treasury claimed that the Cape still owed His Majesty's government £182,978.12.4 for the refund of war-related customs duties; but again it found itself essentially weaponless and finally surrendered. "With regard to the outstanding balance . . . due from the Cape Government in respect of supplies," the guardians of the public purse tiredly wrote the Colonial Office, "my Lords do not propose to press for further payment of this sum."[27] As Robert Lowe (later Lord Sherbrooke), Gladstone's first Chancellor of the Exchequer, wrote, "Instead of taxing them as our forefathers claimed to do, we, in the matter of this military expenditure, permit them in a great degree to tax us . . . ."[28]

While it might be argued that the Anglo-Boer War was of sufficient magnitude to be judged an imperial responsibility, no such justification can be found in the case of New Zealand at the time of the Maori War or in that of Canada under threat of internal strife prompted by Louis Reals's uprising on the Red River. New Zealand, at least, spent more on defense than any other self-governing colony; however, while the colonists there happily accepted British support in the Maori Wars, they ended hostilities as soon as the aid was withdrawn. As Lord Lyttelton, the colonial reformer, wrote to his brother-in-law Gladstone: " . . . The colonists have been so long carried in nurses arms they cannot stand on their own feet. My belief is that this war against some 2,000 aborigines has cost John Bull the best part of £3,000,000. There's a perfect caricature of political relations . . . ."[29]

The British tried for years without success to collect some repayment of the funds they had spent to put down the Red River rebellion. And in 1863 with an American army poised on their border, the best response the Canadians could muster to the British appeal for support was the assertion that "the best defense for Canada is no defense at all."[30] At that time the British were spending almost £900,000 per year on Canadian defense, a level that was maintained until 1868.[31] Nor were those attitudes tempered by the passage of time, as the immediate pre-World War I period will attest.

Not only did the self-governing colonies refuse to pay for their own defense, but they also importuned the British government to underwrite military operations designed solely to expand the Empire in directions that the colonists thought profitable. In the 1880s, for example, the Australians were interested in increasing their sphere of influence in the South Pacific. Lord Derby, in discussing the Australian attitudes, invoked a comparison to the Monroe Doctrine. " . . . but there is one essential difference," he wrote Gladstone, "the colonists expect us to do their fighting for them." More generally he felt: " . . . colonists are always willing to help us and stand by us provided we will pay all the money and take all the risks."[32]

Whitehall was not, however, totally without recourse. It somehow forced the Straits Settlements to bear all costs of the Perak War of 1875, and British troops were in time recalled from most of the self-governing colonies. The "withdrawal of the legions," initiated in New Zealand in the 1860s, culminated in 1871 when the last British troops marched out of the Quebec Citadel, while the band played "Good-bye, Sweetheart" and "Auld Lang Syne."[33]

The withdrawal, however, did not imply that British forces no longer continued to serve in imperial fortresses or that, from time to time, they did not appear in beleaguered parts of the self-governing Empire. Moreover, even withdrawal was not costless. The support of the white settlers was important, and ways had to be found to sweeten an otherwise bitter pill. Thus, at the same time as British troops were leaving the some 250,000 settlers in New Zealand to face the Maoris alone (although there were thought to be many more, the census of 1858 placed their number at 56,000 and that of 1896 at 35,000), Edward Cardwell, Secretary of State for the Colonies, urged Parliament to grant the colony an imperially guaranteed loan of £1,000,000.[34]

Attempts to shift the defense burden continued, and financial pressure was sometimes employed to encourage the recalcitrant. In 1880, for example, the Treasury wrote the Colonial Office that it was its understanding that Lord Kimberley, the Secretary of State for the Colonies, had authorized Natal to raise a loan only on condition that it recognized its pecuniary responsibilities regarding the Zulu War.[35]

Natal got the loan, but the manner in which the colony recognized its responsibilities may not have been what Kimberley had in mind.

In general, the stronger the representative institutions of a colony, the better it was able to resist the Treasury; but a colony as small and basically insignificant as Mauritius was, like Bermuda, able to reduce, if not totally repulse, the demand for a military contribution. In 1891 the Legislative Council voted only £20,000 of the £25,000 demanded by Whitehall. Impotent, the Treasury informed the Colonial Office that "Her Majesty's Government remonstrated vainly."[36]

One thing is certain: In case of doubt, the imperial authorities (that is, the British) paid. Discussing the impending assumption of control over the Transvaal in 1878, Sir Garnett Wolseley wrote:

> . . . we must make up our mind to rule over a country in which at present the majority and for a long time hereafter a large proportion of the people, are and will be discontented . . . to enable us to hold our own we must be prepared to maintain a large garrison of British troops here, the expense of which must be defrayed by the Imperial exchequer.[37]

To which Sir Michael Hicks-Beach roared in frustration, "Now I confess this seems to be a position that can hardly be maintained. I feel pretty confident that if the next general election placed the Liberal party in power, they would not maintain it . . . ."[38]

In many ways, Great Britain seemed a helpless giant as it faced its self-confident and often arrogant offspring. When Queensland threatened to intervene in the affairs of New Guinea, Lord Selborne, in writing to Gladstone, expressed himself as strongly opposed to any annexation: " . . . I am, at present, unable to conceive of any necessity, or justification, for taking the whole of this immense country that can be made and I should consider such an act impolitic in a very high degree, and also morally unjustifiable . . . ." But his Lordship conceded that "if New Guinea must come under the British flag, colonial sovereignty would be unacceptable and the British would have to act themselves."[39] Three years later, Edward Stanhope at the Foreign Office wrote Randolph Churchill:

> I am sorry to have to trouble you about New Guinea . . . I am afraid that the English Government is so far committed that it will be already compelled to make a considerable Imperial contribution . . . toward starting New Guinea. I hate . . . [this] as much as you . . . but the obligations of this country will force it upon us.[40]

Fiji too came under British jurisdiction, largely as a consequence of Australasian pressure. Yet, when Lord Carnarvon had the temerity to ask for a financial contribution from Australia and New Zealand to help defray the costs, the request was unhesitatingly rejected. Lord Normanby, the Governor of New Zealand, wrote Carnarvon reflecting the view of his prime minister, Julius Vogel:

> He believes that underlying the replies of all the colonies there have been two feelings: first, that the Mother Country was drifting into an entirely new colonial, or rather anti-colonial policy, that in times past she did not hesitate to incur colonial expenditures, that assuming possession of Fiji was analogous to many previous cases; that to ask contributions from the colonies was a novel proceeding connected only with the presumed policy of casting off the colonies, and that to acquiesce in it would argue an acceptance by the colonies of the new position it was desired to assign to them.[41]

In 1885, Derby wrote Gladstone about the designs of Natal on Zululand: "All the world waits for us to take Zululand, only because it is next door . . . . This passion for annexation and consequent contempt for the economy is not more to my taste than yours . . . ."[42] But the world's perception was correct and Zululand was annexed.

Whatever controversy prevailed over the appropriate role for the self-governing and dependent colonies, most critics of Empire smiled on India, though some with more insight continued to question its contribution to the public weal. It was pointed out that India did not draw directly on the British exchequer, and the expenses not only of the Indian army but of British regiments stationed on the subcontinent were drawn from the Indian revenues. Indian regiments were also used in hostilities conducted beyond the bounds of the subcontinent in campaigns that were clearly imperial rather than purely Indian responsibilities. Indian troops served in Persia, 1856–7, twice in China, 1857–60, and during the Boxer Rebellion of 1900, where they shared in the relief of Peking. They participated in the Abyssinian campaign of 1864, the Afghan War of 1878–80, the operations in Egypt during 1882–5, and they fought in East and Central Africa in the years 1897–8. Further service in Africa occurred during the Anglo-Boer War and in the East African and Somaliland campaigns of 1902–4. The Indian army mounted the invasion of Tibet in 1903–4, and during World War I, India provided purportedly the largest volunteer army in history in aid of the Allied cause – notably in Mesopotamia and on the Western Front.

When the Indian army was used in imperial wars, the British exchequer at times defrayed the costs. But this was not always the case. India bore both the ordinary and extraordinary costs of the Persian campaign; and the heavy expense of the second Afghan War, despite its imperial implications, fell exclusively on the Indian budget. More surprisingly, in the Abyssinian campaign of 1864, the pay of troops and the charges for vessels employed in the expedition "which would have been charged under the Revenues of India if such troops or vessels had remained in that Country or Seas adjacent," Parliament declared, "shall continue to be so charged . . . ."[43]

To a succession of British viceroys and liberal politicians the evidence was incontrovertible. London, they argued, had successfully transferred a significant portion of the home defense burden to the Indians. Lawrence's response to the 1864 decision was one of outrage, and nothing that occurred later changed his mind.[44] A few years later he argued:

> India is . . . required to pay all the expenses of every British soldier required in India, and even to supply a sum which will cover the cost of keeping up this force; and yet when a portion of these troops leaves the country, they are still charged to India.[45]

Furthermore, he pointed out:

> India is treated differently from the colonies. No one would think of asking any of the latter to pay a portion of the expenses of Afghanistan, no statesman would charge Canada or Australia . . . .[46]

It was the start of a debate that was to span the rest of the century. An attempt by Parliament to saddle India with the imperial costs of the Egyptian campaign prompted Lord Ripon to vent his spleen:

> I think if you will try to realise what the condition of a human being must be who has to live on £2–14–0 a year, you will not be surprised that I feel it my bounden duty to resist to the utmost of my power the imposition of any fresh burden upon him on account of the objects in which he is not directly interested.[47]

To these men the case was clear. India was a poor country and it was being asked to subsidize imperial defense out of all proportion to its position. Not only was it being forced to bear a substantial portion of the costs that should have fallen on the other parts of the Empire, but it was being asked to shoulder a portion of the British burden as well. India paid the direct costs of both Indian and British troops in India, as well as some fraction of the costs of Indian troops used in largely imperial adventures. The subcontinent thus supported a military reserve for the entire British Empire. A popular piece of contemporary doggerel seemed to support the government of India's view:

> We don't want to fight
> But by Jingo if we do
> We'll stay at home and mind the store
> And leave it to the mild Hindoo

Nevertheless, there were Britons who thought the evidence less than conclusive; and, as the quantitative evidence indicates, they were correct. Gladstone, for example, failed to see India as a great asset to imperial defense:

> I am one of those who think that to the actual, as distinguished from the reputed, strength of the empire, India adds nothing. She immensely adds to the responsibilities of Government and I am rather moving toward the belief that by our army arrangements we [at home] have made her . . . [the basis for expenditures] which might have been avoided.[48]

And even Kimberley averred: "But for India, I feel certain that no Egyptian expedition would ever have taken place . . . ."[49] The rulers of India, in the East and in London, continued to press for reductions in the "unjust" Indian military contribution. However, as Lord George Hamilton, the Secretary of State for India, recognized: " . . . I am not unlikely for the future to find myself in a minority of one in the Cabinet as regards India's contribution."[50]

II. Attempts at cooperation through consultation

The increasing power of the continental European states combined with periodic war scares lent urgency to the government's attempts to gain greater monetary contributions from all the constituent parts of the Empire. The possibility of war with Russia in 1878 resulted in the appointment of a Royal Commission under the chairmanship of Lord Carnarvon "to enquire into the defence of British possessions and commerce abroad." Six years later, an interdepartmental committee, soon to be known as the Colonial Defence Committee, was created and served until it was superseded by the more broadly based Imperial Defence Committee.

Queen Victoria's Golden Jubilee was the occasion for the calling of the first of the Colonial (later Imperial) Conferences that were to become a regular consultative mechanism for the British community. Defense and particularly the naval situation in Australasian waters was high on the agenda of the first conference. The discussions were long and on the whole barren. The Australasian colonies, and for that matter, all the self-governing parts of the British Empire were reluctant to contribute to a military establishment over which they had no control. Finally an agreement was reached. The Australian squadron of the Royal Navy would be increased by the addition of five fast cruisers and two torpedo gunboats to protect "the floating trade in Australian waters."[51]

The decision, however, was not a complete triumph for British diplomacy. Even though two of the cruisers and one of the torpedo boats were to be held in reserve, the colonies refused to fund the enterprise in its entirety. The imperial government agreed to advance £850,000 toward the initial costs of the vessels and to pay the capital expenses of commissioning the reserve squadron in time of war. The colonies were to see to general maintenance and pay interest on the capital cost up to a limit of £35,000 annually. The naval agreement was one of the few concrete achievements of the conference and it appears that the Australasian colonies had achieved a remarkably good bargain. For a very modest price they were guaranteed that these ships would remain in the vicinity of Australia both in times of peace and war; and, in addition, the British also agreed to keep two British warships in New Zealand waters on all occasions.

A decade later, the conference once more devoted much of its energy to imperial defense. The Australian colonies and New Zealand undertook to raise £226,000 a year toward the maintenance of a Royal Navy squadron in the Pacific; and that contribution was later increased to £240,000.[52] Although the actual cost was £670,000, Australia was far from satisfied with the new arrangement. Alfred Deaken, the Prime Minister, later wrote:

> While fully recognising the paramount importance of 'unity of control' for all the naval forces of the Empire, the people regard the present contribution of £200,000 to the cost of the Imperial Navy as being somewhat in the nature of a tribute, and it is therefore desirable, if possible, to find some means by which Australia can assist the Admiralty in the naval defence of the Empire without offence to the constitutional doctrine that the Government levies taxation and should be responsible for the expenditures and management.[53]

Outside of Australasia, the conference proved even less productive from the British point of view. The other colonies offered no contributions during the nineteenth century, but they made some small concessions in the twentieth. In 1902, Newfoundland agreed to pay a capital sum of £1,800 plus £3,000 a year for inaugurating and maintaining a branch of the Royal Naval Reserve. Cape Colony pledged the price of a battleship but later commuted this undertaking into a yearly subsidy of £50,000, and Natal agreed to contribute £35,000 annually.[54] The cost of the South African squadron was, however, £1,155,454 per year and £2,104,076 out of the Naval Works Loan Account had been spent on harbor works at Simonstown.[55] All in all, colonial contributions toward imperial defense continued to be very small. As Sir William Jervois, who during his years of service was governor of both South Australia and New Zealand, wrote to the Colonial Office,

> It is with these governments as with popular governments else-where; if war appears likely they are for the time being very energetic, but as the probability of hostility wanes, their ardour decreases . . . they do not much care to expend money on objects from which they derive no popularity.[56]

Lord Minto, the former Governor-General of Canada, wrote Sir Wilfrid Laurier asking for Canadian assistance in the impending war in South Africa to which Laurier stonily replied:

> . . . the present case does not seem to be one, in which England if there is war, ought to ask us, or even expect us to take part, nor do I believe that it would add to the strength of the imperial sentiment to assent at this juncture that the colonies should as-sume the burden of military expenditures.[57]

It was the old story repeated again. British politicians were harsh in their judgment of the senior Dominion. " . . . Canada," Chamberlain wrote, "claims to be part of the Empire and shares in all its privileges . . . . She asks for control of Imperial negotiations when her interests are concerned, full preference in Imperial contracts, and for special consideration in Imperial negotiation. On the other hand, she repudiates her share of Imperial defence . . . ."[58] Hicks-Beach found it "especially intolerable that Canada, which calls herself a nation, should do absolutely nothing to defend her coast."[59] In writing to Salisbury he took his reasoning one step further. "I think both Canada and Australia should be warned that in the event of our being engaged in a naval war, our navy will have other things to do than provide for their defence."[60] But the rhetoric was all so much empty bluster.

The conference of 1907 built on the limited progress achieved at preceding gatherings. As a consequence of the general sense of alarm the British government conveyed to the Dominion leaders, a plan for an expanded Pacific fleet was formulated. The new fleet was to consist of three squadrons – East Indies, Australia, and China. Each would include one battle cruiser, three light cruisers, six destroyers, and three submarines. The total capital expenditure was estimated at more than £11 million. Australia agreed to maintain its squadron and to underwrite most of the cost of the battle cruiser. New Zealand would finance the battle cruiser for the China squadron and would raise its annual maintenance contribution from £40,000 to £100,000. In 1910, the battle cruisers *Australia* and *New Zealand* and two of the light cruisers for the Australian squadron were laid down in Britain. It was agreed that dominion warships should remain under the control of their respective governments in peacetime, but would be used at the discretion of the British Admiralty during war. Canada, on the other hand, limited itself to pointing to its Fisheries Protection Service. That service, the Canadian government argued, cost £50,000 per annum, maintained an armed boat on the Great Lakes, and would soon place one in service on the Pacific coast and all at no cost to the British taxpayer![61] In 1906, Canada did, however, assume responsibility for Halifax at an annual cost of £31,600 and three years later did the same for Esquimalt at a cost of an additional £27,300 per annum.[62]

At the Imperial Conference of 1911, Sir Edward Grey addressed the assembled prime ministers and informed them war was imminent. It had little effect on the self-governing recalcitrants. On the other hand, the Federated Malay States presented a capital ship, the H.M.S. *Malaya*, to the Royal Navy in 1912.[63]

Gaining voluntary contributions from the Dominions proved almost impossible; extracting them from the dependent colonies was, the Federated Malay States aside, only marginally easier. In the years before 1895, the British government attempted to conclude agreements with each dependent colony covering its and the colonies' contributions to the cost of land defenses. The negotiations were an unedifying process filled with recriminations, petty accounting controversies, and financial bickering. How much could a colony afford to pay? What could be excluded from the calculation of the revenue "defense base"? What was the proper rate of exchange? Who had responsibility to underwrite repairs of military capital? At the end of the century, a policy setting contributions at a flat percentage of gross revenue replaced the negotiation procedure. The figure for the Straits and Hong Kong was 17.5 percent (later raised to 20); for Ceylon, 7.5 percent (raised to 9.5); and for Mauritius, 5 percent.[64] In the previous decade, the Straits had actually contributed 19 percent of its gross revenue toward defense; Hong Kong, 15; Ceylon, 6; and Mauritius, 3 percent.[65]

Harold Cox, in a House of Commons debate on February 15, 1907, placed the military expenses of the United Kingdom at £66,000,000 and those of the colonies at £887,000. Figures quoted by the Treasury in 1912 indicated that in terms of actual cash, the Straits contributed £190,000; Hong Kong, £118,000; Ceylon, £138,000; and Mauritius, £25,000. These four colonies, plus Egypt (£150,000), provided £471,000 of a total Empire defense contribution of £621,000.[66] As for the other dependent colonies, no orderly process seemed ever to have been devised, and the vagaries of constitutional development, income, and administrative policy produced a very diffuse pattern of contributions. Thus, at the beginning of the century, the garrison of Jamaica cost £200,000 a year, but the colony contributed nothing!

III. Defense expenditure patterns

How did diplomatic and political policy translate into expenditures (see Table 5.1)? The data indicate that in the late nineteenth and early twentieth centuries, Great Britain maintained the highest levels of per capita defense expenditures in the world. The fifty-three-year average of £1.14 reflects levels that rose from £.76 in the 1860s to £1.56 in the last pre-war decade. The average for the first thirteen years of the present century stood at £2.04. By comparison, the German average per capita figure was £.77 and the French £.85. Defense represented 37 percent of total home expenditures, while the figure for the rest of the developed world was under 30.

That Britain itself disproportionately supported the defense of the Empire was clear to many in Parliament and Whitehall, but even the initiated were unaware of the dimensions of the defense subsidy. The government of India (and hence the Indian taxpayer) underwrote the direct costs of military expenditures actually incurred on the subcontinent and, in addition, contributed armies, in part supported by these same Indian revenues, to the defense of the Empire as a whole. This evidence might seem to indicate that from the point of view of defense India was totally self-supporting, and indeed it came closer to achieving this – from the point of view of the Treasury and the British taxpayer – desirable state than any other colony. It is, however, important to emphasize that even in the case of India, local contributions fell short of what may be assumed to have been the "true" costs of Indian defense. Indian defense expenditures were significantly less than those of comparable independent nations – although higher than the Princely States – and the gap was growing. Karl Marx was aware of the problem. He wrote:

TABLE 5.1

DEFENSE EXPENDITURES

(Railroads Excluded)

	United Kingdom	Responsible Government	Dependent Colonies	India	Princely States	Special Princely States*	Foreign Developed	Foreign Underdeveloped
			PANEL A:	COLONY WEIGHTED £'s PER CAPITA				
1860-64	0.76	.02	.02	.13	.01	.02	.35	.26
1865-69	0.72	.07	.03	.13	.01	.03	.32	.26
1870-74	0.61	.10	.03	.11	.03	.05	.30	.19
1875-79	0.69	.08	.02	.11	.02	.03	.27	.17
1880-84	0.74	.12	.02	.13	.04	.04	.32	.24
1885-89	1.00	.14	.01	.08	.02	.02	.44	.26
1890-94	0.95	.13	.02	.06	.02	.03	.43	.19
1895-99	1.27	.14	.02	.07	.02	.03	.52	.19
1900-04	2.78	.21	.03	.07	.02	.03	.54	.16
1905-09	1.59	.13	.03	.08	.02	.02	.58	.23
1910-12	1.56	.18	.03	.07	.02	.02	.61	.26
AVG(d)	1.14	.12	.02	.10	.02	.03	.42	.22
			PANEL A:	COLONY WEIGHTED PERCENTAGES OF BUDGET				
1860-64	36.4	1.2	1.9	39.5	6.6	15.4	35.1	40.1
1865-69	35.5	2.6	2.8	35.2	5.5	17.7	30.0	36.1
1970-74	32.7	4.0	2.9	27.8	9.8	19.9	30.1	29.6
1975-79	33.0	4.0	1.9	27.4	8.9	15.4	28.4	30.4
1880-84	30.9	3.9	1.7	31.3	11.4	16.2	27.1	26.4
1885-89	35.2	3.9	1.0	32.9	5.7	9.1	27.0	28.5
1890-94	33.5	3.3	1.0	34.3	6.3	11.4	25.1	26.6
1895-99	36.3	2.9	3.7	33.8	6.0	9.0	25.2	23.7
1900-04	54.5	3.4	5.7	31.2	6.0	10.9	28.4	24.5
1905-09	41.1	3.9	4.9	33.4	5.1	7.6	27.1	23.5
1910-12	37.8	3.6	3.7	30.3	4.8	6.9	28.5	23.9
AVG(d)	37.0	3.3	2.8	32.5	7.0	12.9	28.4	28.7
			PANEL B:	POPULATION WEIGHTED £'s PER CAPITA				
1860-64	.76	.02	.02	.13	.02	.02	.43	.14
1865-69	.72	.06	.05	.13	.01	.03	.41	.20
1870-74	.61	.08	.05	.11	.01	.02	.34	.12
1875-79	.69	.07	.03	.11	.01	.02	.27	.13
1880-84	.74	.11	.03	.13	.04	.04	.28	.14
1885-89	1.00	.15	.02	.08	.04	.04	.40	.20
1890-94	.95	.13	.04	.06	.04	.04	.46	.18
1895-99	1.27	.16	.05	.07	.04	.04	.59	.21
1900-04	2.78	.21	.05	.07	.03	.04	.63	.18
1905-09	1.59	.15	.04	.08	.03	.03	.71	.27
1910-12	1.56	.20	.03	.07	.02	.03	.59	.24
AVG	1.14	.12	.04	.10	.03	.03	.46	.18
			PANEL B:	POPULATION WEIGHTED PERCENTAGES OF BUDGET				
1860-64	36.4	1.2	3.5	39.5	10.8	11.8	47.8	35.4
1865-69	35.5	3.4	7.2	35.2	8.0	14.3	37.4	41.3
1970-74	32.7	4.2	7.3	27.8	8.7	15.0	34.3	29.1
1975-79	33.0	3.1	5.2	27.4	7.1	11.5	29.2	29.7
1880-84	30.9	3.6	4.5	31.3	14.4	17.1	25.3	32.5
1885-89	35.2	4.1	2.8	32.9	15.1	16.9	25.3	32.9
1890-94	33.5	3.6	4.3	34.3	13.8	15.4	26.6	34.0
1895-99	36.3	3.8	7.0	33.8	14.2	16.1	27.9	33.3
1900-04	54.5	4.7	10.1	31.2	12.3	14.1	32.4	25.6
1905-09	41.1	4.6	8.9	33.4	11.2	12.7	34.5	25.7
1910-12	37.8	5.6	6.5	30.3	9.6	11.1	27.8	28.8
AVG	37.0	3.7	6.1	32.5	11.5	14.3	31.8	31.7

*Defense and military contribution to Britain.

It is evident that individuals gain largely by the English connection with India, and of course their gain goes to increase the sum of national wealth. But against this a very large offset is made. The military and naval expenses paid out of the pocket of the people of England on Indian account ... and it may be doubted whether, on the whole, this dominion does not threaten to cost quite as much as it can ever be expected to come to.[67]

Indian expenditures in 1912 were only about half what they had been in 1860. Moreover, although by Empire standards Indian military expenditures were high (£.10 per capita average and about a third of total expenditures) and greater than those of the Princely States, they were slightly less than the average for the self-governing colonies. They were also very low, if the appropriate standard is the underdeveloped world, although the possible economies of scale rooted in India's vast population must be borne in mind. Indian defense expenditures were, over the last twenty-eight years of the study, about half of those of a typical underdeveloped nation. Among the list of twenty-five underdeveloped countries only four (Colombia, Tunisia, Costa Rica, and Liberia) spent less, and Tunisia was not exactly independent.

Of the colonies with responsible government, the average, while rising, amounted to only £.12 over the entire period, and even in the last decade, with World War I on the horizon, it was less than £.20. Overall, these colonies spent just less than 4 percent of their budgets on defense. In the developed countries the fifty-three-year average was about £.45 – a figure that rose from about £.40 in the first decade to close to £.60 in the last, and it represented about 30 percent of all expenditures both early and late. In the underdeveloped-foreign sector the comparable numbers were about £.20 and again about 30 percent; however, as a fraction of total expenditures their military commitment was declining. Of all the colonies with responsible government, only New Zealand spent at a rate even vaguely commensurate with its constitutional status. There the annual per capita average was £.28, less than that of the developed countries but more than that of the underdeveloped. The six Australian colonies averaged but £.12 (and the Commonwealth only £.11), those in South Africa £.10, Canada £.09, and Newfoundland less than £.01. The Australian propensity to spend at near modern rates on administration, capital improvement, business, and almost everything else, while depending in part on a willingness to tax and borrow, rested also on the colonies' ability to avoid committing resources to the military.

In the case of the dependent colonies the Australian story is repeated. Those colonies on average spent about £.03, a figure that represents at most 6 percent of their expenditures. Of the sixty-four such colonies, only thirteen spent more than £.05 and only six (Pehang, the Falkland Islands, the Straits Settlements, Hong Kong, Southern Rhodesia, and the Somali Coast Protectorate) more than £.15. A mere handful, seven, spent more than Siam (£.10) and only five expended as much as the "typical" underdeveloped country.

In fact, only about a third of the dependent colonies spent as much as the average of the three lowest amongst that group of countries.

It can be argued that the British maintained two military and naval establishments: one for home defense and a second for imperial protection. In Table 5.2, British military and naval expenditures are allocated between home and imperial defense.[68] The home estimates indicate levels of defense expenditure slightly higher than the average of all developed countries, but about equal to those of France and Germany. The second British military and naval establishment was designed to protect the Empire, and it cost somewhat less but still substantially more than a typical developed country spent.

Table 5.3 provides a measure of defense costs from the point of view of the British taxpayer. A shift of 'the defense burden to the Empire excluding India would have eased the tax load on the average Briton somewhat; but a policy that would have raised Indian military and naval expenditures to a level equivalent to that maintained by the average underdeveloped country would have placed the British taxpayer in a very favorable position indeed. He would have paid on average only one-third instead of almost three times as much as his peers in the developed sector. Nor did British success in recapturing a greater proportion of defense costs from the Empire improve with time. The data indicate that the "subsidy" to the Empire increased during the period under consideration. In the years 1900–12, the per capita British "subsidy" for both the colonies with and without responsible government was £.20, and it was £.07 for India. In the decade of the '60s the figures had been £.06, £.03, and £.63.

Although the precise prediction depends crucially on the assumed counterfactual, it can be conjectured that, in the absence of Empire, tax loads on the British taxpayer could have been reduced, or resources made available for more productive investment with no decline in the level of consumption. If, for example, all British possessions had assumed levels of defense expenditures equal to those borne by countries at similar stages of development, the tax burden on the average Briton could have been reduced by £1.04 a year, or a total amount equal to about 20 percent of savings. If Britain had possessed no Empire and had spent at the level of France and Germany on the military establishment, the savings would have been £.63 per capita per year or about 12 percent of savings.

While the British taxpayers paid, their colonial confreres prospered – at least those in the colonies of white settlement. It may be no coincidence that Canada, New Zealand, and Australia were among the "nations" that devoted the highest proportion of their incomes to education and social overhead investment.[69] For the dependent

TABLE 5.2

IMPERIAL DEFENSE EXPENDITURES, PER CAPITA FOR UNITED KINGDOM COLONIES, AND SELECTED FOREIGN COUNTRIES
1860-1912

Period	UK Total	UK[1] Home 1[2]	UK[1] Home 2[3]	France & Germany	Foreign Developed	Colonies w/ Responsible Government	UK[1] Imperial 1[2]	UK[1] Imperial 2[3]	Foreign Undeveloped	India	Dependent Colonies	Dependent Colonies (Including Police)
1860-69	.74	.30	.35	.39	.34	.05	.44	.39	.26	.13	.02	.14
1870-79	.65	.32	.34	.52	.29	.09	.33	.31	.18	.11	.03	.14
1880-89	.87	.41	.47	.58	.38	.13	.46	.40	.25	.10	.01	.14
1890-99	1.11	.49	.61	.80	.47	.14	.62	.50	.19	.06	.02	.18
1900-12	2.04	.86	1.06	.77	.57	.17	1.17	.98	.21	.07	.03	.14
1900-04	2.78	1.15	1.34	.79	.54	.21	1.63	1.54	.16	.07	.03	.15
1905-12	1.58	.70	.90	.76	.59	.15	.88	.68	.24	.08	.03	.14
1860-1912	1.14	.50	.60	.62	.42	.12	.64	.54	.22	.10	.02	.15

[1] Allocation between UK-Home and Imperial Expenditures: Army by troops on station / Navy by ships on station

[2] Mediterranean fleet included in Imperial expenditures

[3] Mediterranean fleet included in Home expenditures

TABLE 5.3

HYPOTHETICAL UNITED KINGDOM DEFENSE EXPENDITURES

(Assumes Colonies Spent Amounts Equal to Those Spent
by Similar Non-Empire Political Units)

Period	(1) Responsible Governments As Foreign Developed	(2) Dependent Governments As Foreign Undeveloped	(3) India As a Foreign Undeveloped	(4) (1)+(2)	(5) (1)+(2)+ (3)	(6) Foreign Developed	(7) Actual UK
PANEL A:	REDUCTIONS IN UK ANNUAL AVERAGE PER CAPITA EXPENDITURES (Constant £'s)						
1860-69	-.06	-.03	-.63	-.09	-.72		
1870-79	-.05	-.03	-.36	-.08	-.44		
1880-89	-.06	-.10	-.98	-.16	-1.14		
1890-99	-.10	-.10	-.97	-.20	-1.17		
1900-12	-.20	-.20	-.97	-.40	-1.37		
PANEL B:	NEW LEVELS OF UK ANNUAL AVERAGE PER CAPITA EXPENDITURES (Constant £'s)						
1860-69	.68	.71	.11	.65	.02	.34	.74
1870-79	.60	.62	.29	.57	.21	.29	.65
1880-89	.81	.77	-.11	.71	-.27	.38	.87
1890-99	1.01	1.01	.14	.91	-.06	.47	1.11
1900-12	1.84	1.84	1.07	1.64	.67	.57	2.04

Empire the benefits are more obscure. They contributed less than independent countries at similar stages of development, but it is not clear what the weight of their defense burden would have been had there been no expansionist European powers.

6   *British subsidies to the Empire: the nondefense component*

The subsidization of imperial defense was not the only way that the British government used resources supplied by the taxpayers to support colonial governments and, indirectly, the imperial enterprise in general.

I. Loans and interest

Government loans, underwritten by either formal or informal parliamentary guarantees, provided funds for the development of the Empire. A parliamentary loan guarantee was a useful policy tool since it did not directly involve the disbursement of tax revenues. It did, however, provide a significant subsidy: With a guarantee a colony could gain access to borrowed funds at substantially reduced interest rates (see Appendix 6.1). Most often these guarantees were made to help provide finance for a particular project that the Colonial Office felt was not a part of the regular governmental process. The British government, for example, considered making loans to Jamaica because of hurricane damage, to Barbados to counteract the threat of political disturbance, to Newfoundland to purchase French fishing rights, and to the Sudan for development of the cotton-growing industry.[1] Such loans were not normal and it was not only the Treasury that tended to object. In the case of the Barbados loan, for example, Northcote wrote:

> ...I feel I cannot encourage you in this matter. We must not make the P.W. [public works] loan fund the resource of everyone who is in distress, otherwise we shall soon be in trouble. There are many meritorious classes in England who are suffering from the complaint of a temporary impecuniosity, and whom it would be very tempting to assist by loans of public money at low interest, but where could we stop? I am sure that a loan to the Barbadians would be a very dangerous precedent .... [2]

Nor was Parliament always blind to the differential advantage afforded by imperial guarantees. Bonar Law, in opposing the Transvaal loan guarantee bill of 1907, averred that:

> ...it was generosity at the expense of other people, not only at the expense of Great Britain but of the self-governing colonies

166

which desired to borrow money but which had not the inestim-
able advantage of being the particular pet of His Majesty's
Government.[3]

In terms of magnitude, the second largest component of the imperial subsidy was almost certainly the savings in interest costs on
these guaranteed loans. In the late nineteenth century the British
capital market was the largest and most sophisticated in the world,
and most of the finance that passed through it was saved by British
subjects. Those savers reflected the characteristics of the market
itself. They were willing to finance gold mines in Africa, cattle
ranches in Colorado, and gasworks in Bombay at a time when even
Wall Street tycoons felt that government bonds and a few railroad
issues were the limits of prudence. The inclination to look to the far
corners of the earth for potentially profitable investments did not,
however, imply that the British investor thought that all securities
were alike. The evidence indicates that British savers demanded
substantial risk and uncertainty premiums before they were willing
to make their accumulations available to enterprises about which
they had some doubts. In the thirty years between 1882 and 1912,
for example, while British consols were yielding about 3 percent,
investors were regularly demanding four to five times that amount
from the governments of Argentina, Mexico, and Greece and even
more from some others.

Investors viewed the Empire in a different light. Intellectually it
might be difficult to conclude that Bombay bonds were safer than
those of New York City, or that British Honduras was substantially
different from independent Honduras, but the evidence shows that
British investors continually drew these distinctions. Upon occasion
they seem to have been based on faith alone, but at other times de
jure guarantees were certainly persuasive and de facto commitments
at least partially effective. Indian government bonds, for example,
were backed by the full faith and credit of the British government.
The official chronicle of the London Stock Exchange listed Indian
issues with "British Funds." On the other hand, the Colonial Office
or Treasury might have prevented a nonguaranteed issue by the
government of Barbados from going into default, but Winnipeg City
bonds were guaranteed by no one.

In general, the colonies of the dependent Empire were, as compared with their self-governing brethren, in a distinctly disadvan-
tageous position when it came to raising loans. The acceptance of
any direct aid voted by Parliament brought with it increased Treasury
scrutiny and control; and almost every possession consequently

found itself scrutinized by an agency whose propensity for extreme caution and conservatism all too often interfered with the successful conclusion of the complex and cumbersome process leading to a guaranteed loan.

While loans without official guarantees were sometimes floated by political units in the dependent Empire, it was not until the passage of the Crown Colonies Loan Act of 1899 and the Colonial Stock Act of 1900 that the dependent colonies gained almost free access to funds at highly subsidized rates. As an example of the immediate value of the loans act of 1899, the Treasury in a letter of August 21, 1899, was able to write the Colonial Office regarding the financial crisis in Jamaica: "It seems obvious from these figures, that if the Colonial Loans Bill had not been introduced, Jamaica could not, in its present circumstances, have obtained a loan on the open market."[4] As it was, given certain guarantees, the Treasury was prepared to countenance loans of £150,000, £110,000, and £88,000 at the low rate of 2.75 percent. A further loan of £750,000 (and a grant of £200,000) was provided in 1901 for earthquake relief.[5]

But despite the passage of the two acts, the Treasury continued to exercise considerable control over colonial borrowing; and, even after 1900, there are few instances where it permitted a colony to borrow any sum unless the object of the loan appeared productive enough to support both interest charges and eventual repayment. Even the satisfaction of these criteria did not always guarantee the Treasury's approval. In 1911, for instance, Lewis Harcourt, the Secretary of State for the Colonies, armed with several excellent East African projects (including the Thika Tramway and the Mombasa Waterworks), asked the Treasury for permission to raise a £250,000 loan. As he put it: "This also was declined at first, but after great insistence, the Secretary of the Treasury offered to give me £80,000 for any of the three projects, on condition that I did not mention the other two to the Treasury for at least two years to come."[6]

But these administrative policies had an effect on potential investors, and it was one of which the British government was not unaware. A 1901 letter from the Colonial Office to the Treasury discussed the subject in detail:

> The debts of the Crown Colonies . . . have been incurred with the full sanction of the Secretary of State, who not only controls the estimates and taxation of these colonies, but decides whether they shall borrow, to what extent, on what terms, and for what purpose, and it is this control which justifies the attitude of Her Majesty's Government in relation to the debts of the Crown Col-

onies, an attitude which has become marked and more publicly
recognised in recent years.[7]

The financial records of the dependent colonies were matters of
public record. Budgets were almost always in balance, and there
was little chance that funds raised to build lighthouses or waterworks
could be diverted to support military adventures or to pay administrative expenses. The reins of the Colonial Office and Treasury
were tight indeed. For the dependent colonies, occasional guarantees coupled with a history of prompt payments and an expectation
that those policies would be continued were sufficient to convince
the British investor that, even if colonial issues were not quite as
safe as consols, they were much closer to that ideal than the issues
of foreign governments in Asia or South America or, at times, even
across the Channel. Thus, the loans issued on behalf of the dependent colonies rose from a total of £7,414,730 in the decade 1890–
9 to £18,453,730 in the years 1900–9.[8]

The colonies with responsible government enjoyed greater independence from scrutiny than their dependent confreres, but through
the 1870s at least they continued to depend on imperial guarantees.
As the century progressed the guarantee became less important and
by the late 1870s, most of the self-governing colonies found that
they had sufficient credit to borrow on the open market without
direct British governmental support. Indirect assistance through parliamentary intercession was nonetheless still needed, and it came in
the form of the Colonial Stock Act of 1877. That act allowed colonies
to replace debentures chargeable to a particular source of revenue
with stock inscribed in London and thus easily traded on the London
Stock Exchange. Subsequently, the trustee status accorded most colonial issues made them even more marketable.

It may well have been that the recognition of continuing governmental scrutiny helped make the issues of the dependent colonies
attractive to investors; however, it is not so clear why those investors
maintained confidence in dominion issues. Yet the figures on indebtedness indicate they did. In 1890, for example, the total outstanding debt (in millions of pounds) for Australia was 143.4, for
Canada 58.7, for New Zealand 38.8, for the Cape 23.7, and for Natal
5.0. In that year in the dependent Empire, India owed 192.6 million,
the West Indies 2.8, Ceylon 2.5, and Mauritius .7.[9]

Julius Vogel, Prime Minister of New Zealand, discovered the joys
of painless growth through borrowing and launched that colony on
a public-works spree that was to last through most of the century.
There is seldom a shortage of policy makers willing to imitate suc-

cessful new technologies, and Vogel's spread rapidly across the Tasman Sea and somewhat more slowly into Canada and South Africa. Between 1870 and 1900 annual per capita borrowing rose from £30.6 to £65.5 in New Zealand and from £17.1 to £53.0 in Australia, and these figures do not include the issues of the local authorities. Of all the government issues, UK local, foreign, and Empire, included in a detailed study of selected years between 1885 and 1912, just less than £1 out of 7 (£127 million out of £944 million) went to Australia.

Given the number and size of these offerings it is surprising that British investors appear to have examined them with less jaundiced eyes than they used to examine the prospectus of an Argentine offering in support of the railroads or a Greek government loan based on the revenues of the tobacco monopoly. The British government certainly expressed doubt about the quality and quantity of those Empire issues. In 1875, for example, Northcote wrote: "Herbert has told me of Vogel's request for a guarantee to a £4,000,000 loan and I write one line of precaution, as I know of Vogel's character, to say that in my opinion the proposal is simply inadmissible . . . ."[10]

Despite these concerns, the colonies with responsible government borrowed on terms that, although perhaps not quite as favorable as those received by India and the dependent colonies, were still far below the rates charged even the most advanced nations.[11] The ability of these colonies to raise large blocks of capital at very low rates came as something of a surprise to the British government during the heady days of Vogel's spending and borrowing extravaganza when most officials were making dire predictions about the long-run outcome of this massive violation of fiscal orthodoxy. In 1875, for example, the then Secretary of State for the Colonies, Lord Carnarvon, wrote:

> I am not surprised that you are rather startled at the Treasury at the financial speed at which New Zealand is traveling. At the same time the crisis may not come yet - it may even be indefinitely postponed – and you have probably observed the last loan has been obtained by the Colony on very favorable terms . . . .[12]

Nor does the distance of a century make the explanation of the British investor's willingness to underwrite these activities any more apparent. One can never be certain what it was that motivated the investors to act as they did, but the explanation cannot lie in legal guarantees nor in effective Treasury control. The Treasury prevented the dependent colonies from diverting loan funds to unauthorized uses; but for the colonies with responsible government, that check was lacking even when the loans carried British guarantees. As Carnarvon observed:

> ... The point to which I am anxious to look is this: Parliament guarantees a loan for a certain purpose, and charges the Treasury with the duty of seeing that the money raised under the guarantee is applied to the purpose for which the guarantee was given. If it should, in whole or in part, be diverted to other purposes, Parliament should be justly angry with the Treasury. Some years ago, I think, Canada raised a loan under imperial guarantees for a railroad and proceeded to apply a portion to fortifications ... and there was a row about it in the House of Commons.[13]

A row, perhaps, but the guarantee was not rescinded. Two facts are certain. First, even in the absence of legal guarantees the colonies with responsible government were able to borrow and borrow heavily at rates only slightly above those available at home. Second, except for a single New Zealand Harbour Board Loan, no Empire issue appeared on the Council of Foreign Bondholders' list of bonds in default, from the formation of that organization in the early 1870s until the outbreak of World War I.

That the Empire received favorable treatment in the capital market has been well recognized. Thus far, however, there have been few attempts to determine the size of the imperial interest subsidy. How exactly did the system of guarantees, control, and investor faith affect the prices that India, the colonies, and the dominions had to pay? Each year, the *Stock Exchange Annual Yearbook* reported the new issues that had been added to the Stock Exchange's Official List, and these can provide some evidence on the question. In most but not all cases the initial report included information on the size of the issue, the maturity, and initial price.[14] The focus here is on those accepted new issues for which complete information is reported. Data were accumulated on all such issues during eighteen of the thirty-one years between 1882 and 1912.[15] In those years there were a total of 944 issues: 308 from the United Kingdom, 339 from the Empire, and 297 from the rest of the world. (Table 6.1 shows the distributions of the loans examined.)

To convert issue prices into yields, it is necessary to know the maturity of the loan in question. In the nineteenth century the term "maturity" was somewhat ambiguous. Some issues were, of course, for a specified period of time (five, twenty, or fifty years), and for those there is no confusion. For the majority, however, the creativity of the issuing agencies appears limitless. There were consols – never to mature; there were bonds that could be redeemed any time at

TABLE 6.1

DISTRIBUTION OF GOVERNMENT LOANS INCLUDED

Number of Loans

	Pre-1901			1901-1912			All Years		
	Country or Colony	Province, City or Local Authority	Total	Country or Colony	Province, City or Local Authority	Total	Country or Colony	Province, City or Local Authority	Total
United Kingdom	6	233	239	9	60	69	15	293	308
Responsible Governments	90	66	156	46	83	129	136	149	285
Dependent Colonies	23	3	26	9	0	9	32	3	35
India	8	0	8	7	4	11	15	4	19
Foreign Developed	45	12	57	33	24	57	78	36	114
Foreign Underdeveloped	88	20	108	45	30	75	133	50	183
TOTAL	260	334	594	149	201	350	409	535	944

the discretion of the borrower (sometimes with a minimum period, sometimes with a maximum, and sometimes with neither); there were issues with a set fraction redeemed each year by lottery; there were some with a fixed minimum and a fixed maximum maturity, but with the additional provision that a certain portion be redeemed by lottery in each intervening year. Nor is this list exhaustive; there were other permutations too numerous to mention. Because of this ambiguity, two sets of calculations, based on average and maximum maturities, are presented.[16]

Table 6.2 reports the results of a number of regressions designed to uncover the relation between the type of government issuing the security and its yield. While the exact specification changed from trial to trial, they were in general of the form:

$$\text{Yield} = a + b_1 \text{ (UK consol rate at time of issue)} + b_2 \text{ (amount of issue)} + b_3 \text{ (average maturity)} + b_4 \text{ (government type)} + b_5 \text{ (date)}$$

Government type is, of course, a dummy variable, and the base against which it is measured is the yield on the issues of UK local authorities.[17]

A comparison of the two panels of Table 6.2 suggests the importance of being a part of the Empire from the point of view of public borrowing. Taking all years together, the model explains only about 15 percent of the variation in yields when the data encompass all countries and colonies. When the focus is restricted to the Empire, the "explanatory" power of the model rises to over 60 percent. Moreover, the British consol rate made only a marginal contribution

TABLE 6.2A

REGRESSION RESULTS
YIELDS ON GOVERNMENT LOANS

(Railroad Loans Excluded)

	"A" All Years				ALL GOVERNMENTS "B" Pre-1900				"C" Post-1900			
	Maximum Maturity		Average Maturity		Maximum Maturity		Average Maturity		Maximum Maturity		Average Maturity	
Variables	P*	T**	P	T	P	T	P	T	P	T	P	T
Consol Rate	1.36	1.82	.48	.43	1.73	2.09	.76	.23	-.98	.25	-2.76	.65
Amount	-.00002	1.37	-.00008	3.12	-.00001	2.04	-.00007	2.77	-.00005	1.01	-.00010	1.69
Average Maturity	-.020	1.74	-.104	6.22	.00029	.06	-.114	5.74	-.053	1.84	-.096	3.04
Year	.002	.14	-.04	1.67	.017	.55	-.041	.33	.13	.69	.14	.69
Government:												
Responsible	1.14	1.03	2.66	1.61	.99	1.21	3.33	1.02	1.55	.79	2.26	1.06
Dependent	.85	.67	1.66	.88	.90	1.06	2.22	.65	1.19	.44	1.82	.62
India	.64	.45	2.80	1.32	.25	.26	4.03	1.03	1.12	.44	1.92	.69
Developed	2.04	1.83	6.32	3.79	2.37	2.87	9.43	2.85	1.97	1.00	3.74	1.76
Underdeveloped	4.26	3.91	5.25	3.23	4.24	5.21	5.96	1.83	4.53	2.35	4.85	2.31
Borrowing Unit:												
Country	-.39	.35	1.53	.93	-.31	.38	-2.54	.78	-.71	.36	-1.10	.52
Province	-.78	.62	1.72	.92	.03	.04	-2.74	.80	-2.37	.98	-1.68	.64
City	-.75	.52	2.70	1.55	-.28	.34	-3.95	1.18	-1.36	.65	-2.02	.90
r^2	.13		.15		.54		.23		.08		.10	

*Parameter Value
**"T" Value

TABLE 6.2B

REGRESSION RESULTS
YIELDS ON GOVERNMENT LOANS - EMPIRE ONLY

(Railroad Loans Excluded)

	"A" All Years				"B" Pre-1900				"C" Post-1900			
	Maximum Maturity		Average Maturity		Maximum Maturity		Average Maturity		Maximum Maturity		Average Maturity	
Variables	P*	T**	P	T	P	T	P	T	P	T	P	T
Consol Rate	1.17	12.09	1.15	11.83	1.29	3.70	1.32	3.69	.52	1.76	.61	3.74
Amount	-.00002	2.58	-.00002	2.28	-.00003	1.43	-.00002	.70	-.00002	1.98	-.00002	2.15
Average Maturity	-.0039	2.63	-.0046	3.09	-.0028	1.19	-.0040	1.63	-.0043	2.31	-.0047	2.58
Post-1900	-.162	4.14	-.166	4.22								
Government Type:												
Dependent	.052	.91	.043	.75	-.021	.29	-.024	.32	.149	1.61	.127	1.39
India	-.335	4.45	-.315	4.15	-.502	3.60	-.475	3.32	-.222	2.78	-.218	2.77
Government Level:												
Country	-.519	12.96	-.513	12.73	-.486	7.56	-.488	7.40	-.561	11.22	-.552	11.17
Province	-.407	6.02	-.402	5.90	-.426	4.57	-.417	4.35	-.347	3.78	-.339	3.74
Date					-.013	1.06	-.011	.85	.015	.88	.007	.45
r^2	.62		.61		.66		.64		.65		.65	

*Parameter Value
**"T" Value

to the explanation of the variation in the all-government yields, but it becomes a very powerful explanatory tool for Empire borrowing.[18]

Within the Empire, India consistently paid less for capital than either the dependent colonies or those with responsible government. Between the dependent colonies and those with responsible government there is little to choose, although it appears that in the years before 1901 the former may have paid slightly less and in the later years somewhat more.[19] Although the assumptions are relatively strong, these data make it possible to estimate the Empire interest subsidy; but, unfortunately, they do not provide a measure of the proportion of that subsidy that fell back onto the British taxpayer. The model used to estimate the Empire subsidy assumes two separate capital markets for government funds: one for "safe" United Kingdom securities and one for "unsafe" securities from elsewhere in the world (see Appendix 6.1). Under reasonable assumptions the transfer of Empire financial demand from the unsafe to the safe market should cause the rates in the former to fall and those in the latter to rise. If the colonies with responsible government are assumed to be comparable to the developed nations and those with dependent status similar to underdeveloped ones, the differences in the interest rates charged to Empire and non-Empire borrowers (responsible less-developed and dependent less-underdeveloped) should provide a minimum estimate of the interest gain accrued through Empire membership. Under certain, perhaps less defensible, assumptions the amount of that subsidy can be estimated by multiplying the interest gain by the quantity of funds borrowed.

The shift in demand from the unsafe to the safe market was not, however, without cost to the British whether they were taxpayers, consumers, or businesspeople. The new demand for funds caused the interest rate to rise and thus increased the costs of borrowing to the British central government and local authorities (to say nothing of domestic business firms); and it rationed certain projects out of the market. That increase and its effects are not the product of some twentieth-century economists' imagination; they were well recognized by contemporary observers. In the words of the foreign correspondent for the *New York Daily Tribune*:

> It is true that successive loans by the India Company in the London market would ... prevent ... the further fall in the rate of interest; but such a fall is exactly required for the revival of British industry and commerce. Any artificial check put upon the downward movement of the rate of discount is equivalent to an enhancement in the cost of production and the terms of credit, which in its present weak state, English trade feels itself unable to bear.

Hence the general distress of the announcement of the British loan.[20]

Since it is not possible to determine by how much the rate increased, it is very difficult to estimate the costs to Britain of that transfer.

What were the benefits to the Empire? There are data on the average maturity of Empire loans (thirty-four years for colonies with responsible government, thirty-one years for dependent colonies, and thirty years for India). The product of the annual interest subsidy and the average maturity is an estimate of the total savings to the residents of the Empire on government borrowing alone. Of course that total would be inflated by any reduction in private rates resulting from the transfer of government demand from the local to the London market.

In these calculations the regression parameters of the government variable were used as proxies for the differences between the levels of interest rates prevailing in each part of the world (Empire and foreign). In conformity with the usual practice, the colonies with responsible government were assumed to be similar to the developed countries, and interest differentials were estimated by subtracting the parameter value of the responsible government dummy variable from the value of the developed country dummy. India and the dependent colonies were deemed comparable to the countries in the underdeveloped world, and the price component of their subsidy was estimated by the appropriate subtractions. The figures on Empire borrowing are taken from the data used to support the study of financial flows. One observation: The use of average maturities and loan data, beginning in 1865 and ending in 1914, means that a part of the subsidy actually accrued after 1914 and that there is an unestimated portion of the subsidy in the early years.

No attempt has been made to include that portion of the subsidy that was accrued after 1915. For the earlier period, it was assumed that the level of governmental borrowing by the dependent colonies and those with responsible government was the same for the years 1850 to 1864 as it was for the five-year period 1865–9. While that assumption probably overstates the level of borrowing in that fifteen-year period, it certainly underestimates the level over the previous decade and a half (for that period it has been assumed that the level was zero). As to India, the average for 1865–9 was assumed to have prevailed in the years from 1858–64, and that assumption certainly underestimates Indian borrowing.

The figures in Table 6.3 indicate that across the entire Empire savings averaged about £.02 per capita per year; however, they were not evenly distributed.[21] The colonies with responsible government

TABLE 6.3

INTEREST SUBSIDY

(Railroad Loans Excluded)

	RESPONSIBLE GOVERNMENT			DEPENDENT COLONIES			INDIA		
	Total	Annual Average	Annual Per Capita	Total	Annual Average	Annual Per Capita	Total	Annual Average	Annual Per Capita
	(1,000s £'s)		(£'s)	(1,000s £'s)		(£'s)	(1,000s £'s)		(£'s)
1865-69	1,686	337	.06	591	118	.03	0	0	0
1870-74	2,226	445	.06	686	137	.03	185	37	.00
1875-79	3,960	792	.10	886	177	.03	3,333	667	.00
1880-84	6,420	2,284	.15	1,425	285	.02	5,810	1,162	.01
1885-89	9,221	2,844	.19	1,608	322	.02	8,410	1,682	.01
1890-94	10,807	2,161	.20	2,073	415	.02	11,168	2,234	.01
1895-99	11,503	2,301	.19	2,481	496	.02	13,661	2,732	.01
1900-04	12,224	2,445	.17	5,718	1,144	.03	14,896	2,979	.02
1905-09	13,048	2,610	.12	11,748	3,450	.07	14,539	2,908	.01
1909-15	14,728	2,946	.12	13,591	2,718	.05	17,459	3,492	.01
ALL YRS	85,823	1,716	.17	40,807	816	.04	89,461	1,789	.01

received the most (£.17), even though the amount of the subsidy per pound borrowed was not high. (If the basis for comparison had been foreign-underdeveloped rather than foreign-developed countries the savings would have been more than £.50.) The dependent colonies benefited to the extent of about £.04 a year, or approximately 5 percent of their tax bill. The explanation of the relatively small level of savings rests not with the price component of the subsidy (3.4 percent) but with the colonies' hesitancy to use the London market before the turn of the century. The Indian subsidy, although the largest of the three in terms of value, was distributed across a very large population, and savings amounted to only about £.01 per person per year. Even that figure, however, was the equivalent of about 6 percent of the annual tax bill. Moreover, the reader should bear in mind these are minimum estimates. All benefits from loans to railroads and short-term borrowing have been excluded. In addition the assumptions about debt in place implies that the total debt outstanding in India was zero in 1865, despite the fact that there were Indian loans floated between 1858 and 1865. All in all, it appears that, from this point of view, the imperial connection was quite remunerative, although it was certainly more profitable to be a member with voting privileges.

As to the other aspects of the interest subsidy, there are no estimates, only speculations. In the case of foreign borrowers, it appears that there must have been some gain. That there was an infinite amount of "risky" finance available at the market rate of interest, and that an increase in demand of £13.5 million a year (the level of actual Empire governmental borrowing) in that market – or even a half or a third that amount – would not have raised interest rates, are inconceivable.

In the case of the United Kingdom, loan rates must have been higher because of the addition of Empire demand, but it is impossible to tell how much so. To the extent that enterprise in Britain competed with foreign borrowers in the risky market, their gains from lower interest rates should be offset against the losses incurred by firms or government bodies borrowing at higher rates in the safe market. In the years from 1865 to 1914 almost two-thirds of safe loans were made to Empire borrowers. Still, the higher rates cannot be viewed as a total deadweight loss to the British. Some domestic projects were almost certainly "rationed out" by the higher rates, and to the extent that the net benefits from those projects are not all captured by the interest charges, there would have been some social loss. In addition, to the extent that the holders of British bonds lived outside the United Kingdom, the loss in interest charges was a loss to Britain. As for the bondholders domiciled in the United Kingdom, the effect was not a loss but a transfer. Taxpayers paid more, but that extra income was received by these bondholders. The best estimates indicate that the bulk of the tax bill was paid by the middle classes and the majority of the bonds were held by the upper classes. To the extent that the two groups – bondholders and taxpayers – differed, the costs of the interest subsidy were borne by one group but a fraction of those costs were received as income by another.

Interest payments can be viewed as the ghost of Christmas past. They are not a burden passed from one generation to another, but they do represent real claims that some members of society must pay to others. In a world where balanced budgets were the order of the day and the commitment to the gold standard made any long-term deviation from the position difficult, interest payments represented a real draw on present resources and limited the governments' expenditure options. In India, for example, the need to pay interest – even on loans made for such worthy purposes as famine relief – played a major role in dictating the functional profile of the budget.

Compared to the underdeveloped world the total amount of funds borrowed by the colonies of the dependent Empire was low (see Table 6.4). In foreign-underdeveloped countries, funds raised by loans were ofttimes used to support military adventures, to prevent civil revolution, or merely to cover administrative deficits. In the dependent Empire, the loans that were approved provided funds to build highways or railroads, repair hurricane destruction, put in gas, water, or sewage plants, or, perhaps, to underwrite immigra-

TABLE 6.4

GOVERNMENT EXPENDITURE: INTEREST PAYMENTS

(Railroads Excluded)

	UK National	UK Total	Responsible Government	Dependent Colonies	India	Princely States	Foreign Developed	Foreign Underdeveloped
	PANEL A: COLONY WEIGHTED (£'s Per Capita)							
1860-64	.77	--	.14	.01	.07	.00	.10	.06
1865-69	.74	.81	.30	.01	.08	.00	.14	.05
1870-74	.70	.86	.34	.01	.06	.00	.20	.10
1875-79	.71	.95	.41	.01	.04	.00	.22	.07
1880-84	.77	1.06	.50	.01	.04	.00	.26	.18
1885-89	.81	1.18	1.53	.01	.03	.00	.38	.18
1890-94	.72	1.12	2.50	.02	.02	.00	.37	.17
1895-99	.75	1.26	3.41	.01	.03	.00	.40	.17
1900-04	.67	1.28	3.30	.02	.02	.00	.32	.13
1905-09	.60	1.41	.47	.01	.02	.00	.32	.14
1910-12	.47	1.31	.56	.01	.02	.00	.28	.14
AVG(d)	.71	1.12	1.25	.01	.04	.00	.27	.11
	(Percentage of Budget)							
1860-64	37.1	--	6.6	0.8	19.9	0.0	13.5	8.4
1865-69	36.8	34.9	10.3	0.8	21.2	0.0	15.2	7.9
1870-74	37.5	31.1	10.4	0.7	14.6	0.0	22.1	16.3
1875-79	34.0	27.7	11.6	1.2	9.4	0.1	22.5	12.0
1880-84	32.2	26.6	11.7	1.2	11.0	0.6	20.7	14.7
1885-89	28.9	24.7	15.7	1.0	12.2	0.4	20.1	13.2
1890-94	25.7	22.4	23.1	1.1	12.4	0.4	20.0	14.0
1895-99	21.4	19.4	26.6	0.7	12.2	0.1	18.3	15.2
1900-04	13.7	14.5	21.9	1.0	7.6	0.5	16.0	14.3
1905-09	15.5	17.0	11.1	1.0	7.4	0.8	15.4	11.7
1910-12	11.6	15.3	10.7	1.1	8.2	0.3	12.9	12.2
AVG(d)	27.3	23.7	14.7	0.9	12.5	0.3	18.1	12.2
	PANEL B: POPULATION WEIGHTED (£'s Per Capita)							
1860-64	.77	--	.23	.02	.07	.00	.12	.03
1865-69	.74	.81	.26	.01	.08	.00	.19	.03
1870-74	.70	.86	.29	.01	.06	.00	.21	.04
1875-79	.71	.95	.38	.02	.04	.00	.24	.03
1880-84	.77	1.06	.44	.02	.04	.00	.27	.05
1885-89	.81	1.18	.62	.02	.03	.00	.38	.06
1890-94	.72	1.12	.85	.01	.02	.00	.37	.05
1895-99	.75	1.26	1.04	.01	.03	.00	.40	.08
1900-04	.67	1.28	.99	.01	.02	.00	.25	.12
1905-09	.60	1.41	.72	.01	.02	.00	.23	.09
1910-12	.47	1.31	.69	.02	.02	.00	.17	.08
AVG(d)	.71	1.12	.59	.01	.04	.00	.26	.06
	(Percentage of Budget)							
1860-64	37.1	--	14.2	3.1	19.9	0.0	13.6	7.5
1865-69	36.8	34.9	15.6	2.0	21.2	0.0	18.9	7.3
1870-74	37.5	31.1	15.6	1.7	14.6	0.0	21.6	9.3
1875-79	34.0	27.7	16.7	2.5	9.4	0.3	25.7	8.5
1880-84	32.2	26.6	14.0	2.4	11.0	1.2	23.9	12.3
1885-89	28.9	24.7	16.5	2.4	12.2	1.3	23.7	10.5
1890-94	25.7	22.4	23.4	1.2	12.4	1.6	20.9	10.2
1895-99	21.4	19.4	25.4	0.7	12.2	0.7	19.1	12.1
1900-04	13.7	14.5	22.1	2.7	7.6	1.2	13.0	16.5
1905-09	15.5	17.0	20.9	2.3	7.4	1.6	11.1	9.0
1910-12	11.6	15.3	19.4	3.3	8.2	0.9	8.3	6.9
AVG(d)	27.3	23.7	18.5	2.2	12.5	0.8	18.5	10.1

Dash (--) = No Data

tion. These activities were at times profitable in their own right, but whether that was true or not, they almost always raised the level of private profits for those businessmen who did not bear all the interest costs.

The United Kingdom was a heavy borrower, and while the level of interest payments declined somewhat, it averaged about £.71 per capita (25 percent of all expenditures). Among the developed countries, as borrowing became a habit, the level rose, but it averaged only slightly over £.25, a figure that represented only about a fifth of the total. In the Empire the colonies with responsible government paid heavily, but how heavily depends on the weight chosen. Using colony weights the figure is £1.25, but with population weights the figure falls to £.59 – lower than the United Kingdom but more than twice the foreign-developed sector. The average of the responsibly governed colonies was again biased upward by the island continent. Those six colonies on average paid £1.39, but when the Commonwealth was organized the figure fell to £.57. The New Zealand average was also high but, despite Julius Vogel, less than the United Kingdom figure. In South Africa, only the Cape engaged in any significant borrowing, and the average was a paltry £.15. On the North American continent, Canada averaged £.36 and Newfoundland £.14. While Australia clearly paid more than anyone else, Canada paid about 40 percent more than a typical developed country and New Zealand almost two and one-half times as much.

The self-governing colonies borrowed heavily and were subject to substantial debt charges. Government supervision meant that the dependent colonies did not and were not. If the standard is foreign-underdeveloped countries (at most £.11 per capita and 12 percent of budget), they can be said to have borrowed hardly at all. In the colonies without responsible government the average per capita interest payment was only £.01 per annum with a budget share of about 1 percent. Of the sixty-four dependent colonies, thirty-three spent no money at all on interest. In India the level was higher, and interest absorbed about 12 percent of the budget. However, the average was only £.04 per capita, less than the level prevailing in the underdeveloped countries. While both level and share were doubling in the latter countries, in India they were falling. They averaged £.07 and 20 percent in the 1860s, but by 1910 those figures had decreased to £.02 and 8 percent.

Britain has long had a history of dependence on the capital market, but in those parts of the Empire over which it exercised some substantial control, the Treasury remained firm in its resolve that they should not follow the home precedent. For better or worse and despite the subsidized rates, the burden of debt rested lightly. It seems possible to conclude that as far as public borrowing was concerned, being a British colony, whether self-governing or dependent, provided a privileged entree to the London capital market. In ad-

TABLE 6.5

GREAT BRITAIN
MISCELLANEOUS ADMINISTRATIVE SUBSIDIES

(1,000s of £'s)

	Total	Annual Average	Per Capita UK Subsidy Per Year
1880–84	645	129	.004
1885–89	839	168	.005
1890–94	3,169	6,341	.017
1895–99	1,760	352	.009
1900–04	6,545	1,309	.031
1905–09	5,998	1,200	.027
1910–14	6,703	1,341	.030
1880–1914	25,659	733	.018

Source: Richard M. Kesner, Economic Conditions
and Colonial Development, pp. 34–43.

dition, it involved a hidden subsidy paid in part by the British taxpayer. On the other hand, dependent colonies were constrained
from exercising that privilege too frequently.

II. Direct assistance

Parliament, with the usually grudging acquiescence and recommen-
dation of the Treasury, was prepared from time to time to come to
the financial assistance of British colonies and not require repayment
(see Table 6.5). A disbursement might be voted in support of the
budget of a colony whose resources were insufficient to support the
normal functions of government, or the vote might be specifically
directed toward the salary of the governor and his staff. Most frequently grants-in-aid were designed to attack specific problems: a
public works project, disaster relief, or native education, to cite three.

Often the Colonial Office saw the need for a grant-in-aid to a
colony but was opposed by the Treasury. In 1882, for instance,
Kimberley at the Colonial Office wrote Gladstone:

> I wish to make an appeal for mercy from the Treasury in the case
> of Malta. The Maltese complain bitterly (1) of the governor's sal-
> ary, (2) the expensive drainage works which they say are only
> required for the garrison and ought not be paid from local funds,
> (3) the drawbacks on stores for the troops . . . . It must I think be

a matter of interest to us that the Maltese should be well effected
by this country. The safety of the fortress in times of war would
be seriously endangered if they were hostile. I am sorry to say
there is amongst them a chronic and growing discontent.[22]

As a means of improving communication within an Empire in
which defense was a major concern, the British government, occasionally with the colonies playing a subordinate but financially supportive role, provided subsidies for shipping lines that carried the
mail and for all-British cable services. Shipping subsidies totaled
almost a million pounds annually as early as the 1860s. At that time,
close to £900,000 went to three lines: P and O, Royal Mail, and
Cunard.[23] A great expansion both in service and subsidy resulted
from the passage of the Imperial Penny Postage Act of 1899. The
law was designed to provide an increased volume of mail and better
imperial communication as a concomitant of lower postage rates,
and this indeed was the result. The implementation of the act, however, required increased government subsidies.[24]

The process of financing, to say nothing of constructing, trans-
oceanic cables was often tortuous. The great Pacific cable designed
to link Australia with Canada was first proposed at the Colonial
Conference of 1887, but negotiations leading to its construction were
not completed until 1900, and it did not come into operation until
1903. For much of the time the Treasury, concerned with limiting
British liability, constituted the chief obstacle. Finally, an acceptable
formula was agreed upon; Parliament would advance £2,000,000 to
a consortium consisting of Australia, New Zealand, and Canada.
Those Dominions pledged, in turn, to raise a loan on the open
market and to use the proceeds to repay the British government. It
was hoped that the revenues generated by the line would pay for
the sinking fund, interest, and operating costs. Any deficits or surpluses would be shared by the three contracting parties and Britain
itself on the basis of Australia 6, Canada 5, New Zealand 2, and
Britain 5.[25] The line opened in 1903, and the first year's operating
deficit of £87,500 was shared according to the agreed formula. The
same was true for the next several years; however, in time the cable
did become self-supporting. The total cost to Britain of this one
venture, including interest costs on capital during construction of
about £116,000 and an operating subsidy that had totaled £130,000
by 1914, was in excess of £250,000. The Pacific cable was not the
only such enterprise to receive an operating subsidy. In 1904, for
example, eight British companies serving the Empire received direct

support totaling £85,475. The largest award was £25,000 to the Pacific Cable Company and the smallest £3,500 to the Eastern and South African Telegraph Company.[26]

The total funds disbursed by the British government in direct support of the dependent colonies increased over the years. In 1879, the figure amounted to only £99,411, but by 1900 it was ten times that amount. Of this latter sum, £414,635 went to the Gold Coast, whose budget had fallen into deficit because of the colony's new responsibilities in its northern territories and hostilities against the Ashanti. In 1911, when the total had risen to £1,416,408, the largest single contribution was £369,111 to the Uganda Railway.[27] The construction of that railroad was begun in 1895 and completed in 1902. Construction costs constituted an imperial expense of £5,550,000. The line did not even begin to pay its running costs until 1906 and earnings certainly never covered expenditures. Between 1895 and 1914, the British taxpayers' contribution to the interest costs and sinking fund of the railroad amounted to an additional £3,351,000 (a figure not included in the estimate of miscellaneous administrative subsidies shown in Table 6.5), and of that total more than £2,000,000 were incurred after the line was completed!

The Uganda Railway was one of the most controversial undertakings ever sponsored by Whitehall.[28] It was apparently star-crossed from the first. The meter-gauge line, which ran from Mombasa to Kisumu on Lake Victoria, covered 587 miles and traversed a mountain escarpment 7,000-feet high. Built largely by Indian labor, not the least of its troubles was the campaign waged against the construction gangs by a pride of people-eating lions. Henry Labouchere, the Little-England Radical, was probably more right than wrong when he satirically declaimed:

> What will it cost no words can express;
> What is its object no brain can suppose;
> Where it will start from no one can guess;
> Where it goes nobody knows.
> What is the use of it none can conjecture;
> What it will carry there's none can define;
> And in spite of George Curzon's superior lecture,
> It clearly is naught but a lunatic line.[29]

At times direct aid constituted a significant fraction of a colony's total revenue. In Nigeria, between 1900 and 1912, the figures ranged between 12 and 44 percent; and in 1901 direct aid constituted 88 percent of the Gold Coast's revenue. Usually, however, the ratio was less than £1 in 20.[30] As far as the British taxpayer was concerned the direct payments between 1880 and 1914 averaged £733,000 per year and cost every resident British subject £.02 per year.

III. The Crown Agents

The indispensable agency for the marketing of colonial securities and much else besides was the Crown Agents Department. The roots of that institution lay in the eighteenth century. At that time, the colonies began to maintain agents in London to pursue their commercial, political, and financial interests. The British government also appointed officials to supervise colonial expenditures under parliamentary grants. In time the situation became sufficiently confusing to force reform, and in 1833 the Colonial Office and the Treasury determined on the appointment of just two Crown Agents. Rather than being housed in the Colonial Office, they were separately established, albeit supervised first by the Treasury and then, after 1880, by the Colonial Office, with the Treasury lurking in the background for consultation on "extraordinary occasions."[31]

By 1880, the Crown Agents had become the purchasing agents and loan negotiators for the dependent colonies. In 1874, the Colonial Office decreed that all goods imported for the public service of the Crown Colonies had to be purchased through the Crown Agents. At first they represented all colonies; however, in 1880, the Crown Agents were deprived of the right to represent self-governing colonies in most dealings. These increasingly autonomous entities were to maintain individual agents in London, but this official change had only a limited effect.[32] In the year 1908, for example, the Crown Agents acted on behalf of twenty-four colonies, eleven protectorates, and Zanzibar, and they still continued to conduct certain financial undertakings for Cape Colony, Natal, New Zealand, Western Australia, the Orange River Colony, and the Transvaal.[33]

Although there were only two Crown Agents, the support they were accorded was not insignificant. In 1900, the staff of well over 200 included a secretary, 8 department heads, 11 deputy department heads, 23 section heads, 65 clerks, 52 copyists, 20 typists, and a dozen miscellaneous functionaries.[34] The Colonial Office in contrast had an establishment of only 125. The areas of Crown Agents' concern were seemingly endless. They took a major role in the construction of colonial public works and particularly railroads. They drew up all contracts, placed all orders for plants and stores, supervised the execution of contracts and inspections, arranged for the shipment of goods, recruited engineers for colonial construction projects, and saw to the design of colonial currencies and stamps. They provided their clients with pistols, saddles, tropical headgear, perambulators, fezzes, "arctic footwarmers," money clips, zouave jackets, sewing machines, gin, and so on, ad infinitum. The office in 1908, for example, processed 9,000 orders requiring 24,000 separate contracts.[35] Railway equipment was always a major responsibility for the Crown Agents. In the year 1904, for example, they saw to the purchase of railway locomotives to the value of £139,825.[36] In that same year, the total of commercial, railway, and general business stores purchased and shipped amounted to £2,541,936, while financial transactions, loans, and miscellaneous business conducted on behalf of the colonies came to £22,903,901.[37]

There are few remaining records of the actual purchases made by the Crown Agents during the period in question, but over the first years of the present century the annual total appears to have ranged from £2 to £2.6 million.[38] If the ratio between those figures and the total expenditures of the dependent colonies provides a reasonable index, it appears that the purchases made by the agents for the colonies totaled almost £125 million over the period. That is not a huge figure, but even if the agents' bargaining ability netted only about a conjectured 10-percent price reduction (many of the purchases were for railroad and other specialized equipment, and those markets were probably not competitive), the colonial savings would have averaged £233,000 a year.

It is remarkable that all this activity was generated by an office whose employees " . . . have no formal Constitution and who are not part of the United Kingdom Civil Service or of the United Kingdom Government machine . . . . Their functions are not anywhere laid down except inferentially by reference to certain Colonial Regulations. . . . In general their position rests entirely on useage . . . ."[39] In his study of the Crown Agents, A. W. Abbott, former Senior Crown Agent, placed their importance in perspective when he pointed out that "over a total period of 140 years the Crown Agents have bought or sold £2,000 million worth of equipment, invested over £3,000 million worth of funds, and issued and managed £300 million of market loans . . . ."[40]

How did the Crown Agents go about their business? When it came to purchasing, the list of firms qualified to bid for contracts was determined by the Crown Agents. In 1904, for example, thirty-five firms including some foreign ones were invited to bid on £135,549-worth of rail contracts. On the other hand, only nine companies were given the opportunity to tender bids for the £139,825 in locomotive contracts. For a small contract involving £4,664 for telegraph insulators, the Crown Agents felt two competing bids would be sufficient.[41] While concerns about bias were surprisingly rare, in at least one instance a colonial client was worried that British companies were being favored over local firms. The evidence, however, was not compelling.[42]

In the case of loan flotations the borrowing colony established the highest permissible rate of interest, fixed the amount desired, and set what other conditions it saw fit. The secretary of state then authorized the Crown Agents to seek the loan on the best terms possible. At first (circa 1860) advertisements were filed for tenders for debentures carrying a stated rate of interest. Offers were subject to a minimum price – one that was as a rule not disclosed until the tenders were opened. Later, debentures were offered at a fixed price and "success" was assured by having the issues underwritten by private agencies who could comply with the regulations contained in the Colonial Stocks Acts of 1877 and 1900. Underwriting arrangements were placed in the hands of a regular group of brokers on whom the Crown Agents felt they could rely. The brokers were expected not only to place the underwriting in "substantial hands" but also to confine it, insofar as possible, to institutions that could be relied upon to hold the bonds until the market could absorb them without breaking. Underwriters normally received a commission of 1 percent on colonial stock and the brokers .25 percent.[43]

Between 1860 and 1914 the Crown Agents acting through one of several private brokers (most often Scrimegour and Co.), successfully marketed almost £85 million in long-term government securities. That total does not, of course, include the short-term loans the agents made directly to the colonies. Slightly over half of the £85 million represented issues of colonies that either had or were soon to be granted responsible government; however, some £40 million were issued by colonies with dependent status (see Table 6.6).[44] The colonies with responsible government often preferred to utilize the services of the Crown Agents because of their low cost, but Colonial Office policy gradually forced them to employ their own agents.[45]

It is difficult to estimate the savings in flotation costs generated by the agents, but the reluctance displayed by colonies such as New Zealand to abandon the agency's good offices suggests that they were substantial. What is certain is that the dependent colonies paid brokerage and other flotation fees that were no higher than those charged by firms who underwrote the issues of the world's most developed nations. In commenting on the role of the Crown Agents, the chronicler of the early twentieth-century capital market wrote:

TABLE 6.6

EMPIRE LOANS HANDLED BY THE CROWN AGENTS

(1,000s £'s)

	"A" Empire Totals			"B" Colony Totals		
Date	Total	Annual Average	Colony	Total Amount	Colony	Total Amount
1860-64	5,153	1,031	Antigua	143	Mauritius	3,030
1865-69	5,140	1,028	Bahamas	56	Montserrat	207
1870-74	6,311	1,262	Barbados	375	Natal	9,405
1875-79	19,768	3,954	British Columbia	300	New Zealand	21,141
1880-84	9,158	1,832	British Guinea	720	St. Helena	19
1885-89	3,344	669	British Honduras	189	St. Kitts-Nevis	79
1890-94	6,183	1,237	Cape Colony	13,193	St. Lucia	181
1895-99	1,423*	356	Ceylon	5,966	St. Vincent	5
1900-04	4,248*	1,062	Dominica	36	Sierre Leone	2,341
1905-09	14,206	2,841	Fiji	150	Straights Settlements	7,850
1910-13	9,009**	2,252	Gibralter	24	Southern Nigeria	8,099
			Gold Coast	2,098	Tasmania	3
TOTAL	83,943	1,614	Granada	141	Trinidad	1,350
			Hong Kong	1,886	Vancouver	40
			Jamaica	1,687	Western Australia	1,229
			Lagos	2,000		
					TOTAL	83,943

*No records for years 1899 and 1900.
**No loans 1912.

Source: Records of the Crown Agents

> It would, perhaps, be more exact to say that he [the broker] *allots* the underwriting, for it seems probable that the parties with whom he places it, would usually accept their quotas even though such a commitment happened at the moment to be particularly unwelcome.[46]

It was not only the colonies with responsible government that displayed an inclination to continue to employ the Crown Agents. Even today the Agents continue to act for several countries that, although dependent colonies in the nineteenth century, are now independent. Writing in 1921, Lavington shows why this may be true:

> It seems tolerably certain that Colonial and Indian securities are sold to the public at a fair price and a modest cost ... [and] that there is little scope for abuse in the marketing of highly reputable stocks.[47]

That the Crown Agents had immense power in their capacity as agents to choose brokers for loans and to assign contracts for the purchase of equipment is too evident to need elaboration. Charges against them were frequent, and as a consequence a major parliamentary enquiry was completed in 1909. After an extensive investigation, the report suggested only minor organizational changes; and the Crown Agents' conduct was found to be, in general, above reproach. Given the amounts of money with which the Crown Agents dealt, it is not surprising that accusations of such alleged offenses as "accepting return commissions" were levied against them.[48] Cases of dishonesty were, however, remarkably rare.

The Agents' colonial customers were, of course, not always satisfied. For instance, in 1902 the manner in which a Ceylon 3-percent loan was handled came under severe criticism. The payment of what was deemed an extra dividend and the fact that the issue fetched only 91.2 percent lay at the heart of the dissatisfaction.[49] Again, when in 1910 the Crown Agents negotiated a second installment of an authorized £7,861,457 3.5 percent loan on behalf of the Straits Settlements for 95.5 percent, the governor, Sir John Anderson, was furious. He accused the Crown Agents of having failed to consult with his government and, as a consequence, of having negotiated too small a loan at an inappropriate rate.[50] R. C. Antrobus, one of the agents, denied the allegations and defended his office's position: "We claim . . . that the Colony has been well served by us in this matter and we cannot help feeling disappointed that our success in the conduct of this very important and responsible business should . . . have failed to obtain for us any expression of approval . . . ."[51]

Aside from their direct economic function, at times the Crown Agents were able to assist the British government in effecting its foreign policy. A loan raised by the Crown Agents for Hong Kong in 1906 was then loaned by Hong Kong to Hukuan and Lianghuang in China.[52] Previously, in 1905, a direct loan had been made to the viceroy of Wu Chang, who was apparently considered more reliable than the Chinese government itself, to make it possible for him to repurchase the concession for the Kowloon-Canton Railway from the King of Belgium. In a letter of September 22, 1905, the Colonial Office thanked the Crown Agents for their "valuable assistance."[53]

The Crown Agents' files provide evidence of the diversity of their financial endeavors. In 1891, for instance, they were involved in raising a loan for the tiny Caribbean Island of St. Kitts. The funds were designed to cover a new water supply for the windward side of the island, completion of the public library, the construction of new treasury buildings, renovation of the medical baths, construction of a leper asylum, the opening of new cemeteries, improvements of public roads, hospital refurbishment, and enlargement of the prison of Besseterre – and all of that for only £23,500.[54] Even this loan was far from the smallest marketed by the agents. In 1879, they raised a 5-percent waterworks construction loan of £3,000 for the Montserrat government. As an aside, it might be mentioned that the second installment of that loan was only £300![55] At the other extreme, the Crown Agents managed a £35,000,000 loan designed to cover a number of post-Boer War exigencies including £19,000,000 for railway construction in the Transvaal.[56]

The Crown Agents' services were not provided free to the colonies; the Agents demanded and received recompense for their undertakings. Colonies were charged a flat 1 percent commission for stores purchased on their behalf by the Crown Agents. In addition, an annual contribution (in 1908, for example, it ranged from £30 to £650) was assessed against colonies conducting over £100,000 worth of nonloan business through the office.[57] A .5 percent commission was also charged on the issue and repayment of loans and .25 percent on the payment of interest. Overdrafts had to be settled at bank rates, but never at less than 3 percent. From this income, which amounted to as much as £100,000 per annum, the Crown Agents paid all office expenses including their own salaries. Surpluses were invested to cover possible future deficits.[58] The records indicate no instance of colonial complaint at these charges. The benefits provided by the Office of the Crown Agents for the Colonies in the vital areas of purchasing and loan management were too evident to bear more than petty carping.

It appears almost impossible to quantify with any precision the contribution of the Crown Agents to the colonial subsidy, but it does appear possible to speculate about its magnitude. In comparison to defense and interest subsidies it was probably not great; but if the Agents' monopsony power yielded as little as 10 percent on the purchases of the dependent colonies, and their monopoly power, 1 percent on the flotation costs of security issues, the subsidy would have totaled £136 million, an average of £2.5 million a year. Even cutting that figure in half suggests a subsidy of well over £1 million per annum or about £.04 for each resident of England and Scotland to whom otherwise the bulk of these rents would almost certainly have accrued.

IV. Trade

Although a discussion of trade is not within the purview of this book, some mention of it should be made in the context of British subsidies to the Empire. All colonies had easier access to the British market than they would have, had there been no financially assisted railroads or subsidized steamship lines. Australia and New Zealand, for example, particularly benefited when the British government provided cold-storage facilities on mail vessels. In an era of free trade, British markets were largely unencumbered by tariff restrictions. On the other hand, the so-called Dominions were, for their part, free to erect barriers against the importation of British goods, and many did so with a vengeance. Alexander Galt's Canadian tariff act of 1859, the initial protective tariff in the Empire, was only the first of a long list of such enactments.

Whatever the case, it must have been a comfort to the imperial community to have the British market as a first and last resort. While few colonies were as completely dependent on the home market as South Africa, it can be said with considerable assurance that the availability of a free British market and a subsidized communications network were vital to the health and welfare of possessions such as Australia and New Zealand. For other colonies the imperial connection was less important. To Britain the Empire was significant but not crucial.

A more detailed scrutiny of these trade flows is instructive.[59] The heavy dependence of some colonies on the British market is reflected in their trade statistics. Sixty-six percent of South African exports went to the United Kingdom in 1860–2, 92 percent in 1885–7, and 91 percent in 1910–12. In the case of New Zealand, the totals were 38 percent in 1860–2, 68 percent in 1885–7, and 83 percent in 1910–12. Comparable figures for Canada were 41, 49, and 43 percent; and for Newfoundland, 31, 24, and 26 percent. Thus, 48 percent of all exports from the colonies with responsible government found their destination in Great Britain in 1860–2, 53 percent in 1885–7, and 60 percent in 1910–12.

Surprisingly, particularly for those who accept Lenin's arguments, the figures for the dependent Empire are much smaller – 43 percent in 1860–2, 26 percent in 1885–7, and 43 percent again in 1910–12. Nor was the total for India substantially different: 44 percent in the first period, 40 in the second, and 30 in the third. In contrast, only 11 percent of British exports went to the colonies with responsible government in 1860–2, and no more than 15 percent in 1885–7 and 1910–12. For India, the comparable figures were 11, 17, and 12 percent, and for the dependent Empire, 4, 3, and 5 percent. The vast majority of British exports went to other independent countries: 75 percent in 1860–2, 65 percent in 1885–7, and 68 percent in 1910–12.

While exports to the Empire were relatively small from Britain's point of view, these goods were of much greater importance to the Empire itself, although the British share of the market was falling in India and the responsibly governed colonies during the last years of the study period. India received 62 percent of its imports from Britain in the first period, 71 in the second, and 55 in the third. The figures for the self-governing Dominions were 52, 48, and 38 percent.

For the dependent colonies, on the other hand, dependency was apparently increasing. The figure for 1910–12 was 38 percent, whereas in 1885–7 it had totaled a mere 19.

Overall, with the exception of India, Great Britain maintained a fair balance between its Empire exports and imports. Among its main Empire trading partners were Canada, New Zealand, and Australia. For Canada the average annual balance of trade, while a substantial negative £1,194,000 in the years 1860–2, had become slightly positive (£29,000) in 1885–7, and by 1910–12 the account showed a considerable surplus of £2,576,000. For New Zealand the figures were not dissimilar: £630,000, £113,000, and £98,000. Nor does the Australian case differ substantially [the deficits were large through the 1880s, -£2,473,000 and -£5,636,000, but the account had also gone surplus by the end of the first decade of the present century (+£4,492,000)]. India, however, continued to run massive trade deficits. The averages for the three periods were: -£8,377,000, -£16,101,000, and -£24,336,000. It appears reasonable to conclude that access to the British market was of great importance to most colonies; that India depended heavily on Britain for its imports; but that this was less true for the dominions and dependent colonies. As for Great Britain itself, trade with the Empire was not of overwhelming significance; and from the most independent of its offspring, the unencumbered welcome of their products into the United Kingdom earned, not reciprocity, but not-inconsiderable tariff barriers.

Interimperial trade was largely insignificant. As late as the triennium 1910–12, India sent less than 3 percent of its exports to the colonies with responsible government and only 8 percent to the rest of the dependent Empire. At the same time, imports from these sources amounted to only 5 and 4 percent of the Indian total. In those years the colonies with responsible government directed 3 percent of their exports to India, 5 percent to other responsibly governed colonies, and only 1 percent to the dependent colonies. The comparable import figures were 5, 4, and 3 percent. The dependent colonies sent 6 percent of their exports and received 17 percent of their imports from India. The figures for their trade with the colonies with responsible government were 5 and 3 percent, and for trade with other dependent colonies, some 4 percent. Again, analysis of the figures for 1910–12 indicates that of all Empire trade, 33 percent originated in Britain; 9 percent in India; 5 percent in Australia; 3 percent in Canada and South Africa; 1 percent in New Zealand (a total of 12 percent in the responsibly governed colonies); and 5 percent in the dependent colonies. A very substantial 41 percent originated in the foreign sector.

In summation, Great Britain provided both visible and invisible subsidies to the Empire. In the former category are grants-in-aid and subsidies for steamship and telegraph communication; in the latter, defense, trade advantages, and subsidized interest rates. From a strictly economic point of view being a part of the Empire was profitable – or more correctly the British taxpayer paid and the colonies benefited. The value of those benefits was high for the colonists in the colonies of white settlements, although a part of the subsidy did accrue to those British residents who invested in the British overseas. For the remainder of the Empire, the returns are less obvious. Given the behavior of the independent underdeveloped countries, there is no reason to believe that the inhabitants of the dependent Empire, had they possessed similar liberties, would have selected the particular market basket of public goods that the Colonial and India Offices chose on their behalf. For India and the dependent colonies one cannot rule out the conclusion that everyone (Briton and Indian) lost – a true Pareto *pessimum*.

APPENDIX 6.1

Consider the following very simplistic model diagram in Figure 6.1A. It is assumed that there are two distinct markets for government funds: a market for "safe" and a market for "risky" securities. Let i^s stand for the interest rate in the safe market and i^r the rate in the risky market; and let B^{uk}, B^{for}, and B^{emp} stand for the amount of funds borrowed by the United Kingdom, foreign countries, and the Empire, respectively; D^{uk}, D^{for}, D^{emp} refer to UK, Empire, and foreign demand; and S^s and S^r to safe and risky supply. Let the subscripts 1 and 2 refer to time periods. In the initital position (time period 1), it is assumed that only the United Kingdom has access to the safe market. In this counterfactual world, India and the colonies lie outside the Empire and must compete with the foreign countries in the risky market. Under these hypothetical assumptions one would expect that rate i^s_1 would prevail in the safe market and i^r_1 in the risky one; moreover, one would expect that $i^r_1 > i^s_1$. The United Kingdom would borrow B^{uk}_1; foreign countries B^{for}_1; and the Empire, B^{emp}_1. Next, assume that the Empire is "created" and that gives India and the colonies access to the safe market. The transfer of the Empire demand from one market to the other raises the rate in the safe market and causes the rate to fall in the risky one. The new equilibriums occur where the new safe demand ($D^{uk} + D^{emp}$) equals the safe supply (S^s) and where foreign demand (D^{for}) equals the risky supply. The beneficiaries of the "Empire subsidy" are the residents of the Empire (where rates have fallen from i^r_1 to i^s_2) and the citizens of other countries who now are required to pay less for their capital ($i^r_1 > i^r_2$). If we assume that Empire demand is interest inelastic, then the annual value of the subsidy to persons in the Empire is equal to the difference between the rate that they previously had to pay and that which they now have to pay ($i^r_1 - i^s_2$) multiplied by the amount that they borrow (B^{emp}). The annual gain to foreigners is measured by their interest differential ($i^r_1 - i^r_2$) multiplied by the amount they initially borrowed (B^{for}_1) plus the gain in consumer surplus associated with the increase in the level of their borrowing ($B^{for}_2 - B^{for}_1$). On the diagram the amount is represented by the area of the rectangle (i^r_2, A, C, i^r_1) plus the triangle ABC.

The annual costs of the subsidy borne by the British taxpayer are measured by the difference in interest they had to pay ($i^s_2 - i^s_1$), multiplied by the amount they borrowed at these new high interest rates (B^{uk}_2) plus the loss in consumer surplus associated with the reduced level of borrowing ($B^{uk}_1 - B^{uk}_2$). On the diagram that amount is equal to the area of the rectangle (i^s_1, D, F, i^s_2) plus the area of the triangle DEF.

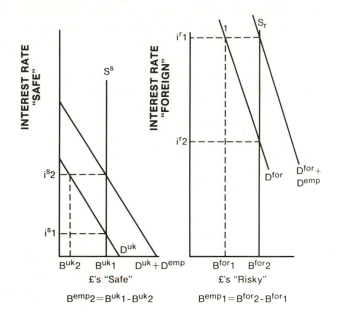

Figure 6.1A

The analytics of the model are relatively straightforward; however, it is not possible to make all the calculations required to actually estimate the three parts of the subsidy. In the real world (at least that of the nineteenth century), it is never possible to observe the hypothetical rates i^s_1 and i^r_1 nor their associated quantities B^{for}_2, B^{emp}_1, B^{uk}_1. All that can be observed is the final equilibrium rates (i^s_2 and i^r_2) and quantities (B^{for}_2, B^{emp}_2, and B^{uk}_2). Thus neither the amount of the Empire subsidy accruing to citizens of other countries nor the cost of that subsidy to the British taxpayer can be estimated. However, with a few not too controversial assumptions, it is possible to produce a minimum estimate of the value of the subsidy to the Queen-Empress's colonial subjects.

First, assume that the Empire demand for funds is interest inelastic. This assumption is very strong, but given the pyrotechnics of Vogel and his imitators it may not distort reality too far. Second, assume that the demand for funds in the foreign and Empire sectors is not upward sloping (i.e., that persons will borrow the same amount or less at higher rates of interest) and that the supply of funds in both the safe and the risky markets is not downward sloping (at lower rates investors will supply less or the same but not more funds to the market). In addition we know that the difference between the observed rate in the risky market (i^r_2) and the observed rate in the safe market (i^s_2) is a minimum estimate of the price component of the interest subsidy. It is a minimum estimate, because the rate that would have prevailed in the risky market in the absence of the Empire is almost certainly higher than that which did prevail, because India and the colonies were able to borrow in the safe market. Only if the supply of risky funds were completely interest inelastic would the shift of Empire demand not reduce the rate in that market.

Given these facts and assumptions it is possible to measure the minimum price-break advantage that Empire citizens received, and in addition the data on actual borrowing levels are available (B^{emp}_2). By multiplying these two figures together, the annual value of the Empire interest subsidy is obtained.

7 The shareholders in imperial enterprises

I. Introduction

The Empire was profitable for some; and even when it was not, losses were lower than they would have been had the British not shouldered the burden of the Empire subsidy. If the Empire investors were not the same people who paid the taxes, imperialism, at least in part, can be viewed as a process of income transfer from British taxpayers to imperial investors. To test this hypothesis both the imperial investors and the British taxpayers must be identified. Then it is necessary to determine whether as a group the imperial investors differed substantially from those who put their accumulations to work in the domestic and foreign sectors. In this chapter the occupational and geographic composition of a sample of imperial shareholders is compared with the distribution of the stockholders of a sample of foreign and domestic firms.

The Company Acts of 1856 and 1862 required that corporations annually file a statement of their equity structure and a list of their stockholders. The latter included not only names, but most often addresses and occupations as well. It is these annual reports to the Board of Trade that provide the basis for the study. The three samples (domestic, foreign, and Empire firms) were drawn from the corporations listed in the *Stock Exchange Annual Yearbook (SEAYB)* at some time between 1883 and 1907. For each company an attempt was made to choose a list three to five years after charter to capture the "public" imperialists as opposed to the promoters. Companies were placed in one of the three sectors on the basis of information in that chronicle, the original prospectuses, and the financial press. Firms were classified by industry on the basis of the classifications made by the editors of the *SEAYB*.[1]

The industries were the same as those used by the editors in the year 1903 except that no insurance firms were included. The industries are (1) commercial banks, (2) breweries and distilleries, (3) canals and docks, (4) commercial and industrial, (5) financial, land, and development, (6) financial trusts, (7) gas and light, (8) iron, coal and steel, (9) mines, (10) railroads, (11) shipping, (12) tea and coffee, (13) telephone and telegraphs, (14) tramways and omnibuses, and

TABLE 7.1

STOCKHOLDERS
FIRMS IN SAMPLE BY LOCATION & INDUSTRY

	Home	Foreign	Empire	Total
Commercial Banks	4	5	6	15
Breweries and Distilleries	6	6	6	18
Canals and Docks	5	2	1	8
Commercial and Industrial	13	9	22	44
Financial Land and Development	7	10	21	38
Financial Trusts	2	6	4	12
Gas and Light	4	3	8	15
Iron, Coal and Steel	7	6	11	24
Mining	5	4	15	24
Railroads	0	6	11	17
Shipping	1	4	1	6
Tea and Coffee	0	0	10	10
Telephone and Telegraph	0	4	2	6
Trams and Omnibuses	5	5	5	15
Waterworks	0	5	3	8
TOTAL	59	75	126	260

(15) waterworks. The Stock Exchange lists, however, include only Empire tea and coffee companies and nothing but foreign and Empire telephone and telegraph companies and waterworks. Moreover, no United Kingdom (home) railroads were included in the sample.[2] Table 7.1 displays the number of firms in each location and industry. There were a total of 260 firms, with 79,944 stockholders, in the sample. Of that total 15,220 invested in British, 25,044 in foreign, and 39,680 in Empire enterprises.

The occupational categories are largely self-explanatory. Appendix 7.1 lists all occupations included in each category. Initially all stockholders were classified into thirty-three occupational categories. The thirty-three were divided into twelve superoccupations, and the twelve were again subdivided into the general categories business, elites, and others.[3] There were some (less than 2 percent) multiple occupations. In those cases, any occupation took precedence over deceased or retired, all but deceased and retired took precedence over "woman," all but those three took precedence over peers and gents, and all but those four took precedence over Member of Parliament (MP). Thus, a Baronet who was also retired and a shipbuilder was included as a shipbuilder (manufacturer). Anyone who was listed as an MP had no other classification except, perhaps, deceased, retired, or peers and gents; however, a separate listing includes the holdings of all MPs regardless of their occupations. For other joint occupations, the first listed was given precedence, but dividing the shares between occupations does not affect the results. Shares held jointly by several persons were divided equally between the occupations of the joint holders.

One additional caveat. There are some problems with nominee holders.[4] They did exist, and they are difficult to identify. The phrase "and another" is easy, but that classification is significant only in the case of railroads.[5] In addition, it is clear that stocks were often held in the name of a banker, a stockbroker, solicitor, an employee, a wife, or a relative; and these present a more difficult dilemma. Subsidiary studies indicate that the problem may not be too serious. Nominee holders were less common than on the continent, and when they did exist they tended to be most often used by peers and gents and shareholders in Empire and foreign firms. For those firms there may be some overstatement of the proportion held by brokers, women, clerks, and bankers and an underenumeration of the holdings of peers and gents. It has probably become evident by now that the taxonomy was designed to minimize the holdings of the elites and to maximize those of the business community. Thus, any conclusions about elite participation can be viewed as reflecting the "worst case" (i.e., it is a minimum estimate of their investment). On the other hand, statements concerning business participation may overstate the contributions of that group.

For the analysis of the geographic distribution of stockholders, England has been divided into nine regions (the North, Yorkshire, Lancashire, Midlands industrial, West, East, South and Southwest, Home Counties, and London).[6] Within London, EC (the City) addresses present a problem. Not only was it the most common location of nominee holders, but more importantly, shareholders often used their banks and brokers as convenience addresses. Therefore, London averages have been calculated both with and without that district. The former probably overstates the importance of the metropolis, but since there were many shareholders who lived or worked in EC, the latter certainly understates it. If the record listed only a city or town and no county, and if there was more than one place with that name, the address was, in the absence of other information, assigned to the town with the largest population.[7]

The basic index utilized in this analysis is the fraction of the total value of a firm's capital stock that is owned by a particular occupational group or by the residents of some specific region.[8] Clearly, since a focus of this study is on the relationship between stock ownership and economic and political behavior, this index is not ideal. A measure that reflected either the relative or absolute importance of a class of investments (i.e., home, foreign or Empire) to a group of holders might, to cite two of the possible alternatives, provide a better measure.[9] Since the focus of this study is the effects of stock ownership on economic and political behavior, ideally one would want a measure of the importance of each class of securities to each group of holders [e.g., the amount of income (dividends plus capital gains) on Empire investments as compared with the total income earned by members of the group in question]. Unfortunately, since some data are not available, the measure employed herein is at best a proxy. As such, however, the measure chosen has at least one desirable characteristic. It is generally recognized that the members of the middle class were far more numerous than their counterparts in the upper class. R. Dudley Baxter, for example, estimated that only 3 out of 100 Britons, not in the working class, were actually in the upper class, but no one is likely to believe that the ratio was any lower than 5 or 10 to 1.[10] Thus, if the upper class held a larger fraction of the equities of Empire business, it is almost certain that the income arising from those shares must have been on average greater for each member of that class than it was on average for a middle class shareholder.

Yet, the concentration of major wealth in the late nineteenth century shifted from the traditional upper class, most of whose holdings were in land and who until about 1880 constituted around half of the really rich people in Britain, to businesspeople. W. D. Rubenstein points out that in Britain this meant persons engaged in commerce and finance rather than manufacturing and industry, but, at least for the period under study, his data suggest that the conclusion may be too strong. Although the actual proportions varied from decade to decade, of the 189 nonlanded millionaires enumerated between 1860 and 1919, 49 percent earned their fortunes in trade and commerce and 51 percent in the two industrial categories – manufacturing and "food, drink, and tobacco." A further breakdown of those figures indicates that of the total, 11 percent were from engineering and iron and steel, 12 percent from brewing and distilling, 12 percent from textile manufacturing, and 20 percent from commercial and merchant banking.[11]

II. The occupational distribution of shareholders

Table 7.2 reports the occupational composition of the stockholders, the value of each group's holdings, and the average investment in the 260 firms, classified by location (domestic, foreign, and Empire).[12] The all-firms enumeration provides some general insight into the types of persons who held shares in the three classes of firms and provides a standard against which to compare the distributions of particular industries. The average investment in all enterprises was £1,908. Domestic investments were on average smaller than foreign, and foreign smaller than Empire. Moreover, while there was some difference in level, that ordering holds for both elites and

TABLE 7.2

MEAN OF PERCENTAGE OF SHARES HELD BY EACH OCCUPATION CATEGORY IN EACH COMPANY

Occupations	Number of Shareholders			Total Value of Shares (in £'s)			Value of Average Holdings (£'s)				Percent of Value Held[1] Firm Weights			
	UK	FOR	EMP	UK	FOR	EMP	UK	FOR	EMP	ALL	UK	FOR	EMP	ALL
Trade & Commerce	3,055	2,353	4,228	1,248,090	7,055,735	7,971,800	409	2,998	1,885	2,689	15.4	16.5	14.7	15.3
Manufacturing	1,356	729	1,314	1,606,589	1,298,837	1,846,629	1,185	1,782	1,405	1,398	19.4	5.7	5.3	8.6
Professions	1,299	1,554	2,828	765,631	1,664,645	4,153,823	598	1,071	1,469	1,159	10.1	5.8	6.2	7.0
Misc. Business	666	262	653	385,654	972,326	1,304,048	579	3,711	1,997	1,684	5.9	2.9	2.7	3.5
Total Business	6,376	4,898	9,023	4,005,964	10,991,543	15,276,309	628	2,244	1,693	1,491	50.8	30.9	28.9	34.4
Finance	743	1,244	2,274	495,848	3,757,116	4,285,626	667	3,020	1,885	2,004	3.9	8.1	7.8	7.0
Military	613	760	1,292	490,743	1,010,420	3,107,686	801	1,330	2,405	1,729	1.5	2.5	2.2	2.1
Misc. Elite	340	933	1,494	228,698	1,437,809	4,807,901	673	1,541	3,218	2,340	2.4	3.6	2.2	2.7
Gents & Peers	2,960	5,958	12,697	3,032,550	9,991,583	41,840,932	1,025	1,678	3,295	2,539	21.0	25.2	25.1	24.2
Total Elites	4,656	8,895	17,757	4,247,839	16,202,928	54,042,145	912	1,821	3,043	2,379	28.8	39.4	37.2	36.0
Labor	734	450	1,328	135,900	209,183	398,413	185	465	300	296	1.7	0.4	1.0	1.0
Miscellaneous	1,111	6,026	4,979	450,399	6,694,826	8,022,812	405	1,111	1,611	1,252	6.7	14.9	12.4	11.8
Public Companies	51	230	267	386,020	2,383,092	13,279,702	7,569	10,361	49,737	29,286	4.0	8.4	14.3	10.2
Women	2,292	4,545	6,326	544,602	2,475,934	12,757,961	238	545	2,017	1,199	8.0	5.9	6.2	6.5
Total Other	4,188	11,251	12,900	1,516,921	11,763,035	34,458,888	362	1,046	2,671	1,685	20.4	29.7	33.9	29.6
GRAND TOTAL	15,220	25,044	39,680	9,770,724	38,957,506	103,777,342	642	1,555	2,615	1,908	100.0	100.0	100.0	100.0

UK: United Kingdom
FOR: Foreign
EMP: Empire

[1]Percentage calculated for each firm in sample and those figures averaged across all firms. This procedure is utilized so that every firm, regardless of size, is given equal weight.

others, but not for businesspeople. Their foreign investments were larger on average than their Empire ones.

Within the business community, all groups except merchants had a much greater affinity for domestic than foreign or Empire shares. On average businesspeople held about 50 percent of domestic, but only 30 percent of overseas shares. Among businesspeople, only merchants held as high a proportion of overseas as domestic shares; for the professions and agriculture and mining, the ratio was about one to two and for manufacturers, one to three. Given the importance of overseas commerce in the British economic matrix and the proclivity of businesspeople to invest in "what they know," it is hardly surprising that the merchants seem to have behaved somewhat differently than their confreres from other business activities.

The second group, the elites, appears to have pursued a markedly different investment strategy. They held less than 30 percent of domestic, but almost 40 percent of foreign and Empire shares. Peers and gents, the most numerous group, held about a fifth of the value of domestic, but a quarter of foreign and Empire securities. Smaller but still substantial proportions were held by the financial community – 4 percent of domestic, 8 percent of foreign and Empire. The other subgroups were much less important, but it is interesting to note that the military displayed a slightly greater preference for foreign than for Empire investment.

The third general group, others, is very diverse and generalizations have little meaning. However, the pattern displayed by some of its constituent elements appears worthy of note. The tiny holdings of laborers indicate that "people's capitalism" had made very little headway in the late nineteenth century, but it is interesting that workers held any shares at all. "Other firms" held 4 percent of domestic, 8 percent of foreign, and 14 percent of Empire shares. While at times these represented interfirm holdings of nascent multinationals, such was not usually the case. Instead, they were most often blocks of shares held by commercial and private banks; financial, land, and development companies; and financial trusts. Together these financial firms accounted for more than one-half of interfirm holdings. Lastly, women held almost 8 percent of domestic, 5 percent of foreign, and 6 percent of Empire shares. (See Table 7.3 for a summation of group industrial holdings by location.)

What can be inferred about the contrasting record of business and elites vis-a-vis the investments they did make in the Empire? There are at least two possible measures of the demonstrated industrial "taste" of the two groups. On the one hand it is possible to compare holdings in a single industry in the Empire with average holdings in that industry across all sectors (see Table 7.4). On the other, within one industry, one can contrast Empire with domestic investment (Table 7.4). To the extent that both measures lead to similar results, and in this case they do, it should be possible to conclude something about the investment choices of the two groups; and therefore, perhaps, learn something about their interest in the Empire.

In the case of the business sector, it is quite clear that, to the degree that businesspeople invested in the Empire at all, their proclivities ran strongly to shipping and commercial and industrial, and to canals and docks, and mines, and tea and coffee plantations as well. Mines and mealtime beverages aside, it appears that when businesspeople turned their attention to the Empire, they tended to place their resources in activities related to their businesses at home. Concomitantly, it would seem that the group showed a strong disinclination to invest in commercial banks; financial, land, and investment companies; railroads; telephone and telegraph companies; and trams and omnibuses. The unifying principle is less clear, but there seems to have been a hesitancy to invest in financial enterprises and transportation.

It is possible to extend the argument by examining the relationship between investment in these "outlying" industries in the Empire and investments by the same groups in the foreign sector. Given the demonstrated inclination to invest in some and not in other activities, were these tendencies a reflection of Empire-related factors or just of overseas investment in general? Businesspeople displayed no particular affinity for Empire as opposed to overseas investment in general. On the other hand, while they tended to stay away from commercial banks and canals and docks in the Empire, they were more willing to invest in those activities in the foreign sector.

The elites showed a preference for Empire investment in financial, land, and investment companies; commercial banks; breweries; gas and light companies; railroads; iron, coal, and steel companies; and waterworks. At the same time they seemed to have been less willing to invest in canal and dock companies, mines, shipping lines, and tea and coffee plantations. In the case of the commercial and industrial sector, their behavior was mixed. If the measure is domestic habits, then Empire investments were high; but in terms of "normal" elite investment behavior in the Empire, their commitments to trade and commerce were very low.

A comparison of elite overseas patterns indicates that of the seven "favored" activities, the Empire appeared particularly attractive for investments in financial, land, and investment; commercial banks;

TABLE 7.3A

VALUE OF AVERAGE SHAREHOLDING
(£'s)

OCCUPATIONS	ALL				1 COMMERCIAL BANKING				2 BREWERIES & DISTILLERIES				3 CANALS & DOCKS			
	UK	FOR	EMP	ALL	UK	FOR	EMP	ALL	UK	FOR	EMP	ALL	UK	FOR	EMP	ALL
Trade & Commerce	409	2,998	1,885	1,689	990	1,630	996	1,197	235	438	403	327	519	1,066	253	604
Manufacturing	1,185	1,782	1,405	1,398	1,949	1,156	680	1,429	1,561	507	3,303	1,474	827	4,771	7,093	2,088
Professions & Management	589	1,071	1,469	1,159	881	859	818	836	2,371	333	236	972	508	395	--	494
Misc. Business	579	3,711	1,997	1,684	409	805	692	607	194	171	382	231	1,560	110,415	--	2,992
Total Business	628	2,244	1,693	1,491	1,203	1,405	874	1,090	917	407	939	728	931	5,245	2,866	1,554
Finance	667	3,020	1,885	2,004	900	2,081	911	1,316	233	515	445	426	249	2,523	794	680
Military	801	1,330	2,405	1,729	1,233	671	1,379	1,302	537	289	490	390	--	1,364	40	1,364
Misc. Elites	673	1,541	3,218	2,340	652	1,242	915	917	510	203	595	356	325	3,232	--	1,564
Peers & Gents	1,025	1,678	3,295	2,539	2,010	1,427	981	1,122	555	504	609	542	3,695	3,976	454	3,307
Total Elites	912	1,821	3,043	2,379	1,672	1,561	1,008	1,143	491	471	575	504	1,949	3,538	527	2,388
Labor	185	465	300	296	332	99	346	316	144	105	62	108	101	18	1,500	183
Miscellaneous	405	1,111	1,611	1,252	1,253		1,001	1,057	372	451	348	428	720	329	620	641
Other Firms	7,569	10,361	49,737	29,286	--	58,202	3,291	24,645	300	4,723	1,568	3,795	11,400	18	--	5,709
Women	238	545	2,017	1,199	373	528	514	508	224	198	7,435	1,899	238	2,697	850	662
Total Other	362	1,046	2,671	1,685	416	2,346	585	743	248	526	3,817	1,106	424	1,784	917	670
ALL	642	1,555	2,615	1,908	1,258	1,610	856	1,028	632	477	1,565	764	937	3,519	1,528	1,502

OCCUPATIONS	4 COMMERCIAL & INDUSTRIAL				5 FINANCIAL, LAND & INVESTMENT				6 FINANCIAL TRUSTS				7 GAS & LIGHT			
	UK	FOR	EMP	ALL	UK	FOR	EMP	ALL	UK	FOR	EMP	ALL	UK	FOR	EMP	ALL
Trade & Commerce	263	1,364	2,747	1,396	2,818	2,821	474	1,492	650	7,213	34	5,257	272	898	1,181	971
Manufacturing	1,157	3,228	1,665	1,438	478	1,236	250	556	465	1,532	32	1,289	204	5,992	1,416	1,683
Professions & Management	258	274	814	563	342	754	679	668	33	1,413	108	1,208	162	550	1,153	945
Misc. Business	46	343	1,574	669	2,709	1,810	183	899	486	1,015	0*	903	129	305	587	408
Total Business	415	1,466	2,017	1,169	1,367	1,934	508	1,044	720	3,328	62	2,640	217	2,064	1,190	1,098
Finance	221	2,325	1,316	1,059	2,260	1,467	682	1,040	2,869	6,279	90	4,701	218	523	1,559	1,302
Military	100	5,241	1,178	1,664	279	1,190	659	860	988	1,409	111	1,155	433	674	2,917	2,160
Misc. Elites	568	1,241	1,125	930	4,157	2,486	1,121	1,769	646	864	0*	829	300	538	1,995	1,784
Peers & Gents	1,146	1,422	1,748	1,567	8,214	1,842	1,654	2,251	937	2,183	158	1,842	266	946	978	942
Total Elites	802	1,804	1,551	1,396	6,25	1,666	1,311	1,770	1,109	2,298	123	1,898	266	865	1,332	1,178
Labor	87	53	306	214	128	84	66	75	681	976	2	844	88	368	258	291
Miscellaneous	416	226	982	631	294	1,054	583	789	963	801	59	770	324	919	3,562	2,305
Other Firms	980	1,941	17,566	9,505	10,565	2,900	11,449	7,670	15,444	15,979	1,314	10,870	183	23,728	5,554	14,951
Women	226	533	482	378	179	352	370	326	724	580	59	572	125	314	952	539
Total Other	277	336	919	600	413	929	670	760	1,174	768	144	766	192	911	2,486	1,607
ALL	435	978	1,529	1,042	1,760	1,208	836	1,060	1,069	1,659	112	1,486	219	979	1,740	1,371

OCCUPATIONS	8 IRON, COAL & STEEL				9 MINES/EXTRACTIVE				10 RAILROADS				11 SHIPPING			
	UK	FOR	EMP	ALL	UK	FOR	EMP	ALL	UK	FOR	EMP	ALL	UK	FOR	EMP	ALL
Trade & Commerce	376	1,503	487	699	723	2,573	1,669	1,632	--	17,392	5,121	6,984	101	1,021	3,830	1,252
Manufacturing	1,244	1,173	727	1,057	1,021	8,685	268	1,931	--	282	3,330	3,102	181	694	822	554
Professions & Management	404	432	350	387	716	1,966	283	726	--	1,274	6,632	6,087	67	654	679	430
Misc. Business	1,225	262	1,237	1,151	164	6,957	335	1,951	--	5,120	13,966	13,203	190	9,661	1,826	5,362
Total Business	702	1,076	532	725	750	3,801	1,068	1,441	--	10,161	5,987	6,483	122	3,044	2,334	1,785
Finance	594	886	558	684	559	3,110	698	1,006	--	4,056	7,296	6,931	144	1,049	1,338	678
Military	478	432	528	491	775	622	278	459	--	2,298	7,793	7,407	267	832	1,360	888
Misc. Elites	358	428	232	312	113	2,413	213	861	--	1,462	13,517	12,414	14	12,493	667	4,610
Peers & Gents	525	1,064	663	747	785	340	526	430	--	3,041	10,991	10,350	425	810	1,909	956
Total Elites	530	928	584	677	695	507	552	540	--	3,007	10,626	9,986	247	1,539	1,586	1,123
Labor	304	240	77	162	58	43	113	97	--	357	816	809	120	58	580	156
Miscellaneous	592	461	388	453	476	6,278	426	1,080	--	14,168	14,012	14,045	44	3,272	--	1,268
Other Firms	2,467	4,070	22,429	8,778	34,572	20,288	23,570	23,487	--	26,945	107,613	97,933	--	669	--	669
Women	223	399	178	240	118	332	409	347	--	2,716	7,356	7,113	33	919	460	600
Total Other	343	655	741	619	1,145	2,644	918	1,320	--	9,479	12,540	12,221	58	1,564	520	776
ALL	557	874	613	676	825	1,297	849	1,002	--	6,056	10,460	10,075	117	2,320	2,019	1,335

OCCUPATIONS	12 TEA & COFFEE				13 TELEPHONES & TELEGRAPHS				14 TRAMWAYS & OMNIBUSES				15 WATERWORKS			
	UK	FOR	EMP	ALL	UK	FOR	EMP	ALL	UK	FOR	EMP	ALL	UK	FOR	EMP	ALL
Trade & Commerce	--	--	2,619	2,619	--	1,533	--	1,394	76	345	511	253	--	1,214	407	1,249
Manufacturing	--	--	227	227	--	2,149	--	1,303	123	4,420	1,027	931	--	928	776	1,985
Professions & Management	--	--	620	620	--	1,253	--	974	138	1,879	403	520	--	2,597	722	1,320
Misc. Business	--	--	1,147	1,147	--	429	--	461	70	170	365	253	--	--	597	251
Total Business	--	--	1,580	1,580	--	1,375	--	1,121	101	1,565	513	436	--	1,323	692	1,323
Finance	--	--	403	403	--	7,112	--	5,922	45	2,281	385	693	--	3,838	1,014	2,385
Military	--	--	613	613	--	5,146	--	1,416	88	296	1,167	537	--	1,316	705	1,452
Misc. Elites	--	--	182	182	--	13,177	--	3,902	37	505	672	321	--	1,086	673	974
Peers & Gents	--	--	691	691	--	3,545	--	1,169	116	4,177	931	895	--	2,253	767	1,896
Total Elites	--	--	571	571	--	4,859	--	1,431	105	3,426	860	804	--	2,264	759	1,864
Labor	--	--	421	421	--	755	--	593	77	46	120	87	--	40	270	215
Miscellaneous	--	--	639	639	--	5,521	--	2,352	159	418	348	360	--	1,999	639	2,583
Other Firms	--	--	42,752	42,752	--	9,660	--	13,761	838	9,361	41,537	18,294	--	6,070	20,099	64,683
Women	--	--	199	199	--	1,150	--	436	91	427	230	209	--	364	264	516
Total Other	--	--	858	858	--	3,949	--	1,668	97	731	811	518	--	1,256	819	4,028
ALL	--	--	930	930	--	3,984	--	1,460	102	1,879	761	679	--	1,620	760	2,141

Dash (--) = No Data

*Less than L.05

TABLE 7.3B

PERCENTAGE OF NOMINAL VALUE OF SHARES HELD

OCCUPATIONS	ALL				1 COMMERCIAL BANKING				2 BREWERIES & DISTILLERIES				3 CANALS & DOCKS			
	UK	FOR	EMP	ALL	UK	FOR	EMP	ALL	UK	FOR	EMP	ALL	UK	FOR	EMP	ALL
Trade & Commerce	15.4	16.5	14.6	15.3	20.9	31.5	14.8	22.0	14.5	10.1	6.7	10.4	10.2	13.4	1.9	10.0
Manufacturing	19.4	5.7	5.3	8.6	22.1	3.2	1.3	7.5	29.8	5.4	20.5	18.6	13.3	13.8	15.0	13.6
Professions & Management	10.1	5.8	6.2	7.0	7.1	3.5	6.0	5.5	24.4	5.5	2.8	10.9	5.7	1.3	4.7	4.5
Misc. Business	5.9	2.9	2.7	3.5	3.8	3.0	1.4	1.8	0.5	0.3	0.5	0.4	27.2	16.0	0.0	21.0
Total Business	50.8	30.9	28.9	34.4	54.0	38.7	23.5	36.7	69.2	21.4	30.5	40.3	56.3	44.5	21.6	49.0
Finance	3.9	8.1	7.8	7.0	4.3	20.9	5.5	10.3	2.1	5.3	4.0	3.8	1.5	7.1	5.5	3.4
Military	1.5	2.5	2.2	2.7	1.4	2.1	9.1	4.4	1.6	1.8	2.0	1.8	0.0	1.4	5.5	0.4
Misc. Elites	2.4	3.6	2.2	2.7	2.6	2.1	4.1	3.0	0.7	1.1	1.8	1.2	1.5	6.1	0.0	2.5
Peers & Gents	21.0	25.2	25.1	24.2	33.1	17.8	37.8	29.9	15.7	28.5	32.3	25.5	16.0	29.8	9.4	18.6
Total Elites	28.8	39.4	37.2	36.0	41.3	41.8	56.6	47.6	20.0	36.7	40.1	32.3	19.0	44.4	14.9	24.8
Labor	1.7	0.4	1.0	1.0	1.1	0.1	0.9	0.7	0.9	0.2	0.4	0.5	0.7	0.0	2.1	0.7
Miscellaneous	6.7	14.9	12.4	11.8	0.0	3.7	7.5	4.6	4.6	22.5	3.9	10.3	5.7	1.8	53.9	10.8
Other Firms	4.0	8.4	14.3	10.2	0.0	12.5	0.9	4.5	0.0	14.5	5.0	6.5	11.4	0.0	0.0	7.1
Women	8.0	5.9	6.2	6.5	2.3	3.2	10.5	5.9	5.3	4.7	20.2	10.1	6.9	9.2	7.6	7.6
Total Other	20.4	29.7	33.9	29.6	4.7	19.5	19.9	15.7	10.8	42.0	29.4	27.4	24.7	11.1	63.5	26.1

OCCUPATIONS	4 COMMERCIAL & INDUSTRIAL				5 FINANCIAL, LAND & INVESTMENT				6 FINANCIAL TRUST				7 GAS & LIGHT			
	UK	FOR	EMP	ALL	UK	FOR	EMP	ALL	UK	FOR	EMP	ALL	UK	FOR	EMP	ALL
Trade & Commerce	18.2	25.3	27.2	24.2	7.6	13.1	5.3	7.8	32.1	7.7	3.1	10.2	27.8	7.4	10.1	14.3
Manufacturing	32.6	4.5	8.4	14.8	10.4	2.5	1.3	3.3	1.2	3.9	0.9	2.4	18.5	20.1	10.0	14.3
Professions & Management	10.3	12.5	5.6	8.4	10.5	7.4	7.9	8.3	5.2	10.4	20.8	13.0	5.9	4.3	6.8	6.0
Misc. Business	5.4	0.2	6.0	4.6	0.8	1.1	0.1	0.5	2.7	0.9	0.0	0.9	4.2	0.0	0.5	1.4
Total Business	66.5	42.5	47.2	51.9	29.3	24.1	14.7	19.9	41.2	22.8	24.7	26.5	56.4	31.9	27.4	36.0
Finance	2.5	7.6	6.5	5.5	3.1	6.8	15.8	11.1	8.7	8.5	7.7	8.3	4.1	0.5	4.7	3.7
Military	0.4	6.5	1.3	2.1	0.2	3.0	1.3	1.5	15.2	2.1	0.7	3.8	1.1	1.2	3.9	2.6
Misc. Elites	1.4	0.7	1.3	1.3	9.3	3.9	3.5	4.7	0.7	4.9	0.0	2.6	0.6	0.3	3.2	1.9
Peers & Gents	10.9	22.2	15.1	15.3	23.9	24.5	24.6	24.4	11.9	20.3	26.0	20.8	16.2	15.6	34.3	25.7
Total Elites	15.1	37.0	24.5	24.3	36.5	38.2	45.3	41.8	36.5	35.8	34.4	35.5	22.0	17.6	46.1	34.0
Labor	1.0	1.7	1.3	1.1	0.7	0.1	2.3	1.5	3.6	0.7	0.0	1.0	1.3	0.8	0.7	0.8
Miscellaneous	9.5	9.9	13.9	11.8	13.0	28.9	19.2	20.6	0.9	19.9	13.9	14.7	9.1	15.8	14.4	13.3
Other Firms	0.6	4.5	9.1	5.7	6.1	4.4	14.5	10.3	4.7	5.6	21.6	10.8	0.8	24.3	5.1	7.8
Women	7.4	4.4	4.3	5.3	14.5	4.2	4.0	6.0	13.0	15.1	5.3	11.5	10.4	9.5	6.4	8.1
Total Other	18.4	20.5	28.4	23.8	34.2	37.7	40.0	33.3	22.3	41.3	40.8	38.0	21.6	50.5	26.5	30.0

204

OCCUPATIONS	8 IRON, COAL & STEEL				9 MINES/EXTRACTIVE				10 RAILROADS				11 SHIPPING			
	UK	FOR	EMP	ALL	UK	FOR	EMP	ALL	UK	FOR	EMP	ALL	UK	FOR	EMP	ALL
Trade & Commerce	11.5	22.0	10.9	13.9	9.6	6.5	24.1	18.2	--	32.4	9.6	17.6	19.3	8.0	55.7	17.8
Manufacturing	19.9	7.3	7.8	11.2	6.3	11.6	2.8	5.0	--	0.7	2.0	1.5	12.9	8.1	4.6	8.3
Professions & Management	7.8	3.8	6.4	6.2	10.8	4.8	3.9	5.5	--	1.9	3.0	2.6	4.4	2.8	4.0	3.3
Misc. Business	10.0	0.1	2.2	4.0	1.2	10.8	1.4	2.9	--	1.6	0.0	0.8	10.4	26.5	13.1	21.6
Total Business	49.3	33.2	27.3	35.2	27.9	33.7	32.2	31.6	--	36.5	15.0	22.6	47.0	45.3	77.4	51.0
Finance	9.7	6.4	5.6	7.0	2.8	4.8	9.9	7.6	--	11.8	6.8	8.5	9.1	4.4	5.4	5.4
Military	1.0	1.2	2.0	1.5	1.2	3.4	0.9	1.4	--	1.9	1.6	1.7	1.7	1.6	2.1	1.7
Misc. Elites	1.7	1.6	2.9	2.2	1.2	3.6	0.4	1.1	--	1.2	1.7	1.5	0.2	7.9	0.6	5.4
Peers & Gents	21.4	34.8	33.7	30.4	40.0	29.0	14.0	21.9	--	20.9	36.8	31.1	22.5	7.8	12.9	11.1
Total Elites	33.8	44.0	44.2	41.1	45.2	40.8	25.1	31.9	--	35.7	46.7	42.8	33.4	21.8	21.0	23.6
Labor	1.6	1.0	1.6	1.5	1.7	0.0	0.6	0.7	--	0.0	0.8	0.5	9.3	0.1	0.9	1.7
Miscellaneous	6.8	8.9	3.6	5.9	2.5	6.7	16.5	11.9	--	19.7	4.5	9.9	6.8	21.6	0.0	15.5
Other Firms	1.8	8.1	19.1	11.3	20.3	15.7	21.4	20.2	--	2.6	28.6	19.4	0.0	0.5	0.0	0.3
Women	6.6	4.8	4.2	5.1	2.4	3.2	4.1	3.6	--	5.5	4.4	4.7	3.4	10.7	0.7	7.8
Total Other	16.9	22.8	28.5	23.7	26.9	25.5	42.6	36.5	--	27.8	38.3	34.6	19.5	32.8	1.6	25.4

OCCUPATIONS	12 TEA & COFFEE				13 TELEPHONES & TELEGRAPHS				14 TRAMWAYS & OMNIBUSES				15 WATERWORKS			
	UK	FOR	EMP	ALL	UK	FOR	EMP	ALL	UK	FOR	EMP	ALL	UK	FOR	EMP	ALL
Trade & Commerce	--	--	18.4	18.4	--	2.8	2.0	2.5	14.1	2.2	4.8	7.1	--	31.5	17.8	26.4
Manufacturing	--	--	0.3	0.3	--	2.1	10.5	4.9	10.3	10.9	8.0	9.7	--	2.6	2.8	2.7
Professions & Management	--	--	7.5	7.5	--	2.1	7.3	3.8	8.2	4.4	3.4	5.3	--	5.3	7.8	6.3
Misc. Business	--	--	12.2	12.2	--	0.4	1.8	0.9	2.1	0.1	1.3	1.2	--	0.0	0.1	0.0
Total Business	--	--	38.4	38.4	--	7.4	21.5	12.1	34.7	17.7	17.5	23.3	--	39.4	28.6	35.3
Finance	--	--	4.8	4.8	--	8.2	0.8	5.7	3.0	11.2	1.9	5.4	--	6.6	8.3	7.3
Military	--	--	2.9	2.9	--	4.2	2.0	3.4	3.0	0.6	5.0	2.9	--	1.2	1.3	1.2
Misc. Elites	--	--	2.1	2.1	--	22.1	1.9	15.3	3.0	1.5	3.2	2.5	--	1.4	3.3	2.1
Peers & Gents	--	--	18.1	18.1	--	42.5	42.5	42.5	32.8	29.9	28.9	30.5	--	31.9	31.7	31.9
Total Elites	--	--	28.0	28.0	--	76.9	47.2	67.0	41.8	43.2	39.0	41.3	--	41.1	44.7	42.5
Labor	--	--	0.2	0.2	--	0.1	0.6	0.7	5.4	0.1	0.6	2.0	--	0.0	1.0	0.4
Miscellaneous	--	--	17.4	17.4	--	7.8	6.6	7.4	3.3	9.5	5.9	6.2	--	11.0	2.2	7.7
Other Firms	--	--	3.6	3.6	--	4.8	19.1	9.5	0.4	22.9	30.2	17.8	--	5.1	19.0	10.3
Women	--	--	12.3	12.3	--	3.0	5.3	3.8	14.4	6.6	6.8	9.3	--	3.4	4.6	3.8
Total Other	--	--	33.5	33.5	--	15.6	31.3	20.9	23.5	39.2	43.5	35.4	--	19.5	26.7	22.2

Dash (---) = No Data

Note: Percentage calculated for each firm in sample and those figures averaged across all firms. This procedure is utilized so that every firm, regardless of size, is given equal weight.

TABLE 7.4

RELATIVE ATTRACTIVENESS HOME, FOREIGN AND EMPIRE INDUSTRIES:
TWO MEASURES

INDUSTRIES	BUSINESS						ELITES						OTHER					
	UK[1]	UK[2]	FOR[1]	FOR[2]	EMP[1]	EMP[2]	UK[1]	UK[2]	FOR[1]	FOR[2]	EMP[1]	EMP[2]	UK[1]	UK[2]	FOR[1]	FOR[2]	EMP[1]	EMP[2]
Commercial Banking	112	100	123	103	79	66	131	100	105	78	152	111	23	100	67	222	61	227
Breweries & Distilleries	143	100	68	44	103	66	63	100	92	142	108	163	53	100	144	208	90	146
Canals & Docks	117	100	141	113	73	57	61	100	112	180	40	63	121	100	38	24	193	138
Commercial & Industrial	138	100	135	91	158	106	48	100	93	188	66	132	90	100	70	59	87	83
Financial, Land & Development	61	100	76	117	50	75	117	100	96	81	122	101	168	100	130	59	122	63
Financial Trusts	85	100	73	79	83	96	117	100	90	75	92	76	109	100	142	99	124	98
Gas & Lighting	117	100	101	81	92	73	70	100	45	62	124	171	106	100	173	125	80	66
Iron, Coal & Steel	102	100	105	96	91	82	107	100	111	100	119	107	83	100	79	72	87	91
Mines	58	100	107	173	108	172	144	100	103	69	67	46	132	100	88	51	130	88
Railroads	--	--	116	--	50	--	--	--	90	--	126	--	--	--	96	--	116	--
Shipping	98	100	144	137	260	246	106	100	54	50	56	51	96	100	112	90	5	
Tea & Coffee	--	--	--	--	129	--	--	--	--	--	75	--	--	--	--	--	102	--
Telephones & Telegraphs	--	--	24	--	72	--	--	--	193	--	127	--	--	--	54	--	95	--
Trams & Omnibuses	72	100	56	73	59	75	133	100	109	79	105	76	115	100	135	89	132	99
Waterworks	--	--	125	--	96	--	--	--	103	--	120	--	--	--	67	--	81	--

[1]Relative to all investments.
[2]Relative to UK investments.
[Both measures scaled to average 100]

Dash (--) = No Data

gas and light companies; canals; breweries and distilleries; and waterworks, and somewhat attractive for railroad investment. When it came to the commercial and industrial sector, the Empire was apparently far less appealing than the foreign sector. In general, it appears that the Empire attracted investment of the elites in railroads, public utilities, and banking, but that if they were interested in directly supporting the production and distribution of commodities, they looked elsewhere.

A word might be in order about the stockholders in the sample whose shareholdings were of considerable value and about whom biographical information is available. Nineteen such investors held shares in a single company valued at between £25,000 and £50,000; twenty-two had holdings between £50,000 and £100,000; and thirty-five held securities worth more than £100,000. Of this last group, twenty-two were peers and gents; ten, merchants; and three, bankers. The single largest investment was £804,000 in Dalgety and Company, and not surprisingly it was held by Frederick G. Dalgety. The most popular security for the large investors was, however, the Bengal Nagpur Railroad. No less than eighteen of the over-£100,000 group invested in the line, and all but two of the eighteen were peers and gents. Joseph Christy and James Alexander were the two largest holders, with shares valued at £600,000 each. Thomas Sutherland, chairman of the board of the Pacific and Orient, held £400,000, and two prominent British Jews had large holdings as well. Nathan de Rothschild, the first of his religion to be created a peer and the son of Lionel de Rothschild, the first Jew to take a seat in the House of Commons and the man responsible for generating the short-term funds necessary for the British purchase of the controlling interest in the Suez Canal, owned shares to the value of £200,000. Leonard Lionel Cohen, the son of another early Jewish member of Parliament, owned shares valued at £300,000.

The second most popular investment for the £100,000-plus cohort was the Merchant's Trust. Included on its share list were seven men – four merchants, two bankers, and a "gentleman" each of whom controlled between £100,000 and £150,000. Among those seven were two members of the Gibbs family – Alban and Vicary – both partners in Antony Gibbs and Sons, and Sir John Willoughby (the "gent"), fifth baronet, a soldier who served in Egypt and Matabeleland and who accompanied Dr. Jameson on his famous and ill-fated raid into the Transvaal.

Of the twenty-two investors who reported holdings in the £50 to £100,000 range, eight were peers and gents; four, bankers; four, businesspeople or manufacturers; and one, a soldier. The latter, Major General John Clark, had served primarily in India, and he too put a part of his fortune (£94,800) to work in the Bengal and Nagpur Railroad. The favorite investment of this group, however, was again the Merchant's Trust. Among the seven who held shares in that firm was Sir Everard Hambro, one of the directors of the Bank of England and the son of the noted banker, Baron Hambro. He owned shares in the company worth £94,500. John Hays Hammond, the mining engineer, who had served as the special expert for the U.S. Geological Survey team that surveyed the California gold fields and had later worked as a consultant to Cecil Rhodes, invested £90,000 in the Bulwayo Waterworks. Of the nineteen shareholders in the £25,000 to £50,000 range, nine were peers and gents, and among that group railroads were the favorite choice.

It is evident that experience in the Empire helped motivate investment in the colonies, usually in an area where the investor had served. Thus, General Clark, who had been stationed in India, held shares in the Bengal Nagpur Railroad. Sir John Willoughby, long involved in Rhodesia, invested in the Bulwayo Waterworks as did Rhodes's advisor, John Hammond. James Alexander, who held the largest block of Bengal Nagpur stock, had been the last agent for India in London. Thomas Russell, although residing in Eaton Square, had been defense minister for New Zealand. He held £82,258 worth of shares in the New Zealand Mines Trust. Lieutenant General George Jackson, who had served in the Punjab, however, preferred to place his trust in London's Maypole Dairy!

Of the total of almost 80,000 shareholders in all the companies, at least 323 had sat in the House of Commons at some time between 1860 and 1912 (out of the total of 3,768). At first blush this seems a small number; but they represented not only 8 percent of the total membership, but also 1.5 percent of the value of all outstanding stock in the sampled companies. It is difficult to judge exactly the degree to which MP participation compares with the involvement of other groups in similar circumstances, but it appears to have been substantially higher. Virtually none of the great names of British politics appear on the roster of stockholders, and even when they do their holdings were usually small. To be sure, the wealthy Joseph Chamberlain showed his faith in the Empire of which he was the leading prophet by investing £15,000 in the Royal Niger Company, £9,500 in the National Africa Company, and £500 in the Kleksdorp Estate. Arthur Balfour, a man of great means, limited himself to £3,000 in the Floating Dock of St. Thomas and £636 in the Colonies Securities Trust. Henry Labouchere, the fierce opponent of Empire, held £12,500 worth of stock in the Boston Consolidated Mine.

Of the 15,000 stockholders in sample domestic companies, 29 were MPs, and they held shares to the value of £208,000 (1.3 percent of the outstanding shares and 2.1 percent of their value). This figure is in some sense reduced, however, when it is realized that one of their number, William Cuthbert Quilter, the innovative accountant, owned £100,000-worth of securities in a single company, the Railway Rolling Stock Trust. Just over 2 percent of the value of shares (£715,000) in sample foreign companies were held by MPs. Eighteen owned 3.8 percent (£26,000) of the outstanding stock in the Peking Syndicate, and three held 19 percent (£44,000) of the Chile Telephone Company; but again, £348,000 of the £715,000 was held by Quilter.

It must be reiterated that of the some 104 firms in which MPs held shares, only 14 were domestic (about one-fourth of the total). Foreign investment was more popular; there were 113 MP shareholders in 39 different companies. However, 181 owned shares (valued at £1,520,000) in 51 Empire firms, out of a total of close to 40,000 stock-holders who had invested almost £118 million in 126 firms. Of the MPs' investment, £1,115,000 was invested in the Bengal Nagpur Railroad alone. Of that total, Bernhard Samuelson held £400,000-worth of shares; William Henry Smith, £300,000; and Frederick Thorpe Mappin, £200,000.

In interpreting this data, it soon becomes clear that because of the large holdings of a few individuals, the value of shares held by MPs is not a very useful measure. In terms of the location chosen by MPs for their investment, the foreign and Empire sectors certainly held

TABLE 7.5

GEOGRAPHIC DISTRIBUTION OF SAMPLE STOCKHOLDERS
BY FRACTION OF VALUE HELD

(Percents)

STOCKHOLDER RESIDENCE	FIRM LOCATION			
	United Kingdom	Foreign	Empire	All
Asia	0.0	1.1	*	.3
Europe	.4	8.4	2.5	3.7
North Africa & Middle East	*	.1	*	*
North America	*	5.5	*	1.6
South & Central America	*	1.6	.1	.5
Other Empires	0.0	*	*	*
Total Foreign	.4	16.7	2.6	6.1
Dependent Government	0.0	.1	1.8	.9
Responsible Government	.1	*	4.9	2.4
India	.0	*	1.8	.9
Total Empire	.1	.1	8.5	4.2
London EC	9.9	33.7	38.6	30.7
London Other	10.9	17.2	19.9	17.1
Total London	20.8	50.9	58.5	47.7
Home	4.2	4.3	6.4	5.3
Lancashire	9.6	8.0	2.1	5.5
Midlands	8.1	2.3	2.5	3.7
Rural East	2.5	.8	1.1	1.4
Rural West	6.4	2.8	3.2	1.9
South & Southwest	9.0	2.8	3.7	4.6
North	5.1	1.7	.5	1.9
Yorkshire	14.2	3.1	1.7	4.9
Non-Metropolitan England	59.1	25.8	21.2	30.8
TOTAL ENGLAND	79.9	76.7	79.7	78.8
Scotland	8.6	4.5	7.6	7.0
Ireland	1.4	1.1	.9	1.1
Wales	9.5	.6	.6	2.6
Total Celtic Fringe	19.5	6.2	9.1	10.7
TOTAL UNITED KINGDOM	99.4	82.9	88.8	89.5
Known Total	100.0	99.7	99.9	99.8
Unknown Total	0.0	.3	.1	.2
All Total	100.0	100.0	100.0	100.0

*Less than .05 percent

pride of place over the domestic. As to the percentage of companies with MP shareholders, the foreign sector has the highest figure with 53 percent, followed by Empire with 40, and domestic with 23. When it comes to the percentage of MP shareholders in the total, the results are similar – foreign, 0.5; Empire, 0.4; and the United Kingdom, 0.2 percent.

III. The geographical distribution of stockholders

Table 7.5 displays the geographic distribution of shareholders. No matter whether "east Londoners" (EC) are included or not, the data place the most important conclusions into sharp focus.[13] Any thought that British domestic firms depended on overseas investors is immediately dispelled; and the contribution of those investors to British enterprise in the foreign and Empire sectors, while large, was far from dominant. Under the most generous assumption (removal of all EC residents), overseas shareholders accounted for less than .5 percent of domestic, about one-third of foreign, and 22 percent of Empire issues. If EC owners are included, the overseas proportions of firms located in the foreign sector is about one-sixth and Empire firms no more than one in ten.

In the Celtic fringe, Irish investment in no sector exceeded 1.5 percent. The Welsh and the Scots, however, made a substantial contribution to domestic industry, and the Scots owned almost 5 percent of foreign and more than 7 percent of Empire securities as well. The pattern suggested by the Scottish and Welsh experience is underscored when attention is focused on England. Depending on how one treats the City of London, as much as one-fifth or as little as one-tenth of domestic shares were held in London, and the rest were owned by stockholders living outside the metropolis. Domestic shares were very broadly held, with stockholders spread fairly evenly from Land's End to John O'Groats. There were greater-than-average concentrations in the South and Southwest, in Yorkshire, and in the North and less than typical concentrations in the Home Counties and the East; but British industry was truly domestic industry.

In the case of the foreign sector, other than London, only Lancashire stands out. Residents of the capital, however, held less than 20 percent of the foreign shares if the City is excluded and more than one-half if it is not. In the case of the Empire, there was no secondary concentration in Lancashire, and, depending on the measure, the London proportion ranges from one-fifth to three-fifths of the total. If holdings are adjusted for population differences, it appears that a Londoner was more likely to invest in equities than his "country" cousin, but there was also a sharp contrast between London and the rest of the country when it came to selecting where to invest. A Londoner was about twice as likely as a non-London resident to make an investment in domestic equities, but the population-adjusted index for London was only slightly higher than the Yorkshire (the next highest) figure. Those same Londoners, however, were twelve times as likely to buy foreign securities as their non-London countrymen and eighteen times as likely to buy Empire securities. Nor were there other regions with indices close to London's. In the foreign sector, Lancashire residents displayed the second highest investment propensity (thanks to the citizens of Manchester and Liverpool), but that figure was only one-sixth the London number. In the case of the Empire, the scenario is repeated. Residents of the Home Counties bought Empire shares more frequently than any other non-London group (and one can wonder whether many were not actually Londoners), but their average was only one-seventh that of London.

One conclusion is obvious. While Britain was a very important market for equities, it was not one capital market but two.[14] Domestic firms enjoyed the savings of London residents, but they could not have survived without the accumulations of investors in Cornwall, Birmingham, and rural Rutland. In 1901, 26 million of England's 31 million people lived outside the capital, but, in terms of foreign equities, the contribution of that 26 million was only one and one-half times as large as that of the residents of greater London, even if the entire holdings of EC residents are removed from consideration. Moreover, in the case of the Empire, the total contributions of the two groups (the one, five and a half times as large as the other) were almost equal. If the EC residents are counted, then the 4.6 million London residents contributed twice as much to foreign, and two and three-quarters times as much to Empire finance as all the rest of England. To help place the foregoing in context, it might be useful to point out, based on geographical location at time of death, that of the some 57 millionaires in Great Britain who died in the period 1880–99, 11 were situated in the City and 10 elsewhere in London. The next largest contingents were 8 at Merseyside; 4 at Clydeside; and 4 in the Nottingham-Derby area. There were only two millionaires listed for greater Manchester.[15]

IV. Conclusions

The analysis presented in this chapter is designed to uncover any differences between the composition of stockholders who invested in the Empire and those who chose domestic or foreign equities. It appears that there were substantial contrasts between investors in domestic enterprises and those who bought shares in overseas companies, and even considerable differences between investors who chose the Empire and those who preferred investments in lands not owing fealty to the British Crown. Given the way that the data were collected, it is difficult to investigate the composition of the "investment portfolios" of the occupational groups; however, Table 7.6 provides an index of relative holdings for the elite and business classes.[16]

While there were some important interoccupational differences, businesspeople as a whole were twice as likely to invest in domestic as in Empire securities and about a sixth more likely to invest in domestic than in foreign securities. Of that group, merchants held the highest proportion of their "portfolios" in overseas investments, but as far as the Empire was concerned, their proportions were still below those held by any elite subgroup except the military, and it was equal to that. Such behavior was, however, not typical of their

TABLE 7.6

INDEX OF RELATIVE HOLDINGS BY OCCUPATIONS
UK = 100

Occupation	UK	Foreign	Empire
Merchants	100	173	76
Manufacturers	100	24	13
Professional and Management	100	66	64
Miscellaneous Business	100	100	41
All Business	100	86	45
Financiers	100	228	97
Military	100	63	76
Miscellaneous Elite	100	200	260
Peers and Gents	100	97	166
All Elites	100	115	153

foreign investments. Merchants displayed a very strong affinity for those securities; and financiers and miscellaneous elites aside, they were more likely to invest in the foreign sector than any other group. Removal of the merchants from the calculations, for example, reduces that foreign index for the business group from 86 to 53. Manufacturers, on the other hand, displayed the least interest in overseas and particularly Empire investment. Members of that group were eight times as likely to invest in domestic as in Empire securities.

The elites appear to have been somewhat more inclined to invest in foreign issues (the index is about 15 percent higher) but very much more likely as a whole to invest in Empire than in domestic issues. In the latter case the index was more than half again the domestic figure. Oddly enough, the military seem to resemble the business group far more than the other elites. They displayed a fairly strong preference for domestic as opposed to any overseas investments. The financiers appear to have much preferred foreign investment, and their index for Empire commitments was slightly below their domestic baseline. Miscellaneous elites showed the strongest preference for overseas investment; they acquired foreign securities at rates more than twice as high as domestic, and Empire shares at rates two and a half times as great. Finally, the numerically largest group, the peers and gents, display no particular predilection for foreign shares (their index was slightly less than 100), but a strong (more than 60 percent above domestic) preference for Empire investments.

The conclusions are quite clear. Businesspeople did invest abroad, but their major interest was the domestic economy. While the merchants should have been interested in foreign political developments, they, like the rest of the businesspeople, were more oriented toward domestic than Empire problems. For the elites the opposite was true, although military officers were an exception. If, however,

TABLE 7.7

RELATIVE ATTRACTIVENESS, ELITES/BUSINESSMEN BY INDUSTRY

	UK	Foreign	Empire
Commercial Banks	135	85	188
Breweries and Distilleries	51	135	102
Commercial & Industrial	40	68	40
Financial Land & Development	219	124	239
Financial Trusts	157	123	108
Gas and Light	68	44	131
Iron, Coal and Steel	121	105	127
Mines	285	95	60
Railroads	--	77	242
Shipping	125	37	21
Tea and Coffee	--	--	56
Telephone and Telegraphs	--	813	172
Trams and Omnibuses	213	193	172
Waterworks	--	81	121
Canals and Docks	59	78	53

*Source: Table 7.4

the success of Empire ventures was linked to political policies at home, the elites (and particularly the miscellaneous and peers and gents) must have been more concerned with the shape of those policies than their counterparts in the business sector.

There were, of course, some substantial interindustry deviations from the all-firms average. Businesspeople were more heavily involved in some industries, and the elites in others. A measure of relative affinity is presented in Table 7.7. A number larger than 100 suggests that the industry was relatively attractive to the elites and relatively unattractive to the business community. For numbers less than 100, the opposite holds.

The elites' interest in Empire was strongest in railroads; commercial banks; and financial, land, and development companies; and the "public utilities" – gas and light, telephones and telegraphs, tramways and omnibuses, and waterworks. Businesspeople, however, tended to focus their Empire investments in the "private" sector: in shipping, commercial and industrial, and tea and coffee plantations. While the Empire connection was important, these were competitive industries, and profits must have depended far less directly on the particular form of the political structure. As Schumpeter has observed:

> . . . where free trade prevails no class has an interest in forceable expansion . . . . Where the cultural backwardness of a region makes normal intercourse dependent on colonization, it does not matter, assuming free trade, which of the civilized nations undertakes the task of colonization. Dominion of the seas, in such a case, means little more than a maritime traffic police. Similarly, it is a matter of indifference to a nation whether a railway concession in a foreign country is acquired by one of its own citizens or not – just as long as the railway is built.[17]

TABLE 7.8

INDEX OF RELATIVE HOLDINGS BY LOCATION

Residence of Stockholder	Location of Firm		
	UK	Foreign	Empire
Non-UK	100	1018	471
London EC	100	198	164
London Other	100	106	154
London Total	100	156	161
Home	100	90	176
Lancashire	100	122	47
Midlands	100	23	29
Rural East	100	229	187
Rural West	100	63	82
South & Southwest	100	48	72
North	100	23	12
Yorkshire	100	12	12
Non-London England Total	100	50	52
Total England	100	92	96
Scotland	100	86	159
Ireland	100	120	93
Wales	100	12	14
Celtic Total	100	58	89

It has also been possible to examine the geographic distribution of stockholders, and those distributions are summarized in Table 7.8.[18] Overseas residents showed little inclination to invest in domestic securities; those in foreign countries placed most of their accumulations in foreign concerns, and shareholders who lived in the colonies turned almost entirely to Empire firms. Ninety percent of the shareholders, however, resided in the United Kingdom, and it is their spatial distribution that is of most interest. The average figures for Scotland, Ireland, and Wales would suggest that investors there looked much like the typical Briton living outside the capital, but that average masks very different behavior by the citizens of the three Celtic "nations." The Welsh were more English than the English and seldom invested in any nondomestic securities. The Irish were, as might be expected, far more catholic in their tastes; on the average, however, they preferred domestic to Empire, and foreign to domestic shares. The Scots displayed a little more interest in foreign equities than the typical non-London English, but they still preferred domestic investment. On the other hand their preference for Empire shares was as strong as a resident of the City – and that is a strong preference indeed.

Interest, however, must center on the English investors since they accounted for more than 90 percent of UK and 80 percent of all holdings; and there were clearly two Englands: London and the Provinces. To the extent that equity holdings provide an adequate measure of total investments, a Londoner's portfolio held less than one-quarter domestic, more than one-third foreign, and almost two-fifths Empire securities. Within Greater London the EC residents

TABLE 7.9

RELATIVE ATTRACTIVENESS OF INDUSTRIES

London
Non-London

Industry	UK (1)*	UK (2)*	Foreign (1)	Foreign (2)	Empire (1)	Empire (2)
			Location of Firm			
Commercial Banks	55	73	88	95	57	67
Breweries and Distilleries	35	43	110	116	52	68
Canals and Docks	54	32	422	475	282	282
Commercial and Industrial	76	81	84	96	98	87
Financial Land and Development	329	306	111	95	127	161
Financial Trusts	184	238	38	35	93	75
Gas and Light	82	80	244	275	62	67
Iron, Coal and Steel	56	61	104	72	83	78
Mines	163	170	68	59	202	143
Tea and Coffee	--	--	--	--	61	51
Railroads	--	--	125	140	189	220
Shipping	102	81	14	16	86	107
Telephone and Telegraph	--	--	118	133	40	56
Trams and Omnibuses	139	112	359	380	101	117
Waterworks	--	--	394	448	178	178

*(1) Non-London is England
*(2) Non-London is UK

were strongly attracted to foreign investments and relatively strongly attracted to the Empire (the portfolio ratios were 22, 43, and 35). In London, outside the City, the Empire was very popular; but those investors appear to have been largely indifferent when it came to choosing between home and foreign investment.

In the "country," both the Empire and foreign indices are about twice the domestic. The foreign-sector figure was much inflated by the residents of Lancashire and the rural east, while that latter area and the Home Counties kept the Empire index as high as it was. The areas outside London were not, however, all identical. In the North, in Yorkshire, and in the Midlands the domestic proportions ranged from more than two-thirds to four-fifths and averaged about three-quarters. Elsewhere, the domestic figure, though much lower, was still far above ratios recorded in London. Empire proportions average 14 percent of all investment in the four northern regions (the North, Lancashire, Yorkshire, and the Midlands), but they were over two times that level in the four southern (Home, East, West and South, and Southwest). Even in the country, the "London disease" appears to have infected the contiguous regions.

Table 7.9 provides an indication of the relative attractiveness of particular industries to London and provincial investors (figures greater than 100 indicate a London bias and less than 100 a provincial bias).[19] The index compares holdings in a particular industry with the typical all-industry holdings of Londoners and those outside the metropolis. The results are also less sharp than for the occupational distributions, but in the Empire, Londoners had a propensity to invest in canals and docks; financial, land, and investment com-

TABLE 7.10

RELATIVE ATTRACTIVENESS HOME, FOREIGN AND EMPIRE
BY OCCUPATION AND LOCATION
BUSINESS AND ELITES ONLY

(Ratio is London to Non-London)

Occupation	Location of Firm		
	UK	Foreign	Empire
Merchants	19	135	110
Manufacturers	44	140	162
Professional	22	114	126
Miscellaneous Business	2	40	635
Total Business	17	122	142
Financiers	61	105	103
Military	132	108	94
Miscellaneous Elites	152	129	90
Gents and Peers	49	102	105
Total Elites	62	106	102

panies; and mines, in the unregulated sectors; and railroads, trams and omnibuses, and waterworks, among the public utilities. The non-London investors, while gazing abroad far less frequently than their London peers, looked in different directions when their eyes did turn outward. In the Empire their investments, with the exceptions of gas and light and telephones and telegraphs, clustered about the nonregulated part of the economy. They displayed above-average indices for three of the five goods-producing sectors (brewing, iron, coal and steel, and tea and coffee), and in addition they invested above-typical amounts in commercial banks and shipping. In the "public" sector they showed greater-than-average interest in gas and light and telephone and telegraph companies.

Finally, given the two-nation character of imperial investment, it appears useful to examine the composition of the occupational "portfolios" in the two regions. In that way it may be possible to determine if London investors in the Empire came from an occupational distribution similar to country investors or if members of the same occupational group behaved differently if they lived in London. Table 7.10 provides some insights into that question. An entry greater than 100 indicates that Londoners had a stronger preference for the sector's securities than their provincial cousins, and a number less than 100 manifests a country-investor preference.[20] If the behavior of the investors was similar in both regions, the ratios should be close to 100.

In the case of businesspeople, it is apparent that Londoners behaved very differently. In every subcategory, London businesspeople invested far less often in domestic industry and far more frequently in the Empire. The miscellaneous business category aside, the same preference appears to hold for foreign investments as well. In the business sector as a whole, the ratio of London to non-London indices stood at less than one-fifth for domestic and almost one and one-half for Empire investment.

For the elite group, the urban-rural differences are much less clearly marked. Every subgroup appears somewhat more willing to invest in the foreign sector than were their counterparts outside London, but there is no such uniformity of feelings in the domestic and Empire sectors. In the former, although the overall elite ratio for London is well below that for the provinces, both the military and miscellaneous groups tended to invest in domestic activities relatively more often than their country counterparts. In the case of Empire investment, the rates were similar for Londoner and non-Londoner alike. In London, financiers and peers and gents appear to have viewed such investment as slightly more attractive than did their rural confreres, but the opposite was true for the other two groups.

Altogether it appears that the London bias toward overseas investment, while in part accounted for by the somewhat greater concentration of elite investment in the metropolis (peers and gents accounted for about 5 percent more of London than of rural investment), can in large measure be traced to the attraction of that overseas investment for London businesspeople. Clearly that lure was less strong outside the capital, and the farther one traveled north from London the weaker it became.

APPENDIX 7.1

OCCUPATIONAL GROUPS

BUSINESS

1. Trade and Commerce
   Merchants
   Sales and Agency
   Retail and Business Services

2. Manufacturing
   Manufacturers
   Engineering and Construction
   Brewers and Distilleries

3. Professions
   Management
   Medicine
   Education
   Creative Arts
   Legal Professions
   Entrepreneurs
   Publishing

4. Miscellaneous Business
   Agriculture
   Marine, Transportation
     and Communication
   Mining

ELITES

1. Finance
   Bankers

2. Military
   Military Officers

3. Miscellaneous Elites
   Government and Civil Service
   Ecclesiastical
   Members of the House of Commons (with no other occupation)
   Land and Property Owners

4. Peers and Gents
   Peers and Gents

OTHERS

1. Labour
   Craftsmen
   Unskilled Labour
   Personal Service
   Skilled Labour

2. Miscellaneous
   Retired
   Deceased
   Unknown
   Unknown Abroad

3. Miscellaneous Public Companies
   Miscellaneous Public Companies
   Banks

4. Women
   Women

APPENDIX 7.2

UNITED KINGDOM REGIONS AND CONSTITUENT COUNTIES

ENGLAND

The North
    Cumberland
    Durham
    Northumberland
    Westmorland

Yorkshire

Lancashire

Midlands Industrial
    Derbyshire
    Leicestershire
    Nottinghamshire
    Staffordshire
    Warwickshire

Rural Western
    Berkshire
    Buckinghamshire
    Cheshire
    Gloucestershire
    Herefordshire
    Northamptonshire
    Oxfordshire
    Shropshire
    Worcestershire

Rural Eastern
    Bedfordshire
    Cambridgeshire
    Hertfordshire
    Huntingdonshire
    Lincolnshire
    Norfolk
    Rutland
    Suffolk

South and Southwest
    Cornwall
    Devonshire
    Dorset
    Hampshire
    Somersetshire
    Sussex
    Wiltshire
    Channel Isles

Home Counties
    Essex
    Kent
    Middlesex
    Surrey

London
    E
    EC
    N
    NE
    NW
    S
    SE
    SW
    W
    WC

WALES

North Wales
    Anglesey
    Brecknockshire
    Carnarvonshire
    Cardiganshire
    Denbighshire
    Flintshire
    Merionethshire
    Radnorshire

South Wales
    Carmarthenshire
    Glamorganshire
    Monmouthshire
    Pembrokeshire

SCOTLAND

The Highlands
    Argyllshire
    Buteshire
    Caithness-shire
    Dumbartonshire
    Inverness-shire
    Orkney
    Ross and Cromarty
    Shetland
    Stirlingshire
    Sutherlandshire

Northeast
    Aberdeenshire
    Banffshire
    Clackmannanshire
    Fifeshire
    Forfarshire
    Kincardineshire
    Kinross-shire
    Moray
    Nairnshire
    Perthshire
    Elginshire

South
    Ayrshire
    Berwickshire
    Dumfriesshire
    Edinburghshire
    Haddingtonshire
    Kirkcudbrightshire
    Lanarkshire
    Linlithgowshire
    Peeblesshire
    Renfrewshire
    Roxburghshire
    Selkirkshire
    Wigtownshire

IRELAND

Ulster
    Antrim
    Armagh
    Cavan
    Donegal
    Down
    Fermanagh
    Londonderry
    Monaghan
    Tyrone

Leinster
    Carlow
    County Dublin
    Kildare
    Kilkenny
    Kings
    Leix
    Longford
    Louth
    Meath
    Offaly
    Westmeath
    Wexford
    Wicklow
    Queens

Munster
    Clare
    Cork
    Kerry
    Limerick
    Tipperary
    Waterford

Connaught
    Galway
    Leitrim
    Mayo
    Roscommon
    Sligo
    Connaught

The shareholders in imperial enterprises

APPENDIX 7.3

VALUE AND STANDARD DEVIATION OF AVERAGE SHAREHOLDINGS BY LOCATION AND OCCUPATION

	HOME			FOREIGN			EMPIRE		
	$\bar{x}$	σ	$\sigma/\bar{x}$	$\bar{x}$	σ	$\sigma/\bar{x}$	$\bar{x}$	σ	$\sigma/\bar{x}$
Trade & Commerce	409	1,597	3.91	2,998	20,372	6.79	1,885	15,949	8.49
Manufacturing	1,185	4,732	3.99	1,782	7,052	3.96	1,405	5,888	4.19
Professions	589	4,428	7.51	1,071	3,730	3.48	1,469	7,476	5.08
Misc. Business	579	3,283	5,67	3,711	23,792	6,41	1,997	16,734	8.38
Total Business	628	3,345	5.32	2,244	15,559	6.93	1,693	12,726	7.52
Finance	667	2,375	3.56	3,020	13,479	4.46	1,885	11,351	6.02
Military	801	1,718	2.15	1,330	5,687	4.28	2,405	9,643	4.01
Misc. Elite	673	5,526	8.21	1,541	12,096	7.85	3,218	23,725	7.27
Gents & Peers	1,025	5,664	5.53	1,678	7,635	4.55	3,295	23,061	7.00
Total Elites	912	4,891	5.36	1,821	9,097	4.99	3,043	21,239	6.98
Labour	185	626	3.39	465	1,425	3.07	300	1,425	4.75
Miscellaneous	405	1,799	4.44	1,111	15,393	13.85	1,611	8,644	5.36
Public Companies	7,569	16,642	2.20	10,361	37,686	3.64	49,737	166,025	3.34
Women	238	746	3.14	545	2,503	4.60	2,017	15,771	7.82
Total Other	362	2,278	6.29	1,046	12,661	12.11	2,671	27,687	10.36
All Shareholders	642	3,671	5.72	1,555	12,205	7.85	2,615	22,094	8.45

8   The sources of government revenues

I. Introduction

Empire investors appear to have come from the ranks of the elites and the London merchants and, outside London, what has traditionally been regarded as the British middle class (where the term is used to encompass both factory and shopowners) does not seem to have been heavily involved.[1] If the two former groups were the recipients of the imperial subsidy, who paid the bill? There is no more powerful policy tool available to a government than its budget, but the ability to spend is based to a large extent on the revenues raised through taxation. These imposts are the subject of this chapter. Empire shareholders found the Empire valuable, but some of that institution's worth depended on the imperial subsidy. Its size was substantial, and its benefits not spread evenly. The middle class, particularly those living in the Midlands and the North, received substantially less than their proportionate shares, while the financiers, government officials, the leisure classes, and London merchants received more. In the Empire indigenous entrepreneurs fared even better since they paid none of the subsidy but received full measure of its rewards. It seems natural, therefore, to analyze the tax structure and discover who paid and who was relieved from those costs. Neither task can be effected with complete precision, but the data yield some very suggestive hypotheses which have a substantial measure of support.[2]

II. The Empire

Table 8.1 provides a summary of revenues received by the "central" governments. While most revenues came from taxes, a significant proportion originated in nontax sources. In the United Kingdom such sources accounted for less than 15 percent of the total, but in the Empire the proportion was more than twice as great. The trends in the total revenue series are somewhat unexpected. Over time, revenues rose in the United Kingdom, in the colonies with responsible government, and in the foreign sectors, but there is no evidence of such an increase in the dependent Empire. On average the largest

221

TABLE 8.1A

TOTAL GOVERNMENT REVENUE

(£'s Per Capita; Railroads Out)

	Colony Weights								Population Weights							
	UKN	UKT	RG	DC	India	PSts	FD	FU	UKN	UKT	RG	DC	India	PSts	FD	FU
1860-64	2.11	--	2.70	1.00	.31	.16	0.77	0.77	2.11	--	1.58	.66	.31	.18	.71	.41
1865-69	1.87	2.18	2.92	1.01	.31	.17	0.91	0.64	1.87	2.18	1.64	.65	.31	.18	.94	.43
1870-74	1.84	2.59	2.98	0.98	.29	.23	0.88	0.78	1.84	2.59	1.84	.62	.29	.17	.87	.44
1875-79	1.98	3.04	3.36	0.91	.31	.20	0.97	1.13	1.98	3.04	2.19	.61	.31	.17	.95	.60
1880-84	2.20	3.46	3.79	0.89	.33	.27	1.28	1.15	2.20	3.46	2.56	.67	.33	.27	1.23	0.57
1885-89	2.72	4.33	6.11	1.09	.23	.20	1.73	1.04	2.72	4.33	3.13	.76	.23	.27	1.61	.69
1890-94	2.95	4.79	5.09	1.25	.18	.19	1.69	0.94	2.95	4.79	3.11	.72	.18	.26	1.70	.75
1895-99	3.56	6.23	6.19	1.23	.20	.21	2.05	0.98	3.56	6.23	3.43	.57	.20	.27	2.08	.87
1900-04	4.19	7.07	5.66	1.12	.23	.35	2.09	0.72	4.19	7.07	3.65	.42	.23	.31	1.95	.87
1905-09	4.01	7.52	3.29	1.04	.23	.35	2.20	0.99	4.01	7.52	3.14	.38	.23	.32	2.10	1.16
1910-12	4.02	7.54	3.47	1.10	.22	.40	2.39	1.03	4.02	7.54	3.51	.39	.22	.32	2.23	.95
AVG(d)	2.82	4.76	4.17	1.05	.26	.24	1.51	.92	2.82	4.76	2.68	.59	.26	.24	1.46	.69

UKN: United Kingdom National   PSts: Indian Princely States
UKT: United Kingdom Total   FD: Foreign Developed Countries
RG: Responsible Government   FU: Foreign Underdeveloped Countries
DC: Dependent Colonies

revenues were raised in the colonies with responsible government (£2.68, population weights – £4.76, colony weighted), but the number for the United Kingdom was still £2.82. That for the dependent colonies was probably less than £1.00. The latter figure was below the average of the foreign-developed countries and probably less than the average of the foreign-underdeveloped sector as well. In India, however, average revenues were well below those of the foreign-underdeveloped countries and the dependent colonies but about equal to the figures for the Indian Princely States.

While the focus of this chapter is on tax revenues, given the important role played by nontax earnings in the Empire, they deserve a brief comment. Both dependent and self-governing colonies drew heavily from licenses and fees – charges that averaged about £.16 per person per year. That figure compares with an average of £.08 among developed and £.02 among underdeveloped countries. However, the bias toward licenses and fees, while accounting for a substantial portion of the extra nontax revenues in the case of the dependent colonies, was a much less significant contributor to the colonies with responsible government. For them (and to a lesser extent in the dependent colonies) it was revenues from natural resources and particularly from public land sales that in large measure accounted for the high level of nontax receipts.

Table 8.2 summarizes the receipts from land sales and leases and from mining royalties. While the colonies with responsible government were clearly the greatest beneficiaries from the vastness of the imperial lands, the entire non-Indian Empire drew on these "public" resources far more than the rest of the world. In the case of land, revenues were highest in Australasia. They averaged £1.78 per capita

TABLE 8.1B

SOURCES OF GOVERNMENT REVENUE - POPULATION WEIGHTS

(£'s Per Capita)

	United Kingdom National			Responsible Government			Dependent Colonies			India			Princely States		
	Total	Taxes	Misc	Total	Taxes	Misc	Total	Taxes	Misc	Total	Taxes	Misc	Total	Taxes	Misc
1860-64	2.11	1.97	.14	1.58	.79	.79	.66	.35	.31	.31	.19	.12	.18	.16	.02
1865-69	1.87	1.70	.17	1.64	.90	.74	.65	.34	.31	.31	.19	.12	.18	.16	.02
1870-74	1.84	1.62	.22	1.84	1.09	.75	.62	.33	.29	.29	.18	.11	.17	.14	.03
1875-79	1.98	1.69	.29	2.19	1.18	1.01	.61	.32	.29	.31	.18	.13	.17	.13	.04
1880-84	2.20	1.87	.33	2.56	1.51	1.05	.67	.36	.31	.33	.19	.14	.27	.21	.06
1885-89	2.72	2.26	.46	3.13	2.01	1.12	.76	.43	.33	.23	.16	.07	.27	.21	.06
1890-94	2.95	2.46	.49	3.11	1.99	1.12	.72	.43	.29	.18	.13	.05	.26	.21	.05
1895-99	3.56	3.00	.56	3.43	2.19	1.24	.57	.37	.20	.20	.15	.05	.27	.21	.06
1900-04	4.19	3.59	.60	3.65	2.33	1.32	.42	.26	.16	.23	.16	.07	.31	.22	.09
1905-09	4.01	3.37	.64	3.14	2.11	1.03	.38	.24	.14	.23	.16	.07	.32	.23	.09
1910-12	4.02	3.31	.71	3.51	2.22	1.29	.39	.27	.12	.22	.15	.07	.32	.24	.08
AVG(y)	2.82	2.41	.41	2.68	1.65	1.03	.59	.34	.25	.26	.17	.09	.25	.19	.06

	Foreign Developed			Foreign Underdeveloped		
	Total	Taxes	Misc	Total	Taxes	Misc
1860-64	.71	.43	.28	.41	.31	.10
1865-69	.94	.59	.35	.43	.31	.12
1870-74	.87	.65	.22	.44	.35	.09
1875-79	.95	.73	.22	.60	.49	.11
1880-84	1.23	.90	.33	.59	.47	.12
1885-89	1.61	1.17	.44	.72	.56	.16
1890-94	1.71	1.14	.57	.76	.55	.21
1895-99	2.08	1.36	.72	.87	.52	.35
1900-04	1.95	1.18	.77	.87	.71	.16
1905-09	2.10	1.17	.93	1.18	.92	.26
1910-12	2.24	1.29	.95	.97	.76	.21
AVG(y)	1.48	.96	.52	.71	.54	.17

(Percents)

	United Kingdom National		Responsible Government		Dependent Colonies		India		Princely States	
	Taxes	Misc	Taxes	Misc	Taxes	Misc	Taxes	Misc	Taxes	Misc
1860-64	93.3	6.7	50.1	49.9	53.6	46.4	61.7	38.3	93.3	6.7
1865-69	91.1	8.9	55.1	44.9	52.5	47.5	61.9	38.1	87.9	12.1
1870-74	88.0	12.0	59.5	40.5	53.3	46.7	63.6	36.4	83.8	16.2
1875-79	85.4	14.6	54.0	46.0	53.4	46.6	57.5	42.5	76.2	23.8
1880-84	85.0	15.0	58.9	41.1	54.0	46.0	57.6	42.4	77.1	22.9
1885-89	83.1	16.9	64.1	35.9	56.4	43.6	69.7	30.3	80.2	19.8
1890-94	83.6	16.4	64.0	36.0	60.3	39.7	72.4	27.6	81.1	18.9
1895-99	84.3	15.7	63.8	36.2	64.2	35.8	74.3	25.7	78.1	21.9
1900-04	85.6	14.4	63.9	36.1	61.8	38.2	70.2	29.8	72.3	27.7
1905-09	83.9	16.1	67.4	32.6	62.3	37.7	69.2	30.8	72.3	27.7
1910-12	82.0	18.0	63.2	36.8	68.3	31.7	69.0	31.0	74.5	25.5
AVG(y)	86.1	13.9	60.3	39.7	57.8	42.2	66.0	34.0	79.6	20.4

	Foreign Developed		Foreign Underdeveloped	
	Taxes	Misc	Taxes	Misc
1860-64	60.7	39.3	75.6	24.4
1865-69	62.1	37.9	72.6	27.4
1870-74	75.1	24.9	80.0	20.0
1875-79	77.2	22.8	82.3	17.7
1880-84	73.6	26.4	80.4	19.6
1885-89	72.8	27.2	78.2	21.8
1890-94	67.3	32.7	72.2	27.8
1895-99	65.4	34.6	60.3	39.7
1900-04	60.3	39.7	81.5	18.5
1905-09	55.7	44.3	77.9	22.1
1910-12	58.4	41.6	79.9	20.1
AVG(y)	66.4	33.6	76.4	23.6

in New South Wales, £1.57 in Queensland, and only in Victoria (£.72) and Tasmania (£.49) did the level fall below £1.00 per person per year. In the rest of the colonies the numbers were much smaller, but they averaged more than £.15 in the Cape, and only on the North American continent were they as low as £.02. Of the dependent colonies five averaged more than £.20, sixteen more than £.02, and only twenty received nothing at all. Among the developed

TABLE 8.2

LAND RELATED REVENUES

(£'s Per Capita)

	LAND SALES				MINING ROYALTIES			
	RG	DC	FD	FU	RG	DC	FD	FU
	PANEL A:		COLONY WEIGHTS					
1860-64	.90	.03	.01	.00	.02	.00	.00	.00
1865-69	.83	.04	.01	.00	.04	.00	.00	.00
1870-74	.69	.03	.01	.00	.03	.00	.00	.00
1875-79	1.02	.03	.01	.02	.02	.00	.00	.00
1880-84	.94	.02	.01	.01	.01	.00	.00	.00
1885-89	1.46	.03	.01	.00	.01	.00	.01	.00
1890-94	.85	.04	.01	.00	.01	.00	.01	.00
1895-99	.75	.03	.01	.01	.04	.00	.01	.00
1900-04	.63	.02	.01	.00	.18	.00	.00	.00
1905-09	.16	.03	.00	.04	.10	.00	.00	.00
1910-12	.13	.03	.02	.01	.16	.00	.00	.00
AVG(d)	.78	.03	.01	.00	.00	.00	.00	.00
	PANEL B:		POPULATION WEIGHTS					
1860-64	.33	.04	.02	.00	.01	.00	.00	.00
1865-69	.34	.05	.02	.00	.02	.00	.00	.00
1870-74	.34	.04	.01	.00	.01	.00	.00	.00
1875-79	.60	.04	.01	.00	.01	.00	.00	.00
1880-84	.50	.03	.01	.00	.01	.00	.00	.00
1885-89	.40	.03	.01	.00	.01	.00	.00	.00
1890-94	.38	.03	.01	.00	.01	.00	.02	.00
1895-99	.36	.02	.01	.00	.01	.00	.02	.00
1900-04	.33	.01	.01	.00	.03	.00	.00	.00
1905-09	.23	.01	.01	.04	.05	.00	.00	.00
1910-12	.25	.01	.05	.01	.09	.00	.00	.00
AVG(d)	.38	.03	.01	.00	.02	.00	.01	.00

RG: Responsible Government
DC: Dependent Colonies
FD: Foreign Developed Countries
FU: Foreign Underdeveloped Countries

countries only five averaged as much as £.01, and of the underde-veloped countries, just four – Argentina, Siam, Guatemala, and Venezuela.

When it comes to mining royalties, earnings were far less, but not surprisingly the figure for the Transvaal was £.58 and New Zealand, Queensland, and Western Australia averaged more than £.02 as did Australia after the formation of the Commonwealth. In the ranks of the dependent colonies, Southern Rhodesia and the Pacific posses-sions (Labuan, Sarawak, and the Gilbert and Ellice Islands) averaged more than £.02. Beyond the Empire, Norway, Russia, Greece, and Spain earned more than £.01, but only Bulgaria of the underdevel-oped countries recovered anything near that amount. It is readily apparent that the colonies with responsible government benefited from the unoccupied lands within their borders and were able to turn those "free resources" into funds to support public expendi-tures without having to increase the burden of taxes.

The important questions, however, concern income derived from tax levies (Table 8.3). Empire residents paid relatively high taxes, but they were less than might have been expected given comparative levels of expenditures. The trend in per capita taxes was generally

TABLE 8.3A

TAXES BY TYPE

(£'s Per Capita - Population Weighted)

	Total	Customs	Excises	Income	Inher-itance	Assessed	Special & Misc	Total	Customs	Excises	Income	Inher-itance	Assessed	Special & Misc
	UNITED KINGDOM NATIONAL							RESPONSIBLE GOVERNMENT						
1860-64	1.97	.68	.54	.41	.13	.10	.11	.79	.71	.03	.00	.00	.01	.04
1865-69	1.70	.62	.56	.17	.14	.09	.12	.90	.80	.06	.00	.00	.00	.04
1870-74	1.62	.54	.62	.15	.13	.08	.10	1.09	.91	.12	.00	.01	.00	.05
1875-79	1.69	.51	.71	.15	.15	.06	.11	1.19	.96	.13	.00	.01	.01	.08
1880-84	1.87	.52	.70	.28	.18	.08	.11	1.51	1.20	.15	.00	.01	.05	.10
1885-89	2.27	.62	.80	.37	.24	.10	.14	2.01	1.54	.21	.00	.02	.08	.16
1890-94	2.46	.61	.89	.42	.31	.07	.16	1.99	1.51	.24	.00	.02	.07	.15
1895-99	3.00	.68	1.03	.53	.45	.08	.23	2.19	1.57	.31	.05	.02	.08	.16
1900-04	3.59	.86	1.06	.86	.51	.07	.23	2.33	1.65	.29	.05	.04	.10	.20
1905-09	3.37	.86	.92	.84	.47	.07	.21	2.11	1.39	.29	.09	.05	.05	.24
1910-12	3.31	.75	.85	.88	.56	.06	.21	2.23	1.56	.30	.10	.06	.07	.14
AVG(d)	2.42	.66	.79	.44	.29	.08	.16	1.64	1.24	.19	.02	.02	.05	.12
	DEPENDENT COLONIES							INDIA						
1860-64	.36	.28	.03	.00	.00	.01	.04	.20	.02	.04	.01	.00	.12	.01
1865-69	.32	.25	.03	.00	.00	.00	.04	.18	.01	.04	.00	.00	.12	.01
1870-74	.33	.24	.03	.00	.00	.01	.05	.18	.01	.04	.00	.00	.12	.01
1875-79	.33	.24	.03	.00	.00	.01	.05	.17	.01	.04	.00	.00	.11	.01
1880-84	.35	.25	.04	.00	.00	.02	.04	.19	.01	.05	.00	.00	.12	.01
1885-89	.43	.27	.07	.00	.00	.04	.05	.15	.00	.04	.00	.00	.10	.01
1890-94	.43	.28	.05	.00	.00	.04	.06	.13	.00	.04	.00	.00	.08	.01
1895-99	.36	.24	.04	.00	.00	.03	.05	.15	.01	.04	.00	.00	.09	.01
1900-04	.26	.17	.03	.00	.00	.01	.05	.15	.01	.04	.01	.00	.08	.01
1905-09	.24	.16	.02	.00	.00	.01	.05	.17	.02	.04	.01	.00	.08	.02
1910-12	.27	.18	.02	.00	.00	.01	.06	.15	.02	.03	.01	.00	.07	.02
AVG(d)	.35	.24	.04	.00	.00	.02	.05	.16	.01	.04	.00	.00	.10	.01
	PRINCELY STATES							FOREIGN DEVELOPED						
1860-64	.16	.00	.02	.00	.00	.14	.00	.42	.09	.18	.01	.00	.10	.04
1865-69	.15	.00	.03	.00	.00	.12	.00	.60	.16	.24	.04	.00	.11	.05
1870-74	.14	.01	.03	.00	.00	.10	.00	.65	.17	.23	.03	.01	.14	.07
1875-79	.14	.01	.03	.00	.00	.09	.01	.73	.17	.29	.02	.01	.15	.09
1880-84	.21	.01	.03	.00	.00	.16	.01	.89	.24	.35	.02	.01	.16	.11
1885-89	.21	.02	.03	.00	.00	.15	.01	1.17	.34	.46	.04	.01	.18	.14
1890-94	.21	.02	.04	.00	.00	.14	.01	1.13	.35	.41	.05	.01	.21	.10
1895-99	.21	.02	.04	.00	.00	.14	.01	1.35	.40	.46	.07	.02	.28	.12
1900-04	.23	.03	.04	.00	.00	.15	.01	1.18	.36	.45	.06	.01	.18	.12
1905-09	.23	.03	.04	.00	.00	.15	.01	1.17	.39	.43	.06	.01	.16	.12
1910-12	.24	.02	.05	.00	.00	.16	.01	1.30	.35	.43	.08	.03	.19	.22
AVG(d)	.20	.02	.03	.00	.00	.14	.01	.96	.27	.36	.04	.01	.17	.11
	FOREIGN UNDERDEVELOPED							UNITED KINGDOM TOTAL						
1860-64	.32	.14	.02	.00	.00	.12	.04							
1865-69	.31	.14	.02	.00	.00	.12	.03	1.90	.62	.56	.17	.14	.29	.12
1870-74	.36	.16	.02	.00	.00	.15	.03	2.11	.54	.62	.15	.13	.57	.10
1875-79	.49	.19	.05	.01	.00	.20	.04	2.28	.51	.71	.15	.15	.65	.11
1880-84	.48	.21	.05	.00	.00	.18	.04	2.58	.52	.70	.28	.18	.79	.11
1885-89	.57	.26	.07	.00	.00	.18	.06	3.20	.62	.80	.37	.24	1.03	.14
1890-94	.55	.26	.06	.00	.00	.17	.06	3.46	.61	.89	.42	.31	1.07	.16
1895-99	.52	.23	.06	.00	.00	.13	.10	4.52	.68	1.03	.53	.45	1.60	.23
1900-04	.71	.39	.09	.00	.00	.10	.13	5.05	.86	1.06	.86	.51	1.53	.23
1905-09	.93	.51	.11	.00	.00	.14	.17	5.06	.86	.92	.84	.47	1.76	.21
1910-12	.76	.44	.09	.00	.00	.11	.12	4.98	.75	.85	.88	.56	1.73	.21
AVG(d)	.54	.26	.06	.00	.00	.15	.07	3.32	.65	.79	.44	.29	.98	.16

upward, and that movement marked the United Kingdom imposts as well. Not only was the tax burden increasing, but taxes in the home country remained among the highest in the world. Overall the "national" figure averaged about £2.40 per person per year, but in the twentieth century the assessment was £3.44. In those parts of the Empire with responsible government the average values are very high when compared to almost any place in the world except Great Britain and a very few of the developed countries (the population-weighted figure for those colonies is £1.64, the colony-

TABLE 8.3B

TAXES BY TYPE

(Percents of Total Taxes - Population Weighted)

	Customs	Excises	Income	Inher-itance	Assessed	Special & Misc	Customs	Excises	Income	Inher-itance	Assessed	Special & Misc
	UNITED KINGDOM NATIONAL						RESPONSIBLE GOVERNMENT					
1860-64	34.5	27.4	20.8	6.6	5.1	5.6	89.9	3.8	0.0	0.0	1.3	5.1
1865-69	36.5	32.9	10.0	8.2	5.3	7.1	88.9	6.7	0.0	0.0	0.0	4.4
1870-74	33.3	38.3	9.3	8.0	4.9	6.2	83.5	11.0	0.0	0.9	0.0	4.6
1875-79	30.2	42.0	8.9	8.9	3.6	6.5	80.7	10.9	0.0	0.8	0.8	6.7
1880-84	27.8	37.4	15.0	9.6	4.3	5.9	79.5	9.9	0.0	0.7	3.3	6.6
1885-89	27.3	35.2	16.3	10.6	4.4	6.2	76.6	10.4	0.0	1.0	4.0	8.0
1890-94	24.8	36.2	17.1	12.6	2.8	6.5	75.9	12.1	0.0	1.0	3.5	7.5
1895-99	22.7	34.3	17.7	15.0	2.7	7.7	71.7	14.2	2.3	0.9	3.7	7.3
1900-04	24.0	29.5	24.0	14.2	1.9	6.4	70.8	12.4	2.1	1.7	4.3	8.6
1905-09	25.5	27.3	24.9	13.9	2.1	6.2	65.9	13.7	4.3	2.4	2.4	11.4
1910-12	22.7	25.7	26.6	16.9	1.8	6.3	70.0	13.5	4.5	2.7	3.1	6.3
AVG(d)	27.3	32.6	18.2	12.0	3.3	6.6	75.6	11.6	1.2	1.2	3.0	7.3
	DEPENDENT COLONIES						INDIA					
1860-64	77.8	8.3	0.0	0.0	2.8	11.1	10.0	20.0	5.0	0.0	60.0	5.0
1865-69	78.1	9.4	0.0	0.0	0.0	12.5	5.6	22.2	0.0	0.0	66.7	5.6
1870-74	72.7	9.1	0.0	0.0	3.0	15.2	5.6	22.2	0.0	0.0	66.7	5.6
1875-79	72.7	9.1	0.0	0.0	3.0	15.2	5.9	23.5	0.0	0.0	64.7	5.9
1880-84	71.4	11.4	0.0	0.0	5.7	11.4	5.3	26.3	0.0	0.0	63.2	5.3
1885-89	62.8	16.3	0.0	0.0	9.3	11.6	0.0	26.7	0.0	0.0	66.7	6.7
1890-94	65.1	11.6	0.0	0.0	9.3	14.0	0.0	30.8	0.0	0.0	61.5	7.7
1895-99	66.7	11.1	0.0	0.0	8.3	13.9	6.7	26.7	0.0	0.0	60.0	6.7
1900-04	65.4	11.5	0.0	0.0	3.8	19.2	6.7	26.7	6.7	0.0	53.3	6.7
1905-09	66.7	8.3	0.0	0.0	4.2	20.8	11.8	23.5	5.9	0.0	47.1	11.8
1910-12	66.7	7.4	0.0	0.0	3.7	22.2	13.3	20.0	6.7	0.0	46.7	13.3
AVG(d)	68.6	11.4	0.0	0.0	5.7	14.3	6.3	25.0	2.0	0.0	62.5	6.3
	PRINCELY STATES						FOREIGN DEVELOPED					
1860-64	0.0	12.5	0.0	0.0	87.5	0.0	21.4	42.9	2.4	0.0	23.8	9.5
1865-69	0.0	20.0	0.0	0.0	80.0	0.0	26.7	40.0	6.7	0.0	18.3	8.3
1870-74	7.1	21.4	0.0	0.0	71.4	0.0	26.2	35.4	4.6	1.5	21.5	10.8
1875-79	7.1	21.4	0.0	0.0	64.3	7.1	23.3	39.7	2.7	1.4	20.5	12.3
1880-84	4.8	14.3	0.0	0.0	76.2	4.8	27.0	39.3	2.2	1.1	18.0	12.4
1885-89	9.5	14.3	0.0	0.0	71.4	4.8	29.1	39.3	3.4	0.9	15.4	12.0
1890-94	9.5	19.0	0.0	0.0	66.7	4.8	31.0	36.3	4.4	0.9	18.6	8.8
1895-99	9.5	19.0	0.0	0.0	66.7	4.8	29.6	34.1	5.2	1.5	20.7	8.9
1900-04	13.0	17.4	0.0	0.0	65.2	4.3	30.5	38.1	5.1	0.8	15.3	10.2
1905-09	13.0	17.4	0.0	0.0	65.2	4.3	33.3	36.8	5.1	0.9	13.7	10.3
1910-12	8.3	20.8	0.0	0.0	66.7	4.2	26.9	33.1	6.2	2.3	14.6	16.9
AVG(d)	10.0	15.0	0.0	0.0	70.0	5.0	28.1	37.5	4.2	1.0	17.7	11.5
	FOREIGN UNDERDEVELOPED						UNITED KINGDOM TOTAL					
1860-64	43.8	6.3	0.0	0.0	37.5	12.5						
1865-69	45.2	6.5	0.0	0.0	38.7	9.7	32.6	29.5	8.9	7.4	15.3	6.3
1870-74	44.4	5.6	0.0	0.0	41.7	8.3	25.6	29.4	7.1	6.2	27.0	4.7
1875-79	38.8	10.2	2.0	0.0	40.8	8.2	22.4	31.1	6.6	6.6	28.5	4.8
1880-84	43.8	10.4	0.0	0.0	37.5	8.3	20.2	27.1	10.9	7.0	30.6	4.3
1885-89	45.6	12.3	0.0	0.0	31.6	10.5	19.4	25.0	11.6	-7.5	32.2	4.4
1890-94	47.3	10.9	0.0	0.0	30.9	10.9	17.6	25.7	12.1	9.0	30.9	4.6
1895-99	44.2	11.5	0.0	0.0	25.0	19.2	15.0	22.8	11.7	10.0	35.4	5.1
1900-04	54.9	12.7	0.0	0.0	14.1	18.3	17.0	21.0	17.0	10.1	30.3	4.6
1905-09	54.8	11.8	0.0	0.0	15.1	18.3	17.0	18.2	16.6	9.3	34.8	4.2
1910-12	57.9	11.8	0.0	0.0	14.5	15.8	15.1	17.1	17.7	11.2	34.7	4.2
AVG(d)	48.1	11.1	0.0	0.0	27.8	13.0	19.9	23.8	13.3	8.7	29.5	4.8

weighted, £2.38). The tax burden was below that in the United Kingdom in the early years, but it rose very rapidly and, when colony weights are chosen, it peaked at nearly £4.00 in the last half of the 1890s. Even when the Australian colonies are given less weight, the level more than doubled between 1860 and 1912.[3] Only Western Australia, New Zealand, and Queensland of the colonies with responsible government levied as much per head as did the United Kingdom; however, these three display levels almost £1.00 above those at home. Of the others, Tasmania, Australia, Victoria, and the

TABLE 8.3C

TAXES BY TYPE

(£'s Per Capita - Colony Weights)

UNITED KINGDOM NATIONAL

	Total	Customs	Excises	Income	Inheritance	Assessed	Special & Misc
1860-64	1.97	.68	.54	.41	.13	.10	.11
1865-69	1.70	.62	.56	.17	.14	.09	.12
1870-74	1.62	.54	.62	.15	.13	.08	.10
1875-79	1.69	.51	.71	.15	.15	.06	.11
1880-84	1.87	.52	.70	.28	.18	.08	.11
1885-89	2.27	.62	.80	.37	.24	.10	.14
1890-94	2.46	.61	.89	.42	.31	.07	.16
1895-99	3.00	.68	1.03	.53	.45	.08	.23
1900-04	3.59	.86	1.06	.86	.51	.07	.23
1905-09	3.37	.86	.92	.84	.47	.07	.21
1910-12	3.31	.75	.85	.88	.56	.06	.21
AVG(d)	2.41	.66	.79	.44	.29	.08	.16

RESPONSIBLE GOVERNMENT

	Total	Customs	Excises	Income	Inheritance	Assessed	Special & Misc
1860-64	1.20	1.12	.01	.00	.00	.03	.04
1865-69	1.41	1.31	.02	.00	.00	.01	.07
1870-74	1.49	1.35	.04	.00	.01	.00	.09
1875-79	1.71	1.47	.05	.00	.01	.01	.17
1880-84	1.98	1.68	.08	.00	.01	.08	.13
1885-89	3.38	2.90	.10	.00	.02	.16	.20
1890-94	3.08	2.61	.11	.00	.02	.15	.19
1895-99	3.84	3.15	.23	.07	.03	.15	.21
1900-04	3.48	2.68	.18	.06	.05	.20	.31
1905-09	2.38	1.56	.14	.08	.04	.09	.47
1910-12	2.08	1.48	.13	.09	.04	.11	.23
AVG(d)	2.38	1.95	.10	.03	.02	.09	.19

DEPENDENT COLONIES

	Total	Customs	Excises	Income	Inheritance	Assessed	Special & Misc
1860-64	.47	.42	.03	.00	.00	.01	.01
1865-69	.50	.44	.03	.00	.00	.01	.02
1870-74	.52	.46	.03	.00	.00	.01	.02
1875-79	.51	.44	.03	.00	.00	.02	.02
1880-84	.51	.44	.04	.00	.00	.02	.01
1885-89	.59	.47	.06	.00	.00	.05	.01
1890-94	.65	.51	.07	.00	.00	.04	.03
1895-99	.65	.53	.05	.00	.00	.04	.03
1900-04	.64	.54	.04	.00	.00	.04	.02
1905-09	.59	.49	.03	.00	.00	.04	.03
1910-12	.65	.54	.04	.00	.00	.02	.05
AVG(d)	.57	.48	.04	.00	.00	.03	.02

INDIA

	Total	Customs	Excises	Income	Inheritance	Assessed	Special & Misc
1860-64	.20	.02	.04	.01	.00	.12	.01
1865-69	.18	.01	.04	.00	.00	.12	.01
1870-74	.18	.01	.04	.00	.00	.12	.01
1875-79	.17	.01	.04	.00	.00	.11	.01
1880-84	.19	.01	.05	.00	.00	.12	.01
1885-89	.15	.00	.04	.00	.00	.10	.01
1890-94	.13	.00	.04	.00	.00	.08	.01
1895-99	.15	.01	.04	.00	.00	.09	.01
1900-04	.15	.01	.04	.01	.00	.08	.01
1905-09	.17	.02	.04	.01	.00	.08	.02
1910-12	.15	.02	.03	.01	.00	.07	.02
AVG(d)	.17	.01	.04	.00	.00	.10	.01

PRINCELY STATES

	Total	Customs	Excises	Income	Inheritance	Assessed	Special & Misc
1860-64	.14	.01	.02	.00	.00	.11	.00
1865-69	.14	.01	.03	.00	.00	.10	.00
1870-74	.15	.01	.02	.00	.00	.12	.00
1875-79	.13	.01	.02	.00	.00	.10	.00
1880-84	.19	.01	.02	.00	.00	.16	.00
1885-89	.14	.01	.01	.00	.00	.11	.01
1890-94	.14	.01	.02	.00	.00	.10	.01
1895-99	.14	.01	.02	.00	.00	.10	.01
1900-04	.19	.01	.03	.00	.00	.14	.01
1905-09	.22	.02	.03	.00	.00	.15	.02
1910-12	.28	.01	.03	.00	.00	.23	.01
AVG(d)	.16	.01	.02	.00	.00	.13	.01

FOREIGN DEVELOPED

	Total	Customs	Excises	Income	Inheritance	Assessed	Special & Misc
1860-64	.49	.14	.14	.01	.01	.13	.06
1865-69	.59	.18	.18	.03	.01	.13	.06
1870-74	.63	.21	.17	.03	.01	.14	.07
1875-79	.71	.22	.20	.03	.02	.13	.11
1880-84	.90	.27	.27	.04	.02	.16	.14
1885-89	1.20	.37	.38	.05	.02	.21	.17
1890-94	1.18	.38	.32	.06	.02	.25	.15
1895-99	1.39	.48	.33	.08	.02	.30	.18
1900-04	1.36	.43	.41	.08	.02	.24	.18
1905-09	1.45	.49	.41	.09	.02	.24	.20
1910-12	1.46	.49	.41	.09	.03	.22	.22
AVG(d)	1.02	.33	.29	.05	.02	.19	.14

FOREIGN UNDERDEVELOPED

	Total	Customs	Excises	Income	Inheritance	Assessed	Special & Misc
1860-64	.44	.37	.01	.00	.00	.04	.02
1865-69	.46	.34	.02	.00	.00	.09	.01
1870-74	.56	.43	.02	.00	.00	.09	.02
1875-79	.71	.52	.07	.00	.00	.08	.04
1880-84	.91	.52	.15	.00	.00	.17	.07
1885-89	.85	.56	.07	.00	.00	.13	.09
1890-94	.76	.46	.08	.00	.01	.14	.07
1895-99	.77	.49	.09	.00	.00	.11	.08
1900-04	.73	.45	.11	.00	.00	.09	.08
1905-09	.91	.55	.13	.00	.01	.12	.10
1910-12	1.01	.59	.15	.00	.01	.14	.12
AVG(d)	.73	.48	.08	.00	.00	.11	.06

UNITED KINGDOM TOTAL

	Total	Customs	Excises	Income	Inheritance	Assessed	Special & Misc
1860-64							
1865-69	1.90	.62	.56	.17	.14	.29	.12
1870-74	2.11	.54	.62	.15	.13	.57	.10
1875-79	2.28	.51	.71	.15	.15	.65	.11
1880-84	2.58	.52	.70	.28	.18	.79	.11
1885-89	3.20	.62	.80	.37	.24	1.03	.14
1890-94	3.46	.61	.89	.42	.31	1.07	.16
1895-99	4.52	.68	1.03	.53	.45	1.60	.23
1900-04	5.05	.86	1.06	.86	.51	1.53	.23
1905-09	5.06	.86	.92	.84	.47	1.76	.21
1910-12	4.98	.75	.85	.88	.56	1.73	.21
AVG(d)	3.13	.59	.74	.41	.28	.97	.14

Transvaal all received more than £2.00 per capita per year, and except for Natal (£.70), taxes in the others ranged between £1.29 (Canada) and £1.99 (New South Wales).

These figures are in sharp contrast to the levels that prevailed in the foreign-developed countries, where the rate of increase was also rapid, but the average was less than £1.00. Of the sixteen countries in that group, none levied taxes that on average were as high as £2.00 and only nine (six in western Europe and the United States) reached £1.00. The others ranged from £.25 (Portugal) to £.91 (Norway). In the colonies with responsible government, where citizens were free to choose the weight of their tax burden, they appear to have been willing to shoulder very heavy loads. Natal aside, the voters in every one of the other colonies opted to pay taxes that were at minimum a third higher than the average of all developed countries.

In the dependent colonies, the local residents had less voice; and the battles most often were fought between the London bureaucracies interested in a self-supporting Empire and the local governor, whose views frequently reflected his own or local opinion. Over the period, the tax burden rose but little; however, there is every evidence that there was no single policy for the colonies. Intercolony policy differences are reflected in the two averages (£.57 colony weighted, and £.35 population weighted). It is not surprising that residents in each of the dependent colonies paid some taxes, but it is worthy of note that the citizens of eleven paid more than £1.00 (the foreign-developed average), another twenty, more than £.50, and only sixteen paid less than £.10. The latter were almost all in Central Africa or the Pacific. However, while the most heavily taxed were concentrated in the Caribbean, they included Gambia and Sierra Leone as well. In comparison, the average level of foreign-underdeveloped taxes was about £.60; that burden was increasing; and there was much less intercountry dispersion. Only three countries (Uruguay, Argentina, and Bulgaria) received on average as much as £1.00 (one in eight as compared with one in six in the Empire), and only two (Liberia and Haiti) averaged less than £.10.[4]

India differed markedly both from the rest of the dependent Empire and from the underdeveloped sector, but less sharply from the Princely States. Tax levies were much lower and, if there was any trend, it was downward. The average assessment was £.17 (£.19 in the 1860s and £.16 in the twentieth century). The Princely States, on the other hand, received somewhat more; that series trends upward and is characterized by very wide state-to-state variation. Some (like Jobat, Manipur, and Dhar) averaged £.03 or less – below all but two dependent colonies – while three (Rampur, Baroda, and Jam Khandi) averaged more than £.30. The analysis of public expenditures leads to the conclusion that, to the extent service was correlated with cost, the level of public services provided by the government of India was quite meager. It is, however, equally clear that the taxes levied to support those services were also low. The average burden was, for example, only about one-third the £.43 levied in neighboring Siam.

On average, throughout the dependent Empire the level of taxes was not high, although some colonies were marked by quite substantial tax burdens. Since taxes do not fall equally on all social groups, it is important to examine the Empire tax structure. In the decade following the death of Victoria, the free-trade debate raged in Britain. In the colonies with responsible government, however, the issue had long been settled. Throughout the last four decades of the nineteenth century and despite continual pleas from the home country – at first for free trade and later for at least imperial preference – those colonies were at least as protectionist as Germany and the United States. In every colony, customs revenues were by far the most important source of tax revenue. On average, receipts between £1.24 (population weights) and £1.95 (colony weights) per person per year were derived from taxes on foreign trade, and that figure represented over three in every four pounds of tax income. While the trend in the proportion of customs in total taxes was downward (it fell from 90 to about 70 percent), the average burden had climbed, depending on the measure chosen, to at least £1.65 and perhaps £2.68 by the end of the nineteenth century. The evidence indicates that the tariffs were a matter of continual concern to the colonies' chief trading partner, the United Kingdom. As noted previously, Kimberley in 1871 had lamented the impact of proposed legislation in New Zealand.[5]

The dependence on customs differed somewhat from colony to colony, but in none did the ratio of tariffs to total taxes fall much below 60 percent. Newfoundland aside (tariffs were almost the only source of tax revenue in that colony), the dependence was greatest in Australasia, although after the birth of the Commonwealth that reliance was reduced somewhat. The figures for the six Australian colonies ranged from a high of 95 percent in Western Australia to a low of 78 percent in New South Wales.[6] In New Zealand, the source of Kimberley's concern, the proportion was only 80. Elsewhere dependence was less. After the formation of the Union of South Africa, the fraction there was about equal to that in the Commonwealth (60 percent). Earlier, however, the figures ranged from 70 percent in the Cape to a mere 57 percent in the Orange River Colony. Canada lay somewhere between the extremes; that average was just over 75 percent.

It is interesting to note that differential customs actually acted as a deterrent to consolidation in South Africa. In 1880 Bartle Frere wrote:

> ... Natal has a low tariff. The Cape has raised its rates .... the difference and separation of interests has a bad effect on com-

> merce in general and benefits only a few traders in Natal by
> enabling them to under-sell the Cape in quarters whose natural
> channel of supply would be via the Cape ports .... This is an
> obstacle to any union or confederation .... Natal does not want
> to give up its extensive power of lowering its rates, and thereby
> attracting a trade that would not otherwise come to its ports .... [7]

The responsibly governed colonies stand in stark contrast to the
developed world, even though the latter is usually assumed to have
been not only very protectionist but increasingly so. There the fraction of customs among all tax revenues averaged somewhere from
20 to 30 percent, and while the trend was upward, the movement,
at least after 1880, was small. In per capita terms, of course, the
customs burden was increasing; however, that figure, which on
average was perhaps £1.50 in the responsibly governed Empire,
stood at only about £.30 for the developed countries. While no colony
with responsible government raised less than 55 percent of its taxes
from customs duties, only two developed countries (Switzerland
and Norway) depended that heavily on them. Among the others,
only three received as much as one-half of their tax revenues from
this source (Denmark, Germany, and the United States) and six
received less than one-fifth (France, Netherlands, Italy, Belgium,
Austria-Hungary, and Japan).

Without question, the dependence of the colonies with responsible
government on customs revenues had implications for the imperial
system. Much to Britain's chagrin, faith in the wonders of free trade
was limited to Britain itself. The taxes were, of course, ultimately
paid by the colonial consumers, but a substantial income must have
found its way into the hands of local businesspeople, rentiers, and
workers able to operate under the protective umbrella. At the same
time, British exporters and their employees faced sluggish sales as
their products, burdened by taxes, became less competitive in the
Empire markets.

While tariffs found much favor in the self-governing colonies,
other excises did not. Where the government of the United Kingdom
depended on these levies for about a third of its tax income, and
the figure for developed countries was between 30 and 40 percent,
the colonies with responsible government drew little more than 10
percent. Excises produced no more than £.20 per capita a year.
Moreover, although dependence on those sources was increasing,
at the end of the period the average was still much below the burden
in the developed world. In Canada excises accounted for 23 percent

of all taxes, and in the Australian Commonwealth the figure was about half that amount. Those Dominions aside, however, no other self-governing colony drew more than £1 in 12 and in six the level was £1 in 50 or less.

In contrast, despite the fact that the total tax burden was no more than three-fifths of that in the Empire of white settlement, excises in the foreign-developed sector were almost half again as great. Only three countries turned to domestic excises for less than 12 percent (the responsible government average) of their total tax revenues, and five received more than £2 in 5. In the Empire, foreign producers (most often English) were heavily taxed, but the burden on domestic products was very light. Outside the Empire there were tariffs, but there were also domestic excises. In the case of alcohol taxes, for example, the colonies with responsible government received £.03 per person per year while the foreign-developed countries earned more than twice that amount.

As the nineteenth century wore on, the United Kingdom and, to a lesser extent, other developed countries turned increasingly to income and inheritance taxes. In the United Kingdom over the last four decades of that century, the national government derived about one-quarter of its total revenues from those taxes, but in the twentieth century the figure was almost two-fifths. In the foreign-developed sector the change was more gradual, but the figures were still significant (something less than 5 percent in the nineteenth century and about a third more in the twentieth). In the colonies with responsible government income taxes were almost nonexistent before the late 1890s, but thereafter the per capita levies were about equal to those in the foreign-developed sector. In the case of the inheritance tax, levels, at least after 1895, were higher than in the developed countries. Together, income and inheritance taxes produced somewhat in excess of £.01 per capita in the years before 1895 and £.11 thereafter.

The end of the period was, however, marked by a movement toward income and higher inheritance taxes, particularly in the Commonwealth of Australia and the Union of South Africa. In the twentieth century, the former received 13 percent of its revenues from these sources and the latter, 8. The shift in colonial revenues toward greater dependence on income taxes produced concern in the British Treasury. It noted that a British investor whose holdings were in South Africa was subject to double taxation, while a South African who invested in the United Kingdom was subject to only the UK income tax. Nor did there appear to have been any easy way out of the problem as long as Britain had no voice in dominion tax policy.

> ... The profits made by Englishmen in our colonies are subject
> to local income tax, that our income tax does not apply, is knock-
> ing a big hole in our revenue, while the reciprocity extended by
> the colony is negligible . . . . There is no uniformity in the colonies.
> For instance, there is an income tax at the Cape and none in
> Canada. If we exempted a colony like the Cape from income tax
> in England, we should be giving a pull to the Cape; but Canada
> who chooses to raise her revenue in other ways than income tax,
> would get nothing.[8]

These two "super" possessions aside, the only other colonies to
utilize these sources significantly were the Orange Free States and
Victoria (they accounted for about 5 percent of total taxes) and New
Zealand and Tasmania (the figure was about 3 percent). Three responsibly governed colonies had no income or inheritance taxes. In
the foreign-developed sector, Belgium and Italy displayed ratios (although not levels) only slightly less than those prevailing in the
United Kingdom, nine nations drew at least 3 percent from such
taxes, and only one drew no revenues at all.

The other important tax was the levy on property, and here the
history in the colonies with responsible government was markedly
different from the countries in the foreign-developed sector. The
trend in per capita revenues was upward for both groups, but the
levels were much higher for the latter. In those parts of the Empire
allowed to choose their own tax patterns, the property tax on average
brought in at most £.09 per capita (about 3 or 4 percent of the total).
The British government expressed concern with the disinclination
to tax property. In the case of the Orange River Colony, for example,
Milner pointed out to the colony's treasurer that:

> ... having regard for the fact that the Orange River Colony
> though a bad subject for taxation, has hitherto had very little that
> could be called taxation at all. I do not think for example, that a
> charge of one shilling on every 100 acres should be called a tax,
> and indeed I believe it is not. . . . It may be worth considering as
> we have to restart the agriculture of the whole colony, [that] the
> opportunity might be taken for insuring some larger permanent
> revenue to the State from the land. . . .[9]

In the developed countries, property tax revenues rose from £1 in
10 in the 1860s to about £.20 at the turn of the century. In percentage
terms, property taxes declined from about a quarter to a seventh of

the total, but they remained an important component of the revenue package. In the Empire, on the other hand, of the colonies with responsible government, only South Australia, New Zealand, and Tasmania derived more than 6 percent of their tax revenues from property, and eight colonies received less than one percent. Only four of the developed countries derived no income from property levies, and nine garnered more than a fifth of their tax revenues from this source.

Miscellaneous taxes accounted for at least 12 percent of all tax revenues of the colonies with responsible government, and the bulk of that came from the stamp tax and later the innovation of the native-hut tax in Africa. The former was not important on the North American continent, but it produced £.20 or more per capita in Queensland, New Zealand, and the Transvaal. The hut tax (an almost exclusively African institution) brought in only £.02 in the Cape (with few indigenous Africans); however, it produced £.08 in Natal, £.11 in the Orange Free States, £.17 in the Union of South Africa, and £.35 (17 percent of all revenues) in the Transvaal. Originally the tax had been designed not only to force Africans into the labor force, but also to convince the white settlers that they were not the only source of government revenues. In 1875 Wolseley wrote to Carnarvon:

> ... There will be little difficulty passing the land tax on the property of the white settlers when it is understood that the natives will have to bear a small proportion of the burden imposed upon the Colony by railway construction. The hut tax imposed by the Cape upon our neighboring province of Basutoland is £1 per hut and elsewhere in the Cape Colony it is 10 shillings a hut .... [10]

Among the developed countries miscellaneous taxes increased at about the same rate as taxes in general, and also accounted for about £1 in 10 of tax income. As in the Empire, the category is a broad one, but the most important single component was the stamp tax. While not every country depended to any important extent on stamp taxes, to some it represented a sizeable source of income. That tax brought in about £.30 per capita in France and the Netherlands and more than £.05 in nine more countries.

The conclusions are obvious. The colonies with responsible government depended very heavily on customs duties and made limited use of domestic excises. These findings stand out whether the yardstick for comparison is the United Kingdom or the foreign-developed sector. Given the importance of Great Britain in the pattern of Empire trade, it is hardly surprising that two generations of British politicians continually railed against colonial tariffs. The countries in the underdeveloped-foreign sector depended on customs duties for between one-half and two-thirds of their tax revenues. That figure contrasts with one-quarter in the United Kingdom and only slightly more in the foreign-developed sector. Dependence on customs revenues were highest in South America (Uruguay and Argentina averaged more than £1.50), where no country except Peru fell much below £.50 per capita per year. At the other end of the spectrum, several countries (including Tunisia, Siam, and Haiti) drew no revenues from foreign commerce. The Central American countries fell about halfway between these extremes while Turkey, Liberia, and Japan were concentrated toward the lower end.

Since the British had granted the responsibly governed colonies control of their own finances, they were unable to force them to adopt a more acceptable fiscal package. In the dependent Empire, however, given British economic interests, it would have been expected that the colonies would have displayed far less dependence on tariffs than the underdeveloped nations, but such was not the case. In fact, the dependent colonies drew somewhat more heavily on this source although their reliance was slightly less than their self-governing brethren. Over the period, the colony-weighted average indicates that the typical colony drew about 70 percent of its taxes from tariffs, and there is no evidence of any decline in their importance. (The population-weighted figures, on the other hand, do decline as the Central African colonies were added to the Empire.) Moreover, while six of the dependent colonies (including Hong Kong, the Federated Malay States, and Egypt) raised no money at all from customs, ten raised £1.00 or more. There was almost certainly less opportunity for direct import substitution in the dependent colonies than in the dominions, and therefore these tariffs probably provided less protection for indigenous entrepreneurs. Still, such imposts must have cost British businessmen some sales. Despite an official commitment to free trade, simplification of collection and minimization of political turmoil appear to have carried more weight with the Treasury and Colonial Office than the words "comparative advantage" as enunciated by John Stuart Mill.

The private papers of officials are replete with complaints from the colonial governors about the difficulty of imposing their fiscal views on the colonies they governed. For example, in 1871 Hamilton Gordon, the Governor of Mauritius, lamented:

> . . . You know that I am no financier, but I am appalled by the incidence of taxation on the island. It falls almost wholly on the

poor, who are made to pay in almost every conceivable way, while the rich are pretty well exempt from taxation.

If, for my sins, I am compelled to remain any time in this detestable place (which I devoutly trust I may not be) I shall feel compelled to make an attempt to remedy this evil. It will be difficult work as the whole of the membership of the Legislative Council are directly interested in keeping up the present system, and I shall . . . encounter the most violent opposition . . . . [11]

Costs had to be kept down and local grievances were often more immediate than discontent in the British hinterlands.

In the foreign-underdeveloped sector, domestic excises produced something more than 10 percent of all tax revenues, and these levies became more important after the mid–1870s. In the dependent colonies not only were the average levels lower, but excises appear to have become less important after the turn of the century. Among the foreign-underdeveloped countries, five (23 percent) derived less than £.01 from domestic excises and five received more than £.20 from that source. Of the dependent colonies, no less than forty-one (65 percent) earned less than £.01, and only five (8 percent) derived more than £.20. The latter group included the Territory of the North Borneo Company, Egypt, Trinidad, Honduras, and St. Lucia.

Income and inheritance taxes were not a significant part of the fiscal package of any dependent colony, and the same can be said for the underdeveloped nations. That latter group of countries, however, did turn to property levies as the major supplement to customs receipts. The property taxes produced more than £.15 per capita and accounted for about £1 in 4 of tax revenues. In the dependent colonies the reliance was much smaller. The level was only a fifth of that in the underdeveloped sector, and those imposts accounted for less than 6 percent of tax revenues. While, at the lower end of the scale, about the same proportion of colonies and countries received no property tax income, at the upper, five times as large a proportion of underdeveloped countries received more than £.20.

Finally, special and miscellaneous taxes were somewhat less significant in the budgets of the dependent colonies than they were in those of the underdeveloped countries. The stamp tax was slightly more important among the underdeveloped countries but the differences are not marked. Even in the case of taxes as innocuous as the stamp levy, the governors did not face a compliant citizenry. From the Bahamas the governor wrote:

. . . I propose . . . to ask the assembly to sanction the imposition of a stamp duty as far as cheques are concerned . . . . It is the end

> of the wedge and once people have gotten used to it, the duties
> can be extended to receipts, bills of lading, etc., and be made a
> very fruitful source of income.[12]

The native-hut tax, however, absent from the budgets of the underdeveloped countries, produced £.01 or more in twelve colonies.
Moreover, for two (Swaziland and Southern Rhodesia) the yield was
more than £.30 and for another three (Basutoland, Bechuanaland,
and Fiji), more than £.14.

It is worth reiterating that the most striking feature of the tax
history of the dependent colonies is the reliance on tariffs. These
levies were important in the underdeveloped nations, but those
countries were interested in protecting local business. In the dependent Empire the protective walls were raised in large part against
British business, and the British business community, to the extent
it objected to these discriminatory levies, must have gone largely
unheard.

For Britain, however, India was another matter. As the British
spread their influence across the subcontinent they also assumed
existing institutional baggage which included a significant fiscal component. Moreover, they were forced to deal with an Indian elite with
strongly held views on appropriate tax policies. India was not Africa
or the sugar islands of the Caribbean. By the standards of most of
the dependent Empire, it was relatively well developed; and most
importantly it had a business community that was prepared to compete with the British in providing a wide range of products and
services and that was nearly competitive even in some manufacturing industries - particularly cotton textiles. India not only exported
entrepreneurial talent to many corners of the dependent Empire,
but had, by the end of the period, begun to compete with the British
even in such traditionally British industries as steel. Finally, it was
a "country" that had a significant (and certainly very vocal and
political) group of British "temporary expatriates" who had definite
ideas about an appropriate fiscal structure. These institutional constraints, coupled with a population near and often pushed over the
margin of subsistence by floods and famines, produced schizophre-
nia in a succession of otherwise very able viceroys and a fiscal apparatus that was unlike anything else in Britain or the rest of the
Empire.

The Indian fiscal system can, perhaps, best be viewed as a re-
volving prism reflecting the subcontinent, Parliament, and the India
Office. The British were concerned with the regressivity of the tax
structure, but attempts to alter that structure ran into both legal and

political problems. John Lawrence captured the view of the Indian elite: " . . . At present the ideas of many influential men are in practice to increase the taxation on the poor and to spare those that are well off . . . . "[13] In a similar vein the technical difficulties were summarized by another frustrated British official:

> . . . what weighs heavily on my mind is the fact that taxation in India presses with undue severity on the poorer classes. The reason no doubt in part that it is so difficult to apply taxation in the East; you have to hit your man where you can hit him, through salt in India . . . . Salt and cotton duties press on the poor man, customs and income tax are largely paid by Europeans, your wealthy native does not contribute his fair share, I have been considering whether you could get at him through death duties, but the structure of native societies precludes this . . . . [14]

The goals of British policy appeared straightforward and simple: " . . . The aim of our measures has been, and must be, to make each section of the community (with the exception of the European officials who are exempted for special reasons) contribute fairly and in just proportion towards the necessities of the state, each according to his means . . . . "[15] Even there, however, the European exemption was not based on moral principle, but was merely a reflection of political reality. Mayo outlined the problem in a discussion of a vote on a new tax bill in the legislative council: " . . . The official members of the council . . . much more bitter than the non official. This serves to show how much the European opposition comes from the employees of government who dislike the tax merely because they have to pay it . . . . "[16] Or as Lawrence had earlier observed: " . . . The English community in India is really much more intolerant of taxation than are the natives. There is none to which they will submit, if they can help it. But they do not mind the natives being taxed, if they are themselves exempted . . . . "[17]

Policies were one thing, effecting them another. Existing agreements sorely limited the British in their attempt to tax the Zamindars of Bengal and the threat of political upheaval made them tread very warily in their attempts to increase the taxes on other wealthy Indians. Both constraints were much on the mind of Lytton when he asked:

> . . . permission to extract from the Zemindars of Bengal a somewhat fairer proportional contribution than they have made, towards the necessities of the State. This would be quite in accordance with the principle which I think you are disposed to

approve of, in endeavoring to put at least some portions of the
burden of taxation more directly on the wealthy classes. Professor
Rojli's postulate that the native princes ought to be taxed is very
plausible . . . but I have been led to the conclusion that such a
policy is not practical; and the attempt to carry it out might, I
think (as you suggest), be dangerous. . . . [18]

The frustrated pleas of Randolph Churchill two and a half decades
later showed the continuing resistance to change:

> . . . They [the Zamindars] surely may be required to pay a rea-
> sonable amount of taxation for the military protection of the free
> trade and prosperity which they enjoy while contributing a mere
> fraction to the public revenue. The difficulty of taxing them will
> not decrease with the delay which creates the idea of a prescriptive
> right to immunity.[19]

And in the background was the business community in Britain ready
to bring pressure directly on Whitehall (or Downing Street) should
Indian tax policy threaten to adversely affect their profits. Curzon
warned of the effects of these political decisions:

> . . . One thing the home government must be particularly careful
> to avoid, and that is to make the fiscal system of India the sport
> or victim of political or fiscal exigencies at home. Public opinion
> has never gotten over the excise duty placed on our cotton man-
> ufacture in order to placate the Lancashire members, and any
> revision of Imperial policy which tends to place India more instead
> of less under the hands of the Great Britain would excite bitter
> and hostile feelings here . . . . [20]

The result of all these pressures and counterpressures was a hybrid
fiscal system very different from any other. Policy was almost always
sacrificed to expediency because in the words of John Lawrence:
" . . . There is no doubt that direct taxation in India is especially
odious, while indirect taxation beyond what we have now, is almost
impractical . . . . "[21] and it produced decisions like the one to raise
the export duty on corn because: " . . . such a measure would be
popular with the natives, and not unpopular with the English merchants who don't engage much in this trade . . . . "[22]

The Indian government, like its counterparts in the dependent
Empire, was usually more than willing to solve the continuing financial crises through the imposition of tariffs on imported products;
however, attempts to place even small imposts were met with loud
and frequently effective complaints from British manufacturers and

merchants. In "free-trade" England, customs duties accounted for about one-quarter of all tax revenues; in the increasingly protectionist developed sector, the figure was 30 percent; in the foreign-underdeveloped countries it probably averaged over 50 percent, and in the dependent colonies it was higher than that. In India, on the other hand, tariffs represented but 6 percent, and just briefly at the beginning and end of the period did they reach £.02 per capita per year.

The conflict between the need for revenues and the interests of the Midlands manufacturers and merchants is best captured in the history of the cotton duties. From 1859 to 1869 they were set at 10 percent, but because of political grumbling they were then cut in half. Even that low level did not satisfy the Lancashire business-people, and in 1877 a House of Commons resolution demanded their abolition. Two years later they were gone, and in 1882 all import duties were abolished. Within a decade, however, India's financial position was critical and, as Kimberley wrote Gladstone:

> ... The financial position of India is such that we shall be compelled, if the exchange does not rise, to increase taxation or borrow .... Everyone is agreed that to increase taxation would be most dangerous politically, nor could we get any sigificant addition to revenue, except by raising the salt tax, a hateful expedient and one that would deprive us of our only resource in the event of war or other great emergency. I put out of the question recurrence of import duties, in India their reimposition would, it is true, be generously approved, but the Lancashire opposition would be too strong, not to mention the economic objections to such duties .... [23]

But the pressures did not abate, the exchanges did not improve, and the British government was forced to reassess its position. Opposition was, as predicted, strong and the outcome was a compromise. In Northbrooke's words: " ... As I gather from his [Fowler's] budget speech, the government are disposed to withdraw their objections to imposing import duties on cotton manufacture if an equivalent excise is put on Indian manufacture .... "[24] As Curzon later remarked, the decision was not a popular one in India, but the tariff and the countervailing excise were introduced.

It is interesting to note that while on average customs duties produced only a slightly smaller fraction of revenue in India than they did in the Princely States, the time pattern is very different. In the Princely States tariffs were a regular part of the budgetary package, and tariff revenues appear in the budgets year in and year out. In

India they were temporary measures and subject (as the history of the cotton duties indicates) to substantial year-to-year variation. There were no tariff revenues in the Indian budget in the second half of the 1880s nor in the first half of the 1890s, but they constituted 12 percent of all taxes over the last eight years of the study.

The absence of a customs base meant that the Indian government had to look to other revenues, and to a large extent they turned to the same source that had supported the Mogul princes in the days before the *Raj*: the land tax. At home land taxes counted for only 3 percent of "national" revenues; in those parts of the Empire with responsible government the figure was about the same; and in the dependent colonies it was less than 6 percent. In the foreign sector it was more important, accounting for perhaps a quarter of the tax revenues in the underdeveloped sector and about one-fifth in the developed. In India, however, the average was £.10 per person per year – more than £3 in every £5. The figure would probably have been even larger had the government not been constrained by earlier agreement with the Bengal taxfarmers. As Lytton searched for revenue sources to replace the cotton duties he complained:

> . . . But the Bengal Zemindars, who virtually constitute the British Indian Association, are the most pampered, pretentious, disloyal set of rascals in India. That unfortunate permanent settlement of Lord Cornwallis has deprived the government of India of probably not less than 3 million of revenue, which it can ill afford to forgo, in a time of financial difficulty at the present, and from the remission of which the country in general derives absolutely no benefit . . . . [25]

Only in the Princely States, where such taxes yielded upward of 70 percent of all revenues, was there greater dependence on the "fruits of the land." In India, however, some changes were underway, and the taxes that had supported emperors and princes centuries before the arrival of the British declined from about £.12 in the 1860s to £.08 in the twentieth century. In terms of importance, the fall was from almost two-thirds to less than half.

The second most important source of Indian taxes was the domestic excises. The salt tax in particular produced about three-fourths of the £.04 per person per year garnered from this source. While officials in the government of India spoke against the incidence of the salt tax, they also recognized that it was a tax that could "hit" the Indians where they could be hit and which could be depended upon to produce revenue when needed. As Lytton wrote:

> To no one do I dare openly reveal the full importance which,
> personally, I attach to a *low uniform* salt duty; as being in the
> absence of an income tax (and more prolific than any *possible*
> income tax) permanently the source of revenue which at any
> moment, we can augment almost indefinitely without any ap-
> preciable pressure on the community, by simply turning on
> the screw, *anna per anna.* Even the recognition of such a possi-
> bility, however, must not be whispered in any of the cities of
> Philistia . . . . [26]

Taken together, the excises accounted for about one-fourth of tax
revenues – a proportion that, while below typical levels in the United
Kingdom, was well above those prevailing elsewhere in the Empire
or, for that matter, in the underdeveloped sector. The Indian excise
levels were also somewhat above those levied in the Princely States,
whether the measure is the per capita charge or the proportion of
the total tax bill.

There were no inheritance taxes on the subcontinent, but the
income tax had a stormy history. Because of the difficulties of assessment and a series of agreements and protocols, the tax fell most
heavily on members of the British community (traders and government officials) and that was not a group that acceded easily to any
taxation. The tax was levied in the early 1860s (it produced £800,000
in 1860 and £692,000 in 1865), but because of the objections of British
expatriates it was dropped.[27] A succession of viceroys, each concerned with the perennial problem of balancing the budget, agitated
for reimposition of the tax, despite the objections of the British businesspeople and officials in India. Within three years of the abolition,
Mayo lobbied for parliamentary action on a bill that would tax not
only incomes in India but would "subject the whole of the Indian
debt and all salaries paid out of Indian funds at home to income
tax," and this despite his recognition of the "very strong feeling that
exists in Council against the income tax in any shape and which I
believe is shared by the majority of the people able to form an opinion
on such subjects."[28] As it turned out, these opinions were too strong
to ignore. A few years later Lytton again toyed with the idea of
reimposing the tax, but once more he was forced to conclude that
the political problems were too difficult to overcome. In 1876 he
declared:

> I believe that the country can very well bear two millions worth
> of additional taxes; and, if we can succeed in devising some form
> of imperial taxation which will directly meet the purpose of the
> income tax without directly exciting from the European and of-

ficial community the opposition to which the income tax was
sacrificed . . . the object could be met.[29]

But finding no acceptable way to mask such a tax he wrote in the
next year:

> . . . As regards to the rest of Salisbury's program, you know I have
> always regretted the abolition of the income tax, but I am quite
> confident that to reimpose it now, with the European community
> here so hard hit by the depreciation of the exchanges, would be
> a practical impossibility.[30]

As the financial crises deepened, the government turned its
thoughts time and again to the income tax, but each approach from
London brought complaints from high officials in India. For example, in 1885 the governor of Bombay wrote Churchill:

> The increase of taxation would certainly be unpopular but I am
> not convinced that the outcry against it would not have reason
> on its side . . . . The fall of the rupee hits all Englishmen who have
> to remit for the education of their children or the support of
> relatives very hard, and an income tax on salaries would con-
> tribute more or less to a grievance to them . . . . [31]

Nevertheless, the income tax was reimposed in 1886, but agricultural
incomes were to a large extent exempted. In the first decade of the
present century, an average of more than 6 percent of all taxes were
drawn from the income tax, and while it was never a major source
of revenue, it did produce more than £1 million a year at the end
of the period.

Despite increasing progressivity in the tax structure at home, the
Indian income tax remained proportional. It was not that the government was uninterested in generating more tax revenues and in
shifting the tax burden to the upper income groups; rather, it was
just a question of who paid the tax. In 1911 Hardinge wrote to Crewe:

> Montague has written to Fleetwood Wilson suggesting the im-
> position of a graduated income tax. I wish to keep an open mind
> to the subject until I have received full information as to what its
> effects and results would be. Since I have been here I have heard
> on all sides that the income tax which produces at present about
> one million sterling, is levied almost entirely upon Government
> officials and European traders. None of the landed aristocracy
> pay anything although they are the richest people in the land,
> while it is impossible to ascertain what is the income of the native
> traders.[32]

One thing is clear, while the government of India was more sensitive to the interests of the British business community than the India Office appears to have been, the fiscal package that was adopted reflected the interests of the Indian elites and the British in India at least as much as it did the opinions of the midlands manufacturers. It appears that it was only the welfare of the Indian peasants that was not represented, but they received at least some benefits from the insistence of the Lancashire businesspeople on something approximating free trade.

In the Empire the principal sources of revenue were consumption taxes. In the absence of the imperial subsidy, would the colonies have increased domestic imposts or would they have reduced spending? If they chose the former course, to what sources would they have turned? In the colonies of white settlement, the colonies that, after all, profited the most from the generosity of the British taxpayer, it is likely that there would have been some reduction in spending as well as tax increases. If the experience of the developed nations offers any clue, domestic excises would have been increased. In addition, the imposition of direct taxes (income and inheritance) would likely have been accomplished with greater alacrity and at higher levels than actually maintained. Whatever the case, the colonial business community and its British partners would have had to shoulder a greater fraction of the tax burden.

Again, if the underdeveloped countries provide a touchstone, it would appear that the dependent colonies would have followed the strategy that prevailed in the underdeveloped sector and was similar to that likely to have been forced on their autonomous confreres – cuts in spending and increases in domestic excises and property taxes. Even had these colonies chosen to develop new instruments like the hut tax, designed to increase the tax burden on persons not normally a part of the market economy, it is difficult to see how these innovations would have prevented indigenous and British businesspeople from paying at least somewhat more for the services of government.

In India the situation would probably have developed quite differently. It seems evident that, had the Indian elites had a greater voice in the nature of the subcontinent's tax structure, they would have raised tariffs. Such a change would, at least in the short run, have produced an increase in business profits and, in the long run, a greater proportion of resources devoted to the production of commodities, particularly those like textiles, that were directed toward the mass market. Since these new firms and industries would have been high-cost producers in comparison to their foreign (that is,

British) competitors, both the increase in short-run profits and the rise in long-term prices would have raised the "tax" burden disproportionately on the lower classes. If those tariffs would, by permitting the exploitation of scale economies, have produced an efficient and competitive domestic manufacturing sector, as some Indian nationalists contended, then the benefits of British policy that appear to have accrued to the peasants would have become in fact real costs instead. However, there is little evidence that, for the industries in question, protection would have produced a comparative advantage where none had existed before.

III. The United Kingdom

As the subsidy was funded in Britain, the analysis of the incidence of taxes in the United Kingdom becomes particularly important. Taxes were high, £2.40 per capita as compared with an average of about £1.00 elsewhere in the developed world. They were about three and a half times those of the developed countries in the 1860s and still about two and a half times as large in 1912.

In terms of structure, the two sectors (United Kingdom and foreign-developed) look similar, but there were some important differences. Both depended on customs receipts for about 25 percent of their tax revenue, but while that figure was increasing in the developed sector, it was falling at home. Tariff receipts accounted for about one-third of all taxes in the 1860s but less than one-quarter in the years from 1905 to 1912. Moreover, tobacco aside, the decline was spread across most other taxed imports. Between 1860 and 1908 the duty on tea declined from 17 to 5d per pound, that on coffee from 3d to 2d, and that on sugar from 16s to less than 2s a 100-weight (and there was *no* sugar tariff between 1874 and 1902).[33] A contemporary observed that by the end of the period duties on necessities had been largely abolished. He may or may not have been correct, but they certainly had been reduced.

Dependence on domestic excises was probably somewhat less in the United Kingdom than in the foreign-developed sector, although the foreign excises were frequently on products subject to the tariff in Britain. There does not seem to have been a significant trend, but in the United Kingdom revenues were subject to substantial year-to-year fluctuations. The most important of the domestic excises were the taxes on beer and spirits, and both rose over the period. The spirit duty increased by a moderate 10 percent, but the beer duties rose by a substantial 40 percent.[34] While one can argue that beer is not a necessity, it is obvious that the increase in the beer levies fell to a large extent on the lower income groups.[35]

The most striking difference between the United Kingdom and the countries that made up the foreign-developed sector, however, was the dependence in Britain on direct income and inheritance taxes. In the foreign-developed sector these levies gradually increased in importance from less than 5 percent of the total tax bill in the 1860s to something less than twice that figure at the outbreak of the First World War. In Britain, in contrast, the figures were 27 and 43 percent. Before the middle of the nineteenth century most British taxes had been indirect and very regressive. In 1846 in a speech on the Corn Laws Sir Robert Peel had argued:

> ... It is inevitable with a system of indirect taxation that families earning less than 30s a week must pay heavily; but I know if the burden presses unjustly upon them, it is not from want of sympathy on the part of the gentlemen of England; it is, however, inevitable. We must raise a great part of our taxation by indirect taxes and the burden will be unequally distributed .... [36]

The country had experimented with both income and inheritance taxes; the former was viewed as at best a temporary measure and the latter as no more than a minor income source. The inheritance tax antedated the American Revolution, but it was so unimportant that the revenues were not officially segregated from the stamp duties until 1870. The income tax was almost as old. It was first imposed in 1799 as an emergency measure to help finance the Napoleonic Wars, and it was repealed soon after Waterloo. In the 1840s the political profile of Britain began to change, and with it the tax structure. Once that process had begun, politicians found it impossible to stop, let alone reverse. The first permanent income tax was imposed in 1842, and nine years later the tax became not only permanent but heavy. Moreover, in that latter year Gladstone also introduced legislation designed to expand the domain of the death duties to encompass real as well as personal property. So far had the system proceeded by 1874 that Northcote complained to Disraeli: " ... The truth is that the income tax has lost its terrifying character and become a fixed element in our financial system .... "[37]

In the case of the income tax, although rates were proportional to income, exemptions and abatements meant that almost none of the tax fell on working-class incomes.[38] It is, for example, estimated that only 850,000 out of a population of 43 million paid the tax in 1903.[39] More importantly, from the viewpoint of those at the lower end of the income distribution, the exemptions and abatements increased. The Act of 1853 had exempted all incomes below £100, but that figure was increased to £150 in 1877 and to £160 in 1893. In addition, abatements on higher incomes were permitted, and by 1897 they provided at least some relief for incomes as high as £700.[40]

Death duties did not increase from 1853 to 1888, and even then the changes were small. In 1894, however, a progressive rate was imposed, and the total tax structure changed dramatically. The graduated scale began at 1 percent on estates valued at £100 and went up to 8 percent on those over £1,000,000. Progressivity was extended in 1907, and any estate over £3,000,000 was charged £300,000 plus 15 percent of the excess above £1,000,000.

The new direct taxes had become, as Northcote feared, a permanent part of the fiscal system, and politics dictated that they should remain so. In a review of changes in tax policy over the previous twenty years Bernard Mallet, in 1907, noted:

> ... It is interesting to see how the tendency all through until the Boer War, was to substitute direct for indirect taxation increasingly; avowedly because of the disproportionate pressure of the latter on the poorer classes. To turn our back on this seems really impossible. The working classes know too much about it in this country .... [41]

So far, in fact, had the circle come that some politicians saw the new tax policy as a benefit for the wealthy. In 1908 Haldane wrote:

> The more boldly such a proposition is put the more attractive, I think, it will prove. It will recommend itself to many people as a bulwark against Nationalization of wealth .... [42]

Over the entire period, revenues from the income tax averaged £.44 and those from the estate duties £.29 per person per year, and in the years 1910 to 1912 the figures were £.88 and £.56. The total of £1.44 was more than the entire tax bill in the foreign-developed sector.

The shift away from customs and excises and toward income and inheritance taxes meant that taxes were becoming less regressive and that the burden was shifted away from the working classes. Chart 8.1 (estimates of the percentage of income paid in taxes by various income groups in 1863–4, 1883–4, and 1903–4) provides a picture of these changes.[43] The figures for the latter year can be taken as the best available; and while the earlier are certainly less reliable, they do appear to provide some very useful insights.[44] In every year tax rates were highest in the lowest income groups, a reflection of the customs and excise duties that continued to fall most heavily on the lowest-income earners. There was, however, a

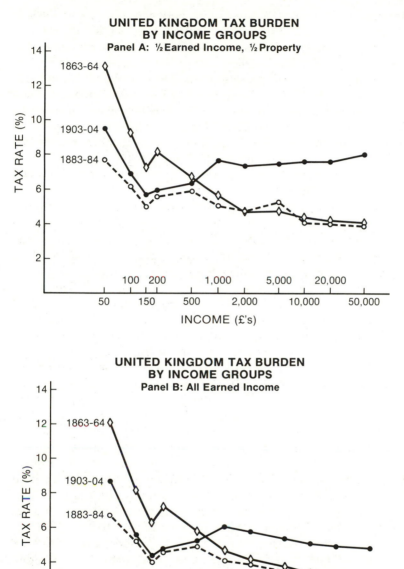

Chart 8

substantial reduction of those burdens between 1863–4 and 1883–4, and even the increases imposed during the Boer War left the relative exaction well below the level of the 1860s. In every year there is also a secondary peak in the average rate in the middle-income group. (Depending on the year chosen, the income to which these rates apply rose from £200, to £500, to £1,000.) For higher incomes, rates fell as income rose, although the decline was tempered for incomes over £10,000. The sole exception to this pattern is the rate on half-earned-half-property income in 1903–4. In that instance, after some decline for incomes between £1,000 and £2,000, rates gradually edged upward, and the charge on incomes in excess of £50,000 actually exceeded the £1,000 rate.

There is clear evidence of increasing progressivity (or at least declining regressivity). In 1863–4 every income category except £200 paid at a lower rate than the one below it. By 1903–4 that was true only for classes below £150. In the years from the 1860s to the 1880s the increase in progessivity was achieved largely through decreases in rates charged the lowest- and middle-income groups. There was essentially no change in the rates on upper incomes. In the second period (1884–1904), however, rates charged at the more prosperous end of the middle groups increased substantially, and those charged the upper classes rose even more precipitously. Evidence that these changes reflect the new estate duties can be found in a comparison of the rates on incomes of £50,000 or more. Between 1884 and 1904 the effective rate for all-earned income rose only by 65 percent, but the rate on part-earned-part-property income more than doubled.

In 1869 R. Dudley Baxter estimated the fraction of the total tax burden that fell on the working classes on the one hand and on the middle and upper classes on the other. Somewhat later Leon Levi provided new estimates for both earlier and later years. For a period when there are few estimates of the distribution of the tax burden, Baxter's and Levi's work is considered speculative, somewhat flawed, but fairly reliable. Baxter's data indicate that in 1867 the British population consisted of 23,000,000 persons in the working class and 6,700,000 persons in the middle and upper classes. From an analysis of the tax burden he also concluded that the former paid 29,112,000 in taxes (35 percent) and the latter two groups 54,000,000, or 65 percent of the total.[45] Levi's estimate places the latter share of the national taxes alone at 55 percent in 1862 and of national and local at 59 percent in 1882.[46] While their figures are almost certainly subject to substantial error, those mistakes would have had to be massive to reverse the central finding: That it was to the middle- and upper-income groups that the government turned for at least

one-half and perhaps as much as two-thirds of its financial requirements. A number of studies have indicated that the proportion of
total national income earned by the working classes did not change
significantly between the 1860s and 1912.[47] Given the shifts in the
incidence of taxes between 1867 and the end of the period, it seems
reasonable to assume that the proportion borne by the middle and
upper classes was no lower and almost certainly higher at the later
date. For the central argument of this study the important question
still remains: How was the burden distributed between the middle-
and upper-income groups?

That task is not easy; however, it appears that some conclusions
can be drawn, if the reader will accept some fairly strong assumptions. The most critical is taxonomic and concerns the definition of
"middle" and "upper" classes. As generally perceived and as used
in this study those classifications carry certain sociological connotations, but the evidence is cast in terms of income groups. Baxter
divides his nonworking classes into middle (97 percent) and upper
(3 percent), but his criterion is income, not social standing or occupation.[48] There is, at best, an imperfect correlation between the
economic and the sociological definitions. There were impoverished
aristocrats, and there were more than a few merchants and manufacturers with incomes well in excess of £5,000 a year.[49] Still, it
appears that the upper class tended to be concentrated at the higher
and the middle class at the lower end of the income scale. If one is
willing to assume that income provides an adequate if not perfect
guide to class, it is possible to construct an index of the proportion
of the total tax bill borne by the two groups.

Baxter for 1867, Levi for 1880, and Williams for 1906 provide estimates of the income accruing to various income groups, and those
estimates are the basis for the following calculations.[50] The latter
two, however, do not attempt to estimate incomes accruing to members of the middle class with incomes below the exemption level.
In 1867, that group constituted almost one-half (49 percent) of the
middle class and accounted for about one-quarter of *all* taxes paid
by the middle and upper classes combined. For the later period no
similar estimates exist, but the size of the intermediate or lower
middle class was apparently not insignificant. While the exemption
level varied, ten separate studies placed the share of income accruing
to that group as between 16 and 29 percent of the total earned by
all members of the middle and upper classes.[51] (The lower figures
are for the period when the exemption level was reduced to £100.)
The 1880 rates from Table 8.4 were applied to the adjusted income
under the assumption that the taxpayers distributed themselves

TABLE 8.4

GREAT BRITAIN TAX RATES (ALL TAXES) & TAX BURDEN
MIDDLE & UPPER CLASSES

(A) 1867			(B) 1880				(C) 1906			
Income	Tax Rate	% Paid	Income	Tax Rate	% Paid		Income	Tax Rate	% Paid	
				MIDDLE CLASSES						
Less than £100	12.03	25.0	Less than £150	6.20	23.4		Less than £100	6.90	22.0	
£100 to £299	8.80	28.5	£150 to £199	5.08	11.7		£100 to £199	5.90	14.7	
£300 to £999	6.77	17.1 70.6	£200 to £499	5.69	24.7		£200 to £499	6.10	32.7	
			£500 to £999	5.65	10.8 70.6		£500 to £999	7.10	13.7 83.1	
				UPPER CLASSES						
£1000 to £4999	4.99	16.8	£1000 to £1999	5.02	7.6		£1000 to £1999	7.60	7.2	
£50,000 & Upward	4.37	12.6 29.4	£2000 to £4999	4.58	8.0		£2000 to £4999	7.50	4.5	
			£5000 to £9999	4.24	4.6		£5000 to £9999	7.60	1.8	
			£10,000 to £49,999	4.02	6.5		£10,000 to £49,999	7.80	2.3	
			£50,000 & Upward	3.90	2.8 29.4		£50,000 & Upward	8.00	1.0 16.9	

among the income groups in the same proportion as tax assessments.[52] In addition, again in keeping with conventional wisdom, it was assumed that the unassessed middle class constituted 49 percent of that group and paid 25 percent of all taxes paid by the combined middle and upper classes. Given these assumptions, it was possible to construct an estimate of the relative tax burden by income group; and the resulting proportions were in turn applied to the estimated total tax bill paid by the middle and upper classes (that total assumed to be 62 percent of all taxes, an average of the Baxter and Levi estimates). The result is an estimate of the actual taxes paid by each income group (see Table 8.5).

In the 1860s Baxter drew the line between middle and upper classes at £1,000. As incomes grew over the next half century, that figure probably rose, and calculations based on Baxter's figure should provide a minimum estimate of the middle class burden. Levi, writing a decade and a half later, for example, places the dividing line at £2,000. For 1867 and 1880 the results are remarkably similar. They indicate that the middle class contributed almost two and one-half times as much to the governmental coffers as did the upper class. For 1906 the figure is even more extreme; and, if it is to be believed, the middle-class contribution was close to five times that of the upper class. These figures are certainly subject to substantial error, but again those mistakes would have to be massive to reverse the central finding: The middle class paid substantially more taxes than the upper class. A pound is a pound is a pound, and there is no way to link particular receipts to particular expenditures. Still, there is a strong implication that the middle class paid far more than its share of the imperial subsidy, and given the evi-

TABLE 8.5

TAX BURDENS AND INCOME ESTIMATES FOR MIDDLE AND UPPER CLASSES, 1906

Income Group	Assessment Weight	Tax Rate[1]	Average Income (£'s)	Burden (%)	Taxes Paid (£'s Millions)	Estimated Income (£'s Millions)
Less than £160	548,244	.062	129	25.0	20.2	325.8
£160 to £199	226,463	.059	185	14.1	11.4	193.2
£200 to £499	297,658	.061	304	31.5	25.4	416.4
£500 to £999	46,500	.071	700	13.2	10.7	150.7
Cumulative Total				83.8	67.6	1086.1
£1,000 to £1,999	11,224	.076	1,423	6.9	5.6	73.7
£2,000 to £4,999	3,408	.075	3,002	˙4.4	3.5	46.7
£5,000 to £9,999	567	.076	7,226	1.8	1.5	19.7
£10,000 to £49,999	269	.078	18,624	2.2	1.8	23.1
£50,000 and Over	24	.080	88,086	.09	.07	8.8
Cumulative Total				16.2	13.1	172.0

[1]Assumes tax rate at 1/2 earned 1/2 property. Rates are midpoint averages.

dence on the composition of stockholders, it should be apparent that they did not receive an equal share of its benefits.

It is possible to obtain a "feel" for the magnitude of these interclass transfers through an exercise in "synthetic history." The evidence presented in Chapter 7 indicates that Empire equities were held by the three occupational groups (businesspeople, elites, and others) in the ratio of 37.2:28.9:33.9. Of the last group, 1 percent was held by laborers and should be excluded. As to the remaining groups in the others category, it appears that they can be distributed between the businesspeople and elites in the same proportion as the initial distributions (28.9:37.2). It is, however, also true that 11.1 percent of Empire shares were owned by persons who were not citizens of the United Kingdom. Adjustments for other and overseas holders suggest that businesspeople held 38.4 and elites 49.4 percent of Empire shares.

The Empire subsidy has been estimated at between £.71 and £.95 per capita (see Chapters 5 and 6). The former figure includes only out-of-pocket costs (defense and subsidies) while the latter encompasses interest and Crown Agent contributions as well. If these subsidies (an annual total of between £30.8 and £41.2 million) are subtracted from total tax receipts, the residual should be the domestic proportion of taxes. That figure for 1906 would fall between £88.9 and £99.3 million since total taxes were £130 million.

The estimates presented in Table 8.5 suggest that the income of the elites was £172 million, on which they paid taxes of £13.1 million. If they received 49.4 percent of the Empire subsidy, their share should have been somewhere between £15.2 and £20.4 million. The value of that subsidy exceeded their total tax bill by an excess of between £2.1 and £7.3 million. Thus the elites were net winners, even if the domestic component of the tax provided them with no benefits; and, to the extent that those benefits were positive, they paid nothing for them.

For the middle classes, however, the scenario suggests a bleaker conclusion. Their share of the subsidy should have yielded between £11.8 and £15.8 million, while at the same time, they paid taxes of £67.6 million. A simple subtraction indicates that they paid "domestic taxes" of between £51.8 and £55.8 million. If they received non-Empire benefits in proportion to their numbers, their share should have been between £19.8 and £22.1 million; and, even if benefits were associated with income rather than numbers, their share would have only been between £47.6 and £53.1. Thus, under even the most extreme assumptions, the middle classes were net losers to the extent of something more than £2.5 million; and, if the distribution of benefits reflected an average of population and income position, the figure is some seven times that amount.

9 *Empire, the special interests, and the House of Commons*

Despite those wags who conjectured that the British Empire had been conceived in a fit of absence of mind and that its progress was solely dictated by the whims of the man on the spot without benefit of a coherent governing philosophy, Parliament, and especially the House of Commons, in fact, scrutinized the affairs of Britain's far-flung possessions with some care. No major change in fiscal or administrative policy could in practice be effected without the House's scrutiny. But power is never absolute, especially in a democracy, and it is the purpose of this chapter to determine, to the degree possible, the extent to which special interests modulated and influenced the decisions of the representatives of the people.

I. The special interests

Firms, acting independently or in concert through trade associations and chambers of commerce, continuously bombarded Parliament with pleas for action on all fronts. If the firms included in this study are representative, the most active were the utilities and transportation companies. They maintained a drumfire of pressure for the extension of their powers, the limitation of governmental control, and the curtailment of competition. In 1871, the Sunderland and South Shields Water Company "bent every effort" to protect the firm from proposed legislation that would have limited its ability to lay pipe over certain bridges; later it demanded that Parliament defeat the Sunderland Corporation Act and, later still, it acted against the Durham County Electricity Supply Bill. Success was sporadic, but in the latter case the company's solicitor did report that the bill's agents had assured him the measure would be amended before it reached the second house.[1] Generally, gas companies resented the introduction of electricity, the street-railroad companies fought the advent of the underground, and the established railroads attacked the chartering of new ones. Although Parliament usually smiled on requests for recapitalization and the expansion of service, it was less cooperative in other directions.

Collieries and steel companies were also frequently involved in lobbying Parliament. Samuel Fox, the steelmaker, felt endangered

253

by removal of water from the Little Don River, and in August 1874, the directors reported that the company had successfully opposed two bills that would have reduced the available water. More than two decades later the issue was still not resolved, but the company's officers were again able to report that new legislation had been amended to their satisfaction.[2] It was, however, labor legislation that most concerned these companies. When the iron industry lost the battle against the Workmen's Compensation Act, the management of the Shotts Iron Company lamented, "This obnoxious act of Parliament comes into operation on January 1."[3] The directors of the Stavely Coal and Iron Company urged strong opposition to the establishment of a minimum pay scale for miners and suggested the organization of a unified crusade on the national level.[4]

Breweries fought continuously against government regulation, and that battle was particularly vicious when the Liberals were in power. The Barclay Perkins Brewery, threatened by licensing legislation, urged its customers to write their MPs: "We would press on you the desirability of your urging your members to support any action in Parliament which has as its object the *equitable protection of licensed property* and the recognition of the *principal that all interest in a license, taken away for no fault of the licensee shall be fully compensated.*"[5] The breweries may have slowed the process, but like the iron and steel companies they largely failed to halt government's determination to control them and their clientele. Still, the Conservative Party drew substantial financial support in the process.

Not suprisingly, the more a firm's business depended on a particular property right, vested by a government license or a charter, the more determined it was to bend the direction of government policy in its favor; and the more formidable its base of support, the greater were the chances of success. At the 1906 meeting of the proprietors of City and West End properties, it was reported:

> Last year the County Council introduced a bill in Parliament entitled "London Builders Act of 1894, Amendment Act." This bill was of a very far reaching and drastic nature and your directors carefully studied it once they saw that if the bill was carried it might interfere largely with some of your properties and more likely cause considerable expense. We therefore drew up a petition which was presented to the City of London and enlisted their sympathies. They, with their powerful backing, opposed the bill in Parliament and as you know, I dare say, the result of the discussion was that the bill was withdrawn . . . .[6]

For those well placed in the establishment, the technique was familiar and direct. Alban Gibbs of the international banking and commercial house of Antony Gibbs and Sons was able to write the prime minister, Arthur Balfour, on familiar terms. "My Dear Arthur," he wrote, "I am sorry to have to trouble you with a long letter, but the state of irritation and strain in the City is such as I feel compelled to do so." Gibbs then proceeded to complain about the Port of London, Employment of Children, Education, and Preferential Tariff measures before Parliament and to declare that he did not want a free-trade candidate winning in the City in the next election.[7]

Perhaps more telling, a member of the same firm wrote the prime minister, Herbert Asquith: "You may remember that when you were good enough to lunch with me back at the Savoy to meet some City friends, you gave me permission to inform them that I would send you the list of subscribers to the General Election Appeal. In fulfillment of that promise I therefore enclose my list, the total of which is £134,887,110 . . . . "[8]

Some two years later, Herbert Gibbs attempted to call in the debt:

> There is one thing which I think necessary to make an appeal for funds a success, and that is that we should know that when Ministers come to power they will devise some permanent constitutional check on the unlimited power of the House of Commons over the money of the rich.
>
> The death duties have done much damage to the country and the uncertainty as to their increase has done and is doing more and from a business point of view it is not good business to spend money in supporting a Party which does not take the matter up, but I think people will agree that it *was* good business to support a party that did . . . .[9]

The income tax law of 1912, however, suggests he was not entirely successful.

Shortly thereafter Herbert Gibbs gained an interview with Lloyd George, then the Chancellor of the Exchequer. His concern was the tax then imposed on nitrate companies' depreciation funds. Gibbs reported that the chancellor was at first not very sympathetic but that after a prolonged discussion, he had finally admitted that the effects were a "bit stiff." Gibbs concluded that his arguments had convinced George that the heavy amortization of nitrate gounds was linked to their short life (as compared with, for example, coal mines) not to an attempt by the companies to earn unfair profit. The chancellor agreed to review the situation.[10]

The explosion of economic activity in Britain during the last half of the nineteenth century produced not only the limited-liability company and the worldwide flows of symbolic capital, but numerous attempts to lessen the competitive edge of the laissez faire environment through the organization of voluntary cooperative associations. Workers pursued their goals through trade unions, and management and investors expressed their interests through chambers of commerce and trade associations.

In the years after 1860, the chambers had grown greatly in number; and, as Clapham noted, they "were always more concerned with dealing than with making."[11] The chambers attempted to influence both government policy and specific legislation; and the Empire and foreign sectors were very important to some business at least. In 1877, the Association of Chambers of Commerce of the United Kingdom resolved: " . . . that a memorial be sent to the First Lord of Her Majesty's Treasury, calling the attention of the government to the very unsatisfactory position of the long pending project of a direct land route for commerce between Rangoon . . . [and] the southwest frontier of China."[12] Similarly, on June 12, 1896, and following earlier resolutions of the Manchester and the London chambers, the association urged the government to support railway construction in Uganda and West Africa.

Any expansion of the Empire that might benefit business and commerce was usually favored by the chambers, although the degree of ardor varied with the importance of colonial trade in the region's economy. London and the port cities tended to be the most vocal. In 1885, for example, the Glasgow Chamber of Commerce advocated the British annexation of Upper Burma and inveighed against the dangers of Chinese commercial competition.[13] The closer the bonds of Empire, and the more fully developed the precepts of imperial reciprocity, the better it was for business. Hence, the Liverpool chamber urged that "with the feeling of imperial citizenship throughout the Empire, and the sense of union already obtained between the Mother Country and her colonies" an imperial consultative assembly representing Britain and its colonies be formed at the earliest possible date.[14] In addition, the Liverpudlians recommended the appointment of a Royal Commission with members drawn from Britain, India, and the colonies to consider the enhancement of trade relations between the various parts of the Empire.[15] In 1903, the fifth Congress of Chambers of Commerce of the British Empire was convened in Montreal. Its policy resolutions, dealing with imperial defense, improved trade relations within the Empire, imperial reciprocity, and the need for improved communications, reflected closely those placed previously on the record both by the Association of Chambers of Commerce and the various municipal chambers.

The chambers supported measures designed to increase Empire trade and demanded a greater mercantile presence on appointed organs of government (the India Council, for example). Profits were, however, profits, and domestic policy also occupied some fraction of their time. They scanned proposed legislation with a watchful eye and became increasingly restive as political and social reform captured an ever larger fraction of the legislative agenda. Any improvement in the lot of the working man (or woman or child), if it might cost a farthing (and sometimes even if it did not), was frowned upon by the chambers. In 1872, for example, the Glasgow chamber fought against a bill aimed at restricting the hours children could work.[16] Political rights for the proletariat, working conditions and hours of labor, and the right to organize were issues the chambers were prepared to combat with all the political power at their command.

A detailed perusal of the records of the Glasgow, Birmingham, Liverpool, Manchester, and London Chambers of Commerce manifests the underlying homogeneity of the British mercantile community. Free trade was perceived as the basis of British prosperity, and it was the cornerstone of the chambers' philosophic position. Thus, laws judged to be in restraint of trade in whatever guise, whether domestic, colonial, or foreign, were continuingly attacked. No measure was too insignificant to arouse the chambers' ire. The London Chamber railed against the Death Duties Act in New South Wales. Birmingham noted with concern French tariffs on "velocipedes" and brass fittings for umbrellas, and protested against a Natal law requiring the payment of a tax by commercial travelers.[17] London was more interested in questions of imperial cohesion and defense than the others, but those were fairly common themes in most of the port cities. As the issues expanded from Empire to overseas trade, the other chambers raised their voices with increasing frequency. Questions regarding the opening of the Congo, West Africa, and China to British commerce; the construction of railways in Africa, India, and China; and opposition to foreign subsidies for shipping and sugar all appeared on the list of resolutions supported by a variety of local chambers. Trade yes, politics maybe – as Schumpeter has noted, in a world of free trade it makes no difference to business who opens new markets or constructs new railroads as long as the markets are opened and the railroads built.

It is difficult to provide a precise measure of the effectiveness of the chambers in their attempts to influence imperial policy; but it is clear that sometimes, at least, they proved quite persuasive agencies of political manipulation. The best example of a successful exercise of political power on a matter of imperial concern can be found in the chambers' campaign to eliminate the Indian duties on British cotton. In that case the organizations were pitted against the entire Indian establishment. The government of India wanted the tariffs for fiscal purposes, and the Indian business community hoped to expand domestic enterprise behind those barriers.

In the early 1860s, the government of India had imposed a tariff of 10 percent on all imports. Although this figure was reduced in 1864 and again in 1875, the Midlands textile interests remained outraged. Morley wrote Lytton in 1876: "At this moment . . . not a seat in Lancashire can beget a man who did not go for total and immediate repeal of the import duty on cotton . . . ."[18] At a time when the government majority was 52 and the Lancashire and Yorkshire seats totaled 71, Gathorn-Hardy wrote Lytton in a similar vein:

> A great deputation from Lancashire on the cotton duties has just left me and they are backed by a formidable force. The question occupies the minds of manufacturers and operatives and the import duties are looked upon as the main cause of their distress. The subject may materially influence the Lancashire elections at present so much in our favour . . . .[19]

Increasingly alarmed, Gathorn-Hardy again wrote the viceroy: "I continue to be picked upon about the cotton duties. Mr. Chancellor of the Exchequer has just sent over four Lancashire letters which speak of the loss of fourteen seats as inevitable unless remission is commenced . . . ."[20]

Responding to the determination of the chambers, the manufacturers, and the Lancashire members, the House of Commons denounced the Indian duties on cotton as protective and demanded their abolition. Succumbing to the pressure, the government of India removed the duty on the coarser grades of cotton (the most common import) and later abolished virtually all tariffs. As has been previously noted, revenue shortfalls prompted by these "reforms" forced the Indian authorities to reinstitute a general 5-percent duty in 1894; but to mollify the critics, an equivalent excise tax was levied on all cotton goods manufactured in India. Even that compromise proved politically unacceptable, and in 1896 both the import and the excise taxes were reduced.

In this instance, both the legislative and bureaucratic response would have pleased even the most resolute chamber member; however, it is far from clear that the same result would have been

achieved on a different issue. The policy flew in the face of a generally accepted view on the efficacy of free trade; but the chambers
were allied with a highly vocal group of manufacturers and workers
who were capable of bringing very focused electoral pressure to bear
on a government whose working majority was not large. Besides,
the issue did not adversely affect any other significant British interest
group. The lesson is quite clear: Parliament could under certain
circumstances be influenced. In the main, however, successful manipulation demanded considerable political muscle and sympathetic
opinion in Parliament.

The chambers' attack on tariffs both in the Empire and abroad
was hardly less vociferous; but, because of a lack of support in the
Empire and the obvious constitutional limitations on the power of
Parliament, it was largely doomed to failure. Of the various chambers, Birmingham's was clearly the most concerned about the tariff
issue (almost one-fourth of that chamber's resolutions between 1863
and 1910 dealt with tariffs in the responsibly governed Empire) but
Liverpool was only somewhat less so. Both took great exception to
the behavior of the Canadian, Australian, New Zealand, and South
African governments. No perceived affront was beneath notice. In
1907, the Birmingham chamber, for example, resolved to contact the
Colonial Office in regard to the customs duty charged by the South
African colonies on the importation of British catalogs and price lists.
While other cities worried less about the Empire, foreign tariffs were
of greater general concern. In London, a third of all deliberations
concerned that latter issue, and for the chambers as a whole, the
figure was almost one-fifth. The attacks were numerous, but in both
the Empire and foreign sectors they appear to have met with little
success.

If the London chamber's greatest concern was with imperial unity,
its Glasgow counterpart was the most bellicosely expansionist. It
strongly supported British advance into New Guinea, Swaziland,
and the Northern Gold Coast and inveighed against the Germans
in the Cameroons. There is no doubt, however, that the London
chamber manifested a more continuing and stronger interest in imperial affairs than did any of its provincial counterparts. Over the
years 1891 to 1912, for example, the city's index of imperial activity
stood at one and one-half times the all-UK average. In contrast, the
figure for Manchester was 132 (but 42 percent of the resolutions
dealt with Indian duties, primarily on cotton, with a secondary and
somewhat surprising emphasis on the cost of Empire), for Liverpool
94, for Glasgow 80, and for Birmingham but 78. (See Table 9.1.) In
a broader context, the chambers directed about one-fifth of their

TABLE 9.1

RELATIVE IMPORTANCE OF DOMESTIC, IMPERIAL AND FOREIGN ISSUES
IN THE DELIBERATIONS OF LOCAL CHAMBERS OF COMMERCE*

(All UK Average Equals 100)

	Domestic	Imperial	Foreign
London	40	155	34
Birmingham	134	78	116
Manchester	63	132	64
Liverpool	99	94	115
Glasgow	110	80	136

*It should be noted that there is great disparity between the
various chambers vis-a-vis years in existence and frequency of
meetings.

TABLE 9.2

RELATIVE IMPORTANCE OF LOCAL CHAMBERS OF COMMERCE
RESOLUTIONS AND DISCUSSIONS,
TOPICS OF FOREIGN AND EMPIRE ECONOMIC INTEREST*

	Extension of Foreign and Colonial Trade Including Railroad Construction	Imperial Defense	Indian Laws, Tariffs, etc., in Constraint of British Trade	Dependent Government Laws, Tariffs, etc., in Constraint of British Trade	Responsible Government Laws, Tariffs, etc., in Constraint of British Trade	Costs of Empire
London	122	400	0	49	82	167
Manchester	76	67	347	47	38	333
Glasgow	122	33	127	147	88	0
Birmingham	81	0	25	112	159	0
Liverpool	99	0	0	0	132	0

*Topics of purely local interest or concerning labor reform excluded.

efforts (if discussions and resolutions can be used as a proxy for
effort) in support of the extension of foreign and colonial trade, and
another one-fifth urging subsidies for mail and telegraph communications and general government support of business. Empire tariffs and imperial preference, although of relatively little interest to
London and Glasgow, were very important to Liverpool and the
other Midlands chambers. Indian tariffs on British textiles were almost the sole imperial concern of the Manchester chamber in the
1870s, and the subject occupied a surprising 41 percent of all its
deliberations for the entire period. (See Table 9.2.)

As with the chambers of commerce, so with the trade associations,
although each had its own specific policy agenda. The associations
covered many fields of enterprise, and their number greatly increased in the last half of the century. Although occasionally interested in questions of broad imperial policy, they became intimately

involved only when specific legislation appeared to directly affect their prospects and profits. Not surprisingly, the Oldham cotton spinners, for example, were immersed in the protest against Indian tariffs. More often, however, their concerns were domestic but no less narrow. Most of the association's efforts were devoted to specific pieces of legislation, to opposition to foreign competition, and to the design of institutional arrangements that could allow them to effectively control wages and maintain monopoly prices.

Trade associations varied in their levels of effectiveness and organization. Some were so loosely knit that they met only once a year and then to little purpose. Others were active not only in rhetorical efforts to effect wage and price controls but in attempts to limit production as well. Examples of the associations span the industrial spectrum. They include: the Master Cotton Spinners' Association of Oldham, the Midland Flint Glass Manufacturers, the London Master Printers, the London Master Builders, the Cleveland Ironmasters' Association, the South Staffordshire Association (iron), the Steam Coal Association of Tyneside, the Lancashire Cornish Boilerplates Association and the Dundee Spinners' and Manufacturers' Association.

Purely regional trade associations were followed by more broadly based ones – a development that paralleled the evolution of the chambers of commerce. On March 2, 1899, for example, the North Staffordshire, the Lancashire, and the North Wales Colliery Owners' Associations met to merge their organizations and one representing Cheshire into a single unit. The aim was to broaden the effectiveness of their political activity. The General Builders' Association, the North of England Iron Manufacturers' Association, the Association of Tin Plate Manufacturers, the Wire Trade Association, the English and Scottish Steelmakers (founders), the Scottish Steelmakers, the Association of Steel Rail Makers, the Tire and Axlemakers Association, the Steel Smelters' Association, the Steel Plate Manufacturers' Association, the Steel Wheel Centers Association, and organizations representing sugar refiners, alkali manufacturers, leather manufacturers, and paper makers were all examples of cooperation along increasingly comprehensive lines.

II. Interaction between Whitehall and British business overseas

Later in this chapter, an attempt will be made to provide some quantitative measure of the success enjoyed by individual firms and cooperative pressure groups in their attempts to influence parliamentary action. For the moment, however, in order to provide some qualitative assessment and flavor, it seems appropriate to examine the interrelationship of government (in this case Whitehall more than Westminster) and business in the imperial sector and in those parts of the foreign overseas where British influence was sufficiently strong to possibly deem them parts of Robinson and Gallagher's conception of an "informal Empire."

Although the government of India tended to prefer public to private enterprise, there was an inclination, even under free-trade policies, to favor British over foreign business. In 1903, Lord Kilbracken wrote St. John Brodrick, the Secretary of State for India:

> ... We constantly get from foreign firms tenders which are far below those from English firms in respect to price, which as to quality we are often told there is little or nothing to choose . . . . Lord George Hamilton was always most unwilling to place an order abroad; and as a rule we have managed to avoid it, though occasionally it is by no means easy to do so . . . . At the same time the charge thrown upon interior revenue is sometimes very heavy . . . . [21]

When Standard Oil competed for a contract in India, it was turned down and Hamilton wrote Curzon that despite the undoubted benefits which would have accrued to the consumer due to lowered prices,

> ... I think you are perfectly correct in refusing the concession to the American Standard Oil Company. Great commercial organizations such as Standard Oil, become the depository of gigantic potential forces, which might at any moment be used to the detriment of some vast community or nation which those managing the monopoly wish either to spite or squeeze . . . . [22]

And this xenophobic view was also reflected in a Parliament that was ready to rise in wrath against the implementation of a mild import duty on British cotton imports into India. " . . . This outcry against protection," Godley wrote Elgin, "comes very ill from a House of Commons which is ready to pass a vote of censure on the Secretary of State, if the guaranteed Indian Railway Companies are allowed to save £1,500 on an order of steel sleepers by placing it in Belgium."[23] Clearly, free trade was not the eleventh commandment and was only worshipped when it did not interfere with profits and self-interest. Either the right hand did not know what the left was doing or India was sui generis and treated like no other colony. The previous discussion of the Crown Agents indicated that they made purchases for India's imperial brethren at the best price, even if the vendor of choice were foreign!

The history of the debate over the Indian tariffs has already been related. Despite their victory, the textile manufacturers did not relax their vigilance. Somewhat incredulously, Cross wrote Lansdowne that a large deputation from Lancashire had called upon him to protest the passage of the Indian factory acts. The secretary of state was not sure he had convinced his callers "that the purpose of the acts was to protect women and children and not trade."[24] Similarly Lord Hardinge, the Viceroy, understood that the Indian cotton duties despite being smaller than the British free-trade government's equivalent could not survive because the Indian tariff had hurt firms whose parliamentary support the government needed.[25]

But India appears to have been an exception. In general, when it came to British business operating abroad, the official attitude was different. Overseas, Whitehall manifested great reluctance to support British commercial enterprises. With few exceptions, British diplomats were willing to offer their good offices, but little else. An official philosophy that asked only the protection of international law and equal but not favored treatment for British subjects, and the prejudices of the day both played a role. Laissez faire was the state religion at least outside India, and government's interference on behalf of business was anathema. In addition, most government bureaucrats were drawn from a social class that looked down on commerce as not altogether respectable. Philosophy and prejudice together produced a set of policies neatly summarized in a letter from Sir Robert Morier to Rosebery: "No rule has been more absolutely insisted upon in the dealings of Her Majesty's Missions abroad than this one, that, unless there is a denial of justice, or treatment of British subjects engaged in mercantile transactions contrary to Treaties, or to the spirit of Treaties, no assistance shall be rendered to further private interests."[26] Three years later, the Treasury expressed essentially the same view when it said in a letter to the Foreign Office: "It has been and is My Lords' conviction that it is unsound commercial policy to seek to assist the British enterprise in its struggle with foreign rivals out of the pocket of the general taxpayer."[27]

So-called foreign bondholders were held in particular contempt as they were deemed to have diverted useful resources for the unilateral benefit of a foreign state.[28] Thus, their cries for support and protection from foreign default tended to go unheeded and to evoke little sympathy. The voluminous records of the Council of Foreign Bondholders, the association formed to protect their interests, show little evidence of government sympathy. In a letter to the Earl of

Ripon, Robert Meade (an undersecretary in the Colonial Office) reflected prevailing official opinion when he wrote: "H.M.'s Government must expect pressure from the bondholders who will like to
be relieved of their bad investment and this pressure they must be
prepared to resist."[29]

Very rarely, however, the government did provide some assistance to British business operations in the foreign sector. When trouble erupted at Antony Gibbs and Sons' nitrate works in Quique,
Peru, the company requested a British naval presence. Whether as
a consequence of the company's efforts or mere happenstance, Herbert Gibbs was able to write Louis Mallet at the Foreign Office in
December, 1907: " . . . I have just received your letter telling me that
the Admiralty are sending a ship at once, and I can only confess
the gratitude of my firm and the Nitrate Industry for the kind assistance of the Foreign Office in the protection of our interest."[30]
The Gibbs family, of course, had very good political connections,
and the records provide few other examples.

More representative of the support that would normally have been
expected was, however, an incident described in the minutes of the
board of directors of the Peruvian Corporation:

> Acting upon instructions received from this government, the Brit-
> ish legation in Lima addressed the Peruvian minister of foreign
> affairs upon the date of 7 January, 1898, in a letter intimating that
> Her Majesty's Government could not consent to the infraction of
> British rights of property involved in the decision and degrees of
> the Peruvian government . . . .[31]

No doubt fully aware that the British lion had no intention of un-
sheathing his claws, the Peruvian minister of foreign affairs duly
acknowledged the communication but "at the same time reiterated
the views held by the Peruvian government on the subject." And
the minutes concluded: "There the matter at present rests," and
would continue to rest.[32] As Salisbury had declared when pressed
to intervene in South America, Her Majesty's Government was not
willing to relinquish the principle of nonintervention that had been
in operation since the time of Canning. "We have been pressed . . .
to undertake the part of arbitrator, of compulsory arbitrator, in quar-
rels in the west of South America . . . . We have been earnestly
pressed, also . . . to undertake the regeneration of Argentine finance.
On neither of these subjects are Her Majesty's Government in the
least degree disposed to encroach on the function of providence."[33]

When British interests in Chile's Atacama Desert seemed threatened, the government would offer only "tacit diplomatic support"
and no gunboats.[34] In the case of British economic relations with

Uruguay, "even the Baring Crisis of 1890, where greater British economic interests were at stake than in Egypt a decade before, did not lead to British intervention."[35] The records of the Lautaro Nitrate Company are filled with reports of litigation in Chilean courts with no evidence of British intervention or even diplomatic pressure on the firm's behalf. As D.C.M. Platt concludes: "In practice, Government assistance was insignificant."[36]

Nor do China and Thailand offer frequent examples of political support of British commercial activities. In the case of the former, Whitehall resisted the blandishments of business and refused to support British investment in China when it became convinced, "that the China trade would never be worth the expense of war or sovereignty . . . ."[37] As one expert wrote, "Economic criteria . . . may be applied as important determinants of the existence of informal empire . . . [but] for China the evidence suggests that such factors did not exist."[38] The official position on intervention is underscored by the reaction to an apparently innocent request from the British legation in China for assistance in obtaining copies of imperial decrees that had authorized certain loans made by British financiers. On May 22, 1885, the British chargé d'affaires in Peking was peremptorily ordered not to cooperate and instructed in no way "however remotely" to assist the representatives of British finance in China.[39]

Writing about Thailand, James Ingram concludes that: "The British desire to keep Thailand as a buffer state between British and French possessions in British hands, was largely responsible for the use of British diplomacy to preserve the independence of Thailand . . . ."[40] And indeed Rosebery had written Gladstone: "Our interest in Siam is twofold: for we do not desire to see her absorbed by France, a circumstance which would place . . . their great military power on our eastern frontier, and as we have practically a monopoly of Siamese commerce we do not wish to see our trade destroyed by the tariff the French erect around their possessions."[41] The imperialism of free trade is an elusive concept, and perhaps never more so than in Thailand.

Turning to Africa, it appears that, even in the dependent Empire outside of India, British business did not fare well. The Bathurst Company, with its primary operations in West Africa, frequently importuned Whitehall for intervention on its behalf. Rather than offering support, Her Majesty's government ceded the port of Yarbutenda on the Gambia River to the French. The directors of the company could but dejectedly note: "The monetary interests which the company has created on the River Gambia in the firm belief . . .

that the colony in its entirety would always remain under the sovereignty of the British Crown has been adversely affected by the unexpected concession."[42] Other examples abound. Sir William MacKinnon, the President of the Imperial British East Africa Company, pointed to the vast support afforded their respective imperial enterprises by the Germans and Belgians and how niggardly in contrast was that of the British government.[43] But the company was not above using every means of improving its position. George Mackenzie wrote Sir Murdoch Smith:

> ... it has occurred to me that perhaps you might be able to find some influential party ... to get some leading men, personally known either to Lord Rosebery or Mr. Gladstone, to approach them, as entirely outside the Company, without in any way indicating that they were inspired from here as to the desirability of Government now coming forward to give some support .... [44]

The Pacific Steam Navigation Company, too, seldom ceased to bemoan the lack of government help against foreign competition. At the general meeting of May 29, 1899, the chairman reported: "I am sorry to say, with the exception of the Foreign Office, it is Inland Revenue, with its refusal to allow a just deduction for depreciation, and imposition of taxes on transfer, or the Agriculture Department, who do all they can to prevent us carrying sheep and cattle; or the Post Office ... or the Board of Trade .... They are all alike it seems to me ...."

Apparently driven to the limits of tolerance, the National Africa Company at a meeting of its board on September 23, 1885, resolved:

> And whereas the Directors have in ways that are well known to H.M.G. already made as great a sacrifice as they could justify to their shareholders in order to make the Niger a British river, and to keep open to British influence and to British freight, the only practical commercial river route to the vast populations of the Central Sudan, and whereas after unexampled patience and mature consideration, the directors cannot but conclude to their deep regret that H.M.G. will continue to procrastinate (although admittedly long convinced of the necessity of immediate action) until after the occurrence of a complete catastrophe, the forerunning disturbances of which had long since been reported to them. Resolved: that negotiations be opened with a foreign power with the following objects, a) the transfer to the foreign power of the independent treaties of the company; b) the effective occupation of the countries thus transferred; c) the placing of the country under the

flag of a foreign power; and d) the obtaining of such conditions as
shall be most advantageous to the shareholders . . . .

There was no doubt a good deal of bluff in this series of threats,
coming as they did at a time when the negotiations for a Royal
Charter for what was to become the Royal Niger Company were
underway, but there was an element of real frustration as well.

The entire position on foreign investment was neatly summarized
by Salisbury: "On general principles," he wrote, "Her Majesty's
Government always decline to place the power of the country at the
disposal of individual investors to secure investments which they
may think fit to make in the territory of another power."[45] In the
Empire formal and informal, India aside, the same attitude seems
to have prevailed.

III. Voting behavior in the House of Commons

It is now appropriate to attempt to determine the degree to which
pressure groups with vested imperial interests affected the House
of Commons, the font of British power. To reach this end, it is
necessary to examine the voting behavior of the 3,768 men who
served in the Commons between January 1, 1860 and December 31,
1912. In particular, an attempt to "explain" that behavior in terms
of an individual MP's personal idiosyncrasies, the socioeconomic
characteristics of his constituency, and certain political factors seems
in order. Ideally, at the personal level those traits would include
measures of occupation, wealth, imperial holdings, education, and
social relations. At the constituency level it would be desirable likewise to explore the effects of income, home ownership, rural/urban
proportions, the industrial composition of economic activity, religion, and education. In the political arena, questions of party and
the level of election competition should be considered. Between
reality and that ideal there is, however, a considerable gap. Thus
these are very preliminary explorations, and the conclusions should
be taken as at best tentative.

For this analysis the divisions on 377 bills of both imperial and
domestic concern were gathered.[46] The domestic measures were included to provide a standard against which to assess behavior on
imperial questions. Initially, every division, save those on the most
trivial or parochial issue, was examined. That list was reduced by
the deletion of most third readings, which are essentially pro forma.
All remaining divisions were categorized as to subject and importance (measured by the number of members actually voting) and
then stratified according to these selected variables.

Although there was considerable Parliament-to-Parliament variation, for the entire period 1859 to 1910, 44 percent of the imperial divisions dealt with military matters, 38 percent with loans and other nonmilitary subsidies, and 18 percent with administrative and tax matters.[47] More than a third of the issues involved India; about a fourth, the responsibly governed dominions; and somewhat more than two-fifths, the dependent colonies.

For the forty-two Indian divisions, military matters were the subject of more than one-half, slightly less than one-third concerned administration and taxes (half of those, the cotton duties), and only 14 percent involved questions of loans and subsidies. For the thirty divisions relating to the responsibly governed colonies, loans and subsidies accounted for 57 percent, defense was the subject of less than a fourth, and administrative and tax matters were taken up only slightly less often. In the fifty-three divisions involving the dependent colonies, loans and subsidies accounted for just less than half, military matters accounted for 45 percent (twelve of these twenty-four involved Egypt and the Sudan), but administration and taxes only about one in twelve.

By and large the honorable members tended to go home when a motion dealing with the overseas Empire came to the floor. For those that remained, however, the chief issues in the ten divisions of the 1859–65 session were financial-military expenses and loans. Five imperial divisions marked the next Parliament, and the majority dealt with steamship subsidies and railway construction. It was, however, loans that again dominated the subsequent (1868–72) session. The twenty-one divisions on imperial matters in Disraeli's Parliament (1874–80) dealt with concerns over the Afghan and Zulu wars, the annexation of Fiji, Indian cotton duties, and other Indian administrative and tax matters. Gladstone's subsequent session was limited largely to questions of Egypt and the Sudan.

The Parliament of 1886–92 saw the newly reapportioned members dividing eleven times on imperial matters, and questions of naval defense provided the most significant single issue. The Empire appears to have receded in parliamentary importance between 1892 and 1895; only five divisions were recorded. Of that small total, four dealt with loans and subsidies to India and the dependent colonies in East Africa. The Empire reemerged in the next session (1895–1900), and an early concern with the financial affairs of Cyprus and railway construction in Uganda was replaced by the growing crisis in South Africa. In the new century the South African situation continued to be important, but concern for defense in the dominions also drew attention. Finally, of the five imperial divisions that occurred between 1906 and 1910, two dealt with free trade and imperial preference and two with loans for the Transvaal and India.

It must be borne in mind that many parliamentary decisions were made without a formal division. Moreover, it was next to impossible to discover all imperial issues hidden in supply and ways and means votes. The 120 divisions forming the basis for analysis in this chapter should, however, provide a substantial index to parliamentary behavior and its causes.

It should be possible to develop the data necessary to explain MP political behavior better than has been the case to date. For an individual member, wealth (at least at death) should be discoverable in the probate records; here the proxies (number of club memberships held and number of residences reported) do not serve very well. Occupational information is available for most members, and the same is true for education. Social connections were proxied by club membership.[48] A member's party identification is readily accessible, and it is possible to use "winning margin" to measure the "safeness" of his seat.[49] The greatest problem arises in attempts to measure the sociodemographic character of the constituency. In this analysis geographic location is the sole proxy used to capture these effects. The unit of measurement is an individual member's voting behavior in the particular Parliament.

For each such member a measure of his relative support of imperial issues was calculated. That measure was the ratio of the proportion of times that the member supported the pro-imperial position on the set of imperial bills divided by the percentage of support his party gave those same bills in a given Parliament. For all calculations the party's position is defined as that taken by the majority of the party on the issue in question.

The late nineteenth century was a period of growing party discipline (see Appendix 9.3), but there was still a significant fraction of defections, particularly among the Liberals and the Irish Nationalists, even at the end of the period. Moreover, the rate of defection appears to have been higher for imperial than for domestic legislation.

The measure of relative support on imperial issues was taken as the index of MP behavior, and an attempt was made to explain that behavior on the basis of individual, party, and constituency influences (see Appendix 9.4). A number of separate regressions were run and the results are reported in the next section. In general, however, an individual member's behavior on imperial issues was related to (1) his willingness to bow to party discipline on nonimperial matters, (2) his party, (3) the safety of his seat, (4) his occupation (see Appendixes 9.5 and 9.6), (5) his education (see Appendixes 9.7 and 9.8), (6) his club membership (see Appendix 9.9), (7) his wealth, (8) and the location of his constituency.

IV. MP support on imperial questions

In establishing the statistical base for a discussion of MP political behavior on imperial matters, it must be remembered that members often did not attend parliamentary sessions; and that fact raises some questions about the treatment of MPs who were frequently absent. If a member did not vote because he was sick or had better things to do, it would be wise to ignore him. If he did not appear because he was indifferent, it might be best to treat him as one-half in favor of an issue and one-half opposed. If he failed to vote because he opposed the party's stance, but did not want to overtly breach its discipline, he should be counted as opposed to the party's position. There is, of course, no way to resolve this puzzle totally; but in an attempt toward a solution, the regressions have been run in three different ways: (1) ignoring members who did not vote, (2) counting their position as one-half in favor and one-half opposed, and (3) counting them as having voted against the party position. In those cases where the three yield the same result, the questions raised by absenteeism can probably be ignored, and in general this is the case. It is not, however, always so; and that fact, too, raises some additional questions of interpretation. The treatment of both imperial and nonimperial abstentions as antiparty votes greatly enhances the positive association between the two and increases in turn both the explanatory power of the model and the significance of the party-support coefficient. For that reason only the yes/no results have been reported, but in general, the party-support measure aside, there is little difference between the three specifications.

It should be emphasized that the explanatory power of the model is not great. There was obviously a great deal more that underlay a member's voting behavior than the factors that are captured in this model explain. Moreover, there is also a considerable degree of inter-Parliament variation in the power of the model. The r^2s across the ten Parliaments average .11 for Conservatives and .15 for Liberals, but the range is from .04 to .22. The model has three continuous independent variables: support on nonimperial issues, winning margin, and number of club memberships. It also has a number of discrete independent variables. They include (1) seven occupational categories (three business and four elite) that are treated as dummies and measured against the behavior of the barristers and solicitors in parliament; (2) two educational variables (last school: university, last school: a major public school) that are again treated as dummies and compared with all other educational histories; (3) membership in five types of clubs (Empire and foreign, social, literary, other, and no club), dummied and measured against the behavior of those MPs who belonged to political clubs; and (4) five regions (Scotland and Wales, Ireland, the North and Lancashire, rural and South, and London and Home Counties). In this latter instance the comparison is against the industrial Midlands. In the overall regression, each Parliament is treated as a discrete independent variable. In this case, the base line of behavior is provided by the first Parliament (1859–65).

The standard tests indicate that while the explanatory power is not high, the model seems to provide a suggestive analytical tool.[50] In the case of the all-years–all-parliaments regressions, for the Conservatives the nonimperial support score is positively (and significantly) associated with imperial support; however, for the Liberals the relationship is even more significant and runs in the other direction. Liberal members who were most loyal to the party on domestic issues tended to defect most frequently on imperial ones. The winning margin is weakly associated with the strength of a member's pro-imperial position, but the relationship is not strong, particularly for the Liberals. The number of club memberships (a proxy for wealth) is positively associated, but only mildly, with that position for both Liberal and Conservative members.

For Conservative businessmen, occupation does not appear to have distinguished them from their peers in the legal profession. For Liberals of similar background, however, merchants were somewhat, and miscellaneous business and professional people substantially, less interested in imperial aggrandizement. Among the Conservative elites, financiers and peers and gents were mildly less and miscellaneous elites somewhat more strongly in favor of imperial adventures than the barristers and solicitors in their party. Among the Liberals, on the other hand, financiers, military men, and peers and gents were all less devoted to imperial principles.

University education appears to have turned the members away from imperialism, and that relationship is particularly strong for the Liberals. The impact of attendance at a major public school, however, depended upon the party chosen. For Conservatives such attendance was strongly associated with an anti-imperial position, but for a Liberal, the relationship ran in the other direction.

Club membership for a Liberal does not appear to have been related to his position on imperial matters, but for Conservatives such membership was associated with a pro-imperial stance. Before 1895, Liberal MPs who belonged to political clubs tended to be more pro-imperial than did those who chose to join nonpolitical clubs or no clubs at all. After 1900, although the relationship is weak, the opposite may be true.

Regional differences in imperial attitudes tended to be more marked among Liberals than Conservatives. For members of that former party, when measured against the votes of the representatives of the industrial Midlands, those from Ireland, the Southwest and rural Midlands, and from Scotland and Wales voted less often for imperial legislation, while those from London and the Home Counties voted somewhat more frequently. Among the Conservatives, only those from Ireland appear less and those from London and the home counties more imperialistic than the members from Birmingham and Manchester.

Broadly speaking, the Conservatives as opposed to the Liberals were the pro-imperial party, and from 1868 to 1906 (the years 1886 and 1895 aside) their assumption of this position was a strong one. In the last Parliament, however, the party appeared to have reversed its previous stand and assumed a strongly anti-imperial position.

The Liberals were essentially anti-imperial. Only in the last Parliament, as the Conservatives adopted an anti-imperial stance, did they display a moderately pro-imperial attitude.

Given the interparliamentary differences, it appears logical to examine voting behavior in each Parliament. The reader should, however, bear in mind that as the focus narrows, the number of observations declines and the power of the model becomes less certain. Clearly, more work is needed to distinguish between domestic and overseas businessmen, to better measure wealth and imperial investment, and to distinguish more finely between the socioeconomic characteristics of the members' districts. Still, the results are suggestive.

The party-support variable attempts to capture a component of a member's idiosyncratic behavior, and the results are somewhat surprising. It might have been expected that an MP who tended to support his party on nonimperial issues would also have been inclined to support it on imperial issues. Indeed that was sometimes but not always the case. In more than half of the Parliaments the relationship ran the other way, and most of this reversal can be attributed to the behavior of the Liberal members. For them, the reverse relationship was particularly strong in the fourth (1874–80), sixth (1886–92), eighth (1895–1900), and ninth (1900–6) Parliaments – all periods of imperial war or impending hostilities. Among the

Conservatives, the relative strength of party support on imperial as opposed to domestic issues was strong and only in the second Parliament (1865–68), which dealt largely with colonial loans and subsidies, is there any significant negative relation. Returning to the Liberals, there was a significant positive relationship only in the first (1858–65), fifth (1880–5), and tenth (1906–10) Parliaments. For the last, no doubt support for the financial measures to rebuild the war-ravaged lands of the losers in the South African War the Liberals had opposed played a major part, along with the defense of free trade against legislative attack.

It has already been noted that to the extent that one can generalize about party positions in the nineteenth century, it is possible to identify the Conservatives as more pro-imperial than the Liberals. It is not surprising that those Liberals who most strongly supported the party's position on domestic affairs, in other words the really true believers, also opposed bellicose and imperialistic tendencies when they discerned them in the positions taken by a party whose manifestos had traditionally opposed war and overseas expansion. Analysis of the party-support scores also indicates that from time to time groups of Liberal MPs emerged who opposed the party's domestic policy and supported imperialism. This was certainly true in the Parliaments that ran from 1865 to 1885 and from 1886 to 1892. It was, however, a phenomenon that occurred but rarely, and the numbers involved were never great. Neither interpretation of the data, however, explains the strong positive association between party support and imperialism during the fifth Parliament which was dominated by measures supporting war in Egypt and the Sudan and hostilities in Burma. No really credible explanation is close at hand. Possibly, even the staunchest Liberals, who were in spite of everything still patriots, found these events sufficiently threatening to rally round the flag. It is interesting to note that the Liberals joined the Conservatives in strongly supporting resolutions of thanks to those officers responsible for British victories and in defeating a resolution regretting the overthrow of the Mahdi. On the other hand, they voted 270 to 3 favoring the withdrawal of British forces from southern Afghanistan, while the Conservatives strongly backed the continued British presence. Both parties voted unanimously in favor of an additional £1,000,000 for the army. But whereas the Conservatives opposed the guarantee of a £135,000 loan to Egypt for essentially peaceful purposes 28 to 193, the Liberals overwhelmingly voted in favor, 243 to 3.

The degree of electoral competition affected Conservative voting behavior before the 1886 redistricting. In those early years, it appears that a pro-imperial stance was associated with the safeness of a member's seat. Thereafter, there is little association, although in the eighth Parliament (1894–1900), marked by the erruption of the Anglo–Boer War, it was the members who had survived the closest elections who tended to support imperial issues the most fervently. For the Liberals there is some association, but no pattern is readily apparent.

Club membership is admittedly a very poor proxy for wealth, but the fourth Parliament (1874–80) aside, it does appear to have been related to voting behavior in the manner that this argument would predict – the greater the wealth of a member, the more pro-imperial his attitude. That general conclusion rests, however, almost entirely on the behavior of the Conservative members. For the Liberals the signs are generally similar, but the coefficients hardly significant. For the Conservatives, the fourth Parliament is, however, an anomaly. Although Disraeli was the prime minister, and the issues were colonial wars and the Indian tariffs, the coefficient on numbers of clubs is negative and significant.

As already indicated, a member's occupation was not strongly related to imperial support. In the business sector, merchants appear to have supported imperial measures somewhat less frequently than the lawyers who provide the standard of comparison. The first Parliament aside, the relationship tends to be weak except for Liberal MPs in the second and eighth Parliaments. Surprisingly, it was steamship and railroad subsidies (issues one might have thought of particular concern to the commercial community) that dominated the first agenda. In the second case, the Anglo–Boer War appears to have affected all Liberal businessmen in much the same way – they became substantially less imperialistic than their legal counterparts. It can be said, in regard to that vital watershed in British imperial history and its aftermaths, that Liberal businessmen truly hated the war, and the Conservatives the subsequent reparations.

For manufacturers the pattern is somewhat more interesting. In eight of the ten sessions there is little to choose between the behavior of that group and the lawyers. In the fourth and sixth Parliaments, however, they adopt a marginally more pro-imperial stance than the barristers and solicitors of the same party. But even in those sessions, it was the Conservative manufacturers who adopted the strong pro-imperial position.

For the elites, there is no evidence to support the conclusion that they were more imperialistic than the "typical" member. If the fourth Parliament is excluded, the three major groups (financiers, military officers, and peers and gents) were almost certainly less pro-imperial than the lawyers who provide the baseline, at least as far as the Conservatives are concerned. The anti-imperial sentiment appears particularly strong in the second and seventh Parliaments and, even in the fourth, the shift toward a position more favorable to imperialism is more in evidence if absentees are counted than it is for the members who actually voted. In conformity with previous observations, it is the Liberals who provide what differences there were. While there was some session-to-session variation, in general, to be a Liberal and a member of the elites meant, after 1880, voting somewhat less often for imperial measures than was the case for Liberal lawyers.

The relationship between imperialism and education was basically similar on both sides of the political aisle, but the relationship for the Liberals appears stronger. It is worthy of note, however, that for the Conservatives both university-educated members and those who had ended their education in public school were more strongly anti-imperial in the seventh Parliament (1892–95) than their colleagues with different educational backgrounds. University-educated Liberal MPs were the most anti-imperial of any group when education is the measure, but Liberal Old Boys from public schools who did not go on to university were more favorable to imperialism than the Liberals with other educational backgrounds.

In some Parliaments there was a relationship between club membership and voting behavior; however, the effects seem to have been largely unrelated to the category of club the member had chosen to join. For Conservatives, membership appears to have been a slight positive association with a pro-imperial stance in the sixth Parliament and a significant negative link in the first and anomalous fourth. For the Liberals, the connection is less marked, but there is evidence of a fairly strong positive sign in the fourth Parliament and a negative one in the fifth. It should be re-emphasized, however, that whatever effect is discernible remains constant across type of establishment and that clubs associated with the Empire had no more influence on MP behavior than did those devoted to literary or political debate or even ones limited to social exchange or leisure activities.

For the regional analysis, the standard was the industrial Midlands. In comparison, Conservatives in Scotland and Wales were more pro-imperial in the first, second, and third Parliaments and mildly more anti-imperial from the sixth Parliament on. Liberals in the region were generally anti-imperial when compared to the industrial Midlands, with the exception of the fifth and sixth Parliaments. Ireland was generally more anti-imperial; and in Lancashire and the North, the Conservatives were slightly more pro-imperial and the Liberals weakly anti-imperial, with the exception of the fifth and tenth Parliaments, when the sign is positive. For Liberals it appears that after the redistribution of 1886, London and Home members were marginally more pro-imperial than the Midland representatives.

V. Conclusion

Individual companies, the chambers of commerce, and the trade associations were interested in politics only in relation to questions involving trade and commerce. In that arena, the evidence leaves little room for doubt that firms operating either individually or in concert (often through formal organizations like the chambers of commerce and trade associations, and occasionally through informal and frequently short-lived coalitions) were at times able to influence government policy. The essential elimination of Indian tariffs on textiles is a case in point. On the other hand, the number of resolutions on colonial and foreign tariffs and regulations adverse to business that were not followed by government action, and the number of times a minister noted that he had been called on by a delegation of businessmen to whom he offered nothing but sympathy, indicate that their success was very far from complete. Questions of tariffs in the responsibly governed colonies and imperial preference together were the subject of almost a third of the chambers' Empire business, and to little effect.

Although the evidence is not totally compelling, it seems possible to speculate about the explanation of the relative success of some, but not all, business-supported lobbying. It is clear that the British government displayed a greater willingness to deploy its services in support of Indian rather than foreign-sector activities. In the case of the remainder of the dependent Empire the evidence is much less clear. In large part, whatever tendency to intervene maintained was the result of domestic political realities, but it may also have reflected the much lower cost of Empire involvement, and some official questioning of the usefulness of foreign as opposed to imperial or domestic investment. It may, on the other hand, also have been indicative of something more fundamental. During the time when Britain was powerful enough to interfere in the foreign sector without engendering serious responses from other developed countries, there was a general, and almost certainly correct, belief that its commerce and industry were sufficiently competitive to allow its business people to triumph, if guaranteed equal access. On the question of the right to compete unimpeded, the government was firm. By the turn of the century, however, the right to compete was no longer a guarantee of success, but by then the costs of intervention had risen substantially. It is interesting to note that the Indian examples of government interference all come from the later years.

By and large, complaints by disgruntled British investors were directed toward the foreign sector, not the Empire. In the Empire, the government had already adopted a set of policies that protected the investors' interests almost as well as any set of regulations they themselves might have designed. Indian debt was British debt, and elsewhere there were certain de facto guarantees in the years before 1900 and de jure ones thereafter. In its relations with the private sector, in India, at least, the government did informally act to reduce foreign (that is, non-British) competition.

Neither in India nor elsewhere, however, is there evidence that markets were not open to all British and indigenous entrepreneurs. Moreover, over most of the period the British competitive advantage in manufactures was so great that foreign exclusion, if it existed, must have entailed, at most, trivial costs. After the turn of the century, such was no longer the case.

The Indian government may have acted to stifle foreign competition, but the same was not true in the dependent colonies. The Crown Agents, when acting as colonial purchasing agents, actively sought foreign bids when they thought domestic prices "out of line." Finally, when it came to those parts of the Empire with responsible government, the business lobbyists were almost uniformly unsuccessful. Despite the continued pleas of a succession of groups of manufacturers and almost every chamber of commerce, the dominions continued to increase the level of those tariffs aimed at excluding British business from colonial markets. In the words of one member of the free-trade Manchester school: "The worst offenders against us are our own kinsfolk, whom we have defended in their infancy at our cost, and who retort on us by repudiating all the projects of our industry but our money . . . ."[51] Or as it was more stridently put by an economist arguing for dissolution of the Empire: " . . . Retain our colonies? What is there left to retain? Retain the privilege of spending nearly 4,500,000 pounds sterling on their prohibitive tariffs and 'ironical allegiance.' "[52] British businesspeople could call on their representatives and the chambers could rally and rail, but colonial response was higher, not lower, tariffs. All that was left was for a laissez-faire economist to bemoan the granting of self-government to colonies – a privilege accorded without restrictions on the ability of colonial Parliaments to protect infant industries through the erection of "mischievous tariff barriers."[53] Britain had indeed attempted to tie the hands of the Canadian Parliament, to no avail. No dominion had higher tariffs than Canada.

It appears that three conditions characterize the most successful lobbying operations of the business community. First, the agitation had to be focused: That is, a substantial concentration of affected businesses capable of commanding a pivotal coalition needed to be concentrated in some geographic area. Second, the probability of achieving the desired end was greatest when there was no countervailing pressure within the United Kingdom. Third, the chances of gaining governmental support tended to be highest when the costs of the effort were low, as, for example, in cases where demands were consistent with established British policy.

It has been noted that 3,768 men served in the House of Commons in the period January 1, 1860 and December 31, 1912. Of this number, in the area of occupational categories 47 percent can be placed in the elite classification (finance, peers and gents, military officers, civil service, clergy, and miscellaneous elites); 29 percent in business (including the professionals); 22 percent in association with some facet of the law; and only 2 percent in labor. Before 1885 there was a marked dominance by the elites in the House but, after that date, their numbers decline, while members associated with the legal profession increase still further along, with professional men. Not surprisingly the elites were predominantly Conservative, and businessmen, even more devoutly Liberal. The lawyers were fairly evenly divided between the two parties.

If any further proof is required of the intensely upper-class nature of the House of Commons in the period under study, it is provided by the record concerning education. Over 40 percent of the cumulative membership attended either Oxford, Cambridge, Edinburgh, or Trinity College Dublin. Thirty-five percent attended a major public school and 22 percent studied law. Again, the years after 1885 mark a change with a shift away from Oxbridge education to a somewhat more egalitarian pattern. For instance, University College London in these later years trained 65 future MPs, a number well in excess of nearly all the Oxford and Cambridge colleges.

Even more dramatic than the evidence on education is that on club membership. The men who served in the House of Commons during the period covered by this study held 8,537 club memberships between them – or an average of well over two per member – and this figure did not change appreciably after 1885.

When an attempt is made to relate MP characteristics to individual political behavior, the results are tantalizing but not compelling. Using the device of "member support score," it can be determined that the Liberals were much more perverse than the Conservatives. Individual members not infrequently voted against their party's established position on issues concerning the Empire, especially when it was pro-imperial. But then, the Conservatives were customarily the party concerned with foreign affairs and the imperial overseas, and to many traditional Liberals who strongly supported their party's domestic policies, official party advocacy of Empire, when it occurred, must have been close to heresy.

The safeness of an individual member's seat does not appear to be too useful a guide to his voting pattern. Club membership as a proxy for wealth seems to indicate that for the Conservatives the greater their riches the more pro-imperial they tended to be [with the exception of the fourth Parliament (1874–80)]. A member's occupation turned out not to be strongly related to his enthusiasm for Empire. Likewise, education provides few keys, although it is safe to say that university-educated Liberals were the single most anti-imperial group of MPs. Turning to geographical regions, only in Ireland did both parties incline to be more anti-imperial than their Midland colleagues. The Liberals from other regions (except perhaps London and the Home Counties) tended to be less pro-imperial than the members from Manchester and Birmingham. However, for the Conservatives, although the pattern is somewhat obscure, it seems that the Midlands representatives were on the average less imperially minded.

It is possible that further research into the business histories of individual members of Parliament and a more detailed scrutiny of their holdings of foreign and domestic securities may yield a more significant relationship between an MP's economic self-interest and his voting behavior. On the other hand, nothing new might be gleaned, and it would have to be concluded that economic self-interest was not the driving force behind parliamentary support of Empire. Although it is highly unlikely, the bulk of the members were possibly too wealthy for the usual economic incentives to operate. At any rate, at this moment in time, the hypothesized connection between self-interest and voting behavior is not proved – at least not when it comes to imperialism. Unless further research provides startling new evidence, one must either look elsewhere for the mechanism that translated self-interest into support of Empire or conclude that the Empire's development was largely unrelated, at least in the political sphere, to the search for economic profit.

APPENDIX 9.1

IMPERIAL DIVISIONS IN STUDY
1860-1910

Parliament	Party Strength		Bill Number and Title	Conservatives Aye	Conservatives Nay	Liberals Aye	Liberals Nay
I	Conservative	307	1 European Forces India Bill	95	26	157	21
(1859-65)	Liberal	347	2 Fortifications--Provision for Expenses	51	3	68	24
			3 Fortifications--Provision for Expenses	66	10	75	42
			5 Fortifications--Provision for Expenses	54	12	70	42
			7 Ashanti War, Health of Troops Critical	17	188	192	16
			8 New Zealand Guarantee of Loan	29	11	45	16
			9 Indian Medical Service	5	26	36	14
			10 Indian Army Officers Grievances	32	6	12	27
			1008 New Zealand Guarantee of Loan	33	8	47	20
			2008 New Zealand Guarantee of Loan	22	21	59	29
II	Conservative	299	13 Counsel to the Secretary of State for India	0	47	32	6
(1865-68)	Liberal	359	14 Canada Railway Loan	157	3	55	35
			17 East Indian Troops & Vessels, Abyssinian Campaign	109	2	62	17
			18 India, China & Japan Mails	42	0	8	12
			1018 India, China & Japan Mails	11	75	176	2
III	Conservative	279	21 Canada Loan--Rupert's Land	12	1	46	8
(1868-74)	Liberal	379	24 Emigration--Paupers to Colonies	23	27	20	113
			26 Common Nationality--Colonies	53	10	8	94
			27 East India Opium Revenue	11	53	29	85
			30 East India Company Claims of Former Officers	94	11	10	76
			33 Canada Guarantee of Loan	24	3	36	12
			40 Fiji Protectorate	69	56	8	73
			43 Canada Loan Guarantee	36	2	74	12
			501 East India Loan Bill	22	22	55	16
IV	Conservative	352	47 Gold Coast Withdrawal	207	14	77	49
(1874-80)	Liberal	300	52 India Councils	127	6	26	39
			53 Fiji Annexation Approval	62	5	13	20
			54 P&O Contract Approval	108	1	27	15
			55 East India Home Government	116	8	3	57
			63 Council of India Professional Appointments	110	4	25	30
			69 Appointment Select Committee Indian Finances	10	154	94	2
			70 Supplementary £40,500 for Colonial Expenses	7	128	74	4
			71 Supplementary £44,500 for Colonial Expenses	4	103	48	5
			77 Notion £23,176 to Defray Colonial Expenses	2	90	10	34
			83 Indian Vernacular Press Act	10	176	127	6
			84 Afghan Expenses of Military Operations Charged to India	206	7	7	104
			85 Zulu War, Regret British Actions	20	271	202	4
			87 Afghan War Expenses not to Delay Remission of Indian Cotton Duty	11	145	64	4
			88 Reduction in Cotton Duties, Good First Step	7	139	49	6
			89 Lytton Condemned for Actions Against Indian Population	137	1	57	30
			91 Thanks Lytton/Haines for Afghan War--Lytton Exclud Amend	103	2	26	24
			92 Vote of Thanks to Lytton & Haines for Afghan War	101	2	20	19
			502 Against India Trade Licences Tax	11	127	73	13
			503 Regrets Increased Salt Duty in Bombay & Madras	8	130	70	13
			504 India Overcharged for Afghan War	117	13	4	98

APPENDIX 9.1 (Continued)

Parliament	Party Strength	Bill Number and Title	Conservatives Aye	Nay	Liberals Aye	Nay
V (1880–86)	Conservative 238 Liberal 414 Election of 1885: Conservative 250 Liberal 334 Irish Nationalist 86	100 India Office Sale of Superfluous Land	0	23	3	44
		103 Afghanistan Against Withdrawal from South	191	29	3	270
		107 Vote of Thanks for Haines Afghan Military Operations	136	0	139	5
		112 India to Bear Costs of Her Troops in Egypt	35	3	94	13
		113 Thanks to Seymour for Attack on Alexandria	148	0	174	4
		114 Thanks to Wolseley for Tel El Kebir	85	2	124	8
		115 Condemning Additional Financial Burdens Due to Egypt	21	4	66	11
		116 £274,000 More for Navy Due to Egypt	6	30	6	114
		120 Reduce Indian Expenditure--Adjournment of Debate	33	8	35	0
		132 £324,000 for Navy in Egypt	12	0	48	4
		135 East India Expenses--Military Expedition to Sudan	12	3	65	7
		136 Guarantee of £315,000 Loan for Egypt	28	193	243	3
		505 Army Supply 1,000,000 for Nile Expedition for Year Ending 0385	12	0	56	0
		506 Replace $330,000 for Building New Ships Because of Nile by $80,000	0	12	2	48
		507 3,000 Extra Men for the Army	0	1	0	8
		508 Replace Proposed 35,000 New Men for the Army with 12,000	1	72	7	14
		510 Regrets Use of Power to Overthrow Mahdi	4	210	63	186
		511 Government's Sudan Policy Does Not Justify Confidence of House	198	25	10	238
VI (1886–92)	Conservative 316 Liberal 191 Irish Nationalist 85 Liberal Unionist 78	144 Criticism of Indian Frontier Policy	4	115	51	4
		148 U.K. Australasia Naval Defence Pact Ratification	86	0	4	33
		149 £185,000 for Vessels Under Australasian Agreement	127	0	84	35
		150 £2,600,000--Imperial Defense, Ports, Coaling Stations	180	0	21	41
		155 £2,130,000 for Navy	217	1	26	56
		156 £21,500,000 for Navy	198	1	7	91
		157 Naval Defence	250	0	14	113
		158 Telegraph Contract, Halifax & Bermuda	1	140	23	5
		509 Indian Revenues for Burma Expedition	169	5	112	57
		513 $28,375 for Telegraph Subsidy	69	0	1	23
		1151 Indian Revenue Accounts	1	101	21	3
VII (1892–95)	Conserative 268 Liberal 271 Irish Nationalist 81 Liberal Unionist 47 Labor 3	192 East India Loan £100,000,000	2	63	102	2
		515 $50,000 for Uganda	99	1	96	30
		516 India Pays Excessive Military Costs	8	18	61	5
		517 $29,000 for Cyprus	109	1	111	15
		518 $80,000 for IBEAC	128	1	93	34

APPENDIX 9.1 (Continued)

Parliament	Party Strength	Bill Number and Title	Conservatives Aye	Conservatives Nay	Liberals Aye	Liberals Nay
VIII (1895-1900)	Conservative 341 Liberal 177 Irish Nationalist 82 Liberal Unionist 70	207 Naval Works	204	1	42	17
		208 Naval Works	157	0	22	14
		214 Uganda Railway	200	1	22	56
		226 Recent Hostilities Beyond India not to be Charged	3	170	62	4
		229 Expendient that Loan of £798,802 to Egypt Not to be Repaid	134	5	3	58
		235 Thanks for Sudan Expedition	231	0	92	
		236 To Disallow Indian Tariff Act	7	254	113	
		241 Royal Niger Company	150	0	13	5
		242 Colonial Loans	102	0	5	4
		248 War Loan	183	0	65	
		250 Uganda Railway	157	0	45	3
		519 $182,432 for Uganda, West & Central Africa and Uganda Railroad	119	0	9	3
		520 $1,000 for Cyprus	120	1	7	2
		521 $104,000 Grant for Uganda East & Central Africa	144	0	8	2
		522 Approves Uganda Railway and Votes $3,000,000	210	0	23	5
		523 India to Pay for Its Troops in Africa	242	21	1	13
		524 India to Pay for Its Troops in Africa (Main Q)	226	5	1	6
		525 $1,000 Grant for Cyprus	119	0	8	2
		526 $154,463 for Uganda, East & Central Africa and Uganda Railroad	94	1	1	2
		527 $1,000 for Cyprus	176	1	12	4
		528 $1,000 for Cyprus	174	2	2	5
		530 $805,000 for Payments to Niger Co. (Orig)	193	1	4	7
		531 $805,000 for Payments to Niger Co. (Orig)	194	1	3	9
		550 $10,000,000 for India	175	0	32	6
		551 $120,000 for Army and $13,000,000 for War in South Africa	191	0	58	
		552 Supplemental $11,500,000 for Army in China and South Africa (Against)	0	74	1	
		1551 Colonial Supply	158	0	36	
		2551 Colonial Supply	128	0	28	
IX (1900-06)	Conservative 334 Liberal 184 Irish Nationalist 82 Liberal Unionist 68 Labor 2	261 Colonial Loan	193	0	7	
		262 Thanks to Imperial Forces in South Africa	238	1	108	
		272 Sugar Convention	201	10	5	10
		275 Brussels Sugar Convention, Negative View	6	182	97	
		279 East Indian Revenues for Any Tibet Expense	210	1	35	
		289 Cunard Agreement Money	124	1	4	
		305 Naval Works	190	2	1	
		553 $5,000,000 for Army for South African War	166	0	38	
		554 Vote for Land Forces of 420,000	176	0	7	
		555 $1,016,000 for Colonial Services Inc. Grants	146	0	2	
		556 $26,500 for Colonial Expenses Inc. Grants	162	1	4	
X (1906-10)	Conservative 156 Liberal 374 Irish Nationalist 83 Labor 52	309 Anti-Free Trade	101	2	1	30
		336 Favors Imperial Preference	81	4	6	33
		339 Transvaal Loan Guarantee	1	49	172	
		368 East India Loans	6	21	96	
		557 $29,050 for Colonial Expenses Inc. Grants	3	69	265	

APPENDIX 9.2

IMPERIAL DIVISIONS ANALYZED
1859-1910

NUMBER OF DIVISIONS

Parliament	INDIA Military	INDIA Loans and Non-Military Subsidies	INDIA Admin. and Taxes	RESPONSIBLE GOVERNMENT Military	RESPONSIBLE Loans and Non-Military Subsidies	RESPONSIBLE Admin. and Taxes	DEPENDENT GOVERNMENT Military	DEPENDENT Loans and Non-Military Subsidies	DEPENDENT Admin. and Taxes	ALL EMPIRE Military	ALL EMPIRE Loans and Non-Military Subsidies	ALL EMPIRE Admin. and Taxes	EMPIRE TOTAL	DOMESTIC TOTAL	ALL BILLS TOTAL
1859-65	6	0	0	0	3	0	1	0	0	7	3	0	10	2	12
1865-68	0	2	1	0	1	2	1	0	0	1	3	1	5	6	11
1868-74	1	0	0	0	4	0	0	0	2	1	4	4	9	21	30
1874-80	5	0	8	0	1	0	2	4	1	7	5	9	21	27	48
1880-86*	4	1	1	3	0	0	11	1	0	15	2	1	18	30	48
1886-92	2	0	2	0	1	0	3	1	0	8	2	2	12	36	48
1892-95	1	1	0	4	0	0	0	3	0	1	4	0	5	20	25
1895-1900	3	1	1	0	6	0	2	15	1	9	16	2	27	29	56
1900-06	1	0	0	0	1	2	4	0	0	5	6	2	13	36	49
1906-10	0	1	0	0	0	2	0	1	0	0	3	2	5	45	50
All Parliaments	23	6	13	7	17	6	24	25	4	54	46	23	125	252	377

PERCENT OF IMPERIAL DIVISIONS BY PARLIAMENT

Parliament	INDIA Military	INDIA Loans and Non-Military Subsidies	INDIA Admin. and Taxes	RESPONSIBLE GOVERNMENT Military	RESPONSIBLE Loans and Non-Military Subsidies	RESPONSIBLE Admin. and Taxes	DEPENDENT GOVERNMENT Military	DEPENDENT Loans and Non-Military Subsidies	DEPENDENT Admin. and Taxes	ALL EMPIRE Military	ALL EMPIRE Loans and Non-Military Subsidies	ALL EMPIRE Admin. and Taxes	EMPIRE TOTAL
1859-65	100	0	0	0	100	0	100	0	0	70	30	0	100
1865-68	0	67	33	0	33	67	100	0	0	20	60	20	100
1868-74	100	0	0	0	100	0	0	0	100	12	44	44	100
1874-80	38	0	62	0	100	0	33	67	5	33	24	43	100
1880-86*	67	17	16	75	25	0	92	8	0	83	11	6	100
1886-92	50	0	50	0	100	0	75	25	0	66	17	17	100
1892-95	50	50	0	100	0	0	0	100	0	20	80	0	100
1895-1900	60	20	20	0	100	0	11	83	6	32	60	8	100
1900-06	100	0	0	0	33	67	100	0	0	38	46	15	100
1906-10	0	100	0	0	0	100	0	100	0	0	60	40	100
All Parliaments	55%	14%	31%	23%	57%	20%	45%	47%	8%	44%	38%	18%	100%

*Includes both 1880-35 and 1835-86 sessions.

APPENDIX 9.3

AVERAGE PARTY SUPPORT ON NON-IMPERIAL ISSUES

(Percents)

PARLIAMENT	CONSERVATIVE	LIBERAL
1859-65	.704	.740
1865-68	.913	.871
1868-74	.880	.936
1874-80	.930	.789
1880-85	.878	.892
1886-92	.943	.892
1892-95	.950	.929
1895-1900	.947	.895
1900-06	.949	.965
1906-10	.917	.913

MP SUPPORT SCORES

CONSERVATIVES

Parliament Number	R²	SNI	WM	# Clubs	BUSINESS Comm	Bus/Mfg	OB	ELITES Fin	Mil	Aris	OE	EDUCATION Univ	MPS	CLUBS Emp	Soc	Lit	No Clubs	Other	REGIONS S&W	Ire	N&L	RS	L&H
1	17		+.22		+	+		-.46		-.16	-.65		-.29	+	-.29		+.73	-.19	+		+	+.17	+.31
2	13	-.32	+.27								+.26				+		+	+.13	+		+	+.17	-
3	15	+.60		+.04		+.18					+.26	+		+.14	+	+.29	+.44	+	+.37	-.20	+		
4	09	+.45	+.13	-.04					-	-	+		-		-	-	-	-		-			-
5	04	-			-	+		-	+	+		-	-		+	+	-.11	+	-		+		
6	06	+.14			-	+		+	+					+	+		+						
7	17		+		-	-		+	-	+				+	+			+					
8	07	+.15	-.05		+.04	+.03		+.09	+	+	-.34	-.68	+	+		+		-.03	+	+.31		-.02
9	09	+.15	+			+			-	+		+.06	+	-			-	+	+	+.41		+
10	11				-	-.61			-	-				-		-			-				

LIBERALS

Parliament Number	R²	SNI	WM	# Clubs	BUSINESS Comm	Bus/Mfg	OB	ELITES Fin	Mil	Aris	OE	EDUCATION Univ	MPS	CLUBS Emp	Soc	Lit	No Clubs	Other	REGIONS S&W	Ire	N&L	RS	L&H
1	25	+.20	+.62	+.06	-.20	+.25	+.30	-.39	+	-.24	+.17		+	-.32		-	-.19	+		-.14			+
2	10	-.02	-.25	+.04		+	-	-1.07	-.18	+	+		-	-	-.19	+.13	-					+
3	06					+			+								+						
4	18	-.34				+	-	+.25	-.20	+.23	-	-.13	+.14	-.09	-.15	-.32	-.13	+	-.21	-.25	-.30	-.30
5	17	+.39				-	-	-.47	-.39	-	-.22	+.53	-.37	-	-	-.11	+.09	-.25	+.10	-.36	+
6	12	-.78	-.59	+.07					+	+			+				-.23		+			
7	20	-.68	-		-.28	-.25		-	-	-.33	-.25	+	-.23	+		-.23	-.19				+
8	16	-.67	+.67			-	-.29	-	-	-.41	-	+.34	+	-	-	-.26	-.21	+		
9	09	+.49	+.25	+		+	+.12	-	+	+.08	+.14	+	+	+.12	+	+.11	+				

Aris: Aristocrats
Bus/Mfg: Business and Manufacturing
Clubs: Number of Club Memberships
Comm: Commerce
Emp: Empire
Fin: Finance
Ire: Ireland

L&H: London and Home Counties
Lit: Literary
Mil: Military
MPS: Major Public Schools
N&L: North and Lancashire
OB: Other Business
OE: Other Elites

RS: Rural South
S&W: Scotland and Wales
SNI: Support on Non-Imperial Issues
Soc: Social
Univ: Universities
WM: Winning Margin

APPENDIX 9.5

MP OCCUPATIONS

PANEL A: FREQUENCIES

OCCUPATIONS	ALL YEARS			1860-1885 ALL MPs ELECTED BEFORE 12/85 AND SITTING			1886-1910 ALL MPs SITTING			1886-1910 MPs ELECTED FIRST TIME AND SITTING		
	A	B	C	A	B	C	A	B	C	A	B	C
Medical	48			25			38			23		
Education	71			30			63			41		
Newspapers	158			64			134			94		
Miscellaneous Professions	32			11			27			21		
Professions Group Subtotal	(309)	297		(130)	128		(262)	250		(179)	169	
Merchants	316			196			186			120		
Retail & Business Services	40			19			35			21		
Sales & Agency	36			22			25			14		
Trade & Commerce Group Subtotal	(392)	382		(237)	231		(246)	238		(155)	151	
Miscellaneous Manufacturing	309			177			202			132		
Engineering & Construction	70			35			49			35		
Brewers & Distillers	51			33			32			18		
Manufacturing Group Subtotal	(430)	425		(245)	241		(283)	280		(185)	184	
Marine, Transport, etc.	62			34			41			28		
Management	3			2			2			1		
Agriculture	48			16			42			32		
Mining	56			31			44			25		
Business Unspecified	90			24			83			66		
Misc. Business Group Subtotal	(259)	256		(107)	107		(212)	209		(152)	149	
BUSINESS CLASS TOTAL	((1390))	(1360)	1199	((719))	(707)	605	((1003))	(977)	870	((671))	(653)	594
Finance	112			69			72			43		
Peers & Gents	1030			751			458			279		
Military	559			375			265			184		
Civil Service	118			63			82			55		
Clergy	20			10			16			10		
ELITES CLASS TOTAL	((1839))	(1839)	1815	((1268))	(1268)	1257	((893))	(893)	875	((571))	(571)	558
Barristers	771			449			495			320		
Solicitors	124			51			100			75		
LEGAL CLASS TOTAL	((895))	(895)	883	((500))	(500)	495	((595))	(595)	584	((395))	(395)	388
Labor Leaders	41			2			40			39		
Laborers	62			23			59			39		
LABOR CLASS TOTAL	((103))	(103)	87	((25))	(25)	24	((99))	(99)	83	((78))	(78)	63
ALL CLASSES TOTAL	4227	4197	3984	2512	2500	2381	2591	2564	2412	1715	1697	1603

PANEL B: PERCENTS

OCCUPATIONS	ALL YEARS			1860-1885 ALL MPs ELECTED BEFORE 12/85 AND SITTING			1886-1910 ALL MPs SITTING			1886-1910 MPs ELECTED FIRST TIME AND SITTING			RELATIVE ELECTED PRE-1885 ELECTED POST-1885		
	A	B	C	A	B	C	A	B	C	A	B	C	A	B	C
Medical	1.1			1.0			1.5			1.3			77		
Education	1.7			1.2			2.4			2.4			50		
Newspapers	3.7			2.5			5.2			5.5			45		
Miscellaneous Professions	0.8			.8			1.0			1.2			33		
Professions Group Subtotal	(7.3)	7.1		(5.2)	5.1		(10.1)	9.8		(10.4)	10.0		(50)	51	
Merchants	7.5			7.8			7.2			7.0			111		
Retail & Business Services	.9			.8			1.4			1.2			67		
Sales & Agency	.9			.8			1.0			.8			112		
Trade & Commerce Group Subtotal	(9.3)	9.1		(9.4)	9.2		(9.5)	9.3		(9.0)	8.9		(104)	103	
Miscellaneous Manufacturing	7.3			7.0			7.8			7.7			91		
Engineering & Construction	1.7			1.4			1.9			2.0			70		
Brewers & Distillers	1.2			1.3			1.2			1.0			130		
Manufacturing Group Subtotal	(10.2)	10.1		(9.8)	9.6		(10.9)	10.9		(10.8)	10.8		(91)	89	
Marine, Transport, etc.	1.5			1.4			1.6			1.6			88		
Management	.1			.1			.1			.1			100		
Agriculture	1.1			.6			1.6			1.9			32		
Mining	1.3			1.2			1.7			1.5			80		
Business Unspecified	2.1			1.0			3.2			3.8			26		
Misc. Business Group Subtotal	(6.1)	6.1		(4.3)	4.3		(8.2)	8.2		(8.9)	8.8		(48)	49	
BUSINESS CLASS TOTAL	((32.9))	(32.4)	30.1	((28.6))	(28.3)	25.4	((38.7))	(38.1)	36.1	((39.1))	(38.5)	37.1	((73))	(74)	68
Finance	2.6			2.7			2.8			2.5			108	108	
Peers & Gents	24.3			29.8			17.7			16.3			183	183	
Military	13.2			14.9			10.2			10.7			139	139	
Civil Service	2.8			2.5			3.2			3.2			78	76	
Clergy	.5			.4			.6			.6			67		
ELITES CLASS TOTAL	((43.5))	(43.8)	45.5	((50.4))	(50.7)	52.8	((34.5))	(34.8)	36.3	((33.3))	(33.6)	34.8	((151))	(151)	152
Barristers	18.3			17.8			19.1			18.6			95	95	
Solicitors	2.9			2.1			3.7			4.3			47	47	
LEGAL CLASS TOTAL	((21.2))	(21.3)	22.2	((19.9))	(20.0)	20.8	((23.0))	(23.2)	24.2	((23.0))	(23.3)	24.2	((87))	(86)	86
Labor Leaders	1.0			.1			1.5			2.3			4	4	
Laborers	1.5			.9			2.3			2.3			40	39	
LABOR CLASS TOTAL	((2.5))	(2.5)	2.2	((1.0))	(1.0)	1.0	((3.9))	(3.9)	3.4	((4.6))	(4.6)	3.9	((22))	(22)	26

COLUMN A reflects the distribution of MP occupations across 25 career categories, with each MP counted once for each career in a different category (but no more than once in any one category). Computed on this basis, the subtotals for each occupational group (excluding those which consist of only one category) are given, enclosed by a single set of parenthesis. The class totals computed on this basis are also given, enclosed in a set of double parentheses.

COLUMN B contains the group subtotals, and the class totals (enclosed in a single set of parentheses) for MP occupations, counting each MP no more than once for multiple occupations held within the same group, regardless of any distinctions which are made at the category level.

COLUMN C contains class total figures only, counting each MP no more than once in any of the four classes, regardless of any distinctions made at either the group or category level.

APPENDIX 9.6

MP OCCUPATIONS BY PARTY

PANEL A-1: ALL YEARS FREQUENCIES

OCCUPATIONS	CONSERVATIVES			LIBERALS			LABOR			IRISH NATIONALISTS			OTHERS		
	A	B	C	A	B	C	A	B	C	A	B	C	A	B	C
Medical	8			28			2			10			0		
Education	14			46			1			10			0		
Newspapers	33			78			6			41			0		
Miscellaneous Professions	12			18			0			2			0		
Professions Group Subtotal	(67)	65		(170)	164		(9)	9		(63)	59		(0)	0	
Merchants	80			200			1			35			0		
Retail & Business Services	17			13			0			10			0		
Sales & Agency	11			18			0			7			0		
Trade & Commerce Group Subtotal	(108)	107		(231)	228		(1)	1		(52)	46		(0)	0	
Miscellaneous Manufacturing	92			204			5			8			0		
Engineering & Construction	27			34			4			5			0		
Brewers & Distillers	30			14			0			2			0		
Manufacturing Group Subtotal	(149)	149		(251)	253		(9)	9		(15)	15		(0)	0	
Marine, Transport, etc.	32			28			0			2			0		
Management	2			0			0			1			0		
Agriculture	6			14			0			28			0		
Mining	20			34			0			2			0		
Business Unspecified	40			45			0			5			0		
Misc. Business Group Subtotal	(100)	97		(121)	121		(0)	0		(38)	38		(0)	(0)	
BUSINESS CLASS TOTAL	((424))	(417)	372	((779))	(766)	668	((19))	(19)	17	((168))	(158)	142	((0))	(0)	0
Finance	67			65			2			2			0		
Peers & Gents	586			407			2			35			0		
Military	394			159			3			6			0		
Civil Service	55			55			3			6			0		
Clergy	0			19			1			1			0		
ELITES CLASS TOTAL	((1102))	(1102)	1083	((683))	(683)	678	((5))	(5)	5	((49))	(49)	49	((0))	(0)	0
Barristers	356	358		375	378		1	0		33	33		0	0	
Solicitors	43	40		67	64		0	0		20	20		(1)	(1)	
LEGAL CLASS TOTAL	((399))	(398)	394	((442))	(442)	435	((1))	(1)	1	((53))	(53)	52	((1))	(1)	1
Labor Leaders	2			9			26			4			1		
Laborers	2			29			27			5			0		
LABOR CLASS TOTAL	((4))	(4)	4	((38))	(38)	34	((53))	(52)	40	((9))	(9)	9	((1))	(1)	1
ALL CLASSES TOTAL	1929	1921	1853	1942	1929	1815	78	77	63	279	269	252	1	1	1

PANEL A-2: 1859-1885 FREQUENCIES; ALL MPs ELECTED BEFORE 12/85 AND SITTING

Category	1	2	3	4	5
Medical	3	18	0	4	0
Education	4	24	0	2	0
Newspapers	10	32	0	22	0
Miscellaneous Professions	4	6	0	1	0
Professions Group Subtotal	(21) 21	(80) 78	(0) 0	(29) 29	(0) 0
Merchants	51	130	0	13	0
Retail & Business Services	6	7	0	6	0
Sales & Agency	8	11	0	3	0
Trade & Commerce Group Subtotal	(65) 64	(150) 148	(0) 0	(22) 19	(0) 0
Miscellaneous Manufacturing	46	129	0	2	0
Engineering & Construction	12	21	0	1	0
Brewers & Distillers	20	12	0	1	0
Manufacturing Group Subtotal	(78) 78	(162) 158	(0) 0	(5) 5	(0) 0
Marine, Transport, etc.	19	15	0	0	0
Management	1	0	0	2	0
Agriculture	1	9	0	6	0
Mining	9	22	0	1	0
Business Unspecified	9	14	0	1	0
Misc. Business Group Subtotal	(39) 39	(60) 60	(0) 0	(8) 8	(0) 0
BUSINESS CLASS TOTAL	((203)) (202) 175	((452)) (444) 376	((0)) (0) 0	((64)) (61) 54	((0)) (0) 0
Finance	42	27	0	0	0
Peers & Gents	421	315	0	15	0
Military	249	123	0	3	0
Civil Service	27	43	0	3	0
Clergy	0	9	0	0	0
ELITES CLASS TOTAL	((739)) 730	((508)) 506	((0)) 0	((21)) 21	((0)) 0
Barristers	186	244	0	15	0
Solicitors	21	25	0	9	1
LEGAL CLASS TOTAL	((207)) 205	((269)) 266	((0)) 0	((24)) 23	((0)) 1
Labor Leaders	0	2	0	3	0
Laborers	0	20	0	0	0
LABOR CLASS TOTAL	((0)) 0	((22)) 21	((0)) 0	((3)) 3	((0)) 1
ALL CLASSES TOTAL	1149 1147 1110	1251 1243 1169	0 0 0	112 109 101	1 1

PANEL A-3: 1886-1910 FREQUENCIES; ALL MPs SITTING

OCCUPATIONS	CONSERVATIVES A	B	C	LIBERALS A	B	C	LABOR A	B	C	IRISH NATIONALISTS A	B	C	OTHERS A	B	C
Medical	8			18			2			10			0		
Education	14			38			1			10			0		
Newspapers	30			59			6			39			0		
Miscellaneous Professions	11			14			0			2			0		
Professions Group Subtotal	(63)	61		(129)	123		(9)	9		(61)	57		(0)	0	
Merchants	43			108			1			34			0		
Retail & Business Services	15			10			0			10			0		
Sales & Agency	8			10			0			7			0		
Trade & Commerce Group Subtotal	(66)	66		(128)	126		(1)	1		(51)	45		(0)	0	
Miscellaneous Manufacturing	65			125			5			7			0		
Engineering & Construction	19			21			4			5			0		
Brewers & Distillers	20			10			0			2			0		
Manufacturing Group Subtotal	(104)	103		(156)	154		(9)	9		(14)	14		(0)	0	
Marine, Transport, etc.	21			18			0			2			0		
Management	1			0			0			1			0		
Agriculture	5			9			0			28			0		
Mining	18			24			0			2			0		
Business Unspecified	39			39			0			5			0		
Misc. Business Group Subtotal	(84)	81		(90)	90		(0)	0		(38)	38		(0)	0	
BUSINESS CLASS TOTAL	((317))	(311)	282	((503))	(493)	433	((19))	(19)	17	((164))	(154)	138	((0))	(0)	0
Finance	45			25			2			33			0		
Peers & Gents	263			160			2			5			0		
Military	206			54			0			5			0		
Civil Service	43			31			3			5			0		
Clergy	0			16			0			0			0		
ELITES CLASS TOTAL	((557))	(557)	52	((286))	(286)	283	((5))	(5)	5	((45))	(45)	45	((0))	(0)	0
Barristers	256			208			1			30			0		
Solicitors	30			51			0			19			0		
LEGAL CLASS TOTAL	((286))	(286)	22	((259))	(259)	253	((1))	(1)	1	((49))	(49)	48	((0))	(0)	0
Labor Leaders	2			8			26			4			0		
Laborers	2			27			27			4			0		
LABOR CLASS TOTAL	((4))	(4)	4	((35))	(35)	31	((53))	(52)	40	((8))	(8)	8	((0))	(0)	0
ALL CLASSES TOTAL	1164	1158	110	1083	1073	1000	78	77	63	266	256	239	0	0	0

PANEL A-4: 1886-1910 FREQUENCIES; ALL MPs ELECTED FIRST TIME AND SITTING

Category	(1)	(2)	(3)	(4)	(5)
Medical	5	10	2	6	0
Education	10	22	1	8	0
Newspapers	23	46	8	19	0
Miscellaneous Professions	8	12	1	1	0
Professions Group Subtotal	(46) 44	(90) 86	(12) 12	(34) 30	(0) 0
Merchants	29	68	5	22	0
Retail & Bus.Services	11	6	2	4	0
Sales & Agency	3	7	0	4	0
Trade & Commerce Group Subtotal	(43) 43	(81) 80	(7) 7	(30) 27	(0) 0
Miscellaneous Mfg.	46	75	9	6	0
Engineering & Construction	15	13	4	3	0
Brewers & Distillers	10	7	1	1	0
Manufacturing Group Subtotal	(71) 70	(95) 95	(14) 14	(10) 10	(0) 0
Marine, Transport, etc.	13	13	1	2	0
Management	1	0	0	0	0
Agriculture	5	5	1	22	0
Mining	11	12	0	2	0
Business Unspecified	31	31	0	4	0
Misc. Business Group Subtotal	(61) 58	(61) 61	(2) 2	(30) 30	(0) 0
BUSINESS CLASS TOTAL	((221)) 197	((327)) 292	((35)) 31	((104)) 88	(0) 0
Finance	25	16	2	2	0
Peers & Gents	165	92	7	20	0
Military	145	36	0	3	0
Civil Service	28	21	5	3	0
Clergy	0	10	0	0	0
ELITES CLASS TOTAL	((363)) 353	((175)) 172	((14)) 14	((28)) 28	(0) 0
Barristers	170	131	5	18	0
Solicitors	22	42	1	11	0
LEGAL CLASS TOTAL	(192) 189	(173) 169	(6) 6	(29) 29	(0) 0
Labor Leaders	2	7	26	4	0
Laborers	2	9	26	2	0
LABOR CLASS TOTAL	(4) 4	(16) 13	(52)	(6) 6	(0) 0
ALL CLASSES TOTAL	780 743	658 653	78 77	167 151	0 0

APPENDIX 9.6 (Continued)

PANEL B-1: ALL YEARS PERCENTS

OCCUPATIONS	CONSERVATIVES			LIBERALS			LABOR			IRISH NATIONALISTS			OTHERS		
	A	B	C	A	B	C	A	B	C	A	B	C	A	B	C
Medical	0.4			1.4			2.6			3.6			0.0		
Education	0.7			2.4			1.3			3.6			0.0		
Newspapers	1.7			4.0			7.7			14.7			0.0		
Miscellaneous Professions	0.6			0.9			0.0			0.7			0.0		
Professions Group Subtotal	(3.5)	3.4		(8.7)	8.5		(11.6)	11.7		(22.6)	21.9		(0.0)	0.0	
Merchants	4.2			10.4			1.3			12.5			0.0		
Retail & Business Services	0.9			0.7			0.0			3.6			0.0		
Sales & Agency	0.6			0.9			0.0			2.5			0.0		
Trade & Commerce Group Subtotal	(5.6)	5.6		(12.0)	11.8		(1.3)	1.3		(18.6)	17.1		(0.0)	0.0	
Miscellaneous Manufacturing	4.8			10.5			6.4			2.9			0.0		
Engineering & Construction	1.4			1.8			5.1			1.8			0.0		
Brewers & Distillers	1.6			1.3			0.0			0.7			0.0		
Manufacturing Group Subtotal	(7.7)	7.7		(13.6)	13.1		(11.5)	11.7		(5.4)	5.6		(0.0)	0.0	
Marine, Transport, etc.	1.7			1.4			0.0			0.7			0.0		
Management	0.1			0.0			0.0			0.4			0.0		
Agriculture	0.3			0.7			0.0			10.0			0.0		
Mining	1.0			1.8			0.0			0.7			0.0		
Business Unspecified	2.1			2.3			0.0			1.8			0.0		
Misc. Business Group Subtotal	(5.2)	5.1		(6.2)	6.3		(0.0)	0.0		(13.6)	14.1		(0.0)	0.0	
BUSINESS CLASS TOTAL	((22.0))	(21.7)	20.1	((40.5))	(39.9)	36.8	((24.4))	(24.7)	27.0	((60.2))	(58.7)	56.4	((0.0))	(0.0)	0.0
Finance	3.5	3.5		2.2	2.3		0.0	0.0		0.7	0.7		0.0	0.0	
Peers & Gents	30.4	30.5		21.0	21.1		2.6	2.6		12.6	13.0		0.0	0.0	
Military	20.4	20.5		8.2	8.3		0.0	0.0		2.1	2.2		0.0	0.0	
Civil Service	2.8	2.9		2.8	3.7		3.8	3.8		1.8	1.8		0.0	0.0	
Clergy	0.0	0.0		1.0	0.0		0.0	0.0		0.4	0.4		0.0	0.0	
ELITES CLASS TOTAL	((57.1))	(57.4)	58.4	((35.2))	(35.4)	37.4	((6.4))	(6.4)	7.9	((17.6))	(18.2)	19.4	((0.0))	(0.0)	0.0
Barristers	18.5	18.6		19.3	19.6		1.3	1.3		11.8	12.3		100.0	100.0	
Solicitors	2.2	2.1		3.4	3.3		0.0	0.0		7.2	7.4		0.0	0.0	
LEGAL CLASS TOTAL	((20.7))	(20.7)	21.3	((22.7))	(22.9)	24.0	((1.3))	(1.3)	1.6	((19.0))	(19.7)	20.6	((100.0))	(100.0)	100.0
Labor Leaders	0.1	0.1		0.5	0.5		33.3	33.8		1.4	1.5		0.0	0.0	
Laborers	0.1	0.1		1.0	1.5		34.6	33.8		1.8	1.9		0.0	0.0	
LABOR CLASS TOTAL	((0.2))	(0.2)	0.2	((1.5))	(2.0)	1.9	((67.9))	(67.6)	63.5	((3.2))	(3.4)	3.6	((0.0))	(0.0)	0.0
ALL CLASSES TOTAL	100.0	100.0	100.0	99.9	100.0	100.1	100.0	100.0	100.0	100.1	100.0	100.0	100.0	100.0	100.0

PANEL B-2: 1859-1885 PERCENTS; ALL MPs ELECTED BEFORE 12/85 AND SITTING

Medical	0.3	1.4	0.0	3.6	0.0
Education	0.3	1.9	0.0	1.8	0.0
Newspapers	0.9	2.6	0.0	19.6	0.0
Miscellaneous Professions	0.3 1.8	0.5 6.3	0.0 0.0	0.9	0.0 0.0
Professions Group Subtotal	(1.8)	(6.4)	(0.0)	(25.9)	(0.0)
Merchants	4.5	10.4	0.0	11.6	0.0
Retail & Business Services	0.5	0.6	0.0	5.3	0.0
Sales & Agency	0.7 5.6	0.9 11.9	0.0 0.0	2.7	0.0 0.0
Trade & Commerce Group Subtotal	(5.7)	(11.9)	(0.0)	(19.6)	(0.0)
Miscellaneous Manufacturing	4.0	10.2	0.0	1.8	0.0
Engineering & Construction	1.1	1.6	0.0	1.8	0.0
Brewers & Distillers	1.7 6.8	1.0 12.7	0.0 0.0	0.9	0.0 0.0
Manufacturing Group Subtotal	(6.8)	(12.8)	(0.0)	(4.5) 4.6	(0.0)
Marine, Transport, etc.	1.6	1.2	0.0	0.0	0.0
Management	0.1	0.0	0.0	0.9	0.0
Agriculture	0.8	0.7	0.0	5.3	0.0
Mining	0.8	1.8	0.0	0.0	0.0
Business Unspecified	0.8 3.4	1.1 4.8	0.0 0.0	0.9	0.0 0.0
Misc. Business Group Subtotal	(3.4)	(4.8)	(0.0)	(7.1) 7.3	(0.0)
BUSINESS CLASS TOTAL	((17.7)) (17.6) 15.8	((35.9)) (35.7) 32.1	((0.0)) 0.0	((57.1)) (56.0) 53.5	((0.0)) 0.0
Finance	3.7 3.7	2.2 2.2	0.0 0.0	0.0 0.0	0.0 0.0
Peers & Gents	36.6 36.7	25.2 25.3	0.0	13.4 13.8	0.0
Military	21.7 21.7	9.8 9.9	0.0	2.7 2.8	0.0
Civil Service	2.3 2.3	2.7 3.5	0.0	1.8 2.7	0.0
Clergy	0.0	0.7	0.0	0.9	0.0
ELITES CLASS TOTAL	((64.3)) (64.4) 65.8	((40.6)) (40.9) 43.3	((0.0)) 0.0	((18.8)) (19.3) 20.8	((0.0)) 0.0
Barristers	16.2 16.4	19.9 19.7	0.0	13.4 13.8	100.0 100.0
Solicitors	1.8 1.6	1.8 1.8	0.0	8.0 8.2	0.0 0.0
LEGAL CLASS TOTAL	((18.0)) (18.0) 18.5	((21.8)) (21.6) 22.8	((0.0)) 0.0	((21.4)) (22.0) 22.8	((100.0)) (100.0) 100.0
Labor Leaders	0.0 0.0	0.2 0.2	0.0	0.0 0.0	0.0 0.0
Laborers	0.0 0.0	1.5 1.6	0.0	2.7 2.7	0.0 0.0
LABOR CLASS TOTAL	((0.0)) (0.0) 0.0	((1.7)) (1.8) 1.8	((0.0)) 0.0	((2.7)) (2.7) 3.0	((0.0)) (0.0) 0.0
ALL CLASSES TOTAL	100.0 100.0	100.0 100.0	0.0 0.0	100.0 100.1	100.0 100.0

PANEL B-3: 1886-1910 PERCENTS; ALL MPs SITTING

OCCUPATIONS	CONSERVATIVES			LIBERALS			LABOR			IRISH NATIONALISTS			OTHERS		
	A	B	C	A	B	C	A	B	C	A	B	C	A	B	C
Medical	0.7			1.7			2.6			3.8			0.0		
Education	1.2			3.5			1.3			3.8			0.0		
Newspapers	2.6			5.4			7.7			14.7			0.0		
Miscellaneous Professions	1.0			1.3			0.0			0.8			0.0		
Professions Group Subtotal	(5.4)	5.3		(11.9)	11.5		(11.6)	11.7		(22.9)	22.3		(0.0)	0.0	
Merchants	3.7			10.0			1.3			12.8			0.0		
Retail & Business Services	1.3			0.9			0.0			3.8			0.0		
Sales & Agency	0.7			0.9			0.0			2.6			0.0		
Trade & Commerce Group Subtotal	(5.7)	5.7		(11.8)	11.7		(1.3)	1.3		(19.2)	17.6		(0.0)	0.0	
Miscellaneous Manufacturing	5.6			11.5			6.4			2.6			0.0		
Engineering & Construction	1.6			1.9			5.1			1.9			0.0		
Brewers & Distillers	1.7			0.9			0.0			0.8			0.0		
Manufacturing Group Subtotal	(8.9)	8.9		(14.3)	14.4		(11.5)	11.6		(5.3)	5.5		(0.0)	0.0	
Marine, Transport, etc.	1.8			1.7			0.0			0.8			0.0		
Management	0.1			0.0			0.0			0.4			0.0		
Agriculture	0.4			0.8			0.0			10.5			0.0		
Mining	1.6			2.2			0.0			0.8			0.0		
Business Unspecified	3.4			3.6			0.0			1.9			0.0		
Misc. Business Group Subtotal	(7.2)	6.7		(8.3)	8.4		(0.0)	0.0		(14.3)	14.8		(0.0)	(0.0)	
BUSINESS CLASS TOTAL	((27.2))	(26.9)	25.4	((46.3))	(46.0)	43.3	((24.4))	(24.6)	27.0	((61.7))	(60.2)	57.7	((0.0))	(0.0)	0.0
Finance	3.9			2.3			0.0			0.8			0.0		
Peers & Gents	22.6			14.8			2.6			12.4			0.0		
Military	17.7			5.0			0.0			1.9			0.0		
Civil Service	3.7			2.9			3.8			1.9			0.0		
Clergy	0.0			1.5			0.0			0.0			0.0		
ELITES CLASS TOTAL	((47.9))	(48.1)	48.8	((26.5))	(26.6)	28.3	((6.4))	(6.5)	7.9	((16.9))	(17.6)	18.8	((0.0))	(0.0)	0.0
Barristers	22.0			19.2			1.3			11.3			0.0		
Solicitors	2.6			4.8			0.0			7.1			0.0		
LEGAL CLASS TOTAL	((24.6))	(24.7)	25.4	((24.0))	(24.2)	25.3	((1.3))	(1.3)	1.6	((18.4))	(19.1)	20.1	((0.0))	(0.0)	0.0
Labor Leaders	0.2			0.7			33.3			1.5			0.0		
Laborers	0.2			2.5			34.6			1.5			0.0		
LABOR CLASS TOTAL	((0.3))	(0.4)	0.4	((3.2))	(3.2)	3.1	((67.9))	(67.6)	63.5	((3.0))	(3.1)	3.4	((0.0))	(0.0)	0.0
ALL CLASSES TOTAL	100.0	100.0	100.0	100.0	100.0	100.0	100.0	100.0	100.0	100.0	100.0	100.0			

PANEL B-4: 1886-1910 PERCENTS; ALL MPs ELECTED FIRST TIME AND SITTING

	(1)	(2)	(3)	(4)	(5)
Medical	0.6	1.3	2.6	3.6	0.0
Education	1.3	3.2	1.3	4.8	0.0
Newspapers	3.0	6.7	7.7	11.4	0.0
Miscellaneous Professions	1.0	1.7	0.0	0.6	0.0
Professions Group Subtotal	(5.9) 5.7	(13.1) 12.5	(11.6) 11.7	(20.4) 18.8	0.0
Merchants	3.7	9.8	1.3	13.2	0.0
Retail & Business Services	1.4	0.9	0.0	2.4	0.0
Sales & Agency	0.4	1.0	0.0	2.4	0.0
Trade & Commerce Group Subtotal	(5.5) 5.6	(11.7) 11.7	(1.3) 1.3	(18.0) 16.9	0.0
Miscellaneous Manufacturing	5.9	10.9	6.4	3.6	0.0
Engineering & Construction	1.9	1.9	5.7	1.8	0.0
Brewers & Distillers	1.3	1.0	0.9	0.6	0.0
Manufacturing Group Subtotal	(9.1) 9.0	(13.8) 13.8	(11.5) 11.6	(6.0) 6.2	0.0
Marine, Transport, etc.	1.7	1.9	0.0	1.2	0.0
Management	0.1	0.0	0.0	0.0	0.0
Agriculture	0.6	0.7	0.0	13.2	0.0
Mining	1.4	1.7	0.0	1.4	0.0
Business Unspecified	4.0	4.5	0.0	2.4	0.0
Misc. Business Group Subtotal	(7.8) 7.5	(8.8) 8.9	(0.0) 0.0	(18.0) 18.7	0.0
BUSINESS CLASS TOTAL	((28.3)) (27.8) 26.5	((46.9)) (46.9) 45.2	((24.4)) (24.6) 27.0	((62.3)) (60.6) 58.3	0.0
Finance	3.2	2.3	0.0	1.2	0.0
Peers & Gents	21.2	13.3	2.6	12.5	0.0
Military	18.6	5.2	0.0	1.9	0.0
Civil Service	3.6	3.0	3.8	1.9	0.0
Clergy	0.0	1.4	0.0	0.0	0.0
ELITES CLASS TOTAL	((46.6)) (46.9) 47.5	((25.2)) (25.5) 26.6	((6.4)) (6.5) 7.9	((16.8)) (17.5) 18.5	0.0
Barristers	21.8	19.4	1.3	11.2	0.0
Solicitors	2.8	5.8	0.0	6.9	0.0
LEGAL CLASS TOTAL	((24.6)) (24.8) 25.5	((25.1)) (25.2) 26.2	((1.3)) (1.3) 1.6	((17.4)) (18.1) 19.2	0.0
Labor Leaders	0.3	1.3	33.3	2.5	0.0
Laborers	0.2	1.3	34.6	1.3	0.0
LABOR CLASS TOTAL	((0.5)) (0.5) 0.5	((2.3)) (2.4) 2.0	((67.9)) (67.6) 63.5	((3.6)) (3.8) 4.0	0.0
ALL CLASSES TOTAL	100.0	100.0	100.0	100.0	100.0

APPENDIX 9.6 (Continued)

PANEL C-1: RELATIVES; SITTING PRE-1885 / SITTING POST-1885 (Percents)

A = Relatives B = Sitting Pre-1885 C = Sitting Post-1885

OCCUPATIONS	CONSERVATIVES			LIBERALS			LABOR			IRISH NATIONALISTS			OTHERS		
	A	B	C	A	B	C	A	B	C	A	B	C	A	~	C
Medical	43			82			0			95					
Education	25			54			0			47					
Newspapers	35			48			0			133					
Miscellaneous Professions	30			38			0			113					
Professions Group Subtotal	(33)	34		(54)	55		(0)	0		(113)	119				
Merchants	122			104			0			91					
Retail & Business Services	39			67			0			139					
Sales & Agency	100			100			0			104					
Trade & Commerce Group Subtotal	(100)	98		(102)	102		(0)	0		(102)	99				
Miscellaneous Manufacturing	71			88			0			69					
Engineering & Construction	69			84			0			95					
Brewers & Distillers	100			111			0			113					
Manufacturing Group Subtotal	(76)	76		(90)	88		(0)	0		(85)	84				
Marine, Transport, etc.	89			71			0			0					
Management	100			0			0			225					
Agriculture	25			88			0			51					
Mining	50			82			0			0					
Business Unspecified	24			32			0			47					
Misc. Business Group Subtotal	(47)	51		(58)	57		(0)	(0)		(50)	49				
BUSINESS CLASS TOTAL	((63))	(65)	62	((78))	(78)	82	((0))	(0)	0	((93))	(93)	93			
Finance	95	95		96	96		0	0		108	107				
Peers & Gents	162	162		170	170		0	0		142	140				
Military	123	122		196	198		0	0		95	135				
Civil Service	62	62		93	80		0	0		0	0				
Clergy	0	0		47	0		0	0							
ELITES CLASS TOTAL	((134))	(134)	135	((153))	(154)	153	((0))	(0)	0	((111))	(110)	111			
Barristers	74	74		104	100		0	0		119	118				
Solicitors	69	62		46	42		0	0		113	111				
LEGAL CLASS TOTAL	((73))	(73)	73	((91))	(89)	90	((0))	(0)	0	((116))	(115)	113			
Labor Leaders	0	0		29	29		0	0		0	0				
Laborers	0	0		60	64		0	0		180	169				
LABOR CLASS TOTAL	((0))	(0)	0	((53))	(56)	58	((0))	(0)	0	((90))	(87)	88			
ALL CLASSES TOTAL	100	100	100	100	100	100	0	0	0	100	100	100			

296

PANEL C-2: RELATIVES; ELECTED PRE-1885
                        ELECTED POST-1885

(Percents)

	PRE-1885				POST-1885
Medical	50	0	93	0	100
Education	23	0	54	0	38
Newspapers	30	0	39	0	172
Miscellaneous Professions	30	0	29	0	150
Professions Group Subtotal	(31) 32	(0) 0	(49) 50	(0) 0	(127) 142
Merchants	122	0	106	0	88
Retail & Bus.Services	36	0	67	0	221
Sales & Agency	175	0	90	0	113
Trade & Commerce Group Subtotal	(104) 100	(0) 0	(102) 102	(0) 0	(109) 103
Miscellaneous Mfg.	68	0	94	0	50
Engineering & Construction	58	0	79	0	100
Brewers & Distillers	131	0	100	0	150
Manufacturing Group Subtotal	(75) 76	(0) 0	(93) 92	(0) 0	(75) 74
Marine, Transport, etc.	94	0	63	0	0
Management	100	0	0	0	0
Agriculture	17	0	100	0	40
Mining	57	0	106	0	0
Business Unspecified	20	0	24	0	38
Misc.Business Group Subtotal	(44) 45	(0) 0	(55) 54	(0) 0	(39) 39
BUSINESS CLASS TOTAL	((63)) 60	(0) 0	((77)) 78	(0) 0	((92)) 92
Finance	116	0	96	0	0
Peers & Gents	173	0	189	0	112 / 110
Military	117	0	188	0	150 / 147
Civil Service	64	0	90	0	100 / 142
Clergy	0	0	50	0	0
ELITES CLASS TOTAL	((137)) 139	(0) 0	((161)) 163	(0) 0	((112)) (110) 112
Barristers	74	0	105	0	124
Solicitors	64	0	31	0	121
LEGAL CLASS TOTAL	((71)) 73	(0) 0	((87)) 87	(0) 0	((123)) (122) 119
Labor Leaders	0	0	20	0	0
Laborers	0	0	115	0	0
LABOR CLASS TOTAL	((0)) 0	(0) 0	((74)) 90	(0) 0	((75)) (71) 75
ALL CLASSES TOTAL	100	0	100	0	100

COLUMN A reflects the distribution of MP occupations across 25 career categories, with each MP counted once for each career in a different category (but no more than once in any one category). Computed on this basis, the subtotals for each occupational group (excluding those which consist of only one category) are given, enclosed by a single set of parenthesis. The class totals computed on this basis are also given, enclosed in a set of double parentheses.

COLUMN B contains the group subtotals, and the class totals (enclosed in a single set of parenthesis) for MP occupations, counting each MP no more than once for multiple occupations held within the same group, regardless of any distinctions which are made at the category level.

COLUMN C contains class total figures only, counting each MP no more than once in any of the four classes, regardless of any distinctions made at either the group or category level.

APPENDIX 9.7

MP EDUCATION
LAST SCHOOL ATTENDED

PANEL A: TOTAL NUMBERS

Last School Attended	ALL YEARS						ELECTED 1860-1885						ELECTED 1886-1912					
	Cons	Lib	Lab	Nat	Other	Total	Cons	Lib	Lab	Nat	Other	Total	Cons	Lib	Lab	Nat	Other	Total
Medical School	5	14	1	5	0	25	1	9	0	3	0	13	4	5	1	2	0	12
Law School	372	394	2	33	1	802	200	262	0	15	1	478	172	132	2	18	0	324
Oxbridge, etc.	520	353	3	18	0	894	317	229	0	6	0	552	203	124	3	12	0	342
British Universities	50	89	1	20	0	160	19	47	0	9	0	75	31	42	1	11	0	85
Foreign Universities	36	38	1	6	0	81	10	14	0	1	0	25	26	24	1	5	0	56
Military Education	30	8	0	1	0	39	14	5	0	0	0	19	16	3	0	1	0	20
Major Public Schools	262	106	0	0	0	368	148	70	0	0	0	218	114	36	0	0	0	150
Other Schools	119	261	36	78	0	494	67	127	0	22	0	216	52	134	36	56	0	278
Private Education	42	82	2	14	0	140	11	19	0	5	0	35	31	63	2	9	0	105
Unknown	335	361	10	59	0	765	287	327	0	31	0	645	48	34	10	28	0	120
Total	1771	1706	56	234	1	3768	1074	1109	0	92	1	2276	697	597	56	142	0	1492

PANEL B: PERCENTAGES

Last School Attended	ALL YEARS						ELECTED 1860-1885						ELECTED 1886-1912					
	Cons	Lib	Lab	Nat	Other	Total	Cons	Lib	Lab	Nat	Other	Total	Cons	Lib	Lab	Nat	Other	Total
Medical School	0.3	0.8	1.8	2.1	0.0	0.7	0.1	0.8	--	3.3	0.0	0.6	0.6	0.8	1.8	1.4	--	0.8
Law School	21.0	23.1	3.6	14.1	100.0	21.3	18.6	23.6	--	16.3	100.0	21.0	24.7	22.1	3.6	12.7	--	21.7
Oxbridge, etc.	29.4	20.7	5.4	7.7	0.0	23.7	29.5	20.7	--	6.5	0.0	24.3	29.1	20.8	5.4	8.5	--	22.9
British Universities	2.8	5.2	1.8	8.6	0.0	4.3	1.8	4.2	--	9.8	0.0	3.3	4.5	7.0	1.8	7.8	--	5.7
Foreign Universities	2.0	2.2	1.8	2.6	0.0	2.2	0.9	1.3	--	1.1	0.0	1.1	3.7	4.0	1.8	3.5	--	3.8
Military Education	1.7	0.5	0.0	0.4	0.0	1.0	1.3	0.5	--	0.0	0.0	0.8	2.3	0.5	0.0	0.7	--	1.3
Major Public Schools	14.8	6.2	0.0	0.0	0.0	9.8	13.8	6.3	--	0.0	0.0	9.6	16.4	6.0	0.0	0.0	--	10.1
Other Schools	6.7	15.3	64.3	33.3	0.0	13.1	6.2	11.5	--	23.9	0.0	9.5	7.5	22.5	64.3	39.4	--	18.6
Private Education	2.4	4.8	3.6	6.0	0.0	3.7	1.0	1.7	--	5.4	0.0	1.5	4.5	10.6	3.6	6.3	--	7.1
Unknown	18.9	21.2	17.9	25.2	0.0	20.3	26.7	29.5	--	33.7	0.0	28.3	6.9	5.7	17.9	19.7	--	8.0
Total	100.0	100.0	100.0	100.0	100.0	100.0	100.0	100.0	--	100.0	100.0	100.0	100.0	100.0	100.0	100.0	--	100.0

Dash (--) = No Data

Cons: Conservative   Lab: Labor
Lib: Liberal   Nat: Irish Nationalist

MP EDUCATION

PANEL A: ALL SCHOOLS ATTENDED

	ALL YEARS						ELECTED 1860-1885						ELECTED 1886-1912					
	Cons	Lib	Lab	Nat	Other	Total	Cons	Lib	Lab	Nat	Other	Total	Cons	Lib	Lab	Nat	Other	Total
Medical School	6	22	2	9	0	39	2	16	0	5	0	23	4	6	2	4	0	16
Law School	395	416	3	38	2	854	208	275	0	18	2	503	187	141	3	20	0	351
Oxbridge, etc.	839	647	4	29	1	1520	488	429	0	11	1	929	351	218	4	18	0	591
British Universities	99	191	2	45	0	337	38	103	0	22	0	163	61	88	2	23	0	174
Foreign Universities	77	110	5	18	0	210	17	44	0	7	0	68	60	66	5	11	0	142
Military Education	76	27	0	2	0	105	29	12	0	1	0	42	47	15	0	1	0	63
Major Public Schools	860	442	1	6	0	1309	469	285	0	1	0	755	391	157	1	5	0	554
Other Schools	329	672	50	172	0	1223	145	309	0	57	0	511	184	363	50	115	0	712
Private Education	68	116	2	18	0	204	16	27	0	7	0	50	52	89	2	11	0	154
Unknown	335	361	10	59	0	765	287	327	0	31	0	645	48	34	10	28	0	120
Total	3084	3004	79	396	3	6566	1699	1827	0	160	3	3689	1385	1177	79	236	0	2877

PANEL B: PERCENT OF PARTY

	ALL YEARS						ELECTED 1860-1885						ELECTED 1886-1912					
	Cons	Lib	Lab	Nat	Other	Total	Cons	Lib	Lab	Nat	Other	Total	Cons	Lib	Lab	Nat	Other	Total
Medical School	0.2	0.7	2.5	2.3	0.0	0.6	0.1	0.9	--	3.1	0.0	0.6	0.3	0.5	2.5	1.7	--	0.6
Law School	12.8	13.9	3.8	9.6	66.7	13.0	12.2	15.1	--	11.3	66.7	13.6	13.5	12.0	3.8	8.5	--	12.2
Oxbridge, etc.	27.2	21.5	5.1	7.3	33.3	23.2	28.7	23.5	--	6.9	33.3	25.2	25.3	18.5	5.1	7.6	--	20.5
British Universities	3.2	6.4	2.5	11.4	0.0	5.1	2.2	5.6	--	13.8	0.0	4.4	4.4	7.5	2.5	9.8	--	6.1
Foreign Universities	2.5	3.7	6.3	4.6	0.0	3.2	1.0	2.4	--	4.4	0.0	1.8	4.3	5.6	6.3	4.7	--	4.9
Military Education	2.5	.9	0.0	0.5	0.0	1.6	1.7	0.7	--	0.6	0.0	1.1	3.4	1.3	0.0	0.4	--	2.2
Major Public Schools	27.9	14.7	1.3	1.5	0.0	19.9	27.6	15.6	--	0.6	0.0	20.5	28.2	13.3	1.3	2.1	--	19.3
Other Schools	10.7	22.4	63.3	43.4	0.0	18.6	8.5	16.9	--	35.6	0.0	13.9	13.3	30.8	63.3	48.7	--	24.8
Private Education	2.2	3.9	2.5	4.6	0.0	3.1	0.9	1.5	--	4.4	0.0	1.4	3.8	7.6	2.5	4.7	--	5.4
Unknown	10.9	12.0	12.7	14.9	0.0	11.7	16.9	17.9	--	19.4	0.0	17.5	3.5	2.9	12.7	11.9	--	4.2
Total	100.0	100.0	100.0	100.0	100.0	100.0	100.0	100.0	--	100.0	100.0	100.0	100.0	100.0	100.0	100.0	--	100.0

PANEL C: RELATIVES

	Cons	Lib	Lab	Nat	Other	Total
Medical School	33	180	--	182	--	100
Law School	90	126	--	133	--	111
Oxbridge, etc.	113	127	--	91	--	123
British Universities	50	75	--	141	--	72
Foreign Universities	23	43	--	150	--	37
Military Education	50	54	--	29	--	50
Major Public Schools	98	117	--	73	--	106
Other Schools	64	55	--	94	--	56
Private Education	24	20	--	163	--	26
Unknown						
Total	483	617	--		--	417

Dash (--) = No Data

Cons:	Conservative	Lab:	Labor
Lib:	Liberal	Nat:	Irish Nationalist

MP CLUB MEMBERSHIPS

PANEL A: NUMBER OF MPs

MEMBERSHIP	ALL YEARS						ELECTED 1860-1885						ELECTED 1886-1912					
	Cons	Lib	Lab	Nat	Other	Total	Cons	Lib	Lab	Nat	Other	Total	Cons	Lib	Lab	Nat	Other	Total
Political	2428	2356	7	89	0	4880	1388	1392	0	33	0	2813	1041	964	7	56	--	2068
Empire	274	187	0	4	0	465	180	149	0	4	0	333	94	38	0	0	--	132
Military	316	117	0	1	0	434	195	97	0	1	0	293	121	20	0	0	--	141
Business	54	38	1	1	0	94	31	28	0	1	0	60	23	10	1	0	--	34
Educational	203	165	0	2	0	370	131	136	0	0	0	267	72	29	0	2	--	103
Social	423	169	1	8	0	601	181	99	0	6	0	286	242	70	1	2	--	315
Literary	360	304	4	12	0	680	216	229	0	8	0	453	144	75	4	4	--	227
Regional	398	92	3	28	0	521	255	72	0	7	0	334	143	20	3	21	--	187
Sports & Recreation	250	132	0	13	0	395	56	24	0	3	0	83	194	108	0	10	--	312
Unclassified	41	50	0	4	0	95	14	34	0	3	0	51	27	16	0	1	--	44
No Clubs	89	185	47	138	1	460	65	140	0	53	1	259	24	45	47	85	--	201
Total	4836	3795	63	300	1	8995	2712	2400	0	119	1	5232	2124	1395	62	181	--	3763

PANEL B: PERCENT DISTRIBUTION BY PARTY

MEMBERSHIP	ALL YEARS						ELECTED 1860-1885						ELECTED 1886-1912					
	Cons	Lib	Lab	Nat	Other	Total	Cons	Lib	Lab	Nat	Other	Total	Cons	Lib	Lab	Nat	Other	Total
Political	50.21	62.08	11.11	29.67	0.00	54.25	51.18	58.00	0.00	27.73	0.00	53.77	49.01	68.53	11.29	30.94	--	54.63
Empire	5.67	4.92	0.00	1.33	0.00	5.17	6.64	6.20	0.00	3.36	0.00	6.36	4.43	2.70	0.00	0.00	--	3.51
Military	6.53	3.08	0.00	.33	0.00	4.82	7.19	4.04	0.00	.84	0.00	5.60	5.70	1.43	0.00	0.00	--	3.75
Business	1.12	1.09	1.58	.33	0.00	1.05	1.14	1.16	0.00	.84	0.00	1.15	1.08	.71	1.61	0.00	--	.90
Educational	4.20	4.34	0.00	.67	0.00	4.11	4.83	5.65	0.00	0.00	0.00	5.10	3.39	2.07	0.00	1.10	--	2.74
Social	8.75	4.45	1.58	2.67	0.00	6.68	6.67	4.13	0.00	5.04	0.00	5.47	11.39	5.01	1.61	1.10	--	8.37
Literary	7.44	8.01	6.34	4.00	0.00	7.56	7.96	9.54	0.00	6.72	0.00	8.66	6.78	5.37	6.45	2.21	--	6.03
Regional	8.23	2.42	4.76	9.33	0.00	5.79	9.40	3.00	0.00	5.88	0.00	6.38	6.73	1.43	4.83	11.60	--	4.97
Sports & Recreation	5.17	3.47	0.00	4.33	0.00	4.39	2.06	1.00	0.00	2.52	0.00	1.59	9.13	7.74	0.00	5.52	--	8.29
Unclassified	.85	1.31	0.00	1.33	0.00	1.06	.52	1.41	0.00	2.52	0.00	.97	1.27	1.14	0.00	.55	--	1.17
No Clubs	1.84	4.87	74.60	46.00	100.00	5.11	2.40	5.83	0.00	44.54	100.00	4.95	1.13	3.22	75.80	46.96	--	5.34
Total	53.76	42.19	.70	3.34	.01	100.00	51.83	44.87	0.00	2.27	.02	100.00	56.44	37.07	4.81	4.81	--	100.00

PANEL C: PER CAPITA BY PARTY

MEMBERSHIP	ALL YEARS						ELECTED 1860-1885						ELECTED 1886-1912					
	Cons	Lib	Lab	Nat	Other	Total	Cons	Lib	Lab	Nat	Other	Total	Cons	Lib	Lab	Nat	Other	Total
Political	1.37	1.38	.13	.38	.0	1.30	1.3	1.26	--	.36	--	1.3	1.49	1.61	.13	.39	--	1.39
Empire	.15	.11	0.00	.02	.0	.12	.17	1.3	--	.04	--	.17	.13	.06	.00	.00	--	.09
Military	.18	.07	0.00	.00	.0	.12	.18	.09	--	.01	--	.18	.17	.03	.00	.00	--	.09
Business	.03	.02	.00	.00	.0	.02	.03	.03	--	.01	--	.03	.03	.02	.02	.01	--	.02
Educational	.11	.10	0.00	.00	.0	.10	.12	.12	--	.09	--	.10	.10	.05	.02	.01	--	.07
Social	.24	.10	.02	.03	.0	.16	.17	.09	--	.07	--	.16	.35	.12	.07	.03	--	.21
Literary	.20	.18	.07	.05	.0	.18	.20	.21	--	.08	--	.18	.21	.13	.05	.15	--	.15
Regional	.22	.05	.05	.12	.0	.14	.24	.06	--	.03	--	.14	.21	.03	.00	.07	--	.13
Sports & Recreation	.14	.08	0.00	.06	.0	.10	.05	.02	--	.03	--	.05	.28	.18	.00	.01	--	.21
Unclassified	.02	.03	0.00	.02	.0	.03	.01	.03	--	.03	--	.01	.04	.03	.00	.01	--	.03
No Clubs	--	--	--	--	--	--	--	--	--	--	--	--	--	--	--	--	--	--
Total	2.60	2.11	.29	.69	0.0	2.27	2.47	2.04	--	.71	--	2.04	3.02	2.26	.29	.67	--	2.39

Dash (--) = No Data

Cons: Conservative   Lab: Labor
Lib: Liberal   Nat: Nationalist

10 *Imperium economicus – in retrospect*

M. K. Gandhi, an unlikely imperialist, once wrote, "Though Empires have gone and fallen, this Empire perhaps may be an exception." That opinion was based on the conviction that the British Empire was "not founded on material but on spiritual foundations."[1] The future Mahatma was no more correct than the rhetoricians who saw the Empire as the expression of Britannia's divine mission. "Wherever her [Britain's] sovereignty has gone," one writer averred, "two blades of grass have grown where one grew before. Her flag wherever it has advanced has benefited the country over which it floats; and has carried with it civilization, the Christian religion, order, justice and prosperity."[2] Other observers were not so certain. In response to Betsy Prig's comment, " . . . ain't it lovely to see 'ow Britannia improved her position, since Benjy picked up the dropt threads of England's imperial tradition," Cleo, less sure, in an 1878 issue of *Punch* replied:

> Fine phrases and flatulent figures (sez she) are the charlatan's tools.[3]

This book is essentially about the "flatulent figures" and the often eloquent message they carried. However difficult it may be to disentangle figures and messages, it is possible to measure one aspect of the Empire: its costs and its revenue. Even Disraeli, the great avatar of Britain's conquering might, in a brief incarnation as Chancellor of Exchequer referred to "Those wretched colonies . . . " as "a mill stone around our neck."[4] A few years later, Karl Marx, an observer of a different political stripe, filed a supportive brief in the *New York Daily Tribune* in which he wondered whether "this dominion does not threaten to cost quite as much as it can ever be expected to come to."[5]

For whatever reason, Empire to many Britons seemed not only politically desirable but hypnotically alluring. Disraeli thundered: " . . . no Minister in this country will do his duty who neglects the opportunity of reconstructing as much as possible of our colonial empire . . . ."[6] So potent was the message that the ordinarily archliberal Gladstone was forced to dissemble and to protest: " . . . Gentlemen, while we are opposed to imperialism we are devoted to empire."[7] While he proclaimed that "nothing will induce

301

me to submit to these colonial annexations," he nevertheless ordered the bombardment of Alexandria and the virtual annexation of Egypt.[8] To conclude that Disraeli had suddenly discovered that Empire was costless is wrong. He merely felt that other considerations were of greater importance than cost-effectiveness. Even in the Crystal Palace Speech, he admitted that: ". . . It has been proved to us that we have lost money on our colonies. It has been shown with precise, with mathematical demonstration, that there never was a jewel in the Crown of England that was so costly as the possession of India."[9]

Although not alone, Joseph Chamberlain stands out as a latter-day prophet who actually espoused the principle that the Empire should be a source of monetary profit to the home country. Not only did he believe in imperial reciprocity between Britain and the dominions, but he urged that "we should maintain firmly and resolutely our hold over the territories we have already acquired, and we should offer freely our protection to those friendly chiefs and people who are stretching out their hands to us."[10] A decade later a cynic might have inquired which chiefs in the Transvaal and Orange Free State were "stretching out their hands."

The move toward closer colonial association and imperial federation found support on both sides of the political spectrum. Not unexpectedly, on the one side were Salisbury, Balfour, and Hicks-Beach, joined later by Joseph Chamberlain. Across the aisle they found allies not only among the Roseberys, the Milners, and the "rad imps" (the latter group included not only Gladstonian free traders of the like of Harcourt and Campbell-Bannerman, but the young intellectuals such as G. K. Chesterton, G. M. Trevelyan, and Gilbert Murray), but even among such "rad libs" as Asquith, Edward Grey, and Haldane, to cite only three. Support was widespread, but because of the intransigence of the dominions it was never possible to discover if the idea had any substance at all.

No one can sanely argue that there were not British politicians dedicated to maintaining and expanding the Empire, nor that there were not businessmen who recognized that such policies might redound to their profit. It may well have been that both groups increased in size after the mid-1880s, as political and economic competition from the Continental powers and the United States increased, exacerbating the rising protectionist sentiment both in the newly competitive nations and in the Dominions. Chamberlain, himself, bought Canadian Pacific Railroad bonds and lost £50,000 in an ill-fated attempt to grow sisal in the Bahamas.[11] Nevertheless, Lenin went too far when he concluded that, "leading British bourgeois politicians fully appreciated the connection between what might be called purely economic and the political–social roots of imperialism."[12]

Few of the nineteenth-century proponents and critics of Empire thought that the enterprise was without expense. Adderley had railed against the colonies' refusal to pay their just share of expenses, and Marx doubted that the Empire would ever carry its own financial weight. Disraeli, even as he proposed further imperial expansions, acknowledged that the Empire was costly and that India was a particularly expensive undertaking. Chamberlain, although he looked at imperial expenditures as potentially profitable investments, admitted that they required money; and Hicks-Beach at the Treasury had threatened his resignation when presented with the estimated expenses of one of the Colonial Secretary's development schemes. For those, like Chamberlain, who argued that the Empire was good business for the British, imperial costs had still to be offset against private profits in any calculation of social gain, a point Marx had recognized as early as 1858. Even if the claim was only that the Empire was good for a few but not for the many, the question still remains: How much did it cost the many to enrich the few?

Both Marx and Adderley emphasize the major, but not the only, element in the British subsidy to the imperial investor. The former, in reference to India, had pointed to "the military and naval expenses made by the people of England on Indian account," and the latter, speaking of a British colony, to the exemption "in purse and person from the cost of its own defense."[13] Despite the widespread recognition of the absurdity of the situation – an appreciation that had already in 1861 led to the creation of a parliamentary select committee – there is no evidence that the situation was significantly better in 1914 than it had been in that earlier year. The same Canadians who in 1862 with an American invasion army poised on their borders had said, "the best defense for Canada is no defense at all," in 1911 argued that the Canadian Fisheries Protection Service with its one (soon to be two) armed gunboat(s) on the Great Lakes was a sufficient contribution to imperial naval defense.[14]

The failure of a long succession of governments to distribute the defense burden between home and Empire in some more equitable fashion lay rooted in history, in the law, in the bureaucratic mire, and in the pressing nature of defense requirements. The colonies with responsible government argued that they did not have to contribute; the dependent Empire said that it could not afford to pay; and, hence, who but the British taxpayer was left to redress the balance? An attempt to ameliorate the situation had cost England the American colonies, and that piece of history can never have been far from the politicians' minds. In the dependent colonies, the appointed representatives of the Crown often appeared to side more with the local taxpayers than with their nominal masters in Whitehall. Even in India – a dependency that probably assumed a greater fraction of the cost of its own defense than any other – a succession of viceroys strenuously resisted London's pressure to increase the subcontinent's commitment; "... it is my bounden duty," Ripon wrote, "to resist to the utmost of my power the imposition of any fresh burden ...."[15]

Nor was the peculiar inequity in the distribution of the burden a figment in the minds of British politicians. The expenditure figures suggest that, if anything, the magnitude of the problem was underestimated. On average, in the late nineteenth and early twentieth centuries, the cost of British defense was about two and a half times as great as that borne by the citizens of a typical developed country and almost twice that of the French and Germans. The denizens of the colonies with responsible government, meanwhile, assumed a fiscal responsibility only a quarter that of the resident of a foreign–developed country; and in the dependent colonies, the impost was less than one-quarter of that demanded from inhabitants of underdeveloped nations. India paid relatively more, but even its figures do not appear high if the comparison is made not with the Empire but with the rest of the world. Indian per capita expenditures were substantially more than those of either the dependent colonies or the Indian Princely States, and they were only slightly less than the levels of expenditure maintained by the colonies with responsible government. At the same time, per capita defense costs were only about half as much as those of the foreign–underdeveloped countries, and by the end of the period, only a third. During a comparable period, Siam, for example, paid three times as much.

The evidence indicates that Britain actually maintained two defense establishments: one for the home islands and a second for the Empire. If the British burden is allocated between home and Empire on the basis of ships and men on station, domestic expenditures are about equal to those of Germany and France, and Empire ones slightly more than those of a typical developed country. If the British had been somewhat more exploitative – so coercive that they could have forced British subjects in the Empire to assume a burden *equal* to what they would have paid had they been independent – their savings would have amounted to twice that figure – a full one-fifth of savings.

Although defense was the largest single component in the total imperial subsidy, it was by no means the only one. De facto and de jure loan guarantees made it possible for Empire governments to borrow at rates much below those available to non-Empire nations. The gains were not spread evenly over the Empire but, given the actual level of borrowing, the differentials meant that the residents of the colonies with responsible government saved about 10 percent of their tax bill and those of the dependent Empire, about one-half that amount.

The British government also provided regular administrative subsidies to the dependent colonies and a substantial additional amount of direct support on an irregular basis. At times, those latter grants were relatively small. (Newfoundland, for example, received a grant of £260 in 1906 to help offset the effects of a severe depression in the fishing industry.) At other times, however, they were not. The Gold Coast received more than £400,000 in 1900, and the Ugandan railroad cost the British taxpayer almost £9 million between 1896 and 1914.

The fact that the sun never set on the Empire may well have provided vicarious pleasure to many inhabitants of the home islands; however, the global dispersion of dominions and colonies did present serious problems of administration and control. To help provide the links necessary to hold the Empire together, the government found it necessary to subsidize both telegraphs and steamship lines. The British, for example, paid a quarter of a million pounds to help finance a cable connection between Australia and Canada; and, even in the 1860s, Empire shipping subsidies were running over a million pounds a year.

Finally, the British government founded and underwrote the operations of the Crown Agents. This organization acted as the marketing agency for the sale of colonial securities and as the purchasing agent for colonial supplies. Acting as an effective monopolist in the market for colonial issues and as a monopsonist in the market for the supplies used by those colonial governments, the Agents obtained very favorable marketing arrangements for bond issues and equally favorable prices for the goods and services destined for their colonial customers.

It is difficult to measure precisely the total cost to the British of the nondefense component of the imperial subsidy, but it appears unlikely to have been less than one-fifth of the defense subsidy and it may have been twice that. Although the actual amount of Empire investment is unknown, the best estimates indicate that it amounted on average to about £17.40 per capita in prices of 1913.[16] The defense subsidy alone amounted to at least £.54 per year for every British man, woman, and child, and it could have been as high as £.64, more than 10 percent of national savings. The minimum figure suggests that private Empire returns would have to have been reduced by more than 3 percent to provide an estimate of the social returns, even if the nondefense components of the subsidy were zero. At the other extreme, assuming the larger defense figure and a very generous £.20 for the nondefense component, the adjustment would be almost 5 percent. Even the lower charge is sufficient to reduce Empire returns below levels that could have been earned at home or in the foreign sector.

The British as a whole certainly did not benefit economically from the Empire. On the other hand, individual investors did. In the Empire itself, the level of benefits depended upon whom one asked and how they calculated. For the colonies of white settlement the answer is unambiguous: They paid for little and received a great deal. In the dependent Empire the white settlers, such as there were, almost certainly gained as well. As far as the indigenous population was concerned, while they received a market basket of government commodities at truly wholesale prices, there is no evidence to suggest that, had they been given a free choice, they would have bought the particular commodities offered, even at available bargain-basement rates.

It is clear that imperial exactions placed on the British taxpayer enabled the colonists and residents of the dominions and the dependent Empire to pay fewer taxes and to devote a substantial proportion of the taxes they did pay to a variety of projects that did not include defense and interest. The Empire was a political system, and it should have been possible to align the pattern of colonial expenditures so as to increase the level of support for business and to guarantee that the revenues required to command those resources were charged not to those businesses but to the taxpayers at large.

The potential for government subsidization is vast, and such subsidies can take as many forms as Jacob's coat had colors. Some, involving nothing but the manipulation of political decisions, would have been difficult to discover even at the time, and are probably impossible to uncover a century later. Many subsidies, however, involve government expenditures, and for those, the government budget provides a paper trail that can be followed. It is possible to measure the impact of government policy on expenditures on law and justice (costs incurred, in part at least, in maintaining property rights and enforcing contracts), public works (the real capital component of social overhead investment), science and human capital (the nontraditional component), and direct business support.

Whether it is the total package or its individual components that is analyzed, the pattern is the same. Great Britain spent somewhat more than other developed countries, but hardly more than that nation's advanced state of development would suggest. The same is not true for the colonial Empire whether dependent or blessed with responsible government. On average the latter group of colonies spent at levels about twice those prevailing in Britain, the former, at rates not much different from those at home; but that figure is remarkable given the fraction of a colony's total expenditures that were involved, the relative state of development of the colonies in question, and the amounts spent by countries in the underdeveloped world.

In India, however, the record was different. The decision to finance a railroad network aside, there were few policies designed to provide support for business; and at times even the railroad expenditures appear to have been made more because of considerations of famine relief or military necessity than because of a desire to increase the earnings of the business sector. Not only were expenditures on all levels of business support much below those observed in the underdeveloped world but, excluding railroads, they were below those of the Indian Princely States as well.

In general, the colonial Empire provides strong evidence for the belief that government was attuned to the interest of business and willing to divert resources to ends that the business community would have found profitable. That behavior is not necessarily evidence that the British used the political process to distort the allocation of governmental resources. Expenditures that benefited business were greatest in the colonies with responsible government, where even the British government (let alone British business) had almost no influence. They were next highest in the dependent colonies, where the British did have a very substantial voice in policy making. Within that set, however, expenditures tended to be larger in those colonies with some local participation in political decision making and smaller in those with little or no consultation. Finally, expenditures were lowest in India, where British influence was strongest and where there were no representative institutions at the national level.

Perhaps the explanation for this ordering lies not with the British but with the local business community. Those merchants and manufacturers may have been quite willing and able to bend the structure of government expenditures to their own benefit. If that is correct, except in India, where financial crisis and the threat of famine overrode all other considerations, they appear to have been successful.

It cannot be denied, however, that the policies adopted, perhaps under local business pressure, served the interest of British investors as well as their colonial cousins.

In the late nineteenth century the London capital market acted as a conduit for the greatest international movement of private capital in the history of the world. Nevertheless, most of the flow of funds that passed through the Stock Exchange was not destined for the Empire. Of the almost £5 billion total, less than 70 percent passed out of Britain and almost two-thirds of that amount went to Europe and other parts of the world not pledging fealty to the House of Hanover. The largest single recipient was the United States, but a not insubstantial portion (more than a quarter) was directed to the underdeveloped but politically independent countries of South America. In fact these Latin countries received substantially more than all the funds destined for the dependent Empire. Although the Empire as a whole absorbed nearly a quarter of the total, two-thirds of that amount went to the colonies of white settlement; and those colonies were, at least in matters economic, not likely objects for British exploitation. They were colonies that, since the middle of the nineteenth century, had been pursuing a strongly protectionist policy – one aimed explicitly at British manufacturers and traders.

If Britain itself absorbed 30 percent, if the nations over which the British exercised no political control drew an additional 45, and if the colonies over which its control was, at best, limited took an additional 16, less than £1 in 10 remained for all of India and colonies (such as St. Kitts, the Bahamas, the Falklands, the Gold Coast, Malta, and Rhodesia) that had few representative institutions. Certainly, the amount of finance that was directed to the dependent Empire was substantial enough (it averaged more than £8 million per year) to ensure that some Englishmen could have become rich, but it appears doubtful (unless the "exploitative" profit rate was higher than even Lenin dreamed) that the total was sufficient – even if there were no offsetting social costs – to make the average British subject substantially better off.

Perhaps profits were very high, or possibly the dependent Empire was good business for the few but not for the many. In either case, financial flows were not evenly distributed across the world or across the industrial map. Of the £415 million received by India and the colonies of the dependent Empire, Asia received 65 (India alone, 56) and Africa an additional 19 percent. In India that investment was largely associated with railroads and, to a lesser extent, government finance. In the dependent colonies the relative concentrations of British investment were in the agriculture and extractive industries, in finance (the financial, land, and development companies), and in government. Just how profitable were these investments?

Although the measures of "the" rate of return are only approximate, the general outlines confirm the individual industry comparisons and are similar no matter which measure is chosen. Questions of timing and level are still open, but it would take a massive reversal of the evidence to alter the general conclusions. If the standard is domestic earnings, it appears that in the years before 1885 Empire returns were substantially higher than domestic. While some of the observed differences may reflect the small size of the sample and the mix of firms included in the study, it would be very difficult to argue that colonial profits were any less than domestic and they were almost certainly substantially higher. In the case of the returns on manufacturing and commercial investments, for example, Empire returns through 1880 were one and one-quarter of domestic – and that measure is the most favorable for the home economy. Over time, the advantage eroded, and for the last half of the period Empire returns were substantially below those available at home. There was, however, some recovery in Empire earnings after the turn of the century, and in the last decade they may well have equaled domestic.

As Marx had predicted, profits were falling; however, they were declining more rapidly in the Empire than in the foreign sector and faster in the latter than in the domestic. It is, of course, not the trend but the home–Empire differential that is important for the Hobson–Lenin argument. In the same way it is difficult to deny that the Empire was *relatively* very profitable in the earlier years. It is even more difficult to conclude that profits in the colonies were substantially above those at home in the later ones.

The explanation of the trends in relative returns can in large measure be traced to two phenomena. First, early entrants into new markets and regions had distinct advantages. To the extent that property rights were well defined and enforced they may have been able to acquire the potentially most profitable lands at bargain prices. Secondly, they frequently had an initial monopoly position that allowed them to exploit those new opportunities until, in Schumpeter's terms, the "herd like movement" of the imitative entrepreneurs undercut their profits. Evidence of these initial advantages can be found in the history of colonial agriculture and mines and even among the trading companies operating in the African wilderness. The Assam Tea Company, for example, had a long, fairly profitable history despite growing world competition, because of the location of its plantations. Similarly, the records of the African traders are full of references to attempts to re-establish their earlier monopoly through the negotiation of an almost endless series of formal cartels. Their success was never great, and each new attempt was launched with a lament for the "good old days" before increased competition had blunted the position of the original traders. The Board of Directors of the African Association bemoaned the lack of cooperation between traders and asserted "the powers granted to the Royal Niger Co. will give them a virtual monopoly" at the expense of British enterprise in East Africa; but the company nonetheless continued its efforts to induce collaboration.[17] A few years later the directors were able to report that "In cooperation with other firms, efforts have been made, attended with partial success, to induce those interested in the trade of the Niger Protectorate District to unite in measures for placing prices of produce upon a profitable basis."[18]

Nor was initial advantage and later erosion limited to the Empire. The Liebig Extract of Meat Company found its profits falling because of competition from George Johnston's Bovril. In the United Kingdom, Huntley and Palmers learned that, although they could produce an acceptable chocolate biscuit before their competitors, and although they were very adept at discovering how to tap the new mass consumer market, other firms could imitate their recipes and repeat their organizational innovations. While profits rooted in property rights could last as long as the political structure was undisturbed, the record indicates that in the absence of some legally enforced institutional arrangement, a firm could expect less than a decade of extra profits from its initial advantage.

The relative trends can in part be explained by the surprising energy displayed by the domestic economy, a vigor many historians have overlooked. Kuznets long ago pointed out that no single industry can continue to grow indefinitely; and, if the British economy had remained wedded to traditional lines, it probably would have declined as rapidly as its critics charge it did. Instead, however, new industries emerged, and the post-1880s prosperity was led by firms serving the mass consumer market in Britain. They included Huntley and Palmers in the domestic sector, Liebig's in the foreign, and the Assam Tea Company in the Empire. Of course there were more of these firms at home than abroad.

If domestic performance is the yardstick, and the period scrutinized one for which comparable data is available, the most profitable Empire activities were financial trusts, the agricultural and extractive industries, and waterworks. If the focus is narrowed to the present century, that list is modified by the addition of trams and omnibuses and gas and light companies and by the disappearance of financial trusts – they had become hardly more profitable than domestic alternatives.

The contrast between the initial profits of Empire public utilities and those observed later may have been associated with problems inherent in establishing a new service – it takes time to dig gas mains and lay tram tracks.[19] However, relative Empire profits rose in large measure because of increasing regulation and mounting intertechnological competition at home. In the Empire, home electricity arrived still later than in England and even at the end of the period trams still faced little competition from subways or gasoline-powered omnibuses.

No matter what time period is chosen, after the mid–1880s, high Empire returns, to the extent that they existed at all, tended to be concentrated in the agricultural and extractive and in the public-utility sectors. The great surprise is the relatively poor performance of colonial railroads. It may be that in the Empire – as in the United States – expansion into underdeveloped regions meant a long period of low profits. It has been argued that the American railroad network went bankrupt three times in the nineteenth century; and, even if that is something of an overstatement, it was a long time before those roads began to show regular profits.[20] In the Empire, railroad earnings had, by the present century, almost equaled the profits earned at home; however, both were still well below those available abroad.

Still, railroads aside – and for some Indian railroads the government did guarantee returns to their bond, if not their equity, holders – the pattern of Empire profits is intriguing. Commercial and industrial returns were high in absolute terms, but after the mid-1880s, no higher than domestic. The most profitable Empire activities were those that depended, at least to some extent, on the political structure. In the case of the agricultural and extractive sector, profits were rooted in well-defined and -enforced property rights; and British firms operating in the foreign sector frequently found those rights to be less than secure. The president of the Lautaro Nitrate Company, for example, voiced a common complaint when he said:

> Our lawsuits . . . are again the subject of a part of the Report. . . .
> I regret to say that our last year's expectations have proved correct, viz. during the year there has been no abatement in the tax against the Company. Incited . . . by the increased value of the nitrate grounds . . . persons of influence in the country, tempted by the profits to be realised on shares of new undertakings, have thrown themselves in with the parties who tried to upset our titles. . . .[21]

The experience of Antony Gibbs and numerous other companies operating in South America was similar. In the case of public utilities which were natural or quasinatural monopolies, it was the ability to acquire and retain a charter on favorable terms that made it possible to earn any profits at all. That ability was, again, not totally divorced from the vagaries of local politics. It is only necessary to glance at the history of the Rosario Gas Company to understand how difficult it must have been to maintain that quasimonopoly position in countries with a non-British legal and political environment.

While some stockholders clearly benefited from the imperial connection, the evidence indicates that probably at no time, and certainly not after the 1870s, were Empire profits sufficient to underwrite *British* prosperity. However, for the shareholders in the agricultural and extractive and the public-utility sectors – and perhaps others as well – where competition was blunted, or enforced property rights pushed potential competitors onto inferior lands, the Empire was important, and it was profitable. One can readily conclude that there should have been some economic imperialists. How many and who they were is a different matter.

In 1892 Edward Weatherley, meat merchant and poulterer and master of the London Fishmongers and Poulters Company, died. At his death his estate was valued at £156,000. The estate inventory indicated that he owned, in addition to the usual real and personal property and £98,000 in British consols, bonds of New Zealand in the Empire, and of Argentina, Brazil, Chile, China, Egypt, Greece, Hungary, the Ottoman Empire, Russia, Spain, and Uruguay, outside. In addition, it listed issues of British local authorities in Billingsborough, Hounslow, Chingford, and Birchington; of Quebec City and Ottawa in Canada; of Wellington and New Plymouth in New Zealand; and of Santa Fe in Argentina. Also included were railroad securities from the Cordoba Central, the Great Indian Peninsula, the Quebec Latre de John, the Royal Trans Africa, the Russian Consolidated, the Scinde Punjab and Delhi, and the Temiscanta. There were also shares of the Brentford Gas, the London General Omnibus, the London and Provincial and the London Joint Stock Banks, and the Scottish Widows' Fund, in Britain, and of the Daira Sanieh Corporation, the Oceania and Transvaal Land Companies, and the East India Tramway, overseas.

It is difficult to determine how typical a middle-class investor Weatherley was. Suffice it to say, by the turn of the century the habit of investing in symbolic capital had become deeply rooted in both the upper and middle classes and, in response to this potential demand, paper securities streamed forth from firms and governments eager for finance. The opportunities, or at least the alternatives, were enormous. A saver could choose between shipbuilding in Glasgow, coal mining in Wales, aluminum manufacture in Canada, diamond mining in the Cape, oil exploration in California, railroad transport in China, the ground-nuts trade in West Africa, or cotton spinning in Russia. Those shares might have ended in the hands of a small poultry merchant, a great London trader, a railroad contractor, or a cousin to the Queen. They could be held in rural Rutland, in Aberdeen, in Manchester, in the City, or in Chelsea. Wentworth Blackett Beaumont, first Baron Beaumont, was in background and social status significantly removed from the world of Edward Weatherley. He died leaving an estate worth £3,189,144, yet the diversity of his holdings was less than Weatherley's, although his portfolio included the Union Pacific Railway, the Atchison Topeka and Santa Fe, the Bank of England, the Great Western Railroad, the Cordoba Central Railway, and the Southern Pacific Railway. The question still remains, however: Did members of different occupational and social classes and the residents of different parts of the United Kingdom display similar tastes for home, foreign, and Empire? What can be said about the demonstrated investment proclivity of those groups that, together, composed the British investing public?

A separation of investors into businesspeople and elites (peers, gentlemen, financiers, and the like) indicates that, place of residence aside, businesspeople were less likely to invest in foreign securities than were their elite counterparts. Moreover, they were *far* less inclined to invest in Empire than foreign enterprise; and among all businesspeople, only merchants displayed any significant willingness to invest beyond the seas. In the Empire the elites were most willing to invest in commercial banks; in financial, land, and development companies; in iron, coal, and steel firms; and in the public utilities. To the extent that they entrusted their resources to the Empire at all, businesspeople tended to put their funds to work in the private sector – competitive and less dependent on government charters or licenses – industries, in short, much less dependent on political control.

The geographic distribution of shareholder "tastes" indicates that there were two very different groups of investors: those who lived in London and those who made their homes in the provinces. A typical Londoner's portfolio was composed of about one-quarter domestic, one-third foreign, and two-fifths Empire shares. Outside London, the portfolio was more than one-half domestic and contained less than one-quarter each of foreign and Empire shares. Within London, those who gave the City as their address preferred Empire to domestic securities, but much preferred foreign to Empire. Beyond the Wall, however, London investors appeared largely indifferent between home and foreign issues, but displayed a very strong preference for Empire over both. The London connection was particularly well illustrated in the case of South African gold mines, and even Rhodes turned to London investors when he needed further capital.[22]

Further exploration of the two-England hypothesis indicates that Empire investors in London were drawn from a different socioeconomic background than were the Empire investors who lived outside the capital. While London elites do not appear to have behaved substantially differently than their provincial counterparts, London businesspeople acted very differently than their confreres residing elsewhere. London merchants, manufacturers, professionals, and managers all invested far less frequently in home and far more frequently in Empire activities. On average, London businesspeople were only one-fifth as likely to invest in domestic securities as those businesspeople who lived in places like Sheffield or Manchester, but they were half again as likely to put their resources to work in the Empire.

Overall, Empire investors tended to be drawn from two groups: elites, wherever they lived, and businesspeople (particularly merchants) who resided in London. The attractiveness of the Empire seemed to decline almost exponentially the farther one traveled north from the City. In terms of the socioeconomic background of its participants, the British capital market was clearly two markets, and it is from one of those segments, elites and London businesspeople, that the most strident Empire support could have been expected to come.

Finally, to the extent that the Empire investments were less profitable than home and foreign alternatives, it would have been expected that the elites, while continuing to rally political support for the Empire, would gradually have attempted to divest themselves of those securities and to reinvest their assets in other more viable enterprises. Although the data do not permit an exact test of this hypothesis, they do allow a less precise examination. If the firm sample is split at 1890 and the two parts compared, the ratio of elite to business investors is substantially lower in the second period. The decline, however, is not related to a rise in business holdings (in fact, they fell as well), but to an increase in the "other" owners – including women, children, and retirees.

Both Gladstone and Disraeli had served an apprenticeship at the Treasury, and both recognized the power of the purse and, more importantly, the dependence of the exchequer on the state's power to tax. For a government to be effective, it must command resources, and those resources must in large measure be derived from taxes. Very early in his tenure as Chancellor, Disraeli had noted: " . . . We cannot distinguish Indian from English finance ultimately: we cannot permit the Indian government to go bankrupt. I need not point out the ultimate consequence on our exchequer."[23] Later, as the leader of the Conservative opposition and faced with looming demands for increases in defense and social expenditures, he fought hard and successfully against Gladstone's plans for abolishing the income tax.[24] Gladstone also recognized the powers inherent in the government's ability to tax, but as a true nineteenth-century Liberal he fought to hold taxes down. "All taxation operated in the restraint of trade, and, therefore, in order to reduce prices, in order to secure full employment, it was necessary to keep taxation and public expenditure at a minimum."[25] The income tax was, he argued, particularly pernicious since, "it tempted statesmen to expansion, it tempted taxpayers to fraudulent evasions."[26] In the last decade of his life these views put him in violent opposition to Joseph Chamberlain and those who saw in the state's power to tax the solution to the problem of imperial expansion *and* increased social legislation.[27]

Despite Gladstone's protestations, England had been and continued to be the most heavily taxed nation in the world. In 1776, a large part of Britain's Empire had exploded into war over the home government's attempt to increase slightly the tax burden on the American colonists – settlers who must have been almost the most lightly taxed group in the civilized world. In the words of one historian: "The British Americans enjoyed a lighter tax burden than any [other] people in the western world except Poland and one knows what happened to Poland."[28] The cost and outcome of the American war appear to have remained fresh in the minds of British policy makers, for there is little evidence that they ever seriously attempted to make their "new" dependent Empire pay its own way.

At home, taxes at the national level averaged just less than £2.50 per person, and if local imposts are added, the total reaches nearly £3.50. The former figure contrasts with an average of less than £1 for a typical developed country. In the Empire the colonies with responsible government (particularly those in Oceania) tended to emulate the home country. Depending on how one counts, the average tax level in those colonies lay somewhere between £1.65

and £2.40. Even the lesser figure was almost twice the level prevailing in the foreign–developed sector. Moreover, three-quarters of those taxes were raised through tariffs; and while they were paid by the colonists, they were taxes aimed in the main at British manufacturers and merchants. Taxes in the dependent Empire were some 20 to 40 percent less than in the underdeveloped world, and in India they were even lower than those levied in the Princely States. In the dependent colonies the greatest proportion of tax revenue was again raised by tariffs; however, in India the Lancashire textile manufacturers were successful in minimizing, if not eliminating, those trade barriers.

If the residents of the dependent Empire spent little on taxes, the British, as we have already seen, spent a great deal. Even the citizens of the colonies with responsible government, who chose to tax themselves more heavily than they might, were largely freed of defense costs and thus able to devote the vast bulk of their resources to more directly productive ends. In the United Kingdom, however, the real tax level increased by about two-thirds over the half century in question, and as a fraction of per capita national income it rose by about one-sixth.[29] In England the tax structure historically had depended very heavily on consumption taxes, and it was certainly regressive. As the second half of the century wore on, however, regressivity declined, as customs and excises were replaced by increases in the income and inheritance taxes. The latter sources together had produced only about one-quarter of the total when Disraeli first became prime minister but had risen to account for more than two pounds in five by the election of 1911. Over the same period, consumption taxes had declined from more than three-fifths to less than one-half of all the imposts. Over Gladstone's protests, the income tax had "lost its terrifying character" and by the mid-1890s, again despite Gladstone's reservations, death duties had begun to bite.

Even with the very regressive tax structure of the 1860s, three-fifths or perhaps two-thirds of British taxes were paid by the middle and upper classes. Given the increasing reliance on income and inheritance taxes, it seems reasonable to conclude that this proportion did not decline and may have risen as the century wore on. Of more direct interest, the fraction that fell on the middle classes was probably close to two and a half times the amount paid by the upper classes. It is hardly surprising that the Gladstonian Liberals opposed higher taxes while the upper classes found that, if the resources gained by tax increases could be used for "productive purposes," they would not only countenance but support such levies. The middle class bore far more than its share of the imperial subsidy and, as is so apparent in the stockholder figures and those in the previous chapter, they did not share equally in its benefits. The profits of Empire accrued largely to the upper class.

When it came to the formulation and execution of official policy toward the Empire, the responsibility of course rested fundamentally with Parliament and particularly the House of Commons. It was a quintessentially patrician legislative body dominated by the elite classes, business, and the professions. The members had attended the ancient universities and the major public schools and they were "club men" with a vengeance. It is this homogeneity that makes it difficult to explain individual political behavior. In general, on imperial issues, the member support score indicates that Liberals deviated more from established party positions than Conservatives and that university-educated Liberals were particularly anti-imperial. The safeness of a member's seat, his club memberships, his profession, his level of education, and his regional identification seem to provide very little help in explaining voting patterns in a legislature, in which the lack of diversity complicates the process of explanation and analysis. On the fundamental question of the degree to which economic self-interest affected voting behavior on imperial issues, no intimate connection appears to exist between the two, although further research may prove otherwise. In the political arena, the behavior of members of the House of Commons on matters concerning Empire was actuated by motivations other than those economic.

Parliament, much as any other democratic legislative body, was subject to considerable outside pressure. Individual companies, the chambers of commerce, the trade associations, and a fluctuating array of usually short-lived commercial coalitions all tried to influence the course of events. Although not usually successful in the foreign arena, due to long-established British disinclination to interfere on behalf of private businesspeople, they were more so in the case of India – the cotton tariffs being a case in point. Tariffs in the self-governing colonies attracted considerable attention from the various pressure groups, but constitutional inhibitions and lack of parliamentary sympathy precluded the implementation of the desired policy. Even in the dependent colonies, the Crown Agents actively sought foreign bids when they felt domestic ones were excessive.

Much no doubt remains to be said concerning the relationship between Empire and economics. But perhaps, when all is said and done, Cecil Rhodes came closest to summing the whole thing up when he said, not totally in jest, that imperialism was nothing more than philanthropy plus five percent! But philanthropy for whom?

Official documents

Colonial Office, original correspondence

(Appropriate registers and entry books were consulted but are not listed.)

C.O. 323, Colonies, General, Correspondence.
C.O. 337, Colonies, General, Correspondence.
C.O. 417, South Africa, Correspondence.
C.O. 551, South Africa, Correspondence.
C.O. 553, South Africa, Blue Books.
C.O. 418, Australia, Correspondence.
C.O. 560, Australia, Blue Books.
C.O. 13, South Australia, Correspondence.
C.O. 17, South Australia, Blue Books.
C.O. 18, Western Australia, Correspondence.
C.O. 22, Western Australia, Blue Books.
C.O. 23, Bahamas, Correspondence.
C.O. 27, Bahamas, Blue Books.
C.O. 28, Barbados, Correspondence.
C.O. 33, Barbados, Blue Books.
C.O. 37, Bermuda, Correspondence.
C.O. 41, Bermuda, Blue Books.
C.O. 531, British North Borneo.
C.O. 42, Canada.
C.O. 47, Canada, Blue Books.
C.O. 48, Cape of Good Hope, Correspondence.
C.O. 53, Cape of Good Hope, Blue Books.
C.O. 54, Ceylon, Correspondence.
C.O. 59, Ceylon, Blue Books.
C.O. 60, British Columbia, Correspondence.
C.O. 64, British Columbia, Blue Books.
C.O. 67, Cyprus, Correspondence.
C.O. 456, Cyprus, Blue Books.
C.O. 71, Dominica, Correspondence.
C.O. 76, Dominica, Blue Books.
C.O. 78, Falkland Islands, Correspondence.
C.O. 81, Falkland Islands, Blue Books.

C.O. 87, Gambia, Correspondence.
C.O. 90, Gambia, Blue Books.
C.O. 91, Gibraltar, Correspondence.
C.O. 95, Gibraltar, Blue Books.
C.O. 96, Gold Coast, Correspondence.
C.O. 100, Gold Coast, Blue Books.
C.O. 101, Grenada, Correspondence.
C.O. 106, Grenada, Blue Books.
C.O. 111, British Guiana, Correspondence.
C.O. 116, British Guiana, Blue Books.
C.O. 123, British Honduras, Correspondence.
C.O. 128, British Honduras, Blue Books.
C.O. 129, Hong Kong, Correspondence.
C.O. 133, Hong Kong, Blue Books.
C.O. 137, Jamaica, Correspondence.
C.O. 143, Jamaica, Blue Books.
C.O. 533, Kenya, Correspondence.
C.O. 543, Kenya, Blue Books.
C.O. 144, Labuan, Correspondence.
C.O. 146, Labuan, Blue Books.
C.O. 147, Lagos, Correspondence.
C.O. 151, Lagos, Blue Books.
C.O. 152, Leeward Islands, Correspondence.
C.O. 157, Leeward Islands, Blue Books.
C.O. 158, Malta, Correspondence.
C.O. 163, Malta, Blue Books.
C.O. 167, Mauritius, Correspondence.
C.O. 415, Mauritius, Blue Books.
C.O. 179, Natal, Correspondence.
C.O. 183, Natal, Blue Books.
C.O. 188, New Brunswick, Correspondence
C.O. 193, New Brunswick, Blue Books.
C.O. 194, Newfoundland, Correspondence.
C.O. 206, Newfoundland, Blue Books.
C.O. 422, British New Guinea/Papua.
C.O. 201, New South Wales, Correspondence.
C.O. 206, New South Wales, Blue Books.
C.O. 209, New Zealand, Correspondence.
C.O. 213, New Zealand, Blue Books.
C.O. 444, Niger Coast Protectorate, Correspondence.
C.O. 464, Niger Coast Protectorate, Blue Books.
C.O. 446, Northern Nigeria, Correspondence.
C.O. 465, Northern Nigeria, Blue Books.

C.O. 520, Southern Nigeria Protectorate, Correspondence.
C.O. 473, Southern Nigeria Protectorate, Blue Books.
C.O. 217, Nova Scotia and Cape Breton, Correspondence.
C.O. 221, Nova Scotia and Cape Breton, Blue Books.
C.O. 525, Nyasaland, Correspondence.
C.O. 452, Nyasaland, Blue Books.
C.O. 224, Orange River Colony, Correspondence.
C.O. 598, Orange River Colony, Blue Books.
C.O. 225, Western Pacific.
C.O. 226, Prince Edward Island, Correspondence.
C.O. 231, Prince Edward Island, Blue Books.
C.O. 234, Queensland, Correspondence.
C.O. 238, Queensland, Blue Books.
C.O. 239, St. Christopher, Correspondence.
C.O. 243, St. Christopher, Blue Books.
C.O. 247, St. Helena, Correspondence.
C.O. 252, St. Helena, Blue Books.
C.O. 253, St. Lucia, Correspondence.
C.O. 258, St. Lucia, Blue Books.
C.O. 260, St. Vincent, Correspondence.
C.O. 265, St. Vincent, Blue Books.
C.O. 530, Seychelles, Correspondence.
C.O. 471, Seychelles, Blue Books.
C.O. 267, Sierra Leone, Correspondence.
C.O. 272, Sierra Leone, Blue Books.
C.O. 535, Somaliland, Correspondence.
C.O. 607, Somaliland, Blue Books.
C.O. 273, Straits Settlements, Correspondence.
C.O. 277, Straits Settlements, Blue Books.
C.O. 280, Tasmania, Correspondence.
C.O. 284, Tasmania, Blue Books.
C.O. 285, Tobago, Correspondence.
C.O. 290, Tobago, Blue Books.
C.O. 291, Transvaal, Correspondence.
C.O. 476, Transvaal, Blue Books.
C.O. 295, Trinidad, Correspondence.
C.O. 300, Trinidad, Blue Books.
C.O. 536, Uganda, Correspondence.
C.O. 613, Uganda, Blue Books.
C.O. 305, Vancouver Island, Correspondence.
C.O. 478, Vancouver Island, Blue Books.
C.O. 309, Victoria.
C.O. 521, Wei-Hai-Wei.

C.O. 318, West Indies.
C.O. 321, Windward Islands.
C.O. 431, Accounts Branch, Correspondence.
C.O. 442, Colonial Statistical Tables.
C.O. 532, Dominions, Correspondence.
C.O. 806, Africa, Confidential Prints.
C.O. 807, North America, Confidential Prints.
C.O. 808, Australia, Confidential Prints.
C.O. 809, Eastern, Confidential Prints.
C.O. 810, Mediterranean, Confidential Prints.
C.O. 811, West Indies, Confidential Prints.
C.O. 812, Miscellaneous, Confidential Prints.

Board of Trade - Companies Registration Office

Records of Extant Companies in Companies Registration Office

B.T. 1, Files of Dissolved Companies, Scotland (in Edinburgh).
B.T. 31, Files of Dissolved Companies, 1856–1948

Treasury

T. 1, In Letters and Files (Treasury Board Papers).
T. 2, In Letters and Files (Registers of Papers).
T. 7, Out Letters (Colonial Affairs).
T. 27, Out Letters (General).
T. 39, Accounts (Treasury Chest).

Parliamentary papers and records of the Committee on Imperial Defense and the Crown Agents for the Colonies, as indicated in the text.

Miscellaneous original series

Records of the Council of Foreign Bondholders.
Records of the Birmingham, Glasgow, Liverpool, London, and Manchester Chambers of Commerce and the Associated Chambers of Commerce of the United Kingdom.
Records of Trade Associations.

Private papers

Arber Papers, NRA 13205, Birmingham University Library.
Asquith Collection, NRA 12685, Bodleian Library.
Blackburn Papers, British Museum, ad. ms. 51020.
Bonar Law Collection, NRA 19286, House of Lords Record Office.
Brand Collection, NRA 6114, House of Lords Record Office.
Bryce Collection, NRA 6716, Bodleian Library.
Bulwer-Lytton Collection, British Museum, ad. mss. 59611–59613.
Burns Papers, British Museum, ad. mss. 46282.
Cairns Papers, NRA 10007, Public Record Office 30/51.
Cardwell Papers, Public Record Office 30/48.
Carnarvon Papers, Public Record Office 30/6.
Chamberlain Papers, NRA 12604, Birmingham University Library.
Churchill Collection, NRA 13273, Churchill College, Cambridge.
Clarendon Papers, NRA 6302, Bodleian Library.
Crewe Papers, Cambridge University Library.
Cromer Papers, Public Record Office FO 633.
Cross Collection, British Museum, ad. mss. 51263–51289.
Cross Collection, India Office Library E243.
Curzon Collection, India Office Library F111, F112.
Devonshire Papers, India Office Library Microfilm Reels 794, 944, 945.
Dale Papers, NRA 13202, Birmingham University Library, RWD.
Davidson Manuscripts, Rhodes House Ind. Ocean, S217.
Disraeli Papers, British Museum, ad. mss. 58210.
Dufferin Papers, India Office Library, mss. F130.
Elgin Papers (Earl), India Office Library F84.
Escott Papers, NRA 16926, British Museum, ad. mss. 58774–58801.
Fergusson, Sir James, Public Record Office FO 800.
Fraser Papers, British Museum, ad. mss. 44913.

Gedge Papers, NRA 13161, Rhodes House, Oxford Mss. British Empire S290.

Gladstone Papers, British Museum, ad. mss. 44086–44385.

Granville Papers, NRA 8654, Public Records Office 30/29.

Grey of Fallodin Mss., Public Record Office FO 800/35 to 113.

Grey of Howick, Rhodes House, Afr. T6.

Hamilton Papers, NRA 81956, British Museum, ad. mss.

Hamilton Collection, NRA 10867, India Office D508–510.

Hamilton Papers, Public Record Office T168.

Harcourt Manuscripts, NRA 3679, Bodleian Library 75/23.

Hardinge Manuscripts, NRA 3853Bk, Cambridge University Library.

Hardinge of Penshurst Manuscripts, NRA 8909, Kent County RO (Maidstone) U297.

John Holt and Company, NRA 19042, Rhodes House, ms. afr. s.1525.

Iddesleigh Papers, NRA 5873, British Museum 50013–50064 and 50209–50210.

Kilbracken Papers, British Museum, ad. mss. 44900–44902.

Kilbracken Papers, India Office Library F102.

Kitchener Papers, Public Record Office 30/57.

Lagden Papers, Rhodes House, mss. Afr. s.142–214.

Laird Mair Papers, NRA 11215, India Office Library F90.

Lansdowne Collection, India Office D558.

Lansdowne Collection, Public Record Office FO 8003115–8003146.

Lloyd-George Papers, NRA 15700, House of Lords, Historical Collection 192.

Lowe Manuscripts, Bodleian Oxford, English Letters D148.

Lyttelton Collection, NRA 19700, Churchill College, Cambridge.

Lytton Manuscripts, MSA 4598, Hereford County Records Office D/EK.

Lytton Papers, India Office Library E218.

MacMillan Papers, British Museum, ad. mss. 55055–55057.

Matacong Island Papers, NRA 14049, Birmingham University Library.

Mayo Papers, NRA 10522Bk, Cambridge University Library.

McKenna, NRA 12034, Churchill College, Cambridge.

Middleton Manuscripts, British Museum, ad. mss. 50072–50077.

Middleton Manuscripts, Public Record Office 30/67.

Milner Manuscripts, NRA 14300, Bodleian Library.

Morley Papers, NRA 10208Bk, India Office D573.

Muller Manuscripts, NRA 12354, Bodleian Library D165, 166, 170.

Nathan Manuscripts, NRA 8981, Rhodes House, 231–656.

Northbrooke Collection, NRA 11213, India Office Library, mss. Eur. C144.

Ommaney Manuscripts, Rhodes House, ms. af. s.26.

Onslow Manuscripts, NRA 1088, Surrey County Monument Room, Guildford, FO 173.

Paget Collection, British Museum.

Ponsonby Collection, NRA 18634, Bodleian Library, ms. Eng. hist. c.652–662.

Ripon Papers, British Museum, ad. mss. 43512–43617.

Russell Papers, Public Record Office 30/22.

St. Aldwyn Manuscripts, NRA 3526, Gloucester ROD2455.

Sandars Collection, Bodleian Library, Eng. hist. 921, c.713–733.

Sanderson, Lord, Public Record Office, FO 800.

Saunders Collection, Churchill College, Cambridge.

Selborne Collection, NRA 17810, Bodleian Library, ms. 74/15.

Selborne Papers, NRA 11918, Lambeth Palace Library.

Spender Papers, British Museum, ad. mss. 46387.

Strachey Collection, House of Lords Historical Collection 196.

Swayne Manuscripts, Rhodes House, mss. British Empire S279.

Temple Collection, NRA 11216, India Office F86.

Wilberforce Manuscripts, NRA 7132, Bodleian Library, D36, D38.

Wolseley Letter Book, British Museum, ad. mss. 41324.

Company records

FIRMS, DATA FROM WHICH IS UTILIZED IN THE STUDY

A. Random Sample of Corporations Whose Shares were Traded on the London Stock Exchange, 1883–1912

Aberdeen Cattle & Farm Produce Association
Acol Collieries
African & United Supply & Cold Storage
African City Properties Trust
African Lakes Trading Corp.
Alexandria Water Co.
Allynugger Tea Co.
Amazon Telegraph Co.
American Trust Co.
Anamalay Coffee Co. Ltd.
Anglo Californian Bank
Anglo Egyptian Bank
Anibiri Wassau Exploration
Anterior Matabele Gold Mines
Antwerp Tivoli Breweries
Ardilla Copper Mines
Ashton Vale Iron Co.
Assets Founders' Share Co.
Auckland Electric Tramways
Australian Chilling & Freezing
Azoff Coal Co.
Bank of Mauritius
Bank of Tarapaca & London
Bankers' Investment Trust
Barran, John & Sons
Bell's Asbestos Co.
Bengal Iron & Steel Co.
Bengal Nagpur Railroad
Beyrouth Water Works
Bolivar Railroad
Bombay Gas Co.

Bombay Tea Co.
Booth Steamship Co.
Boston Consolidated Copper & Gold Mining Co.
Bradford Banking Co.
Brahmapootra Tea Co.
Brazilian Street Railroad
Bridgetown & St. Andrews Railroad Co.
Bright's Light & Power
British Columbia Canning
British Columbia Electric Railway
British Columbia Telephones
Buenos Ayres Gas Co.
Buenos Ayres Southern Dock
Bulawayo Water Works
Burgon & Ball
Bute Shipbuilding, Engineering & Dock Co.
Calcutta Electric Supply Corp.
Calcutta Tramways
Calico Printers Assoc.
Cambrian Consolidated Mines
Cape Asbestos Co.
Cardiff District & Penarth Harbour Tramway
Cardiff Junction Dry Dock & Engineering Co.
Carrizal Share Trust Ltd.
Carter, Milner & Bird
Carthagena & Herrerias Steam Tramway
Cedar Valley Land & Cattle Co.
Chesapeake & Ohio Steamship Co.
Chiapas Zone Exploration
Chicago Breweries
Chile Telephone Co.
Chilean National Ammunition Co.
Chinese Engineering & Mining Co.
Chubwa Tea Co. of Assam
Clitters United Mine
Colombo Electric Tramways & Lighting
Colombo Gas & Water Co.
Colonial Securities Trust
Combined Rhodesia Syndicate
Consolidated Rand Rhodesia Trust & General Exploration
 Co.
Consolidated South Rand Mines Deep Ltd.
Consolidated Water Works of Rosario

Cornish Adventurers
Cornish Bank
Costa Rica Electric Light & Traction Co.
Costa Rica Railroad Co.
Daira Sanieh Sugar Corp.
Dalgety & Co.
Deary & Co.
Delhi & London Bank
Dindicolle & Gaudin
Dominion Breweries
Dominion Carpet Co.
Dorman, Long & Co.
East India Coal Co. Ltd.
East India Tramways
Eastern Extension Australasia & China Telegraph Co.
Eastern Mortgage & Agency Co.
Edinburgh North American Investment
Emu Bay & Mount Bischoff Railway
Falkland Islands Meat
Floating Dock Co. of St. Thomas
Foreign & Colonial Investment Trust
Franco African Exploration & Investment Co.
Friary Holroyd's & Healy's Brewery
Glamorgan Public House Trust
Gleesons Success Gold Mines Ltd.
Globe Telegraph & Trust Co.
Goebel Brewing Co. Ltd.
Gold Ore Treatment Co. of West Australia
Goomera Tea Estates
Great Boulder Proprietory Gold Mines
Great Western of Brazil Railroad
Halifax Brewery
Halifax Graving Dock
Harmony Proprietory Co.
Hart & Levy
Heritable Investment Bank
Hood & Moore's Stores
Huon Timber Co.
Imperial Tramway Co.
Indian Midlands Railway
Indianapolis Breweries
International Bank of London
International Lighting Assoc.

International Line Steamship
Kalgoorlie Electric Power & Lighting
Kanan Devan Hills Produce Co.
Kimberley Waterworks Co.
Klerksdorf Estates
Klip Colliery
La Capital Tramways Co.
Labuan & Borneo Ltd.
Lagunas Syndicate
Lancashire & Yorkshire Bank
Land Mortgage Bank of North Western America
Lands Trust Co.
Lea Bridge District Gas, Light & Coke
Leicester Real Property
Linkwood Glenlivet Distilleries
Liverpool & North Wales Steamship Co.
Liverpool Commercial Investment Co.
Liverpool Nitrate
London & Hanseatic Bank
London & San Francisco Bank
London & South Western Bank
London Bank of Australia
London House Trust
London Paris & American Bank
London Platino Brazilian Telegraph Co.
Lucia Silver Mines
Main Colliery Co. Ltd.
Majuli Tea Co.
Malayan (Pahang) Exploration Co.
Malta & Mediterranean Gas Co.
Manitoba Mortgage & Investment Co.
Marbella Iron Co.
Marianao & Havana RR
Mashonaland RR Co.
Maxim, H. Electrical & Engineering
Maypole Dairy
Melbourne Brewery & Distillery
Mercantile Bank of India
Mercantile Pontoon Co.
Merchants Trust
Mersey Forge
Metropolitan Coal Co. of Sydney
Mexican Electric Tramways

Mexican Electric Works
Middleburg Steam Coal & Coke
Mining Investment Co. of Glasgow
Mona & Parys Mines
Montevideo Water Works
Montserrat Co.
Mount Carbon Co.Natal Steam Coal Co.
Natal Zululand RR
National Bank of New Zealand
New Cape Central
New Cimbula Co.
New Ravenswood
New Theatre Cambridge
New Zealand Mines Trust
Newbury's Ltd.
Nitrate Producers Steamship
Nitrate Railways Co.
Noakhali (Bengal) Railway Co.
North Alabama Assets Co.
North Borneo Trading
North Cachar Tea Co.
North Eastern Banking Co.
Nottingham Brewery
Ocean Minerals
Ohlsson's Cape Breweries
Orient Produce Co.
Orient Steam Navigation Co.
Oriental Gas Co.
Parchoca Iron Ore & RR Co.
Parish Lighting
Peking Syndicate
Portsmouth United Brewery
Provincial Tramways Co.
Queensland Smelting Co.
Railway Rolling Stock Trust
Railways & Metropolitan Omnibus
Rand Central Electric Co.
Reynolds Bros.
Rhodesia Breweries
Rhodesia Gold Reefs (Purdon's) Ltd.
River Plate Gas Co.
Riverside Gold Mines
Rohilkund & Kumaon RR

Royal Niger Co.
Russian Engineering Co.
Salar del Carmen Nitrate Syndicate
San Francisco Brewery
San Jacinto Land Co.
Seville Water Works
Shanghai Waterworks Co.
Sheffield Forge & Rolling Mills Co.
Smith's Dock Co. Ltd.
South African Brewery
South African General Syndicate
South African Lighting Assoc. Ltd.
South African Super Aeration
Southern Coal Co. of New South Wales
Southern Mahratta Railroad
Spencer, Turner & Boldero
St. Pauli Breweries
Stroud Brewery Co.
Sydney Harbour Collieries
Tarkway Whim Gold Syndicate
Trust & Agency Co. of Australasia
Tyne Pontoons & Dry Docks
United Trust Co.
Val de Travers Asphalt Co.
Warner Estates
Weardale Lead Co.
West Coast of Africa Oil & Fuel Co.
West Prussian Mining Co.
West's Patent Press
Western Australia Proprietary Gold Mines
Western Railway of Santa Fe
White Pass & Yukon RR
Wrexham Gas & Coke Co.
Wynaad Tea Co.
Yangtse Valley Co.
York Tramways Co.
Yorkshire Electric Power Syndicate
Yorkshire Indigo Scarlet & Colour Dye

B. Companies with more Complete Records, 1860–1912

Aberdare & Aberaman Consumers Gas Co.
African Association Ltd.

Alison, James & Sons.
Alley Mclelland Ltd.
Alliance Investment Co.
American Hawaiian Steamship
American Investment Trust
Anderson & Robertson Ltd.
Anderston Foundry
Anglo-Russian Cotton Mills
Arroll, William & Co.
Ashanti Goldfields Corp.
Assam Co.
Associated Omnibus Co. Ltd.
Barclay, Curle & Co.
Barclay, Perkins & Co.
Barnet District Gas & Water
Barry Dock Cottage Co.
Bathurst Trading Co.
Baxter Bros. & Co., Ltd.
Beardmore, William
Bell, Thomas & Sons
Benson, Robert & Co.
Bertram, James & Sons
Birmingham Small Arms & Metal
Black Dyke Mills
Blaenavon Co.
Bolckow, Vaughan & Co.
Brentford Gas Co.
Bridgend Gas & Water
Bristol City Lines
British Slate Co. Ltd.
Brooke-Bond Tea
Brynmawr & Blaina Gas Co.
Burgess, John & Son
Burnyeat, Brown & Co.
Calder & Hubble Navigation
Calder Navigation
Carlton Main Colliery
Carney & Barrow
Carney & Barrow II
Champdany Jute
Cheltenham Original Breweries
Chilworth Gunpowder Co.
City and West End Properties

City of London Gaslight & Coke
City Bank
Clifton & Kersley Coal Co.
Clydebank Engineering & Shipbuilding
Colville Steel
Commercial Gas Co.
Connock Chase Colliery Co.
Consett Iron Co.
Consett Spanish Iron Ore Co.
Cook, Thomas
Copland & Lye
Cossall Colliery
Courage & Co.
Courtauld, Samuel & Co.
Cox Bros.
Cumberland Union Bank
Cunard Steamship
Darlington Forge
Davey, Paxman & Co.
De La Rue Co.
Dowanhill Estate
Dowlais Iron Co.
Dudley Gas Co.
Duston Iron Ore
Eagle Oil Co.
Eagle Oil Transport Co.
East Cannock Colliery
Economic Life Assurance Soc.
Edmund Swaithe Colliery Co. Ltd.
Ellis & Everard Ltd. II
Ellis, Joseph & Sons (Ellis and Everard I)
Extract Wool & Merino Co.
F. Kendall & Sons
Fairfield Shipbuilding & Engineering
Farnham United Brewery
Finlay Clarke & Co.
Finley, James
Fish, J. Ltd.
Fitton & Sons
Flintshire Oil & Cannel
Flower & Sons Ltd.
Ford-Ayrton
Fordham, E.K. & H.

Foreign, American & General Investment Trust
Fox, Samuel & Co.
Fulham Pottery Co.
Gas Light & Coke
General Hydraulic Power Co.
Gibbs, William - Australia
Gibbs, William - Liverpool
Gibbs, William - South American
Giggal & Clay
Gilroy & Sons
Glasgow Steamshipping Co.
Glenanvon Gawr Collieries
Gold Coast Machinery & Trading
Gowrock Ropeworks
Grand Junction Canal
Gray & Sons - Chelmsford
Gray & Sons, Maldon
Great Central Gas Consumer Co.
Greg & Greg Mill
Grierson, Robert & Co.
Hadden & Co.
Hallamshire Steel & File Co.
Hammersmith & City RR
Hampstead Colliery
Hardy & Padimore
Harrow & Stanmore Gas
Harrow Electric Light & Power
Hartley, John & Sons
Hepworth, J & Sons
Hills Plymouth & Co., Ltd.
Hirst, George & Sons
Hodgsons Kingston Brewery
Hopewell Tea
Horseley Co.
Huddersfield Banking
Hull Dock Co.
Hunt & Winterbotham
Huntley & Palmers
Huth & Co. – Valparaiso
Ibbotson Bros. & Co.
Imperial British East Africa Co.
Indemnity Mutual Marine Assurance
International Financial Society
Isleworth Brewery

Jacquard
Jardine Matheson and Co.
Jessop Bros.
John Foster & Sons
Jowett, Robert & Sons
Kendall (Lille)
Kleinwort, Drake & Cohen
Lautaro Nitrate
Lee, Nephew & Sons
Leon & Sons
Liebig Extract of Meat
Limtott Spirits Co.
Lister & Co.
Little, David
London Assurance Co.
London General Omnibus
London Joint Stock Bank
London Road Car Co.
London, Buenos Ayres, and River Plate Bank (Lloyd's Bank
    International)
Lovell, J & Sons
Macclesfield Silk Manufacturing Co.
Maciver, W. B. & Co.
Main, A & J
Metropolitan District Railway
Metropolitan Tower Construction
Mexican Mines of el Oro
Midlands Bank
Mitchell Main Colliery
Nettlefold's Ltd.
New Charleston Colliery
New Zealand & Australia Land Co.
Newstead Colliery Ltd.
Noakes & Co.
North & South Wales Bank
North Metropolitan Electric Power Supply
North Metropolitan Power Distribution Co.
North Metropolitan Tram
Northern Assurance Co.
Ocean Coal & Wilsons Ltd.
Ocean Marine Insurance Co.
Orr Ewing & Co.
Pacific Steam Navigation Co.
Palatine Insurance Co.

Peek, Frean & Co.
Pennycook Patent Glazing & Engineering
Peruvian Corporation
Phillips, J & B
Pirie, Alexander & Sons
Quarry Bank Mill
Ramsden, T & Sons
Redbourne Hill Co.
Reffel Bexley Brewery
Roper, J. G. & Sons
Royal Brewery Brentford
Royal Mail Steam Packet
Royston Water Co.
Sandwell Park Colliery
Sao Paolo Brazilian RR
Sheepsbridge Coal & Iron
Shotts Iron Works
Sloane, William & Co.
South Durham Steel & Iron
Spears & Jackson
Spen Valley Brewing Co.
Spencer, John Ltd.
Stavely Coal & Iron
Steel Co. of Scotland
Sterling, William & Sons
Stewarts & Lloyds
Sun Fire Insurance
Sunderland & South Shields Water
Swanzy, F & A
Tarapaca Nitrate Co.
Tarkwa Trading Co.
Tehuantepec National Railway
Tenbury Wells Improvement Co.
Tetley Brewery
Theatre Royal Leicester
Thompson, James & George
Thwaites & Reed
Tod, John & Sons
Townsend, Eli
Turnbull Co.
Tyser Line
Veracruz Electric Light Power and Traction
Veracruz Land & Cattle

Vickers, Sons & Maxim Ltd.
Walker, Harry
Walsall Wood Colliery
Wardle & Davenport
Wearmouth Coal Co.
Wembly Park Estates
West Riding Steam Ploughing, Cultivating, and Threshing
   Co.
Western Railroad of Havana
Wharcliffe Colliery
Whitechapel & Bow Railway
Whitworth, W. G. Armstrong
Wiggins Teape & Co.
Wilkins, R. F.
Wolverhampton Gas
Woolley Coal Co.
Wordie & Co.
Wordie Property Co.
Yorkshire & Derbyshire Coal & Iron
Yorkshire Banking Co.

C. *British Railways*

Caledonian Railway (Scotland)
Furness Railway (England)
Great Central Railway (late Manch. Sheff. Linc.)
Great Eastern Railway (England)
Great Northern Railway of Ireland
London and Northwestern Railway
Midland Railway (England)

Notes

Chapter 1

1   See J. S. Galbraith, "The Turbulent Frontier as a Factor in British Expansion," *Comparative Studies in Society and History*, II (2), January 1960.

2   Joseph M. Schumpeter (ed.) *Imperialism, Social Classes: Two Essays*, (New York: Meridian Books, 1955), 72; and David Landes, "Some Thoughts on the Nature of Economic Imperialism," *Journal of Economic History* (December 1961), 511.

3   John A. Hobson, *Imperialism – A Study* (London, 1954), 59.

4   V. I. Lenin, *Imperialism, the Highest State of Capitalism* (New York, 1934), 30.

5   G. Bernard Shaw, *Plays Pleasant and Unpleasant* (New York, 1898), vol. II, "The Man of Destiny," 334–6.

6   H. M. Stanley, *The Autobiography of Sir Henry Morton Stanley, G. C. B.* (London, 1909), 237.

7   Jack Simmons, *Livingstone and Africa* (London, 1955), 79.

8   Bentinck Papers (Nottingham University), William Astall to Bentinck, January 20, 1828.

9   The Report of the Inter-Imperial Relations Committee, Imperial Conference, 1926, cited in A. B. Keith, *Speeches and Documents on the British Dominions 1918–1931* (London, 1948), 160.

10   *Hansard*, 3rd series, volume 176 (February 21, 1865), 536–48.

11   *Parliamentary Papers*, 1865, volume 412.

12   *Hansard*, 3rd series, volume 181 (February 8, 1866), 193–95.

13   Disraeli's speech at the Crystal Palace, June 24, 1872, cited in George Bennett, *The Concept of Empire, Burke to Atlee, 1774–1947* (London, 1953), 258.

14   Acquired during Disraeli's governments: Basutoland, Fiji, Perak, Selangor, Sungei-Ujong, Cyprus; new territories added to the Empire under Gladstone: North Borneo Co. Territory, Egypt, British New Guinea, Somali Coast Protectorate, Niger Coast Protectorate, Northern Nigeria, Bechuanaland, British Solomon Islands, Northern and Northwestern Rhodesia, Uganda.

15   Throughout this book, a system of classifications is used under which the Empire is divided into four classifications: Britain itself, colonies with responsible government, all other colonial possessions regardless of the state of constitutional development, and India. Thus the term "dependent Empire" includes India, but the classification "dependent colonies" does not.

16   Cited in Robert A. Huttenback, *The British Imperial Experience* (New York, 1966), 20.

338

[17] Lord Durham's Report on the Affairs of British North America, cited in A. B. Keith, *Speeches and Documents on Colonial Policy 1763–1917* (London, 1953).

[18] Richard Kesner tells us that while virtually all the senior officials of the Treasury had attended public schools, less than half of their Colonial Office counterparts had done so. On the other hand, nearly all, as was the case with the Treasury, had taken degrees at universities. In Chamberlain's time, for example, only two had not. Two had attended Woolwich Military Academy, two were from Scottish universities, 31 from Oxford, and 13 from Cambridge. Richard M. Kesner, *Economic Control and Colonial Development* (Westport, 1981), 64, 245, fn 41.

[19] Cited in Ann M. Burton, "Treasury Control and Colonial Policy in the Late Nineteenth Century," *Public Administration*, volume 44 (Summer, 1966), 170.

[20] Robert V. Kubicek, *The Administration of Imperialism: Joseph Chamberlain at the Colonial Office* (Durham, 1963), 70.

[21] Burton, op. cit., "Treasury Control," 189.

[22] Ibid., 191.

[23] T 7/23, 3587/85, Treasury to Colonial Office, March 2, 1885.

[24] T 7/23, 2374/86, Treasury to Colonial Office, February 12, 1866.

[25] T 7/26, 2768/89, Treasury to Colonial Office, March 27, 1889.

[26] T 7/23, 11002/89, Treasury to Colonial Office, July 14, 1886.

[27] T 7/27, 15971/93, Treasury to Colonial Office, November 11, 1893.

[28] T 7/23, 18236/86, Treasury to Colonial Office, December 7, 1886.

[29] T 7/26, 20183/87, Treasury to Colonial Office, January 20, 1888.

[30] T 7/26, 30738/88, Treasury to Colonial Office, March 2, 1888.

[31] For an explanation of the calculations and assumptions underlying this table, see Chapter 4, pp. 120–2 and Appendix 4.1. Throughout this volume, the following governmental taxonomy has been adopted:

(a) The British Empire (or the overseas Empire or just Empire) is used to refer to the entire area nominally under British control outside the British Isles. Thus, it includes the colonies with responsible government, the dependent colonies, and India. The term "responsible government" is used to refer to Australia and the seven colonies that became the Commonwealth, Canada and the eleven provinces that formed the Dominion, Newfoundland and its two provinces, New Zealand, and the Union of South Africa and its four constituent colonies. The term "dependent colonies" is used to refer to colonies listed under that heading in Appendix 1.1. For technical reasons, the Anglo–Egyptian Sudan has been excluded. India does not include the Princely States. The term "dependent Empire" is used to refer to the dependent colonies plus India.

(b) For the British Isles (England, Scotland, Wales, and Ireland) two terms are used: "UK national" refers to the expenditures and revenues of the central government. "UK total" includes both the fiscal activities of the central government and those of the county and local governments as well.

(c) The foreign sector refers to all of the world outside of the United Kingdom and the Empire. It has been subdivided into three subsectors: foreign–developed, foreign–underdeveloped, and the Princely States. The precise assignments are enumerated in Appendix 1.3.

[32] Asquith papers, vol. II, letter 252, Churchill to Asquith, December 29, 1908.

[33] See Appendix 4.1 for a general discussion of the data. These four countries are reported in the annual parliamentary report on statistics of foreign countries.

[34] $$\text{Admin} = \frac{.185 - (1.918^{-15}) \, (\text{pop})^2}{30.765 - 4.528}$$

[35] The ratio was .0000103:.248.

[36] Charles Lucas to Sir Robert Herbert, 1891, cited in Brian L. Blakely, *The Colonial Office 1868–1892* (Durham, 1972) 135.

[37] The term Dominion was at first only applied to Canada but soon become a generic term for the colonies of white settlement practicing responsible government – Canada, Australia, New Zealand, and South Africa.

[38] M. Edelstein, "Foreign Investment and Empire 1860–1914," in F. Floud and D. Mccloskey (eds.), *The Economic History of Britain Since 1700* (London: Cambridge University Press, 1981), vol. II, p. 90.

[39] For example, it is assumed that the foreign and domestic sectors were large enough to have absorbed a substantial repatriation of Empire capital without triggering a significant decline in earnings. Again, the assumption is made that in the absence of Empire a colony would have behaved as an independent country at the same stage of development. The first argument implies some very strong assumptions about the elasticities of the supply and demand for capital – elasticities that we know almost nothing about. Thus, no formal model with carefully drawn parameter estimates justifies the assumption. The second presumption assumes that colonies and independent nations were truly comparable (but who would make this argument in regard to Siam and India?) and that a colony's government did not take the imperial connection into account when making its governmental decisions. Better theory would produce better and more relevant counterfactuals. In the absence of a usable general equilibrium model of the world, it appears that use of counterfactuals that at first glance may appear better specified can lead to serious errors rooted in the fallacy of misplaced concreteness.

Chapter 2

[1] J. A. Schumpeter, *Business Cycles: A Theoretical and Statistical Analysis of the Capitalist Process* (New York, 1939) 2 vols., vol. I, 398, 430–1.

[2] Ibid., 430–1.

[3] J. S. Mill, *Principles of Political Economy* (London, Longmans Green, 1907), 739.

[4] Karl Marx, *Capital: A Critique of Political Economy* (Chicago: 1909), 3 vols., vol. III, 278–9, 300.

[5] Marx, *Capital*.

[6] Alfred Marshall, *Memorials* (London, 1890), 415–6.

[7] J. A. Hobson, *Imperialism: A Study* (Ann Arbor, 1967), 40.

[8] F. Engels, *Engels on Capital* (New York, International Publishers, 1937), 117. Rosa Luxemburg, quoted in K. J. Tarbaum, *The Accumulation of Capital – An Anti-Critique;* and Nicolai Bukharin, *Imperialism and the Accumulation of Capital* (New York, 1972), 253. V. J. Lenin, *Imperialism, the Highest State of Capitalism* (New York, 1972), 253.

[9] Lenin, *Imperialism,* 64.

[10] Ibid., 89.

[11] Joseph Chamberlain, speech to the Birmingham jewelers and silversmiths quoted in *The Times*, April 1, 1895.

[12] R. V. Kubicek, *The Administration of Imperialism: Joseph Chamberlain at the Colonial Office* (Durham, 1969), 68–91. For a detailed discussion of British subsidies to the colonies, see: Richard M. Kesner, *Economic Control and Colonial Development: Crown Colony Financial Management in the Age of Joseph Chamberlain* (Westport, 1981).

[13] Matthew Simon, "The Pattern of the British Portfolio Foreign Investment, 1865–1914," in A. R. Hall, *The Export of Capital from Britain* (London, 1968); Herbert Feis, *Europe, The World's Banker* (London, 1930); Leland Jenks, *The Migration of British Capital to 1875* (New York, 1927); Alexander Cairncross, *Home and Foreign Investment, 1870–1913* (Cambridge, 1953); Harvey Segal and Matthew Simon, "British Foreign Capital Issues," *Journal of Economic History* (December 1961). For a useful overview, consult J. C. Woo, *British Economists and the Empire* (New York, 1980).

[14] M. Edelstein, *Overseas Investment in the Age of High Imperialism* (1982) 313–14. Depending on the measure chosen, the correlation between the series ranges from .74 to .80, with associated r^2s between .54 and .64.

[15] D. C. M. Platt, "British Investment Overseas at the End of 1913," *Economic History Review*, forthcoming.

[16] An analysis of all bond issues for eighteen of the thirty-one years between 1882 and 1912 shows that for government bonds there is little to choose between home, responsible colonies, and the dependent Empire. Maturities between 1885 and 1912 averaged about 34.5 years (the dependent Empire was highest, at 35.4, and the colonies with responsible government lowest, at 33.4 years). Foreign-government maturities were much lower (22.4 years). In the private sector, however, the United Kingdom aside, the results were very different. In the case of railroads, for example, maturities averaged 29.8 in the dependent Empire, 31.2 in the colonies with responsible government, 26.0 in India, but 56.2 in the foreign sector.

[17] In the case of the inferred calls, if the first report is on the third call of an issue, we assume that the first and second calls were made in the

months preceding. Similarly, if calls two and five are reported, we assume that three and four were made during the intervening period.

[18]   Platt, "British Investment."

[19]   Based on the records of 482 British firms dealing on the domestic, foreign, and imperial markets.

[20]   It might be noted that both half-decades fall in the period covered by Simon's extension.

[21]   It is very difficult to determine what fraction of these loans was actually financed by the British. C. K. Hobson, for example, reports that in the case of the indemnity loan of 1872 the amount was "covered five times over by the French capitalists and seven times over by foreign subscriptions, principally from England and Germany" [*The Export of Capital* (London, 1919), 138]. Simon claims his adjustments are more accurate, but does not explain how they were made. For the entire period the ratio of intermediate to minimum and maximum to minimum was:

	I/M	M/M
UK	123	123
Foreign	126	153[a]
Empire	121	123
RG	119	120
DG	136	146
India	119	120

[a]122 without 1865–74.

[22]   Peter J. Buckley and Brian R. Roberts, *European Direct Investment in the USA Before World War I* (New York, 1982), 12–13.

[23]   Finance imperialism, in the context of this chapter, refers to the Marxist formulation in which ever-increasing flows of capital pour into the colonies of the dependent Empire as capitalists desperately seek new markets. In the familiar words of J. A. Hobson: ". . . the financial interest has those qualities of concentration and clear-sighted calculation which are needed to set imperialism to work . . . ."

[24]   The intermediate measure indicates a slight increase in the share of the domestic and foreign sectors and a small decline in that of the Empire sector. The maximum measure displays an overall increase of about 5 percent for the foreign sector with a decline in domestic of 2.5, and in Empire, of about 3 percent.

[25]   The European sector includes all of Russia and excludes the United Kingdom and Ireland. Mexico is considered part of North America, and

Africa is defined to include also the Ottoman Empire, Syria, Persia, and
Aden.

26   Simon relatives by continent
     (All-continents average of minimum and maximum = 10)

Year	Europe	North America	South America	Africa	Asia	Australasia
1865–9	86	103	92	101	125	93
1870–4	173	85	87	44	60	82
1875–9	187	54	138	139	101	145
1880–4	53	122	97	121	126	126
1885–9	74	98	141	74	102	86
1890–4	63	120	86	92	91	118
1895–9	49	144	66	125	109	105
1900–4	86	93	89	115	111	87
1905–9	100	88	99	127	113	105
1910–14	114	113	86	99	93	72
Avg., All years	93	93	91	110	107	102

27   Edelstein, *Overseas Investment*, 270–87.
28   C. Lewis, "British Railway Companies and the Argentine Government,"
     in D. C. M. Platt (ed.), *Business Imperialism* (Oxford, 1977), 412.
29   Carnarvon Papers, PRO 30/6, vol. 17 (6), no. 21, Carnarvon to W. H.
     Smith, March 25, 1877.
30   A correction for that political revision would raise the share of the foreign
     sector to something well in excess of one-half.
31   Gladstone Papers, British Library, Add. MS., 44224, F.137, Kimberley
     to Gladstone, May 22, 1871.
32   Lenin, *Imperialism*, 78.
33   For a government engaged in a wide variety of activities there is no clear
     connection between the funds received and the uses to which they are
     put. Since most governments are engaged in a great many activities it
     is simple to sell bonds for one purpose, use those funds to replace some
     existing expenditure, and utilize the funds released for any purpose at
     hand. A study of South American finance in the nineteenth century
     suggests just how creative those governments could be. Only a study
     of the government budgets can provide a clue as to the redirections of
     economic activity within the government sector. Of course, a similar
     shift within a budget can distort private allocations as well. However,
     it is only recently, with the rise of the conglomerate, that we have seen
     funds raised for the steel industry invested in petroleum production.

[34]   Percentage of private finance by industry, 1865–94

	Agricultural & extractive	Manu-facturing	Trans-portation	Finance & public utilities	All else
Capital call (minimum)	10.0	4.1	66.3	18.3	1.3
Segal/Simon	9.4	3.5	68.3	17.4	1.3

[35]   As noted: Many of the private issues had government guarantees. The history of the government guarantees of the railroads in India is well known; however, there was hardly a foreign railroad outside the United States that was not the recipient of some government guarantee or subsidy. Some lines, even within the United States, were assisted in this way. These arrangements were not always honored; however, the pervasiveness of these guarantees is suggested by the fact that, as late as 1903, of the 121 non-U.S. foreign railways whose issues traded on the London exchange, 74 still had some official support.

[36]   Cited in Clark C. Spense, *British Investments and the American Mining Frontier 1860–1901* (Ithaca, 1958), 86. The firm was the Cassels Gold Extracting Company.

[37]   *The Statist*, July 18, 1885, cited in W. Turrentine Jackson, *The Enterprising Scot* (Edinburgh, 1968), 154.

[38]   Ibid., 137.

[39]   Ibid., 154.

[40]   Of the total foreign railroad investment, North America accounted for 44 percent and South America for an additional 20 percent.

[41]   Typescript manuscript, "The Forty Years of the Peruvian Corporation, 1896–1936," deposited with the Records of the Peruvian Corporation at University College, London.

[42]   Ibid., 21–2.

[43]   That surge was attributable to the activities of Canadian telephone (particularly Bell of Canada) and electric utilities (including Toronto, Northern, and Canadian Western).

Chapter 3

[1]   Sir John Clapham, *An Economic History of Great Britain* (Cambridge, 1952), II, 1.

[2]   Ibid., II, 39.

[3]   Ibid., III, 202–3.

[4]   Michael Edelstein, "Foreign Investment and Empire, 1860–1914," in McCloskey, D. and Floud, R. (eds.), *The New Economic History of Britain Since 1700* (Cambridge, 1981); Cairncross, *Home and Foreign Investment;* Albert Imlah, *Economic Elements in the Pax Britannica* (Cambridge, Mass., 1958).

5   Bernard Shaw and H. M. Stanley. Refer to discussion in Chapter 1.
6   R. A. Lehfeldt, "The Rate of Interest on British and Foreign Invest-ments," *Journal of the Royal Statistical Society*, January 1913, March 1914, and May 1915. George Paish, "Great Britain's Investment in Other Lands," *Journal of the Royal Statistical Society*, LXII, 1909.
7   R. L. Nash, *A Short Inquiry into the Profitable Nature of Our Investments* (London, 1880). Alexander Cairncross, *Home and Foreign Investment* (Cambridge, 1953). D. C. M. Platt contends that the figure for total British investment abroad, placed at four billion pounds by Imlah and Paish, is about 35 percent too high. "Britain's Investment Overseas in 1913," unpublished manuscript.
8   British capital was directed toward the British dominions and colonies by the Colonial Stock Act. By this measure as revised in 1900, the se-curities duly registered in the United Kingdom by the British colonial and dominion governments, which observed the applicable Treasury orders, were made eligible for inclusion among "Trustee Securities." Herbert Feis, *Europe, the World's Banker 1870–1914* (New Haven, Conn., 1930), 93.
9   Michael Edelstein, "Realized Rates of Return on U.K. Home and Over-seas Portfolio Investment in the Age of High Imperialism," *Explorations in Economic History*, 13 (1976), 283–329. Also, Michael Edelstein, *Overseas Investment in the Age of High Imperialism: The United Kingdom, 1860–1914* (New York, 1982).
10 The reports of these 241 firms are on deposit in the Guild Hall Library of the City of London. The list of all 482 firms and the years covered by the study can be found in the appendix to this chapter. By decade, the number of firm years in each location was as follows:

	Domestic	Foreign	Imperial
1860–9	55	12	7
1870–9	72	15	10
1880–9	123	47	44
1890–9	176	85	107
1900–9	202	98	130
1910–12	163	72	106

11 The Exchange required that firms listed provide annual information on profits and on assets and liabilities. Most firms filed the required report, although it appears that in cases of particularly poor profits they tended at times to "forget." There is, however, no evidence that failure to report was associated with their location.
12 In addition, the complete records of twelve firms in the stockholder sample were also utilized. For these we have *both* sets of records (re-ported and actual).

13 The two most extreme sets of estimates were calculated for all industries. The low series were based on the narrowest definition of profits. They include as costs all interest charges; all payments to owners, trustees, and managers except those labeled dividends or profit distribution; all depreciation or asset revaluations; and all sums allocated to any reserve. The high series is based on a somewhat broader definition of profits. It includes as profits all payments of interest and salaries to owners, management bonuses and directors and trustee fees, all transfers to any but strictly business reserves, and all irregular depreciation charges and asset revaluations, but it still excludes interest payments to nonowners.

14 As before, a number of alternative measures have been calculated (including good will, gross rather than net assets, etc.), but the results again appear insensitive to the choice of measure.

15 Although the Stock Exchange classified Antony Gibbs as a bank, its various branches tended more to resemble commercial and industrial enterprises, and in this study they have, consequently, been so classified.

16 Records of the Metropolitan Tower Construction Company, Board of Directors Meeting, August 1906.

17 Tarkwa Trading Co., General Meeting of May 7, 1908.

18 Ibid.

19 Liebig Co., Annual General Meeting, 1900.

20 Ibid., 1909.

21 Antony Gibbs and Sons Records, 11041, Antony Gibbs and Sons to the Japanese Ambassador in London, November 3, 1911.

22 Ibid., E. Yamaza, Japanese Chargé D'Affairs, to Gibbs and Co., London, November 7, 1911.

23 Donald McCloskey, "Did Victorian Britain Fail?," *Economic History Review*, 2nd series, vol. XXIII, no. 3 (December 1970).

24 The rates reported for British rails and for Indian roads before 1885 are estimated from the partial balance sheets reported in the *Investors Monthly Manual*, and Parliamentary Papers provide the data for the later period.

25 The Cunard Co. Annual Meeting of the Board of Directors, 1902.

26 Ibid.

27 E. J. Hobsbaum, *Labouring Men: Studies in the History of Labour* (Newport, 1969), Chapter 9; and T. I. Williams, *A History of the British Gas Industry* (Oxford, 1981).

28 L. Hannah, *Electricity before Nationalization* (Baltimore, 1979), 177.

29 Platt, *Business Imperialism, 1840–1930* (Oxford, 1977); Jones and Greenhill, "Public Utility Companies," 86–7.

30 To compound the difficulty, it is not even clear what constitutes the appropriate set of industry weights. Be that as it may, this first measure attempts to adjust for differences in capital structure by including in returns all returns to capital (both debt and equity) instead of merely returns to equity. The numerator includes all interest payments in ad-

dition to the returns to equity. The numerator is the same measure of adjusted assets that has been used through most of this chapter.

[31] The numerator of this measure sums all returns to ownership (i.e., partner's interest plus preference dividends plus amortization and sinking fund plus P&E writeoff plus capital expenditure plus transfer to other reserves plus redemption of debenture and loan plus income taxes plus unrecorded capital assets plus irregular depreciation plus ordinary dividends plus good will writeoff plus capitalized expense plus deposit capital interest plus net profits plus windfall gains plus gains of sale of securities plus miscellaneous revenues plus premiums on new shares issues, unaccounted transfer, miscellaneous transfer plus government subsidy plus premiums, minus debenture interest minus miscellaneous interest minus bond interest minus depreciation regular minus asset writeoff miscellaneous minus investment writeoff minus bad debt writeoff minus losses minus transfer to business reserves minus trade association payments minus general and miscellaneous expenses as profit distribution minus miscellaneous loss and charges minus capital losses minus insurance funds, pension funds). The denominator is the value of contributed equity (i.e., unincorporated capital plus deposit capital plus ordinary shares plus preferred shares plus other shares plus premium shares, minus good will).

[32] The second measure is the rate of return (high) on the book value of symbolic capital less the book value of good will or, in the case of partnerships or sole proprietorships, the returns on invested capital less ploughbacks and good will, if any (there seldom was). The third measure is similar to the measures reported in the earlier sections of this chapter – the rate of return on total assets less good will. The sector is a merged conglomerate of the three goods-producing industries: commercial and industrial, brewing and distilling, and iron and steel.

[33] It would, of course, be preferable if the industries were weighted to reflect their importance in the economies of the three regions. Unfortunately, we do not know enough about the economic structures of the regions to produce a reasonable set of weights. For the United Kingdom such a set of weights could be produced, but we know nothing of the economic structure of the foreign and Empire sectors.

Chapter 4

[1] The colony-weighted figure weights each colony or country equally (it is a simple average). The population-weighted figure weights each colony or country by its population:

$$\text{PW average} = \frac{E\,(\text{Budget item x Population})}{E\,\text{Population}}$$

Neither measure is without its problems. The colony-weighted measure is affected by the very small colonies. It appears that there existed some minimum level of expenditure and, no matter how small the colony, expenditures never fell below that amount. Thus the Falkland Islands present as much of a problem to imperial quantitative historians as they do to Argentine admirals. As to the population-weighted measure, Egypt with its 7,000,000 people tends to distort expenditures in the dependent colonies. Thus two adjustments have been made. For the colony-weight measure, the top and bottom 5 percent of colonies in any expenditure category have been screened out, and for the population-weighted measure, Egypt has been excluded.

2   Because of the wide spectrum of the public–private mix in railroad ownership and the range of maturities of loans, all are reported net of the capital and working expenses of railroads and of debt repayment.

3   The latter category was included partly for convenience – it is sometimes very difficult to separate educational from religious expenditures – and in part because policy makers often viewed religious instruction as an integral part of the investment in human capital.

4   Per capita GNP in Australia in 1901–3 was about £53.

5   Iddesleigh Papers, Northcote to Disraeli, November 17, 1866.

6   Ibid.

7   Charles Holt, *The Role of State Government in the 19th Century American Economy: 1820–1902* (New York, 1977), 107–11, 268–71, and 311–12. John Legler, *Regional Distribution of Federal Receipts and Expenditures in the 19th Century: A Quantitative Study*, Ph.D. dissertation, Purdue University, 1967, 86.

8   Milner Papers, Milner to R. Churchill, September 8, 1902.

9   John Holt Papers, December 18, 1902.

10 John Lawrence Papers, F.90, vol.30, no.62, Lawrence to Wood, October 19, 1865.

11 Ibid., Lawrence to Northcote, January 18, 1868.

12 Ibid., vol.31, no.31, Lawrence to Cranbrook, August 31, 1866.

13 Iddesleigh Papers, 50048, Northcote to Sir A. Cotton, January 18, 1868.

14 Bulwer-Lytton Papers, E 218/3/3, Lytton to Cranbrook, June 2, 1878.

15 Devonshire Papers, Devonshire to Ripon, January 14, 1881.

16 Ripon Papers, no.43575, viceregal minutes, July 4, 1881.

17 Curzon Papers, F.111/158, no.2–21, Curzon to Hamilton, February 16, 1899.

18 This fact is almost certainly a reflection of the nature of the sample – because there was some railway construction in the Princely States. In the early years, the government of India had been cool to their desire to build railways, but later, for political reasons, it, in some cases, actively encouraged construction. Hyderabad, for example, was urged to build a state railway and to do so with British support. Even in our sample, Cochin, Rampur, and Mysore all devoted some funds to state-owned railroads.

19 The U.S. statistics are from *Historical Statistics of the United States: Colonial Times to 1870* (Washington, D.C., 1975), part II, series Y752, 1131; and

Y821, 1134. Prussian figures are from *The Stateman's Yearbook*, 1913 (London, 1913), 920.

20 For early evidence of this, see John Lawrence Papers, F.90, vol.25, no.55, Wood to Lawrence, October 15, 1864; Mayo Papers, vol.37, no.289, Mayo to C. Saunders, October 10, 1869.

21 Mayo Papers, vol.44, no.199, Mayo to Argyll, September 1, 1871.

22 Gladstone Papers, vol.44286, no.253, Ripon to Gladstone, October 22, 1881. A similar opinion was expressed in Devonshire Papers, 794, Devonshire to Ripon, July 1, 1881.

23 Randolph Churchill Papers, no.1011, memorandum of October 1885.

24 Crewe Papers, Hardinge to Crewe, February 9, 1911.

25 Davidson Papers, Davidson to Colonial Office, November 3, 1908.

26 Ripon Papers, 43567, memorandum of August 4, 1882.

27 Morley Papers, D.573–17, Folio 41, Minto to Morley, June 17, 1908.

Chapter 5

1 *Hansard*, May 31, 1860. Other similar debates were held on June 28, 1860; March 5, 1861; March 4, 1862; June 27, 1864; July 25, 1864; February 21, 1865.

2 Donald C. Gordon, *The Dominion Partnership and Imperial Defense, 1870–1914* (Baltimore, 1965), 14.

3 *Hansard*, March 4, 1862.

4 Onslow Papers 173–9, statement by the Rt. Hon. Richard Seddon on the defences of the colony, 1900.

5 CO 48/513, Treasury cutting, Cape 9123, Treasury to Colonial Office, May 27, 1886.

6 CO 48/520, minuting by Meade addressed to Edward Wingfield, October 27, 1886.

7 Clarendon Papers, Cardwell to Granville, No. GO-C500, received 1/69.

8 CO 129/243, Treasury to Colonial Office, September 26, 1889. Ibid., draft Colonial Office to Treasury, October 17, 1887.

9 Gregory to Colonial Office, 1841, cited in J.K. Chapman, *The Career of Arthur Hamilton Gordon, First Lord Stanmore* (Toronto, 1964), 310.

10 CO 273/163, Colonial Office to Treasury, September 18, 1889.

11 Ibid., minuting August 17, 1889.

12 By 1900 the Treasury Chest made £700,000 available annually at 17 sites: Kesner, 167.

13 CO 267/456, War Office to Treasury, December 3, 1900.

14 CO 267/509, War Office to Colonial Office, May 27, 1908; CO 267/514, War Office to Colonial Office; CO 267/514, War Office to Colonial Office, October 25, 1909.

15 Sanderson Papers, FP 800, Salisbury to Sanderson, no date, probably sometime in 1897.

16 Ibid., minute of September 21, 1807.

17 T.7/11, Treasury to Colonial Office, March 22, 1862.

18 Ibid., Treasury to Colonial Office, April 26, 1862.

[19] Hicks-Beach Papers, Hicks-Beach to Frere, December 25, 1878.
[20] Hicks-Beach Papers, Wolseley to Hicks-Beach, February 2, 1880.
[21] T.7/20, Treasury to Colonial Office, September 27, 1880. T.7/21, Treasury to Colonial Office, January 23, 1882.
[22] Hicks-Beach Papers, Frere to Hicks-Beach, February 3, 1879.
[23] Ibid., Frere to Hicks-Beach, August 26, 1879.
[24] T.7/21, Treasury to Colonial Office, January 23, 1882.
[25] T.7/20, Treasury to Colonial Office, January 22, 1881.
[26] T.7/27, Treasury to Colonial Office, March 20, 1891.
[27] CO 48/599, Treasury to Colonial Office, January 8, 1908.
[28] Lowe to Gladstone, cited in C.P. Stacey, *Canada and the British Army, 1866–71* (New York, 1936), 125.
[29] Gladstone Papers, Lyttelton to Gladstone, No. 95, July 27, 1865.
[30] Newcastle Papers, Newcastle to Sir Charles Monk, Governor General of Canada, June 30, 1863.
[31] Stacey, *Canada and the British Army*, 128–9.
[32] Gladstone Papers 44142, Derby to Gladstone, July 7, 1883.
[33] A British presence continued at Esquimalt and Halifax, two imperial fortresses until Haldane's reforms of 1906–7.
[34] *Hansard*, June 13, 1866.
[35] T.7/20, Treasury to Colonial Office, November 30, 1880.
[36] T.7/27, Treasury to Colonial Office, May 11, 1894.
[37] Hicks-Beach Papers, D. 2455/PCC 8/5, Hicks-Beach to Wolseley, November 11, 1879, quoting Wolseley.
[38] Ibid.
[39] Selborne Papers MS 1868, 192–4, Selborne to Gladstone, April 22, 1883.
[40] R. Churchill Papers, No. 2046, Stanhope to Churchill, November 22, 1886.
[41] CO 209/235, Normanby to Carnarvon, April 27, 1876.
[42] Gladstone Papers, 44142, No. 122, Derby to Gladstone, April 1, 1885.
[43] *Hansard*, November 28, 1868, moved by Sir Stafford Northcote and passed.
[44] John Lawrence Papers, Lawrence to Northcote, November 4, 1867.
[45] Ibid., Lawrence to Northcote, January 2, 1868.
[46] Iddesleigh Papers, Lawrence to Northcote, January 20, 1868.
[47] *Hansard* (Lords), July 25, 1882, and Northbrooke Papers, C.144/2, Ripon to Hartington, July 26, 1882.
[48] Northbrooke Papers, C.144/2, 43513, Gladstone to Ripon, November 21, 1881.
[49] Ibid., 143523, Kimberley to Ripon, January 11, 1883.
[50] Curzon Papers, Hamilton to Curzon, February 27, 1903.
[51] E.A. Benians, et al., *Cambridge History of the British Empire* (Cambridge, 1959), III, 239.
[52] *Hansard* (Lords), July 30, 1907. The increase took effect in 1902. Of the £240,000, Australia was to contribute £200,000 and New Zealand £40,000. The First Lord of the Admiralty, Lord Tweedmouth, placed the annual cost of the squadron at the low figure of £581,954.

53 CAB 5 (Cabinet Papers), Colonial Defence, 1909.
54 *Hansard*, February 29, 1904.
55 *Hansard* (Lords), July 30, 1907, Lord Tweedmouth.
56 CO 201/590, Jervois to Mead, December 1, 1879.
57 Chamberlain Papers, JC 9/2/lk/4, Minto to Laurier, June 19, 1899. Ibid., JC 9/2/lk/5, Laurier to Minto, July 30, 1899.
58 Ibid., Chamberlain to Fielding, April 2, 1903.
59 Ibid., Hicks-Beach to Chamberlain, no date, but some time in 1901–2.
60 Hicks-Beach Papers, D. 2455/PCC/34, Hicks-Beach to Salisbury, September 13, 1901.
61 Richard Jebb, *The Imperial Conference* (London, 1911), II, 160. At the time of the 1911 conference, colonial naval subsidies were as follows: Australia, £200,000; New Zealand, £40,000; Cape Colony, £50,000; Natal, £35,000; Newfoundland, £3,000; Canada, 0.
62 *Hansard* (Lords), July 30, 1907, Lord Tweedmouth. Background material in Cabinet S/1, Committee of Imperial Defence, vol. I, Colonial Defence, May 1903.
63 The cost of a capital ship was £1,700,000 or more.
64 The increase occurred in 1897 for Mauritius, 1898 for the Straits, and 1900 for Hong Kong. CO 273/208, Treasury to Colonial Office, June 14, 1895; CO 129/303, Treasury to Colonial Office, June 15, 1900; T.7/381, Treasury to Colonial Office, March 11, 1911.
65 CO 273/208, Treasury to Colonial Office, June 14, 1895.
66 CO 273/391, Straits 1420, Treasury to Colonial Office, January 31, 1912.
67 K. Marx, *The New York Daily Tribune*, no. 5123, September 21, 1857; reprinted in K. Marx and F. Engels, *The First Indian War of Independence 1857–1859*, 86–90 (London, 1960).
68 The allocations are made on the basis of the location of manpower. The two estimates differ because of the allocation of the Mediterranean fleet. In "1" it is placed in the Empire while in "2" it is considered part of home defense. The naval allocation for the period 1893–1912 is made on the basis of the distribution in 1893.
69 Some problems are raised by the experience of World War I. This study stops in 1912. One might, therefore, argue that the colonies always recognized a finite probability that they would be called upon to contribute to a major campaign, and that the dating of the study (encompassing as it does the period when benefits were high but excluding the period of very high costs) badly distorts the cost/benefit calculation. Certainly the real costs of the First World War were substantial. Of the 867,000 Empire military dead, 726,000 were from the United Kingdom, 119,000 from the colonies with responsible government, and 22,000 from India. Still the evidence suggests that the argument is probably not correct. In the first place there was never any direct coercion by the British in raising resources (human and otherwise) from the Empire. Moreover, although there was a military draft in the United Kingdom after 1915, the Empire troops (with the exception of a few engendered by an archaic Canadian conscription bill passed toward the end of that

year) were volunteers throughout. In the second place, although Britain had the power to commit the Empire to war in 1914, the speed at which the colonies with responsible government entered the Second World War – at a time when Britain had lost that power – was no less than it had been in 1914. It was clearly the close cultural (rather than the political) relations that brought about entry in 1914 and 1939 rather than (as with the United States) 1917 and 1941. Samuel Dumas and Ko Vedel-Petersen, *Losses of Life Caused by War* (London, Oxford Press, 1923), 135–9.

Chapter 6

[1]   Regarding the Sudan loan see Edward Grey Papers, FO 800/48, 88. On the Newfoundland loan see Gladstone Papers, 44227, no. 175, Kimberley to Gladstone, June 12, 1882; 44545, no. 151, Kimberley to Gladstone, June 14, 1882. With reference to Barbados, Carnarvon Papers, PRO 30/6, vol. 7(3), no. 78, Carnarvon to Northcote, July 4, 1876.

[2]   Carnarvon Papers, PRO 30/6, vol. 7(3), no. 79, Northcote to Carnarvon, July 6, 1876.

[3]   *Hansard*, August 15, 1907.

[4]   CO 137/606, Treasury to Colonial Office, August 21, 1899.

[5]   CO 137/660, Treasury to Colonial Office, May 7, 1901.

[6]   Harcourt Papers, Box 483, no. 2, Harcourt to Sir Percy Girouard, Governor of the East African Protectorate, March 9, 1911.

[7]   Milner Papers, Box 169 (deposit 46), vol. 44, Colonial Office to Treasury, 1901.

[8]   Crown Agents Records, CA (17) 60, cited in Kesner, 86.

[9]   *Statistical Abstract for the Several Colonies and Possessions of the United Kingdom*, cited in E. A. Benians, et al., *The Cambridge History of the British Empire* (Cambridge, 1959), III, 197.

[10] Carnarvon Papers, PRO 30/6, vol. 7(3), no. 43, Northcote to Carnarvon, February 9, 1875.

[11] A comparison of Indian and colonial issues with rates paid by UK local authorities indicate that there was no significant difference between the Indian and UK rates after 1900, but there was before that date. In the case of dependent colonies there was a significant difference before 1900 and probably one thereafter. For those colonies with responsible government there was a significant difference both before and after. In no case, however, were the differences large. They amounted in the most extreme cases to about .7 percent, but most were smaller. In each case, responsible governments paid more than the dependent colonies, and after 1900 that difference appears to have been significant. However, the differences were about 1/7 of 1 percent in the years before 1900 and about .2 percent thereafter. See Table 8.2 for the exact figures. As compared with foreign–developed countries, however, the differences ran the other way and may have been as much as 3 percent before 1900 and probably about 1 percent thereafter. Again see Table 8.2.

12 Carnarvon Papers PRO 30/6, vol. 17(6), no. 21, Carnarvon to W. H. Smith, March 25, 1875.

13 Ibid., vol. 7(4), no. 98, Carnarvon to Northcote, January 8, 1877.

14 It should be noted that the issue date of the shares does not always conform to the date of acceptance on the Official List. In general, acceptance took a few months, so that it was normal for shares issued in the last three or four months of the year to appear on the list for the following year. In the case of some foreign issues, however, the delay could be as much as a decade or more, although this was rare.

15 The years selected were 1882, 1885, 1887, 1891, 1893, 1894, 1895, 1896, 1898, 1899, 1900, 1903, 1904, 1905, 1906, 1909, 1910, and 1912.

16 Calculations based on minimum maturities produced results that often made no sense. Few shareholders, apparently, believed that a country was prepared to exercise its right of immediate redemption. If it had been otherwise, it would be difficult to explain payments substantially more than par on issues with a zero minimum maturity.

17 Initial runs included a dummy variable for countries (or colonies), cities, and states (or provinces). These results are not reported since they add nothing to the question of the imperial subsidy. Local units appear to have had to pay more than national units, but the difference seems to be independent of membership in the Empire. In some runs, data were at times continuous; in some, a dummy for pre- and post-1900; and, in some, the sample was split at the end of 1900. Runs were made both with and without average maturity since there was concern about the use of maturity in the yield calculations.

18 The coefficient is significant at the 7-percent level in the maximum case, but only at the 67-percent level in the average case.

19 The levels of significance on those differences are not great in any case, but the latter may be marginally significant at levels researchers are likely to quote. The latter result is somewhat surprising in light of the supposed effects of the new Colonial Stock Act, but it probably reflects the growing esteem that investors felt for the issues of Canada, Oceania, and South Africa and underlines the importance of the act if the dependent colonies were to retain their previous position.

20 Karl Marx, *New York Daily Tribune* #5243, February 9, 1858. Reprinted in *The First Indian War of Independence 1857–1859*, 124–8.

21 Calculations of the interest subsidy: (1) The amount of loans outstanding was calculated for each government class for each year by summing the issues for a number of previous years (thirty-four for colonies with responsible government, thirty-one for dependent colonies, and thirty for India). Those numbers are the average maturities for the new issues on the London market 1882–1912. The data on annual issues are from Chapter 2. For the years before 1865 Indian debt was assumed to be zero. For the colonies borrowing 1850 to 1864 was assumed to have been at the average level 1865–9. For the years before 1850 it was assumed to have been zero. (2) The rate subsidy was calculated by subtracting the implied rate differential between Empire and foreign borrowing from

the maximum maturity estimated presented in Table 6.2A. For India the subtraction was foreign–underdeveloped (4.26) less India (.64); for the dependent colonies it was foreign–underdeveloped (4.26) less dependent (.85); and for the colonies with responsible government it was foreign–developed (2.04) less responsible (1.14). The implied rate subsidies are then: responsible government, .90; dependent colonies, 3.41; and India, 3.62 percent. [If the rate differentials implied by the average instead of the maximum maturities had been used, the figures would have been responsible government, 3.66; dependent colonies, 4.59; and India, 2.45. This alternative would have increased the subsidies accruing to the colonies with responsible government and the dependent colonies, but reduced the Indian subsidy. Overall the total estimate would have increased substantially (from £210,091 to £464,483 or from £.02 to £.04 per capita).] (3) For each year the rate subsidy was multiplied by the estimate of the volume of loans outstanding.

[22] Gladstone Papers, 4427, Kimberley to Gladstone, June 22, 1882.

[23] Howard Robinson, *Carrying British Mail Overseas* (New York, 1964), 234–5.

[24] Kesner, 122–6.

[25] Ibid., 142–5.

[26] Ibid., 136.

[27] It should be remembered that these totals do not include implicit interest payments on capital advances nor do they reflect any payment to India or the colonies with responsible government.

[28] Kesner, 34–43.

[29] Sir Andrew Cohen, *British Policy in Changing Africa* (Evanston, 1959), 12.

[30] Kesner, 51–2.

[31] The number was temporarily raised to three in 1895. Brian Blakeley, *The Colonial Office 1868–1892* (Durham, 1972), 94–5.

[32] C. 3073, Papers Explanatory of the Functions of the Crown Agents for the Colonies, August, 1881, no. 6, Colonial Office to Treasury, November 26, 1880.

[33] C. 4473, February, 1909, Report of the Committee of Enquiry into the Organization of the Crown Agents' Office, V.

[34] Kesner, 61.

[35] Ibid., 57.

[36] House of Commons Papers, 194, June, 1904, "Return showing how many Firms were invited by the Crown Agents to Tender for the Supply of each of the following Articles, etc."

[37] Ibid.

[38] The figures were £2,541,936 for 1904; £2,455,066 for 1909; £2,104,104 for 1910; £2,216,787 for 1911; and £2,536,844 for 1912. Parliamentary Papers (194 of 1904; Cd 5391 of 1909; Cd5774 of 1910; Cd 6279 of 1911, and Cd 6862 of 1912).

[39] A. W. Abbott, *A Short History of the Crown Agents and Their Office* (London, 1952), 1–2.

[40] A. W. Abbott, "The Crown Agents as an Issuing House" (unpublished), Chapter 1, p.8.

[41] Blakely, 94–5.

[42] Milner Papers, Milner to Lyttelton, September 3, 1904.

[43] Kesner, 85–6.

[44] New Zealand marketed £21 million; the Cape, £13 million; Natal, £9 million; and Western Australia, more than £1 million.

[45] The last issues handled by the Crown Agents were, for example, 1881 for the Cape, 1883 for New Zealand, and 1902 for Natal. See Crown Agents Papers.

[46] F. Lavington, *The English Capital Market* (London, 1921), 197.

[47] Ibid., 199.

[48] Records of the Crown Agents, File 42A, Malaya, 1906–7.

[49] Records of the Crown Agents, File A.6.

[50] Ibid., File A.67, Anderson to Crewe, October 18, 1910.

[51] Ibid., Crown Agents to Colonial Office, December 23, 1910.

[52] Records of the Crown Agents, File A.50, Blake to Sir Matthew Nathan, February 9, 1906.

[53] Ibid., A. W. Abbott, File 60, "The Crown Agents as an Issuing House."

[54] Records of the Crown Agents, File A.100, 1891.

[55] Ibid., Abbott, "Issuing House," File 60.

[56] Ibid., Records of the Crown Agents, File A.100, 1903.

[57] Cd. 4473, 1909, App. III.

[58] Kesner, 85–6.

[59] Figures are drawn from Parliamentary Papers LXX (1867–68), LXVIII (1870), LXXIV (1885–7), Cd. 7241, 1914 (1910–12), and CO. 442.

Chapter 7

[1] All firms listed in the index in any year ending in three or seven were brought together and duplicates eliminated. This purged master list became the universe from which the three samples were drawn. For firms still in existence in 1973 the records remain in the Companies Record Offices (CRO) in London and Edinburgh. For them, although some files had been misplaced, no serious problems were encountered in finding the records of the firms selected. The same was true for a small number of now defunct firms whose records still remain in the possession of the CRO. The records of most defunct firms, however, had been turned over to the Public Record Office (PRO). For firms registered in Britain and Wales, records are held in London and constitute the basis for PRO series BT-31. Records of Scottish firms are held in Edinburgh as PRO series BT-2. For these latter (Scottish) firms, all records had been preserved, and there was no problem in finding the desired stockholder lists. In the case of defunct British and Welsh companies, however, there were serious problems. In the first place, records had been saved for only every fifth year. In the second place, for "small" firms the PRO had retained only a 5-percent sample of firms registered.

For concerns whose records had been destroyed, replacement was made by choosing the firm of similar location and industry nearest to the originally selected firm in the *Yearbook* that first listed the selected firm. Moreover, since our interest was in "public imperialists" (as opposed to persons who organized imperial enterprises), the focus was on the lists three or four years after the date of incorporation. In the case of the defunct British and Welsh companies, however, the PRO's selection procedure limited the choice. As a result, some lists are from firms only two years old and some from firms as old as six.

2   Most of the major UK railroads were chartered and in operation well before 1862 (the exceptions were a few small lines like "The Lizard") and it was difficult to produce a sample that was comparable to the foreign and Empire roads.

3   See Appendix 7.1. The category "peers and gents" includes anyone who had a title, an honorary title (e.g., JP or DL), or who classified himself as a "Gent."

4   At times the shares "owned" by one person were held in the name of another (the nominee).

5   Often the railroad shares were listed as owned, for example, by J. R. T. Hughes, accountant, and another.

6   A complete enumeration of the counties included in each region is contained in Appendix 7.2.

7   If, for example, the company was the Aberdeen Land and Cattle Company, and, if one of the towns in question was in Aberdeen, it was chosen. Similarly, if the stockholder in question appeared next to another entry with the same town name, but with county included, that county was chosen. The sources for county classifications were John Bartholomew, *The Survey Gazeteer of the British Isles*, 8th edition (Edinburgh, 1932) and *Cassell's Gazeteer of Great Britain and Ireland*, 3 vols. (London, 1899).

8   In this context, the value and total value refer to the amount actually raised, not the face value of the security. For each firm the percentage is calculated and then those percentages are averaged across all firms in an industry–location. Thus each firm, no matter what its size, carries equal weight.

9   The income (dividends plus capital gains) from a class of securities received by an occupational group or that income as compared with the total income of the group are examples of such alternative measures.

10 R. Dudley Baxter, *The Taxation of the United Kingdom* (London, 1869).

11 By period the figures were:

	1860–79	1880–9	1900–19	Total
Manufacturing	12	23	27	62
Food, distilling, tobacco	1	14	19	34
Commerce/finance	16	23	54	93

If half-millionaires are included, the totals are 337 (mfg.) and 344; W. D. Rubinstein, *Men of Property* (London, 1981), 61–7.

[12] Appendix 7.3 displays average shareholdings and measures of their distribution by location and occupation.

[13] See page 209.

[14] It should be clear that the term "two markets" is used to describe the geographic composition of stockholders in home and overseas enterprise, not the degree of economic separation between the London and non-London markets. Clearly, there were many stockholders in both London and the provinces who bought both home and overseas shares, thus there is no reason to suppose that there was not an effective arbitrage mechanism between the two. In fact, in both cases the market is the London Stock Exchange – a single economic entity.

[15] Rubenstein, 103.

[16] The data are constructed by first calculating the home, foreign, and Empire distribution of the "average stockholder." Second, the holdings of each occupational group were expressed as a fraction of that "typical" precentage; and finally, the foreign and Empire figures were compared with domestic.

$$\frac{\% \text{ industry-elite}}{\% \text{ in ``all'' industry-elite}} \Bigg/ \frac{\% \text{ in industry-business}}{\% \text{ in ``all'' industry-business}}$$

[17] Joseph Schumpeter, *Imperialism, Social Classes: Two Essays* (New York, Noon Day Press, 1955), 74–7.

[18]
$$\frac{\% \text{ of the value of shares sectors F or E held in location X}}{\% \text{ of the value of shares of all UK securities held in location X}}$$

[19]
$$\frac{{}^{19}\% \text{ of UK F or E in industry X held in London}}{\% \text{ of UK F or E in ``all'' industries held in London}}$$

$$\frac{\% \text{ of UK F or E in industry X held in non-London}}{\% \text{ of UK F or E in ``all'' industries held in non-London}}$$

[20]
$$\frac{\text{Value held by non-London merchants in UK}}{\text{Total value held by non-London merchants in UK, F and E}}$$

$$\frac{\text{Value held by London merchants in UK}}{\text{Total value held by all London merchants in UK, F and E}}$$

Chapter 8

[1] Although the term "middle class" has not been precisely defined in all contexts it is used here in much the same context as it is used by Hobs-

bawn in *Labouring Men*. While public officials and the clergy have been assigned to the elite category, the middle class includes shopkeepers, billposters, printers, bookmakers, boardinghouse keepers, insurance agents, commercial travelers, and clerks. See E. J. Hobsbawn, *Labouring Men* (New York, Anchor Books, 1967), 316–17.

2   Unless otherwise noted, the data are drawn from the same sources used to analyze the composition of public expenditures (Chapter 4). The reader should approach this work with the same caveats regarding the size of the political unit.

3   The largest part of the post-1890s decline, however, is a statistical artifact reflecting the changes in weights that accompanied the formation of the Commonwealth of Australia. It is much less apparent in the population based series.

4   The coefficient of variation is .88 for the colonies and 1.07 for the underdeveloped countries.

5   Gladstone Papers, 4424, 137, Kimberley to Gladstone, May 22, 1871.

6   The Commonwealth broadened its revenue sources and the rates declined to about 62 percent.

7   Hicks-Beach Papers, D2455, PCC/3/4, Bartle Frere to Hicks-Beach, January 17, 1880

8   Carnarvon Papers, PRO 30/6/7, 164, Carnarvon to the Chancellor of the Exchequer, October 27, 1874.

9   Milner Papers, Milner to Browne, September 18, 1904.

10 Carnarvon Papers, PRO 36/6/38 (18), 375, Wolseley to Carnarvon, August 27, 1875.

11 Gladstone Papers, 44320, 112, Hamilton Gordon to Gladstone, May 3, 1871.

12 Carnarvon Papers, PRO 30/6/41 (19), 73, W. Robinson to Carnarvon, February 14, 1875.

13 John Lawrence Papers, F.90/32A, 7, Lawrence to Cranborne, January 21, 1867.

14 Kilbracken Papers, F102/1, 95, Dawkins to Kilbracken, December 7, 1879.

15 Bulwer-Lytton Papers (3) E.218/3/2, pp. 1034–5, Sales to Lytton, November 23, 1877.

16 Mayo Papers, 42, Mayo to Argyll, March 22, 1871.

17 John Lawrence Papers, 42, Lawrence to Northcote, July 16, 1867.

18 Bulwer-Lytton Papers (8) E.218/3/4, pp. 394–5, Lytton to Cranbrook, September 18, 1877.

19 Randolph Churchill Papers, memo 1011, October 28, 1903.

20 Curzon Papers, F.111/162, 2–269–70, Curzon to St. John Brodrick, October 28, 1903.

21 John Lawrence Papers, F.90/31, no. 13, p. 3., Lawrence to Lord De Grey, March 20, 1860.

22 Ibid., F.90/31, Letter no. 60, Lawrence to Cranborne, December 22, 1866.

23 Gladstone Papers, 44229, 92, Kimberley to Gladstone, June 11, 1893.

24 Kilbracken Papers, F.102/5, 74, Northbrooke to Kilbracken, August 19, 1894.

[25] Bulwer-Lytton Papers (2–2) E.218/514/4, p. 347, Lytton to Cranbrook, May 12, 1879.

[26] Ibid., (4) E.218/3/3, p. 635, Lytton to Stanhope, September 8, 1878.

[27] Iddesleigh Papers, 50023, 37, Lawrence to Northcote, March 25, 1867.

[28] Mayo Papers, 34, Mayo to Argyll, February 21, 1869.

[29] Bulwer-Lytton Papers (2–1) E.218/518/1, p. 312, Lytton to Salisbury, July 22, 1876.

[30] Ibid. (3) E.218/3/2, pp. 1042–3, Lytton to Sir Louis Mallet, November 30, 1877.

[31] Randolph Churchill Papers, 1010, Reay to Churchill, October 29, 1885.

[32] Crewe Papers, C/17, 59, Hardinge to Crewe, September 14, 1911.

[33] For the rest of this chapter the specific information on tax rates is drawn from either John Noble, *The Queen's Taxes: an Inquiry into the Amount, Incidence and Economic Results of the Taxation of the United Kingdom, Direct and Indirect* (London: 1870) or from W.M.J. Williams, *The King's Revenue, Being a Handbook to the Taxes and the Public Revenue* (London, 1908).

[34] Between 1860 and 1880 there were no specific excises on beer, but there was an excise duty on malt and, given contemporary brewing methods that worked out to 5s 5d a 36-gallon barrel. R. Dudley Baxter, *National Income: The United Kingdom* (London, 1869), 32.

[35] Figures from the Committee on National Debt and Taxation indicate that in 1913–14 the per capita consumption of beer was eight times as high for a family with an income of £50 a year than it was for a family earning £2,000. *Report of the Committee on National Debt and Taxation*, Cmd. 2800 1927, 90–2.

[36] Sir Robert Peel, speech of March 27, 1840; cited in John Noble, *The Queen's Taxes*, 221.

[37] Iddesleigh Papers, 50016, 158, Northcote to Disraeli, January 25, 1874.

[38] In 1902, the tax rate varied from a low of 2d to a high of 15d per pound.

[39] This figure compares with 1,190,000 in 1913–14 and 1,262,000 in 1868 (when the exemption was only £100 as opposed to the £160 in the later years). Of those reporting, income averaged £770. J. C. Stamp, *British Incomes and Property: The Application of Official Statistics to Economic Problems* (London, 1916), 432 and 449.

[40] The reader should be reminded that over the period 1860–1914 national income per head (in prices of 1900) rose from 19.4 to 43.7 [B. R. Mitchell and Phyllis Dean, *Abstract of British Historical Statistics* (Cambridge, 1962), 367–8].

[41] Cromer Papers, FO 633/18, 11, Bernard Mallet to Cromer, December 10, 1907.

[42] Asquith Papers, 11, 1624, Haldane to Asquith, August 9, 1908.

[43] In Chart 8.1, Panel A refers to incomes one-half earned and one-half from property and Panel B to earned income alone. The progressive estate duty makes a substantial difference in the two series for 1903–4, but the outlines are similar in the earlier years.

[44] The estimates for 1903–4 were made by the Committee on National Debt and Taxation and are as near to official as are available. For the earlier years, the distributions are hypothetical based on the weights used in

the 1903–4 figures, and the rates that prevailed in the years in question. No attempt has been made to estimate actual consumption levels for the earlier years. It is assumed they were the same as those prevailing in 1903–4. In the case of sugar, for example, these are clearly unrealistic. The effect is certainly to overstate the relative tax burden on the lower income group. In addition, no adjustment has been made either for the increase in per capita income or for changes in the price level.

[45]   Baxter, 119.

[46]   Leone Levi, *Wages and Earnings of the Working Classes* [Shannon, Ireland, 1971 (first edition London, 1885)], 63–5.

[47]   Twelve separate studies (including Baxter's) place the working classes' share of income between .36 and .43, with an average value of .395. That compares very closely to Baxter's .39 estimate. The latest study (1908) puts the share at .38. See Stamp, 427.

[48]   Baxter, 36.

[49]   Of the thirty-three largest British fortunes probated between 1860 and 1912, twenty-eight were businessmen. While this preponderance largely reflects the inheritance laws, it does suggest that there were many rich businessmen. W. D. Rubenstein, "The Victorian Middle Classes: Wealth, Occupation, and Geography," *Economic History Review*, 2nd series, vol. XXX, no. 4 (November 1977).

[50]   Baxter, 36; Leone Levi, 48; and Williams, Income Tax Acts 1842–53, Classes 4 and 5, UK Schedules L and D 1905–6, 186–7.

[51]   In chronological order the estimates are: Levi, .22, 1867; Baxter, .19, 1867; Levi, .20, 1881; Giffen, .16, 1883; Levi, .19, 1883; Money, .21, 1904; Bowley, .20, 1907; Bowley (revised) .27, 1907; and Whittaker, .29, 1907. See Stamp, 427.

[52]   The ratio of assessments to taxpayers has been variously estimated between 1.8 to 3.0. See Stamp, *British Incomes*, 430–65. The 1906 assessment data are from Williams, *King's Revenue*, 186–7.

Chapter 9

[1]   Minutes of the Meetings of the Directors of the Sunderland and South Shields Water Co., February 15 and March 17, 1899.

[2]   Minutes of the Meetings of the Directors of Samuel Fox and Co., Ltd., August, 1896.

[3]   Minutes of the Annual Meetings of Shotts Iron Co., November, 1880.

[4]   Minutes of the Meetings of the Directors of Savely Coal and Iron Co., April 27, 1912.

[5]   Minutes of the Meetings of the Directors of the Barclay Perkins Brewery, April 23, 1903.

[6]   Minutes of the Meetings of the Proprietors of the City and West End Properties Co., May 11, 1906.

[7]   Records of Antony Gibbs and Co., no. 11039, Alban Gibbs to Balfour, July 2, 1905.

[8] Ibid., Hunsdon to Asquith, February 21, 1909.

[9] Ibid., 1041/2, Herbert Gibbs to Steel-Maitland, October 26, 1911.

[10] Ibid., 1042/1, Herbert Gibbs to Lomax, August 8, 1913.

[11] Clapham, II, 145.

[12] Minutes of the Meetings of the Associated Chambers of Commerce of the United Kingdom, February 21, 1877.

[13] Minutes of the Meetings of the Glasgow Chamber of Commerce, December 22, 1885.

[14] Minutes of the Meetings of the Liverpool Chamber of Commerce, October 31, 1903.

[15] Ibid.

[16] Minutes of the Meetings of the Glasgow Chamber of Commerce, May 12, 1872.

[17] Minutes of the Meetings of the London Chamber of Commerce, May 8, 1900. Minutes of Meetings of the the Birmingham Chamber of Commerce, May 20, 1891 and October 16, 1907.

[18] Lytton Papers, E.218/517/1, no. 201(a), Morley to Lytton, April 20, 1876.

[19] Ibid. (5) E.218/516/4, no. 8, Gathorn-Hardy to Lytton, February 4, 1879.

[20] Ibid. (6) E.218/516/4, no. 14, Gathorn-Hardy to Lytton, February 23, 1879.

[21] Kilbracken Papers, F.107, Kilbracken to Brodrick, October 23, 1903.

[22] Curzon Papers, F.111/161, no. 272, Hamilton to Curzon, August 13, 1902.

[23] Elgin Papers, F.84/299, no. 12, Godley to Elgin, March 2, 1894.

[24] Cross Papers, E.243/19, p.64, Cross to Lansdowne, March 22, 1889.

[25] Hardinge of Penshurst Papers, V, 927/Vc5, no. 291, Hardinge to Chirol, February 16, 1911.

[26] Winfried Baumgart, *Imperialism* (New York, 1982), 130.

[27] John S. Galbraith, *MacKinnon and East Africa 1878–1895* (Cambridge, 1972), 161.

[28] Platt, *Business Imperialism*, 1–14.

[29] Ripon Papers, Meade to Ripon, December 31, 1894.

[30] Records of Antony Gibbs and Sons, Herbert Gibbs to Mallet, 1041, December 23, 1907.

[31] Minutes of the Meetings of the Board of Directors of the Peruvian Corporation, December 1, 1898.

[32] Ibid.

[33] D. C. M. Platt, "The Imperialism of Free Trade: Some Reservations," *Economic History Review*, 2nd series, vol. XXI, no. 2, 1888.

[34] D. P. M. McCarthy, "The British in the Atacama Desert," *Journal of Economic History*, vol. 35, no. 1 (March 1975), 122.

[35] Peter Winn, "British Informal Empire in Uruguay in the Nineteenth Century," *Past and Present*, vol. 73 (November 1976), 115.

[36] D. C. M. Platt, *Latin America and British Trade 1800–1914* (London, 1972), 163.

[37] Nathan A. Pelcovits, *Old China Hands and the Foreign Office* (New York, 1948), VII.

[38] Dean Britten, "British Informal Empire: The Case of China," *The Journal of Commonwealth and Comparative Politics*, vol. XIV, no. 1 (March 1976).

[39] David McLean, "Commerce, Finance and British Diplomatic Support in China, 1885–1886," *Economic History Review*, vol. 26, no. 3 (August 1973), 464.

[40] James C. Ingram, *Economic Change in Thailand, 1850–1970* (Stanford, 1971), 2.

[41] Gladstone Papers, 44290, no. 176, Rosebery to Gladstone, August 26, 1893, quoted in Ian Brown, "British Financial Advisors in Siam in the Reign of King Chulalongkorn," *Modern Asian Studies*, vol. 12, no. 1 (February 1978), 200.

[42] Minutes of the Meetings of the Directors of the Bathurst Trading Co., June 3, 1904.

[43] Records of the British Imperial East Africa Co., MacKinnon to Salisbury, December 17, 1898.

[44] Ibid., Mackenzie to Smith, September 10, 1892.

[45] R. Robinson and J. Gallagher, *Africa and the Victorians* (London, 1961), 221.

[46] Appendix 9.1 displays the total of imperial and nonimperial bills by Parliament. Appendix 9.2 analyzes the imperial bills.

[47] There were no imperial bills or motions that went to division in either the short 1910 Parliament or in the first two years of the very long 1911 to 1919 session. Although not strictly accurate, the term session is synonymous with Parliament in this chapter.

[48] The sources included M. Stenton (and for volumes II and III, S. Lees), *Who's Who of British Members of Parliament* (London: 1976, 1978, 1979); *Who's Who* (London, 1959–); *Who Was Who* (London, 1897–); *The Dictionary of National Biography* (Oxford, 1926); *Burke's Genealogical and Heraldic History of the Landed Gentry* (London, 1892–); *Burke's Genealogical and Heraldic History of the Peerage, Baronetage and Knightage* (London, 1907–).

[49] Constituency data were drawn from J. Vincent and M. Stenton (eds.), *McCalmont's Parliamentary Poll Book 1832–1918* (Brighton: Harvester Press, 1971); F. W. S. Craig, *British Parliamentary Election Results 1832–1885 and 1885–1918* (London, 1977 and 1974); and Michael Kinnear, *The British Voter* (Ithaca, 1968). Winning margin is defined as the margin over the most successful losing candidate (there were some multimember districts) divided by the total number of votes cast in the district.

[50] The r^2's in the case of the all-parliaments regressions are .10 for the Conservatives and .09 for the Liberals; the "F" values, however, are 9.28 and 6.86, respectively.

[51] J. E. T. Rogers, *The Economic Interpretation of History, Lectures Delivered at Worcester College Hall, Oxford, 1887–8* (London, 1888), 380.

[52] J. E. Cairnes, "Colonization and Colonial Government," reprinted in *Essays in Political Economy Theoretical and Applied* (London, 1873).

[53] J. E. T. Rogers, op. cit., 378–439, cited in John C. Wood, *British Economists and Empire* (New York, 1983), 59.

Chapter 10

1   M. K. Gandhi, *The Collected Works of Mahatma Gandhi* (Delhi, 1958), XII,
    505.

2   David Wells, "Great Britain and the United States: Their True Relations,"
    North American Review, CLXII (April 1896).

3   Punch, August 17, 1878, cited in Koebner and Schmidt, *Imperialism* (Cam-
    bridge, 1965), 148.

4   Letter to Lord Malmesbury cited in W. F. Monepenny and G. E. Buckle,
    August 13, 1852, *The Life of Benjamin Disraeli, Earl of Beaconsfield* (London,
    1914), IV (1868–1876), 385.

5   K. Marx and F. Engels, *The First Indian War of Independence 1857–1859*
    (London, 1960), 86–90, *New York Daily.Tribune*, no. 5123, September 21,
    1857.

6   Speech to the National Union, June 24, 1872, cited in Buckle, V (1868–
    1876), 195.

7   P. Magnus, *Gladstone, A Biography* (London, 1954), 237.

8   Ibid., 287.

9   Buckle, *Disraeli*, V, 195.

10 Speech to London Chamber of Commerce, May 14, 1888, cited in James
    L. Garvin, *The Life of Joseph Chamberlain* (London: 1933), II (1885–1895),
    465.

11 Kubicek, 11–12.

12 V. I. Lenin, *Imperialism, the Highest Stage of Capitalism*, 78.

13 Marx and Engels, *The First Indian War*, 86–90, *New York Daily Tribune*,
    no. 5123, September 21, 1887. C. Adderley, May 31, 1860.

14 Newcastle Papers, Newcastle to Sir Charles Monk, June 30, 1863 and
    Jebb, II, 160.

15 *Hansard (Lords)*, July 25, 1882, and Northbrooke Papers, C144/2, Ripon
    to Hartington, July 26, 1882.

16 The overseas capital estimates are from C. H. Feinstein, *National Income
    Expenditure and Output of the United Kingdom 1855–1965* (Cambridge,
    1972), Table T 50. The Empire proportion is estimated by summing the
    Empire component of overseas finance (see Table 2.1) and dividing that
    figure by the accumulated total of all overseas finance.

17 The African Association, Minutes of the Board of Directors, June 22,
    1892.

18 Ibid., September 30, 1897.

19 The Calcutta Electric Supply Company, for example, had revenues of
    only £600 its first year of operation and £2,000 the second.

20 The history of American railroads is captured in the bankruptcy statistics
    of the late nineteenth century. In 1872, the list included the Erie, the
    Kansas Pacific, the Northern Pacific, and several lesser roads; in the
    1890s, it involved railroads controlling 30 percent of the nation's mileage
    (the Burlington, the Norfolk and Wester, the Santa Fe, the Frisco, the
    Union Pacific, the Northern Pacific, and the Georgia Central); and in

the first decade of the twentieth century, the Pere Marquette, the Chicago and Eastern Illinois, the Rock Island, the Missouri Pacific, the Kansas, Missouri and Texas, and the Frisco all sought the protection of the federal bankruptcy laws.

[21] Lautaro Nitrate Co., Minutes of the Board of Directors, July 1907.

[22] See Kubicek.

[23] Disraeli to Derby, August 31, 1852, in Buckle, III (1846–1853), 397–8.

[24] G. E. Buckle, V (1868–1876), 272, 306–7; the election of 1874 was fought largely on that issue.

[25] Magnus, 149–50.

[26] Ibid., 112–13.

[27] Michael Barker, *Gladstone and Radicalism: The Reconstruction of Liberal Policy in Britain, 1885–1914* (New York, 1975), 50, 250–1.

[28] Robert R. Palmer, *The Age of Democratic Revolution: A Political History of Europe and America 1760–1800* (Princeton, 1959), 156.

[29] National income figures are from Feinstein, *National Income*, Table 17.

Bibliography

Books and periodical literature

Abbott, A. W., *A Short History of the Crown Agents and Their Office*, Private Printing in London, 1959. Reprinted at Portsmouth, 1971.

Abbot, G. C., "A Re-examination of the 1929 Colonial Development Act," *Economic History Review*, second series, 25 (2), February 1971, pp. 68–81.

Adler, Dorothy R., *British Investment in American Railways*, Muriel E. Hidy (ed.), Charlottesville, 1970.

Adler, J. H. (ed.), *Capital Movements and Economic Development*, London, 1967.

Aish, G. P., "Great Britain's Capital Investment in Other Lands," *Journal of the Royal Statistical Society*, 1909, LXXII, pt. III, 465–80. Also 1911, and the *Statist*, 1914.

Albion, Robert G., "Capital Movement and Transportation," *Journal of Economic History*, XI (4), fall 1951, pp. 361–74.

Aldcroft, D. H. (ed.), *The Development of British Industry and Foreign Competition, 1875–1914*, London, 1968.

"McCloskey on Victorian Growth: A Comment," *Economic History Review*, second series, XXVII (2), May 1974, pp. 271–4.

Allen, G. C. and A. Donnithorne, *Western Enterprise in Indonesia and Malaya*, New York, 1957.

Anderson, B. L., "Law, Finance and Economic Growth in England. Some Long-Term Influences," in Barrie M. Ratcliffe (ed.), *Great Britain and Her World, 1750–1914: Essays in Honor of W. D. Henderson*, Manchester, 1975.

Antony Gibbs & Sons, Ltd., *Merchants and Bankers, 1808–1958*, London, 1958.

Antrobus, H. A., *A History of the Assam Company, 1839–1953*, Edinburgh, 1957.

A History of the Jorehaut Tea Company Ltd., London, 1947.

Armstrong, F. E., *The Book of the Stock Exchange*, London, 1934.

Arndt, E. H. D., *Banking and Currency Developments in South Africa*, Capetown, 1928.

Atkinson, T., "Rupee Prices in India, 1870–1908," *Journal of the Royal Statistical Society*, LXXII, 1909, pp. 499–502.

Aydelotte, William O., "The Disintegration of the Conservative Party in the 1840s: A Study of Political Attitudes," in Aydelotte, et al. (eds.),

The Dimensions of Quantitative Research in History, Princeton, 1972, pp. 319–46.

"Voting Patterns in the British House of Commons in the 1840s," *Comparative Studies in Society and History*, V, 1962–3, pp. 135–63.

Ayres, G. L., "Fluctuations in New Capital Issues in the London Capital Market 1899 to 1913," M.Sc. Econ. thesis, London, 1934.

Baden-Powell, G., "Colonial Government Securities," Royal Colonial Institute, *Report of Proceedings*, XVIII, 1886–7, pp. 253–95.

Bagchi, A. K., *Private Investment in India 1900–1939*, Cambridge, 1972.

Bailey, John Donnison, "Australian Borrowing in Scotland in the Nineteenth Century," *Economic History Review*, second series, XII (2), December 1959, pp. 268–79.

"Australian Company Borrowing 1870–1893: A Study in British Overseas Investment," Ph.D. thesis, Oxford, 1957.

A Hundred Years of Pastoral Banking. A History of the Australian Mercantile Land and Finance Company 1863–1963, Oxford, 1966.

Barclay, Parkings & Co. Brewery, *The History of a Famous Brewery*, London, 1910.

Three Centuries – The Story of Our Ancient Brewery, London, Anchor, 1951.

Barclay's Bank, *Barclay's Bank: A Banking Centenary (Dominion, Colonial and Overseas) 1836–1936*, London, 1938.

Baron, Stanley, *Brewed in America*, New York, 1972.

Baster, A. S. J., "A Note on the Colonial Stock Acts and Dominion Borrowing," *Economic History Review*, II, 1933, pp. 602–608.

The Imperial Banks, London, 1929.

Basu, S. K., *The Managing Agency System in Prospect and Retrospect*, Calcutta, 1958.

Baumgart, Winfried, *Imperialism*, New York, 1982, 130.

Baxter, A. B., *Banking in Australasia from a London Official's Point of View.*

Baxter, Dudley, *The Taxation of the United Kingdom*, London, 1869.

Beer, Samuel, *Treasury Control*, second edition, Oxford, 1957.

Bell, Sidney Smith, *Colonial Administration of Great Britain* (reprint), Kelley, New York, 1970.

Benians, E. A., J. Butler, and C. E. Carrington, "Finance, Trade and Communications, 1870–1895," in *The Cambridge History of the British Empire*, III, *The Empire Commonwealth*, Cambridge, 1959, pp. 181–229.

Bennett, George, *The Concept of Empire, Burke to Attlee, 1774–1947*, Adam and Charles Black (eds.), London, 1953.

Birnberg, Thomas and Stephen A. Resnick, *Colonial Development; An Econometric Study*, New Haven and London, 1975.

Blainey, Geoffrey, "A Theory of Mineral Discovery: Australia in the Nineteenth Century," *Economic History Review*, second series, XXIII (2), August 1970, pp. 298–313.

Blakeley, Brian L., *The Colonial Office, 1868–1892*, Durham, North Carolina, 1972, pp. 20, 64–5.

Blaug, Mark, "Economic Imperialism Revisited," *The Yale Review*, L (3), March 1961, pp. 335–49.

Bodelson, C. A., *Studies in Mid-Victorian Imperialism*, Copenhagen, Gyldendals Forlagstrykkeri, 1924.

Bordo, Michael David, "The Income Effects of the Sources of New Money: A Comparison of the United States and the United Kingdom, 1870–1913," *JEH*, 14 (1), January 1977.

Bose, A., "Foreign Capital," in V. B. Singh (ed.), *Economic History of India 1857–1956*, Bombay, 1965, pp. 485–527.

Bose, S. K., *Capital and Labour in the Indian Tea Industry*, Bombay, 1954.

Boulding, K. E. and J. Mukerjee, *Economic Imperialism*, Ann Arbor, 1972.

Brayer, H. O., "The Influence of British Capital on the Western Range Cattle Industry," *Journal of Economic History*, supplement, IX, 1949, pp. 85–98.

Breckenridge, R. M., *The Canadian Banking System 1817–1890*, New York, 1895.

Broadridge, Seymour, *Studies in Railway Expansion and the Capital Market in England 1825–1873*, London, 1970.

Brody, Richard and Benjamin Page, "Indifference, Alienation and Rational Decisions," *Public Choice*, XV, summer 1973, pp. 1–17.

Brown, A. J., "Britain and the World Economy 1870–1914," *Yorkshire Bulletin of Economic and Social Research*, XVII (1), May 1965, pp. 46–60.

Brown, Hilton, *Parry's of Madras, A Story of British Enterprise in India*, Madras, 1954.

Brown, Ian, "British Financial Advisers in Siam in the Reign of King Chulalongkorn," *Modern Asian Studies*, XII, part 2, February 1978, pp. 193–215.

Brown, Michael B., *After Imperialism*, London, 1963.
The Economics of Imperialism, Harmondsworth, 1974.

Brown, Phelps and S. J. Handfield-Jones, "The Climacteric of the 1890s: A Study in the Expanding Economy," *Oxford Economic Papers*, IV (3), October 1952, pp. 266–307.

Brown, Phelps and Bernard Weber, "Accumulation, Productivity and Distribution in the British Economy, 1870–1938," *The Economic Journal*, June 1953, pp. 263–88.

Brunschwig, H., *French Colonialism 1871–1914*, London, 1966.

Buchanan, D. H., *The Development of Capitalist Enterprise in India*, New York, 1934.

Buckley, Peter J. and Brian R. Roberts, *European Direct Investment in the USA before World War I*, London, 1982.

Burdon, R. M., *King Dick*, London, 1955.

Burnham, T. H. and G. O. Hoskins, *Iron and Steel in Britain*, London, 1962.

Burton, Ann M., "Treasury Control and Colonial Policy in the Late Nineteenth Century," *Public Administration*, XLIV, summer 1966, pp. 169–92.

Bushell, T. A., *Royal Mail – A Centenary History of the Royal Mail Line, 1839–1939*, London, 1939.

Butlin, Noel G., *Australian Domestic Product, Investment and Foreign Borrowing*, Cambridge, 1962.
  "Company Ownership of the NSW Pastoral Stations 1865–1900," *Historical Studies: Australia and New Zealand*, Melbourne, 1950.
  Investment in Australian Economic Development 1861–1900, London, 1964.
Butlin, S. J., *Australia and New Zealand Bank*, Melbourne, 1961.
Buxton, Sydney, *Finance and Politics: An Historical Study 1783–1886*, London, 1888.
Byatt, I. C. B., *The British Electrical Industry 1874–1914. The Economic Returns to a New Technology*, Oxford, 1979.
Cable, B., *A Hundred Years History of the P&O*, London, 1937.
Cain, N., "Squatting in N.S.W., 1880–1905: The Pastoral Finance Company View," unpublished Ph.D. dissertation, Australian National University, Canberra, 1964.
Cain, P. J., *Economic Foundations of British Overseas Expansion 1815–1914*, Hong Kong, 1980.
Cairncross, A. K., "The English Capital Market Before 1914," *Economica*, XXV (98), May 1958, pp. 142–6.
  "Investments in Canada 1900–1913," in A. R. Ford (ed.), *The Export of British Capital 1870–1914*, London, 1968.
  Home and Foreign Investment 1870–1913 – Studies in Capital Accumulations, England, 1953.
Cairns, J. E., *Essays in Political Economy Theoretical and Applied*, London, 1873.
Callis, H. G., *Foreign Capital in South East Asia*, New York, 1942.
Cameron, Sir Donald, *My Tanganyika Service and Some Nigeria*, London, 1939.
Cannadine, David, "Aristocratic Indebtedness in the Nineteenth Century: The Case Reopened," *Economic History Review*, second series, XXX (4), November 1977, pp. 624–50.
Capie, Forrest and K. A. Tucker, "British and New Zealand Trading Relationships, 1841–1851," *Economic History Review*, second series, XXV (2), May 1972, pp. 293–301.
Carrington, C. E., *The British Overseas: Exploits of a Nation of Shopkeepers*, Cambridge, 1950.
Cassell, G., T. E. Gregory, T. E. Kuczinski, and K. Norton, *Foreign Investments*, Chicago, 1928.
Cell, John W., *British Colonial Administration in the Mid-Nineteenth Century: The Policy-Making Process*, New Haven, 1970.
Channon, Geoffrey, "A Nineteenth-Century Investment Decision: The Midlands Railway's London Extension," *Economic History Review*, 25, August 1972, pp. 448–470.
Chapman, J. K., *The Career of Arthur Hamilton Gordon, First Lord Stanmore*, Toronto, 1964.
Chaudhuri, N. C., *Jute in Bengal*, Calcutta, 1933.
Checkland, S. G., *The Mines of Tharsis: Roman, French and British Enterprise in Spain*, London, 1967.

"The Mind of the City," *Oxford Economic Papers*, IX (3), October 1957, pp. 261–78.

Scottish Banking: A History, 1695–1973, Glasgow and London, 1975.

Chester, D. N., *Central and Local Government Financial and Administrative Relations*, London, 1951.

Childers, Spenser, *Life and Correspondence of the Rt. Hon. C. E. Childers*, 2 vols., London, 1901.

Chi-Ming, Hou, *Foreign Investment and Economic Development in China 1840–1937*, Cambridge, 1965.

Chubb, Basil, *The Control of Public Expenditure*, Oxford, 1952.

Church, Roy (ed.), *The Dynamics of Victorian Business*, London, 1980.

Kenricks in Hardware: A Family Business 1791–1966, Newton Abbot, 1969.

Clark, Grover, *The Balance Sheets of Imperialism*, New York, 1936.

A Place in the Sun, New York, 1936.

Cobb, H. S., "Sources of Economic History amongst the Parliamentary Records in the House of Lords Records Office," *Economic History Review*, 19, April 1966, pp. 154–74.

Cochran, Thomas C. and Ray Ginger, "The American–Hawaiian Steamship Company," *Business History Review*, XXVIII, 1954, pp. 343–65.

Cocks, Sir Barnett, *Erskine May's Treatise on the Law, Privileges, Proceedings and Usage of Parliament*, London, 1971.

Coleman, D. C., "Courtaulds and the Beginning of Rayon," in Barry Supple (ed.), *Essays in British Business History*, Oxford, 1977, pp. 88–100.

Courtaulds: An Economic and Social History. Vol I: The Nineteenth Century. Silk and Crepe. Oxford, 1969.

Coleman, James, "The Possibility of a Social Welfare Function," *American Economic Review*, LVI (5), December 1966, pp. 1105–22.

"Internal Processes Governing Party Positions in Elections," *Public Choice*, XI, fall 1971, pp. 35–60.

Converse, Philip E., "The Nature of Belief Systems in Mass Publics," in David Apter (ed.), *Ideology and Discontent*, New York, 1964.

Cook, Arthur Norton, *British Enterprise in Nigeria*, Philadelphia, 1943.

Cooke, Sidney Russell and Ernest Harold Davenport, *Imperial Finance: A Study of the Loan Policy of the British Commonwealth of Nations*, London, 1929.

Cooney, E. W., "Capital Exports and Investment in Building in Britain and the USA 1856–1914," *Economica*, XVI (64), November 1949, pp. 347–54.

Cotrell, P. L., *British Overseas Investment in the Nineteenth Century*, London, 1975.

Industrial Finance 1830–1914, London, 1980.

Coughlan, T. A., *A Statistical Account of Australia and New Zealand 1903–1904*.

Cox-George, N. A., *Finance and Development in West Africa: The Sierra Leone Experience*, London, 1961.

Cozley, T. A. B., *Quaker Enterprise in Biscuits: Huntley & Palmers of Reading 1822–1972*, London, 1972.

Craig, F. W. S., *Boundaries of Parliamentary Constituencies 1885–1972*, Political Reference Pubs., Chichester, 1972.
  British Parliamentary Elections, 1832–1883, London, 1977.
  British Parliamentary Elections, 1883–1918, London, 1974.

Crammond, E., "British Investments Abroad," *Quarterly Review*, 1911, 215, 50.

Crick, W. F. and J. E. Wadsworth, *A Hundred Years of Joint Stock Banking*, London, 1936.

Crouchley, A. E., *The Investment of Foreign Capital in Egyptian Companies and Foreign Debt*, Ministry of Finance, Technical Paper No. 12, Cairo, 1936.

Crouzet, Francois, "Trade and Empire: The British Experience from the Establishment of Free Trade until the First World War," in Barrie M. Ratcliffe (ed.), *Great Britain and Her World, 1750– 1914*, essays in honor of W. O. Henderson, Manchester, 1973.

Currie, A. W., "British Attitudes toward Investment in North America," *Business History Review*, XXXIV (2–3), summer 1960, pp. 194–215.

Dantwala, M. L., *A Hundred Years of Indian Cotton*, Bombay, 1948.

Danvers, Sir Juland, *Indian Railways*, London, 1877.

Darwin, Bernard, *British Clubs*, London, 1947.

Dasgupta, A., "The Jute Textile Industry," in V. Singh (ed.), *Economic History of India 1857–1956*, New York, 1965.

Davies, P. N., *Sir Alfred Jones. Shippping Entrepreneur par Excellence*, London, 1978.
  The Trade Makers: Elder Dempster in West Africa 1852–1972, London, 1973.
  Trading in West Africa 1840–1920, New York, 1976.

Davis, Otto and Melvin Hinich, "On the Power and Importance of the Mean Preference in a Mathematical Model of Democratic Choice," *Public Choice*, V, fall 1968, pp. 59–72.
  "Some Results Related to a Mathematical Model of Policy Formation in a Democratic Society," in J. Bernd (ed.), *Mathematical Applications in Political Science*, 3, Charlottesville, 1967.

Dean, Britten, *China and Great Britain: The Diplomacy of Commercial Relations 1860–1864*, Harvard East Asian Monograph No. 50, Cambridge, Mass., 1974.
  "British Informal Empire: The Case of China," *The Journal of Commonwealth and Comparative Politics*, XLV (1), March 1976, pp. 64–81.

Dickson, P. M. G., *The Sun Insurance Office 1710–1960: A History of Two and a Half Centuries of British Insurance*, Oxford, 1960.

Dougan, David, *The Great Gun Maker: The Story of Lord Armstrong*, Newcastle-on-Tyne, 1970.

Downs, Anthony, *Inside Bureaucracy*, New York, 1967.

Drabble, J. H., *Rubber in Malaya, 1876–1922: The Genesis of an Industry*, Kuala Lumpur, 1973.

Drew, Bernard, *The London Assurance – A Chronicle*, London, 1928.
The London Assurance – A Second Chronicle, London, 1949.
Drummond, Ian M., *British Economic Policy and the Empire 1919– 1939*, London, 1972.
Duguid, C., *The Story of the Stock Exchange*, London, 1901.
Duncan, A. J., "South African Capital Imports 1893–1898," *Canadian Journal of Political and Economic Science*, XIV (1), February 1948, pp. 20–45.
Dunning, John H., *Studies in International Investment*, London, 1970.
Dutt, R. C., *The Economic History of India in the Victorian Age*, London, 1904.
Edelstein, M., *Overseas Investment in the Age of High Imperialism*, New York, 1982.
"Rigidity and Bias in the British Capital Markets 1870–1913," in D. McCloskey (ed.), *Essays on a Mature Economy: Britain after 1840*, London, 1971.
Edwards, K. H. R., *Chronology of the Development of the Iron and Steel Industries of the Tees-side*, Newcastle, 1955.
Egypt Ministry of Finance, Department of General Statistics, *Annuaire statistique de l'Egypte*, Cairo, 1910 and 1914.
Elliot, Arthur R. Douglas, *The Life of Sir George Joachim Goschen*, London, 1911.
Elwin, Verrier, *The Story of Tata Steel*, Bombay, 1958.
Emerson, R., *Representative Government in South East Asia*, Cambridge, Mass., 1955.
Engels, F., *Engels on Capital*, New York, 1937.
Ensor, R. C. K., *England 1870–1914*, Oxford, 1952.
Essex-Crosby, A., "Joint Stock Companies in Great Britain, 1890–1930," Ph.D. thesis, London, 1937.
Evans, David M., *Speculative Notes and Notes on Speculation*, London, 1864.
Evans, George Heberton, *British Corporation Finance 1775–1850: A Study of Preference Shares*, Baltimore, 1936.
Farquharson, Robin, *Theory of Voting*, New Haven, 1969.
Farr, D. M., *The Colonial Office and Canada*, Toronto, 1955.
Fawcett, H., *Indian Finance*, London, 1880.
Feinstein, C. H., *National Income Expenditure and Output of the United Kingdom 1855–1965*, Cambridge, 1972.
Feis, Herbert, *Europe, the World's Banker 1870–1914*, New Haven, 1930.
Fenn, Charles, *Compendium of the English and Foreign Funds*, London, 1889.
Ferns, H. S., *Britain and Argentina in the Nineteenth Century*, Oxford, 1960.
"Investment and Trade between Britain and the Argentine in the Nineteenth Century," *Economic History Review*, second series III (2), 1950, pp. 203–18.
Ferrer, A., *The Argentine Economy. An Economic History of Argentina*, California, 1967.
Field, Frederich William, *Capital Investment in Canada, 1902–1912*, Monetary Times of Canada, Montreal, second edition, 1912.

Fieldhouse, D. K., *The Colonial Empires*, New York, 1965.
  Economics and Empire 1830–1914, Ithaca, 1973.
  The Theory of Capitalist Imperialism, London, 1967.
James Finlay and Company Limited, *Manufacturers and East India Merchants 1750–1950*, Glasgow, 1951.
Finnie, D., *Capital Underwriting*, London, 1934.
Firestone, O. J., *Canada's Economic Development 1867–1953*, London, 1958.
Fisk, H. E., "Flow of Capital – Canada," in W. P. M. Kennedy (ed.), *Social and Economic Conditions in the Dominion of Canada*, Montreal, 1923.
Floud, Roderick, *The British Machine Tool Industry, 1850–1914*, Cambridge, 1976.
Flux, W. A., "The Yield of High Class Investments," *Transactions of the Manchester Statistical Society*, 1910–11.
Ford, A. G., "British Investment in Argentina and Long Swings, 1880–1914," *Journal of Economic History*, XXXI (3), September 1971, pp. 650–63.
  "Overseas Lending and Internal Fluctuations 1870–1914," in A. R. Hall (ed.), *The Export of British Capital 1870–1914*, London, 1968, pp. 84–102.
  The Gold Standard 1880–1914: Britain and Argentina, London, 1962.
  "The Transfer of British Foreign Lending, 1870–1913," *Economic History Review*, second series, XI (2), 1958, pp. 302–8.
Frank, Andre Gunder, *Capitalism and Underdevelopment in Latin America: Historical Studies of Chile and Brazil*, New York, 1969.
  Latin America: Underdevelopment or Revolution. Essays on the Development of Underdeveloped and Intermediate Economies, London, 1970.
Frankel, S. Herbert, *Capital Investment in Africa*, London, 1938.
  Investment and the Return to Equity Capital in the South African Gold Mining Industry 1887–1965: An International Comparison, Cambridge, Mass., 1967.
  The Railway Policy of South Africa, Johannesburg, 1928.
  "Return to Capital Invested in the Witwatersrand Gold Mining Industry 1887–1932," *Economic Journal*, XLV (177), March 1935, pp. 67–76.
Frey, Bruno and Lawrence Lau, "Towards a Mathematical Model of Government Behaviour," *Zeitschrift fur Nationalokonomie*, vol. 28, 1968.
Galbraith, J. S., *Crown and Charter – The Early Years of the British South Africa Company*, Berkeley, 1974.
  "Myths of the 'Little England' Era," *American Historical Review*, LXVII (1), October 1961, pp. 34–48.
  "The Turbulent Frontier as a Factor in British Expansion," *Comparative Studies in Society and History*, II (2), January 1960, pp. 150–68.
Gallagher, J. and R. Robinson, "Imperialism and Free Trade," *Economic History Review*, second series, VI (1), 1953, pp. 1–15.
Gann, L. H. and P. Duignan, *Burden of Empire: An Appraisal of Western*

Colonialism in Africa South of the Sahara, Hoover Institution
   Publications, Stanford, California, 1968.

Colonialism in Africa, 1870–1860, vol. 1, Cambridge, 1969.

Gardiner, A. G., *The Life of Sir William Harcourt,* 2 vols., London, 1923.

Garvey, Gerald, "The Theory of Party Equilibrium," *American Political
   Science Review,* LX (1), March 1966, pp. 29–38.

Garvin, James L., *The Life of Joseph Chamberlain,* London, 3 vols., 1933–5.

Gibbs, Norman, *The Origins of Imperial Defense,* Oxford, 1955.

Gilbert, J. C., *A History of Investment Trusts in Dundee,* London, 1939.

Glen Line Ltd., *Glen Line,* London, 1949.

Goldberg, Arthur, "Social Determinism and Rationality as Bases of Party
   Identification," *American Political Science Review,* LXIII (1), March
   1969, pp. 5–25.

Goodhart, C. A. E., *The Business of Banking 1891–1914,* London, 1972.

Goodwin, Crawford D., "British Economists and Australian Gold,"
   Journal of Economic History, 30 (2), June 1970, pp. 405–26.

Gordon, Donald C., "The Colonial Defence Committee and Imperial
   Collaboration: 1885–1904," *Political Science Quarterly,* LXXVII (4),
   December 1962, pp. 526–45.

The Dominion – Partnership – Imperial Defense, 1870–1914, Baltimore,
   1965.

Graham, Richard, *Britain and the Onset of Modernization in Brazil 1850–
   1914,* London, 1968.

Gray, Richard and David Birmingham (eds.), *Pre-Colonial African Trade.
   Essays on Trade in Central and Eastern Africa before 1900,* London, 1970.

Greenberg, Michael, *British Trade and the Opening of China, 1800–42,*
   Cambridge University Press Library Edition, Cambridge, 1969
   (reprint).

Grieser, N., "The British Investor and His Sources of Information," M.A.
   thesis, London, 1940.

Grisewood, Herman, et al., *Ideas and Beliefs of the Victorians: A Historic
   Revaluation of the Victorian Age,* London, 1949.

Habakkuk, H. J., "Fluctuations in Housebuilding in Britain and the
   United States in the Nineteenth Century," in A. R. Hall (ed.), *The
   Export of British Capital 1870–1914,* London, 1968, pp. 103–45.

"Free Trade and Commercial Expansion 1853–1870," in J. H. Rose, A.
   P. Newton, and E. A. Benians, *The Cambridge Economic History of the
   British Empire,* II, *The Growth of the New Empire,* Cambridge, 1962,
   pp. 751–805.

Hall, A. R., "A Note on the English Capital Market as a Source for Home
   Investment Before 1914," *Economica,* XXIV (93), February 1957,
   pp. 59–66.

The Export of Capital from Britain 1870–1914, London 1968.

"The English Capital Market Before 1914 – A Reply," *Economica,* XXV
   (100), November 1958, pp. 339–43.

The London Capital Market and Australia, Canberra, 1963.

Hall, H. L., *The Colonial Office, A History,* London, 1937.

374   Bibliography

Hamilton, Sir Horace, "Treasury Control in the Eighties," *Public Administration*, 33 (1), spring 1955, pp. 13–17.
Hammond, Richard J., "Economic Imperialism: Sidelights on a Stereotype," *Journal of Economic History*, XXI (4), December 1961, pp. 582–98.
Hancock, W. K., *Survey of British Commonwealth Affairs*, II, *Problems of Economic Policy 1918–1939*, London, 1940.
   Wealth of Colonies, Cambridge, 1950.
Hand-in-Hand Insurance Co., *The Origin and History of the Hand-in-Hand Fire and Life Insurance Co.*, London, 1957.
Hannah, Leslie, *Electricity before Nationalism. A Study of the Development of the Electricity Supply Industry in Britain to 1948*, Baltimore, 1979.
Hansard, Parliamentary Debates, 1860–1913.
Hansen, B. and K. Tourk, "The Profitability of the Suez Canal as a Private Enterprise," as yet unpublished article.
Hanson, John R., II, "Diversification and Concentration of LDC Exports: Victorian Trends," *Explorations in Entrepreneurial History*, 1977.
   Trade in Transition – Exports from the Third World, 1840–1900, New York, 1980.
Hardinge, G. M., *The Development and Growth of Courage's Brewery*, London, 1932.
Harley, C. Knick, "The Interest Rate and Prices in Britain, 1873–1913: A Study of the Gibson Paradox," *Explorations in Entrepreneurial History*, 14, 1977, pp. 69–89.
Harlow, Vincent T., *The Founding of the Second British Empire, 1763–1793*, II, *New Continents and Changing Values*, London, 1964.
Harnetty, Peter, *Imperialism and Free Trade: Lancashire and India in the Mid-Nineteenth Century*, Vancouver, 1972.
Harrisons and Crosfield Ltd., *One Hundred Years as East India Merchants*, London, 1943.
Hartland, P., "Canadian Balance of Payments since 1868," *Trends in the American Economy*, National Bureau of Economic Research, 24, Princeton, 1960, pp. 717–53.
Hartman, Raymond S. and David Wheeler, "Schumpeterian Waves of Innovation and Infrastructure Development in Great Britain and the United States: The Kondratieff Cycle Revisited," Boston University Discussion Paper, No. 14.
Heath, Thomas, *The Treasury*, London, 1927.
Henderson, W. O., "British Economic Activity in the German Colonies, 1884–1914," *Economic History Review*, XV, 1945.
   Studies in German Colonial History, London, 1962.
Heussler, Robert, *Yesterday's Rulers: The Making of the British Colonial Service*, Syracuse, 1963.
Hicks, Ursula K., *British Public Finance, 1880–1952*, Oxford, 1954.
Hicks-Beach, Victoria, *Life of Sir Michael Hicks-Beach, Earl St. Aldwyn*, London, 1932.
Hidy, R. W., *The House of Baring in America Trade and Finance*, Cambridge, Mass., 1949.

Hill, John C. G., "Shipshape and Bristol Fashion," *The Journal of Commerce and Shipping Telegraph*, second edition, Liverpool, 1972.

Hinich, Melvin, John Ledyard, and Peter Ordeshook, "A Theory of Electoral Equilibrium: A Spatial Analysis Based on the Theory of Games," *Journal of Politics*, XXXV (1), February 1973, pp. 154–93.

Hirschman, A. O., *Essays in Trespassing, Economics to Politics and Beyond*, New York, 1981.

Hirst, F. W., *The Stock Exchange*, Oxford, 1948.

Hobson, C. K., *The Export of Capital*, London, 1914.

Hobson, J. A., *The Economic Interpretation of Investment*, London, 1910. *Imperialism: A Study*, third edition, London, 1938.

Hockley, G. C., *Monetary Policy and Public Finance*, London, 1970.

Holt, Charles, *The Role of State Government in the 19th Century American Economy: 1820–1902*, New York, 1977.

Holt, John, "The Early Years of an African Trader," pamphlet published for John Holt & Co., Liverpool, 1962.

Hopkins, A. G., *An Economic History of West Africa*, New York, 1973.
"The Creation of a Colonial Monetary System: The Origins of the West African Currency Board," *African Historical Studies*, III (1), 1970, pp. 101–32.
"Economic Imperialism in West Africa: Lagos, 1880–92," *The Economic History Review*, second series, XXI (3), December 1968, pp. 580–606.
"Imperial Business in Africa: Part I: Sources; Part II: Interpretations," *Journal of African History*, XVII (1 & 2), 1976, pp. 29–48; 267–90.

Houseman, Lorna, *The House That Thomas Built - The Story of the De La Rue Co.*, London, 1968.

Hurd, John II, "Railways and the Expansion of Markets in India, 1861–1921," *Explorations in Economic History*, 12 (3), July 1975.

Huttenback, Robert A., *The British Imperial Experience*, New York, 1966.

Hyde, Francis E., *Liverpool and the Mersey*, Newton Abbey, 1971.

Hymer, S., "Economics of Imperialism: Discussion," *American Economic Review*, 60 (2), May 1970, pp. 243–4.

Imlah, A. H., *Economic Elements in the Pax Britannica*, Cambridge, 1958.

Ingram, James C., *Economic Change in Thailand 1850–1970*, Stanford, 1971.

Investors Monthly Manual, 1865–1914.

Irving, R. J., *The North Eastern Railway Company 1870–1914: An Economic History*, Leicester, 1976.
"The Profitability and Performance of British Railways 1870–1914," *Economic History Review*, XXXI (1), February 1978, pp. 46–66.

Islam, Nural, *Foreign Capital and Economic Development Japan, India, and Canada*, Vermont, 1962.

Jackson, H. C., *Sudan Days and Ways*, London, 1954.

Jackson, W. Turrentine, *The Enterprising Scot, Investors in the American West after 1873*, Edinburgh, 1968.

Jefferys, J. B., "The Denomination and Character of Shares, 1855–1885," *Economic History Review*, XVI, 1946, pp. 45–55.

"Trends in Business Organization in Great Britain since 1856," Ph.D. dissertation, University of London, 1962.

Jeffries, Sir Charles, *The Colonial Office*, London, 1956.

Jenks, Leland, *The Migration of British Capital in 1875*, New York, 1927.

Jenkyn, Sir Henry, *British Rule and Jurisdiction beyond the Seas*, Oxford, 1902.

Johnson, Franklyn Arthur, *Defence by Committee: The British Committee of Imperial Defence 1885–1959*, London, 1960.

Jones, E. G., "The Argentine Refrigerated Meat Industry," *Economica*, 1929.

Joslin, D., *A Century of Banking in Latin America, Bank of London and South America Ltd. 1862–1962*, London, 1963.

Katzenbach, Edward L., *Charles-Louis de Saulles de Freycinet and the Army*, University Microfilm, Ann Arbor, 1953.

Kay, G. B., *The Political Economy of Colonialism in Ghana, A Collection of Documents and Statistics*, London, 1970.

Keith, A. B., *Selected Speeches and Documents on British Colonial Policy 1763–1917*, Oxford University Press, London, 1918.

Kennedy, P. M., "Imperial Cable Conventions and Strategy, 1870–1914," *The English Historical Review*, LXXXVI (341), October 1971, pp. 728–52.

Kennedy, W. P., "Foreign Investment, Trade and Growth in the United Kingdom, 1870–1913," *Explorations in Economic History*, XI (4), summer 1974, pp. 415–44.

Kerr, D. G. G., *Sir Edmund Head: A Scholarly Governor*, Toronto, 1954.

Kesner, R. M., "Britain and the Rehabilitation of the Cyprus Economy," *Journal of European Economic History*, VII (1), spring 1978, pp. 169–90.

"Builders of Empire: The Role of the Crown Agents in Imperial Development, 1880–1914," *Journal of Imperial and Commonwealth History*, V (3), May 1977, pp. 310–30.

Economic Control and Colonial Development – Crown Colony Financial Management in the Age of Joseph Chamberlain, Westport, Conn., 1981.

Kidron, M., *Foreign Investments in India*, London, 1965.

Kilbracken, Lord, *Reminiscences of Lord Kilbracken*, London, 1901.

Kindleberger, C. P., "Foreign Trade and Economic Growth: Lessons from Britain and France, 1850 to 1913," *Economic History Review*, second series, XIV (2), 1961, pp. 289–305.

Kinnear, Michael, *The British Voter*, Ithaca, 1968.

Kirby, M. W., *The British Coalmining Industry, 1870–1946. A Political and Economic History*, London, 1977.

Knight, Robert, *India: A Review of England's Financial Relations, Therewith*, London, 1868.

Knorr, Klaus E., *British Colonial Theories, 1570–1850*, London, 1963.

Knowles, L. C. A., *The Economic Development of the British Empire*, London, 1924.

Koebner, Richard, "The Concept of Economic Imperialism," *Economic History Review*, second series, II (1), 1949, pp. 1–29.

Koebner, Richard and Helmut Dan Schmidt, *Imperialism: The Story and Significance of a Political Word, 1840–1960*, Cambridge, 1964.

Kubicek, Robert V., *The Administration of Imperialism: Joseph Chamberlain at the Colonial Office*, Durham, North Carolina, 1969.

Kurth, James R. and Steven J. Rosen, *Testing Theories of Economic Imperialism*, Lexington, 1974.

Landes, David S., *Bankers and Pashas: International Finance and Economic Imperialism in Egypt*, Cambridge, Mass., 1958.

"Some Thoughts on the Nature of Economic Imperialism," *Journal of Economic History*, December 1961.

Lang, Andrew, *Life, Letters and Diaries of Sir Stafford Northcote, First Earl of Iddesleigh*, London, 1890.

Langer, William L., *The Diplomacy of Imperialism, 1890–1902*, New York, 1935.

Lau, Lawrence and Bernard Frey, "Ideology, Public Approval and Government Behavior," *Public Choice*, X, spring 1971, pp. 21–40.

Lavington, F., *The English Capital Market*, London, 1921.

Lee, G. A., "The Concept of Profit in British Accounting, 1760–1900," *Business History Review*, XLIX (1), spring 1975, pp. 6–36.

Legler, John, "Regional Distribution of Federal Receipts and Expenditures in the 19th Century: A Quantitative Study," Ph.D. dissertation, Purdue University, 1967.

Lehfeldt, *Journal of the Royal Statistical Society*, January 1913.

Leland, Hamilton Jenks, *The Migration of British Capital to 1875*, London, 1963.

Lenfant, J. H., "British Capital Export 1900–1913," Ph.D. thesis, London, 1949.

"Great Britain's Capital Formation 1865–1914," *Economica*, XVIII (70), May 1951, pp. 151–68.

Lenin, V. J., *Imperialism, the Highest State of Capitalism*, New York, 1959.

Levi, Leon, *Wages and Earnings of the Working Classes*, London, 1885.

Levine, A. L., *Industrial Retardation in Britain, 1880–1914*, New York, 1967.

Lewis, G. C., *Letters of Rt. Hon. Sir G. C. Lewis*, London, 1870.

Lewis, Roger William, *Imperialism – The Robinson and Gallagher Controversy*, New York, 1976.

Lewis, W. Arthur, *Aspects of Tropical Trade 1883–1965*, Stockholm, 1969.

Tropical Development 1880–1913: Studies in Economic Progress, London, 1970.

Lokanathan, P. S., *Industrial Organization in India*, London, 1935.

Longley, Ronald Stewart, *Sir Francis Hincks: A Study of Canadian Politics, Railways and Finance in the Nineteenth Century*, Toronto, 1943.

Lovell, R. I., *The Struggle for South Africa 1875–1899, A Study in Economic Imperialism*, New York, 1934.

Lowe, C. J., *The Reluctant Imperialists: British Foreign Policy, 1878–1902*, 2 vols., The Documents, London, 1967.

Lowell, A. Lawrence, *The Government of England*, New York, 1909, p. 200.

Lowenfield, H., *All about Investment*, London, 1909.

Lugard, Captain F. D., *The Rise of Our East African Empire*, Edinburgh, 1893.

Luxemburg, Rosa, and Nikolai Bukharin, *Imperialism and the Accumulation of Capital*, ed. by K. J. Tarbuck, London, 1972.

McAlpin, Michelle Burge, "The Effects of Expansion of Markets on Rural Income Distribution in Nineteenth Century India," *Explorations in Entrepreneurial History*, 12 (3), July 1975.

McCarthy, D. M. P., "The British in the Atacama Desert," *Journal Economic History*, XXXV (1), March 1975, pp. 134–7.

McCloskey, Donald, "Did Victorian Britain Fail?," *Economic History Review*, second series, XXIII (3), December 1970, pp. 446–59.

Economic Maturity and Entrepreneurial Decline: British Iron & Steel, 1870–1913, Cambridge, Mass., 1973.

Essays on a Mature Economy: Britain after 1840, Princeton, N.J., 1971.

McCloskey, Donald and Roderick Floud, *The Economic History of Britain since 1700*, New York, 1981.

McDermott, P. L., *British East Africa or Ibea: A History of the Formation and Work of the Imperial British East Africa Company, Compiled with the Authority of the Directors from Company Documents and the Records of the Company*, London, 1893.

McIntyre, W. David, *The Imperial Frontier in the Tropics, 1865–1875*, London, 1967.

McLean, David, "Commerce, Finance and British Diplomatic Support in China, 1865–85," *Economic History Review*, second series, 26 (3), August 1973, pp. 464–76.

"British Finance and Foreign Policy in Turkey: The Smyrna–Aidin Railway Settlement 1913–14," *Historical Journal*, 19 (2), June 1976, 521–30.

"Finance and 'Informal Empire' before the First World War," *Economic History Review*, second series, XXIX (2), May 1976, pp. 291–305.

McLean, I. W., "Anglo–American Engineering Competition, 1870–1914: Some Third-Market Evidence," *Economic History Review*, second series, XXIX (3), August 1976, pp. 452–64.

Macauley, R. H., *The Bombay–Burmah Trading Corporation*, London, 1937.

MacDonagh, Oliver, "The Anti-Imperialism of Free Trade," *Economic History Review*, second series, XIV (3), 1962, pp. 489–501.

MacGregor, D. H., *Enterprise, Purpose, and Profit*, Oxford, 1934.

Mackey, A. L. G., *The Australian Banking and Credit System*, London, 1931.

MacKintosh, John P., "The Role of the Committee of Imperial Defense before 1914," *English Historical Review*, LXXVII (304) July 1962, pp. 490–503.

MacPherson, W. J., "Investment in India Railways," *Economic History Review*, second series, VIII (2), 1955, pp. 177–86.

Magnus, P., *Gladstone, A Biography*, London, 1954.

Mallet, Bernard, *British Budgets, 1887–88 to 1912–13*, London, 1913.

Manning. H. Y., "Who Ran the British Empire – 1830–1850," *Journal of British Studies*, V (1), November 1965, pp. 88–121.

Margetson, Stella, *Victorian High Society*, New York, 1980.

Marsden, Anthony, *The Anatomy of British Sea Power*, New York, 1940.

Marshall, Alfred, *Memorials*, London, 1890.

Marshall, Alfred and Mary Paley Marshall, *The Economics of Industry*, Chicago, 1909.

Marston, Thomas, *Britain's Imperial Role in the Red Sea Area 1800–1878*, Hamden, Conn., 1961.

Martin, A. P., *Life and Letters of Robert Lowe, Viscount Sherbrooke*, London, 1893.

Marwick, W. H., "The Limited Liability Company in Scottish Economic Development," *Economic History*, III, 1937, pp. 415–29.

Marx, K., *Capital: A Critique of Political Economy*, Chicago, 1909, 3 vols.

Marx, K. and F. Engels, *The First Indian War of Independence*, London, 1960.

Mathew, W. M., "The Imperialism of Free Trade: Peru, 1820–70," *Economic History Review*, second series, XXI (3), 1968, pp. 562–79.

Matthew, C. G., *The Liberal Imperialists*, Oxford, 1973.

Mehta, M. M., *Combination Movement in India Industry, A Study of the Concentration of Ownership Control and Management in Indian Industry*, Allahabad, 1952.

Mehta, S. D., *The Cotton Mills of India, 1854–1954*, Bombay, 1954.

Meier, G. M., "Economic Development and the Transfer Mechanism: Canada 1895–1913," *Canadian Journal of Economics & Political Science*, XIX (1), February 1953, pp. 1–19.

"Long Period Determinants of Britain's Terms of Trade 1880–1913," *Review of Economic Studies*, XX (2), 1952–3, pp. 115–30.

Meredith, David, "The British Government and Colonial Economic Policy, 1919–1939," *Economic History Review*, second series, XXVIII (3), August 1975, pp. 484–99.

Middlemas, Robert Keith, *The Master Builders*, London, 1968.

Mill, J. S., *Principles of Political Economy*, London, 1907.

Mitchell, B. R., *European Historical Statistics 1750–1970*, New York, 1975.

Mitchell, B. R. and Phyllis Deane, *Abstract of British Historical Statistics*, Cambridge, 1962.

Mitchell, B. R. and H. Jones, *Second Abstract of British Historical Statistics*, Cambridge University Monograph No. 17, Cambridge, 1971.

Monepenny, W. F. and G. E. Buckle, *The Life of Benjamin Disraeli, Earl of Beaconsfield*, London, 1910–20, 6 vols.

Moore, R. J., "Imperialism and 'Free Trade' Policy in India, 1853–4," *Economic History Review*, second series, XVII (1), August 1964, pp. 135–45.

Morgan, E. Victor and W. A. Thomas, *The Stock Exchange: Its History and Functions*, London, 1962.

Morissey, M. J. and R. Burt, "A Theory of Mineral Discovery: A Note," *Economic History Review*, XXVI (3), August 1973, pp. 497–505.

Morley, John, *Life of Gladstone*, London, 1903, 3 vols.

Morrison, Richard, "A Statistical Model for Legislative Roll Call

Analysis," *Journal of Mathematical Sociology*, II (2), July 1972, pp. 235–47.

Munro, J. Forbes, *Colonial Rule and the Kamba: Social Change in the Kenya Highlands 1889–1939*, Oxford, 1975.

Munting, R., "Ransomes in Russia: An English Agricultural Engineering Company's Trade with Russia to 1917," *Economic History Review*, second series, XXXI (2), May 1978, pp. 257–69.

Murphy, A., *The Ideology of French Imperialism*, Washington, D.C., 1945.

Musgrave, R. A., *Fiscal Systems*, New Haven, 1969.

Nash, Bradley D., *Investment Banking in England*, New York, 1924.

Nash, R. I., *A Short Inquiry into the Profitable Nature of Our Investments*, London, 1880.

Naylor, R. T., *The History of Canadian Business, 1867–1914: Volume I: the Banks and Finance Capital*, Toronto, 1975.

  The History of Canadian Business, 1867–1914: Volume II: the Banks and Finance Capital, Toronto, 1975.

Neale, R. S., *Class and Ideology in the Nineteenth Century*, London, 1972.

Nevil, Ralph Henry, *London Clubs: Their Histories and Treasures 1911–1969*, London 1971.

Newbury, C. W., *British Policy towards West Africa, Select Documents 1875–1914*, London, 1971.

Newlyn, W. T. and D. C. Rowan, *Money and Banking in British Colonial Africa*, Oxford, 1954.

Nightingale, Pamela, *Trade and Empire in Western India, 1784–1806*, Cambridge South Asian Studies No. 9, Cambridge, 1970.

Niskanen, William, *Bureaucracy and Representative Government*, Chicago, 1971.

Noble, John, *The Queen's Taxes: An Inquiry into the Amount, Incidence and Economic Results of the Taxation of the United Kingdom, Direct and Indirect*, London, 1870.

Ogburn, M. E., *Equitable Assurances. The Story of Life Assurance in the Experience of the Equitable Life Assurance Society 1762–1962*, London, 1962.

Ogilvie, Vivian, *The English Public School*, London, 1957.

O'Grada, Cormac, "The Beginnings of the Irish Creamery System, 1880–1914," *Economic History Review*, second series, XXX (2), May 1977, pp. 284–305.

Oliver, Roland, *Sir Harry Johnston and the Scramble for Africa*, London, 1957.

Oliver, Roland and Anthony Atmore, *Africa since 1800*, London, 1967.

Ostrogorski, M., *Democracy and the Organization of Political Parties*, Chicago, 1964 (1902).

Owen, E. R. J., *Cotton and the Egyptian Economy, 1820–1914: A Study in Trade and Development*, Oxford, 1969.

Paish, F. W., "The London New Issue Market," *Economica*, XVIII (69), February 1951, pp. 1–17.

Paish, George, "Great Britain's Capital Investments in Individual Colonies and Foreign Countries," *Journal of the Royal Statistical Society,* LXXIV, 1911, pp. 167–200.

"Great Britain's Capital Investment in Other Lands," *Journal of the Royal Statistical Society,* LXII, 1909.

"The Export of Capital and the Cost of Living," *Statist (Supplement),* February 14, 1914.

Palande, M. R., *Introduction to Indian Administration,* Bombay, fifth ed., 1951.

Pares, Richard H., "The Economic Factors in the History of the Empire, *Economic History Review,* VII (2), May 1937, pp. 119–44.

Parker, R. H., *Management Accounting: an Historical Perspective,* London, 1969.

Parkinson, C., *The Colonial Office from Within, 1909–1945,* London, 1947.

Parnaby, O.W., *Britain and the Labor Trade of the Southwest Pacific,* Durham, N.C., 1964.

Payne, Peter L., *Colvilles and the Scottish Steel Industry,* Oxford, 1979.

"The Emergence of the Large-Scale Company in Great Britain, 1870–1914," *Economic History Review,* second series, XX (3), December 1967, pp. 519–42.

Studies in Scottish Business History, London, 1967.

Pedler, Frederick, *The Lion and the Unicorn in Africa – A History of the Origins of the United Africa Company, 1787–1931,* London, 1974.

Peek, Frean & Co., *A Hundred Years of Biscuit Making, 1857–1957,* London, 1957.

Pelcovits, Nathan A., *Old China Hands and the Foreign Office,* American Institute of Pacific Relations, New York, 1948.

Pentland, H. C., "The Role of Capital in Canadian Economic Development before 1875," *Canadian Journal of Economics and Political Science,* XVI (4), November 1950, pp. 457–74.

Perham, Margery (ed.), *Mining, Commerce and Finance in Nigeria,* London, 1948.

Perkins, Edwin J., *Financing Anglo–American Trade: The House of Brown 1800–1880,* Harvard, 1975.

Perugini, Mark Edward, *Victorian Days and Ways,* London, 1932.

Phimister, I. R., "The Reconstruction of the Southern Rhodesian Gold Mining Industry, 1903–10," *The Economic History Review,* second series, XXIX (3), August 1976, pp. 465–81.

Platt, D. C. M., "British Bondholders in Nineteenth Century Latin America: Injury and Remedy," *Inter-America Economic Affairs,* XIV (3), Winter 1960, pp. 3–43.

Business Imperialism 1840–1930. An Inquiry Based on British Experience in Latin America, Oxford, 1977.

Finance, Trade, and Politics in British Foreign Policy, 1815–1914, Oxford, 1968.

"Further Objections to 'Imperialism of Free Trade' 1830–60," *Economic History Review,* second series, 26 (1), February 1973, pp. 77–91.

"The Imperialism of Free Trade: Some Reservations," *Economic History Review*, second series, XXI (2), August 1968, pp. 296–306.

"British Portfolio Investment Overseas before 1870: Some Doubts," *Economic History Review*, second series, XXXIII (1), February 1980, pp. 1–16.

Latin America and British Trade 1806–1914, London, 1972.

"The National Economy and British Imperial Expansion before 1914," *Journal of Imperial and Commercial History*, II (1), October 1973, pp. 3–14.

"The Role of the British Consular Service in Overseas Trade, 1825–1914," *Economic History Review*, second series, XV (3), April 1963, pp. 484–512.

Pointon, A.C., *The Bombay–Burmah Trading Corporation Ltd., 1863–1963*, London, 1964.

Pollard, Sidney and Paul Robertson, *The British Shipbuilding Industry, 1870–1914*, Cambridge, Mass., 1979.

Ponko, Vincent, Jr., "The Colonial Office and British Business before World War I: A Case Study," *Business History Review*, XLIII (1), spring 1969, pp. 39–58.

"Economic Management in a Free-Trade Empire: The Work of the Crown Agents for the Colonies in the Nineteenth and Early Twentieth Centuries," *The Journal of Economic History*, XXVI (3), September 1966, pp. 363–77.

"History and Methodology of Public Administration: The Case of the Crown Agents for the Colonies," *Public Administration Review*, Journal of the American Society for Public Administration, XXVII (1), March 1967, pp. 42–7.

Pope-Hennessy, James, *Verandah: Some Episodes in the Crown Colonies 1867–1889*, London, 1964.

Porter, Bernard, *Critics of Empire: British Radical Attitudes to Colonialism in Africa 1895–1914*, London, 1868.

Powell, E. T., *The Evolution of the Money Market*, London, 1915.

The Mechanism of the City, London, 1910.

Power, T. F., *Jules Ferry and the Renaissance of French Imperialism*, New York, 1944.

Preston, Richard, *Canada and Imperial Defense*, Durham, North Carolina, 1967.

Price, A. Grenfell, *The Western Invasion of the Pacific and Its Continent*, Oxford, 1963.

Priestly, H. I., *France Overseas, A Study of Modern Imperialism*, London, 1966.

Prosser, Gifford and Wm. Roger Louis, *France and Britain in Africa*, New Haven, 1971.

Purshottamdas, Sir Thakordas, *Note on Indian Military Expenditure*.

Puthucheary, J. J., *Ownership and Control of the Malaya Economy*, Singapore, 1960.

Rae, Douglas, *The Political Consequences of Electoral Laws*, New Haven, 1967.

Rai, Lajpat, *England's Debt to India – A Historical Narrative of Britain's Fiscal Policy in India*, Ministry of Information, Government of India, Delhi, 1967 (1889).

Ramachandran, N., *Foreign Plantation Investment in Ceylon 1889–1958*, Columbo, Central Bank of Ceylon, 1963.

Ray, P. K., *India's Foreign Trade since 1870*, London, 1934.

Raynes, H. E., *History of British Assurance*, London, 1964.

Reader, W. J., *Imperial Chemical Industries: A History*, vol. I, *The Forerunners 1870–1936*, London, 1970.

Reber, Vera Blinn, *British Mercantile Houses in Buenos Aires, 1810–1880*, Cambridge, Mass., 1979.

Redford, A., *Manchester Merchants and Foreign Trade, Vol. II 1850–1939*, Manchester, 1956.

Redlich, Joseph, *The Procedure of the House of Commons*, 3 vols., New York, 1969.

Register of Defunct and Other Companies, Stock Exchange Office Yearbook, 1971.

Reid, G., *The Politics of Financial Control*, London, 1966.

Remer, Charles Frederick, *Foreign Investments in China*, New York, 1933.

Reynolds, Edward, "Economic Imperialism: The Case of the Gold Coast," *Journal of Economic History*, XXXV (1), March 1975, pp. 94–116.

Richardson, H. W., "British Emigration and Overseas Investment," *Economic History Review*, XXV (1), February 1972, pp. 99–113.

Rippy, J. Fred, *British Investments in Latin America 1822–1949*, Hamden, Conn., 1959.

"British Investments in Latin America," *Inter-American Economic Affairs*, IV (3), winter 1950, pp. 16–26.

"Economic Enterprises of the 'Nitrate King' and his Associates in Chile," *Pacific Historical Review*, XVII, 1948, pp. 457–65.

Roberts, Elizabeth, "Working Class Standards of Living in Barrow and Lancaster, 1890–1914," *Economic History Review*, XXX (2), May 1977, pp. 306–19.

Roberts, Stephen, *History of French Colonial Policy 1870–1925*, P. S. King, 1929.

Robinson, Howard, *Carrying British Mails Overseas*, New York, 1964.

Robinson, Ronald, John Gallagher and Alice Denny, *Africa and the Victorians: The Official Mind of Imperialism*, London, 1961.

Rogers, J. E. T., *The Economic Interpretation of History Lectures Delivered at Worcester College Hall, Oxford, 1887–8*, London, 1888.

Rosenberg, W., "Capital Imports and Growth – The Case of New Zealand – Foreign Investment in New Zealand 1840–1958," *Economic Journal*, LXXI (281), March 1961, pp. 93–113.

Rosenthal, Howard and Subrata Sen, "Electoral Participation in the French Fifth Republic," *American Political Science Review*, 76, March 1973, p. 31.

Roseveare, Henry, *The Treasury: The Evolution of a British Institution*, London, 1969.

The Treasury, 1660–1870: The Foundations of Control, London, 1973.

Ross, Victor, *History of the Canadian Bank of Commerce*, Toronto, 1920 and 1922, 2 vols.

Rothstein, Morton, "A British Firm on the American West Coast," *British History Review*, XXXVII (4), winter 1963.

Royal Institute for International Affairs, *The Problem of International Investment*, London, 1937.

Rubenstein, W. D., *Men of Property*, London, 1981.

"The Victorian Middle Classes: Wealth, Occupation and Geography," *Economic History Review*, second series, XXX (4), November 1977, pp. 602–23.

"British Millionaires, 1809–1949," *Bulletin of the Institute of Historical Research*, XLVII (116), November 1974, pp. 202–23.

Rungta, Radhe Shyam, *The Rise of Business Corporations in India 1851–1900*, South Asian Studies No. 8, London, 1970.

Russet, Bruce, "Discovering the Voting Groups in the United Nations," *American Political Science Review*, LX (2), June 1966, pp. 327–39.

Ryder, Judith and Harold Silver, *Modern English Society: History and Structure 1850–1970*, London, 1970, 62–73.

Sainty, J. C. (ed.), *Officeholders in Modern Britain: Treasury Officials, 1660– 1870*, London, 1972.

Sandberg, Lars G., *Lancashire in Decline*, Columbus, Ohio, 1974.

Sanford, C. T., *Economy of Public Finance*, London, 1969.

Saul, S. B., "Britain and the World Trade," *Economic History Review*, second series, vol. VII, no. 1, 1954, pp. 49–66.

"The Economic Significance of 'Constructive Imperialism'," *Journal of Economic History*, XVII (2), June 1957, pp. 173–92.

Studies in British Overseas Trade, Liverpool, 1960.

Scarr, Deryck, *Fragments of Empire: A History of the Western Pacific High Commission, 1877–1914*, Canberra, 1967.

Schilling, Theodore von, *London als Anleihemarkt der Englischen Kolonien*, Stuttgart and Berlin, 1911.

Schumpeter, Joseph A., *Business Cycles: A Theoretical and Statistical Analysis of the Capitalist Process*, New York, 1939.

Imperialism, Social Classes: Two Essays, New York, 1955.

Schuyler, R. L., *The Fall of the Old Colonial System: A Study in British Free Trade, 1770–1870*, New York, 1945.

Scobie, James R., *Revolution on the Pampas. A Social History of Argentine Wheat*, Institute of Latin American Studies Monograph No. 1, Austin, Texas, 1964.

Scott, J. D., *Vickers: A History*, London, 1962.

Scott, T. H. S., *England – Its People, Policy and Pursuits*, London, 1885.

Segal, H. and M. Simon, "British Foreign Capital Issues, 1865–94," *Journal of Economic History*, December 1961.

Semmel, Bernard, *Imperialism and Social Reform: English Social- Imperial Thought, 1895–1914*, New York, 1968.

The Rise of Free Trade Imperialism: Classical Political Economy and the Empire of Free Trade and Imperialism, 1750–1850, Cambridge, 1970.

Sen, Sunil Kumar, *Studies in Industrial Policy and Development of India*, Calcutta, 1964.

Serle, Geoffrey, *The Rush to be Rich: A History of the Colony of Australia*, Melbourne, 1971.

Shah, K. T., *Sixty Years of Indian Finance*, London, 1927.

Shannon, H. A., "The Limited Companies of 1866–1883," *Economic History Review*, IV (3) October 1933, pp. 290–316.

"The Coming of General Limited Liability," *Economic History*, VI, 1931.

"The First Five Thousand Limited Companies and their Duration," *Economic History*, II, January 1932, pp. 396–424.

Shaw, A. G. L. (ed.), *Great Britain and the Colonies 1815–1865*, London, 1970.

Shaw, G. Bernard, *Plays Pleasant and Unpleasant*, II, New York, 1898.

Shehab, F., *Progressive Taxation*, Oxford, 1953.

Shirras, G. F., *India's Finance and Banking*, London, 1920.

Shortt, Adam, "The Early History of Canadian Banking," *Journal of the Canadian Bankers Association*, IV (1–4), and V (1), October 1896 to October 1897.

"The History of Canadian Currency, Banking, and Exchange," *Journal of the Canadian Bankers Association*, VII (3 and 4), and VIII (1–4), April 1900 to July 1901.

Sigsworth, E. M., *Black Dyke Mills*, Liverpool, 1958.

Simkin, C. G. F., *The Instability of a Dependent Economy, Economic Fluctuations in New Zealand 1840–1914*, London, 1951.

Simmons, Jack, *Livingstone in Africa*, London, 1955.

Simon, M., "New British Investments in Canada, 1865–1914," *Canadian Journal of Economics*, 3 (2), May 1970, pp. 238–54.

"The Pattern of New British Portfolio Foreign Investment, 1865–1914," in A. R. Hall (ed.), *The Export of Capital from Britain 1870–1914*, London, 1968, pp. 15–44.

Singh, Shailendra, "Intergovernmental Fiscal Relations," in V. B. Singh (ed.), *Economic History of India: 1857–1956*, Bombay, 1965, pp. 528–62.

Sinha, H., *Early European Banking in India*, London, 1927.

Skelton, Oscar, *Life and Letters of Sir Wilfred Laurier*, Toronto, 1965.

Slaven, Anthony, "A Glasgow Firm in the Indian Market: John Lean and Sons, Muslin Weavers," *Business History Review*, XLIII (4), winter 1969, pp. 496–522.

Snelling, R. C. and T. J. Barron, "The Colonial Office and its Permanent Officials, 1801–1914," *Studies in the Growth of Nineteenth-Century Government*, London, 1972, pp. 139–66.

Spence, Clark C., *British Investments and the American Mining Frontier 1860–1901*, published for the American Historical Association, Ithaca, 1958.

Spinner, Thomas J., *George Joachim Goschen: The Transformation of a Liberal*, Cambridge, England, 1973.

Stacey, Charles Perry, *Canada and the British Army, 1846–1871: A Study in the Practice of Responsible Government*, revised edition, Toronto, 1963.

Stahl, Kathleen M., *The Metropolitan Organization of British Colonial Trade*, London, 1951.

Staley, Eugene, *War and the Private Investor*, Chicago, 1935.

Stamp, J. C., *British Incomes and Property: The Application of Official Statistics to Economic Problems*, London, 1916.

British Incomes and Property, London, 1920.

Stanley, H. M., *The Autobiography of Sir Henry Morton Stanley, G.C.B.*, London, 1909.

The Statesman's Yearbook, London, 1860–1913.

Stillson, Richard T., "The Financing of Malayan Rubber, 1905–1923," *Economic History Review*, second series, XXIV (4), November 1971, pp. 589–98.

Stirling, Everard, *The History of the Gas Light and Coke Company, 1812–1949*, London, 1949.

Stock Exchange Annual Year Book, 1883–1913.

Stokes, Donald, "Spatial Models of Party Competition, "*American Political Science Review*, LVII, June 1963, pp. 368–77.

Stokes, Eric, "Late Nineteenth-Century Colonial Expansion and the Attack on the Theory of Economic Imperialism: A Case of Mistaken Identity," *The Historical Journal*, XII (2), 1969, pp. 285–301.

Stone, Irving, "British Direct and Portfolio Investment in Latin America before 1914," *Journal of Economic History*, XXXVII (3), September 1977, pp. 311–39.

"British Long-Term Investment in Latin America, 1865–1913," *The Business History Review*, XLII, no. 3, autumn 1968.

Strachey, Sir John, *Finances and Public Works in India*, London, 1882.

Sullivan, R. J. F., *One Hundred Years of Bombay*, Bombay, c 1937.

Sun, E-Tu Zen, *Chinese Railways and British Interests 1898–1911*, New York, 1954.

Supple, Barry, *Essays in British Business History*, Oxford, 1977.

The Royal Exchange Assurance. A History of British Insurance 1720–1970, London, 1970.

Sutch, W. B., *Colony or Nation?*, Sydney, 1966.

Sutherland, Gillian, *Studies in the Growth of Nineteenth-Century Government*, London, 1972.

Swainson, Nicola, *Foreign Corporations and Economic Growth in Kenya*.

Tennant, E. W. D., *A Short Account of the Tennant Companies 1794–1922*, London, 1922.

Thernstrom, Stephan, *Poverty and Progress; Social Mobility in a Nineteenth-Century City*, Cambridge, 1964.

Thomas, Brinley, "The Historical Record of International Capital Movements to 1913," in J. H. Adler (ed.), *Capital Movements and Economic Development*, London, 1967, pp. 3–32.

Migration and Economic Growth, London, 1954.

Migration and Urban Development, London, 1972.

Thomas, J. A., *The House of Commons 1832–1901*, Cardiff, 1939.

Thomas, P. J., *The Growth of Federal Finance in India*, Oxford, 1946.

Thorner, Daniel, *Investment in Empire, British Railways and Steam Enterprise in India 1825–1849*, Philadelphia, 1950.

"Great Britain and the Development of India's Railways," *Journal of Economic History*, XI (4), fall 1951, pp. 389–402.

"The Pattern of Railway Development in India," *The Far Eastern Quarterly*, XIV (2), February 1955, pp. 201–16.

Thornton, A. P., *Doctrines of Imperialism*, New York, 1965.

The Imperial Idea and Its Enemies: A Study in British Power, London, 1959.

Townsend, Mary Evelyn, *Origins of Modern German Colonialism, 1871–1885*, New York, 1974.

The Rise and Fall of Germany's Colonial Empire, New York, 1930.

Trebilcock, Clive, *The Vickers Brothers: Armaments and Enterprise, 1854–1914*, London, 1977.

Trevelyan, G. M., *History of England*, III, Garden City, 1952.

Tullock, Gordon, "A Simple Algebraic Logrolling Model," *American Economic Review*, LX (3), June 1970, pp. 419–26.

Tyson, G. W., *The Bengal Chamber of Commerce and Industry, 1853–1953, A Centenary Survey*, Calcutta, 1953.

Tyson, Geoffrey, *100 Years of Banking in Asia and Africa: A History of National and Grindlay Bank Limited, 1853–1953*, London, 1963.

U.S. Bureau of the Census, *Historical Statistics of the United States: Colonial Times to 1957*, Washington, D.C., 1960.

Urquhart, M. C., *Historical Statistics of Canada*, Cambridge, 1965.

Vakil, C. N., *Financial Developments of Modern India*, London, 1924.

van Oss, S. F., *Stock Exchange Values: A Decade of Finance 1885 to 1895*, London, 1895.

Van Zwanenberg, R. M. A. and Anne King, *An Economic History of Kenya and Uganda, 1800–1970*, New Jersey, 1975.

Vere-Hodge, E. R., *Imperial British East Africa Co.*, London (published in association with The East African Literature Bureau), 1960.

Vincent, J. and M. Stenton, *McCalmont's Parliamentary Poll Book*, British Election Results 1832–1918, Brighton, 1971.

Viner, J., *Canada's Balance of International Indebtedness 1900–1913*, Cambridge, Mass., 1924.

Walker, C. H., "Unincorporated Investment Trusts in the Nineteenth Century," *Economic History*, IV, February 1940, pp. 341–55.

Walters, R. H., *The Economic and Business History of the South Wales Steam Coal Industry 1840–1914*, New York, 1977.

Warberg, Joseph, *The Merchant Bankers*, Boston, 1966.

Webb, Sydney and Beatrice, *The History of Trade Unionism*, London, 1950.

Weisberg, Herbert and Jerold Rusk, "Dimensions of Candidate Evaluation," *American Political Science Review*, LXIV (4), December 1970, pp. 1167–85.

Wilkinon, Rupert, *The Prefects, British Leadership and the Public School Tradition*, Oxford, 1964.

Will, H. A., "Colonial Policy and Economic Development in the British West Indies, 1895–1903," *Economic History Review*, second series, vol. 23, no. 1, 1970, 129–147.

Williams, Judith Blow, *British Commercial Policy and Trade Expansion: 1750–1850*, New York and London, 1972.

Williams, W. M. J., *The King's Revenue, Being a Handbook to the Taxes and the Public Revenue*, London, 1980.

Williams-Taylor, Sir Frederick, "Canadian Loans in London," *United Europe*, December 1912.

Wilson, Charles, *The History of Unilever: A Study in Economic Growth and Social Change. Volume I*, London, 1954.

   The History of Unilever: A Study in Economic Growth and Social Change. Volume II, London, 1954.

   "Economy and Society in Late Victorian England, *Economic History Review*, second series, XVIII (1), August 1965, pp. 183–98.

Wilson, Robert, "An Axiomatic Model of Logrolling," *American Economic Review*, 1970.

Wilson, Roland, *Capital Imports and the Terms of Trade*, Melbourne, 1931.

Wingate, Sir G., *Our Financial Relations with India*, London, 1859.

Winn, Peter, "British Informal Empire in Uruguay," *Past and Present* (73), November 1976, pp. 100–26.

Winslow, E. M., *The Pattern of Imperialism*, New York, 1948.

Withers, Hartley, *Stocks and Shares*, London, 1910.

Withers, Hartley, Sir R. H. Inglis Palgrave, et al., *The English Banking System*, Senate Documents, vol. 18, second session, 1909–10, Washington, D.C., 1910.

Wolfe, Martin (ed.), *The Economic Causes of Imperialism*, New York, 1972.

Wolff, Richard D., *The Economics of Colonialism: Britain and Kenya, 1870–1930*, New Haven, 1974.

Wood, John C., *British Economists and Empire*, New York, 1983.

Woods, Sir John, "Treasury Control," *Political Quarterly*, XXV (4), October-December 1954, pp. 370–81.

Woolf, L., *Empire and Commerce in Africa*, London, 1920.

Wright, Maurice, *Treasury Control of the Civil Service, 1854–1874*, Oxford, 1969.

   "Treasury Control, 1854–1914," in Gillian Sutherland (ed.), *Studies in the Growth of Nineteenth-Century Government*, London, 1972, pp. 195–226.

Wright, W. E., "Life Assurance Company Investments," *The Bankers Magazine*, 1897, 71.

Young, D. M., *The Colonial Office in the Early Nineteenth Century*, London, 1961.

Young, L.K., *British Policy in China, 1895–1902*, Oxford, 1970.

Index

Abbott, A. W., 184
Abyssinian Campaign (1864), 154–5
accounting, 80–4
Adderley, Charles, 9, 146, 303
Afghan War (1878–80), 154–5
Africa, 8, 51–2, 69, 125
  Indian troops in, 154
  Hut tax, 233, 236
  government-business relations,
    265–7
  profits, 310
  *see also specific colonies and
    countries*
Agriculture, 61–3
  profits, 102, 104–5, 311
Alexander, James, 206–7
Alley Maclellan (firm), 92–3
Anderston foundry, 96
Antony Gibbs & Sons, 95, (346 *n.*
    15), 207, 264
  see also Gibbs family
Argyll, 8th Duke of, 135
Ashanti War, 150
Asia, 50, 69
  *see also specific colonies and
    countries*
Asquith, Herbert, 255, 302
Assam Tea Company, 309–10
Association of Chambers of Com-
    merce of the United Kingdom,
    256–7
Australasia, 122, 125
  defense spending, 156–7
  public finance, 181
  trade, 190
Australia, 159

banking (profits), 87–8, 103, 105
  see also financial industry
Baxter, R. Dudley, 198, 248–50
Beaumont, Wentworth B., 313
beef, 94
Bengal Nagpur Railroad, 206–7
Board of Control for India, 14

Board of Trade, 195
Boer War, 106, 151
bouillon cubes, 95
Bovril, 95
breweries and distilleries
  lobbying, 254
  profits, 90–1, 103, 105
British Honduras, 125
  see also West Indies
Brodrick, John, 262
Bulwayo Waterworks, 207
business
  profits, 91–6, 103–5
  organization, 73–4
  see also incorporation; industry

Cairncross, Alexander, 33, 75, 78–9
Campbell-Bannerman, Henry, 302
Canada, 11, 43, 47
  defense spending, 152, 159, 303
  public finance, 181
  trade, 190
  see also North America
Cape Colony, 147, 150–1
capital exports
  and economic theory, 30–2
  geographical distribution, 38–52,
    (342–3 *n.* 24–6), 72
  industrial distribution, 53–72,
    (344 *n.* 35)
  statistical analysis, 33
  volume, 37–8, (342 *n.* 21)
  see also foreign investment; impe-
    rial investment
Cardwell, Edward, 9, 148, 152
Carnarvon, 4th Earl of, 154, 170–1,
    233
Ceylon, 23, 148
Chamberlain, Joseph, 32, 158, 208,
    302–3, 315
Chambers of Commerce, 256–60,
    276
Chesterton, G. K., 302

389